TRANSCULTURAL
Realities

TRANSCULTURAL
Realities

Interdisciplinary Perspectives on Cross-Cultural Relations

Editors
Virginia H. Milhouse
Molefi Kete Asante
Peter O. Nwosu

Sage Publications
International Educational and Professional Publisher
Thousand Oaks ■ London ■ New Delhi

For information:

Sage Publications, Inc.
2455 Teller Road
Thousand Oaks, California 91320
E-mail: order@sagepub.com

Sage Publications Ltd.
6 Bonhill Street
London EC2A 4PU
United Kingdom

Sage Publications India Pvt. Ltd.
M-32 Market
Greater Kailash I
New Delhi 110 048 India

Printed in the United States of America

Library of Congress Cataloging-in-Publication Data

Transcultural realities: Interdisciplinary perspectives on
      cross-cultural relations / edited by Virginia H. Milhouse,
      Molefi Kete Asante, Peter O. Nwosu.
         p. cm.
      Includes bibliographical references and index.
      ISBN 0-7619-2375-6 (cloth : alk. paper) —
      ISBN 0-7619-2376-4 (pbk. : alk. paper)
         1. Intercultural communication. 2. Cross-cultural orientation.
      3. Cultural relations. I. Milhouse, Virginia Hall, 1950-
      II. Asante, Molefi K., 1942- III. Nwosu, Peter.
      HM1211 .T73 2001
      303.48'2—dc21   2001000423

01   02   03   04   05   06   10 9 8 7 6 5 4 3 2 1

Acquiring Editor: Margaret H. Seawell
Editorial Assistant: Alicia Carter
Production Editor: Claudia A. Hoffman
Editorial Assistant: Kathryn Journey
Copy Editor: Jacqueline A. Tasch
Typesetter: Marion Warren
Indexer: Molly Hall
Cover Designer: Jane Quaney

Contents

PART II
Historical and Religious
Struggles Within and Between Nations

PART III
Socially Constructed Racial Identities
and Their Consequences for Transculturalism in America

PART IV
The Transformative Effects of Sojourning in Diverse Cultural Environments

PART V
Toward the Fundamentals of Transcultural Research

Acknowledgments

Working on a project of this magnitude has been both a challenging and exciting experience. For us, it has given added meaning to the value of communication in an increasingly transcultural world.

Several people were helpful to us in the refining and development of this project. First, we express much appreciation to our editor, Margaret Seawell, for her assistance throughout the process of the book's development. And, of course, we owe a debt of gratitude to those scholars who, more than 20 years ago, recognized the importance of transculturalism and its benefits to the study of cross-cultural relations.

Certainly, this book could not have happened had it not been for such a diversified group of scholars who share this vision and helped to shape the interdisciplinary nature of the book. We are similarly indebted to those scholars whose comments, during a rigorous blind review process, helped to guide and refine all of the book's chapters. And to those scholars whose original essays appear herein: Guo-Ming Chen, Min-Sun Kim, Bolanle A. Olaniran, Ali Mazrui, Ayman Omar, Ama Mazama, Chevelle Newsome, Richard Allen, Anthony Monteiro, Travis Dixon, Toni-Mokjaetji Humber, Emeka Okoli, Chuka Onwumechili, Joy Okereke-Arungwa, Judith H. Martin, Ruth L. Butler, Donald S. Taylor, Don Rubin, Pam Lannutti, and Cynthia L. Lehman, we express our deep appreciation and gratitude for your tireless efforts and willingness to adapt your chapters while meeting all of the imposed but necessary deadlines. But over and above these acknowledgments, we acknowledge especially the giver of all knowledge, without whom the ideas, perspectives, and principles expressed in this book would not have been possible.

Introduction

This book is a first attempt to dialogue about the importance of transculture in interdisciplinary contexts. Its primary goal is to help readers understand that a state of community or harmony cannot be achieved in the world until we are all ready to accept different cultural forms, norms, and orientations.

But first, because the concept *transculture* may seem somewhat ambiguous to some, it is important, as a point of departure, to offer a clarification of it. In so doing, we intend also to provide an explanation of how the concept is used in this text. For the purpose of this book, *transculture* is defined as a form of culture created not from within its separate spheres but in the holistic forms of diverse cultures. Whereas culture may have the capacity to free us from the dictates of nature—that is, from its restrictions and necessities—the merit and capacity of transculture is to free us

from the conventions and obsessions of culture itself (Epstein, 1995). So many of us human beings live as prisoners of our own cultures and feel bound to act and think in total agreement with their presumptions and teachings, no matter how narrowly defined they may be.

The concept transculture is, therefore, based on the principle that a single culture, in and of itself, for maturity requires interaction and dialogue with other cultures. This principle is clearly proposed in Epstein's (1995) discourse on contemporary culture. In this work, he suggests that "the transcultural world lies not apart from but within all existing cultures, like a multidimensional space which appears gradually over the course of time" (p. 13). And within this space exists realized and unrealized potential, the latter no less meaningful than the former. But the interaction among all existing and potential cultures makes even the totality of known cultural traditions and practices richer. In this sense, transculturalism is about affirming diverse ways of knowing, communicating, and behaving so that when individuals from different cultures come together, there is the potential for each to be enriched by the other.

To do this, we must be willing to tap into the different transcultural experiences we face, both at home and abroad. In his book, *Transcultural Odysseys: The Evolving Global Consciousness,* Shames (1997) tells us that we can expect to have transcultural challenges in our hometowns as well as in our overseas travels. These challenges can give rise to an expanded worldview that is defined not by its borders but by its horizons.

The concept *transculture* is related, therefore, to other cross-cultural concepts, including intra- and interculturalism, internationalism, and postmodernism—in the sense that it rejects the notion that there is only one way of knowing, behaving, or communicating. But over and above these concepts, we believe *transcultural reality* is more closely aligned with the concept of globalism discussed in Janzen's (1997) *Five Paradigms of Ethnic Relations.* In this work, globalism is described as a continuous search for the center through ongoing discussions in regard to commonly accepted principles. "The center itself draws upon the experiential and intellectual traditions of all world cultures" (p. 67); and although there are many reasons why global awareness is promoted—social, economic, religious—the most important reason is the working together peaceably of world citizens. It is important to point out, however, that whereas a centered perspectives may be the primary focus of a transcultural-global model, those enduring qualities and values that separate and distinguish each culture must be held in high regard.

Thus, through a process of ongoing exploration of a multiple centered perspective, all cultures have the power to influence the creation of knowledge and understanding of human behavior. Yet, for this power to be equitable in view of the world's political, economic,

and demographic contexts, a tremendous amount of community building will be required. To the extent that the United Nations is guided by the principles of authentic communication and negotiation, by its ability to deal with difficult issues, to accept and affirm diversity, to bridge differences with integrity, and to relate to all world citizens with understanding and respect, it is both a model of community building and globalism. It is also transcultural, because "it is organized and functions in such a way that the rights of those nations which are [different, or] not as strong militarily, economically, or demographically are still theoretically protected [or held in high esteem]" (Janzen, 1997, p. 67).

This vision of transcultural globalism has heightened the sense of urgency many have about how best to adopt transculturally recognized principles and to be open to ongoing change without destroying cultural experiences and traditions. For us, the sense of urgency involving the transcultural-global model is fueled by the need to rethink contemporary views about the nature of cross-cultural relations and the notion that one model of human interaction or socialization will fit all cultures. As Samovar and Porter (1994) remind us, there are a variety of ways to investigate the subject of communication; various cultures see the issue differently. For decades, scholars of human interaction have wrestled with questions about the nature of transculturalism. For example, some want to understand international and cross-cultural issues that are also transcultural; they ask if religious and historical struggles within and between cultures can be solved through a spirit of transculturalism. Others want to improve their understanding of the consequences, for transculturalism, of socially constructed identities. They may ask how people sojourning in diverse contexts are affected by the dynamics of those contexts. Questions also exist about the fundamentals of transculture research.

This book is about these questions, and it takes an interdisciplinary approach to cross-cultural relations. In this introduction, it is important for us to address trends in the field of communication, because to understand cross-cultural relations or even transculturalism, we must first understand human communication. We believe, for the most part, that the responsibility of helping people understand human communication rests with the field of communication. Scholars who study communication should have some understanding about what happens when humans interact, why they interact, the effects of human interaction, and what we can do as human beings to influence and maximize the outcome of our communication behavior. Therefore, we address succinctly, in this introduction, the historical situation of the field of communication, the intellectual paths it has taken, and the scientific models it has used and tried to emulate. Then, in the last part of the introduction, we address the implications of a centeredness perspective to cross-cultural relations.

▶ The Historical Situation

The present path of knowledge in communication studies—in all of its critical manifestations as an arena of scholarship—is a purely modern-postmodern phenomenon. Although we are all familiar with the ancient roots of communication in the classical cultures of Europe, Africa, and Asia—and we celebrate them, even praising the structured forms of the past—we also acknowledge that, both in practice and in research, communication scholars have made better mergers of modern-postmodern issues than scholars in other fields. We are, by virtue of our immensely dependent relationship on human actions, thrown into an evolving world constantly re-created by humans. Thus, in our practice and theory, bifurcated in the tradition of Europe, we are pre-eminently involved in the trajectory of the modern-postmodern world. At the same time, we are best suited to receive the multifaceted pathways of light that come from other than straight linear sources. All trajectories are lines, some more curvilinear than others.

This set of circumstances complicates our project because we social scientists were meant to explain the modern phenomenon that Bryant, Thronssen Baird, Oliver, Lomas, Burke, Arnold, Kibler, Wichelns, and others saw as persuasion within the context of Western rationality. Theirs was a highly structured world that fought back the intense stream of consciousness movement that predated the fluidity movement of the current era. Indeed, we fought back or ignored the responses to society that were emerging from other cultural perspectives. We appreciate much of what the earlier champions thought and said, but they were so affected by the First and Second World Wars that their notions of human interaction were often martial, psychological, conflictual, theatrical, or rather, staged, and very modern.

In earlier generations, students of human interaction had sought to understand the transition from rural to urban, from county to city, from community to society, by analyzing the cryptic forms in which such a transformation of the social experience as interpersonal or rhetorical manifested itself. It was left, however, to the teachers of the 1950s and 1960s to consolidate the meaning of the field in concrete ways so that the emergence of discrete disciplines constituted an advancement in linear thinking.

In no time at all, the capitalist imperative, a definitive modern enterprise that is central to the persuasive mission, had captured the rhetorical, interpersonal, intercultural, and international sentiments of communication scientists. Their inquiry became associated with intensive interrogations about the meaning of exchanges, and interchanges, of culture and goods and services. During the ascendancy of democracy, communication became so closely related to civilization and development that scholars operating outside the democratic context were declared authoritarian and thus not part of the communicative enterprise. They only followed orders. Yet, within the capitalist model, with its claim to universality, beacons of uncertainty and indeterminacy were revealed, first in the economic and then in the social sphere. Linear thinking must be acknowledged as important; it has created most of the world's structure, as we know it. But like the portions of an iceberg that are underwater, most of what exists is invisible. The structured world is only a fraction of the universe, physically or metaphysically.

However, because most Western scholars were trained to privilege only rationality, the task of communication scholars became to describe or explain as much as possible how cultures could act on themselves and other cultures to transform or modify others so that they would be receptive to effective persuasion. We had wandered far from the road of the ancient Egyptians. According to Xing Lu's (1998) recent book on Chinese rhetoric, the ancient Chinese concentrated on ethics in communication to a degree that even the ancient Greeks, with their more practical approach to human communication, would not recognize the Chinese instructions even if they recognized the form. More than the Greeks and Chinese, the Egyptians indeed seemed to recognize the possibility of appealing to other ways of knowing that were hidden in nonspatial space or nontemporal time. So we are reminded that "it is easy to forget that Egypt, India, Persia, and China were old, old centers of civilization, and that their rich cultures had in fact provided the basis for contemporary Western cultures" (Rogers, 1986, p. 4).

THE INTELLECTUAL PURSUIT

We believe that the intellectual pursuit in communication has been essentially about a social or cultural calculus in three categories: theory, method, and empiricism. Whatever the discrete disciplines of the communication field, each has come to be characterized by emphases in these categories. All are united by the search for a rational explanation of human communication behavior, despite differences in culture, social status, or gender. This has tended to remain constant.

The portrait sketched in the preceding paragraphs has come under sharp scrutiny in the past few years from numerous sources inside and outside of the field. Not only have interculturalists or internationalists questioned the dominant and reigning paradigm that sees the ancient Greeks as the beginning of all that we do in the West, but even those who have accepted that paradigm are now questioning whether or not it considers all human possibilities of knowing, or all there is to know of communication within the Western framework. This is a new and challenging avenue of thought, raising the possibility that we do not know all that we thought we knew of Western communication. Because the 21st century is said to be the century of diverse independent cultures, each with its own unique value (Epstein, 1995, p. 11), we believe the intellectual pursuit in communication, as in other disciplines, requires genuine acceptance and application of interdisciplinary approaches that are grounded in transcultural realities.

THE NATURAL SCIENCES MODEL

One problem that re-emerges here at the beginning of the 21st century is how to deal with the natural sciences model that has migrated into communication studies. What have we learned, and what more do we need to learn from this model? Are the natural sciences relevant to communication studies now, or have they ever been truly relevant? The natural sciences were used as the normative reference for communication, as they were for the social sciences, to the extent that communication scholars tried to imitate the protocols of the natural sciences. However, the Newtonian model was in decline by the time communication scholars tried to imitate it, a decline that perhaps led to the fragmentation of the natural sciences. In the social sciences, we have seen challenges to all types of deterministic reasoning, leading to new alignments and social definitions. Similar challenges confront such disciplines as sociology and anthropology, due to the inability of these disciplines to explore multiple ways of knowing and problem solving. Anthropology is already a field in crisis because it has failed to transform itself in the face of the emerging centrally established models, preferring, it seems, to continue its pursuit of the comparative model, based on the notion of European standards in language, structure, kinship, and so forth. Indeed, the most prolific of cultural anthropologists, Marvin Harris (1998), has recently written a book, *Theories of Culture in Postmodern Times,* that speaks to the bankruptcy of the analytical model promulgated by himself and others, although he fails to make salient the argument of the centeredness perspective within the context of Western society.

THE CONVERGENCE OF AFFIRMATIONS

Four affirmations converged with the decline of Newtonian rationality to solidify the potential in communication study: The affirmation of social and gender heterogeneity and complexity, the affirmation of forms of knowledge distant from scientific knowledge, the affirmation of a plural rather than a totalizing world, and the prevailing influence of the technologies of communication and information. These affirmations are assisted by the new avenues of agency expressed and explored in the work of scholars affirming a multiplicity of perspectives.

In our opinion, the results problematized the communication project by recentering and deterritorializing knowledge. Humans come in many variations and interact in an infinite number of ways. To the degree that we are open to every possibility of human interaction as a potential communicative event, we will be open to the varieties of ways of knowing. No longer, however, must we simply concentrate on issues of subject-object, us-other, or intersubjectivity as the entire corpus of what is done in communication, when looming before us in a clear light are modalities of gen-

der, language, and class, as well as a new advocacy of propriety.

If human communication scholars have any public role, then it must be to bring harmony, order, reciprocity, and justice through criticism to the public practice of communication. However, we can only do this by asking questions such as, How do we make the invisible visible? How do we make the inexplicable explainable? How do we make the ungraspable graspable? How do we make the unheard heard? We believe the answers to these questions will come from many ways of knowing and not only from knowledge that exists outside of us or knowledge that exists inside of us, but from the centeredness of these two ways. This kind of knowing is capable of directing the pathways of light that we have often caught glimpses of in authentic communication forms found in public speeches such as the one given by Nelson Mandela (1994) during his inaugural address. He says, "We were born to make manifest the . . . [light] that is within us. . . . It's not just in some of us [but] in everyone . . . and as we let our light shine, we unconsciously give other people permission to do the same" (p. 35).

What we are looking for is an emancipatory approach to ways of knowing where the relevance of freeing people from subjugation in its different forms becomes meaningful. We believe that for the Israelis and Palestinians, the Albanians and the Serbians, the Rwandans and Congolese, there ought to be enough emancipatory energy based on what we have discovered in our research to allow people who are negotiating to know that what they are seeking in a linear way may be discovered in a nonlinear way, or vice versa. One manifestation of our age is the increase in technological instruments that externalize and modify much of our imagination, memory, insight, and intuition and enlarge everything we say or do. This means that there are new forms of information, new ways of accessing facts, and new styles of reasoning that are neither deductive nor inductive. Open nonlinear ideas, flows of information, interacting spaces or spheres of influence, and uncertain responses are changing the principles on which much of human communication theory was founded.

▶ Organization

We have assembled herein 19 chapters that provide an interdisciplinary perspective about culture and transculture. *Culture* is the deposit of knowledge and experience that shapes the beliefs and behaviors of a group of people over the course of many generations. *Transculture,* on the other hand, is that which has the merits and capacity to free us from the limitations of our culture so that we may participate in and not negate valued traditions of other cultures.

At first glance, it may appear that the authors of the chapters in this book are advocating something other than transculturalism. But as we explain below, each of the chapters, either directly or indirectly, contributes to the primary goal of the book, which is to promote a centeredness perspective without negating those enduring qualities and values that separate and distinguish a culture. During the book's review process, one of the reviewers remarked that "the pastiche of interdisciplinary dialogue about communicative and cultural realities is perhaps the book's greatest strength." Indeed, we believe the strength of this book lies in the particular scholarly assumptions each scholar brings to his or her own chapter and that it is these assumptions that inform the transcultural nature of the book.

PART I: TRANSCULTURAL
ISSUES IN INTERNATIONAL
AND CROSS-CULTURAL CONTEXTS

The book's 19 chapters are organized into five distinct but relevant parts. It is our hope that the chapters in Part I will help readers better understand the principles of transculturalism and why they are important in

these contexts. We also believe that each chapter, both theoretically and philosophically, supports the assumption that a single culture, in and of itself, is incomplete, requiring interaction and dialogue with other cultures. It is, thus, our purpose in this first section to discuss (a) the importance of coming together peacefully as world cultures and (b) the usefulness of a centeredness perspective that embraces the experiential and intellectual traditions of all cultures. Chapter 1, "Perspectives on Human Communication: Implications for Transculture Theory," is an attempt to bring a transcultural perspective to scholarly analyses of human interaction by investigating traditional studies of human communication, which have centered around Western "independent" self-orientations. Here, alternatives to traditional scholarship in human communication are advocated; this author believes that such a change must happen if we are to transcend the limitations imposed on us by our cultural teachings.

We believe the significance of Chapter 2, "Transcultural Communication in the U.S.-Africa Context: Can It Help Africa's Emerging National Development?" to the book's discussion on transculture lies in the assumptions it makes about the relationship between the United States and Africa. Although these two cultures have very different value systems— Africa being a culture that values community and collective participation and the United States being one that values individuality and competition, this chapter assumes synchronization can still be achieved between the United States and Africa, as long as each culture is willing to accept the experiential and intellectual traditions of the other without negating the importance of either. It further assumes that the United States and Africa are ready for bilateral dialogue concerning Africa's national development. This is discussed in more depth in Chapter 2. Also, like Chapter 1, we believe this chapter helps to strengthen the interdisciplinary approach we have taken in this book. In the context of international relations, in particular where national development policies are concerned, this chapter helps to examine the basic processes of transculturalism. The author also makes a case for the interchangeability, especially in the context of international development, of the terms *transcultural communication* and *international involvement.*

Chapter 3 is titled "Toward Transcultural Understanding: A Harmony Theory of Chinese Communication." We chose this chapter not only because it deals with the interdisciplinary aspects of cross-cultural relations but also because it addresses questions that are relevant to a theory of transculturalism. One of these is how do we make the invisible visible. This question was posed in an earlier section of the introduction because we believe many non-Western cultures lack visibility due, in part, to a lack of systematic research about their culture and customs. As a cardinal element of Chinese culture, harmony is the ultimate goal Chinese people pursue in the process of human interaction. In many ways, the Chinese notion of harmony and its ability to bring continuity and transformation to human interaction is similar to the goals of transculturalism.

"Transcultural Realities and Different Ways of Knowing," Chapter 4, is in Part I of the book because it focuses on the need to examine different ways of knowing across cultures. We know, for example, that some cultures tend to rely almost totally on human reasoning or rationality. Others place a greater emphasis on knowledge derived from spiritual, ancestral, and intuitive sources. And some cultures take a holistic approach to knowing, acquiring knowledge from both internal and external sources. Therefore, this author argues that there is no one way of knowing about intercultural communication, rhetoric, philosophy, linguistics, psychology, education, anthropology, and history. He explains that a revision of notions about the ownership of knowledge is not only necessary but also rewarding. On the other hand, if we do not change the way we "see" the world, a weakness in provincial scholarship will re-

main, and this weakness will be an obstacle to transcultural realities.

If the 18th century was the beginning of the age of Enlightenment, the 21st century is the age of computer-mediated communication. But just as the age of Enlightenment brought disruption in the ways people believed and behaved, computer technology presents challenges to transcultural organizations in the 21st century. Our book, therefore, would not be complete without Chapter 5, "The Effects of Computer-Mediated Communication on Transculturalism." In this chapter, the author argues that although there are benefits—namely, productivity and efficiency—attributed to technological development in global organizations, sociocultural challenges are also likely to be present. This chapter explores some of these challenges by examining questions such as, What effects does computer-mediated communication in global organizations have on humanity? How does it affect the development of transcultural realities in the organization? The author cautions that technology has the potential to blur not only geographical boundaries between cultures but lines of communication as well.

PART II: HISTORICAL AND RELIGIOUS STRUGGLES WITHIN AND BETWEEN NATIONS

It is no secret that we live today in a culturally pluralistic world society. This is evident in the rapid increase in the transmission of information as well as the ability to travel the world in just a matter of hours. Coupled with this realization is awareness of the multitude of diverse and conflicting viewpoints humans have about many different issues. Nowhere are these diverse views more apparent than in the area of religion. More than ever before in history, we are aware of religious and historical struggles within and between nations.

Our purpose, therefore, in selecting the chapters in this part was twofold: First we saw a need for studies that explored the differences and similarities in religions. We also felt there was a need to have a better understanding of the historical backgrounds underlying the struggles between certain religions. And, of course, given the role of religion in so many cultures, we felt a book on transcultural reality would be incomplete without some discussion of religion and its historical challenges. Chapter 6, "Historical Struggles Between Islamic and Christian Worldviews: An Interpretation," discusses historical contentions between Christianity and Islam. The author points out that the close relationship of Judaism, Christianity, and Islam is seriously neglected in Western religious teachings. He believes people throughout the world should know that Islam is closer to Christianity than Judaism in some respects. For example, Islam accepts a substantial part of the New Testament, whereas Judaism does not. Also, Islam accepts Jesus as the messiah, whereas Judaism does not. Moreover, most Muslims accept the virgin birth of Jesus, but Judaism does not. This chapter makes many Abrahamic comparisons among the three religions. It discusses Islam as the first Protestant revolution, differences between Western worldviews and Islam on issues of gender and violence, religious biases, and geographical distortions in space and time.

Religion has always been at the core of the political process in Sudan; many Sudanese consider religion a core part of their identity. Deng (1997) posits that "all of the political parties have in one way or another endorsed a religious agenda . . . [but one] would have a hard time finding a political leader willing to say, 'let's put aside religious issues' " (p. 1). Likewise, the author of Chapter 7, "A Historiographical Survey of the Determinants of the North-South Divide in Sudan," tells us that although civil conflicts are generally about the struggle for resources and political power, they also involve the ideas and values that legitimate such struggle. Nowhere is this more the case than when religion is brought into the mix of issues in Sudan. This chapter, therefore, surveys the literature on the historiography of the north-south divide in postinde-

pendence Sudan to assess the historical factors that contributed to the evolution of two distinct and separate identities. The last chapter in this section of the book, "An Analysis of Discourse on the Spoken and Written Words: A Historical Comparison of European and African Views," contrasts the European predilection for the written word with the African preference for the spoken word. This chapter relates to the ovrall goals of this volume by advocating a holistic approach to the language phenomenon. The author points out that it is impossible to appreciate the richness of language without appreciating its oral dimension, which "is the primary manifestation of language, even in so-called literate societies." To separate literary forms of communication from oral forms would be like separating the known from the knower.

PART III: SOCIALLY CONSTRUCTED RACIAL IDENTITIES AND THEIR CONSEQUENCES FOR TRANSCULTURALISM IN AMERICA

In Part III, we move from discussions in the international and cross-cultural contexts to those having to do with ways of socialization and their consequences for transculturalism in America. If it is true that God made only one race, the human race, then where did all the different racial identities come from? What consequences do these identities have for transcultural relations? Some scholars believe that the categorization of people by race is socially constructed. Although this phenomenon affects human beings all over the globe, it is most common in the United States. The biggest distinction made between human beings in the United States is skin color, distinguishing people along "black" and "white" color lines. Over the years, this distinction has become so inbred in the minds and hearts of North Americans that "they are uneasy categorizing people from mixed-race origins as such, but instead make comments like 'you don't look black' or 'you don't look white' " (Martin & Butler, 2001, this volume).

Although problems with racial identity and socialization have been ameliorated since the Kerner Report of the 1960s warned that the racial divide in America was creating two nations, one black and one white, the chapters in this section indicate that remnants of historical experiences between blacks and whites still exist. The chapters deal openly and authentically with the complex social problems faced by mixed-race children in America and the negative portrayals of African Americans and other non-white groups in the mass media. For example, Chapter 9, "Multiple Identities: The Case of Biracial Children," examines questions that have been avoided until now in the cross-cultural literature, for example, where do mixed-race children and adults belong in the world of European Americans, African Americans, Asian Americans, Hispanic/Latino Americans, and Native Americans? What ethnic categorization is assigned to those of a mixed-race origin?

Chapter 10, "A Culturally Based Conception of the Black Self-Concept," provides a historical context for an examination of African Americans' concept of self. It examines the role of culture in the socialization process and suggests that even within the same geographic boundaries, different historical events can lead to demonstrably different cultures, with an identifiable and distinctive influence on the way people view themselves and others. This chapter also reflects the interdisciplinary nature of the book by suggesting an interdisciplinary analytical framework for integrating theory with research about complex social problems.

In Chapter 11, "Communication and Social Scientific Discourse: Toward an Understanding of the Du Boisian Perspective," a contemporary attempt is made to address W.E.B. Du Bois's contribution to the conceptualization of race and modernity. From this perspective, the chapter recognizes social change as being rooted in the worldwide struggle to eliminate racial oppression. The chapter promotes, therefore, a framework for a progressive program of research in the 21st century. The final chapter in this section is "So-

cial Cognition and Racial Stereotyping in Television: Consequences for Transculturalism." After exploring the literature on social cognition and racial stereotyping in the television media, the author of this chapter suggests that television portrayals of African Americans can contribute to a positive or a negative impression. If negative portrayals are allowed to persist, television will continue to serve as a socializing agent that, as it shapes the way African Americans are viewed by others, discourages positive intergroup relations.

PART IV: THE TRANSFORMATIVE EFFECTS OF SOJOURNING IN DIVERSE CULTURAL ENVIRONMENTS

A common theme running through this section of the book is a concern for the lack of cross-cultural adaptation research and programs that deal realistically with issues of predisposition, preparedness, and readjustment. Some people experience problems with cross-cultural adjustment because they leave their home country with one mind-set about the host enviroment only to come face to face with a totally different reality.

For example, at least two of the editors of this book have had the experience of going to Africa for the first time with preexisting notions about the people and their culture. Almost all of what we were taught in school and in the media about Africa was so grossly distorted that no amount of short term predeparture readiness would be enough to erase the images of Africans as spear-carrying people clad in warrior outfits ready to pounce on the undeserving prospect. We left home expecting to see a continent overtaken by ignorance, disease, flawed development, and grave social disorder. We found instead a land steeped in the principles of transculturalism in its approach to people and the material and spiritual culture.

The first chapter in this section, "Intercultural Adaptation: A Stranger But Not Strange," addresses not only issues of prediposition, preparedness, and reentry but a whole host of issues African Americans face when traveling to Africa for the first time. The author points out that many African Americans confront the stereotypes they learned about African people and the continent of Africa throughout their lives in the United States. Growing up in the United States, most children never hear about the magnificence of Kemet (ancient Egypt) and the kingdoms of West Africa or the struggles of African people to rid themselves of colonial intruders.

Instead, African American children are raised learning about King Kong, King Solomon's mine, Tarzan, and Rama of the Jungle—images that grossly distort the way they see African people. This chapter brings the theories we read about in the literature on cross-cultural adaptation to real life situations. For example, the author shares the experience gained from a 6-week journey in West Africa and uses it to explain how some African Americans were able to rid themselves of the dispositions they had learned about Africa. This journey exposed the sojourning African Americans to traditional societies, villages, and modern urban centers, not the wild animals or jungles they had expected to see.

Chapter 14, "The Impact of Cultural Dynamics on the Newcomer to the Organizational Environment," examines the problems some newcomers have adapting to the cultural dynamics of foreign organizations. It explains the role of the organization in the socialization of newcomers and describes the struggles that newcomers encounter as they attempt to reconcile expectations and the realities of the new environment. How well one adapts to the dynamics of the organization determines the length of stay in that environment.

The main goal of Chapter 15, "Research and Training in Cross-Cultural Readjustment: Recommendations for Advancements," was to offer new directions in the field of readjustment. The authors explain that it was first necessary to examine the trends in the field and then divide these into two periods: (a) the earlier period, which covered studies that were done just after World War II until the 1970s; and (b) later trends, which define the current work in the field. Based on this review, several new directions for the future of cultural adjustment were proposed. These address the questions who, what, when, why, and how as they pertain to new directions in the field.

PART V: TOWARD THE FUNDAMENTALS OF TRANSCULTURAL RESEARCH

The chapters in this part of the book challenge a tradition going back, at least, to Plato, that promoted the idea of a privileged knowledge, that body of scientific knowledge which conforms to the positivistic paradigm. This paradigm is based on the premise that only mathematically quantifiable research methods can be regarded as leading to universally verifiable knowledge. However, the four chapters in this part of the book present transcultural research that recognizes other paradigms, including but not limited to subjective, objective, and functional paradigms. Chapter 16, "Toward an Ethic of Intercultural Communication Research," explores ethical issues involved in investigating the communication patterns of others. This chapter first defines research ethics and then describes ethical concerns and contributions of three research traditions or paradigms within intercultural communication scholarship: functionalist, interpretive, and critical. In addition, a conceptual framework is proposed. The philosophical intent of this framework is that if we speak *with* and *to* others instead of speaking *for* others, we would be guided in our ethics by all research traditions. Based on this framework, the chapter lists six guidelines for ethical intercultural communication research.

Chapter 17, "Afrocentric Empiricism: A Model for Communication Research in Africa," points out the functional utility of Afrocentric empiricism. It is the intent of this model to enable researchers to explore the cultural warrants embodied in the persuasive discourse patterns of Africans. Second, it helps researchers to interpret accurately unique ways in which African people think and behave; and third, it is useful to Africans, in that it can provide insight into their own experiences in a variety of contexts—the media, interpersonal relations, leadership, and gender relations. Chapter 18, "Frameworks for Assessing Contact as a Tool for Reducing Prejudice," attempts to examine more closely the contact hypothesis, which states that intergroup prejudice can be reduced if members of opposing groups will get to know each other better. Thus, program developers and policy makers could extract some frameworks for assessing the likelihood of change ensuing from particular contact situations. This chapter concludes with the notion that the effects of intergroup contact can best be anticipated and engineered when the functions of prejudices targeted for reduction are considered. The final chapter, "The Kemetic Paradigm: An Afrocentric Foundation for Rhetorical Theory," is an explication of Kemetic ideals of rhetoric and their usefulness in the construction of new theories, models, and methods of criticism that address core cosmological, epistemological, axiological, and aesthetic issues of African cultures.

▶ Summary and Use

This book is about bringing transcultural principles to a world that, seemingly, has replaced an awareness of harmony and togetherness with a spirit of collective egocentrism, materialism, and exploitation of humanity. It is our hope that the authentic discussions about different experiential and intellectual traditions will help move us closer to that center Janzen (1997) talks about. The affirmation of differences is what frees us from the limitations placed on us by culture.

The book is designed, therefore, to meet three specific needs. First, its interdisciplinary approach to theory and practice in cross-cultural relations makes it useful to several fields of study. We believe it can be used in specific courses, such as intercultural communication and international relations. A concern for social and religious issues also gives the book a more general appeal; therefore, it can be used as a supplemental text for existing tools and basic texts in human relations, psychology, anthropology, philosophy, and sociology, as well as a book for students, business, and lay people traveling abroad.

Second, because the book provides some fundamentals for transcultural research, we hope scholars will also turn to it for up-to-date information about issues of cross-cultural relations that are transcultural in nature.

Finally, whereas the book has focused mostly on African Americans, Africans, Asians, and Europeans, additional research focusing on Hispanics, Native Americans, Arab Americans, and other groups is crucial to a fuller understanding of cross-cultural relations in a transcultural world. However, as stated above, our book is only a first attempt at addressing issues in cross-cultural relations that are transcultural. The task has, therefore, just begun.

▶ References

Deng, F. (1997). *Religion, nationalism, and peace in Sudan.* Washington, DC: U.S. Institute of Peace, PeaceWatch.

Epstein, M. (1995). *After the future: The paradoxes of postmodernism and contemporary Russian culture.* Amherst: University of Massachusetts Press.

Harris, M. (1998). *Theories of culture in postmodern times.* Walnut Creek, CA: Altamira.

Janzen, R. (1997). Five paradigms of ethnic relations. In L. A. Samovar & R. E. Porter (Eds.), *Intercultural communication: A reader* (5th ed., pp. 663-670). Belmont, CA: Wadworth.

Mandela, N. (1994). *The power of acceptance: Building meaningful relationships in a judgmental world* (Inaugural speech). North Hollywood, CA: Newcastle.

Rogers, E. M. (1986). *Perspectives on development communication*. Paper presented at the workshop, Communication Development, Pune University, Pune, India.

Samovar, L. A., & Porter, R. E. (Eds). (1994). *Intercultural communication: A reader* (7th ed.). Belmont, CA: Wadsworth.

Shames, G. W. (1997). *Transcultural odysseys: The evolving global consciousness*. Yarmouth, ME: Intercultural Press.

Xing Lu. (1998). *Rhetoric in ancient China, fifth to third century BCE: A comparison with classical Greek rhetoric*. Columbia: University of South Carolina Press.

Part I

Transcultural Issues in
International and
Cross-Cultural Contexts

Perspectives on Human Communication

Implications for Transculture Theory

MIN-SUN KIM

A fundamental problem in American communication research is that it takes as universal what is essentially a culture-specific phenomenon. Individualistic values are characteristic of U.S. society, and so these are reflected in ethnocentric human communication theories. If we are going to get any further in our understanding of universal and less culture-bound human communication, we must first examine the metaphors and values generating our research. I am writing this manuscript to investigate ways that traditional studies on human communication have centered around Western independent self-orientations and to bring transcultural perspectives to scholarly analyses of human communication.

The study of human communication from a transcultural perspective is of great pragmatic importance for both the individual and society. The current content centers on reflections on selfhood and the cultural conceptions of self in which human communication theories are anchored. The extent to which individualists and collectivists differ in the way they conceive of themselves and others is just beginning to be studied empirically in relation to communication styles. This has consequences both for the ways in which we do research and for our interpersonal interactions with others. In light of the inherent limitations or myopia contained in any single theoretical perspective, a premium is to be placed on theoretical multiplicity. Any theory that has gained preeminence, any ideology that is pervasive throughout the culture, any normative assumptions about social life pose a threat to the understanding of human communication.

NOTE: The material in this chapter was previously presented at the 1999 International Communication Association and was selected as the Top Paper of the Conference Theme session.

3

In recent years, social scientists have become increasingly sensitive to the ways in which their pursuit of knowledge is influenced by their cultural surrounds (e.g., Kagitcibasi, 1996). Researchers can be vitally influenced by the normative assumptions and value investments of the culture in which they participate (Gergen, 1979). Because researchers participate in the presumptive base on which the meaning of scientific conduct is premised, it is difficult for them to forge a body of knowledge independent of this base. Consideration of the linkage between scientific conduct and cultural context raises questions of profound importance. In what specific ways and to what extent do evaluative investments hinder the quest for objective understanding? And what particular influences have shaped what passes for knowledge in present-day communication research?

Most of what is known about the nature and effects of communication variables—at least in Western cultures—is based on the unspoken assumption that people construe themselves in a relatively independent way. Thus, so-called laws or rules of human communication may not apply (or may take a different form) in cultures in which people view themselves as more interdependent. This is a vital issue, considering the following prediction: By the year 2020, racial and ethnic minorities will constitute the majority population of the United States (Sue, Arredondo, & McDavis, 1992). With the advent of multiculturalism as the "fourth force" within the United States (Pedersen, 1991), there has been an increased emphasis on alternative conceptual systems.

The study of human communication in alternative cultural perspectives reveals how cultural frameworks powerfully structure both everyday and scientific understandings. Although a diverse group of European, American, and Asian theorists (e.g., Bond, 1986; Buss, 1979; Ho, 1976; Sampson, 1988) have found fault with the individualist model of self and its ability to reflect and account for social behavior, for the most part, this critique has gone unheeded in theoretical and empirical analyses of communication behavior. This chapter highlights the cultural relativity of social sciences as applied to human communication.

There is little doubt that the individualistic notion of self has been embraced by mainstream human communication research. A fact that appears to be self-evident, or "natural," is not questioned. The acceptance of this normative base for a broad range of social science has made possible the claim of a value-free science. For instance, Kim and Sharkey (1995) noted that, consistent with the continuing emphasis on white male norms in organizational communication, American writers have traditionally defined miscommunication in organizations as failure to be understood; to be authentic, honest, and disclosive; and to establish an open and clear dialogue. The study of human communication has developed within a European American cultural framework; and not surprisingly, it incorporates a web of tacit understandings and implicit assumptions that are shared by researchers. The shared notions include a blend of normative beliefs and moral prescriptions about human nature that are, for the most part, so obvious and taken for granted they are almost never spelled out (see Markus & Kitayama, 1998).

At the outset, we will note the close connection between normative assumptions within the culture and the construction of communication theories. Although all communication occurs in cultural contexts, only a small portion of human communication research attends to this. The preponderance of contemporary human communication research is still designed, conducted, and interpreted as if culture did not matter. Furthermore, constructs developed in interpersonal communication are sometimes blindly adopted in researching intercultural communication.

This chapter hopes to mark the coming of age of an endeavor to internationalize, in a transcultural sense, what was once a narrow Euro-American discipline. Unless an international dimension is introduced, American communication research may remain blind to its culture-bound assumptions and limitations. A similar point was made in social psychology by Berry (1978), who warned that the discipline is so culture bound and culture blind that, as it stands now, it should not be employed in cultures outside the United States. Clearly, the felt need to expand the international dimension of human communication is spreading. I hope that this chapter will help alert mainstream communication researchers of the need to examine communication phenomena across a diverse array of ethnicities within as well as outside the United States. If communication theories are to transcend culture, they must first address culture.

First, we will compare European American models of independence with East Asian models of interdependence, contrasting two very different conceptions of the self and social behavior. We will discuss the ideas of personhood that contemporary Western researchers inevitably bring to their understanding of human communication. Then, we will deal theoretically with individualistic notions of self and question some well-accepted Western theories of human communication. Finally, we will explore several unfortunate effects of this influence and discuss ways to rechannel attempts at unbiased understanding of human communication. Specifically, we will explore how the commonly accepted view of communication theories in the Western model can be modified to engender transcultural perspectives.

▶ The Content of Self in Different Cultures: Independent and Interdependent Self-Construals

The discovery that many social science findings were culturally specific led researchers to argue that culture should be incorporated as a parameter in communication theories (Kim, 1999; Kim & Leung, 2000). What has become apparent is that the European Ameri-

can view of the self and its relation to the collective is only one view. There are other equally powerful but strikingly different collective notions about the self and its relation to the collective. At the very heart of the concept *culture* is the expectation that different people will possess different values, beliefs, and motives reflected in numerous behaviors. Travelers to foreign lands detect these variations quickly, sensing that they are viewing not only different lifestyles but also different attitudes toward life itself (Segall, 1986). A key meaning that distinguishes cultures is the meaning they assign to being a person. Anthropologists, and more recently psychologists (Geertz, 1973; Markus & Kitayama, 1991, 1998), have argued that cultural groups diverge in their understandings of selfhood and personhood.

The ways of being a person are patterned according to the means and practices of a given cultural community, and communities are maintained by these ways of being in the world. Each person is embedded within a variety of sociocultural contexts or cultures (e.g., country, ethnicity, religion, gender, family, etc). Each of these cultural contexts makes some claim on the person and is associated with a set of ideas and practices (i.e., a cultural framework) about how to be a "good" person (Markus & Kitayama, 1998). In describing the culture-specific nature of self, Markus, Mullally, and Kitayama (1997) suggest that cultural and social groups in every historical period have been associated with characteristic patterns of sociocultural participation or, more specifically, with characteristic ways of being a person in the world. They call these characteristic patterns of sociocultural participation *selfways*. The self, then, is an organized locus of the various, sometimes competing understandings of how to be a person, and it functions as an individualized orienting, mediating, and interpretive framework giving shape to what people notice and think about, to what they are motivated to do, and (the focus of this chapter) to how they communicate with others.

In a related finding, self-concepts are the mental representations of those personal qualities used by individuals for the purpose of defining themselves and regulating their behavior (Niedenthal & Beike, 1997). Self-concepts are thought to contain information about the characteristic features of the self in specific situations, temporal contexts, and moods, as well as the relations among the features (Niedenthal & Beike, 1997). Views of the acquisition and structure of self-concepts, however, are based in two philosophical positions. The two positions give different emphasis to the idea that concepts of self derive meaning through relationships with other people. That is, some theorists have argued that identity develops from social relationships and that relationships with others actually constitute identity, whereas other theorists suggest that identity develops as the individual separates from primary relationships and that features and experiences unique to him or her constitute identity.

How do we live with the powerful pulls between the experiences of relatedness and autonomy, connection and separateness? This is not a question about theory only; it speaks to deeply rooted sensibilities regarding what it means to exist as a human being. What it means to be a person is, of course, construed very differently in contemporary Western and Asian cultures. It is crucial, therefore, to pay attention to the cultural assumptions that underlie theories on human communication, which will be discussed throughout this chapter. By understanding the different ways in which different cultures construct the person as connected or separate, we can better understand the limitations of using various theories as a resource.

Recently, Markus and Kitayama (1991) delineated two general *cultural self-schemata* (independent and interdependent). These two images of self were originally conceptualized as reflecting the emphasis on connectedness and relations often found in non-Western cultures (interdependent self) and the separatedness and uniqueness of the individual (inde-

pendent self) stressed in the West. In the independent construal, most representations of the self (i.e., the ways in which an individual thinks of himself or herself) have as their referent an individual's ability, characteristic, attribute, or goal (I am friendly or I am ambitious). These inner characteristics or traits are the primary regulators of behavior. This view of the self derives from a belief in the wholeness and uniqueness of each person's configuration of internal attributes (Johnson, 1985). The normative imperative of such cultures is to become independent of others and to discover and express one's own unique attributes. Thus, the goal of people in such cultures is to "stand out" and to express their own unique internal characteristics or traits. This orientation has led to an emphasis on the need to pursue personal self-actualization or self-development. Individual weakness, in this cultural perspective, is to be overly dependent on others or to be unassertive (Bellah, Madsen, Sullivan, Swidler, & Tipton, 1985). This perspective is rooted in Western philosophical tradition and is linked to a Cartesian view in which the goal of existence is to objectify the self. According to Lebra (1992), the ontological goal of this perspective is to highlight the division between the experiencer and what is experienced, in other words, to separate the individual from the context.

By contrast, in the interdependent construal, the self is connected to others; the principal components of the self are relationships to others (Markus & Kitayama, 1991). This is not to say that the person with an interdependent view of the self has no conception of internal traits, characteristics, or preferences that are unique to him or her, but rather that these internal, private aspects of the self are not primary forces in directing or guiding behavior. Instead, behavior is more significantly regulated by a desire to maintain harmony and appropriateness in relationships. Within such a construal, the self becomes most meaningful and complete when it is cast in the appropriate social relationship. So a person's behavior in a given situation may be a function more of the needs, wishes, and preferences of others than of his or her own needs, wishes, or preferences. Following this interdependent construal of the self, a person may attempt to meet the needs of others and to promote the others' goals. Weakness, in this perspective, is to be headstrong, unwilling to accommodate to the needs of others, or self-centered (Cross & Markus, 1991). According to Lebra (1992), this interdependent view of self can be traced to Buddhist philosophical traditions, within which the very goal of existence is different from the goal assumed in the West. From this view, the core notion is not "objectify the self" but to submerge the self and "gain freedom from the self." The emphasis is on downplaying the division between the experiencer and the object of experience, and connection with, rather than separation from, others and the surrounding context is highlighted.

Cultural differences in self-construal have been well established by recent studies (Gudykunst et al., 1996; Kashima et al., 1995; Kim et al., 1996). Singelis (1994; Singelis & Brown, 1995) developed a measure that taps the independent and interdependent dimensions of the self and found in Hawaii that participants of Asian background were both more interdependent and less independent relative to those with a European background. Similarly, Bochner (1994) found that Malaysian self-construals were more interdependent and less independent than Australian and British self-construals. Recent studies (Kim et al., 1996; Kim & Sharkey, 1995; Kim, Sharkey, & Singelis, 1994) also show that the degree of independent and interdependent construal of self systematically affects the perceived importance of conversational constraints (Kim, 1993, 1995) within a culture as well as across different cultural groups.

Much more could be said about these apparently startling differences in ontological emphasis (see Lebra, 1992; Markus & Kitayama, 1991, for extended discussions of these differences). But our purpose is to underscore that these ways of being are significant elements of the cultural frame, forming the framework for individual experience of communication behavior.

▶ **Cultural Relativity of Communication Constructs: Individualistic Biases on Conceptualizations of Human Communication**

Many of the findings currently regarded as "basic" to human communication may be a function of particular cultural frameworks that are unseen and unexamined because they are shared by investigators and subjects alike. Scientific theories, concepts, categories, and models are based on studies that are designed, conducted, and interpreted with reference to a very particular framework. Communication researchers often disregard the cultural frameworks that are limiting conditions for their results—sometimes tacitly assuming that the social forms and communicative practices of the modern West are representative of the human species. Consequently, most theories of human communication reflect and incorporate a vast set of cultural meanings and practices that are nearly invisible from within its own subculture. In this section, we will review literature that shows dramatic divergence in psychological functioning and communicative behavior between independent and interdependent selves. The distinction between the independent and interdependent modes of cultural participation serves as an initial framework within which many cross-cultural differences in communication behaviors can be understood; it is also a heuristic device to point out the cultural relativity of theories.

PREDISPOSITIONS TOWARD VERBAL COMMUNICATION: COMMUNICATION APPREHENSION AND ASSERTIVENESS

Predispositions toward certain kinds of communication have been a central focus of theory-building efforts in communication for almost three decades. The importance attached to studying communication from this perspective is understandable, given that communication traits and predispositions have been found to account for significant variance in both observed communication behavior and communication-based perceptions (Infante & Rancer, 1996; McCroskey, 1977; Rubin & Rubin, 1992).

Although the constructs associated with each of these labels differ in emphasis, the general thrust of all is the differing proclivity of people to participate in and enjoy, or avoid and fear, social interaction. In their review of the major trends of social-communicative anxiety and related constructs, Daly and Stafford (1984) found considerable evidence suggesting that, by and large, the many different constructs within this area tap a single broad disposition. The average correlation among the various constructs tapping avoidant communication predisposition is relatively high (Kelly, 1982).

Perhaps the most striking feature of the body of research based on the communication apprehension framework is that the outcomes of communication apprehension and avoidance are solely negative. Researchers have found that individuals who are low in emotional maturity, adventurousness, self-control, self-esteem, and tolerance for ambiguity are more inclined to exhibit communication apprehension (McCroskey, Richmond, Daly, & Falcione, 1977). Individuals with high levels of communication apprehension are perceived as less competent, less attractive, less sociable, and less composed than those with lower levels (McCroskey, Daly, Richmond, & Cox, 1975).

Needless to say, the picture of the person with a high level of communication avoidance that emerges from prior studies generally is a negative one. Such a person might be described typically as an introverted individual who lacks self-esteem and is resistant to change, has a low tolerance for ambiguity, and is lacking in self-control and emotional maturity. People at the other end of the communi-

cation apprehension continuum, on the other hand, might be described as typically adventurous, extroverted, confident, emotionally mature individuals with high self-esteem, tolerance for ambiguity, people willing or even eager to accept change in their environment. Based on profiles such as these, many hypotheses have been tested concerning the behaviors and attitudes of people with different levels of communication apprehension and of other people's perceptions of such individuals (see McCroskey, 1977).

On the other hand, assertiveness (representing approach communication motivation) is defined as behaviors that enable people to act in their best interest, to stand up for themselves without undue anxiety, and to express their rights without denying the rights of others (Alberti & Emmons, 1970). At least within the U.S. context, assertiveness has been viewed as a measure of social competence or as an indicator of interpersonal communication competence. Assertive behaviors are perceived as more competent and attractive than unassertive behaviors in the United States (Cook & St. Lawrence, 1990; Henderson & Furnham, 1982).

A consistent personality profile of assertive and nonassertive individuals has emerged in the literature. Assertive behavior is said to be characteristic of individuals who stand up for their rights and are able to express their thoughts, feelings, and beliefs freely, directly, and honestly. Nonassertive people are characterized, on the other hand, as inhibited, submissive, self-deprecating, self-denying, and conforming. Research showed differences in personality profiles, with assertive people, in comparison to nonassertive ones, being more gregarious, adaptable, sensitive, and rational; less subservient, defensive, and self-protecting; more extroverted and less anxious (Ramanaiah & Deniston, 1993).

It would be imprudent to generalize the description of high versus low argumentative individuals (based on studies using subjects from the United States) to people belonging to other cultures. The outcome and perceptions of verbal communication motivation (e.g., assertiveness and communication apprehension) are mostly based on research involving predominantly Anglo-Saxon subjects in the United States whose self-identity is autonomous and bounded. Numerous scholars have noted the propensity for the Western cultural value of individualism to shape theorists' view of psychological functioning (see Gilligan, 1982; Markus & Kitayama, 1991, 1994; Sampson, 1988; Sharkey & Singelis, 1995). If one assumes that the individual should be a bounded, autonomous, self-sufficient social unit independent of others, then nonassertiveness and shyness become deficiencies. Rather than viewing communication avoidance as a personal deficiency, it is possible to view it as a sensitivity to the social context.

Low motivations for verbal communication may stem from two sources: (a) the strength of a person's idealized role identity (as bounded and separate) in interaction and (b) the person's sensitivity to others' evaluations as the interaction unfolds, depending on the degree to which his or her identity is entwined with and dependent on others. Traditionally, communication anxiety or reticence has been attributed to a weak sense of the independent self. Thus, individuals are thought to have an unstable or uncertain sense of their own role identity as bounded and separate from others. This fragile sense of role identity is inherently vulnerable to threats during interaction, which causes communication anxiety. Hypersensitivity to evaluation is related to an uncertain sense of self and the accompanying fear of negative evaluations. This represents the deficit model of verbal communication avoidance (Kim, 1999).

A second way in which a person's social role is threatened also involves others' evaluations. In this case, however, rather than arising from insecurity about the idealized role identity as an independent self during an interaction, a sensitivity to evaluations can result from a more generalized sensitivity to social context. All else being equal, people who are closely in touch with the social identity that surrounds them will be more anxious because

their perceptions of what takes place in the social context are particularly salient. A generalized sensitivity to others' evaluations and "fitting in" is one of the central characteristics of the interdependent self.

The deficit view is ethnocentric in its conceptualization of the self as a bounded, independent, and autonomous entity. Assertiveness is generally linked to healthy personality adjustment in Western psychology, but there is a danger in assuming that nonassertiveness is maladaptive. From the interdependent standpoint, people are expected to defer to authority and are actively discouraged from asserting themselves as individuals. It is likely that high interdependents tend to discourage aggressive communication, regardless of its locus of attack, because it is regarded as negative and disruptive behavior. Accordingly, people of high interdependent self-construals may want to avoid aggressive forms of communication and may feel anxious if they have to be aggressive in communication situations. Although we agree that extreme forms of communication avoidance and lack of verbal assertiveness can be a handicap in any culture, we are critical of the ethnocentric preoccupation with the single Western view of the self that sees sensitivity to social contexts and "fitting in" orientations as a deficit (see Kim, 1999, for further discussion on this issue).

CONFLICT MANAGEMENT STYLES

Some of the most severe problems in intercultural relations arise as a consequence of interpersonal conflicts. Understanding the ways in which people from different cultures approach resolving conflicts is, therefore, of great importance. Researchers have attempted to describe and understand the differences in conflict handling among cultures (e.g., Chua & Gudykunst, 1987; Kim & Hunter, 1995; Lee & Rogan, 1991; Ting-Toomey et al., 1991).

Popular conflict management scales (e.g., Rahim, 1983; Thomas & Kilmann, 1978) rely heavily on Blake and Mouton's (1964) conceptualization of conflict management, which yields a five-style configuration based on self versus other concern. Although researchers vary in their terms, they generally assume a two-dimensional scheme. Regardless of whether one assumes five styles (Rahim, 1983; Thomas & Kilmann, 1978); four styles, leaving out compromise (e.g., Pruitt & Rubin, 1986); or three styles (Putnam & Wilson, 1982; Sillars, 1980), the categorization is still influenced by the two assumed dimensions. Conflict styles based on the two assumed dimensions have been frequently adopted by communication researchers (Brown, Yelsma, & Keller, 1981; Chua & Gudykunst, 1987; Sillars, 1980; Ting-Toomey, 1988; Trubisky, Ting-Toomey, & Lin, 1991).

Several other models also assume two dimensions: Hall (1986) distinguishes between *concern for personal goals* and *concern for relationships.* Pruitt and Rubin (1986) also characterize the dimensions in terms of *concern for one's own outcome* and *concern for the other's outcome.* Thomas (1976) interprets the five-category scheme as combining two independent dimensions: *cooperation,* or attempting to satisfy the other party's concerns, and *assertiveness,* or attempting to satisfy one's own concerns. Brown et al. (1981) propose two dimensions for distinguishing conflict styles: *feelings,* positive or negative; and *task energy,* high expenditure or low expenditure. Similarly, conflict styles are broken down into two dimensions of assertiveness and cooperativeness (Chusmir & Mills, 1989). Assertiveness involves the desire to fulfill the needs of the individual resolving conflict. The cooperativeness dimension involves fulfilling the needs of others.

The models relying on Blake and Mouton's (1964) work conceptualize avoiding (or withdrawal style) as negative and/or destructive. According to Rahim (1983), avoiding styles reflect "low concern for self" and "low concern for others." Putnam and Wilson (1982) also consider avoidance or nonconfrontation as a "lose-lose" style. Thomas (1976) interprets avoiding as unassertive and uncooperative. Brown et al. (1981) claimed that with-

drawing action means negative feelings and low task energy. The flavor of these scales is that confrontation is more desirable than avoidance. Nicotera (1993) highlights possible logical flaws in existing taxonomic structures of conflict strategies. In the three-dimension model (other's view, own view, and emotional/relational valence) inductively derived from the data set, Nicotera (1993), for instance, distinguishes evasive response (which is not disruptive to personal relations) from estranged response (which is disruptive to personal relations).

Traditionally, within the U.S. context, it has been argued that "covert, or hidden, conflict also is destructive in that it leaves issues unresolved and may result in psychological and/or physical estrangement" (Comstock & Buller, 1991, p. 48). Galvin and Brommel (1986) claim that most conflict when avoided leaves nagging tensions unresolved, creates a climate ripe for future overt destructive conflict, and fosters separation among family members. Furthermore, it has been argued that when people use integrative conflict strategies, constructive outcomes result, whereas use of avoidance strategies results in destructive outcomes (see Comstock & Buller, 1991). According to Filley and House (1969), in the lose-lose conflict situation, people are more likely to employ avoidance techniques rather than personally confront the other party. In dealing with children's conflict resolution skills, Bryant (1992) claimed that both anger/retaliation and withdrawal/avoidance are potentially disruptive to social relationships.

Likewise, the work in this area has been biased by the individualistic assumption that confrontation is more desirable than avoidance, which limits a full understanding of the conflict phenomenon. Hsieh, Shybut, and Lotsof (1969) captured the essence of the individualistic ideology in describing mainstream American culture as a culture that emphasizes the uniqueness, independence, and self-reliance of each individual. Among other things, American culture places a high value on the ideology of openness in conflict resolution. Given the general assumption of the desirability of direct confrontation in conflicts, it is not surprising that researchers have conceptualized avoidance styles as reflecting low concern for self as well as low concern for the other. This assumption is taken so much for granted in individualistic cultures that it has rarely been stated explicitly. Similarly, some researchers, while considering argument (direct confrontation of the matter) as a beneficial and prosocial mode of conflict resolution, view avoidance as less socially acceptable (e.g., Infante, Trebing, Shepherd, & Seeds, 1984; Rancer, Baukus, & Infante, 1985). Because of the individualistic bias, researchers have overlooked the potentially positive attributes of conflict avoidance and suppression. Furthermore, they have ignored the dialectic between conflict avoidance and confrontation and the complexity of avoidance as a conflict management strategy (see Kim & Leung, 2000, for further discussion on this issue).

Blake and Mouton's (1964) two-dimensional framework has been accepted among cross-cultural conflict theorists without due caution; these researchers invariably cite the framework as the basis for their own work. Avoidance of conflict can help individuals to control emotion; at times, it may also allow the passive expression of discontentment without the dangers of a direct challenge. Just as messages of silence (extreme forms of indirectness) might be evaluated differently within different relationship contexts (see Tannen, 1985), avoidance (or withdrawal) strategies can be seen as positive or negative by members of different cultural orientations (as it is measured against what is expected in that context). In individualistic contexts, a "demand to interact" seems often to characterize dyadic communication—a built-in assumption that when people are engaged in focused conversation, it is their responsibility to keep verbal communication active. Avoidant conflict styles might, at times, represent a threat to this responsibility. Specifically, avoidance of conflicts among interdependents can be seen as negative politeness—being nice to others by not imposing. On the other

hand, avoidance among independents may be seen as the failure of positive politeness—the need to be involved with others. Among high interdependents with heightened sense of other's face concerns, there will be efforts to minimize antagonisms that unsettle the groups or that place the individual in confrontation with the group.

In sum, we suggest that interdependents may be less openly assertive and emotional in conflict situations due to their heightened sensitivity to others' face needs. Thus, these views naturally lead to the adoption of high compromising and avoiding behaviors and a relatively low preference for competing and assertive postures. Avoiding and compromising styles may serve to dilute antagonisms that might otherwise surface in the immediate situation. The fear of shame as a result of damaging or ruffling the social fabric or damaging someone else's face would also lead interdependents to avoid assertive or direct styles of handling conflicts. These arguments all suggest a likely preference among high interdependents for saving the other's face in conflict management. It may seem better to avoid the possibility of causing the other to lose face by engaging in avoidance behavior.

In sum, whereas past literature in interpersonal and organizational conflict tends to conceptualize the avoidance style as reflecting both low concern for self and low concern for the other, the use of an avoiding style in collectivistic cultures seems to be associated positively with the other-face concern dimension (see Kim & Hunter, 1995; Ting-Toomey, 1988). Such validity problems indicate that the dimensions used to conceptualize and operationalize styles in the U.S. context may not be the generative mechanisms of behavioral choices in different cultures.

COGNITIVE CONSISTENCY: A CULTURAL ASSUMPTION?

One of the powerful motives assumed to fuel the behavior of Westerners is the need to avoid or reduce cognitive conflict or dissonance. The idea that people are motivated toward a resolution of cognitive consistencies has a long and respectable history in social psychology and communication. Although the tendency toward cognitive consistency is often described as a marker of human rationality and therefore has been expected to be widespread or even universal, a cultural perspective suggests that social psychological notions of consistency may be more or less culturally relative.

Cognitive dissonance theory postulates the need for intrapersonally uniform or consistent states. However, a person may accept and tolerate dissonance as natural. Then, one needs to question the basic notion of a need or drive for consonance, a need being postulated as a part of human nature. This question was not asked because the whole research tradition on cognitive dissonance is anchored in an implicit idea of human nature. These implicit assumptions, which are presupposed, can be found in all social scientific theories. They delimit the type of theoretical conceptualization one can achieve.

A predominant feature of the self in European American contexts is the persistent need for consistency and stability. Empirical research on the self reveals that evidence of malleability or variability in the self is often downplayed or actively discouraged. The psychological tendency toward consistency is extremely robust and well-documented and has been discussed as a universal human motive (Markus et al., 1997). The desire for a consistent self is tied to the notion that the self, by cultural definition, is whole, stable, and integrated rather than fragmented and distributed. Furthermore, it is held that individuals should not be bound to particular situations and that personal attributes should transcend particular interpersonal relationships. Doi (1986) has argued that Americans are decidedly more concerned with consistency between feelings and actions than the Japanese. In Japan, there is a virtue in controlling the expression of one's innermost feelings; no virtue accrues from expressing them.

Markus and Kitayama (1991) maintain that different psychological processes are often observed between cultures because pronounced cultural differences exist in the way that the self is typically construed. Because the identity of the independent self rests on a foundation of internal attributes, such as an individual's attitudes and opinions, any dissonance that is experienced involving these attributes is likely to be directed to the core of the self (Heine & Lehman, 1997b). Viewing one's attitudes as inconsistent with one's behaviors, or one's decisions as unsound, then, may pose a significant threat to independent individuals' self-integrity. Such inconsistencies are not likely to be easily compromised, and individuals should be motivated to go to great lengths to reduce the dissonance (Markus & Kitayama, 1991).

In contrast, the core of the identity of the interdependent self lies more within the individual's roles, positions, and relationships. Internal attributes are patently less relevant to identity for such people. Hence, inconsistencies between their attitudes, or thoughts that they may have made a poor decision, are likely to be relatively tangential to self-identity for interdependent types. Thus, interdependents should be less perturbed when their behavior does not follow from a particular belief and therefore might not show the standard cognitive dissonance effects. A recent study by Heine and Lehman (1997b) has provided initial support for such a possibility by using a free-choice paradigm of cognitive consistency. Respondents were given a choice between two equally attractive CDs. After such a choice, some inconsistencies are likely to arise because the chosen CD may have certain negative features, whereas the unchosen CD may have certain desirable features. Hence, there should arise a motivation to eliminate such a dissonant state by changing some of the cognitions involved. Like countless other investigators, Heine and Lehman found that among their North American participants, there was a considerable "spread" of preference after the choice, such that liking for the chosen CD increased and liking for the unchosen CD decreased. However, the comparable effect was not found among the Japanese respondents. This result supports the idea that the requirement of internal consistency may be much weaker for people operating with an interdependent model of the self than for people operating with an independent model of the self.

ATTITUDE-BEHAVIOR CONSISTENCY

The concept of attitude, typically viewed as a stable underlying disposition, has played a central role in explaining communication phenomena, particularly the effects of persuasive messages. Most research in the area of persuasion has centered around attempts to change attitudes toward some object or target, seeking to build theories that accurately explain and predict patterns of complex communication behaviors. Underlying these efforts has been the implicit assumption that behavior toward the object will change automatically with the attitude. Evidence has not always supported this assumption, however, and the difficulty of finding a strong, predictive relationship between attitudes and behavioral tendencies has turned into one of the greatest controversies in the social sciences (Fishbein & Ajzen, 1975; Kim & Hunter, 1993a, 1993b).

Scholars have widely debated the relationship between attitudes and overt behavior. Most researchers on attitudes-behavior consistency lament that in their career, they tackle a messy world in which the same people will make different utterances under different conditions and will behave differently in different situations and will say one thing while doing another (Deutscher, 1966). As early as 1966, Deutscher wrote, "We still do not know much about the relationship between what people say and what they do—attitudes and behavior, sentiments and acts, verbalizations and interactions, words and deeds" (p. 242). Under what conditions will people behave as they talk? Under what conditions is there no relationship? And under what conditions do they say one thing and behave exactly the opposite?

Models of the self and the collective could provide an alternative view of one of psychology's oldest problems—the inconsistency between attitudes and behaviors. From an interdependent perspective, such inconsistencies do not have to be framed negatively and do not have to give rise to great theoretical consternation. Interdependent selves do not prescribe or require consistency between their internal attributes and their actions. In fact, such consistency may reflect not authenticity but a lack of flexibility; it may be interpreted as rigidity or even immaturity (Markus & Kitayama, 1994).

Iwao (1988) offers some suggestive evidence that people in interdependent cultures often sacrifice consistency for the sake of interpersonal accommodation. Iwao asked American and Japanese respondents what they would prefer to do when confronted by various disagreements—try to change the other person's view, change their own view, or feign agreement. Americans preferred to try to change the other person's view more than did Japanese, whereas Japanese were much more likely to prefer to feign agreement. The latter type of behavior among Japanese might seem hypocritical to holders of the independent view of the self, because the Japanese prefer to behave in ways that differ from what they "truly" believe. Given the interdependent view, however, maintaining a good relationship may be much more important than attempting to settle the disagreement, so it would be uncouth and insensitive to contradict or argue (Fiske, Kitayama, Markus, & Nisbett, 1998).

In Japan, there is a virtue in controlling the expression of one's innermost feelings; no virtue accrues from expressing them. Doi (1986) discusses the difference between the Japanese public self and private self. He suggests that in the United States, it is extremely important for these two selves to remain consistent. When the public self deviates from the private self, an individual is considered a hypocrite. In Japan, being polite and maintaining harmony are what is important. An individual's actual feelings about an action are unimportant (Doi, 1986; Triandis, 1989).

Interdependent selves may not prescribe or require such a consistency between their internal atributes and their actions. Consequently, consistency should be much less important and much less bemoaned when not observed. In fact, consistency from an interdependent perspective may reflect a lack of flexibility, insensitivity to the context, rigidity, or immaturity (Markus & Kitayama, 1991). Many American children are also socialized to be "true to themselves" and to stick by their convictions or principles. To do otherwise would be to risk inconsistency and inauthenticity. The desire for a consistent self is tied to the notion that the healthy self is naturally and properly whole, stable, integrated, and consistent (not a contextual or "dividual" person) (Fiske et al., 1998). It is the individuals' roles, statuses, or positions, along with the commitments, obligations, and responsibility they confer, that are the constituents of the self, and in that sense, they are self-defining. One's internal attributes (e.g., private attitudes or opinions) are not regarded as the significant attributes of the self. Furthermore, one's private feelings are to be regulated in accordance with the requirements of the situation. Restraint over the inner self is assigned a much higher value than is expression of the inner self (Markus & Kitayama, 1991).

Cultures that emphasize the importance of the individual place great value on the expression of personal desires and the pursuit of personal goals. In such cultures, people will regard it as hypocritical to fail to act in accord with personal attitudes—despite possible damage to personal relationships. To accommodate others may seem to involve giving in to external constraints and failing to be true to oneself. In line with this possibility, Kashima, Siegel, Tanaka, and Kashima (1992) examined the strength of the belief that attitudes are normally consistent with behaviors and found that this view is much more strongly held among Australians than among Japanese. For interdependent individuals, it may be regarded as selfish, immature, or disloyal to act in accord with personal attitudes or even to express such attitudes if doing so conflicts with the maintenance of a smooth social equilibrium (Fiske et al., 1998).

GROUP CONFORMITY: SUBMISSION OR TACTFULNESS?

Social scientists have long been interested in social influence and conformity. The body of experimental research in this area has spanned more than half a century, dating back to Sherif's (1935) pioneering research on the autokinetic effect. Over this time, researchers have established that a wide range of personality and situational variables affect conformity.

It has been widely discussed that some national groups are stereotyped as conforming and passive whereas other groups are viewed as independent and assertive (e.g., Peabody, 1985). Asch (1952), who conducted seminal research on conformity to group pressure, considered a conformist one who "has failed to develop (or has lost) the possibility of independence" (p. 451). He also felt that conformity can "pollute" the social process and that it is important for a society to foster values of independence in its citizens. The lack of understanding about possibly different values placed on conformity would lead one to misunderstand or misinterpret others' behavior. Understanding why and in what situations certain characteristics of people conform will be certainly an essential requirement for successful intercultural interactions. For instance, if a theorist accepts the notion that the self is constantly striving to defend itself from the collective, then influence by others is viewed as a weakness or a failure. Yet, from the perspective of a model that acknowledges interdependence between the self and the collective, social influence, acknowledgment of others, and the inhibition of private thoughts or feelings, even yielding to others, can be framed quite differently. Such actions can be construed as essential, positive, and mature (see Azuma, 1986).

The cultural conditions underpinning conformity have been a long-standing concern and are important for theories of social influence. Yet, cultural aspects of conformity have been relatively neglected, and only three previous reviews exist (Bond & Smith, 1996; Furnham, 1984; Mann, 1988). Recently, Bond and Smith (1996) conducted a meta-analysis on cross-cultural studies on conformity. They included only studies that used the "Asch-type" line-judgment task, in which participants are asked to name which of three lines is the same length as a standard. They collected a total of 68 reports involving 133 separate experiments with a total of 4,627 participants. Analyses using measures of cultural values derived from Hofstede (1980), Schwartz (1994), and Trompenaars (1993) revealed significant relationships confirming the general hypothesis that conformity would be higher in collectivist cultures than in individualistic cultures. That all three sets of measures gave similar results, despite differences in the samples and instruments used, provides strong support for the hypothesis. In general, people from collectivistic cultures tend to conform more to group pressure than their counterparts from individualistic cultures. They conclude that cultural values are significant mediators of response in group-pressure experiments.

Bond and Smith (1996), however, argue that whereas the method appears a reliable means of assessing responsiveness to group pressure across cultures, it is questionable whether that behavior is always best described as conformity, given the negative connotations of that work, such as yielding, submissive, and so forth. They note that such connotations stem from Western values that stress the importance of self-expression, of stating one's opinion in the face of disagreement with others. In other cultures, however, harmony with others may be valued more highly; agreeing in public while privately disagreeing may be regarded, for example, as a proper display of tact or sensitivity. Viewed from this perspective, conformity in the Asch

(1952) paradigm may be better described as tactfulness or social sensitivity, whereas independence would be seen as tactlessness or insensitivity. Thus, the Asch paradigm may be a fair way of assessing across cultures how people respond to a discrepant group judgment, but its description as conformity may not be cross-culturally appropriate.

Selves, as well as theories of selves that have been constructed within a European American cultural frame, show the influence of one powerful notion—the idea that people are independent, bounded, autonomous entities who must strive to remain unshackled by influences from various groups and collectives (Markus & Kitayama, 1994). This individualist ideal occasions a desire not to be defined by others and a deep-seated wariness, in some instances even a fear, of the influence of the generalized other, of the social, and of the collective (Markus & Kitayama, 1994). From the perspective of an independent self, there is an abiding concern that the social group will somehow overwhelm or disempower the autonomous, agentic self. Social conformity is often presented as being a troublesome aspect of social behavior, in opposition to individual behavior, and as compromising an individual's rights and preferences (Markus & Kitayama, 1994). But many other cultures—indeed, most cultures—place a higher value on interdependence and fostering empathic connections with others. In these cultures, people may gladly emulate their associates and may be responsive to others' wishes to sustain smooth social relationships (see Fiske et al., 1998). Thus, conformity may not reflect an inability to resist social pressure and to stick to one's own perceptions, attitudes, and beliefs (the defining features of the self). Instead, conformity to particular others with whom the other is interdependent can be a highly valued end state. It may signify a willingness to be responsive to others and to adjust one's own demands and desires so as to maintain the ever-important relation.

Indeed, in Japan, giving in to another is typically not a sign of weakness; rather, it can reflect tolerance, self-control, and maturity

(Markus & Kitayama 1994). They argue that "conforming naturally to others" is one of the most important factors underlying humanness among Japanese. In fact, the current theoretical preoccupation with the constraints on the self provided by others and the "natural" desire to resist them may be a product of the European American cultural view that the self is experienced as separate and autonomous from others. The nature of the relationship between cultural values and conformity requires further elaboration and investigation.

INTERNAL CONTROL IDEOLOGY AND INTERPERSONAL COMMUNICATION

This section focuses on theory and research related to the concept of locus of control and its effect on interpersonal communication. The work in this area has been biased by the assumption, explicit or implicit, that internality is more desirable than externality. The dominant concept of personhood in the area of locus of control is a Western ideal of a centralized, equilibrium-based conception of personhood. In this view, the individual is the architect of order and coherence through personal control and mastery.

Locus of control refers to the individual's perception of where the causal agent of an observed environmental change is located. The concept was originally developed in the context of Rotter's (1954) social learning theory as a variable representing people's beliefs about whether or not reinforcement is contingent on their behavior. A belief in external control exists when a reinforcement is perceived by the subject as following some action of his or her own but as being not entirely contingent on his or action. Internal control is defined as the individual's perception that the event is contingent on his/her own behavior or her/his own relatively permanent characteristics (Rotter, 1966). Why might people develop different control orientations? Culturally, society reinforces a certain value system and expects roles to be followed. The assumption

that people with internal control are better adjusted may be true in one culture but not true in another culture (Christy, 1978).

According to Furby (1979), internal ideology consists essentially of the Protestant ethic: the belief that hard work, effort, skill, and ability are the important determinants of success in life. Hsieh et al. (1969) captured the essence of this individualistic ideology in describing American society. "It, among other things, places a high value on personal output of energy for solving all problems; pragmatic ingenuity; individualism, that is, self-reliance and status achieved through one's efforts" (p. 122). It is easy to find explicit references in the literature to the view that an internal locus of control is more desirable than an external locus of control. Both theory and research point to internal control as the more effective model of functioning (Lefcourt, 1966). Internality has been positively related to perseverance (Weiss & Sherman, 1973), creativity (DuCette, Wolk, & Friedman, 1972), self-esteem (Heaton & Duerfeldt, 1973), and a favorable outlook toward the future (Smith, Steinke, & Distefano, 1973). Lefcourt (1966) has indicated that because internal control is a more desirable social and personal orientation, it is important to investigate means by which individuals may gain this orientation.

In reviewing the relation of locus of control to personality, Joe (1971) concluded that the findings depict externals, in contrast to internals, as being relatively anxious, aggressive, and dogmatic, less trustful and more suspicious of others, lacking in self-confidence and insight, having low needs for social approval, and having a greater tendency to use sensitizing modes of defenses. Given this general assumption about the desirability of internal locus of control, it is not surprising that researchers have examined the necessary conditions for decreasing external and increasing internal locus of control (see Furby, 1979, for further discussion on this issue).

Rotter (1975) referred to this tendency in the literature as "the intrusion of the 'good guy—bad guy' dichotomy." He stated, "In spite of fears, and even warnings to the contrary, some psychologists quickly assume that it is good to be internal and bad to be external" (p. 60). However, Furby (1979) points out that, rather than rejecting this basic assumption, Rotter endorsed it and only warned against its extreme form: "Of course, in some senses this [assumption that it is good to be internal] is true, but the problem lies in assuming that all good things are characteristic of internals and all bad things are characteristic of externals" (p. 60).

Then, what is the nature of interaction between locus of control and communication motivation? Rubin and Rubin (1992) found that locus of control is an antecedent to interpersonal communication motivation, especially communicating to control others. They claim that those who believe that chance and powerful others control their lives communicate instrumentally to be included and to escape. Internals are known to be more persuasive and use fewer coercive strategies than externals (Goodstadt & Hjelle, 1973). Furthermore, Patterson (1983) hypothesized that the internally controlled "may be more sensitive (than externals) to interpersonal and environmental changes that require deliberation and management in interpersonal behavior" (p. 178). "People with fatalistic or helpless expectations act in ways that confirm their expectations; they tend to attribute their state to luck, chance, powerful others, fate, or an unjust, difficult, or politically unresponsive world" (Rubin & Rubin, 1992, p. 308).

Brenders (1987) argued that control is essential for competent interpersonal communication. According to Brenders, externals may have a different "interpersonal agenda" than internals, seeking to capitalize on "lucky breaks" and the help of powerful others, and "developing defense explanations for potential social failures, or otherwise pursuing interpersonal strategies that permit some limited mastery of the situation" (p. 109). Furthermore, Brenders suggests that the socially helpless (externals) will become withdrawn and less satisfied with life. According to Berger and Metzger (1984), as compared with externals, internals have more communicative

strategies and are more sensitive to others. Furthermore, they argue that the number of relationships a person establishes with others (externals would have fewer) and resistance to social influence (internals would have more) are social consequences of locus of control.

Several studies have examined the role of locus of control in dyadic social influence processes (see also Brenders, 1987). In an organizational simulation, Goodstadt and Hjelle (1973) found that internals were more likely to use personal persuasion tactics (such as encouragements) and were less likely to use coercion. In interpersonal conflict situations, internality was positively associated with integrative tactics, whereas externality was positively associated with avoidance and sarcasm strategies (see Canary, Cunningham, & Cody, 1988). In marital interactions, internals have been found to be more assertive and persistent than externals (Doherty & Ryder, 1979), whereas in other conversations, externals seem to use more assertive tactics but to lack confident intonation (Bugental, Henker, & Whalen, 1976). In a study of goals and locus of control, Canary, Cody, and Marston (1986) noted that high internals reported greater likelihood of using positive feelings of target, referent influence (i.e., appeals to the relationship) and rationality (i.e., giving reasons); what they called "powerless actors" (externals) relied more on direct requests, manipulation of both positive feelings and negative feelings (i.e., show disappointment, pout, etc.), and avoidance.

There is possible ethnocentrism in conceptual and empirical approaches to locus of control and communication styles. Without cultural bias, we can look carefully at these statements and recognize the large number of ideological assertions. Why is it that internal locus of control has generally been assumed to be desirable? The answer lies in an examination of the social context of our knowledge about locus of control. Gurin, Gurin, Lao, and Beattie (1969) distinguished between *control ideology,* that is, the generally accepted view in the culture about the degree to which individuals control their own lives, and *sense of personal control,* that is, the degree to which individuals feel they have control over their own lives. Control ideology corresponds to the naive psychological knowledge in the culture with respect to locus of control (Furby, 1979). Academic researchers grow up, do research, and develop theories in a society where the ideology of internal control is prevalent. They are as subject to native knowledge as everyone else in society. Thus, it is not surprising that this ideology might influence their academic "knowledge" (Furby, 1979).

A number of cross-cultural scholars have criticized locus of control research on conceptual grounds for its ethnocentric biases, noting that in some situations and cultural contexts, an external locus of control can have adaptive consequences (Ward & Kennedy, 1992). Wortman and Brehm (1975) suggested, "When an organism is confronted by outcomes that are truly uncontrollable, the most adaptive response may be to give up" (p. 330). Dyal (1984) has suggested that in Asian countries with Karmic philosophies, a "giving up" problem-solving approach might diminish the stress of life changes. These conceptual criticisms and the empirical research highlight the importance of cultural sensitivity in interpretations about control orientations and communication styles.

A belief in internal control seems to appear in those societies that value and emphasize individual independence, self-reliance, and personal initiative, as is the case in the United States. Communication research on locus of control developed in a social and cultural context. We have attempted to demonstrate how the individualistic orientation of American culture led researchers to assume that internal locus of control is more desirable because it leads to more effective response (e.g., control communication strategy) in one's environment than does external locus of control. However, this assumption is faulty and is the result of neglecting to examine the dialectic between a culture's control ideology and the individual's sense of personal control. The discussion here has only touched the surface of potentially fruitful analyses in this area, and we hope it will stimulate others to continue in this vein.

STYLES OF SELF-DISCLOSURE: BRAGGING AND NEGATIVE SELF-DISCLOSURE

Is disclosing about our accomplishments a successful strategy? Styles of self-disclosure is one of the fundamental and important processes by which people negotiate identities for themselves in their social world. It appears that there is a strong and pervasive desire to make a positive impression on others (e.g., Tice, Butler, Muraven, & Stillwell, 1995). However, *how* one creates a positive impression may vary depending on how one construes the self, among various other factors. We will illustrate the process whereby cultural views of self are transformed into styles of self-disclosure.

Prior research has witnessed a marked tendency for those in North America to assert and enhance an overall evaluation of the self (i.e., self-enhancing communication) (e.g., Gilovich, 1983; Greenwald, 1980; Solomon, Greenberg, & Pyszynski, 1991; Tesser, 1986). Myers (1987) found that more than 50% of a sample of American college undergraduates reported that they perceived themselves to be in the top 10% in "interpersonal sensitivity." In a highly influential article, Taylor and Brown (1988) surveyed the social psychological literature on the accuracy of social perception (including self-perception). In this survey, mental health was operationalized in most studies by the absence of low self-esteem or depression. Taylor and Brown arrived at the conclusion that mentally healthy individuals show unrealistically positive self-evaluations (self-enhancement), exaggerated perceptions of control or mastery, and unrealistic optimism. They provided the evidence that supported their conclusion: Most people (mostly university students) show the illusion of, for example, self-enhancement.

This conclusion is anchored in a particular individualist approach to the self. From a different orientation, one in which the individual is cast not as an independent entity but as one fundamentally interdependent with others, the self-enhancement or bragging could be understood differently. Kitayama, Markus, Matsumoto, and Norasakkunkit (1997) have suggested, based on initial evidence, that a Japanese tendency to appraise the self in a critical light serves the goal of improving the self vis-à-vis socially shared standards of excellence. Indeed, clear evidence exists that self-criticism in Japan is often a spontaneous, genuinely felt, personal response, although under certain conditions it can also be motivated by a self-presentation concern not to "stand out" in public (Kitayama et al., 1997).

Gilbert and Horenstein (1975) found that respondents in the United States best liked those males who disclosed positive rather than negative information about themselves. Furthermore, men who reveal negative things about themselves were especially likely to be perceived as weak and incompetent (Kleinke & Kahn, 1980). Rudman (1998) also found that self-promoters were perceived as more competent than self-effacers. Thus, the content of the disclosures appears crucial to the receipt of positive interpersonal evaluations. In the U.S. context, it was found that people tend to feel more attracted to, interested in, and affirming about positive compared with negative disclosers (Gilbert & Horenstein, 1975; Jones & Gordon, 1972). Similarly, in studies with American respondents, Miller, Cooke, Tsang, and Morgan (1992) asked respondents to rate characters who disclosed in a boastful, positive, or negative fashion. Boasters and positive dislosers were viewed as more competent than negative disclosers. Compared to the boaster, the positive discloser was rated as more feminine (less masculine) and less competent. Thus, in the European American context, if we would like to be perceived as competent and successful, boasting appears to be a better strategy than disclosing negatively.

Findings from a number of social psychological domains suggest that European Americans show a general sensitivity to positive self-relevant information, which Kitayama et al. (1997) refer to as self-enhancement. American children as young as age 4 believe themselves to be better than their peers. U.S. adults typically consider themselves to be more intelligent, friendlier, and more attractive than the average adult (Myers, 1987). A growing body of literature indicates that the self-enhancement effect is reversed in non-Western groups. The predominant pattern is mainly to explain one's success in terms of effort or luck and one's failure in terms of one's lack of abilities or talents. This sensitivity to negative self-relevant information is referred to as self-criticism. Heine and Lehman (1997a) could not replicate the tendency for people to overemphasize the uniqueness of their positive attributes in Japan, Thailand, or Korea.

It is not likely that the Asian self-reports are due merely to impression-management style. Even when responses are recorded in a manner that maintains the anonymity of Japanese respondents, self-enhancement is still absent or reversed (Kitayama et al., 1997). Instead, it seems likely that the tendency not to self-enhance, or even to self-criticize, may reflect authentic subjective experience. Asian practices may paradoxically be comparable in function to Western tendencies toward self-enhancement. The inclination to self-criticize may be a way to affirm the identity of the self as interdependent by engaging in the process of self-improvement—an important element of the interdependent, Japanese sense of well-being (Fiske et al., 1998). For Japanese interdependent selves, the perceived absence of negative features, rather than the perceived presence of positive features, might be crucial in maintenance of well-being.

Therefore, it is argued that within a Japanese cultural system that is rooted in the importance of maintaining, affirming, and becoming part of significant social relationships, sensitivity to negative self-relevant information is not an indicator of low self-esteem or something to be avoided or overcome. Rather, it has positive social and psychological consequences. Markus et al. (1997) have argued that when selfways emphasize being part of the group, standing out or being different even in a positive sense may not be valued. Instead, selfways may give rise to what, from a Western perspective, appears to be self-effacement (Tanaka, 1987).

Psychological tendencies involving the self, such as self-enhancement (United States) and self-criticism (Japan) are afforded and sustained by the ways in which realities are constructed in each cultural context. On the basis of review here, it is evident that self-enhancement appears obvious and natural in those cultural contexts in which one is encouraged to create a distinct and objectified self. To the extent that the self is interdependent with others, it seems likely that there will be many fewer concerns with enhancing and actualizing one's identity, because the need to create an autonomous self is not a cultural imperative (Kitayama et al., 1997).

This process implies that communication styles result from a collective process through which views of the self are inscribed and embodied in the very ways in which social acts and situations are defined and experienced in each cultural context. Thus, it is proposed that situational definitions that compose the American mainstream cultural context are relatively more conducive to self-enhancement and bragging self-disclosure. Similarly, situational definitions that compose the Japanese cultural context may be relatively more conducive to negative self-disclosure. Thus, independent individuals should be relatively likely to engage in self-enhancing communication styles. Similarly, situational definitions among interdependent individuals should be relatively conducive to self-criticizing communication styles, and they should be relatively likely to engage in negative self-disclosure.

Gender differences in self-enhancement and self-criticism have also been studied. Past research has suggested that women tend to be more interdependent than men. It was also found that self-enhancement in the United States is weaker for women than for men. Recent efforts to acknowledge gender difference in self-presentational tactics have approached the problem intrapsychically (Kacmar & Carlson, 1994). It has been argued that women are unable to self-promote due to low self-esteem (i.e., a belief that "they have nothing about which to brag"; Kacmar & Carlson, 1994, p. 690). Similar negative attributions can be made about interdependent individuals, who may be reluctant to self-promote for fear of violating their normative tasks, which in turn may limit their perceived suitability for many occupations in individualistic societies. Self-presentation strategies undoubtedly influence both career and interpersonal success. The present discussion highlights the normative pressures that may discomfort interdependents when they consider using self-promotion as a means to self-efficacy. Self-promotion may intuitively be more normative and acceptable for independents than for interdependents.

SILENCE

Now we will focus attention on a relatively neglected component of human communication—silence. The term *silence* refers to abstaining from speech or utterance, sometimes with reference to a particular matter, according to the *Oxford English Dictionary*. Silence has typically been considered most often an out-of-awareness phenomenon—the ground against which the figure of talk is perceived (Tannen, 1985). Reversing polarities and treating silence as the figure to be examined against the ground of talk may heighten awareness of this universal aspect of human communication while at the same time emphasizing its complex nature as a cultural phenomenon.

Researchers still favor Descartes in taking the machine as the model of both human cognition and interpersonal interaction. This, in turn, has consequences both for the ways in which we do research and for our interpersonal interactions with people who do not build their understanding of communication on the metaphor of the machine (Scollon, 1985). Studies of communication have tended to look at silence as absence—as absence of sound and therefore as absence of communication. In the Western context, conversational silence appears to be a negative quality. Thus, Feldstein, Alberti, and BenDebba (as cited in Scollon, 1985) find the results of their research intuitively reasonable. They write,

> It does not seem unduly strange that speakers take longer turns when talking with persons who are reserved, detached, and taciturn than with persons who are talkative, cheerful, and cooperative. Nor is it difficult to believe that persons who are reserved, cold, suspicious, insecure, and tense tend to produce longer pauses. (p. 85)

Scollon (1985) noted the implied direction of causation: The researchers have taken the personality characteristics as given and then assumed that they have caused the pausing phenomena. In their view, a suspicious person pauses longer. It seems difficult for either individuals or researchers to give up the idea of the humming conversational machine. Scollon (1985), in his essay on "Silence in the Metaphor of Malfunction," argues that silence is typically heard as the malfunctioning of a machine (the industrial metaphor):

> The normal state of the machine is thought of as a steady hum or buzz, with hesitation or silences indicating trouble, difficulty, missing cogs, and so forth. We see the quality control engineer sitting at a window on the production line overlooking the production of the gross cognitive product as reflected in verbal outputs. (p. 26)

He further argues that changing the metaphor changes the meaning of silence. If we are going to get any further in our understanding of the meaning of silence in conversation, we must first examine the metaphors generating our research and our conversational stance.

Since the time of ancient Greek philosophers, Western thought has emphasized bipolar values and concepts by opposing terms such as black versus white, good versus bad, life versus death, and yes versus no. Speech versus silence has been researched and taught from the same bipolar stance: Speech has a positive connotation, and silence has a negative one (Ishii & Bruneau, 1988). Even though the importance of silence in intra- and intercultural communication has recently been recognized (e.g., Tannen, 1985), only a marginal amount of data is available on their communicative significance. Silence, as well as its functions and meanings in intercultural communication, continues to be a fairly unexplored area.

The study of communication has focused on talk to the relative exclusion of silence. Silence is more acceptable in many parts of the world, a condition some U.S. scholars refuse to acknowledge. Ishii and Bruneau (1988) support this notion. Today's U.S. communication scholars, they contend, view the Western rhetorical tradition uncritically, as being the only way. This tradition perceives silence and ambiguity negatively, especially in social and public relations. Ishii and Bruneau (1988) charged that Western scholars fall prey to a major misconception when they assume silence is completely other than speech, its foreign opposite, its antagonist.

Each culture maintains its own norms concerning acceptable as well as unacceptable or aberrant speech behavior in social interactions. Values regarding appropriate behavior are often reflected in proverbs, popular sayings. In Finland, for instance, some proverbs equate talkativeness with foolishness: "A loud voice shows an empty head" (Sallinen-Kuparinen, 1986, p. 23). The Japanese, another culture respecting silence, similarly cautions against speaking through the use of proverbs: "The cat that does not mew catches rats" (Klopf, 1995, p. 17). In many parts of the world, silence is power, in some cultures, more powerful than the spoken word.

An extensive literature documents cultural differences in communication and beliefs about talk (Giles, Coupland, & Wiemann, 1992). Since the ancient Greeks, Westerners have tended to celebrate talk and rhetoric, construing it as a vehicle for the discovery and expression of truth. In addition, there seems to be an aversion to silence in that people find it awkward and embarrassing. Silence tends to be interpreted variously as lack of interest; an unwillingness to communicate; a sign of hostility, rejection, or interpersonal incompatibility; anxiety or shyness; or a lack of verbal skills (Giles et al., 1992).

The significance of silence is derived by convention within particular speech communities and conveys some information on cultural norms for and attitudes toward loquacity (Saville-Troike, 1985). Attitudes toward silence and speech are among the internalized social and cultural standards against which people measure their own (and others') communicative performance. Saville-Troike (1985) argues that children seem to talk more when they are being enculturated into societies that place a high value on individual achievement (e.g., America and Britain) and to talk less when family and group achievement is more valued (e.g., China and Japan). The latter perspective expects children to be "seen but not heard." Special attention is needed to distinguish between, and properly interpret, the different meanings of silences. Stereotyping and misunderstanding occur when the characteristic use of silence by members of one speech community is interpreted according to the norms and rules held by members of another. Thus, learning appropriate rules for silence is also part of the acculturation process for people attempting to develop communicative competence in a second language and culture (Saville-Troike, 1985).

An adequate description and interpretation of the process of communication requires that we understand the structure, meaning, and functions of silence as well as of verbal strategies. Recently, Kim, Shin, and Cai (1998) posed two hypotheses in their study: (a) For both first- and second-attempt requests, independents would perceive silent communicative acts as less effective than would inter-dependents; (b) For both first- and second-attempt requests, independents would perceive silent communicative acts as less likely to be used than would interdependents. The researchers found that the more pronounced people's independent cultural orientation, the less prone they are to remain silent in either the first- or the second-attempt requests. They argue that we should view silence as itself a valid object of investigation, bounded by cultural orientations. A total theory of communication should be concerned with the ways these two modes of behavior (verbal strategy and silence) are patterned in relation to the culture and social organization of a speech community. Profound differences in cultural metaphors affect interpretations of silence in interaction and even our research agenda. Communication behavior consists of both verbal strategies and silences. Adequate description and interpretation of the process of communication requires that we understand the structure, meaning, and functions of silence as well as of verbal strategies.

▶ Toward a Bidimensional Model of Cultural Identity: Implications for Theory

At this point, readers will appreciate that the development of human communication theory in the United States has been based, in large part, on individualistic orientations and empirical research involving subjects representing the mainstream U.S. culture. The low external validity of such research and theory has been recognized by many researchers, but the proposed solution to the problem frequently has consisted only of recommendations to examine other samples of the population to test generalizability. According to Brockner and Chen (1996), in evaluating whether people from different cultures vary in their psychological makeup, researchers would be well-advised to do more than perform simple cross-cultural comparisons of the mean level of the psychological dimensions in question. For instance, much work has been done to describe and explain cultural similarities and differences of individuals' verbal communication styles (e.g., cross-cultural comparisons of mean differences in communication apprehension). However, such inquiry is, in Kuhn's (1970) sense, wholly within paradigm. That is, it has primarily expanded or elaborated on the accepted paradigm, rather than providing a significant challenge to normative assumptions. From the present vantage point, greater scientific gain lies in the breaking of a paradigm.

Individualism is typically analyzed as the critical element of Western society (Guisinger & Blatt, 1994; Markus & Kitayama, 1998). Lebra (1992) contends that individualism is a function of a Cartesian categorization system that draws a sharp distinction between the self and others. Independent and interdependent orientation may at first sight appear to be conflicting, even mutually exclusive. However, such an interpretation would probably reflect a Western individualistic worldview pitting the individual against the group. Indeed, there is nothing illogical about the coexistence of interdependence and independence orientations, and quite a bit of research and thinking provides evidence for such coexistence (Kagitcibasi, 1996). Theories of European American communication behavior have been extremely influenced by the prevailing ideology of a unidimensional model of cultural identity. The self is often viewed as in tension, or even as in opposition, to the collective. The source of all-important behavior is typically "found" in the unique configuration of internal attributes—thoughts, feelings, motives, abilities—that form the bounded, autonomous whole. As a consequence, the ways in which the self is, in fact, quite interdependent with the collective, and the communicative consequences of that relationship, have been underanalyzed and undertheorized. It is our view that there are important reasons for researchers to go beyond theories that are directly shaped by the cultural ideal of individualism and to consider a broader view of the self (see Markus & Kitayma, 1994).

When a whole culture or society is pigeonholed in dichotomous categories such as masculine/feminine, active/passive, or loose/tight, subtle differences and qualitative nuances that may be more characteristic of these social entities are glossed over. Also, when cultures and individuals are presented in black-or-white terms, not only does this cloud our understanding of them, but it inevitably leads to our making good/bad comparisons.

Models that acknowledge differences without placing them in hierarchy or opposition are thus useful. Gaining cognizance of the normative influences shaping contemporary communication theories may serve as a useful start for change. It has been argued that a single image of human functioning has generated ethnocentric theoretical formulation within the field. Thus, the present question is how to engender a multiplicity of perspectives.

For instance, Kagitcibasi (1996) has proposed a model of family change based on the dual common human needs for agency (autonomy) and communion (relatedness). Here is a recognition of the coexistence of these two basic conflicting needs everywhere. Kagitcibasi (1996) notes that a family culture of relatedness and interdependence is not incompatible with socioeconomic development. It is possible for individual loyalties to coexist with communal-familial loyalties and relations, in a new synthesis; such loyalties need not be mutually exclusive. An interdependent interpersonal perspective does not put the individual against the group and can thus provide scientists with a fruitful base to explore the psychology of relatedness. Similarly, we need to assume a dialectic orientation, given the conflicting nature of the two needs involved. Thus, an independence that does not recognize the need for relatedness and an interdependence that does not recognize the need for autonomy would not do justice to the two basic human needs. A dialectical synthesis of the two would appear to be a more optimal solution for cultural identity.

The first step in expanding theories of the self and the communicative consequences seems to require being deliberately self-conscious about what is being taken for granted in the initial formulation of the problem and about the labels that are used. To develop comprehensive and univeral human communication theories, we need to recognize one major stumbling block: a cultural view that the individual is, a priori, separate and self-contained and must resist the collective. Gates (1993) called this individualist view America's civil religion. In the dominant mentality of contemporary Western culture, self is equated with the autonomous or self-sufficient individual. Therefore, relationship in Western cultures is often constructed as undermining the "right" or most powerful kind of selfhood (Klein, 1995). To the extent that personal creativity and individuality are more valued than relationship in the West, to the extent that autonomy is characterized as the pinnacle of psychological and ethical development, there is the implicit suggestion that caring and a relational style of identity make one less than one might be.

A lot of theories in social sciences are cultural constructions, reflecting a particular orientation to and interpretation of reality. As a whole, the discussion presented here, although disparate and fragmentary, suggests that the content and structure of selves may vary significantly by cultural context. We have adopted the notions of interdependent and independent selfways (Markus et al., 1997) as characteristic patterns of engaging in the social world. These selfways provide a guiding orientation to subjectivity and thus structure patterns of communication. Theoretical analyses of a communication behavior within a cultural context that is different from one's own makes typically invisible selfways become visible.

Our discussion of the communicative consequences has by no means exhausted the range of potential consequences of holding an independent or interdependent construal of the self. But it is enough, we believe, to indicate that the field of communication must consider the idea that communication processes are culturally contingent. One by one, we can analyze the cultural conditions that are necessary for each phenomenon to operate. Then, we can investigate a sample of the world's cultures to see the various culturally limiting conditions of these phenomena. This may be an effective and hence appropriate early strategy for establishing that human communication is culturally contingent, because it will reorient the field and facilitate a paradigm shift.

▶ Implications for Future Inquiry

Although self-construal represents a constellation of variables that differentiate people from varying cultures, it is not the only way to distinguish people from different cultures. Future research needs to examine other psychological variables besides self-construal in an attempt to explain cross-cultural differences in belief and communication behavior. Furthermore, as the content to this point reflects, the majority of research on cultural variations in the self and communication has centered on U.S.-Asian comparisons. In developing a perspective on the cultural grounding of the self, it is obviously useful to analyze a wide variety of cultural contexts. Although much less developed than the work on Asian selves, there is also a growing literature on selves in Indian, Arab, Mexican, and African contexts (Markus et al., 1997; Oyserman, 1993; Sinha & Tripathi, 1994).

We have to post a clear reminder that general trends in culture do not affect all people in the same fashion. Even within highly individualistic Western culture, most people are still much less self-reliant, self-contained, or self-sufficient than the prevailing cultural ideology suggests they should be. Perhaps, Western models of the self are quite at odds with actual individual social behavior and should be reformulated to reflect the substantial interdependence that characterizes even Western individualists (Markus & Kitayama, 1991). Sampson (1988) has argued that the reality of globalization and a shrinking world will force just such a rethinking of the nature of the individual.

Currently, the cross-cultural research is moving away from the crude operationalization of culture as a national citizenship and toward the operationalization of culture in terms of individual differences, such as idiocentrism and allocentrism or independent and interdependent self-construals. This review focusing on self-construals should also be brought back into within-culture research because it goes without saying that every cultural group contains substantial within-culture variance.

Given the "America-centrism" of most social science (Featherman, 1993), this broadening in the cultural base out of which human communication is generated will help universalize our discipline. Future research must take into consideration that individualism and collectivism appear to be a dialectic (see Kagitcibasi, 1996). That is, individualism and collectivism exist in all cultures, and individuals hold both individualistic and collectivistic values. This position is consistent with Schwartz's (1990) contention that individualistic and collectivistic values are not necessarily incompatible; they can coexist. This idea is compatible with several recent discussions of individualism and collectivism. Furthermore, if individualism-collectivism is a dialectic at both the cultural and individual level, as it appears, then it is critical that future research hypotheses involve very specific predictions regarding the linkages between the various aspects of individualism-collectivism and individuals' behavior. A universally applicable theory should concern itself with individual-level as well as cultural-level issues (see Gudykunst et al., 1996; Kim, 1995; Kim et al., 1996).

Because individualism is a matter not just of belief or value but also of everyday practice, including scientific practice, it is not easy for theorists to view social behavior from another cultural frame. And it is probably harder still to reflect a different frame in empirical work. The continued effort to develop culture-universal communication theories may eventually open new and productive possibilities for the understanding and analysis of human communication behavior. Research and theoretical developments such as those discussed above look into new combinations (coexistence, synthesis) of individualist and collectivist orientations. This promises to continuously improve conceptualizations in this area.

Multicultural perspectives seek a new way of experiencing self and world. The alternative perspectives and theories discussed throughout this book can provide creative impetus for the new sensibilities. These and other innovations are only now beginning to emerge, to be conceptualized and integrated into the human communication literature. Smith and Bond (1993) claim that the emergence in social psychology of similar ideas had to await the diffusion of Western psychology to different cultural milieus and the nurturing of local psychologists who are capable of challenging the biases of the discipline in its own terminology, using its established procedures. We in the communication field have now reached this stage. The consequences will be an intellectual synergy that will enable us to transcend the limitations imposed by our cultural origins. We may then be able to claim that we have a more truly universal understanding of human communication behavior.

▶ References

Alberti, R. E., & Emmons, M. L. (1970). *Your perfect right: A guide to assertive behavior.* San Luis Obispo, CA: Impact.

Asch, S. E. (1952). Effects of group pressure on the modification and distortion of judgments. In G. E. Swanso, T. M. Necomb, & E. L. Hartley (Eds.), *Readings in social psychology* (pp. 2-11). New York: Holt.

Azuma, H. (1986). Why study child development in Japan? In H. Stevenson, H. Azuma, & K. Hakuta (Eds.), *Child development and education in Japan* (pp. 3-12). New York: Freeman.

Bellah, R. N., Madsen, R., Sullivan, W. M., Swidler, A., & Tipton, S. M. (1985). *Habits of the heart.* New York: Harper & Row.

Berger, C. R., & Metzger, N. J. (1984). The functions of human communication in developing, maintaining, and altering self-image. In C. C. Arnold & J. W. Bowers (Eds.), *Handbook of rhetorical and communication theory* (pp. 273-337). Boston: Allyn & Bacon.

Berry, J. W. (1978). Social psychology: Comparative societal and universal. *Canadian Psychological Review, 19,* 93-104.

Blake, R. R., & Mouton, J. S. (1964). *The managerial grid.* Houston: Gulf.

Bochner, S. (1994). Cross-cultural differences in the self concept: A test of Hofstede's individualism/collectivism distinction. *Journal of Cross-Cultural Psychology, 25,* 273-283.

Bond, M. H. (Ed.). (1986). *The psychology of the Chinese people.* Hong Kong: Oxford University Press.

Bond, R., & Smith, P. B. (1996). Culture and conformity: A meta-analysis of studies using Asch's (1952b, 1956) line judgment task. *Psychological Bulletin, 119,* 111-137.

Brenders, D. A. (1987). Perceived control: Foundations and directions for communication research. *Communication Yearbook, 10,* 86-116.

Brockner, J., & Chen, Y.-R. (1996). The moderating roles of self-esteem and self-construal in reaction to a threat to the self: Evidence from the People's Republic of China and the United States. *Journal of Personality and Social Psychology, 71,* 603-615.

Brown, C. T., Yelsma, P., & Keller, P. W. (1981). Communication-conflict predisposition: Development of a theory and an instrument. *Human Relations, 34,* 1103-1117.

Bryant, B. K. (1992). Conflict resolution strategies in relation to children's peer relations. *Journal of Applied Developmental Psychology, 13,* 35-50.

Bugental, D. P., Henker, B., & Whalen, C. K. (1976). Attributional antecedents of verbal and vocal assertiveness. *Journal of Personality and Social Psychology, 34,* 405-411.

Buss, A. R. (Ed.). (1979). *Psychology in social context.* New York: Irvington.

Canary, D. J., Cody, M. J., & Marston, P. J. (1986). Goal types, compliance-gaining, and locus of control. *Journal of Language and Social Psychology, 5,* 249-269.

Canary, D. J., Cunningham, E. M., & Cody, M. J. (1988). Goal types, gender, and locus of control in managing interpersonal conflict. *Communication Research, 15,* 426-446.

Christy, L.C.T. (1978). Culture and control orientation: A study of internal-external locus of control in Chinese and American-Chinese women. *Dissertation Abstracts International 39,* 770-A.

Chua, E., & Gudykunst, W. B. (1987). Conflict resolution styles in low- and high-context cultures. *Communication Research Reports, 5,* 32-37.

Chusmir, L., & Mills, J. (1989). Gender differences in conflict resolution styles of managers: At work and at home. *Sex Roles, 20,* 149-162.

Comstock, J., & Buller, D. B. (1991). Conflict strategies adolescents use with their parents: Testing the cognitive communicator characteristics model. *Journal of Language and Social Psychology, 10,* 47-59.

Cook, D. J., & St. Lawrence, J. S. (1990). Variations in presentation format: Effect on interpersonal evaluations of assertive and unassertive behavior. *Behavior Modification, 14,* 21-36.

Cross, S. E., & Markus, H. R. (1991, July). *Cultural adaptation and the self: Self-construal, coping, and stress.* Paper presented at the ninety-ninth annual convention of the American Psychological Association, San Francisco, CA.

Daly, J. A., & Stafford, L. (1984). Correlates and consequences of social-communicative anxiety. In J. A. Daly & J. C. McCroskey (Eds.), *Avoiding communication: Shyness, reticence, and communication apprehension* (pp. 125-143). Beverly Hills, CA: Sage.

Deutscher, I. (1966). Words and deeds: Social science and social policy. *Social Problems, 13,* 235-254.

Doherty, W. J., & Ryder, R. G. (1979). Locus of control, interpersonal trust, and assertive behavior among newlyweds. *Journal of Personality and Social Psychology, 37,* 2212-2239.

Doi, T. (1986). *The anatomy of self: The individual versus society.* Tokyo: Kodansha.

DuCette, J., Wolk, S., & Friedman, S. (1972). Locus of control and creativity in black and white children. *Journal of Social Psychology, 88,* 297-298.

Dyal, J. A. (1984). Cross-cultural research with the locus of control construct. In H. M. Lefcourt (Ed.), *Research with the locus of control constructs* (Vol. 3). New York: Academic Press.

Featherman, D. L. (1993). What does society need from higher education? *Items, 47*(2/3), 38-43.

Filley, A. C., & House, R. J. (1969). *Managerial process and organizational behavior.* Glenview, IL: Scott, Foresman.

Fishbein, M., & Ajzen, I. (1975). *Belief, attitude, intention, and behavior: An introduction to theory and research.* Reading, MA: Addison-Wesley.

Fiske, A. P., Kitayama, S., Markus, H. R., & Nisbett, R. E. (1998). The cultural matrix of social psychology. In D. T. Gilbert, S. T. Fiske, & G. Lindzey (Eds.), *The handbook of social psychology* (pp. 915-981). New York: McGraw-Hill.

Furby, L. (1979). Individualistic bias in studies of locus of control. In A. R. Buss (Ed.), *Psychology in social context* (pp. 169-190). New York: Irvington.

Furnham, A. (1984). Studies of cross-cultural conformity: A brief and critical review. *Psychologia, 27,* 65-72.

Galvin, K. M., & Brommel, B. J. (1986). *Family communication: Cohesion and change.* Glenview, IL: Scott, Foresman.

Gates, H. L., Jr. (1993, September 20). Let them talk. *New Republic,* pp. 37-49.

Geertz, C. (1973). *The interpretation of culture: Selected essays.* New York: Basic Books.

Gergen, K. J. (1979). The positivist image in social psychological theory. In A. R. Buss (Ed.), *Psychology in social context* (pp. 193-212). New York: Irvington.

Gilbert, S. J., & Horenstein, D. (1975). The communication of self-disclosure: Level versus valence. *Human Communication Research, 1,* 316-322.

Giles, H., Coupland, N., & Wiemann, J. (1992). "Talk is cheap . . ." but "My word is my bond": Beliefs about talk. In K. Bolton & H. Kwok (Eds.), *Sociolinguistics today* (pp. 218-243). New York: Routledge.

Gilligan, C. (1982). *In a different voice: Psychological theory and women's development.* Cambridge, MA: Harvard University Press.

Gilovich, T. (1983). Biased evaluation and persistence in gambling. *Journal of Personality and Social Psychology, 40,* 797-808.

Goodstadt, B. E., & Hjelle, L. A. (1973). Power to the powerless: Locus of control and the use of power. *Journal of Personality and Social Psychology, 27,* 190-196.

Greenwald, A. G. (1980). The totalitarian ego: Fabrication and revision of personal history. *American Psychologist, 35,* 603-618.

Gudykunst, W. B., Matsumoto, Y., Ting-Toomey, S., Nishida, T., Kim, K., & Heyman, S. (1996). The influence of cultural individualism-collectivism, self-construals, and individual values on communication styles across cultures. *Human Communication Research, 22,* 510-543.

Guisinger, S., & Blatt, S. J. (1994). Individuality and relatedness: Evolution of a fundamental dialectic. *American Psychologist, 49,* 104-111.

Gurin, P., Gurin, G., Lao, R. C., & Beattie, M. (1969). Internal-external control in the motivational dynamics of Negro youth. *Journal of Social Issues, 25,* 29-53.

Hall, J. (1986). *Conflict management survey: A survey of one's characteristic reaction to and handling of conflicts between himself and others.* Conroe, TX: Teleometrics.

Heaton, R., & Duerfeldt, P. (1973). The relationship between self-esteem, self-reinforcement, and the internal-external personality dimension. *Journal of Genetic Psychology, 123,* 3-13.

Heine, S. J., & Lehman, D. R. (1997a). The cultural constructions of self-enhancement: An examination of group-serving biases. *Journal of Personality and Social Psychology, 72,* 1268-1283.

Heine, S. J., & Lehman, D. R. (1997b), Culture, dissonance, and self-affirmation. *Personality and Social Psychology Bulletin, 23,* 389-400.

Henderson, M., & Furnham, A. (1982). Self-reported and self-attributed scores on personality, social skills, and attitudinal measures as compared between high nominated friends and acquaintances. *Psychological Reports, 50,* 88-90.

Ho, D.Y.F. (1976). On the concept of face. *American Journal of Psychology, 81,* 867-884.

Hofstede, G. (1980). *Culture's consequences: International differences in work-related values.* Beverly Hills, CA: Sage.

Hsieh, T. T., Shybut, J., & Lotsof, E. J. (1969). Internal versus external control and ethnic group membership. *Journal of Consulting and Clinical Psychology, 33,* 122-124.

Infante, D. A., & Rancer, A. S. (1996). Argumentativeness and verbal aggressiveness: A review of recent theory and research. In B. Burleson (Ed.), *Communication yearbook* (Vol. 19, pp. 318-351). Thousand Oaks, CA: Sage.

Infante, D. A., Trebing, J. D., Shepherd, P. E., & Seeds, D. E. (1984). The relationship of argumentativeness to verbal aggression. *Southern Speech Communication Journal, 50,* 67-77.

Ishii, S., & Bruneau, T. (1988). Silence and silences in cross-cultural perspective: Japan and the United States. In L. Samovar & P. Porter (Eds.), *Intercultural communication* (pp. 246-251). Belmont, CA: Wadsworth.

Iwao, S. (1988, August). *Social psychology's models of man: Isn't it time for East to meet West?* Invited address to the International Congress of Scientific Psychology, Sydney, Australia.

Joe, V. C. (1971). Review of the internal-external control construct as a personality variable. *Psychological Reports, 28,* 619-640.

Johnson, F. (1985). The Western concept of self. In A. Marsella, G. De Vos, & F.L.K. Hsu (Eds.), *Culture and self* (pp. 91-138). London: Tavistock.

Jones, E. E., & Gordon, E. M. (1972). Timing of self-disclosure and its effects on personal attraction. *Journal of Personality and Social Psychology, 2,* 348-358.

Kacmar, K. M., & Carlson, D. S. (1994). Using impression management in women's job search processes. *American Behavioral Scientist, 37,* 682-696.

Kagitcibasi, C. (1996). *Family and human development across cultures: A view from the other side.* Hillsdale, NJ: Lawrence Erlbaum.

Kashima, Y., Siegel, M., Tanaka, K., & Kashima, E. S. (1992). Do people believe behaviors are consistent with attitudes? Toward a cultural psychology of attribution processes. *British Journal of Social Psychology, 31,* 111-124.

Kashima, Y., Yamaguchi, S., Kim, U., Choi, S.-C., Gelfand, M. J., & Yuki, M. (1995). Culture, gender, and self: A perspective from individualism-collectivism research. *Journal of Personality and Social Psychology, 69,* 925-937.

Kelly, L. (1982). A rose by any other name is still a rose: A comparative analysis of reticence, communication apprehension, unwillingness to communicate, and shyness. *Human Communication Research, 8,* 99-113.

Kim, M. S. (1993). Culture-based conversational constraints in explaining cross-cultural strategic competence. In R. L. Wiseman & J. Koester (Eds.), *Intercultural communication competence* (pp. 132-150). Newbury Park, CA: Sage.

Kim, M. S. (1995). Toward a theory of conversational constraints. In R. L. Wiseman (Ed.), *Intercultural communication theory* (pp. 148-169). Thousand Oaks, CA: Sage.

Kim, M. S. (1999). Cross-cultural perspectives on motivations of verbal communication: Review, critique, and a theoretical framework. In M. E. Roloff (Ed.), *Communication yearbook* (Vol. 22, pp. 51-89). Thousand Oaks, CA: Sage.

Kim, M. S., & Hunter, J. E. (1993a). Attitude-behavior relations: A meta-analysis of past research—focusing on attitudinal relevance and topic. *Journal of Communication, 43,* 101-142.

Kim, M. S., & Hunter, J. E. (1993b). Relationships among attitudes, behavioral intentions, and behavior: A meta-analysis of past research, part 2. *Communication Research, 20,* 331-364.

Kim, M. S., & Hunter, J. E. (1995, November). *A test of an ethno-cultural model of conflict styles.* Paper presented at the annual meeting of the Speech Communication Association, San Antonio, TX.

Kim, M. S., Hunter, J. E., Miyahara, A., Horvath, A. M., Bresnahan, M., & Yoon, H. (1996). Individual vs. culture-level dimensions of individualism and collectivism: Effects on preferred conversational styles. *Communication Monographs, 63,* 29-49.

Kim, M. S., & Leung, T. (2000). A multicultural view of conflict management styles: Review of past research and critical synthesis. In M. E.

Roloff (Ed.), *Communication yearbook* (Vol. 23, pp. 227-269). Thousand Oaks, CA: Sage.

Kim, M. S., & Sharkey, W. F. (1995). Independent and interdependent construals of the self: Explaining cultural patterns of interpersonal communication in multi-cultural settings. *Communication Quarterly, 43,* 20-38.

Kim, M. S., Sharkey, W. F., & Singelis, T. M. (1994). The relationship between individual's self-construals and perceived importance of interactive constraints. *International Journal of Intercultural Relations, 18,* 117-140.

Kim, M. S., Shin, H. C., & Cai, D. (1998). The influence of cultural orientations on the preferred forms of requesting and re-requesting. *Communication Monographs, 65,* 47-66.

Kitayama, S., Markus, H. R., Matsumoto, H., & Norasakkunkit, V. (1997). Individual and collective processes in the construction of the self: Self-enhancement in the United States and self-criticism in Japan. *Journal of Personality and Social Psychology, 72,* 1245-1267.

Klein, A. C. (1995). *Meeting the great bliss queen: Buddhists, feminists, and the art of the self.* Boston: Beacon.

Kleinke, C. L., & Kahn, M. L. (1980). Perceptions of self-disclosures: Effects of sex and physical attractiveness. *Journal of Personality, 48,* 191-205.

Klopf, D. (1995). *Intercultural encounters: The fundamentals of intercultural communication.* Englewood, CO: Morton.

Kuhn, T. S. (1970). *The structure of scientific revolutions.* Chicago: University of Chicago Press.

Lebra, T. S. (1992). *Culture, self, and communication.* Paper presented at the University of Michigan, Ann Arbor.

Lee, H., & Rogan, R. (1991). A cross-cultural comparison of organizational conflict management behaviors. *The International Journal of Conflict Management, 2,* 181-199.

Lefcourt, H. (1966). Internal versus external control of reinforcement: A review. *Psychological Bulletin, 65,* 206-220.

Mann, L. (1988). Culture and conformity. In M. H. Bond (Ed.), *The cross-cultural challenge to social psychology* (pp. 182-195). Newbury Park, CA: Sage.

Markus, H., & Kitayama, S. (1991). Culture and the self: Implications for cognition, emotion, and motivation. *Psychological Review, 98,* 224-252.

Markus, H. R., & Kitayama, S. (1994). A collective fear of the collective: Implications for selves and theories of selves. *Personality and Social Psychology, 20,* 568-579.

Markus, H. R., & Kitayama, S. (1998). The cultural psychology of personality. *Journal of Cross-Cultural Psychology, 29,* 63-87.

Markus, H. R., Mullally, P. R., & Kitayama, S. (1997). Selfways: Diversity in modes of cultural participation. In U. Neisser & D. A. Jopling (Eds.), *The conceptual self in context* (pp. 13-59). Cambridge, UK: Cambridge University Press.

McCroskey, J. C. (1977). Oral communication: A summary of recent theory and research. *Human Communication Research, 4,* 78-96.

McCroskey, J. C., Daly, J., Richmond, V., & Cox, B. (1975). The effects of communication apprehension on interpersonal attraction. *Human Communication Research, 2,* 51-65.

McCroskey, J. C., Richmond, V., Daly, J. A., & Falcione, R. L. (1977). Studies of the relationship between communication apprehension and self-esteem. *Human Communication Research, 3,* 269-277.

Miller, L. C., Cooke, L. L., Tsang, J., & Morgan, F. (1992). Should I brag? Nature and impact of positive and boastful disclosures for women and men. *Human Communication Research, 18,* 364-399.

Myers, D. (1987). *Social psychology.* New York: McGraw-Hill.

Nicotera, A. M. (1993). Beyond two dimensions: A grounded theory model of conflict-handling behavior. *Management Communication Quarterly, 6,* 282-306.

Niedenthal, P. M., & Beike, D. R. (1997). Interrelated and isolated self-concepts. *Personality and Social Psychology Review, 1,* 106-128.

Oyserman, D. (1993). The lens of personhood: Viewing the self and others in a multicultural society. *Journal of Personality and Social Psychology, 65,* 993-1009.

Patterson, M. L. (1983). *Nonverbal behavior: A functional perspective*. New York: Springer-Verlag.

Peabody, D. (1985). *National characteristics*. Cambridge, UK: Cambridge University Press.

Pedersen, P. (1991). Counseling international students. *The Counseling Psychologist, 19,* 10-58.

Pruitt, D. G., & Rubin, J. Z. (1986). *Social conflict: Escalation, stalemate, and settlement*. New York: Random House.

Putnam, L. L., & Wilson, C. E. (1982). Communication strategies in organizational conflicts: Reliability and validity of a measurement. In M. Burgoon (Ed.), *Communication yearbook* (Vol. 6, pp. 629-652). Beverly Hills, CA: Sage.

Rahim, M. A. (1983). A measure of styles of handling interpersonal conflict. *Academy of Management Journal, 26,* 368-376.

Ramanaiah, N., & Deniston, W. (1993). NEO personality inventory profiles of assertive and unassertive person. *Psychological Reports, 73,* 336.

Rancer, A. S., Baukus, R. A., & Infante, D. A. (1985). Relations between argumentativeness and belief structures about arguing. *Communication Education, 34,* 37-47.

Rotter, J. B. (1954). *Social learning and clinical psychology*. Englewood Cliffs, NJ: Prentice Hall.

Rotter, J. B. (1966). Generalized expectancies for internal versus external control of reinforcement. *Psychological Monographs, 80*(609).

Rotter, J. B. (1975). Some problems and misconceptions related to the construct of internal versus external control of reinforcement. *Journal of Consulting and Clinical Psychology, 43,* 56-67.

Rubin, R. B., & Rubin, A. M. (1992). Antecedents of interpersonal communication motivation. *Communication Quarterly, 40,* 305-317.

Rudman, L. (1998). Self-promotion as a risk factor for women: The costs and benefits of counterstereotypical impression management. *Journal of Personality and Social Psychology, 74,* 629-645.

Sallinen-Kuparinen, A. (1986). Finnish communication: Perception and self-reported behavior. *Studia Philogica Jyvaskylaensia, 19,* 16-18.

Sampson, E. E. (1988). The debate on individualism: Indigenous psychologies of the individual and their role in personal and societal functioning. *American Psychologist, 43,* 15-22.

Saville-Troike, M. (1985). The place of silence in an integrated theory of communication. In D. Tannen & M. Saville-Troike (Eds.), *Perspectives on silence* (pp. xi-xvii). Norwood, NJ: Ablex.

Schwartz, S. H. (1990). Individualism-collectivism: Critique and proposed refinements. *Journal of Cross-Cultural Psychology, 21,* 139-157.

Schwartz, S. H. (1994). Cultural dimensions of values: Towards an understanding of national differences. In U. Kim, H. C. Triandis, C. Kagitcibasi, S. C. Choi, & G. Yoon (Eds.), *Individualism and collectivism: Theory, method, and applications* (pp. 85-119). Thousand Oaks, CA: Sage.

Scollon, R. (1985). The machine stops: Silence in the metaphor of malfunction. In D. Tannen & M. Saville-Troike (Eds.), *Perspectives on silence* (pp. 21-30). Norwood, NJ: Ablex.

Segall, M. H. (1986). Culture and behavior: Psychology in global perspective. *Annual Review of Psychology, 37,* 523-564.

Sharkey, W. F., & Singelis, T. M. (1995). Embarrassability and self-construal: A theoretical integration. *Personality and Individual Differences, 19,* 919-926.

Sherif, M. (1935). A study of some social factors in perception. *Archives of Psychology, 27*(187).

Sillars, A. L. (1980). Attribution and communication in roommate conflict. *Communication Monographs, 47,* 180-200.

Singelis, T. M. (1994). The measurement of independent and interdependent self-construals. *Personality and Social Psychology Bulletin, 20,* 580-591.

Singelis, T. M., & Brown, W. J. (1995). Culture, self, and collectivist communication: Linking culture to individual behavior. *Human Communication Research, 21,* 354-389.

Sinha, D., & Tripathi, R. C. (1994). Individualism in a collectivist culture: A case of coexistence of opposites. In U. Kim, H. C. Triandis, C. Kagitcibasi, S. C. Choi, & G. Yoon (Eds.), *Individualism and collectivism: Theory, method, and applications* (pp. 123-136). Thousand Oaks, CA: Sage.

Smith, C. E., Steinke, J., & Distefano, M. K. (1973). Perceived locus of control and future outlook among psychiatric patients. *Journal of Community Psychology, 1,* 40-41.

Smith, P. B., & Bond, M. H. (1993). *Social psychology across cultures: Analysis and perspectives.* New York: Harvester Wheatsheaf.

Solomon, S., Greenberg, J., & Pyszynski, T. (1991). A terror management theory of social behavior: The psychological foundation of self-esteem and cultural worldviews. In M. P. Zanna (Ed.), *Advances in experimental social psychology* (Vol. 24, pp. 93-159). San Diego, CA: Academic.

Sue, D. W., Arredondo, P., & McDavis, R. J. (1992). Multicultural counseling competencies and standards: A call to the professional. *Journal of Counseling and Development, 70,* 477-486.

Tanaka, T. (1987). Self-deprecative tendencies in self-evaluation through social comparison. *Japanese Journal of Experimental Social Psychology, 27,* 27-36.

Tannen, D. (1985). Silence: Anything but. In D. Tannen & M. Saville-Troike (Eds.), *Perspectives on silence* (pp. 93-111). Norwood, NJ: Ablex.

Taylor, S. E., & Brown, J. D. (1988). Illusion and well-being: A social psychological perspective on mental health. *Psychological Bulletin, 103,* 193-210.

Tesser, A. (1986). Some effects of self-evaluation maintenance on cognition and action. In R. M. Sorrentino & E. T. Higgins (Eds.), *Handbook of motivation and cognition: Foundations of social behavior* (pp. 435-464). New York: Guilford.

Thomas, K. W. (1976). Conflict and conflict management. In M. Dunnette (Ed.), *Handbook of industrial and organizational psychology* (pp. 889-935). Chicago: Rand McNally.

Thomas, K. W., & Kilmann, R. H. (1978). Comparison of four instruments measuring conflict behavior. *Psychological Reports, 42,* 1139-1145.

Tice, D. M., Butler, J. L., Muraven, M. B., & Stillwell, A. M. (1995). When modesty prevails: Differential favorability of self-presentation to friends and strangers. *Journal of Personality and Social Psychology, 69,* 1120-1138.

Ting-Toomey, S. (1988). Intercultural conflict styles: A face-negotiation theory. In Y. Y. Kim & W. B. Gudykunst (Eds.), *Theories in intercultural communication* (pp. 213-235). Newbury Park, CA: Sage.

Ting-Toomey, S., Gao, G., Trubisky, P., Yang, Z., Kim, H. S., Lin, S. L., & Nishida, T. (1991). Culture, face maintenance, and styles of handling interpersonal conflict: A study in five cultures. *The International Journal of Conflict Management, 2,* 275-296.

Triandis, H. C. (1989). The self and social behavior in differing cultural contexts. *Psychological Review, 96,* 506-520.

Trompenaars, F. (1993). *Riding the waves of culture.* London: Economist Books.

Trubisky, P., Ting-Toomey, S., & Lin, S. L. (1991). The influence of individualism-collectivism and self-monitoring on conflict styles. *International Journal of Intercultural Relations, 15,* 65-84.

Ward, C., & Kennedy, A. (1992). Locus of control, mood disturbance, and social difficulty during cross-cultural transitions. *International Journal of Intercultural Relations, 16,* 175-194.

Weiss, H., & Sherman, J. (1973). Internal-external control as a predictor of task effort and satisfaction subsequent to failure. *Journal of Applied Psychology, 57,* 132-136.

Wortman, C. B., & Brehm, J. W. (1975). Responses to uncontrollable outcomes: An integration of reactance theory and the learned helplessness model. In L. Berkowitz (Ed.), *Advances in experimental social psychology* (Vol. 9, pp. 277-336). New York: Academic Press.

Transcultural Communication in the U.S.-Africa Context

Can It Help Africa's Emerging National Development?

VIRGINIA H. MILHOUSE

Transculture communication is said to be the aim, rather than the transmission of policies from one culture to the next. However, in the context of national development, transculture communication means not just being present but being actively involved (Awa, 1989). In this sense, transculture communication is a sociocultural activity deriving from things people say and do to each other. Although this type of activity may begin at the cognitive level, it is manifested in both explicit and implicit behaviors (Samovar & Porter, 1997), including face-to-face interaction, participatory involvement, and the trans-mission of mutually agreed on policies through communication technology.

In fact, several researchers have examined the role of transculture communication in the formulation of national policies and programs and found that it was inextricably linked to policy participation and social change. For example, transculture scholars at an international development conference in Bogota stressed the need to link development with public participation and social change so that a majority of the people of that country could take part in its national development process (UNESCO, 1974). Likewise, researchers associated with the National Summit on Africa concluded that national policies cannot be developed without widespread participation from all segments of society.

Therefore, the literature on national development describes participatory communication as "knowing how to speak the other's language" (Awa, 1989, p. 438), that is, knowing how to behave in ways that promote successful and productive development. For the purpose of this chapter, transculture communication will mean not just talking but being actively involved across cultures. It assumes, therefore, a transcultural relationship between the United States and Africa. In so doing, it discusses ways in which these two very different peoples can rise above the conventions and limitations of their cultures and draw from the experiential and intellectual traditions of the other without negating the values of either, to arrive at commonly accepted goals. In this view of transculturalism, this chapter is linked with the primary goals of the book, which are to promote harmony, interaction, and dialogue between diverse cultures. Also examined in this chapter are issues of national development as they relate to the continent of Africa.

Critical to any discussion about national development is an evaluation of contextual factors, including policies involving education and culture, human rights and democracy, and economic development. The first part of this chapter will provide, therefore, an evaluation of Africa's past and current policies in these areas. Also discussed are ways in which the United States can help with Africa's national development. This discussion takes place in the second part of the chapter, using recommendations proposed by the National Summit on Africa to improve U.S.-Africa relations.

▶ Critical Issues in Africa's National Development

Since the early 1990s, Africa has been experiencing profound social, political, and economic changes in what some describe as a "continental rebirth" (National Summit on Africa, 1996). Others have remarked that this is a particularly exciting time for the United States to be involved with Africa, because the region is emerging from years of benign neglect by American business and U.S. policy makers (Coffman, 1999). In fact, Atwood (1999), administrator of the Agency for International Development, says that "Africa is starting on the superhighway to global economy" (p. 16).

Although Africa's current pace of recovery promises to carry it into the new millennium with greatly improved prospects for peace and security, its quest for national development still faces many challenges. First, Africa needs to help development experts, both at home and abroad, to understand its social, cultural, and economic needs. At the domestic level, Africa's development must focus on capacity building across a broad spectrum of infrastructures including, but not limited to, educational institutions, production, management, social engineering, agribusiness, biotechnology, service industries, and information technology. Nation building of this magnitude will enable people to be more self-reliant in economic production while empowering them to plan, implement, evaluate, and participate in national development programs (Toungara, 1998).

Africa's leaders will also need to help development experts from the United States to understand the needs of their continent. Research shows that the American public, as a whole, is both uninformed and misinformed about the continent of Africa (Hart, 1997). This problem is due in part to incomplete and biased portrayals of Africa in the educational system and the mass media (National Summit on Africa, 1996). American knowledge about Africa also has roots in the colonial era when the United States emphasized a "hands off" and isolationist policy toward Africa, followed by constructive engagement with the repressive system of apartheid in South Africa, corruption in Zaire, dictatorship in Liberia, and human rights abuses in Nigeria. These types of abuses helped to reinforce the image of African people as standard bearers of poverty, ignorance, disease, flawed development, and social disorder. Thus, over the years, Americans have viewed Africa as a region of no strategic value to the United States (Nwosu & Taylor, 1999). It is clear, therefore, that both national and transnational understanding will be important to Africa's national development. But how does Africa, a culture that values community and collective action, bring about cultural synchronization with the United States, which values individuality and competition?

One way is to employ coalition building as a means to promote transculture communication and negotiation between the two cultures. Coalition building helps to shed valuable light on all types of differences (Dupont, 1996), especially in an international setting. Moreover, coalition building seeks to highlight common interests between cultures and reduces the complexity of bilateral transactions, in this case between African and the United States, while offering a level of equanimity in international negotiations. Thus, it is also a away to promote transculture communication.

If cultures with widely different values are to work in harmony, Awa (1989) argues that they must have a common understanding of the idea of national development. National development is a complex process that defies attempts to see it as unidimensional, although this view is often reflected in some descriptions of it. Traditionally, scholars in the development field focused only on economic growth; now, it is conceded that national development is a total process involving not only economic change but social, political, and educational development. Thus, five issues that are critical to national development are: participation, development planning, implementation, evaluation, and decentralization.

Development planning is the application of intelligence to the analysis of current situations and the search for strategies to solve specific problems in a nation (Awa, 1989, p. 432). In Africa, development planning requires the establishment of policies in the areas of de-

mocracy and human rights, education and culture, and economic development. While neither the United States or Africa is a stranger to planning, implementation of a policy plan of action, which requires widespread participation at all levels of society, is often hampered by politics, ethnic loyalties, and ineffective communication between groups within Africa. Also, a national plan of action can be hampered by the degree to which governments are willing to decentralize planning and development functions. In many parts of Africa, there is a movement toward the devolution of specific development functions to district or provincial administrative bodies.

While completing a 1996-1997 Fulbright teaching and research program in South Africa, I took part in its educational development process. An aspect of this was the decentralization of power at the national Department of Education level so that educators at provincial, local, and community levels would have more say about their schools' practices and about teaching and learning decisions. Thus, as a part of a huge group of educators and individuals from local school communities, I witnessed firsthand the process of decentralization, as South Africa adopted its new Schools Act of 1997. Among other policies, this act created new school governance structures and partnerships between the state and all those involved in education, including parents, learners, educators, non-teaching staff, and the community.

As for *participation,* this means different things to different people. For the purposes of this discussion, it is defined as the "mental, physical, and emotional involvement of persons in group situations that encourage them to contribute to group goals and share responsibility for them" (Davis, 1977, p. 140). During my stay in South Africa, I also learned about its view of the importance of involvement and/or participation. Many South Africans today aspire to the Sotho principle of *tiriasano,* which means working together. Although many have participated at the national and community levels, one still gets the sense that participation is more about who they are than about what they do. For most, participation is a way of life. This sense of community participation is modeled from the top down. It was no more unusual to see, then, President Nelson Mandela at *straat* (street) children's homes or community development projects in the townships than to see him at functions for prime ministers or ambassadors. This same sense of community participation has trickled down to the grassroots level in South Africa.

If Africa's quest for development is to be successful, this same spirit of involvement will need to be part of its dealings with the United States. These cultures will need to be involved mentally and emotionally, as well as being physically present. Americans and Africans must be motivated to work with each other and to view their partnership as mutually beneficial. Africa needs U.S. resources: know-how, capital, technology, and political support. On the other hand, the United States is also quite aware of the economic stake it has in Africa. According to Nwosu and Taylor (1999), U.S. trade figures show more than $5 billion in exports to Africa in 1997 alone, surpassing the volume of U.S. trade with countries in the former Soviet Union.

Just how successful the United States and Africa will be at achieving their goals will depend on the readiness of both parties to negotiate. Proponents of the readiness theory argue it can be useful in international negotiations when conditions are ripe. However, both sides must be motivated and optimistic about achieving mutually acceptable outcomes. For example, some theorists believe, had it not been for "motivational ripeness" before the Oslo and Middle East talks and the optimism that developed during the talks, agreement would not have been reached.

Readiness theory would be useful for talks between the United States and Africa because (a) it allows for a circular negotiation process, which is suited to the traditions of Africa; (b) it builds on a steady growth in trust; and (c) it gives the perception that both parties are represented by authentic spokespersons and perceived common ground (Pruitt, 1997).

I am among those who believe that the timing for improved U.S.-Africa relations could not be better. As indicated above, since the beginning of the 1990s, Africa has been experiencing profound social, political, and economic changes. Certainly, when President Clinton announced at Independence Square in Accra, the seat of the Ghanaian government in 1998, that "I want to build a future partnership between our two peoples, and I want to introduce the people of the United States to the new face of Africa" (Nwosu & Taylor, 1999, p. 13), he was signaling that the time was ripe.

One of the first steps in planning, whether or not it focuses on development, is the evaluation of existing problems and the identification of what ought to be done. The ultimate goal of national development is to move from a less desirable state to a more desirable one. Therefore, this part of the chapter evaluates Africa's emerging national development by examining its historical and contemporary policies toward democracy and human rights, education and culture, and economic development. The second part of the chapter addresses the question, how can U. S. involvement (i.e., participatory communication) help Africa's emerging national development.

▶ Africa's Policy Toward Democracy and Human Rights

HISTORICAL PERSPECTIVE

If democracy, as defined by Dewey (1916), is a mode of associated living and participation, then it is not a new concept to Africa. Research shows that during ancient times, African peoples practiced a democracy that was shaped by the complexity and uniqueness of their societies. Although in ancient times, many African societies presented marked features of nonhomogeneity, they valued the devolution of power. In other words, power was systematically distributed throughout local societal units such as territorial divisions, clans, lineages, and extended families. Thus, traditional Africa had a highly developed political system that included empires, kingdoms, and stateless societies. The organizational structure of these systems was hierarchical, beginning with the family unit, and the devolution of power was extended from this point to the lineage, the clan, and various territorial divisions. These ancient systems practiced a democratic process that was both autonomous and participatory: Extended families in villages chose their heads, who together formed a council of elders without which the process could not work, because there was an egalitarian relationship between the council of elders, the chiefs, and the king.

This devolution of power seems rather analogous to some modern day political systems, in which one branch of government shares power with other branches, for example, the executive, legislative, and judicial branches of the U.S. government. It also resembles Awa's (1989) concept of participation, which means being actively involved. As noted by Dia (1996), "the moral order of African management was robustly collective" (p. 41). There was a consciousness of the rights of every individual to contribute and participate in all aspects of society and of the need to maintain cohesion within a society that was also heterogeneous.

As for human rights, Keller (1998) states that "human rights ideals represent a goal that no society has as yet achieved . . . and [they] represent] aspirations that are pursued with varying degrees of success" (p. 7). But Africa is known for its belief in the principle of human rights or *ubuntu,* which embodies a way of life that contributes positively to the sustenance and well-being of a people, community, or society (Sindane, 1994). *Ubuntu,* an ancient African proverb, describes a way of believing, thinking, behaving, and living that promotes the good of the society.

Using the Xhosa spelling of the word, Goduka (1999) explains that *yobuntu* is a morally guiding principle that undergirds the past and present worldviews of indigenous peoples of Africa, Asia, Australia, and North and South America. *Yobuntu* societies live by a set of collective and cooperative values that recognize all peoples as belonging to the same race, the human race. Such values were an integral part of Africa's ancient cultural, social, and spiritual fabric. Thus, basic human rights have always been held sacred by African countries and are embodied in the *African Charter on Human and Peoples' Rights,* which states that all peoples "shall have the unquestionable and inalienable right to self-determination, dignity, freedom, social justice, and respect" (Salim, 1992, p. 4), but society, at the same time, must be conscious of the need to balance individual rights with those of the "overaching" society. Likewise, Makau wa Mutua (1996) explains that

> The concept of group-centered individuals in Africa delicately entwines rights and duties, and harmonizes the individual with the society. Such a concept does not necessarily see society. . . . organized either as the community or the state . . . as the individual's primary antagonist. (p. 591)

RECENT PERSPECTIVE

Africa's recent democratic and human rights policies provide a big contrast to those of ancient times—those pervasive and enduring qualities of humanity, community, and collectivity all but degenerated into a relativistic pretext for authoritarian military rule by the early 19th century.

What were the extenuating circumstances that caused the continent's member states to move from humanitarian societies to the autocratic colonial states that existed between the years 1956 and 1990? Some scholars argue that the core of African society and culture was changed in the early 19th century, when European colonialism interrupted the flow of human life throughout the continent of Africa and introduced institutional mutations that continue to have a profound effect on people today (Entelis, 1998). Although the world was led to believe that colonialism was engaged in a "civilizing" and "humanizing" effort in Africa, it was instead, exploitative, using people mainly for economic purposes (Davidson, 1994; Mazrui, 1995). During the long struggle against colonialism, Africans were treated as less than citizens in their own lands, whereas European settlers were given the benefits and rights of African citizenship as well as the right to retain citizenship in their own land. To compound the problem, the wealth of Africans' land was taken away from them through unscrupulous and inequitable means, leaving the continent ultimately in a virtual state of bankruptcy (Entelis, 1998). But the biggest problem colonialism caused for Africa was to create an infrastructure that no longer embodied African traditions and structures—rendering it insufficient for the challenges of the modern age (Kay, 1975).

Thus, following independence, most African states found themselves using political institutions that were developed and structured by their former rulers. For example, Francophone Africa had adopted France's presidential form of government, which adhered to a rather moderate-autocratic type of leadership; Anglophone Africa continued to follow the parliamentary form of government, which was designed to encourage representative democracy and to monitor the actions of the executive through an assembly of popularly elected delegates to a national assembly (Entelis, 1998). Consequently, Africa's recent political systems came to be built on competitiveness instead of the traditional principles of cooperation, collectivity, and humanitarianism.

Africa's postindependent states had been expected to adopt the "best" Western democratic practices and use them to form even more efficient, effective, and equitable models of their own, but this was not to be. In fact, it was hard for Africans to adopt the ways and customs of the regimes that had oppressed them for so many years. As a result, one after another, African societies began to reject the ways that the West had governed and run its society, trying to create instead hybrid governments more suitable to their own ways and customs (Entelis, 1998). According to Keller (1998), by the mid-1980s, more than half of Africa's 50 independent states had military governments; among the remaining civilian regimes, only 5—Botswana, Gambia, Mauritius, Senegal, and Zimbabwe—had competitive party systems.

Shortly after the competitive party system was replaced by authoritarian military regimes, the state of affairs in Africa began to decline. Frequent coups and civil wars broke out in many countries, acts of genocide were not uncommon in noncivilian states such as Rwanda, and legislation was introduced in South Africa that gave meaning to the colonial system of subjugation of Africans, colored, and Indians. This was, in many ways, the beginning of the apartheid or "apart-hate" regime in South Africa, which introduced a series of anti-democratic and anti-human rights laws, including the Prohibition of Mixed Marriages of 1949, which outlawed marriages between the races; and the Population Registration Act of 1950, which created a legal definition of race and classified everybody into one of four races: white, native or Bantu, colored, and Indian. A law known as the Group Areas Act of 1950 allowed the National Party government to create totally separate living and working areas and prohibited one race of people from owning property in an area reserved for another. This law was followed by the intensification of the British Pass Law or Natives Abolition of Passes Act of 1952, which subjected black people to punishment if they did not have a document called a reference book. The Separate Amenities Act separated the races completely by removing colored, Indians, and natives to the outskirts of urban areas. It also instituted the separation of public facilities such as trains, buses, beaches, and park benches. Last but not least, in 1953, the Bantu Education Act, "one of the most hated aspects of the apartheid regime" (Bradley, 1996, p. 12), was instituted. This act decreed a separate and inferior education for black children, which meant that they would never be able to compete with whites in the labor market (Bradley, 1996).

The following quote by Dr. Salim Ahmed Salim, secretary general of the Organization of African Unity (OAU), best sums up the human rights abuses perpetrated on the peoples of South Africa by the apartheid regime:

> The struggle of our countries in Africa against colonialism and apartheid was given legal expression through such concepts as the right to self-determination. Indeed, in the particular case of apartheid, so strong was our perception, as that of the international community, that it was an evil in need of destruction that it came to be termed a "crime against humanity." It became, in fact more than just a civil breach of the rights of our brethren in South Africa. It became a phenomenon that was not to be tolerated and the apartheid state which was perpetrating all those wrongs against humanity became in consequence an outlawed state against which the international community imposed sanctions. (1992, p. 3)

TODAY'S PERSPECTIVES

Currently, at least one out of every two countries in Africa has begun to establish procedural steps for democracy. This trend is linked to several events, one of which is the emergence of a widespread commitment to civility. In many parts of Francophone Africa, for example, civil society is manifested in the form of national dialogues based on both the traditional principles of village assemblies and the French Estates-General. The first of these conferences took place in Benin, after a group of concerned citizens for consolidated civility forced the Kerekou government to hold a national assembly on political reform. The assembly, which brought together diverse groups and associations, convened for more than a year to plan a new process of democratic laws that would govern relations between the people and the state. The outcome of the Benin assembly produced several path-breaking democratic reforms that would later have widespread ramifications. Perhaps the most important of these was the establishment of legislative and executive bodies to serve during the transitional period leading up to multiparty elections. This political reform spread to other societies such as Niger, Mali, and Zaire.

The second event was the adoption of the 1990 OAU Heads of State Declaration, which clearly establishes precedents for national unity in Africa. In this document, heads of states declared that "it is necessary to promote a political environment which guarantees human rights and the observance of law, the promotion of democratization of our societies, and the consolidation of democratic institutions in our countries" (Salim, 1992, p. 4).

According to political scientists, the success of democratic consolidation can best be judged by how graciously an ousted democratic government accepts its defeat immediately following the implementation of a multiparty system. The test of Africa's commitment to democratic consolidation was, thus, demonstrated in several recent multiparty elections. South Africa's first democratic election was described, for example, as one of the most peaceful government turnovers in history. The process of democratization in South Africa actually began in 1990, when the ban on all political groups was lifted and large numbers of exiles were allowed to return to the country. This was followed by the release of Nelson Mandela, who had been imprisoned for 27 years. And although the events that followed led to difficult negotiations, in the general election of April 1994, "for the first time all adults from diverse backgrounds were eligible to vote to elect a new government democratically" (Goduka, 1999, p. 42).

Although South Africa has just recently emerged from a bitter struggle of racism and colonial oppression, the new government has put in place a number of structures to ensure democracy in South Africa. It has been said that democracy is not something you have but something you do. In 1996, the Constitutional Assembly wrote South Africa's first democratic constitution, which reflects this principle in many ways. The assembly took major steps not only to protect the country's democracy but also to guard against abuses of power. Among other initiatives, the constitution ensures the right of all South Africans to equal protection and benefit under the law. No one, including the government, will be allowed to discriminate against individuals because of race, gender, marital status, origin, color, sexual orientation, age, disability, religion, culture, or language. The new constitution marked the birth of a new nation and ushered in an era of freedom and the dawning of democracy in families, schools, and the entire South African society (Goduka, 1999).

Recent elections in Benin and Madagascar also represent examples of Africa's commitment to consolidated democracy. In Benin, Kerekou, described as a chastened former dictator, was reelected in 1995 in a relatively peaceful and fair election. Similarly, in Madagascar in 1996, another former dictator, Diedier Ratsiraka, also won reelection in a multiparty system. In fact, Ratsiraka is quoted as saying, "My victory is due more to the disillusionment of the Malagasy people toward the old regime than to their enthusiasm for me" (Meldrum, 1997, p. 5).

Even some "second elections" that retain incumbent regimes can express the character of democratic consolidation. This was the case of Ghana's 1996 presidential elections. President Jerry Rawlings, in his first term after the revitalization of multiparty politics, continued to develop Ghana's economic recovery, thus attracting strong international and domestic support. "Rawlings was able to score a huge victory, winning 58 percent of the vote with 75 percent voter turnout . . . clearly demonstrat[ing]. . . . he had forsaken the autocratic ways [which] characterized his rule before 1992" (Entelis, 1998, p. 20). The real test of Ghana's new democracy will come at the end of Rawlings's term, when he is forbidden by law from running again.

In conclusion, Africa's current process of democratization is still in a delicate period of transition. It is experiencing both democratic gains and setbacks, making any sustainable consolidation difficult. On the other hand, there is the promise that the continent will experience its second political liberation and ultimate democratic consolidation—especially, if those forces that had the political will to undermine the autocratic regimes continue to prevail.

▶ Policy Toward Education and Culture

HISTORICAL PERSPECTIVE

Throughout history, Africa, the birthplace of ancient civilization, has influenced a broad range of ideas and ways of knowing. Neter (1990) argues that all fundamental knowledge, skills, and institutions of civilization began with black nations such as Kemet (ancient Egypt), Summer, Babylon, Elam, the Harappa Valley civilization, Kush (Ethiopia), Indus Kush (black India), and Canaan. Drawing from a rich and diverse cultural heritage, African peoples contributed to world civilizations many features, including science and knowledge, art, literature, music, and spirituality. This occurred long before the rise of Western Europe. And although it is true that the Romans and the Greeks built classical civilizations of their own, they were influenced by ancient Africa.

Although Europe and the United States emerged as world powers with the help of Africa's human and natural resources, Africans were viewed by the colonizers as uncivilized peoples. They were described as such because their education did not meet the conditions for acquiring knowledge set by the rational model of science, which was based on the ideology and philosophy of Newton, a physicist, and Descartes, a philosopher. This model dominated the natural sciences and the humanities in the early 19th century and continues to do so.

But the truth about African societies and their provision of systematic programs of education, including children's education, should by now be beyond doubt (Kenyatta, 1978, p. 98). Although there were informal elements in traditional African education, that is, it was not generally conducted by a professional class of educators or in schools as distinct social institutions as we know them today, systematic programs of education with identifiable learning processes and goals were deeply embedded in the African social fabric (Fowler, 1997; Njoroge & Bennaars, 1986).

But the fact that African education lacked a formal structure or Western style professionalism was not the reason why the colonizers viewed it as a primitive form of education. The main reason was because it lacked the learning goals and processes that were characteristic of European education. In other words, African education was not premised on a universal scientific model that engaged in the claims of (a) objective knowledge, (b) rational knowledge (knowledge based on human reasoning), or (c) positivism (empirically verified knowledge).

African traditional education was based, instead, on a different way of knowing. In contrasting the different ways of knowing, Neter (1990) distinguishes three ways. One way tends to rely on the will of the human being for survival and growth. The second way relies on omniscient intelligence and automation, and the third way of knowing is the equilibrium of these ways.

The ways of knowing are not separate or distinct types but a continuous spiral that can best be explained as stages of development. The first stage relates to the first way of knowing, which relies on limited knowledge and capability, such as human reasoning or the rational mind. The second stage relates to the second way of knowing and, as noted above, relies on infinite knowledge and capability, whereas stage three is the equilibrium between the first and second stages. In Stage 1,

human development relies totally on outside or external knowledge and guidance; that is, from educators, missionaries, ministers, tools, machinery, medicines, objective science, and so forth. In Stage 2, human development relies on self-knowledge—spiritual, ancestral, and intuitive knowledge; and Stage 3 is the interrelationship between Stages 1 and 2. Knowledge is systemic, beginning as an inner notion and then reaching levels external to the individual, including institutional, societal, national, and cultural levels.

However, the way in which most cultures acquire knowledge, that is, epistemology, is by cultivating only one of these ways. For the most part, Westerners cultivate knowledge through external ways of knowing. On the other hand, Africans and some Asians have sought to understand life and humankind more from the internal perspective. Only the Kemetians (ancient Egyptians), argues Neter, have been successful in cultivating both ways of knowing—integrating internal and external knowledge. Consequently, ancient Africans had the ability to learn from the internal part of the self, which stores knowledge about the secrets of the world; thus, they were able to intuit—more than 6,000 years ago—the knowledge that forms the basis of our civilization (religion, mathematics, geometry, medicine, astronomy, writing, literature, agriculture, metallurgy, government, architecture, painting, sculpturing, algebra, and science). On the other hand, Western people, being polarized in the cultivation of the external part of the self (rational mind), learned these skills from those cultures that relied most on the intuitive or inner way of knowing (Neter, 1990, pp. 7-8).

Yet, the colonizers, unable to recognize and appreciate existing knowledge and assuming that the rational model was valid anyplace in the world, dismissed the African way of acquiring knowledge as educationally worthless. This wholesale displacement of ancient African (Kemetic) traditions had a significantly devastating effect on its societies. First, it introduced a dissonance in Africa's ways of learning that was irreconcilable. Moreover, by giving primacy to scientific and technocratic knowledge as the values that guide human development, the Western colonizers denied the importance of extraordinary knowledge, such as wisdom, understanding, and intuition.

The irony of this whole situation is that African traditional education incorporated features that many U.S. educators are now seeking to incorporate into their teaching and learning processes, that is, principles such as community, cooperation, unity, real learning (developing the whole person mind, body, and spirit), civic education, and education that re-creates the self by making learning recreational.

TODAY'S PERSPECTIVE

What is the condition of Africa's culture today, and how has it affected African education? Geographically, Africa is the second-largest continent in the world. It covers an area of 11.7 million square miles, occupies about 22% of the world's land mass, and is divided into 54 independent states. Ethnoculturally, the continent is also diverse, consisting of 1,000 different ethnic groups who speak more than 800 different languages or dialects and who practice a variety of religions. Ethnically, the continent's nearly 800 million people form a cross-section of all African groups.

In the 1990s, African culture continues to be defined by African art and music, which capture the historical, social, and political transformation of the continent. Ranging from rock paintings to wood, metal, and stone sculptures, African art expresses deeply rooted philosophical and social values. Currently, at the grassroots level, there has emerged a vibrant culture that marries traditional art forms to both modern art forms and modern themes. In Mozambique, for example, some brilliantly conceptualized and executed paintings depict the extreme suffering of the people who died in the thousands at the hands of violent rebels and from the starvation that

accompanied the fighting. All over Africa, community drama groups have emerged, bringing entertainment as well as education to the people (Toungara, 1998, p. 9).

These aesthetic forms have the unique power to educate about African culture. In particular, the drama groups both entertain and educate about African experiences with human rights abuses, poverty, crime, and antidemocratic practices. Paintings such as Pemba's "Freedom Through Education" reflect the quest for freedom through teaching and learning, as well as the artist's interpretation of the Shell Education Service, a unique program dedicated to enhancing the skills of thousands of African teachers. This piece of art shows that through the production and distribution of teaching resources such as pictures, puzzles, and posters, teachers are empowered to satisfy their students' thirst for knowledge.

However, to create a truly successful culture in the 21st century, Africa will need more than merely passive forays into historical cultural forms. It must mediate the gap between a society that is historically situated in African indigenous systems and the demands of an emerging global world. There is the need, therefore, for widespread application of development technologies as well as major changes in social structures, political systems, and economic organizations. Although most African countries have already begun to make such changes, they lack the strong and dynamic education policies and infrastructure needed to undergird this difficult process. Thus, one of the biggest needs facing the continent in the new century is quality and technological education.

There have been some remarkable improvements in African education over the past three decades, including a major climb in adult literacy, which doubled from 27% to 54%; in primary school enrollment, which increased from 25% to 50%; and in secondary school enrollment, which increased from 13% to 38%. Still, more than half of African children, 80 million, remain out of school. Additional sources point to the fact that in almost every country, African girls account for a small percentage of the total number of children enrolled at the primary and secondary education levels, although they form about 30% of the total population for this age group. In addition, the retention rate for children who start school is not optimal. Only about 1.5% ever obtain university or postgraduate education levels. Over the years, these conditions have produced a group of African youth ages 15 to 30 who are uneducated and unemployed (Toungara, 1998).

South Africa is in the midst of transformation and development. Although it has only recently ended a regime once described as a crime against humanity (i.e., apartheid), the country's economic, political, and social structures are changing very rapidly. Yet, this nation is not without problems. As in other parts of the continent, poverty is both extreme and pervasive in South Africa, with a large segment of the population living in nearly destitute conditions. We have learned from experience that poverty is a precursor to crime, and the crime rate in South Africa threatens to put the entire continent at risk. In addition, relationships between the different ethnic and racial groups continue to be often adversarial; in this sense, the legacy of apartheid lives on. In other words, South Africa is still a deeply divided society in which competition is likely to increase between these groups. Inequity is also rampant, especially in the African segment of the population (O'Hair, Milhouse, Reitzug, & Slabbert, 1999).

To address these issues and continue the momentum of political, social, and economic transformation, South Africa's educational system needs to be transformed. Currently, its educational system reflects the drastic social, cultural, and economic inequities that exist throughout the continent. Rural and township schools, attended mostly by African students, are frequently housed in substandard facilities with limited access to books, learning materials, and technology. Potenza (1998) concedes that "some township schools are hellholes. . . . [there's] no question about it. Parents feel they cannot rely on state education and their anxiety about this is really taking

hold" (p. 50). Equally significant, teachers, parents, and other educators in these areas have limited access to information, knowledge, and the latest research on teaching, learning, and democratic school practices. This puts a ceiling on their professional development. Educators are largely isolated within their own classrooms, homes, and schools, with limited opportunities to learn from each other and from other schools. Parents have been described as treating schools as glorified day care centers and taking little interest in their children's progress (O'Hair et al., 1999).

Meanwhile, many predominantly English and Africaan schools in more urban areas have the latest in technology, facilities, and materials but still work largely in isolation, with little or no sharing of best practices among educators. Thus, they seem to be achieving a degree of success, while continuing the traditional and regimented educational practices that poorly prepare students for life in South Africa's rapidly changing society. This is compounded by the fact that educators at predominately white schools have limited knowledge about the conditions that exist for educators and students in rural and township schools or of the successes these educators and students achieve despite the adverse conditions under which they labor (O'Hair et al., 1999).

▶ Africa's Economic and Sustainable Development

Initially, development experts believed that economic growth was the primary goal of national development. They have since acknowledged that national development is a total process involving not only economic change but social, political, and environmental factors (Awa, 1989). Thus, Africa's success with economic development will depend on how successful it is in all of the national development areas, on how well it balances major social, political, and environmental changes.

Meyer-Weitz (1998) cautions that different cultures hold different views about development. Some tend to treat issues important to development as if they were totally separate. This is partly due to the fragmentation of knowledge that characterizes the Western practice of human science. For example, in Western cultures, development may involve nonhuman entities such as the physical infrastructures of water and sanitation, roads, buildings, schools, hospitals, and houses. On the other hand, issues such as health and nutrition, human resources, natural resources, and education or community participation are treated as separate entities of the development process.

But the truth of the matter is that a society cannot have national development without developing people and, in turn, having people participate in the development of their society. This is consistent with the human development model, which acknowledges that whereas development can be measured in terms of *economic aggregates* or technological and physical achievements, human development is the only dimension of true worth in national development (Awa, 1989). Thus, Africa has begun to teach its people the importance of developing healthy lifestyles, which is a prerequisite to participation in the broader society, including (a) education, i.e., training in basic mathematics, science, and reading; (b) human resource management, including preparing women and children for involvement in decision making in business, families, and communities; (c) advanced scientific and technological revolutions for the development of rural and disparate areas; and (d) nutrition and health. Good health is viewed, therefore, as the cornerstone of society and as a prerequisite to economic and sustainable development, which must be balanced with major political, economic, environmental, and social changes.

In addition, Africa has adopted widespread community participation. Although community participation can take many forms, most African communities employ steps that are aligned with Awa's national participation model: (a) the decentralization of goods and services to regions, provinces, and districts so

that they are accessible to the people; (b) the adoption of a management system in which district personnel play an important part; (c) implementation of primary health care and community-based social development programs; and (d) involvement of stakeholders—both inside and outside the community—in the planning and delivery of services. These steps demonstrate the relevance of economic and sustainable development to the total developmental process.

In summary, Africa's successful management of participatory development is largely responsible for the unprecedented political and economic transformation it is currently undergoing. For example, Coffman (1999) reports that more than 30 countries have held elections during the 1990s, building a climate of business confidence. Awa (1989) says that when program implementation is not hampered by politics, ethnic loyalties, or poor participation, it can ensure that action will be taken and progress made (p. 433).

Thus, following on the heels of its democratic revolution, Africa is experiencing a major surge in economic growth. More than 30 nations have instituted programs of divestiture in discredited state-controlled economic systems, which have been replaced by free enterprise systems. According to the International Monetary Fund, these measures have influenced economic growth throughout the continent. For example, in 1997, sub-Saharan Africa experienced 4.0% real growth, with projections for 1998 and 1999 of 4.1% and 4.8%, respectively. Finally, as its political and economic programs continue to flourish, Africa's global trading system is reaching historic proportions. Between 1993 and 1996, the continent's total exports were up by 45% while the trading figures for imports surged to an all-time high of 32%.

▶ U.S. Involvement in Africa's National Development

In the first part of this chapter, Awa's critical issues of national development were dis-

U.S.-Africa Context ▼ 45

cussed. It was also noted that one of the most important issues of national development was communication, which he describes as "being actively involved" (Awa, 1989, p. 435). Also posed were the questions, What does participation and active involvement have to do with communication between the United States and Africa? How can it help Africa's emerging national development? After studying national development in the Middle East, Iran, and Turkey, Lerner (1966) argued that for transculturalists to gain a true understanding of events occurring in remote places or to get a broad perspective from all segments of a society, they needed to be actively involved in the development process and not just present.

Thus, the United States will need to be actively involved in Africa's quest for national development, providing such resources as technical know-how, capital, technology, and political support. Both cultures must be motivated to be involved; they must view the partnership as mutually beneficial. The United States has an important economic stake in Africa. As stated earlier, U.S. trade figures showed more than $5 billion in exports to Africa in 1997 alone.

Therefore, the time has come for improved relations between the United States and Africa. This is evident at governmental and business levels as well as in other parts of the public sector in America. In fact, Jean Coffman, program adviser to the U.S. Department of Commerce, remarked that Africa is the focus of U.S. government attention today as never before. This was highlighted by President Clinton's visit to Africa in March 1998, as well as by congressional approval of the African Growth and Opportunity Act.

There is also a growing interest in Africa at the grassroots level in the United States. In 1997, Hart surveyed Americans' knowledge and attitudes about the continent of Africa on behalf of the National Summit on Africa. Although it was revealed that Americans knew very little about Africa, they said they wanted to "learn more and [were] supportive of efforts to raise public awareness" (p. 1).

Thus, no longer can it be said that the United States has a hands-off or isolationist policy toward Africa and its peoples. Rather, during his visit to Africa in early 1998, President Bill Clinton emphasized a need for a major shift in U.S. foreign policy toward Africa. For example, he openly expressed the need for mutual respect and partnership between the two cultures. Moreover, President Clinton acknowledged the futility of past developmental approaches and announced that U.S. leadership in the world must be inextricably linked to its strategic interest in Africa. This shift in policy, as we enter the new millennium, would help to ensure America's sustainability both at home and abroad and, at the same time, give Africa the resources, technical know-how, technology, and political support it so strongly needs.

By greatly expanding dialogue between Africa and all segments of American society, the United States can also help Africa's emerging national development. In a speech to the Ghanaian government on March 23, 1998, President Clinton committed to greater U.S. participation in Africa's development when he said, "I want to build a future partnership between our two peoples, and I want to introduce the people of the United States to the new face of Africa" (Nwosu & Taylor, 1999, p. 13). Furthermore, by emphasizing a participatory partnership between the United States and Africa—one based on dialogue and not top-down directives—the president essentially placed the continent of Africa on equal terms with the United States.

Almost immediately following the president's historical visit to the continent of Africa, the National Summit on Africa's Foreign Policy Advisory Committee drafted a Development Plan of Action aimed at guiding U.S. relations with the countries and peoples of Africa. This plan addressed at least three of Awa's (1989) critical issues in national development: evaluation, participation (i.e., communicative involvement), and implementation.

First, it required a survey, that is, evaluation, to assess current knowledge and attitudes of Americans toward Africa. The plan also required broad-based participation. In other words, a series of five regional summits and preparatory meetings were held in which people all over the United States participated in public education activities and engaged in discussion to provide input for the implementation of the national plan for U.S.-Africa relations. This process culminated with the National Summit on Africa (NSOA) in Washington, D.C., from February 16 to 21, 2000.

A discussion of what happened at the National Summit can, in my view, best answer the questions: What does participation and active involvement have to do with transculture communication between the United States and Africa? How can it help Africa's emerging national development? First, the summit provided a forum for six world leaders (from Africa, Europe, and the United States) who presented a lively and thought-provoking discussion about issues of governance, economic development, health care, and conflict resolution. Moreover, participants from every segment of American society—students, homemakers, clergy, doctors, professors, former Peace Corps volunteers, diplomats, community organizers, local government officials, representatives of nongovernment organizations, business people, and immigrants from Africa—joined the debate and discussions.

The discussions were transcultural in the sense that they were guided by the principles of

Authentic communication: Kenya's President Daniel Arap Moi, remarked that "I don't usually attend many international meetings because Africa is not usually an item on the Agenda."

Acceptance and affirmation of diversity: Vice President Al Gore remarked, "If the world had been wiser, they would have taken from Africa not its valuables but its values."

Inclusiveness: In his keynote address, President Bill Clinton remarked that "it is no longer an option for us not to know

about the trials and triumphs of people who share this small planet. We can no longer choose not to know . . . but we can only choose not to act. Americans must choose, when it comes to Africa, to a make a difference."

Ability to relate to others with understanding and respect: The National Summit's president, Leonard Robinson, said, "we must never allow Africa to be marginalized again. . . . as the cradle of human evolution, it deserves our priority attention to help it realize its promise." (all quotes from (*Summit News,* 2000, pp. 1-2).

NSOA RECOMMENDATIONS FOR U.S.-AFRICA RELATIONS

However, the summit wasn't just about being present or giving speeches; it was about active involvement and participation. As one of about 1,800 delegates to the National Summit, I participated in a 3-day intensive process of deliberation in which 239 recommendations were debated and approved to help guide U.S. relations with Africa. In addition, we approved 10 priority recommendations (2 for each of the summit's five thematic sessions) for immediate action and to serve as anchors to the *National Policy Plan of Action for U.S.-Africa Relations in the 21st Century* (National Summit on Africa, 2000). To demonstrate how these recommendations can be used to help guide U.S. involvement in Africa's national development, 1 of 10 priority recommendations for each of the five Summit themes is discussed in the paragraphs below.

One priority recommendation we debated and adopted during the thematic session, Democracy and Human Rights, was

The U.S. government and public and private sectors should make the promotion of democracy and respect for human rights central to their policies toward Africa. The United States should increase support toward existing and emerging institutions that do not violate human rights. U.S. foreign assistance, including trade benefits, security assistance, finance, and logistics should be available on a preferential basis to those that respect human rights. This assistance must include human rights training. To this end, the [United States] should be committed to bringing all Americans, particularly African Americans, to the forefront of discussions, planning, and implementation of all initiatives. (National Summit on Africa, 2000, p. xiii)

Since the early 1990s, there has been a systematic attempt to influence these types of initiatives. At first, this was done primarily through existing programs under the United States Information Service (USIS) and newer programs created by the United States Agency for International Development (USAID). USIS tried to promote civic education and empowerment programs for disadvantaged groups, such as organizations representing women and children, to build democratic institutions, and to promote human rights. USAID also sought to foster democracy in Africa, although it has historically limited its programs to social and economic development (Entelis, 1998).

However, Entelis (1998) argues that the U.S. government's current approach toward democracy focuses less on electoral monitoring and insistence on immediate multiparty electoral competition. Instead, there is a greater emphasis on building institutional capacity and creating enabling environments for the development of a "culture of democracy." As a result, the immediate pressure for democracy from the United States has been somewhat reduced in Africa.

As for human rights policy, the Clinton administration has been particularly conspicuous in tolerating grave human rights violations in some states while being critical of human rights practices in other states. Thus, to ensure just and fair treatment for all African states, participants in the National Summit on Africa further recommended that "the U.S. formulate an alliance of constituencies for Africa, with national, regional, and local repre-

sentation," such as the Rainbow Coalition, TransAfrica, the African-American Institute, and the Congressional Black Caucus. In the past, these organizations have been crucial to the U.S. international policy-making process, and they should be used to encourage proactive and fair human rights policies for Africa. In fact, Nwosu and Taylor (1999) point out the increasing importance of African Americans in the development of U.S. human rights policies toward Africa. More than 30 million Americans trace their origins to Africa, and they are increasingly proud of their ancestral roots.

As a matter of fact, many African Americans trace their roots back to Ghana, which was President Clinton's first stop on his historic 12-day trip to Africa. During the trans-Atlantic slave trade, Ghana was a major trading post. Indeed, recalling the inhumane treatment of millions of Africans who were captured and transported to Europe and the Americas to serve on plantations, President Clinton remarked that "going back to the time before we were even a nation. . . . European Americans received the fruits of the slave trade. And we were wrong in that" (Nwosu & Taylor, 1999, p. 14). If there were human rights policies aimed at giving human beings freedom from torture, arbitrary arrest, and imprisonment, they were not practiced during the enslavement of millions of Africans. Instead, Africans were subjugated and stripped of their national and cultural identities. Entire families were dissolved; small children and teenagers were separated from their families and auctioned off while grieving relatives stood watching.

Thus, President Clinton's acknowledgment of America's wrongdoing regarding slavery can be regarded as a historical event: He is the first U.S. President to make such a declaration. Mazrui (1999), a leading voice on African national development, conceded, for example, that of all U.S. presidents, Clinton came the closest to expressing regret for America's involvement in the slave trade. Mazrui further noted that such remarks, although not an official apology, demonstrate an authentic interest in improving U.S.-Africa relations. Yet, had it not been for the involvement of local and national constituencies, such as the Congressional Black Caucus, in the U.S. political and economic decision-making process, it is not conceivable that a U.S. president or any head of state would have offered such an apology.

In summary, as we enter the new century, it is clear that it is in the U.S. national interest to assist Africa's emerging national development. However, for Africa to become a participant in the global economy, the United States must be actively involved in Africa's quest to build institutional capacity, promote democratic participation, and engender respect for human rights. These goals can be achieved only if the United States makes democracy, human rights, and justice a central part of its foreign policy toward Africa.

Here is another priority recommendation of the National Summit on Africa (2000), this one approved during the thematic session on Economic Development, Trade and Investment, and Job Creation.

> The [United States] should stimulate direct trade and investment between Africa and the United States because, without it, democracy will fail and the needs of the people will not be met. This should be done with particular emphasis on small and medium-sized businesses between Africans and African Americans. There must be support for the African Growth and Opportunity Act in order to foster trade and investment in Africa and enable African countries to develop mutually beneficial partnerships with the United States so as to accomplish these goals. [Supporting] Africa's efforts to expand the volume and content of its exports . . . will in turn make it possible for Africa to import more American goods. (p. xi)

This initiative is important because its stands to benefit the emerging partnership between the United States and Africa. As stated earlier, the United States has an important economic stake in Africa. U.S. exports to Africa were valued at $5 billion in 1997 alone, surpassing U.S. exports to countries in the former Soviet Union. On the other hand, the United States imported twice as much from Africa in the 1990s, especially in the form of crude oil, as it did in the previous decade. In addition, data for 1995 alone indicated that South Africa's economy had absorbed more U.S. exports than all of Eastern Europe combined. The United States has enjoyed tremendous economic growth over the past 5 years, and much of its success can be traced to its policy of global interdependency and, therefore, its emerging partnership with Africa. Africa's size and resources can no longer be left to the exploitation of unscrupulous businesses and governments. African leaders now seek true partners, and the United States through President Clinton is shaping that communicative involvement. With a population of nearly 1 billion (ranking it just behind China and India), Africa is a major market that sits untapped, along with the region's vast deposits of oil, uranium, diamonds, gold, bauxite, cocoa, coffee, and other agricultural products essential to continuing U.S. economic growth and prosperity. Indeed, some estimates suggest that more than 100,000 American jobs depend on U.S. investments in Africa, with continual growth projected (Nwosu & Taylor, 1999).

A third priority recommendation of the National Summit derived from discussion of Sustainable Development, Quality of Life, and the Environment.

> The [United States] should invest in and support African initiatives to provide basic necessities through the development of sustainable infrastructure. Addressing these issues requires commitment to human capital, gender issues (with emphasis on women), education, capacity building, participatory development involving the inclusion of nongovernmental organizations, community-based organizations, reliance on expertise from Africa, [and] establishing linkages with African Americans. All existing and future U.S. government projects, U.S. nongovernmental organizations, and businesses should adhere to the same environmental protection standards that they would need to meet in the United States and should be required to sign on to a list of principles that pro-

mote sustainable utilization of land, water, forest, wildlife, marine, biodiversity, and coastal resources. The United States should strictly enforce the prohibition of transporting, selling, and dumping of toxic and hazardous substances. (pp. xi-xii)

This policy is crucial to the health and well-being of the peoples of Africa because problems with neglect and exploitation have produced an environmental nightmare in the vast majority of the states. Some of these problems can be linked directly to the large international oil companies, such as Shell and Chevron in Nigeria. Shell, one of the world's largest oil companies, struck oil in Nigeria in 1958 and accounts for nearly 50% of the country's daily oil production. According to Nwosu and Taylor (1999), the effects of oil spillage, hydrocarbons, and other poisonous wastes released into the air have created an environmental nightmare for more than 6 million people who live in the oil-producing areas, a region with the highest population density in Africa (1,500 people per square mile). Nearly half a million of them are from Ogoniland, an area that has been hardest hit by the oil pollution. As for Africa's rivers and rain forests, the data suggest that since 1980, about one quarter of the rain forests in Central Africa, regarded as second-largest in the world, have disappeared. The accompanying land degradation poses potential harm to the global environment. The U.S. understands that its programs on environmental protection will be limited unless it can ensure that all regions of the world cooperate. . . . In other words, it cannot have one region in and another region outside looking in on emerging environmental issues.

I served as spokesperson for the Oklahoma delegation to the National Summit's thematic session on Education and Culture. In this area, we recommended strongly that

the United States, including African American educational institutions, should seek equitable partnerships with African professionals, institutions, and communities, to include opportunities

for international exchange, training, research, technology, knowledge transfer, information sharing, and arts and culture. (p. xiii)

Although the education community in the United States has begun to establish partnerships with African people and institutions, we need to make sure these are equitable and reciprocal in nature. An example of this type of partnership is one that I, along with a team of U.S. educators from the University of Oklahoma, was involved in during the summer of 1999. We traveled to South Africa to establish a university-school-community partnership with the University of Pretoria. This partnership reflects the above recommendation in the sense that it promotes an equitable and reciprocal relationship in the areas of research, international exchange programs, and information sharing. It also provided the opportunity to obtain firsthand information about Africa so that U.S. educators can consistently and accurately inform the U.S. public about Africa. At the same time, the program enabled educators from Africa to learn about the United States.

During our research, we found many similarities between the two societies. Like South Africa, the United States also struggles with poverty, crime, inequity, and problematic race relations. For example, the number of young American children living in poverty increased from 3.5 million in 1979 to 5.2 million in 1997. About 22% of young children in America live in poverty, that is, in families with incomes below the federal poverty line, $12,802 for a family of three. The U.S. poverty rate for young children is two to three times higher than that rate in other major Western industrialized nations. And although the young child poverty rate is highest for African Americans and Latinos, by international standards, it is also exceptionally high for young white children (13%) (data from Lickona, 1993).

Crime in American schools is also rampant. In 1992, the National Research Council reported that the United States had become the most violent of all industrialized nations. The Centers for Disease Control (1996) confirms that violent behavior is a problem for young people, reporting between 1994 and 1999, more than 200 incidents of school violence occurred in the United States.

Equally significant is the increasing number of people, coming from many ideological and philosophical perspectives, who believe that U.S. society is in deep moral trouble. The picture is disheartening: the breakdown of the family; the deterioration of civility in everyday life; rampant greed at a time when one in five children is poor; an omnipresent sexual culture that fills our television and movie screens with sleaze, beckoning the young toward sexual activity at ever earlier ages; the enormous betrayal of children through sexual abuse (Lickona, 1997, p. 52). The decline in moral values in the United States doesn't affect only U.S. children. The University of Oklahoma group learned during its South African visit that many children there have been influenced by U.S. moral standards. In fact, it was disconcerting to learn that the students at one school we visited had been negatively influenced after watching U.S. television programs, movies, and videos and listening to violent U.S. music. Some South African students told us, for example, that they learned about "gangs" from watching movies and videos made in the United States.

According to O'Hair and colleagues (1999), the major difference between the social, political, economic, and educational context in the United States and that in South Africa is that the U.S. version of apartheid ended several decades ago with the outlawing of legal segregation of the races. Thus, the extremes of the problems confronted by both countries may be somewhat closer together in the United States than they are in South Africa, because the United States has had several more decades to wrestle with these issues.

Moreover, educators (i.e., teachers, administrators, parents, community members) in both South Africa and in the United States face significant and somewhat similar issues. The greatest education problem in South Africa is probably the disparity in the quality of education for different population groups. This is evident in the funding of education, the pupil-teacher ratio, the qualification levels of

teachers, and the character of buildings and facilities. As one U.S. educator in the University of Oklahoma group remarked, "nothing could have prepared me for the gross inequity between the Africaans and the African schools. There were differences in the physical structure as well as the methods of instructional delivery." We visited schools that were fit for kings and others that didn't even have electricity. Most Africaan and English schools had student-teacher ratios of no more than 15 to 1; in the African schools, that ratio was 45 to 1 or greater.

For both the United States and South Africa, parental involvement in their children's education is also a major issue. In fact, until recently, many U.S. parents were told, "Hands off, you don't know how to do it" (Rich, 1997). Educators in both countries work in schools that are often undemocratic and that are antithetical to preparing students for democratic citizenship. Educators in both countries labor under conditions of isolation that restrict their ability to learn from each other. Essentially, isolationism guarantees that schools will not function as democracies and that they will fall short of preparing students for productive democratic citizenship. What is needed are structures and processes that reduce isolation by connecting school communities within the country and across national boundaries (O'Hair et al., 1999).

The fifth and final thematic area we dealt with at the National Summit concerned Peace and Security. In light of the recent bombings of U.S. embassies in Africa, we felt a major priority should be placed on

U.S. support for peacekeeping and conflict prevention efforts in Africa including timely financial and logistical support. The United States should support humanitarian disaster relief operations and restructure its security forces to promote civilian control and reduce military expenditures. (pp. xii-xiii)

Nwosu and Taylor (1999) believe this is especially urgent where international terrorism and the war on drugs are concerned. For example, they point to the recent bombings at

U.S. embassies in Nairobi, Kenya, and Dar es Salaam, Tanzania. These acts show what terrorists will do if they perceive an area as neglected and easy to attack. When these U.S. embassies in Africa were bombed, the terrorists placed the whole of Africa on the geopolitical map of the world and catapulted the continent into America's strategic interest. By significantly increasing its security and peacekeeping forces in Africa, the United States can deny access or opportunity for terrorists. This point is further illustrated by the words of Susan Rice (1997), the U.S. assistant secretary of state for Africa affairs, who said, "we must defend the United States from the threats [terrorism, crime, weapons, proliferation, narcotics, and disease] to our national security that emanate from Africa, as from the rest of the world." Safety in these areas "will render both Americans and Africans safer and more prosperous" (p. 14).

In discussing the maintenance of U.S. influence in a world with only one superpower, Nwosu notes that, in the past, Africa was viewed as a playground for superpower competition and Cold War rivalry. Things are quite different today, however. Along with the collapse of the former Soviet Union and the demise of the Cold War came a major shift in Africa's national development. Major reforms began to take place all over the continent, especially in countries such as Botswana, Uganda, and Ghana. These markets experienced unprecedented growth rates, and today, Botswana boasts of one of the fastest-growing economies in Africa. So when President Clinton announced that it was important for U.S. leadership in the world to be inextricably linked to its strategic interest in Africa, this meant also being supportive of Africa's continuing prosperity, peace, and security. The president implied as much during his trip to South Africa in 1998, when he said that like Africa, America needs dependable partners to build prosperity and a strategic stake because of 21st century threats to our common security, from terrorism, from international crime, and drug trafficking, from the proliferation of weapons of mass destruction, from the spread of deadly disease and the degradation of our common environment because no nation is immune to these problems.

Susan Rice (1997) echoed similar sentiments when she said, "If Africa can achieve liftoff, then we all, Africans and Americans, will stand to benefit. If Africa fails, then we too will pay the price. The U.S. cannot afford to be a bystander at this pivotal point in time" (p. 20). As stated above, many Africans believe it is time for the United States to become involved in Africa's national development. There appear to be numerous opportunities for the United States to take advantage of this challenge.

▶ **Summary and Conclusions**

This chapter had a two-fold purpose. One goal was to examine Africa's emerging national development using Awa's critical issues of development as a framework. Another purpose was to answer the question, How can transculture communication between the United States and Africa help Africa's national development?

National development was defined as a complex process involving political, social, and economic transformation (Awa, 1989). But successful transformation in these areas depends also on such factors as development planning and evaluation, participation (i.e, communication or involvement), decentralization, and implementation.

Development planning was defined as evaluation or analysis of existing problems and identifying what needs to be done. Thus, the status of Africa's national development is determined by evaluating its historical, recent, and present policies toward the issues of democracy and human rights, education and culture, and economic development.

Africa's current process of democratization is still in the throes of a delicate period of transition. It is experiencing both democratic gains and setbacks, making sustainable national development difficult. However, there is the promise that the continent will experience its second political liberation and ultimate democratic consolidation—especially if those forces that had the political determination to resist the autocratic regimes continue to prevail.

As for education and culture, these issues are key to Africa's attainment of sustainable development. Africa's education policies must first address local and national needs—especially the cultural and political socialization of women and children. Second, to be globally comparable, its indigenous education and cultural systems need to be skillfully mediated with Western knowledge systems, including a widespread application of technological development.

Because Africa's economic development depends on solid policies toward human rights, politics, and social and educational development, the chapter's focus in this area was all-inclusive. It focused on human and nonhuman issues, such as physical infrastructures, health and nutrition, human resources, and community participation. It was concluded that Africa cannot achieve national development without developing its people and, in turn, encouraging its people to participate in the development of society. It was noted, for example, that human development is the cornerstone of society and a prerequisite for economic and sustainable development. It was also noted that development cannot be achieved without community participation. Many African communities had adopted widespread community participation strategies that resemble those proposed in Awa's (1989) national development model. This section of the chapter was concluded by noting that because Africa has been, since the early 1990s, successful in managing participatory development, it is now experiencing unprecedented political and economic transformation.

Finally, the last part of the chapter dealt with U.S. involvement in Africa's national development. The data show that the United States is more involved in Africa's development today than at any other time in history. This is true at all levels—government, business, and society. In fact, the National Summit on Africa was a grassroots effort aimed at ed-ucating the American public about Africa and U.S.-African relations, broadening and strengthening the network of Africa's supporters in the United States, and developing a policy plan of action to guide U.S. relations with the countries and peoples of Africa (National Summit on Africa, 1996). The drafters of this plan made recommendations for U.S. foreign policy toward Africa. They noted, for example, that education policy and development should be based on dialogue and not top-down directives. This is consistent with President Clinton's commitment to Africa: that the United States should develop both a respect and a partnership with Africa and its peoples.

The National Summit on Africa also encourages the United States to help Africa build a culture of democracy. Although democracy is a universal concept, it is important to consider it within the context of African realities, taking into account indigenous values, institutions, and social mores. It is also important to consider Africa's traditional principles of participation and consensus building, which may differ from processes in the United States. Also, the principle of human rights has different universal interpretations and must be considered within the African context. Thus, Africa's participation in its own democracy is integral to the success of its national development.

▶ References

Atwood, B. (1999). Remarks by J. Brian Atwood, Administrator, U. S. Agency for International Development. U.S.-African Ministerial.

Awa, N. E. (1989). National development. In M. K. Molefi & W. Gudykunst (Eds.), *Handbook of international and intercultural communication*. Newbury Park, CA: Sage.

Bradley, C. (1996). *End of apartheid: Causes and consequences*. Austin, TX: Raintree Steck-Vaugh Publishers.

Centers for Disease Control. (1996). *Incidents of school violence*. Washington, DC: Author.

Coffman, J. (1999). U. S. commercial strategy for Africa. *African-watch: The authentic voice, 1*(1), 15.

Davidson, B. (1994). *The search for Africa: History, culture, politics.* New York: Random House.

Davis, K. (1977). *Human behavior at work: Organization behavior* (5th ed.). New York: McGraw-Hill.

Dewey, J. (1916). *Democracy and education.* New York: Free Press.

Dia, M. (1996). *Africa's management in the 1990s and beyond: Reconciling indigenous and transplanted institutions.* Washington, DC: World Bank.

Entelis, J. P. (1998). *Democracy and the state in North Africa.* Bloomington: Indiana University Press.

Fowler, S. (1997). Reality, knowledge, and African education: In the context of a postmodernist world. In P. Higgs, S. Miedema, J. van der Walt, & G. Zecha (Eds.), *Postmodernism and education.* Potchefstroomse, South Africa: Potchefstroomse Universiteit vir Christelike Hoer Onderwys.

Goduka, I. N. (1999). Educating in South Africa. *Democracy and Education, 10*(20), 42-49.

Hart, P. D. (1997). *The National Summit on Africa survey results summary.* Washington, DC: National Summit on Africa.

Kay, G. (1975). *Development and underdevelopment: A Marxist analysis.* London: Macmillan.

Keller, E. (1998). *Democracy and human rights: Thematic working papers.* Washington, DC: National Summit on Africa.

Kenyatta, J. (1978). *Facing Mount Kenya.* Nairobi, Kenya: Heinemann.

Lerner, D. (1966). *The passing of traditional society: Modernizing the Middle East.* New York: Free Press.

Lickona, T. (1997). The return of character education. *Educational Leadership, 51*(3), 6-11.

Makau wa Mutua. (1996). The ideology of human rights. *Virginia Journal of International Law, 36*(3), 589-657.

Mazrui, A. (1995). The blood of experience: The failed state of political collapse in Africa. *World Policy Journal, 2,* 6-21.

Meldrum, A. (1997). Coups no longer acceptable: OAU. *African Recovery, 11*(1).

Meyer-Weitz, A. (1998). Health promotion: Vital link in sustainable development. *Focus Forum, 6*(1), 18-22.

National Research Council. (1992). *Understanding and preventing violence.* Washington, DC: Author.

National Summit on Africa. (1996). *Draft policy plan of action.* New York: Ford Foundation and the Carnegie Corporation.

National Summit on Africa. (2000, February 16-21). *National policy plan of action for U.S.-Africa relations in the 21st century.* Washington, DC: Author.

Neter, M. (1990). *The great oracle of Tehuti and the Egyptian system of spiritual cultivation.* Brooklyn, NY: Khamit.

Njoroge, R. J., & Bennaars, G. A. (1986). *Philosophy and education in Africa.* Nairobi, Kenya: Transafrica.

Nwosu, P., & Taylor, D. (1999). Why the U. S. needs Africa: The new dialogue. *Africanwatch: The authentic voice, 1*(1), 13-15.

O'Hair, M. J., Milhouse, V. H., Reitzug, R., & Slabbert, J. (1999). *International centers for democratic citizenship and human potential.* Unpublished manuscript.

Potenza, E. (1998). The great school trek. In *Syaya.* Cape Town, South Africa: Idasa.

Pruitt, D. G. (1997). Lessons learned from the Middle East peace process. *International Negotiation Journal* (Abstracts), *2*(2).

Rice, S. (1997, November 14). *New partnership for the twenty-first century.* Paper presented at the annual meeting of the African Studies Association, Columbus, OH.

Rich, E. J. (1997). *Partnership for family involvement in education.* Washington, DC: U.S. Department of Education.

Salim, A. S. (1992). Opening address, first Southern African moot court competition. In *From human wrongs to human rights.* Harare: University of Zimbabwe Press.

Samovar L. A., & Porter, R. E. (1997). An introduction to intercultural communication. In *Intercultural communication: A reader* (pp. 5-26). Belmont, CA: Wadsworth.

Sindane, J. (1994, November 1). *Ubuntu and national-building.* Paper delivered at a conference organized by the Ubuntu School of Philosophy, Pretoria, South Africa.

Summit News. (2000). *The Daily newspaper of the National Summit on Africa's dialogue and celebration of Africa.* Washington, DC: National Summit on Africa.

Toungara, J. M. (1998). *Education and culture: Thematic working paper series.* Washington, DC: The National Summit on Africa.

UNESCO. (1974). *Report of the meeting of experts on communication policies in Latin America.* Paris: Author.

Toward Transcultural Understanding

A Harmony Theory of Chinese Communication

GUO-MING CHEN

Abundant studies from different disciplines have indicated that culture and communication have an interdependent and reciprocal relationship (Becker, 1986; Chen, 1995a; Gudykunst & Nishida, 1984; Harnett & Cummings, 1980; Hofstede, 1980; Nakanishi, 1987). According to Chen and Starosta (1998a), whereas communication serves as a carrier of culture, what, where, and how we should talk is regulated by culture. Thus, culture not only conditions our thinking but also is manifested in our communication patterns.

Scholars have also examined the impact of culture on communication behaviors. For example, Hsu (1953) found that in interaction, Americans tend to be more individual-centered and emotion-displayed, whereas Chinese are more situation-centered and emotion-constrained. Ma (1990, 1992) also reported that Chinese are much less explicit in showing their emotions during communication than northern Americans. In addition, studies consistently indicate that a major difference in communication style between Chinese and Americans is that Chinese tend to be less confrontational and direct (Lindin, 1974; Schneider, 1985; Wolfson & Pearce, 1983; Yang, 1978). Finally, Gudykunst and Ting-Toomey (1988) and Hall (1976) summarized the different communication behaviors in high-context versus low-context cultures. According to the authors, people in high-context cultures (a) give less emphasis to explicit verbal messages, (b) transmit important information through contextual cues, (c) highly value harmony, (d) tend to be silent more often and to use ambiguous language, and (e) tend to avoid saying no directly to their counterparts. People in low-context cultures (a) do not emphasize the situational context; (b) transmit important information through explicit verbal messages; (c) highly value self-expression, verbal fluency, and eloquent speech; and (d) tend to express opinions and intentions freely and directly to persuade others to accept their viewpoints.

These studies indicate that to understand a person's communication behavior or to communicate effectively with a person from a different culture, it is necessary to first understand the person's culture. In other words, to reach transcultural realities, people are required to understand a single culture through interaction and dialogue with the culture (Epstein, 1995). The ability to establish transcultural realities is similar to intercultural communication competence, which demands intercultural awareness, intercultural sensitivity, and intercultural adroitness (Chen, 1989; Chen & Starosta, 1996, 1998b, 1999, 2000). This chapter aims to delineate the core values of Chinese culture to help people reach transcultural understanding when interacting with Chinese. Research attempting to help people better understand and communicate with each other by focusing on the study of a specific culture's cultural traits has been increasing over the past years (Benedict, 1946; Broome, 1996; Condon, 1984, 1985; Kapp, 1983; Stewart & Bennett, 1991). However, very few scholars systematically deal with Chinese cultural traits from the communication perspective. To fill this gap, the author develops in this chapter a harmony theory based on cultural traits that can be used to understand Chinese communication behaviors.

▶ **Ontological
Foundations of the Theory**

To understand Chinese communication, it is necessary to recognize the ontological as-

sumptions that guide Chinese beliefs and behaviors. According to Cheng (1987) and Wilhelm (1979), Chinese consider change the only constant phenomenon in the universe. Change is based on the dialectic interaction of two opposite but complementary forces: *yin* and *yang. Yin* represents amiable, yielding, or submissive attributes, and *yang* unyielding or dominant attributes. The interaction of the two forces produces more opposite but interdependent pairs of change, such as empty versus tangible, bright versus dark, moving versus tranquil, large versus small, more versus less, high versus low, distant versus close, and so on. Thus, the universe is forever experiencing change: alteration, movement without rest, and flowing, rising, and sinking without fixed law. To interact successfully, individuals must bring continuity into the process of change, because "when a change runs its course, it will alter; through alteration one achieves continuity; and through continuity one achieves duration. This is the key to being blessed by heaven and bringing in good fortune" (Chu, 1974, p. 106).

Based on the concept of change, Chai and Chai (1969) generated three ontological assumptions that guide Chinese communication behaviors. First, the universe is a great whole in which all is but a transitional process, with no fixed substance to its substratum. Human communication is, then, ever in a state of change and transformation. Second, the transforming process of the universe does not proceed onward but revolves in an endless cycle. Human communication is, then, changing according to this cycle of the universe like the succession of day and night and the periodical ebb and flow of the tide (Liu, 1990, 1992). Third, there is no end to the transforming process of the universe. The process of human communication is, then, never absolutely completed or finished. In this transforming, endless, and cyclic communication process, the role of human beings is vital. The process shows a spirit of enlightenment in which human beings communicate with dignity and influence in a mutual and interdependent network. The process forms a continuous chain of natural sequences without consciously devaluing the dignity of communicator and communicatee (Cheng, 1987; Fang, 1981). These ontological assumptions provide a foundation for reaching a more dynamic, interactive, and responsive notion of human communication. Human communication from the Chinese perspective, then, requires individuals to develop and keep a harmonious relationship between those who interact in a continuously transforming process of mutual dependency. Thus, three theoretical statements in the form of assumptions can be made to summarize Chinese ontological thinking on this subject; these statements serve as fundamental definitions and descriptions from which subsequent theoretical axioms and theorems can be assumed or inferred:

> *Assumption 1:* Human communication is a changing and transforming process.
>
> *Assumption 2:* Human communication is changing according to the endless but orderly cycle of the universe.
>
> *Assumption 3:* Human communication is never absolutely completed or finished.

▶ Formulation of the Harmony Theory

According to Hawes (1975), a substantive theory must consist of a primary statement; a theorem as a secondary statement can be added to the primary statement. An axiom is a primary statement that is assumed to be true with a general scope. From the axiom, a theorem is inferred or derived that is also general in scope and empirically valid. Concepts in a theorem should be observable and operationally definable; if necessary, a series of hypotheses can be derived from the theorem. In other words, a hypothesis is a statement that specifies the necessary conditions of a prediction, and it can be tested directly. These guidelines are followed in this chapter for the development of the harmony theory of Chinese communication.

HARMONY

The Chinese approach to the study of human communication differs from Western approaches in three ways (Chen, 1993). First, it holds that harmony is the end rather than the means of human communication. Conflicts are then considered to be harmful to harmony in the process of communication. Second, whereas many Western scholars treat human communication as a process of the communicators striving to direct the interaction in their own favor, Chinese view it as a process in which the communicators continuously adapt and relocate themselves toward interdependence and cooperation. Third, the Chinese approach suggests that the process of human communication includes an ethical appeal that induces a sense of duty for cooperation between those who interact, not by their strategic words or behaviors but by the sincere display of whole-hearted concern between each other (Chen, 1993). These distinct differences indicate that harmony is the core value of Chinese culture that guides Chinese communication behaviors. As Legge (1955) indicated, Chinese consider that human society can be nourished and flourish only when harmony prevails. Harmony is, then, the most important element Chinese people use to regulate the transforming, cyclic, and never-ending process of human communication. As a result, the ultimate goal of Chinese communication is to pursue a conflict-free interpersonal and social relationship (Chen & Chung, 1994). Thus, the ability to reach a harmonious state of human relationship becomes the main criterion for evaluating whether an individual is competent in the process of Chinese communication. In other words, to Chinese, communication competence means an individual's ability to develop and keep a harmonious relationship between those who interact in a continuously transforming process of mutual dependency (Chen, 1993). An assumption based on the concept of harmony and an axiom from it can be inferred:

Assumption 4: Chinese communication aims to reach a harmonious state of human relationship.

Axiom 1: An increase in the ability to achieve harmony in Chinese communication will increase the degree of communication competence.

To achieve harmony or competence in the process of communication, Chinese develop three sets of guidelines (Chen, 1997; Chen & Chung, 1997; Chen & Starosta, 1997-1998; Hwang, 1987; Shenkar & Ronen, 1987; Wu, 1964; Yum, 1988):

1. Intrinsically, individuals must be able to internalize three principles: *jen* (humanism), *yi* (righteousness), and *li* (rite).
2. Extrinsically, individuals must be able to accommodate three components: *shih* (temporal contingencies), *wei* (spatial contingencies), and *ji* (the first imperceptible beginning of movement).
3. Strategically, individuals must be able to exercise three behavioral skills: *guanxi* (interrelation), *mientz* (face), and power.

Jen (humanism) is an inner force that establishes the close connection between two people. Chen and Chung (1994) pointed out that self-restraint and self-discipline foster this inner force by which people naturally show love, affection, and benevolence to others. It is the heart of seeing all human beings as brothers and sisters. *Jen* helps us to develop and maintain not only ourselves but also others (Fung, 1983). Thus, being empathic is a prerequisite for showing like-hearted feeling toward others and reaching the state of *jen* (Chang, 1992; Chung, 1992; Yum, 1988). Applying this to daily interaction, Chen (1987) summarized that *jen* demands self-discipline toward oneself, filial piety toward one's parents, humanity toward other people,

respect toward elders, commitment to one's work, and trust regarding one's behavior. In other words, *jen* is the collective virtue of showing love or being humane in interactions. Moreover, to reach a harmonious state of human communication, the practice of *jen* must be based on the principle of reciprocity. Only through a mutually dependent process can the light of *jen* be fully emitted. Thus, the ideal of harmony is sustained by the principle of reciprocity, which requires those who interact to show mutual responsibility in the process of communication (Chen & Xiao, 1993). The violation of the reciprocal principle, for example, failing to return goodwill or showing an indifferent attitude, often leads to lack of cooperation in Chinese communication.

Axiom 2: The higher the degree of *jen,* the higher the likelihood that harmony will be developed in Chinese communication.

Axiom 3: The higher the degree of being humane, the higher the likelihood that *jen* will be maintained in Chinese communication.

Theorem 1: The more reciprocal a person is, the more competent the person will be in Chinese communication.

Theorem 2: The more empathic a person is, the more competent the person will be in Chinese communication.

Yi (appropriateness), equivalent with appropriateness or righteousness, is the internal criterion of communication behaviors, stipulating what we ought or ought not to do in the process of social interactions (Chen & Chung, 1994). Chen (1987) indicated that *yi* provides three functions for human communication. First, it guides individuals' behaviors in the communication process. Second, it regulates individuals' behaviors by preventing them from deviating from social norms. Third, it penetrates into all the behaviors that are within the boundary of social norms. That is, all appropriate or righteous behaviors are guided and regulated by the principle of *yi.*

These functions denote that the state of *yi* can be achieved only through appropriate behaviors in the process of communication. Therefore, appropriateness becomes the criterion for examining whether an individual's behavior meets the demands of *yi*. At the same time, appropriate behaviors also refer to flexibility and adaptability toward the situation. In other words, *yi* aims to reach the best outcome of human interaction by adopting the most appropriate reaction toward external stimuli, which include time, space, people, and situation (Chen, 1987). Thus, in human communication, the characteristics of situational orientation embedded in *yi* allow us to look beyond personal profit and contribute to the betterment of common good from the perspective of the original goodness of human nature (Yum, 1988). In sum, to Chinese, a harmonious state of human communication cannot be reached without the guidance of *yi*, which is reflected in appropriate actions, and the appropriate actions are carried out through flexibility and adaptability.

> *Axiom 4:* The higher the degree of *yi*, the higher the likelihood that harmony will be developed in Chinese communication.
> *Axiom 5:* The higher the degree of appropriateness, the higher the likelihood that *yi* will be maintained in Chinese communication.
> *Theorem 3:* The more flexible a person is, the more competent the person will be in Chinese communication.
> *Theorem 4:* The more adaptable a person is, the more competent the person will be in Chinese communication.

Li (rite), holy rite or sacred ceremony, is used as a metaphor to represent the specifically humanizing form of the dynamic relation among people. This form produces a pattern of human behaviors that, in turn, coordinates social interaction in a civilized society. Thus, through the image of *li* we realize that the rites and ceremonies are an emphatic, intensified, and elaborated extension of everyday civilized interaction (Fingarette, 1972). In other words, *li* symbolizes the formality of human interaction. Chinese culture treats this formality not only as a human character or a linguistic character but also as a moral and religious character. In the process of human communication, *li* also refers to norms and rules of proper behavior in a social context. It is an external means to achieve the ideal state of harmony by showing respect or reverence for social norms. Yum (1988) indicated that *li* is "the fundamental regulatory etiquette of human behavior" (p. 378). It connects an individual character and social duties by following the rules of conduct and speech in communication. Thus, individuals ought to follow *li* in social interactions if they are to actively adjust to the harmonious and hierarchical order of society.

This formality can be easily found in the use of honorific language in Chinese daily interactions and in the sense of order, propriety, and appropriate behavior between parents and children, inferiors and superiors, teachers and students, elders and youngsters, as well as among friends (Chen & Starosta, 1998a; Condon & Yousef, 1975). It is also reflected in one of the Chinese characters, *keqi*. This phrase not only denotes the meaning of politeness but also includes personal attributes such as being courteous, modest, humble, understanding, considerate, and well-mannered in the process of human communication (Wei, 1983). Hence, showing aggressive behaviors and being unable to subdue or control one's emotions in public indicate impoliteness that not only violates the principle of harmony but also produces an insult not easily forgiven (Eberhard, 1971). An example of lacking aggressive behavior is the Chinese reluctance to engage in an argument during social interactions. When challenged, Chinese may just keep quiet without rejoining or discussing a point, even when they feel they are right, hoping to save everyone's face and maintain a harmonious relationship between the two parties (Chen & Xiao, 1993). According to Shenkar and Ronen (1987), this kind of formality of social life is a way to avoiding embarrassing confrontations, to handle socially ambiguous situations, and to uphold the group control over egocentric tendencies.

> *Axiom 6:* An increase of the practice of *li* will produce an increase in the development of harmony in Chinese communication.
>
> *Axiom 7:* The higher the degree of formality, the higher the likelihood that *li* will be maintained in Chinese communication.
>
> *Theorem 5:* The more skillful a person is in managing honorific language, the more competent the person will be in Chinese communication.
>
> *Theorem 6:* The more skillful a person is in dealing with hierarchical social relations, the more competent the person will be in Chinese communication.
>
> *Theorem 7:* The more polite a person is, the more competent the person will be in Chinese communication.
>
> *Theorem 8:* The more skillful a person is in controlling emotion, the more competent the person will be in Chinese communication.
>
> *Theorem 9:* The less aggressive a person is, the more competent the person will be in Chinese communication.

These three concepts form the foundation of the inner structure for those who interact in the process of Chinese communication. They are the basis of reaching harmony and communication competence. Individuals are required to internalize these elements to become successful communicators in the Chinese cultural context. However, as the intrinsic and preliminary elements of Chinese communication, *jen, yi,* and *li* must coordinate three extrinsic elements: *shi, wei,* and *ji.* The integration of the intrinsic and extrinsic elements will determine whether a successful Chinese communication in the transforming process can be reached (Wu, 1964).

Shih (spatial contingencies) refers to temporal contingencies in human interactions. Chinese use eight symbols, accompanied with the 24-hour time period, to portray the eight stages of the cyclic process of human relationship development through the process of communication (Chen, 1998; Wilhelm, 1979). Thunder, paralleling with 4:30 a.m. to 7:30 a.m., symbolizes the arousing power for a burgeoning relationship with others. Wind, 7:30 a.m. to 10:30 a.m., symbolizes the continuation of relationship development by a gently penetrating effort. Fire, 10:30 a.m. to 1:30 p.m., symbolizes the desire of those who interact to cling to each other. Earth, 1:30 p.m. to 4:30 p.m., symbolizes the reception of each other's relationship. Lake, 4:30 p.m. to 7:30 p.m., symbolizes the joyous relationship developed by those who interact. Heaven, 7:30 p.m. to 10:30 p.m., symbolizes the sublime stage of success in a relationship. Water, 10:30 p.m. to 1:30 a.m., symbolizes the deterioration of relationship. Finally, mountain, 1:30 a.m. to 4:30 a.m., symbolizes keeping still without further endeavoring to develop or continue the relationship. Knowing the temporal relations and appropriately performing in different stages of human interaction is the function of *shi.* In other words, knowing *shi* requires the ability to decide when is the appropriate time to initiate, maintain, and terminate an interaction. This element is an application of the principle of appropriateness that is embedded in *yi.* It is to explain the importance of knowing the influence due to the change of temporal contingencies in the process of human communication. Chinese believe that being unable to recognize the change of temporal contingencies in interactions is detrimental to the achievement of harmony and therefore leads to a failure of communication.

> *Axiom 8:* An increase of knowing *shi* will produce an increase in the development of harmony in Chinese communication.
>
> *Axiom 9:* The higher the degree of knowing temporal contingencies, the higher the likelihood that *shi* will be maintained in Chinese communication.
>
> *Theorem 10:* The more a person knows when is the appropriate time to act, the

more competent the person will be in Chinese communication.

Wei (spatial contingencies) refers to spatial contingencies in human interactions, that is, the static aspects of human interactions, including social context and communication environment. Wei is like a container carrying *li.* In other words, the application of rites will vary due to the change of social context and communication environment. To Chinese, *wei* is typically reflected in the hierarchical structure of human relationships called the Five Code of Ethics, which traditionally specifies the relationships between ruler and subject, father and son, husband and wife, older brother and younger brother, and among friends (Lin, 1988). This hierarchical structure not only ensures an unequal and complementary relationship in Chinese society but also provides a specific context for Chinese communication. It maximizes differences in age, sex, and role or status and encourages an interdependent relationship between those who interact (Condon, 1977). Thus, knowing spatial contingencies and appropriately performing as one should in different contexts of human interaction is the function of *wei.* In other words, knowing *wei* requires the ability to realize and distinguish who, what, and where to initiate, maintain, and terminate an interaction. Like *shi, wei* integrates the principle of appropriateness to show the impact of spatial contingencies on human communication. Therefore, *wei* also serves as a criterion for measuring the degree of harmony and competence in Chinese communication.

> *Axiom 10:* An increase of knowing *wei* will produce an increase in the development of harmony in Chinese communication.
> *Axiom 11:* The higher the degree of knowing spatial contingencies, the higher the likelihood that *wei* will be maintained in Chinese communication.
> *Theorem 11:* The more a person knows the communication environment, the more competent the person will be in Chinese communication.

> *Theorem 12:* The more a person knows the social context, the more competent the person will be in Chinese communication.

Ji (the first imperceptible beginning of movement) shows the trail of possible consequences of the ongoing interaction (Wilhelm, 1990). Chinese consider that being competent in communication means that one should know what is hidden and what is evident during the interaction. This requires sensitivity by which one can develop a positive emotion toward understanding and appreciating the potential differences due to the variations of temporal and spatial contingencies and further take an appropriate action in the process of communication (Chen & Starosta, 1996). Thus, the ability to recognize the track of movement is a necessary condition for individuals to develop harmony and gain a feeling of complete security in interactions (Chen, 1993). The development of sensitivity or the ability of knowing *ji* is based on sincerity, which represents the internal consistency of individuals who hold a sincere and honest mind toward themselves and others. A sincere and honest mind helps individuals to figure out the trail of movement and to know the right time to behave appropriately to fit in with the environment. It also unites the people who interact as one (Wang, 1989; Wu, 1976). Sincerity is, then, the force integrating *shi, wei, and ji* and the bridge connecting the three elements with *jen, yi,* and *li.*

> *Axiom 12:* An increase of knowing *ji* will produce an increase in the development of harmony in Chinese communication.
> *Axiom 13:* The higher the degree of knowing the trail of possible consequences of an interaction, the higher the likelihood that *ji* will be maintained in Chinese communication.
> *Theorem 13:* The more a person knows the trail of possible consequences of an interaction, the more competent the person will be in Chinese communication.

Theorem 14: The more sensitive a person is, the more competent the person will be in Chinese communication.

Theorem 15: The more sincere a person is, the more competent the person will be in Chinese communication.

Jen, yi, and *li,* as intrinsic elements and the latitude of Chinese communication, and *shi, wei,* and *ji,* as extrinsic elements and the longitude of Chinese communication, together weave the contextual network of Chinese society. In the soil of this contextual network, Chinese develop a variety of strategic behaviors to deal with their daily interactions. Among them, three cardinal and interdependent skills or strategies are found to be most prominent: *guanxi, mientz,* and power (Chang & Holt, 1991; Chen, 1997; Chiao, 1988b; Chu, 1991; Hwang, 1987, 1988, 1997-1998; Jia, 1997-1998; Jocobs, 1979; Ma, 1992). The achievement of harmony in Chinese communication is ultimately based on the exercise of these three concepts.

Guanxi (interrelation) refers to the relationship between two parties. Jocobs (1979) found that at least nine basic patterns of interrelation exist in the Chinese social network. These are formed by the sharing of common background based on geography, blood, work, classmates, sworn brotherhood, surname, teacher-student, economy, and public affairs. Leung (1988) indicated that Chinese are more likely to pursue a conflict with a stranger than with a friend. To Chinese, maintaining these interrelations is necessary for fulfilling the principle of *li,* because a proper interrelation between people is treated as a way to avoid serious conflicts and embarrassing encounters in daily interactions. Moreover, *guanxi* can also be employed as a social resource to resolve conflicts or to produce functions of persuasion, influence, and control in Chinese society (Chang & Holt, 1991; Chung, 1991).

According to Yum (1988), because Chinese people emphasize a hierarchical social structure based on the Five Code of Ethics, those particular human relationships specified by Jocobs are much more likely to be developed in the process of social interaction. Moreover, particular relationships are governed sets of specific communication rules and patterns, which give individuals direction concerning to whom to talk, where, when, and how (Chen & Chung, 1997). As a result, Chinese develop a clear distinction between strangers and friends in the social network. Chinese people would feel more restrained when dealing with strangers and acquaintances but more free and open to express themselves to intimate friends (Chen, 1995c). The ability to distinguish the levels of hierarchical relationships in a social interaction, then, functions to develop a more supportive communication climate and to sustain a harmonious relationship between those who interact. The emphasis of particular relationships also leads to the development of a clear boundary between in-group and out-group members. Chinese tend to distrust out-group members. The "we feeling" among in-group members often affects the outcome of Chinese communication (Gu, 1992). Pye (1982) pointed out that in the case of social, political, or business negotiations, any intention for personal gain is considered to threaten or jeopardize the group's hierarchy and harmony.

Therefore, knowing how to make a good *guanxi* is a prerequisite for the achievement of harmony and competence in Chinese communication. According to Shenkar and Ronen (1987), keeping frequent contacts, developing mutual understanding, giving gifts or favors, and establishing personal trust and mutual interests with one's counterparts are several examples for making a good relation with Chinese people.

Axiom 14: An enhancement of *guanxi* will produce an enhancement in the development of harmony in Chinese communication.

Axiom 15: The higher the degree of establishing particular relationships, the higher the likelihood that *guanxi* will be maintained in Chinese communication.

Theorem 16: The more a person knows how to establish interrelation with others, the more competent the person will be in Chinese communication.

Theorem 17: The more skillful a person is in distinguishing in-group from out-group members, the more competent the person will be in Chinese communication.

Theorem 18: The stronger the "we feeling" a person has, the more competent the person will be in Chinese communication.

Mientz (face) refers to reputation, self-esteem, or face gained from the respect of other people in interactions. It represents an individual's social position and prestige gained from the successful performance of one or more specific social roles that are well recognized by other members in the society (Chu, 1988; Hu, 1944). In Chinese society, to keep a harmonious atmosphere, competent communicators must know how to show due respect for other parties' feelings, or to save their face. Any conscious act of making others lose face in Chinese society will cause not only emotional uneasiness among others but also damage to one's own image or self-humiliation (Hwang, 1987; Jin, 1988). Thus, to maintain one's and others' face means to maintain friendship between each other in the network of *guanxi.* For example, losing control of facework in the process of Chinese negotiations will mean the loss of bargaining power and the denial of any offer (Jia, 1997-1998).

The importance of saving each other's face can explain, especially in a situation of unavoidable conflict, why Chinese people would show courtesy before using force to solve a problem. Moreover, Chinese often use an intermediary to help them solve the problem to save face. This indirect communication pattern leads Chinese to pursue a smooth verbal and nonverbal exchange in social interactions. It also allows Chinese to avoid saying no

openly or directly to another's request or showing aggressive behaviors that are considered to be detrimental to the harmonious atmosphere of interaction and relationship. Consequently, Chinese people would use all possible means to "earn face" or to "make face" for their counterparts to establish a harmonious atmosphere of interactions (Chiao, 1981; Chu, 1983). Communication competence can then be assessed by evaluating the degree of appropriateness or skillfulness with which a person can earn or make face for others (Chen, 1993).

According to Silin (1981) and Pye (1982), as a behavioral skill in daily interactions, face saving is frequently used by Chinese not only to manage a modern social organization but also to conclude a successful business transaction, especially in negotiations.

For example, Shenkar and Ronen (1987) found that Chinese negotiators are likely to make concessions at the end of a negotiation so that they can save each other's face and keep the harmonious relationship. Facework, therefore, becomes one of the most influential elements in the Chinese power game (Wang, 1992).

Strategically, to find or create an opportunity to express *renqin* (i.e., doing a favor) to one's counterparts is the most common method Chinese people employ to "make face" (Hwang, 1988). Through this process, a network of *guanxi* will be developed gradually. However, the practice of *renqin* is regulated by the principle of reciprocity in Chinese society. Hwang (1988) indicated that Chinese often consciously or unconsciously expect to get something in return when they do a favor (e.g., gift giving) to others. Not returning a favor to the giver will cost both parties' face and, in turn, jeopardize their *guanxi* and further disturb the harmonious atmosphere. As mentioned previously, the principle of reciprocity requires people to show mutual responsibility in social interactions. This kind of reciprocally obligatory relationship develops a feeling of indebtedness in which Chinese are always preparing to return a favor to those who give them a favor. As a result, a great dilemma or anxiety often occurs in the process of Chinese communication, because it is usually difficult to predict when, how, and in what situation one's counterparts will return the favor to oneself (Hwang, 1988). Based on the discussion, we can fairly conclude that *mientz, guanxi,* and the interdependent relationship between the two concepts determine largely the success or failure of Chinese communication.

Axiom 16: An enhancement of *mientz* will produce an enhancement in the development of *guanxi* in Chinese communication.

Axiom 17: An enhancement of *mientz* will produce an enhancement in the development of harmony in Chinese communication.

Axiom 18: The higher the degree of respect toward others, the higher the likelihood that *mientz* will be maintained in Chinese communication.

Axiom 19: The higher the degree of *renqin* toward others, the higher the likelihood that *mientz* will be maintained in Chinese communication.

Theorem 19: The more a person knows how to increase others' *mientz,* the more competent the person will be in Chinese communication.

Theorem 20: The more skillful a person is in doing a favor for others, the more competent the person will be in Chinese communication.

Theorem 21: The stronger the indebtedness a person feels, the more competent the person will be in Chinese communication.

Power refers to the control of resources valued by other parties. It is granted by members of a society in which they believe that they should obey the commands and seek the favor and support of specific members (Conrad, 1994). The power one exerts usually sustains moves and countermoves of the participants in social interactions (Folger, Poole, & Strutman, 1993). The basis of power in Chinese society is built on two sources: *guanxi* and the hierarchical structure of the social network.

Conrad (1994) indicated that people with good interrelations are more likely to comply with each other's wishes or requests and tend to perceive each other as being more expert, trustworthy, and powerful. In addition, as previously discussed, *guanxi* not only functions to avoid conflicts and embarrassing encounters but also can be used as a social resource to produce influence and control in the process of Chinese communication. Chiao (1988b) indicated that *guanxi* has penetrated every aspect of Chinese life. For example, *guanxi* helps people gain what they desire in the areas of marriage, funeral, job, housing, medical care, entertainment, and other social, cultural, political, and economic activities.

The Five Code of Ethics in Chinese society dictates a hierarchical and particular structure of human relationships. According to Chen (1997), this specific structure of social network ascribes power to the seniority one holds and authority one possesses. Seniority is considered the locus of power and knowledge in Confucianism-influenced societies. The elders in Chinese society continue to receive high status and respect not only in the family but also in the community and workplace (Bond & Hwang, 1986; Carmichael, 1991). In addition, elders also enjoy relative freedom in initiating and terminating an idea or decision in social interactions. For example, Chung (1996) indicated that elders tend to have a wide range of prerogatives in the situation of conflict resolution and negotiations, and their seniority is treated as equivalent to credibility, which may determine whether a cooperative or competitive stance will be taken in an interaction and often causes changes in social relationships, including control over the interaction process and acceptance of others' influence (Griffin, 1967; Nadler, Nadler, & Broome, 1985).

The hierarchical structure of particular relationships also ascribes to the superior, father, husband, older brother, and those in high status authority to receive more power or control over their counterparts. Thus, it is not surprising to find that in the process of Chinese communication, authority often overpowers knowledge and expertise in the final decision. For example, Cai and Gonzalez (1997-1998) found that although knowledge and expertise served as powerful tools in persuading opponents of the Three Gorges Project in China, the final decision was still made by the political leaders who are culturally accepted as the decision makers and problem solvers. In other words, in Chinese society, people with higher status in the particular relationship structure are considered to be more knowledgeable in the process of problem solving or conflict resolution. Power, in the form of seniority and authority, therefore works with *guanxi* and *mientz* to reinforce the ultimate goal of harmony in Chinese communication.

> *Axiom 20:* An appropriate exertion of power will produce an enhancement in the development of harmony in Chinese communication.
>
> *Axiom 21:* An increase in *guanxi* will produce an increase in the development of power in Chinese communication.
>
> *Axiom 22:* An increase in the degree of seniority will produce an increase in the development of power in Chinese communication.
>
> *Axiom 23:* An increase in the degree of authority will produce an increase in the development of power in Chinese communication.
>
> *Theorem 22:* The more senior a person is, the more competent the person will be perceived in Chinese communication.
>
> *Theorem 23:* The more authority a person possesses, the more competent the person will be perceived in Chinese communication.

Taken together, harmony is the axis of Chinese communication, sustained by nine spokes: *jen, yi, li, shi, wei, ji, guanxi, mientz,* and power. The functions and interrelationships of these concepts form a holistic system of ideal Chinese communication. The interaction and integration of them brings continuity into the endless transforming process of Chinese communication. Based on this the-

ory, we understand that, to the Chinese, harmony is a state of equilibrium representing the fulfillment of competent communication by which four ultimate goals of human communication can be reached: feeling secure, feeling togetherness, feeling the joy of interacting, and benefitting from the interaction (Chen, 1993; Hsu, 1987).

► Discussion and Conclusion

The theory proposed in this chapter is an initial attempt to formally state a general theory of Chinese communication based on the concept of harmony. As a cardinal element of Chinese culture, harmony is the ultimate goal Chinese people pursue in the process of human interaction. It is also the main criterion used to assess communication competence in Chinese society. The principle of harmony is regulated by three holistic ontological assumptions of Chinese culture, including transformation, orderly cycle, and endless movement. The achievement of harmony requires individuals to internalize the principles of *jen, yi,* and *li;* to be able to accommodate *shi, wei,* and *ji;* and to appropriately exercise *guanxi, mientz,* and power. A total of four propositions, 23 axioms, and 23 theorems were generated. The first three propositions state the ontological foundation of Chinese culture. They lead to the fourth proposition, which specifies harmony as the basis of Chinese communication behaviors. Except for the first axiom, which specifies the relationship between harmony and competence and in turn serves as the basis for generating more axioms and theorems, all axioms are primary statements with a universal scope in Chinese society and assert a positive relationship between harmony and the nine concepts. Except for Theorem 9, all the theorems, as secondary statements with a general scope and empirically valid, assert a positive relationship between communication competence and concepts inferred or derived from the nine concepts. To directly test the relationship between concepts to understand Chinese communication, future research can derive a series of hypotheses indirectly from axioms or directly from theorems (Hawes, 1975).

The harmony theory developed in this chapter stipulates a complete approach Chinese people use to bring continuity into the endless transforming process of human communication. This harmony perspective of Chinese communication is quite different from the Western approach. Whereas effectiveness or goal attainment is considered the main element of communication competence in Western cultures, Chinese place much more emphasis on appropriateness and reciprocity; through them, harmony can be reached (Chen & Starosta, 1996). This theory not only serves as a mirror that can reflect potential problems occurring in intercultural communication but also provides a great opportunity for people to better understand Chinese communication to reach transcultural understanding while interacting with Chinese.

Nevertheless, the theory proposed in this chapter should not give readers an impression that culture and communication is a linear process. The dynamic and complex nature of culture suggests that human communication is a multiple faceted process in which a prominent cultural value can be consciously or unconsciously used as a tool to implicitly or explicitly shake other core values. For example, power may be abused in a time of social and political turmoil, producing a negative force that seriously challenges the ethical mandate of harmony (Chen & Starosta, 1997-1998). Powers's (1997-1998) study on conflict genres and management strategies during China's 10 years of turmoil vividly demonstrates how people's behaviors deviate from the ethical principle of Chinese communication. Chen's (1997) study also reflects how the culturally endowed superiority based on seniority can be used for personal gain in the process of decision making.

In addition, the structure of hierarchical and particular relationships consequently leads Chinese to develop a different attitude and behavior toward out-group people. In other words, it is not uncommon to see that the principles of *jen, yi,* and *li* are not followed in the process of Chinese communication. For example, face saving usually becomes a victim of competition with out-group members for scare resources. An abundant record in Chinese literature on compliance-gaining strategies used to achieve one's goal in daily interactions illustrates the opposite side of Chinese communication, in which harmony does not play an influential role in regulating Chinese behavior (Chen, 1995b; Chen & Zhong, 1996; Chiao, 1988a, 1989; Chu, 1991; Cleary, 1988; Li, Yang, & Tang, 1989; Senger, 1988; Wang, 1976). This contradictory phenomenon provides a great opportunity for future research to help people better understand Chinese communication behavior.

Finally, an intriguing aspect of Chinese communication also deserves further investigation. When Chinese feel powerless to control their destiny, they tend to adopt a deterministic attitude and behavior in the process of communication. *Ming* (fate) and *yuan* (destined affinity) represent this aspect of Chinese character (Chen, 1996; Chen & Starosta, 1997-1998). In this situation, to Chinese, to be or not to be connected with others or in other areas of daily life is the function of one's predestined fate (*ming*). In the development of relationship, for example, if one is predestined to be together with the other, it is considered *yao yuan* (having destined affinity). On the other hand, if people are unable to connect with each other, they will consider it *wu yuan* (having no destined affinity). *Ming* and *yuan* continue to display a great impact on the process of developing *guanxi* in Chinese society (Chang & Holt, 1993; Wen, 1988). To further pursue this line of research will make a contribution to the understanding of Chinese communication.

▶ References

Becker, C. B. (1986). Reasons for the lack of argumentation and debate in the Far East. *International Journal of Intercultural Relations, 10,* 75-92.

Benedict, R. (1946). *The chrysanthemum and the sword: Patterns of Japanese culture.* Tokyo: Charles E. Tuttle.

Bond, M. B., & Hwang, K. (1986). The social psychology of Chinese people. In M. H. Bond (Ed.), *The psychology of Chinese people* (pp. 213-226). Hong Kong: Oxford University Press.

Broome, B. J. (1996). *Exploring the Greek mosaic.* Yarmouth, ME: Intercultural Press.

Cai, B., & Gonzalez, A. (1997-1998). The Three Gorges project: Technological discourse and the resolution of competing interests. *Intercultural Communication Studies, 7,* 101-112.

Carmichael, C. W. (1991). Intercultural perspectives of aging. In L. A. Samovar & R. E. Porter (Eds.), *Intercultural communication: A reader* (pp. 128-135). Belmont, CA: Wadsworth.

Chai, C., & Chai, W. (1969). Introduction. In J. Legge (Trans.), *I Ching: Book of changes.* New York: Bantam.

Chang, H.-C. (1992, November). *From words to communication: Some philosophical implications for Chinese interpersonal communication.* Paper presented at the annual convention of Speech Communication Association, Atlanta, GA.

Chang, H.-C., & Holt, G. R. (1991). More than relationship: Chinese interaction and the principle of Guan-hsi. *Communication Quarterly, 39,* 251-271.

Chang, H.-C., & Holt, G. R. (1993). The concept of *yuan* and Chinese interpersonal relationships. In S. Ting-Toomey & F. Korzenny (Eds.), *Cross-cultural interpersonal communication* (pp. 28-57). Newbury Park, CA: Sage.

Chen, D. C. (1987). *Confucius thoughts.* Taipei, Taiwan: Cheng Chuong.

Chen, G. M. (1989). Relationships of the dimensions of intercultural communication competence. *Communication Quarterly, 37,* 118-133.

Chen, G. M. (1993, November). *A Chinese perspective of communication competence.* Paper presented at the annual convention of the Speech Communication Association, San Antonio, TX.

Chen, G. M. (1995a, August). *A Chinese model of human relationship development.* Paper presented at the 5th International Conference on Cross-Cultural Communication: East and West, Harbin, China.

Chen, G. M. (1995b, November). *A classification of Chinese persuasive communication strategies.* Paper presented at the annual convention of the Speech Communication Association, New Orleans, LA.

Chen, G. M. (1995c). Differences in self-disclosure patterns among Americans versus Chinese: A comparative study. *Journal of Cross-Cultural Psychology, 26,* 84-91.

Chen, G. M. (1996, November). *Feng shui: The Chinese art of space arrangement.* Paper presented at the annual convention of the Speech Communication Association, San Diego, CA.

Chen, G. M. (1997, November). *An examination of PRC business negotiation styles.* Paper presented at the annual convention of the Speech Communication Association, Chicago.

Chen, G. M. (1998). A Chinese model of human relationship development. In B. L. Hoffer & H. H. Koo (Eds.), *Cross-cultural communication East and West in the '90s* (pp. 45-53). San Antonio, TX: Institute for Cross-Cultural Research.

Chen, G. M., & Chung, J. (1994). The impact of Confucianism on organizational communication. *Communication Quarterly, 42,* 93-105.

Chen, G. M., & Chung, J. (1997). The "Five Asian Dragons": Management behaviors and organizational communication. In L. A. Samovar & R. E. Porter (Eds.), *Intercultural communication: A reader* (pp. 317-328). Belmont, CA: Wadsworth.

Chen, G. M., & Starosta, W. J. (1996). Intercultural communication competence: A synthesis. *Communication Yearbook, 19,* 353-383.

Chen, G. M., & Starosta, W. J. (1997-1998). Chinese conflict management and resolution: Overview and implications. *Intercultural Communication Studies, 7,* 1-16.

Chen, G. M., & Starosta, W. J. (1998a). *Foundations of intercultural communication.* Needham Heights, MA: Allyn & Bacon.

Chen, G. M., & Starosta, W. J. (1998b). A review of the concept of intercultural sensitivity. *Human Communication, 1,* 1-16.

Chen, G. M., & Starosta, W. J. (1999). A review of the concept of intercultural awareness. *Human Communication, 2*, 27-54.

Chen, G. M., & Starosta, W. J. (2000). Communication and global society: An introduction. In G. M. Chen & W. J. Starosta (Eds.), *Communication and global society* (pp. 1-16). New York: Peter Lang.

Chen, G. M., & Xiao, X.-S. (1993, November). *The impact of "harmony" on Chinese negotiations.* Paper presented at the annual convention of the Speech Communication Association, Miami Beach, FL.

Chen, G. M., & Zhong, M. (1996, November). *Dimensions of Chinese compliance-gaining strategies.* Paper presented at the annual convention of the Speech Communication Association, San Diego, CA.

Cheng, C.-Y. (1987). Chinese philosophy and contemporary human communication theory. In D. L. Kincaid (Ed.), *Communication theory: Eastern and Western perspectives* (pp. 23-43). New York: Academic.

Chiao, C. (1981). *Chinese strategic behavior: Some central principles.* Paper presented at the Conference on Content of Culture, Claremont, CA.

Chiao, C. (1988a). An establishment of a model of Chinese strategic behaviors. In K. S. Yang (Ed.), *The psychology of Chinese people* (pp. 431-446). Taipei, Taiwan: Kuei Guan.

Chiao, C. (1988b). On *guanxi.* In K. S. Yang (Ed.), *The psychology of Chinese people* (pp. 105-122). Taipei, Taiwan: Kuei Guan.

Chiao, C. (1989). Chinese strategic behavior: Some general principles. In R. Bolton (Ed.), *The content of culture: Constants and variants* (pp. 525-537). New Haven, CT: Hraf.

Chu, C.-N. (1991). *The Asian mind game.* New York: Rawson.

Chu, J. L. (1988). The Chinese social interaction: A face perspective. In K. S. Yang (Ed.), *The psychology of Chinese people* (pp. 238-288). Taipei, Taiwan: Kuei Guan.

Chu, R. L. (1983). *Empirical researches on the psychology of face.* Doctoral dissertation, National Taiwan University, Tapei.

Chu, S. (1974). *The interpretation of I Ching.* Taipei, Taiwan: Wen Hua.

Chung, J. (1991, April). *Seniority and particularistic ties in a Chinese conflict resolution process.* Paper presented at the annual convention of Eastern Communication Association, Pittsburgh, PA.

Chung, J. (1992, November). *Equilibrium in the Confucianism-influenced superior-subordinate communication system.* Paper presented at the annual convention of Speech Communication Association, Chicago.

Chung, J. (1996). Avoiding a "Bull Moose" rebellion: Particularistic ties, seniority, and third-party mediation. *International and Intercultural Communication Annual, 20,* 166-185.

Cleary, T. (1988). *The art of war.* Boston: Shambhala.

Condon, J. C. (1977). *Interpersonal communication.* New York: Macmillan.

Condon, J. C. (1984). *With respect to the Japanese: A guide for Americans.* Yarmouth, ME: Intercultural Press.

Condon, J. C. (1985). *Good neighbors: Communicating with the Mexicans.* Yarmouth, ME: Intercultural Press.

Condon, J. C., & Yousef, F. (1975). *An introduction to intercultural communication.* Indianapolis, IN: Bobbs-Merrill.

Conrad, C. (1994). *Strategies of organizational communication.* New York: Harcourt Brace College.

Eberhard, W. (1971). *Moral and social values of the Chinese—collected essays.* Washington, DC: Chinese Materials and Research Aids Service Center.

Epstein, M. (1995). *After the future: The paradoxes of postmodernism and contemporary Russian culture.* Amherst: University of Massachusetts Press.

Fang, T. H. (1981). *Chinese philosophy: Its spirit and its development.* Taipei, Taiwan: Linking.

Fingarette, H. (1972). *Confucius: The secular as sacred.* New York: Harper & Row.

Folger, J. P., Poole, M. S., & Strutman, R. K. (1993). *Working through conflict.* New York: Harper Collins.

Fung, Y. L. (1983). *A history of Chinese philosophy.* Princeton, NJ: Princeton University Press.

Griffin, K. (1967). Interpersonal trust in small-group communication. *Quarterly Journal of Speech, 53,* 224-234.

Gu, Y. J. (1992). Distinction of in-group and out-group. In C. Yiao (Ed.), *The Chinese renqin and mientz* (pp. 24-33). Beijing, China: Chinese Friendship.

Gudykunst, W. B., & Nishida, T. (1984). Social penetration in close relationships in Japan and the United States. In R. Bostrom (Ed.), *Communication yearbook* (Vol. 7). Beverly Hills, CA: Sage.

Gudykunst, W. B., & Ting-Toomey, S. (1988). *Culture and interpersonal communication.* Newbury Park, CA: Sage.

Hall, E. T. (1976). *Beyond culture.* Garden City, NY: Anchor.

Harnett, D. L., & Cummings, I. I. (1980). *Bargaining behavior: An international study.* Houston, TX: Some.

Hawes, L. C. (1975). *Pragmatics of analoguing: Theory and model construction in communication.* Reading, MA: Addison-Wesley.

Hofstede, G. (1980). *Culture's consequences: International differences in work-related values.* Beverly Hills, CA: Sage.

Hsu, F.L.K. (1953). *Americans and Chinese: Two ways of life.* New York: Abelard-Schuman.

Hsu, W. (1987). *The modernization of Chinese management.* Hong Kong: Hsin Lien.

Hu, H. C. (1944). The Chinese concept of "face." *American Anthropology, 46,* 45-64.

Hwang, K. K. (1987). Renqin and face: The Chinese power game. *American Journal of Sociology, 92,* 944-974.

Hwang, K. K. (1988). The Chinese *renqin* relationship. In C. Y. Wen & S. H. Xiao (Eds.), *The Chinese: Their perception and behaviors* (pp. 43-70). Taipei, Taiwan, Taiwan: Ju Lieu.

Hwang, K. K. (1997-1998). *Guanxi* and *mientze:* Conflict resolution in Chinese society. *Intercultural Communication Studies, 7,* 17-40.

Jia, W. (1997-1998). Facework as a Chinese conflict-preventive mechanism: A cultural/discourse analysis. *Intercultural Communication Studies, 7,* 63-82.

Jin, Y. J. (1988). An analysis of face, shame, and Chinese behaviors. In K. S. Yang (Ed.), *The*

psychology of Chinese people (pp. 319-346). Taipei, Taiwan: Kuei Guan.

Jocobs, B. J. (1979). A preliminary model of particularistic ties in Chinese political alliances: Kanching and Juan-his in a rural Taiwanese township. *China Quarterly, 78,* 237-273.

Kapp, R. A. (Ed.). (1983). *Communicating with China.* Chicago: Intercultural Press.

Legge, J. (1955). *The four book.* Taipei, Taiwan: Wen Yo.

Leung, K. (1988). Some determinants of conflict avoidance. *Journal of Cross-Cultural Psychology, 19,* 125-136.

Li, S. J., Yang, S. J., & Tang, J. Z. (1989). *Sun Tze Bin Fa and business management.* Hong Kong: San Lien.

Lin, Y. S. (1988). *The social philosophy of Yi Chuan's Yi Chuan.* Taipei, Taiwan: Shen Wu.

Lindin, O. G. (1974). Harmony with nature in Chinese thought and opposition to nature in Western thought. *The Journal of Intercultural Studies, 1,* 5-9.

Liu, C. L. (1990). The cyclic view of I Ching and Chinese thinking. *China Yi Studies, 123,* 14-16 & *124,* 13-18.

Liu, C. L. (1992). *Chinese wisdom and system thoughts.* Taipei, Taiwan: Shen Wu.

Ma, R. (1990). An exploratory study of discontented responses in American and Chinese relationships. *The Southern Communication Journal, 55,* 305-318.

Ma, R. (1992). The role of unofficial intermediaries in interpersonal conflicts in the Chinese culture. *Communication Quarterly, 40,* 269-278.

Nadler, B. N., Nadler, M. K., & Broome, B. J. (1985). Culture and the management of conflict situations. In W. B. Gudykunst, L. P. Stewart, & S. Ting-Toomey (Eds.), *Communication, culture, and organizational processes* (pp. 87-113). Beverly Hills, CA: Sage.

Nakanishi, M. (1987). Perceptions of self-disclosure initial interactions: A Japanese sample. *Human Communication Research, 13,* 167-190.

Powers, J. H. (1997-1998). Conflict genres and management strategies during China's ten years turmoil. *Intercultural Communication Studies, 7,* 149-168.

Pye, L. (1982). *Chinese commercial negotiation style.* Cambridge, MA: Oelgechlager, Gunn & Hain.

Schneider, M. J. (1985). Verbal and nonverbal indices of the communicative performance and acculturation of Chinese immigrants. *International Journal of Intercultural Relations, 9,* 271-283.

Senger, H. (1988). *The book of stratagems: Tactics for triumph and survival.* New York: Viking.

Shenkar, O., & Ronen, S. (1987). The cultural context of negotiations: The implications of Chinese interpersonal norms. *The Journal of Applied Behavioral Science, 23,* 263-275.

Silin, R. H. (1981). *Leadership and values: The organization of large-scale Taiwanese enterprise.* Cambridge, MA: Harvard University Press.

Stewart, E. C., & Bennett, M. J. (1991). *American cultural patterns: A cross-cultural perspective.* Yarmouth, ME: Intercultural Press.

Wang, B. S. (1989). *Between Confucianism and Taoism.* Taipei, Taiwan: Han Kuan.

Wang, J. D. (1976). *Sun Tze Bin Fa.* Taipei, Taiwan: Chuon Wen.

Wang, Y. L. (1992). *Renqin and mientz.* In C. Yiao (Ed.), *The Chinese renqin and mientz* (pp. 34-45). Beijing, China: Chinese Friendship.

Wei, Y. (1983). The importance of being KEQI: A note on communication difficulties. In R. A. Kapp (Ed.), *Communicating with China* (pp. 71-76). Chicago: Intercultural Press.

Wen, C. I. (1988). An investigation of Chinese national character: A value orientation perspective. In I. U. Lee & K. S. Yang (Eds.), *The Chinese character* (pp. 49-90). Taipei, Taiwan: Kwei Kwan.

Wilhelm, R. (1979). *Lectures on the I Ching: Constancy and change.* Princeton, NJ: Princeton University Press.

Wilhelm, R. (Trans.). (1990). *The I Ching.* Princeton, NJ: Princeton University Press.

Wolfson, K., & Pearce, W. B. (1983). A cross-cultural comparison of the implications of self-disclosure on conversational logics. *Communication Quarterly, 31,* 249-256.

Wu, Y. (1964). The concept of change in I Ching. *Chuon Kuo Yi Chou, 754,* 19-21.

Wu, Y. (1976). *The philosophy of Cheng in Chuon Yuon.* Taipei, Taiwan: Don Da.

Yang, H. J. (1978). Communicative competence in Formosan sociable events: A participant observation study. *Dissertation Abstracts International, 39,* 2622A.

Yum, J. O. (1988). The impact of Confucianism on interpersonal relationships and communication patterns in East Asia. *Communication Monographs, 55,* 374-388.

Transcultural Realities
and Different Ways of Knowing

MOLEFI KETE ASANTE

What has fascinated me is the manner in which most of my colleagues have written theory and engaged in the social sciences and communication in relationship to African people. They have often assumed that their particular "objectivity," a kind of collective subjectivity of European culture, should be the measure by which the world marches. I have seldom fallen in step, insisting that there are other ways in which to experience phenomena rather than viewing them from a Eurocentric vantage point.

My work has increasingly constituted a radical critique of the Eurocentric ideology that masquerades as a universal view in the fields of intercultural communication, rhetoric, philosophy, linguistics, psychology, education, anthropology, and history. Yet, the critique is radical only in the sense that it

suggests a turnabout, an alternative perspective on phenomena. It is about taking the globe and turning it over so that we see all the possibilities of a world where Africa, for example, is subject and not object. Such a posture is necessary and rewarding for both Africans and Europeans. The inability to "see" from several angles is perhaps the one common weakness in provincial scholarship, and this weakness remains the most troubling obstacle to transcultural realities. Those who have delighted us most thoroughly and advanced thought most significantly have been those thinkers who have explored the multiple realities of human communities. They have been the ones who have brought new perspectives.

My objective has always been to present a critique that propounds a cultural theory of society by the very act of criticism (Asante, l980). In other words, to provide a radical assessment of a given reality is to create, *inter alia,* another reality. Furthermore, any criticism of society is, by definition, a criticism of the ruling ideology of that society. I have the insight that comes from having been born black in the United States. That fact puts me in a critical mood within the intellectual and social milieu I share with Eurocentrists. As the critic, I am always seeking to create a new world, to find an escape, to liberate those who see only a part of reality. Similarly, Countee Cullen (1972), the noted poet, could say,

> Inscrutable His ways are, and immune
> To catechism by a mind too strewn
> With petty cares to slightly understand
> What awful brain compels his awful
>   hand?
> Yet do I marvel at this curious thing
> To make a poet black, and bid him
>   sing!

By the very act of being a poet, Countee Cullen was criticizing the society that said a black person could not be a poet. As a writer in cultural and intellectual alignment with basic human needs and values, he was, by definition, in defiance of an oppressive situation.

The crystallization of this critical perspective I have called *Afrocentricity,* which means literally placing African ideals and behaviors in the center of any discourse that involves Africans. This perspective is as valid within the human context as any other. For example, the communication scholar who defines a speech as an uninterrupted spoken discourse demonstrates either a disregard or ignorance of the African tradition of speech, much as Leslie Fiedler (1966) was using a purely European conception of fiction when he contended that romance was the central theme of literature. Fiedler's reaction to literature was essentially a Eurocentric contextual affair. Familiar with the classics of American and British literature, he apparently accepted Western literature as world-defining. Although an able critic of Eurocentric culture, he failed to analyze his genre from a worldwide perspective—or at least, to acknowledge the possibility of such an analysis. Traditionally, African writers are not concerned with the romance variety of literature, but Fiedler, like many Eurocentric writers, gives us no awareness of this fact. We are thus left with his word for literature—a truncated word parading as universal.

Charles Larson (1973) wrote a perceptive essay, "Heroic Ethnocentrism: The Idea of Universality in Literature," in which he examined the European notion of universality. Larson had first come face to face with the problem of universality while teaching an English literature course in Nigeria—a good place, I might add, to come to grips with ethnocentric ideas of all kinds. His students did not understand the idea of kissing in the Victorian novel, and how Larson handled the situation is revealing. He groped for words to explain the work of such a celebrated writer as Thomas Hardy to his African audiences. He learned, of course, how culture shapes the interpretation of literature. But because culture itself is shaped by the constant demands of society and the environment, Larson concluded that kissing and description have not found counterparts in the African novel—not yet, at least. He writes, "Usually, when we try to force the concept of universality on someone who is not western, I think we are implying that our own culture should be the standard of measurement" (Larson, l973, p. 463). Larson is correct to see Fiedler's assertion that the romance is universal as another Western analysis imposed on world literature. Because there are entire cultural areas where the romance is nonexistent, the universality of the genre is doubtful. There are no major African novels where the plot progresses because of a hero's attempt to attract a mate. An Afrocentric discussion of literature, thus, would guard against this ethnocentric promotion of group universality.

The central problem with Fiedler and others who write in this vein is that, just as 15th-century Europeans could not cease believing that the earth was the center of the universe, many today find it difficult to stop viewing European/American culture as the center of the social universe. Thus, the work they produce seldom considers the possibilities of other realities or, indeed, shared realities. A number of scholars have challenged such a narrow view of the arts and the social sciences. Their works speak to the abiding problem of Western formulations based on parochial observations (Hilliard, 1998; Karenga, 1990; Nobles, 1986).

But Robert Armstrong (1975) declares, in a more direct way, that Europeans tend to speak as Fiedler did, tying themselves to all that is supposedly universal, because they have "an ethnocentric crypto-aesthetics" that links them to what they perceive as a "universal cultural phenomenon." What is particularly troubling about these formulations by European and some African and Asian writers, who have been thoroughly trained in Eurocentrism, is that they assume that everyone else should simply acquiesce in their expansive provincialism. Not only do they make their arguments with a bewildering array of tropes, figures, and oxymorons, but they assert them as if there were no other reality, no other perspective.

It is striking that some feminist critics have addressed the same conceptual issue, although from a different point of view. For example, Karen Sacks (1979) has attacked social Darwinist anthropology for its industrial-capitalist bias. In her study of six African societies, she argues that anthropology's inherent hierarchical and competitive dimensions create, as well as reinforce, beliefs in the natural superiority of men over women. According to Sacks, "the center of the struggle lies in changing institutionalized patterns of behaviors and allocations of social roles" (p. 3). Because Marxism does not presume such inequality, Sacks extols its analytic advantages in the feminist movement. Social Darwinist and Marxist theories "are diametrically opposed ways of seeing the same social order(s), and they represent opposed class views and needs" (Sacks, 1979, p. 3). However, her argument, like those of other Marxist theorists, rests on a reaction to the industrial-capitalist

order and must use its language to demonstrate the opposition. Thus, although the opposition is real, the balance is weighted toward social Darwinism.

Although Afrocentric thinkers must also confront presumptions of inequality, Marxism is likewise not helpful in developing Afrocentric concepts and methods because it, too, is a product of a Eurocentric consciousness, which excludes the historical and cultural perspectives of Africa. I am sympathetic to Sacks's view to the extent that she criticizes the social Darwinist perspective and attempts to find, as I have done, a way of seeing based on people's needs and experiences. But because Marxism emerged from the Western consciousness, it is mechanistic in its approach to social understanding and development, and it has often adopted forms of social Darwinism when explaining cultural and social phenomena.

I have challenged the African American Marxists, who have claimed to be radical democrats under the new philosophical regime, in which Marxism appears weakened by the demise of the Soviet formula, to understand that the structural problems they identify in the American system are not primary causes of the economic dislocation of African people. Although it is true that the American system, with its new technological thrust away from the old industrial order, is structurally organized by the energy it gathers to dislocate and disorient African people, it is dependent on the cooperation of systemic racism. In other words, the system exists because of the racism, not the other way round. One cannot claim that the industrial age was any better for Africans than the new structural situation. Furthermore, what appears to Cornel West (1993) and others as evidence of nihilism in the African American community is simply the failure of the American economic system to deliver its goods equitably, not some imperfection in African people. Actually the system, as designed, has worked quite well in marginalizing African Americans and other ethnic populations. Interestingly, in trying to pinpoint the nature of this nihilism in the African

American community, among West, Angela Davis, and Manning Marable, radical democrats all, none has been able to offer a way to eliminate the nihilism, except to argue that there must be some sort of structural change in the American economy. To be sure, Marable (1996) is more specific, calling for a socialism committed to human equality in which liberty is not simply a function of the power and privilege of the wealthy. What I, as an Afrocentrist, am concerned about is not nihilism per se but the underlying problem of a strictly class analysis of the African American situation. I do not accept the thesis that the material condition creates ideas in an absolute sense. One sees this precisely in the manner that race operates differently for the white worker and the black worker. There is no consistent, provocative, revolutionary sentiment, as Harold Cruse (1969) would say, evident in the white proletariat. On the other hand, African Americans want fundamental change in the way we are perceived. It is clear to me that Afrocentricity assists us in understanding how people come to create material realities, whether those realities are based in class or race conditions. Furthermore, it is not true now, nor has it ever been true, that the white poor see themselves as united with the black poor against the white elite in the struggle to bring about a more equitable society. In fact, the white poor and working classes believe (witness the various white separatist and paramilitary groups) that the black poor and the white establishment work in tandem. Although radical democrats argue that the failure of the Soviet Union was not the failure of communism, Soviet communism is the only grand communism that we have known. Such is the limit of class thinking in racial societies.

While inquiring into the nature of the African condition in the Americas, Cornel West concluded that the fundamental problem was the loss of values, a sort of nihilism that has derailed the best intentions of the African American genius. Although West (1993) has expressed this belief in many places, it is especially pronounced in *Prophetic Thought in Postmodern Times,* where he contends that the period between 1965 and 1992 produced "the highest level of forms of destruction known in black history." With the passion that only West can bring to an issue, he reiterates in his unique manner that

> These demons which are at work, the demons of meaninglessness, of hopelessness, a sense of nothingness conjoined with the institutional and structural marginalization of large numbers of black people. . . . But for the most part, it has produced the highest level of self-destruction known to black people since we arrived. (p. 150)

My response to what West sees as nihilism has been to present an Afrocentric vision wrapped in the optimism that remains the attitude of the African multitudes in the United States. By raising some important issues in regard to the loss of values, West has struck the same chord as the African American conservatives from whom he distances himself. They argue that the loss of values means that the African Americans need to acquire the habits and values of the white population to become fully functioning citizens of the United States. To his credit, West does not go this far and indeed has taken issue with the conservatives Glenn Loury and Thomas Sowell, who have made a rather straightforward critique of the conservative position by framing this question of values in terms of individual choices rather than in terms of what the structural dimensions of society have created as choices.

But the concentration on the loss of values by the conservatives, by West, and to a lesser extent by Marable and other radical democrats is misplaced. I have tried to demonstrate that there is no loss of values in the African American community and that the values that we honor and respect are as strong today as they have ever been. Of course, changing economic and political realities do highlight certain antihuman behaviors by some individuals, but these actions are neither acceptable to African Americans nor unprecedented in this nation's past. Although our traditional values, such as harmony, justice, equality, patience, diligence, and good-naturedness, are not foreign to us today, they are rarely represented in the media, which instead produces a flood of images and ideas about how nihilistic we have become. Although I do not dismiss the realities of violence and other destructive behaviors, I believe that the media make them seem more pervasive than ever.

If we have lost anything, it has been our cultural centeredness; that is, we have been moved off of our own platforms. This means that we cannot truly be ourselves or know ourselves or know our potential because we exist in a borrowed space. But all space is a matter of point of view or interpretation. Our existential relationship to the culture that we have borrowed defines what and who we are at any given moment in history. By regaining our own platforms, standing in our own cultural spaces, and believing that our way of viewing the universe is just as valid as any other, we will achieve the kind of transformation that we need to participate fully in a multicultural society. However, without this kind of centeredness, we bring almost nothing to the multicultural table but a darker version of whiteness.

There is, therefore, nothing strange about the Afrocentric idea. All distorted or otherwise negative understandings of it are rooted in the society's manner of viewing Africans. This is not to say that all who reject the Afrocentric idea are racists but rather that their failure to appreciate its context and objectives suggests their seduction by the structural elements of a hierarchical society that fails to recognize African agency. We have, however, arrived at a point at which the entire process of human knowledge is being assessed and reassessed to help us discover what we know about each other. As we open the doors to return to our own platforms, we greatly enrich the world.

What makes Afrocentric concepts more inclusive is that they seek to reorient our worldview in ways that challenge social Darwinism, capitalism, and most forms of Marxism, all of which are grounded in their own particularity. The invalidity of an idea arises not from its exponents but from its own fundamental flaws. This is the point at which the feminist critique converges with the Afrocentric line of reasoning. What I seek to do here is to move closer to a post-Eurocentric idea that makes true transcultural analyses possible; this can be accomplished alongside a postmale ideology as we unlock creative human potential.

It should be clear that although numerous issues remain unresolved in the discourse of Afrocentricity, I am not opposed to any conception of the human being that is rewarding and liberating. Indeed, we can only advance communally in the context of freedom, personal liberty, and collective liberation as conceived by many scholars.

I, as an Afrocentrist, argue the primacy of the cultural crisis in the context of a heterogeneous racist society, but I am aware of the varieties of oppressions in our contemporary situation, and like other Afrocentrists, I believe that it is necessary to confront all forms of discrimination, persecution, and oppressions simultaneously. Without such confrontation we cannot bring about transcultural realities.

But what of the poststructualist and, by extension, postmodernist concern about the perceived restructuralism inherent in Afrocentricity? This question is meant to sharpen the conflict that frequently exists between the postmodernist and the Afrocentrist on the cultural issue. Afrocentricity cannot abandon the structuralisms of modernism without betraying the achievements of culture. African Americans are a preeminently cultured people within American society, and our contributions to what is called "popular American culture" are immense. To seek to transcend the African cultural presence in contemporary society is to quest for anonymity at the very time that African Americans and Africans are most capable of asserting their culture. Robert Farris Thompson (1984, p. 23) has argued that the modern world is fundamentally a world created by the presence of Africans in the Americas. Thus, African presence in art, science, Egyptology, literature, politics, and democracy is a decisive force in the modern world, as it either affirms or rejects that presence. That we Africans have been involved in the construction of the modern world is precisely why Afrocentrists are questioning the abandonment of modernism. We are not, however, running away from ourselves, and although we are in the midst of projecting ourselves to the world, we do not lose sight of the structural ideas of location, place, and stance.

Nevertheless, the quest for transcendence, in the sense of going beyond the simple affirmation or rejection of African presence, does not have to be detrimental to good society: It can be affirming and fulfilling, so long as an Afrocentric agency is constituted in the creation of a new world. We must conclude that modernism's problem is with the *use* of Africans rather than with the *agency* of Africans. If this unsettles some to the point that they question the restructuring of the world, it serves to demonstrate that the deconstruction process was never completed in the first place. If it had been completed, it would have had to serve up the abandoned concepts of white racism on the altar of progressive sacrifice so that we could have a more fully creative world. What needs to be deconstructed are the means by which human beings in the Western world have defined a triumphal vision that diminishes other people. I know that this is a difficult road for those who are committed to the detours of literary analysis and historical speculation, because once again we are in the area of the forbidden when we question the Eurocentric idea about culture.

Unless they are subjected to severe criticism, the Eurocentric myths of universalism, objectivity, and classical traditions retain a provincial European cast. Scholarship rooted in such myths obviously lacks historical or conceptual authenticity. The aggressive seizure of intellectual space, like the seizure of land, amounts to occupying someone else's territory and claiming it as one's own. When this happens, cultural analysis takes a back seat to galloping ethnocentric interpretation of phenomena.

Applied to the African world, such conceptions become limiting, restricting, and parochial. For example, a discussion of African cultural history rarely calls forth African culture in the American context when the discussion is made by Eurocentric writers. Like the literary critics, the historians dismiss the African elements that survived on the American continent as purely temporal. They usually refer to them as "Negro culture," or speak of "the African slave in the New World" or "Negro emancipation." The fact that the spatial referent is Africa is ignored, and *Negro* becomes a cryptoterm that is used to designate our degradation. In this way the Eurocentric writer ties the African to the Negro, a false concept and a false history, separate from any particular spatial reality. The word *Negro* did not exist prior to slavery; both the term and its application were products of the social and economic context of the European slave trade. Consequently, the attachment of the term *Negro* to Africans means a negation of history and culture.

Furthermore, the Eurocentric formulations recognize neither African classical thought nor the African classical past. We are essentially left with a discontinuous history and an uncertain future. By contrast, the Afrocentric analysis reestablishes the centrality of the ancient Kemetic (Egyptian) civilization and the Nile Valley cultural complex as points of reference for an African perspective, in much the same way that Greece and Rome serve as reference points for the European world. Thus, the Afrocentrist expands human history by creating a new path for interpretation, making words like *Negro* and *colored* obsolete and anachronistic. *African* is identified with time, place, and perspective. Without the Afrocentric perspective, the imposition of the European line as universal hinders cultural understanding and demeans humanity.

Such deliberately separatist views carry the false assertion that Africans in the Americas are not Africans connected to their spatial origin. Although differences exist between Barbados and Zimbabwe, these differences are much like the differences between Florence and Brisbane. African American culture and history represent developments in African culture and history, inseparable from place and time. An analysis of African American culture that is not based on Afrocentric premises is bound to lead to incorrect conclusions. In a similar manner, the interpretation of historical data from a strictly Eurocentric perspective can cause serious intercultural conflict, based on wrong premises.

Let me give an example of how cultural misunderstandings can be propagated by different views. In the 19th century, Cecil John Rhodes sought to gain control of a large territory of southern Africa that was ruled by the Ndebele King Lobengula, and he sent emissaries to the powerful king in an effort to secure his consent. After many days of discussion with Lobengula, the white emissaries returned to Rhodes with the king's signature on a piece of paper. They told Rhodes that Lobengula had given him all of his territory, and Rhodes sent a column of soldiers into the area with the instruction to shoot any black on sight. Thus began the country of Rhodesia.

Rhodes may have believed that King Lobengula had given him title to the land, but Lobengula never believed that he had. Thus, their two cultural views of the world clashed, and the Europeans automatically assumed the correctness of their view. An Afrocentric analysis points out that Lobengula could never have sold or given the land away, because it belonged not to him but to the ancestors and the community. He could grant Rhodes permission to hunt, to farm, and even to build a house, but not to own land. Only in this manner could the king follow the discourse of his ancestors. It took nearly 100 years, two revolts, and a 7-year war to correct the situation. A rigid Eurocentrism made Rhodes believe that Lobengula had signed his country over to him.

Similarly, I am certain that Native Americans did not believe they had sold Manhattan Island for $23 worth of trinkets, no matter what the Dutch thought. Native Americans revere the land in much the same way that Africans do. No king or clan leader could sell what did not belong to him. On the basis of European contractual custom, the Dutch may have thought they were purchasing the island from the Indians, but this was obviously a view based on their own commercial traditions.

One has to ascertain other points of view to understand human phenomena. African responses and actions, however, have too often been examined from Eurocentric perspectives. The misunderstandings between Europeans and others have provoked in me an interest in alternative perspectives and an attempt to critically reevaluate social phenomena within transcultural realities.

▶ A Place to Stand

I turn now to a related area of concern. I have been criticized as an essentialist, a bad thing to be, according to deconstructionists. They believe that when one argues for certain characteristics of culture that constitute a given community, one is taking an essentialist position. The problem with such a position, according to these critics, is that it denies the fluidity of cultures and the possibility that cultures can change. In a videotaped debate with me, Cornel West (1995) said, "Molefi Asante believes that one has to be centered, rooted, but I believe that one must go with the flow, move and groove, and be dynamic." My reply was that I, too, believe that one must be "open to the possibilities of dynamism, moving and flowing, but you have to be moving and flowing from some base. Those who do not move from a base are just floating in the air." It is clear to me from my own study of history that cultures do exist and in fact persist for centuries with many basic characteristics hardly changed. This is the nature of human societies operating on the foundations of myths, history, and memories. The African American community is no different from others in this regard. There are certain essential characteristics that identify the contours of our African American community. These are not immutable characteristics, in the sense of being inborn, but rather the fundamental outlines of what we regard and preserve as characteristic of our society.

Thus, although I may answer to being an essentialist, I am not an immutabilist. It is unreasonable to expect African Americans to divest themselves of culture and history when such unilateral divestiture is neither required nor expected of other cultural groups. Imbedded in the suggestion is a notion of power and hierarchy according to which only communities considered of low status are required to abandon their essential characteristics, whereas others seek to preserve their characteristics for generations yet unborn. Look at the degree to which the French are going to preserve their cultural essentials. Look at the concern among Japanese Americans and Jewish Americans that high rates of intermarriage will erase their cultural heritage. To claim an African identity and an Afrocentric place to stand is no more essentialist than the positions taken by critics in feminist, gay/lesbian, and cultural studies and others who challenge established hierarchy.

The Afrocentric critic's chief problem is finding a place to stand—so to speak—in relation to the Western standards that are imposed as interpretative measures on other cultures. I have familiarized myself with the leading proponents of the logic of scientific discovery, only to find their reductionist views of the world incapable of adequately dealing with African cultural data. In fact, I question whether they are able to examine any data that are dynamic and transformational. Because the time-space domain is not stationary and has not been considered to be so since the Newtonian view was shattered by quantum theory's evidence of particle-wave behavior, there needs to be an accommodating, flexible frame of reference that permits the dynamic.

A promising attempt to account for the harmony of opposites and to break down the false dichotomies that occur in much social science and physical science research is found in the work of Thomas Kuhn. It is promising as a heuristic, not an accomplished end, because Kuhn does not question the ground on which he stands. The procedure for scientific discovery, in Kuhn's (1970) view, has two components: verifiability and falsifiability. However,

the Kuhnian paradigm has been considered a copy of Karl Popper's logic of discovery. Kuhn pointed out the similarities and differences between his views and Popper's in a rather lengthy paper that contrasts the logic of discovery and the psychology of research. Although he admits that he and Popper selected the same scientific aspects to investigate, he says they differ in how they perceive these aspects and in how they evaluate their significances. The two agree on the following:

1. Scientific development is a dynamic process.
2. Science is not the accretion of concepts but rather a transformation of conceptual frames.
3. History often provides facts.
4. Outstanding science should be viewed as revolution.

However, Kuhn argues, he and Popper arrive at these conclusions by different analytical modes.

Both Kuhn and Popper are primarily concerned with falsification and verification. Whereas Popper believes that scientific revolutions occur when there is falsification of a theory, Kuhn argues for the joint approach of verification and falsification. The progress of science is supposed to occur when the crises of revolution are resolved. In my view, both the Kuhnian and the Popperian arguments, although certainly powerful within the context of European science, fail to raise the first-order question, which asks for a justification of the scientific endeavor itself. Rather than discuss the relative differences between revolutionary and normal science, one might question the scientific enterprise or perspective itself or, as Stephen Toulmin (1958) did, the notion of the revolutionary when used in connection with science. Yet, it is clear that Kuhn, among the most cited authors of the last century, has introduced a controversial and creative idea, although he must, as he says of scientists, defend his own commitments while assuming a universal role. He cannot question the ground on which he stands. He does not assume any understanding of the transcultural realities of the modern world. His is essentially a materialist view.

▶ An Afrocentric View

The Afrocentric writer knows that oppositional dichotomies in real everyday experiences do not exist. The speaker or the writer is fully engaged in every way, not merely in ways that seem measurable. You may use the computer, but you cannot understand all that is involved in my writing simply by observing my fingers. I may experience hunger, joy, pain, or pleasure while I write. I might even get an electric shock or two, but you would not know that from observing my hands unless I shrieked. I might experience the most delightful romantic thoughts while I strike the keyboard to produce unromantic prose. This flow of energy cannot be accounted for by the mere observation of my physical movements as I write, nor by my report of what I describe in my writings. Nor is it explained by what I say has crossed my mind while I was writing. The interaction of my physical and metaphysical world leads to my behavior at the moment, and this interaction cannot be reduced to separate units of an either/or nature of body-mind. It cannot be assumed that the body causes mental activities or that mental activities cause the body to function. Accounting for different perspectives or allowing them to emerge becomes the principal aim of a truly liberating perspective.

Although the contributions of Eurocentric philosophers and scientists have been important and valuable, they have not been fully expressive of the extent of the power of human ways of knowing. The arguments that have been advanced for the Western formulation of science are not convincing. Marvin Harris (1979), for example, writes as good an apologia as anyone for the value of science:

> Science is a unique and precious contribution of western civilization. . . . No other way of knowing is based on a set of rules explicitly de-signed to transcend the prior belief systems of mutually antagonistic tribes, nations, classes, and ethnic and religious communities in order to arrive at knowledge that is equally probable for any rational human mind. The real alternative to science is not anarchy, but ideology; not peaceful artists, philosophers and anthropologists, but aggressive fanatics and messiahs, eager to annihilate each other and the world if need be in order to prove their point. (p. 28)

Harris characterizes the scientific approach as superior to others and claims that it is uniquely rational among systems. He is perhaps at his Eurocentric best as an interpreter of the nonscientists of other cultures. He readily admits that there are "domains of experience the knowledge of which cannot be achieved by adherence to the rules of scientific method" (Harris, 1979, p. 28). But he sees this "nonscientific" knowledge, particularly "the ecstatic knowledge of mystics and saints; the visions and hallucinations of drug users and of schizophrenics; and the aesthetic and moral insights of artists, poets, and musicians" (p. 28), as beyond his understanding. This is almost fantastic, an admission that he cannot distinguish between the euphoria of drug users and saints or schizophrenics and the insights of artists and poets! Harris's characterization of the Western scientific method is by no means unique. Yet, his ability to denigrate other ways of knowing creates a false impression of science itself. Science does not exclude moral or aesthetic insight. The special disciplines and rigors of the arts and the regularized, methodical procedures of the so-called mystics cannot be easily discounted, for they have added knowledge and richness to the human experience. What Harris and other apologists of this peculiarly narrow version of the scientific adventure argue against is what they perceive as the random, mystical type of discovery. They see it as valuable only when it is transformed by precise, logical verification. Thus, discovery is separate from verification. In effect, Harris's view would dismiss the creative process, divest itself of discovery, and concentrate on the verification process. My desire is to see a paradigm of complementarity that integrates discovery with verification where necessary. In this manner, Afrocentricity expands the repertoire of human perspectives on knowledge. Because the Afrocentric idea is unthinkable without African agency, I feel compelled to resolve the confusion surrounding the terms *Afrocentricity* and *Africanity.* How one approaches these concepts in large measure determines the efficacy of a challenge to hierarchy. The substance of one term is not that of the other, and the consequences of one can create problems for the other. In other words, Afrocentricity seeks agency and action, whereas Africanity broadcasts identity and being. Actually, Africanity refers in its generality to all of the customs, traditions, and traits of people of Africa and the diaspora. On the other hand, Afrocentricity is very specific in its reliance on self-conscious action. To say, for example, that Afrocentricity has no role in Africa because the people there already have an African perspective is to misunderstand the practical dimensions of Afrocentricity. To be African is not necessarily to be Afrocentric. It is possible, however, to develop a nexus between Africanity and Afrocentricity to generate a more productive architectonic African culture of balance and harmony.

A major part of my Afrocentric quest has been to bring the consciousness of rhetorical structure to the study of African communication, particularly discourse. This is why I set a conceptual field for exploring the Afrocentric perspective on discourse in other works as well. Such a conceptual field allowed for the explanation of the rhetorical condition as a phenomenon with an implicit structure and did not negate the position of a metatheory for African communication. The oratory of African Americans could then be examined as the totalization of the Afrocentric perspective, emphasizing the presence of *nommo,* the generative and productive power of the spoken word, in African discourse and in specific instances of resistance to the dominant ideology. In the oratorical experience, much as in the jazz experience, the African person finds the ability to construct a discourse reality capable of calling forth nommo. One can see in this type of quest that different human objectives are derived from different historical and cultural experiences. What occurs in any science or art is a debate over mode, structure, and condition; that is, the guidelines for the valid discussion of discourse are at the center of any polemic. But hearing the voice of African American culture with all of its attendant parts is one way of creating a more sane society and one model for a more humane world.

▶ References

Armstrong, R. P. (1975). *Wellspring: On the myth and source of culture.* Berkeley: University of California Press.

Asante, M. K. (1980). *Afrocentricity: The theory of social change.* Buffalo, NY: Amulefi.

Cruse, H. (1969). *Rebellion or revolution.* New York: William Morrow.

Cullen, C. (1972). *To make a poet black* (Phonodisk; read by Ruby Dee and Ossie Davis). New York: Caedrion.

Fiedler, L. (1966). *Love and death in the American novel.* New York: Stein & Day.

Harris, M. (1979). *Cultural materialism: The struggle for a science of culture.* New York: Random House.

Hilliard, A. (1998). *SBA: The reawakening of the African mind.* Gainesville, FL: Makare.

Karenga, M. (1990). *Introduction to black studies.* Los Angeles: University of Sankore Press.

Kuhn, T. (1970). *The structure of scientific revolution.* Berkeley: University of California Press.

Larson, C. R. (1973). Heroic ethnocentrism: The idea of universality in literature. *American Scholar, 42*(3), 463.

Marable, M. (1996). *Speaking truth to power.* Boulder, CO: Westview.

Nobles, W. (1986). *African psychology.* Oakland, CA: Institute for the Advanced Study of the Black Family.

Sacks, K. (1979). *Sisters and wives.* Westport, CT: Greenwood.

Thompson, R. F. (1984). *The flash of the spirit: African and Afro-American art and philosophy.* New York: Random House.

Toulmin, S. (1958). *Uses of argument.* Cambridge, UK: Cambridge University Press.

West, C. (1993). *Prophetic thoughts for post-modern times.* Monroe, ME: Common Courage Press.

West, C. (1995, May 5). *Afrocentricity and black theology* (Videotape recording). Debate between Molefi Kete Asante and Cornel West at the United Theological Seminary, Dayton, OH.

The Effects of Computer-Mediated Communication on Transculturalism

BOLANLE A. OLANIRAN

Advances in information technology and moves toward globalization are parallel developments that are becoming norms in most organizations and, thus, part of the transcultural realities we live. Information technology developments help fuel globalization developments and vice versa. Globalization is an attempt by organizations to expand beyond their domestic national boundaries. This provides competitive advantages to corporations, and the number of multinational corporations competing in today's business market has increased. According to recent surveys of the world's chief executive officers (CEOs), two thirds believe that foreign markets are a key factor in their organization's future business success and that greater revenues will be generated outside their organization's home country (Adler & Bartholomew, 1992; George, 1995; Hambrick, Korn, Frederickson, & Ferry, 1989; Mesdag, 2000). Information technology adds the flexibility that organizations need for coordinating and managing human resources across different geographical operational settings. Essential to the coordination process is communication with and among organization participants. Opportunities in global markets are enhanced by standards promoted through emerging technologies (Engle, 1999). Thus,

AUTHOR'S NOTE: The author would like to extend his gratitude to Ron Rice (Rutgers University) and Urs Gattiker (University of Lethbridge, CA), for their comments, which aided in the development of the manuscript. Also thanks to Carol Cawyer (University of North Texas), Karla Jensen, Donald Rude, David Williams, and Diane Wood (Texas Tech) for the assistance they provided in editing this manuscript.

the extent to which information technologies aid coordination activities deserves a closer look (Karimi & Konsynski, 1991).

Among several state-of-the-art information technologies popular in the globalization movement is computer-mediated communication (CMC). In general, CMC is a process whereby messages are electronically transmitted from senders to receivers in both synchronous and asynchronous settings (Elton, 1982; Olaniran, 1994). CMC facilitates both dyadic and conference (multiuser) interactions. In the past, meetings and other communications took place within organizations in a traditional face-to-face (FTF) format. Thus, most meetings required that representatives from subsidiary organizations travel some distance to attend. In fact, the literature has stressed the advantage of CMC's lack of dependency on set times and location and the cost savings accruing compared to the traditional FTF system (e.g., Hiltz & Turoff, 1978). Other benefits of CMC technologies are realized in distance education and learning, which represent transcultural realities. Thus, networked computers are able to function as person-to-person communication through various applications such as e-mail, videoconferencing, voice mail, simultaneous chat rooms, and entertainment (see Postmes, Spears, & Lea, 1998). It has being argued that CMC helps to realize the "global village" through the breakdown of traditional social boundaries. At the same time, the prospect of developing new communities (i.e., virtual) and social identities creates new sets of social boundaries as it removes the old traditional boundaries (Postmes et al., 1998).

Previous CMC literature has emphasized the advantages of technology in overcoming geographical barriers and has viewed CMC as a cost-saving medium, but research on implications of CMC across cultural boundaries is practically nonexistent. To fully understand CMC technology as an integral component of information management systems in globalized organizations, the cross-cultural environment in which the medium operates must be taken into account. In essence, *culture* needs

to be explored in both intercultural and multidomestic (intranational) uses of CMC in multinational corporations (Martinsons & Westwood, 1997; Oetzel, 1998). After all, members interacting through an electronic medium bring their self-perception and cultural backgrounds (e.g., Qureshi, 2000). Therefore, this chapter provides a framework to address these issues. It uses social information processing theory (SIPT), which incorporates cultural issues, as a central focus for examining the use and implications of CMC in multinational corporations and transcultural realities of the present time. SIPT incorporates two theoretical perspectives, namely, the social influence model (Fulk, Schmitz, & Steinfield, 1990) and the relational model (Walther, 1992a). The social influence model focuses on subjective information processing based on the "shared" meaning about a medium, or an object that individuals derive from interacting with others. From the social influence perspective, the focus is given to the social context, emphasizing how organizational structure shapes individual perceptions and communication behaviors. Conversely, the relational model emphasizes the individual's cognitive processing of information, which is closely aligned with "impression formation" and the idea that impressions change over time. SIPT draws from the relational perspective by acknowledging that interpersonal relationships among participants influence the degree to which people perceive their interactions as effective; in this regard, time is critical to perceptions.

The central argument of SIPT, as presented in this chapter, is that social contexts and interpersonal relationship development are governed by culture, such that communication behaviors in a medium (CMC or FTF) reflect these cultural factors. As a result, information processing is incomplete when viewed as independent of cultural factors. Furthermore, this chapter attempts to demonstrate how and why cultural factors are important, using some dimensions of cultural variability (see Hall, 1976; Hofstede, 1980) and how cultural factors manifest themselves in different communication media (i.e., CMC and FTF), which leads to specific assumptions and propositions. First, however, the dimension of cultural variability is revisited. Specifically, the concept of high and low context, along with power distance dimensions, is used in the chapter. Later, discussions of applications and implications are also provided for practitioners and researchers.

▶ Culture and Dimensions of Cultural Variability

A theoretical underpinning stresses the interactivity of culture and technology. Walther (1997) for example, contends that "certain social conditions [culture] and technology lead people from different places, who have never and will never see each other, to communicate more affection, to like each other more, to think they look better, and to work harder than people working together under other conditions in CMC or by working together face-to-face" (p. 365). At present, it is fair to say that the modus operandi as far as CMC technology is concerned can be captured in the saying, "if you build it, they will come." Developers create technology with the goal that users will come to realize the benefits and embrace the purpose of design. A major problem with this thinking is the neglect of cultural suitability and effects of such technology. Steingard and Fitzgibbons (1995) argue that the globalization process is one instance of the proliferation of American/Western values in global culture. The authors proceed to explain that the need to market products (e.g., technology) and their accompanying ideologies beyond national boundaries allows the marketplace to subvert the culture in less technologically advanced countries. However, if meanings and interpretations are derived both collectively and individually—collectively, in that meanings are negotiated between communicators, and individually, in that negotiation is mediated by individual perceptions that are subject to one's identity and expectations—they are

guided by culture (e.g., Gudykunst & Kim, 1992; Martinsons & Westwood, 1997). Olaniran (1993) argues that as individuals are socialized into different cultures, they learn and develop norms, values, and ideologies consistent with those cultures. These culturally induced values and norms influence cognitive perceptions and are reflected in the word choices, styles, and meanings that characterize social information in either FTF or CMC settings. The inclusion of culture in SIPT suggests that culture guides the behavioral rules and norms reflected in a communication process. Norms, however, are also subject to negotiation or intersubjective interpretations during interaction (Folger, Poole, & Stutman, 1993). Asian cultures, for instance, in compliance with the norm of saving face, use a text medium such as a memo, which is considered a lean medium, for potentially conflict-causing tasks. For example, in the Japanese *ringi* method of decision making (e.g., Hirokawa, 1981), group members must sign their names to support or modify a proposed decision. This example brings to light the importance of different dimensions of cultural variability in SIPT.

Hall (1976) categorizes cultures by identifying the distinction between high- and low-context communication cultures (see also Hofstede, 1980, 1991). High-context communication characterizes messages where "most of the information is either in the physical context or internalized in the person, while very little is in the coded, explicit, transmitted part of the message" (Hall, 1976, p. 79). Low-context communication, by contrast, represents messages where "the mass of information is vested in the explicit code" (Hall, 1976, p. 70). Characteristics of high-context cultures are suited to collectivistic cultural tendencies, whereas those of low context cultures are suited to individualistic cultural tendencies. Although no culture exists at either end of the continuum, U.S. culture can be categorized as primarily low context, whereas most Asian cultures, such as Japan, would fall at the high-context end of the continuum. People from high-context cultures communicate in an indirect manner (Gudykunst & Kim, 1992; Gudykunst et al., 1996; Triandis, 1995). It is arguable that communicating in an indirect manner necessitates an increased use of social context cues to fill the gaps created by unspoken verbal expression. It is imperative to determine how this tendency affects communication effectiveness in different media. The increased use of and demand for CMC is facilitated by the need to coordinate organizational activities globally. Therefore, one could argue that the need for information, and at a considerable speed (attributes of low context culture), contributes to the proliferation of CMC from such cultures to high-context cultures.

▶ The Social Information-Processing Theory

SIPT embraces perception as a key issue in understanding culture. Perception is described as attitudes, statements, and behaviors about an object (Fulk et al., 1990). For instance, information processing, as presented in the social influence model of media use, gives the impression that job positions and communication networks determine appropriate media. It is implied, then, that occupants of similar jobs have similar perceptions of acceptable media, whereas perceptions differ between job positions (see Rice, 1993). However, SIPT assumes that wider cultural norms also influence shared attitudes and behaviors. Therefore, differences across groups due to different task demands, work socialization, and the culture at large are to be expected in the perception of a medium's appropriateness. For example, CMC capacity to function like any other communication medium because of accessibility, cost, and proclaimed autonomy to engage in interaction regardless of national, ethnic, religious, and status restrictions is known to offer users greater freedom (e.g., Dubrovsky, Kiesler, & Sethna, 1991; Kiesler, Siegel, & McGuire, 1984; Postmes et al., 1998). Nevertheless, the increased freedom and lack of control has the potential to increase antisocial behaviors among CMC users and to decrease the regulatory function of social norms (e.g., Lea, O'Shea, Fung, & Spears, 1992; Postmes et al., 1998; Walther, 1997; Walther, Anderson, & Park, 1994). Postmes et al. (1998) found that the opportunity to be liberated via communication technology does not always lead to the choice or preference for such liberation from social influence. While information processing theory acknowledges differences across groups in the same cultural context, it fails to take the wider societal culture into account as a source of varying perceptions in a group. The effect of societal culture is pertinent given the globalization process, which increases the likelihood that people from different ethnic and national cultures are working together in groups and organizations (Gasner, 1999; Kalawsky, Bee, & Nee, 1999). Also, the lack of strong research support for information processing indicates that the theory, as presented in the social influence model, is insufficient (e.g., Rice & Aydin, 1991; Rice, Grant, Schmitz, & Torobin, 1990; Schmitz & Fulk, 1991). A reason for this may be that perception is culturally based and differs even for individuals in similar job positions.

SIPT moves beyond social influence and relational models by arguing that meanings in communication activities not only are mediated by past interactions and time (Walther, 1992a; Walther & Burgoon, 1992) but are also culture bound. In addition, SIPT accepts that social presence and media richness—the ability of a medium to support or carry multiple cues—influence media perception and that perception of these factors is embedded and reinforced by culture. Social presence, media richness, and media appropriateness, then, are important issues because they emphasize media attributes that vary by context and are influenced by individual differences (Rice, 1993). Simultaneously, individual differences and experiences are rooted in culture, which influences perceptions and interpretations made about media attributes.

If one accepts the idea that meanings are influenced by culture, then, perceptions of CMC media attributes and social interaction would reflect the nuances of cultural differences in norms and beliefs in multinational (intercultural) and multidomestic (cross-cultural) organizations, according to SIPT. In other words, messages can be transmitted among people, but not meanings. For instance, CMC media are conduits and transmitters of symbols, which influence meaning (Sitkin, Sutcliffe, & Barrios-Choplin, 1992). As a result, it is paramount that the culture from which meaning evolves is taken into consideration in studying these technologies (Hiemstra, 1982; Mesdag, 2000). Because interaction in most globalized organizations involves relationships between people from diverse cultures, it can be classified as intercultural, and SIPT takes this into consideration. For instance, CMC offers paralinguistic codes: signs and symbols that express emotion and meaning in written text through icon manipulation, capitalization, parenthetical notes, and exclamation marks (Lea & Spears, 1992). Caution, however, must be exercised with paralinguistic cues in CMC because they have localized meanings (Spitzer, 1986; Turkle & Papert, 1990) and thus can never be given a fixed meaning (Barthes, 1977).

In summary, SIPT is specifically influenced by cultural ideals. First, communication is viewed contextually, indicating that the environment and our perceptions of the environment influence our communication behaviors. Second, culture is considered an essential component of the environment, which in turn influences perceptions and shapes behaviors. Third, meaning represents the core values and shared understandings that are created during communication that defines social interaction. As a result, the meaning attached to encoded messages is a function not only of the message but also of the individuals' encoding and decoding of the message (cognitive patterns) and the cultural context of messages (Gudykunst & Kim, 1992).

The next section presents a theory of culture and communication technology. Culture is examined at both a macro societal level and a micro organizational one. Three key issues are addressed under societal culture: linguistic and symbolic cues, content and relational aspects of messages, and power. Organizational culture is also explored relative to SIPT from control and consensus standpoints.

▶ Toward a Theory of Culture and Communication Technology

First, societal and organizational cultures will be examined to analyze the impact of these variables on CMC according to SIPT. Second, relevant assumptions and propositions will be presented.

SOCIETAL CULTURE

In an intercultural encounter, each individual's life experiences differ, and interpretations drawn from messages and behaviors are not always correct, often resulting in misunderstandings. These cultural differences affect how people process information in communication encounters. Some factors that may influence media use in light of SIPT are presented below.

Linguistic Cues and Symbols

The varying contexts of cultures with CMC media may be explored in terms of the data-carrying capacity (linguistic cue) and symbol-carrying capacity of a communication medium. Data-carrying capacity involves the degree to which a medium is able to convey hard (verbal/written) and soft (social) cues, such as nonverbal and visual data. Symbol-carrying capacity involves the degree to which a medium manifests symbolic meaning (see Daft & Lengel, 1984; Short, Williams, & Christie, 1976; Sitkin et al., 1992). Communication media vary in their capacity to convey both hard and soft data; soft data cannot be conveyed via verbal or written messages (Redding, 1972; Sitkin et al., 1992). As suggested by media richness theory (Daft, Lengel, & Trevino, 1987), a classification by data-carrying capacity of a medium would recognize FTF communication as the richest medium and written text as the least rich. Furthermore, Hiemstra (1982) argues that "as the bandwidth narrows, the communication is likely to be seen as less friendly, emotional, and personal and more serious, businesslike, depersonalized, and task oriented" (p. 881).

The degree to which communication media vary in their capacity to carry different types of message influences their appropriateness for direct or indirect communication styles. For example, a richer medium would be viewed as supplying the greater social context cues necessary in high-context cultures (Hofstede, 1991; Kamel & Davison, 1998). In other words, when there are few nonverbal cues and little awareness of the physical presence of others (as in CMC), message interpretation is reduced to verbal/written cues (Kraus, Apple, Morencz, Wentzel, & Winton, 1981; Kraut & Lewis, 1984; Kraut, Lewis, & Swozey, 1982; Siegel, Dubrovsky, Kiesler, & McGuire, 1986). By implication, this concern about nonverbal and social context cues suggests an across-the-board generalization that nonverbal and other social context cues always have positive consequences. That is not always the case. Nonverbal messages have the potential to be misunderstood, and negative social consequences may also result (see Culnan & Markus, 1987; Hiemstra, 1982; Kamel & Davison, 1998; Lea & Spears, 1992; Walther, 1992a, 1992b). For example, the Japanese preference for a leaner text medium in the *ringi* process illustrates an attempt to overcome negative consequences that richer cues (e.g., FTF medium) might make possible, even though Japan is a high-context culture. Anonymity in CMC is believed to help overcome discrimination due to age, gender, and race (Potsmes et al., 1998). It is argued that such technology facilitates cultural sensitivity and allows for diverse opinions in communi-

cation encounters. The lack of physical cues or presence in CMC helps facilitate cohesion dynamics in international settings, which might not occur in video or FTF encounters (e.g., Gasner, 1999; Postmes et al., 1998; Walther, 1997).

Furthermore, the CMC medium, in addition to conveying meaning and hard data, sometimes becomes a symbol (e.g., of power, competence), which reflects nonverbal and tacit codes embedded in a culture (Sitkin et al., 1992), thus creating another source of problems. The symbol-carrying capacity of a medium influences meaning and interpretation of linguistic cues provided by the data-carrying capacity. It is valuable to explore the reciprocal effects of culture and media and to consider how they might alter communication interactions. To examine media preferences among organization members, a process that distinguishes CMC users from nonusers and explores why they use or refuse to use different media is necessary. Therefore, the first assumption posited is that the choice or preference for a communication medium will be influenced by cultural mandates.

Perhaps no area of communication interaction depicts nuances of high- and low-context cultures more than the linguistic and face-saving strategies. Ting-Toomey (1988) defined face as "a projected image of one's self in a relational situation" (p. 215). Linguistic and face-saving strategies can be used to explore a specific cultural effect in CMC. The linguistic and face strategies are inseparable in that linguistic strategies focus on language use and expression, whereas a face strategy focuses on how language is used to convey a particular expression. Concern for face has been described as the positive social value that an individual clings to relative to others during interaction (Goffman, 1967; Hiemstra, 1982). Face behaviors are potentially problematic in terms of message comprehension due to cultural differences in intercultural CMC. For instance, the use of face-saving strategies can seldom be understood without consideration for culture. Tannen (1993) illustrates that Americans consider directness in communication to be logical and consistent with power, whereas indirectness is equated with dishonesty and submissiveness. Nevertheless, indirectness represents the norm of communication in other cultures. Whether intentional or unintentional, this is overlooked in communicational technology (especially the text-based medium), where users are expected to code their messages more explicitly, hence creating a bias against cultures that prefer indirectness. A case in point is the Japanese culture, where the word *no* is considered to be so face-threatening that negative responses are phrased in positive manner. It is then left to the message recipient to determine if a yes is truly a yes or a polite no. It is evident from this example that indirectness is not necessarily a strategy of subordination and can be used by both powerful and powerless individuals. However, interpretations based on such usage depend on the setting, individual relationship, and the linguistic conventions that are embedded in the cultural context.

Concern for face is believed to be higher in FTF interactions than in CMC. Hiltz and Turoff (1978) claimed that CMC reduces or eliminates the need for face work that occurs in FTF meetings. This claim is questionable, given its assumption that face-saving needs are only displayed nonverbally and that because nonverbal cues are lacking in CMC, face work is automatically absent. First, communication strategies employed by those interacting in the study were never examined to explore how concerns for face were demonstrated textually (see also Hiemstra, 1982). Second, it has been argued that *any* interaction is potentially face threatening, be it positive or negative (Brown & Levinson, 1978). Concern for face is demonstrable by both verbal/written and nonverbal behaviors; hence, participants will demonstrate concern for face, regardless of the communication medium (i.e., CMC and FTF). Hiemstra (1982) found that CMC participants use fewer politeness strategies than participants in FTF settings. The underuse of face strategies reported for CMC may be due to the lack of knowledge

necessary to interpret indirect communication styles in CMC (see Brown & Levinson, 1978, for a fuller discussion of specific face strategies). Thus, the second assumption states that there is a concern for face in CMC interactions. Furthermore, organization members or CMC participants are expected to interact with one another in various ways over a period of time. The nature of such interactions could be based on and guided by previously established relationships among members (Walther, 1992a). Also, interactions via CMC in any organization are constrained by anticipated future interactions among participants (Olaniran, 1994; Walther, 1994). The third assumption contends that face strategies will be determined by one's concern for face, the social context factors within organizations (e.g., the positional power structure among those who are interacting, organizational culture) and the perceived media appropriateness. Based on Assumptions 1, 2, and 3, the following propositions are presented.

Proposition 1: Participants' concerns for face in CMC interaction will deviate from the societal culture when an organizational culture differs and takes precedence over the societal culture.

Proposition 2: The patterns of face work strategies will differ between CMC and FTF communication. Specifically, the pattern of face work in CMC will seem more harsh (less polite) than in FTF communication.

Proposition 3: Concerns about negative face work will positively influence preference for CMC media. For instance, the need to convey negative face work will result in preference for the CMC medium over FTF communication, and this effect will be greater in high-context cultures than in low-context cultures.

Content and Relational Messages

Differences in cultures and their implications for social information processing may also be explained in terms of the two levels from which messages can be interpreted. The two levels include *what is said* (task/content) and *how it is said* (social/relational) (Watzlawick, Beavin, & Jackson, 1967), or how it is perceived in the case of CMC. Gudykunst and Kim (1992) indicate that the content level is usually encoded verbally, whereas the relational level tends to be encoded nonverbally. It would seem that communication in high-context cultures would emphasize the relational level (e.g., nonverbal and social contexts) more than in low-context cultures. However, this view would only reinforce the position that communication is either task or social, a position that contradicts the claim about concurrence of content and social dimensions of messages posited by Watzlawick and associates. Thus, to argue that CMC messages are simply more task oriented than FTF messages is an oversimplification.

Cue-substitution technique explains how messages in CMC can be used to convey social cues similar to those in FTF communication (Sitkin et al., 1992). With cue substitution, communicators develop different symbols for expressing relational messages in CMC, which are otherwise not available due to the lack of nonverbal cues. According to Walther (1992a), "CMC-only partners can be expected to achieve desired immediacy levels normally conveyed nonverbally through the manipulation of verbal immediacy" (p. 77). Relational cues in the form of icons (Asteroff, 1987), electronic paralanguage and lexical surrogates (Carey, 1980), or parenthetical messages that express emotional feelings are a few ways in which relational messages are conveyed in CMC interactions (see also Lea & Spears, 1992; Walther, 1997). For instance, the use of all caps in e-mail is often considered an aggressive tactic equivalent to yelling (see Allen, 1988). In CMC interactions such as voice mail, tone inflection, pitch, and decibel level of verbal messages are used to deduce affective expressions. Thus, all communication media have both data- and symbol-carrying capacity (Sitkin et al., 1992). Impression formation and relational development among those interacting via CMC, however, take a

longer time to recognize, decode, and develop than in FTF communication (Walther, 1992a, 1992b). A longer time is expected in a computer-mediated environment because functions achieved through multichannel cues in FTF communication must be accomplished with fewer cues in CMC. Thus, CMC would require greater message exchange to have the same effect as an FTF message (Bordia & Rosnow, 1998; Olaniran 1995; Walther, 1992a; 1992b). Evidence of socioemotional expression found in long-term CMC interactions attests to this (see Lim & Facciola, 1988; Rice & Love, 1987; Walther, 1997). By implication, previous and ongoing interactions in multinational corporations will provide the basis for impression-formation episodes in the intercultural use of CMC. At the same time, CMC may still be so new that communication norms have not yet been established. Therefore, it may be difficult to determine the extent to which the level of hesitancy and uncertainty in CMC is related to cultural differences or to the novelty of communicating in a new context. The fourth assumption addresses the issue of affective cues and relational history. It is believed that cultural principles guiding traditional communication interactions will direct the use of affective/social cues in CMC interactions. The next two propositions are based on this assumption.

> *Proposition 4:* Participants from high-context cultures are likely to exhibit more social cues in their CMC messages than people from low-context cultures.
>
> *Proposition 5:* In CMC, participants from high-context cultures will use fewer social cues for negative face-threatening interactions than for positive face-threatening interactions.

Power/Status

Hiemstra (1982) indicated that communication mediated by technology may lead to and result from alterations in the symbols and meanings specified by a culture. A case in point is power and how it is used in an organizational setting via mediated communication. Power is viewed from the notion of the power-distance cultural standpoint (Hofstede & Bond, 1984). Hofstede and Bond (1984) defined power distance as "the extent to which the less powerful members of institutions and organizations accept that power is distributed unequally" (p. 419). People from high power-distance cultures view one another differently on the basis of their status, and these cultures stress coercive use of power. People from low power-distance cultures only acknowledge the use of power when it is an expert or legitimate power (positional) (Kamel & Davison, 1998; Martinsons & Westwood, 1997). For example, individuals from high power-distant cultures refrain from addressing each other by first name; rather, they use appropriate titles to acknowledge the difference in status. On the other hand, in low power-distant cultures, individuals normally address each other using first names, even in a superior-subordinate interaction. Furthermore, the underlying assumption with proliferation of technology in the transcultural reality of globalization is that access to technology is evenly distributed, but this is not the case (Steingard & Fitzgibbons, 1995). Experience and data indicate that access to computers and the Internet is common in the United States, but this is seldom the case in developing countries; even in other developed countries, access may be available only through the Internet cafe (e.g., Olaniran, in press; Postmes et al., 1998; Steingard & Fitzgibbons, 1995). Therefore, access to personal computers often creates a status symbol and a digital divide between the "haves" and the "have-nots," where the haves wield the power and control how and when technology such as CMC is used. Another cultural implication deals with the different values placed on power acceptance in a culture and the effect on social information processing. For instance, the CMC literature generally acknowledges that CMC facilitates a more democratic decision-making process. However, looking at the degree to which a culture acknowledges power distance, it would seem that some cultures may show greater readiness to accept authority than to engage in a demo-

cratic decision-making process. This problem is illustrated by Gudykunst and Kim (1992, p. 140) in the following scenario from Vassiliou's (a Greek psychologist) file.

Message/ Behavior	*Meaning/ Attribution*
American: How long will it take you to finish the report?	American: I ask him to participate.
	Greek: His behavior makes no sense. He is the boss. Why doesn't he tell me?

The above scenario took place between a supervisor from the United States (a low-context culture) and a subordinate from Greece (a high-context culture). As one can see, the supervisor wants the employee to take the initiative to participate in a decision-making process (a U.S. norm), whereas the subordinate expects to be told what to do (a Greek norm). This may suggest that democratic participation through CMC may not be acceptable cross-culturally. The situational determinant of democratic participation can be illustrated by a condition where leaders or management in a power-distance culture may use CMC to disseminate information and not use it for the decision-making process. Therefore, the fifth assumption posits that CMC interaction will reflect a culture's power distance. Based on this assumption the next proposition is made.

Proposition 6: CMC interaction will reflect greater formality, stressing participants' status, in high power-distance cultures than in low power-distance cultures.

▶ Organizational Culture

Every organization has its own culture, which is derived to some extent from societal culture but also reflects the philosophy embraced by management and other employees.

Organizational culture embraces factors such as control and consensus when describing the identity of an organization. One must take into consideration the role of organizational culture, given that multinational corporations are increasingly locating in sites where the societal culture is markedly different from the organizational culture.

CONTROL

Research notes that parent organizational partners usually exert control and dominance on the subsidiary affiliates (e.g., Lecraw, 1984; Martinez & Ricks, 1989). Subsequently, the parent multinational corporation often sets managerial standards and relational expectation guidelines that, in essence, dictate organizational culture for the affiliates. Four control strategies depict the attitudes of most multinational corporations: (a) ethnocentrism, (b) polycentrism, (c) regiocentrism, and (d) geocentrism (Perlmutter & Heenan, 1974).

Ethnocentric strategy implies that the multinational corporation uses the home-country culture (i.e., its nationals) to manage the affiliates and subsequently determine the organizational culture. The following statement describes how ethnocentricism may sometimes be embedded within the transcultural realities of globalization process:

We, as Americans, want to spearhead the drive to bring to the "underdeveloped" nations of the world the gifts of capitalism—poverty, illiteracy, family and community disintegration, child labor, violence, political apathy, environmental degradation, and workaholism. . . . Despite its unchallenged and unfettered expansionism, globalization is not a value free, natural phenomenon catapulting the world into a pristine state of progress. The globalization of capitalism is the contemporary manifestation of a system that evolved over several centuries, the primary purpose of which was to be the economic servant of western society. (Steingard & Fitzgibbons, 1995, p. 31)

Ethnocentric views may guide the crusade for the communication technologies that propel the globalization process, which advocates harmonious and homogenous global culture. A case in point was the drive to stress a one-sided view of technology (i.e., the Internet) as giving Japanese women more equality than their male counterparts by helping them to establish their own businesses (*Nightly Business Report,* 2000). This proposal is bound to complicate the Japanese woman's roles, as she has to juggle business responsibilities with the cultural value of raising children. In essence, the drive toward homogenized culture is actually creating a fragmented and malignant world culture (Steingard & Fitzgibbons, 1995). For example, differences in language, distributions, regulations, marketing structure, and cultural features are so enormous that standardization strategies are rendered fruitless as product brands within Europe alone are termed *local* but are neither global nor local (Kapferer, 1992; Mesdag, 2000).

Conversely, polycentric strategy involves using the affiliates' nationals to manage affiliate operations, with the affiliates' cultures subsequently becoming the controlling entity. Regiocentric strategy involves using people from a common market or similar area to manage multinational corporations. Geocentric strategy involves using nationals from various places without emphasis on a particular culture or location to manage multinational corporations. Consequently, interactions in these organizations will reflect the controlling strategy (e.g., ethnocentric, etc.) embraced in an organizational culture (see Proposition 1). CMC may, however, differ from FTF interactions by deviating from the controlling organizational culture when interaction is expected to be one-time or short-lived.

Furthermore, the relational power displayed during communication may be decided by the normative expectations of each organizational culture. Organizational culture has been described as rule-like consensual meanings that guide the symbolic interpretation of meaning in a medium and its use (Putnam,

1983). In other words, normative guidelines influence the symbols attached to a communication medium and the selection and appropriateness of a medium (Sitkin et al., 1992; see also Rice, 1993, for discussion of media appropriateness). Consequently, Assumption 6 indicates that normative guidelines within an organizational culture will reflect an interpersonal display of power in communication encounters.

Knapp (1984) presents forms of address as indicators of relational formality. Such displays can be seen in CMC interaction, as well. For instance, an organization with a formal hierarchical structure and a cultural ethos that emphasizes formality in superior-subordinate interactions would reflect this ethos. Similarly, an organization will need to evaluate the symbolic value attached to a medium and will need to provide direction for modification when an ascribed cultural symbol hinders goal accomplishment. Consequently, there is a need to determine whether organizational culture takes precedence over the societal culture in multinational corporations by looking at the issue of coordination and control.

Coordination and control, often referred to as human resource management, is essential to multinational corporations and most globalized industries (e.g., Adler & Bartholomew, 1992; Adler & Graham, 1989; Konsynski & McFarlan, 1990). The emphasis on coordination focuses on directing organization activities toward goal attainment. Control, on the other hand, determines an organizational culture, which drives the coordination efforts (see Geringer & Herbert, 1989, for review).

CONSENSUS

Consensus is another factor influencing social information processing. Consensus has been viewed as agreement and level of commitment regarding a decision (Fisher & Ellis, 1990). Historically, research indicates that CMC hinders consensus formation in group decision processes (DeSanctis & Gallupe, 1987). However, recent research suggests that CMC does not hinder consensus develop-

ment; rather, it takes longer to achieve a group goal in a CMC environment than in an FTF situation because there are fewer codes (Olaniran, 1994; Walther, 1992a; Weisband, 1992). An unresolved issue about consensus and CMC involves the implications CMC has for consensus in intercultural encounters. It must be realized that different cultures place different emphasis on consensus. For instance, high-context cultures (e.g., Asians) are more consensus seeking than low-context cultures (e.g., Gudykunst et al., 1996; Ho & Raman, 1991; Oetzel, 1998). In the consensus-building decision-making environment that prevails in high-context cultures, emphasis is given to a decision-making process that minimizes internal conflict and maximizes internal group harmony (Hiltz & Turoff, 1978). Ho and Raman (1991) argue that when an electronic meeting system hinders postmeeting consensus, it will violate the cultural norms of the group, resulting in refusal to adopt the system. The manager-subordinate scenario above presents a glimpse of cultural norm violations that are more likely in CMC, especially with the lack of immediate feedback to correct attribution errors. The next proposition examines this issue.

> *Proposition 7:* There will be more normative violations for consensus in CMC than in FTF communication, especially for high-context cultures that emphasize consensus.

SUMMARY

In summary, SIPT, as presented in this chapter, borrows from both social influence (Fulk et al., 1990) and relational models (Walther, 1992a). From the social influence model, the notion of social context was examined. Social context comprises communication behaviors, individuals' perceptions in organizations, and organizational structures that guide behavior. Borrowing from the relational model, SIPT recognizes that interpersonal relationships among interacting parties contribute to the degree to which communication (e.g., CMC or FTF) is perceived on affective or relational dimensions, and that time mediates this effect. The conceptualization of SIPT in CMC is extended to include the fact that all these factors are derivatives of culture. That is, culture guides participants in their communication behavior by setting appropriate expectations and by guiding the type of relationship established in CMC or FTF. Consequently, culture guides both content and relational dimensions of communication, which serve as the basis on which meanings are shared. This view of SIPT is closely aligned with the systems view of communication media (Lievrouw & Finn, 1990), which indicates that culture influences social relationships among communicators to the extent that it affects the message content. Assumptions and propositions have been presented from this perspective. The next section explores cultural issues and policies that are of significance to SIPT and CMC media for multinational corporations. Implications and recommendations are also provided for intercultural and cross-cultural CMC interactions.

▶ Discussion

The social information-processing perspective makes its most significant contribution toward the understanding of media use by the addition of a cultural effect on users' communication behaviors. From this perspective, both organizational culture and societal culture play a significant role in understanding users' communication behaviors and media usage. In essence, SIPT is presented in terms of the cognitive abilities of organization members, both individually and collectively, as they learn, make sense, and make decisions in an organization while being influenced by cultural factors such as beliefs, values, and power (Egelhoff, 1991; Martinsons & Westwood, 1997; Wood & Bandura, 1989). For instance, the issue of silence versus volubility, a dimension that exhibits cultural and power variability, exemplifies the notion of social information processing. Some cultures cherish silence (e.g., high context) over volubility,

and vice versa. At the same time, volubility is often misconstrued as a characteristic associated with those having power. The problem with this general assertion is that the culture and relational factors that guide the display or the use of silence in an interaction must be understood. Therefore, it becomes imperative to examine the cultural or contextual premises of those who are interacting in an intercultural CMC setting.

A potential problem that may occur in CMC, for example, is that CMC requires more explicit and longer conversational styles than FTF communication (Olaniran, 1995; Walther, 1992a). Therefore, the degree to which people valuing silence over volubility are able to adjust to CMC norms regarding silence is essential. A major challenge decision makers face is that cultural problems or technology mismatch are at times disguised as technical problems. For example, according to Suomi and Pekola (1998), in Northern Europe and other economically developed countries where technology is not an issue, people still blame rejection and nonusage on it. It is clear from such examples that there are potential problems when using CMC in multinational corporations. In essence, culture possesses information that allows one to explain users' attitudes, behaviors, and individuals' information-processing mechanisms in CMC environments. For instance, by understanding the dimensions of cultural variability in which CMC technology users operate, one can predict and explain with some degree of certainty the users' attitudes toward CMC media and their communication styles. The rest of the chapter focuses on issues for application of CMC in multinational corporations' cultural settings and implications for managers and researchers.

▶ Issues for the 21st Century and Recommendations for Managers and Other Decision Makers

The transcultural reality is that the application of CMC technology in multicultural settings is inevitable. Efforts to diffuse CMC technologies globally, especially in Africa, Asia, Europe, and elsewhere, have demonstrated that CMC technologies are neither culturally neutral nor communicatively transparent. Different cultural attitudes toward technology and communication—those embedded in current CMC technologies and those shaping the beliefs and behaviors of current and future users—often clash. The clash necessitates the need to address specific cultural problems and offer possible recommendations for decision makers in those settings. Key issues facing decision makers with CMC media include (a) misunderstanding, (b) training, (c) media selection and appropriateness, and (d) ethical considerations.

MISUNDERSTANDING

Different cultural orientations present problems of misunderstanding as people attempt to make sense of transmitted messages in terms of their own cultural milieu. Gudykunst and Kim (1992) expand on different cultural orientations when they argue that we learn most of our behaviors unconsciously; thus, people are usually unaware of their communication behaviors. Williams, Rice, and Rogers (1988) also suggest that information sharing may be psychological, accomplished through perceptual and cognitive processes that may be involuntary (e.g., interpreting message meaning). If communication process involves unconscious behaviors by virtue of cultural orientation, there may be room for misunderstanding when participants attribute different meanings to the same phenomenon. Although misunderstanding may be unavoidable in intercultural use of CMC, the problem can be reduced. The recommendation for transcultural reality is to become more consciously aware of cultural differences that distinguish CMC participants. Sensitivity to these differences would help users engage in meaningful interactions that are free of stereotypes and focus on the goal of becoming interculturally competent. A good start for CMC should begin with the use of

parenthetical comments and paralanguage; these are believed to reduce the chances for misunderstanding in CMC (Asteroff, 1987; Carey, 1980). Even when such comments are absent, the norm in most organizations is multiple media (CMC, FTF, or their combination). Therefore, with culture taken into consideration in the social information process, multiple media use is encouraged as another avenue for reducing communication misunderstanding. Sitkin et al. (1992) note that when normative requirements are ambiguous, the use of multiple media presents "redundancy insurance," which increases the chance that information gets through the medium as intended. Multiple media use, for instance, could help prevent a situation where subordinates from a high power-distant culture may be conveying an agreement message with a superior from a low power-distant culture simply because that's what they believe is expected of them rather than expressing their true intentions (Brislin, Cushner, Cherrie, & Yong, 1986; Oetzel, 1998). The redundancy could help save organization money and time in the long run.

TRAINING

Different cultural patterns dictate rigorous cross-cultural training for multinational corporations to facilitate greater awareness and understanding among members in these organizations. Some executives expressed similar concerns when they indicated that the increased complexity of operating internationally makes their No. 1 need education. More specifically, Deans, Karwan, Golsar, Ricks, and Toyne (1991) indicated that senior managers require training on country-specific issues (emphasizing the role of culture) with regard to political, legal, economic, cultural, and technological environments of affiliate organizations in foreign countries. Such training, it is hoped, will enhance the effectiveness of CMC in terms of conveying messages and making interpretations based on them. Specific training should concentrate on language and metacommunicative rules that define organizational culture and interpersonal communication encounters.

First, language training is essential in multinational corporations for members to understand the guiding principles of cultural communication styles and behaviors (see Gudykunst & Kim, 1992; Gudykunst et al., 1996; Kim, 1988; Lambert, 1963; Triandis, 1995). Whereas it is acknowledged that multinational corporations train their employees, language training is stressed here, including metacommunicative rules and norms guiding its usage (Gudykunst & Kim, 1992). This notion points to the universality of words in a language across cultures, while at the same time it recognizes the cultural differences in meaning ensuing from such words. Training is essential for effective performance with CMC media. For instance, as indicated earlier, word choice and paralanguage in CMC interactions influence meanings (i.e., SCC). Therefore, understanding metacommunicative rules guiding language use enables users to become adept in using surrogate cues to convey social information by attending to cultural variations that could otherwise stand in the way of shared meanings. Consequently, language training must emphasize more than syntax and word choice by focusing on cultural or situational appropriateness of the word choices. Kim (1988) echoes this view by stressing the need to understand semantic and pragmatic rules of language. This has special implications for language and identity. The key to linguistic identity is a sense of belonging or being accepted as an in-group member, which is critical to CMC interactions. Being part of an in-group or being accepted as an insider involves saying the right thing in the right way, while creating a sense of who we are. All of this depends on social cultural group membership, on a particular language, and on the context (Gee, 1996; Miller, 2000). Gee (1996) contends that individuals shift their identity to express solidarity with particular groups, using language variations. Thus, a key to successful interaction in intercultural uses of CMC lies not only in how well participants use language but also in how well they are re-

ceived by others as a part of the group. For example, large network organizations may use ad hoc groups that have no commonality other than being employed by the same organization; this is likely to accentuate group identities and reinforce the boundaries that guide behavior in that environment (Postmes et al., 1998; Scott, 1999). Therefore, users and potential users must be trained in how to get their messages across in a way that enhances receivers' ability to attribute correct meaning to messages. Training is needed on lexical varieties, paralanguages, and relational development techniques in the CMC environment. Thus, CMC media training should stress the use of surrogate cues that help users to address both content and social dimensions of communication simultaneously.

Furthermore, the persistence of global economic integration due to intensified competition demands more equitable international joint ventures of the kind between American and Japanese auto manufacturers. Consequently, transnational organizational cultures, rather than cultures in which subsidiary partners are acculturated into the dominant partner's culture, are becoming the norm (Adler & Bartholomew, 1992; Baker, Sircar, & Schkade, 1998; Martinsons & Westwood, 1997). In essence, training to coordinate multinational corporate activities becomes more pressing, and CMC is central to this issue as scheduling real time FTF communication becomes increasingly difficult. A key advantage of CMC media, facilitating training in a multicultural arena, is the belief that they avoid embarrassment to learners (e.g., when mistakes are made), contrary to traditional FTF communication (Olaniran, 1994). Just as one needs to learn to avoid misunderstanding in FTF interactions where social information is available nonverbally (Lea & Spears, 1992), one must also learn to avoid misunderstanding in CMC messages. In a move in this direction, it may be necessary to adopt a "conversational writing style" in the CMC environment (e.g., computer conferencing, e-mail). This training focus would allow arguments to be laid out a few points at a time rather than in a single note, especially when discussing technical information (Newman & Newman, 1992). Therefore, a combination of mass and individual instruction could help facilitate the training effort, along with an employee reward or incentive program to encourage and maximize technology use and productivity. Verdin (1988) indicates that incorporating the use of information technology into an organization's incentive program (i.e., salaries and promotions) would increase the likelihood of appropriate technology usage (see also Gattiker, 1988). Training needs to be broad based and enforced in a curriculum, given that CMC is being used in education settings such as university classrooms and general distance education and entertainment. The proliferation of CMC makes these media more accessible and necessary for studying (Garcia & Jacobs, 1999). Furthermore, the changing face of the workforce in transcultural reality dictates that students, governments, and corporations join forces to encourage programs of study abroad. Any type of intercultural or international experience that students have provides valuable skills that can help them adapt technology and develop customized technology that is sensitive to their cultural needs and experience. For instance, the way people with international exposure relate to people on return from their travels is different than before they go abroad in that they are more flexible in adapting their communication strategies. These skills are what is needed in global corporations, where teamwork and travel are part of the job description and necessary for organizational success (e.g., Gasner, 1999).

MEDIA APPROPRIATENESS

The socialization process of employees in multinational corporations must stress the social desirability of each medium (i.e., appropriateness). In other words, the symbolic meaning attached to or conveyed through different media, as prescribed by organizational culture, should not only be relayed to employees, but also discussed and identified by employees. For instance, the symbols attributed

to a CMC medium may be different for users by virtue of role expectations, status differences, and various settings (Rice & Shook, 1988; Sitkin et al., 1992). After all, not all companies can afford Ford's strategy of providing employees with personal computers or access to organizational communication technologies. Attention should, therefore, be given to both intraorganizational (e.g., superior-subordinates) and interorganizational usage, where there may be a cultural distinction in terms of symbolic or normative expectations guiding different media use. Attention has been called to both internal and external organizational factors in communication technology (Baker et al., 1998).

Media appropriateness is influenced by time. For instance, e-mail is known to allow individual participants the opportunity to reflect before composing an appropriate response to a given message, thus prolonging the turnaround or feedback time. On the other hand, teleconferencing reduces turnaround time for responses but does not provide as much reflection time as e-mail, especially when elapsed time between message and response is short because all users are on the channel (see also Munter, 1998, for discussion of different communication media). Therefore, communication media must be selected in terms of their time appropriateness. Similarly, it is beneficial to recognize cultural differences attributable to time orientation. Most high-context cultures see time as relatively polychronic (i.e., they have no sense of urgency), whereas low-context cultures operate on monochromic time (they emphasize being on time) (Hall, 1976). Therefore, to avoid intercultural problems, CMC media should be selected according to the time requirement of the message. For example, teleconferencing may be selected over e-mail or voice mail when a sense of urgency is needed. It must also be recognized, however, that differences in cultural appropriateness of CMC media do not exclude the fact that several media may be appropriate for a particular task.

Developments in CMC technologies will continue to expand medium appropriateness, as CMC media continue to interface using multiple channels, such as verbal, written, text, audio, and graphics (e.g., picture phone). As a matter of fact, the move toward virtual reality, where computer conferencing occurs without typing, is something to anticipate. CMC media will continue to present challenges for decision makers in multinational corporations regarding technology innovation and adoption, which would intensify the need to address cultural differences. It is believed that the CMC media revolution will cut across all organizational hierarchies (from the lowest to the highest levels). For instance, people such as janitors who are currently inactive in CMC use will become active as they use the technology to make supply requisitions, to leave messages for their superiors, or to engage in international support groups.

ETHICAL CONSIDERATIONS

It was mentioned earlier that communication technologies, as they break down old traditional boundaries, also erect new ones. It must be recognized that CMC media are tools and like any other tools, they have the potential for misuse, which could have significant cultural implications. Consequently, multinational corporations must be alert to the intentional and unintentional consequences of CMC media on a societal culture.

The use of CMC media as a measure of organizational control poses ethical issues that every organization must address. It is not uncommon for organizations today to listen in on or to use recorded transcripts of interactions between their representatives and customers. This makes privacy issues a concern in some cultures (i.e., low-context cultures) whereas it raises issues concerning lack of trust in other cultures (i.e., high context). Media use that violates certain cultural norms poses a threat of discontinuation and resistance to the media technology. Therefore, multinational corporations will have to find ways to overcome this barrier by either deciding of their own volition to deal with the CMC problems or wait for governmental intervention (Rogers, 1990). Whatever method multinational corporations choose to address the problem would have cultural implications for organizational members in terms of perceived relationships and decisions to adopt or resist CMC technology. Also, policy makers and managers must be aware of their moral obligation, which comes with their indirect role of being cultural change agents through implementation of technology. Their organizational cultures reinvent/affect society's culture. Contrary to popular opinion, some of these cultural changes pose serious threats that may have critical consequences.

► **Recommendations for Cross-cultural CMC Research**

Given the notion of cultural variability, one thing is clear: There are differences in communication behaviors. However, it is uncertain is whether these communication behaviors are self-evident in CMC media behaviors. Scholars (e.g., Hiemstra, 1982; Kamel & Davison, 1998; Li & Ye, 1999; Lievrouw & Finn, 1990; Sitkin et al., 1992) have identified the need to explore culture in CMC; however, empirical research is still scarce. This lack of research has considerable consequences, given the continued growth in technology application.

First, new transnational alliances suggest collaborative cultural learning, which according to Adler and Bartholomew (1992), would put American firms with a low-context cultural perspective at a disadvantage (see also, Hamel, Doz, & Prahalad, 1989; Martinsons & Westwood, 1997). Adler and Graham (1989) found that whereas negotiators in cross-cultural situations generally adapt their behaviors, Americans are the most obstinate; their behaviors were consistent across cultural situations. The low adaptive tendency has been attributed to the fact that Americans and their firms have enjoyed controlling cultural and economic advantage over their international partners (Adler & Bartholomew, 1992; Graham & Gronhaug, 1989; Hamel et al., 1989).

This situation has created a cultural barrier that must be overcome by collaborative cultural learning (Adler & Bartholomew, 1992). For instance, emphasis has focused on the advantages of CMC in promoting certain Western cultural ideals (e.g., freedom, independence, and democracy), which sounds positive. However, these ideals may be viewed differently in cultures that stress norms of status, power, and even consensus. Thus, cultural sensitivity to these differences in use of communication technologies is required. The past and continuous growth in the use of communication technology makes this a necessity. Specifically, emphasis must be given to (a) how cultural factors influence CMC media use (e.g., media selection and preferences) and (b) how cultural variations (high- versus low-context) influence media behaviors (the nature of interaction that occurs in a medium). Along this line, it would be useful to determine how firms are adjusting their communication behaviors in CMC to address cultural differences in transnational alliances. Some specific cross-cultural variables that deserve immediate attention in this area include face work or face strategies, silence, ambiguity, volubility, affective cues, and power, just to mention a few; how these variables are conveyed in intercultural CMC interactions should be studied. These factors would shed light on the linguistic strategies and conversational styles of users and the contextual differences that can be anticipated due to culture. These issues are the focus of the propositions presented in this chapter.

A second area of concern is methodology.[1] A variety of research methods should be implemented to study CMC media effects. In an attempt to capture the extent to which cultural variability influences the communication process, methodological processes cannot be restricted to questionnaire techniques; there is a greater need for methodologies that focus on user interactions. Thus, message transcripts that search for social information messages and face-saving activities rather than message content would provide more insight for determining the effect that dimensions of cultural

variability have in CMC. Furthermore, using interaction analysis would present a clearer picture of adaptation strategies employed to address cultural differences. To aid the interaction analysis, some software applications are suitable for these techniques. For example, WinPhaser, developed by Holmes and Poole (1991), allows researchers to map or identify how a group moves from one conflict phase to another in group interaction. This type of software may be reconfigured to map and categorize interaction on cultural variability (see Krippendorff, 1980; Tesch, 1990, for more on computer-based text analysis tools). Other methods, such as participant observation, interviews, and other ethnographic analysis techniques that investigate users' behaviors at the moment of their occurrence, would provide a detailed understanding of how cultural variations influence user behavior and users' level of satisfaction with the media.

There is a parallel need to address the issue of gender differences. It has been argued that American women possess some of the admired qualities of Japanese management culture, such as a consensus-seeking decision-making style (Steinhoff & Tanaka, 1988). However, this quality has been considered feminine and disadvantageous by American management (Adler, 1988; Adler & Izraeli, 1988; Steinhoff & Tanaka, 1988). The implication from this observation is threefold. One, there is an assumption that American women's cultural communication pattern is high-context (Adler & Izraeli, 1988). Two, if this is true, there is the assumption that American women would make a faster and smoother transition in interacting with people from high-context cultures. For instance, Steinhoff and Tanaka (1988) recommend American women to Japanese managers when they complain about the difficulty of finding capable American men who can fit into their overseas operations. Three, there is the implication that dimensions of cultural variability may be too restrictive to male communication styles in categorizing American culture as low-context. Nevertheless, one must explore the degree to which American women would adjust into high power-distance cultures, giving their cultural emphasis on equal status with men. Specifically, gender differences have been noted in CMC medium usage (e.g., Allen, 1995; Barrett & Lally, 1999). Allen argues that men are likely to compose their e-mail messages with less attention to details or less care than women. In a formal online learning environment, it was found that men sent more messages than women; they wrote messages that were twice as long as women's messages (i.e., volubility); and they made more socioemotional contributions than women. On the other hand, women contributed more interactive messages than men (Barrett & Lally, 1999). Therefore, the extent to which women can manage both high-context and power-distance culture requirements simultaneously must be addressed. Information derived from these issues would provide a basis for training programs in media adoption and effectiveness evaluation, which are needed in global organizations.

► Conclusion

This chapter raised issues of primary importance to multinational corporations as they apply CMC media in their organizing activities. SIPT is presented as a framework for understanding interaction in CMC. Discussion regarding the role of culture and implications for multinational corporations using CMC in the years ahead is presented. The chapter posits that culture represents a central position in the communication process, so that media use, communication styles, and meaning attribution are affected by culture. Implications for global organizations (e.g., training) and researchers are explored. CMC technology presents a new set of challenges for managers in the global economic environment, challenges that extend beyond the technological infrastructure. Some challenges differ from those that managers are accustomed to dealing with in a local or multidomestic setting. The greatest challenge facing organizations and society at large is not whether or not to use communication technology. Rather, CMC is an amplifier of social, cultural, and psychological phenomena, such that the important question is how to use it meaningfully and how to rearrange the social circumstances of its use (Walther, 1997). Different communication outcomes can be expected from group and individual use, and these outcomes vary with context as well. Therefore, to assume that communication strategies (especially mediated communication) that work in one culture will suffice in another would be a fatal error for multinational corporations. More important, whatever role an organization decides to play in the move toward globalization, CMC technology will play a significant part.

► Note

1. Research on gender differences in communication and group interaction addressed some intracultural differences to be expected in consensus building between males and females. For sample works see Eakins and Eakins (1976), Mantovani (1994), and Olaniran (1995).

► References

Adler, N. J. (1988). Pacific Basin managers: A gaijin, not a woman. In N. J. Adler & D. N. Izraeli (Eds.), *Women in management worldwide* (pp. 226-249). New York: M. E. Sharpe.

Adler, N. J., & Bartholomew, S. (1992). Academic and professional communities of discourse: Generating knowledge on transnational human resource management. *Journal of International Business Studies, 23,* 551-569.

Adler, N., & Graham, J. L. (1989). Cross-cultural interaction: The international comparison fallacy. *Journal of International Business Studies, 20,* 515-537.

Adler, N. J., & Izraeli, D. N. (Eds.), (1988). *Women in management worldwide* (pp. 3-16). New York: M. E. Sharpe.

Allen, B. J. (1995). Gender and computer-mediated communication. *Sex Roles, 32,* 557-563.

Allen, T. B. (1988, September). Bulletin boards of the 21st century are coming of age. *Smithsonian,* pp. 83-93.

Asteroff, J. F. (1987). *Paralanguage in electronic mail: A case study.* Doctoral dissertation, Columbia University.

Baker, J., Sircar, S., & Schkade, L. (1998). Complex document search for decision making. *Information & Management, 34,* 243-250.

Barrett, E., & Lally, V. (1999). Gender differences in an on-line learning environment. *Journal of Computer Assisted Learning, 15,* 48-60.

Barthes, R. (1977). The death of the author. In S. Heath (Ed.), *Image, music, text.* New York: Hill & Wang.

Bordia, P., & Rosnow, R. (1998). Rumor rest stops on the information highway: Transmission patterns in a computer-mediated rumor chain. *Human Communication Research, 25,* 163-179.

Brislin, R., Cushner, K., Cherrie, C., & Yong, M. (1986). *Intercultural interactions.* Beverly Hills, CA: Sage.

Brown, P., & Levinson, S. (1978). Universals in language usage: Politeness phenomena. In E. N. Goody (Ed.), *Questions and politeness.* Cambridge, MA: Cambridge University Press.

Carey, J. (1980). Paralanguage in computer-mediated communication. In N. K. Sondheimer (Ed.), *The 18th annual meeting of the Association for Computational Linguistics and parasession on topics in interactive discourse: Proceedings of the conference* (pp. 67-69). Philadelphia: University of Pennsylvania.

Culnan, M. J., & Markus, M. L. (1987). Information technologies. In F. M. Jablin, L. Putnam, K. Roberts, & L. Porter (Eds.), *Handbook of organizational communication* (pp. 420-423). Newbury Park, CA: Sage.

Daft, R. L., & Lengel, R. H. (1984). Information richness: A new approach to managerial behavior and organization design. In B. M. Staw & L. L. Cummings (Eds.), *Research in organization behavior* (pp. 191-233). Greenwich, CT: JAI Press.

Daft, R. L., Lengel, R. H., & Trevino, L. K. (1987). Message equivocality, media selection, and manager performance: Implications for information systems. *MIS Quarterly, 11,* 355-366.

Deans, P. D., Karwan, K. R., Golsar, M. D., Ricks, D. A., & Toyne, B. (1991). Identification of key international information systems issues in U.S.-based multinational corporations. *Journal of Management Information Sytems, 7*(4), 27-50.

DeSanctis, G., & Gallupe, R. B. (1987). A foundation for the study of group decision support systems. *Management Science, 33,* 589-609.

Dubrovsky, V. J., Kiesler, S., & Sethna, B. N. (1991). The equalization phenomenon: Status effects in computer-mediated and face-to-face decision-making groups. *Human-Computer Interaction, 6,* 119-146.

Eakins, B. W., & Eakins, R. G. (1976). *Sex differences in human communication.* Boston: Houghton Mifflin.

Egelhoff, W. G. (1991). Information processing theory and the multinational enterprise. *Journal of International Business Studies, 22,* 341-368.

Elton, M.C.J. (1982). *Teleconferencing: New media for business meetings.* New York: American Management Association.

Engle, S. G. (1999, September). The global future. *Resource, 6*(9), 11-12.

Fisher, B. A., & Ellis, D. G. (1990). *Small group decision making: Communication and the group process*(3rd ed.). New York: McGraw-Hill.

Folger, J. P., Poole, M. S., & Stutman, R. K. (1993). *Working through conflict.* New York: Harper Collins College.

Fulk, J., Schmitz, J., & Steinfield, C. W. (1990). A social influence model of technology use. In J. Fulk & C. Steinfield (Eds.), *Organizations and communication technology* (pp. 117-140). Newbury Park, CA: Sage.

Garcia, A. C., & Jacobs, J. B. (1999). The eyes of the beholder: Understanding the turn-taking system in quasi-synchronous computer-mediated communication. *Research on Language and Social Interaction, 32*(4), 337-367.

Gasner, A. (1999). Globalization: The changing face of the workforce. *Business Today, 36*(3), 43-44.

Gattiker, U. (1988). Where do we go from here? Directions for future research and managers. In U. Gattiker & L. Larwood (Eds.), *Managing technological development: Strategic and human resources issues* (pp. 213-217). New York: Walter de Gruyter.

Gee, J. P. (1996). *Social linguistics and literacies: Ideologies in discourses* (2nd ed.). London: Sage.

George, V. P. (1995). Globalization through interfirm cooperation: Technological anchors and temporal nature of alliances across geographical boundaries. *International Journal of Technology Management, 10,* 131-145.

Geringer, J. M., & Herbert, L. (1989). Control and performance of international joint ventures. *Journal of International Business Studies, 20,* 235-254.

Goffman, E. (1967). On face work. In E. Goffman (Ed.), *Interaction ritual.* New York: Doubleday.

Graham, J. L., & Gronhaug, K. (1989). Ned Hall didn't have to get a haircut: Or why we haven't learn much about international marketing in twenty-five years. *Harvard Business Review, 67,* 160-168.

Gudykunst, W. B., & Kim, Y. Y. (1992). *Communicating with strangers: An approach to intercultural communication* (2nd ed.). New York: McGraw Hill.

Gudykunst, W., Masumoto, Y., Ting-Toomey, S., Nishida, T., Kim, K., & Heyman, S. (1996). The influence of cultural individualism-collectivism, self-construals, and individual values on communication styles across cultures. *Human Communication Research, 22,* 510-543.

Hall, E. T. (1976). *Beyond culture.* New York: Doubleday.

Hambrick, D. C., Korn, L., Frederickson, J. W., & Ferry, R. (1989). *21st century report: Reinventing the CEO.* New York: Korn & Ferry.

Hamel, G., Doz, Y., & Prahalad, C., (1989). Collaborate with your competitors-and win. *Harvard Business Review, 67,* 133-139.

Hiemstra, G. (1982). Teleconferencing, concern for face, and organizational culture. In M. Burgoon (Ed.), *Communication yearbook* (Vol. 6, pp. 874-904). Beverly Hills, CA: Sage.

Hiltz, S. R., & Turoff, M. (1978). *The network nation: Human communication via computer.* Reading, MA: Addison-Wesley.

Hirokawa, R. Y. (1981). Improving intra-organizational communication: A lesson from Japanese management. *Communication Quarterly, 30,* 35-40.

Ho, T. H., & Raman, K. S. (1991). The effect of GDSS and elected leadership on small group meetings. *Journal of Management Information Systems, 8*(2), 109-133.

Hofstede, G. (1980). *Culture's consequences.* Beverly Hills, CA: Sage.

Hofstede, G. (1991). *Cultures and organizations: Software of the mind.* Maidenhead, UK: McGraw Hill.

Hofstede, G., & Bond, M. (1984). Hofstede's culture dimensions: An independent validation using Rokeach's value survey. *Journal of Cross-Cultural Psychology, 15,* 417-433.

Holmes, M. E., & Poole, M. S. (1991). The longitudinal analysis of interaction. In B. Montgomery & S. Duck (Eds.), *Studying interpersonal interaction* (pp. 286-302). New York: Guilford.

Kalawsky, R. S., Bee, S. T., & Nee, S. P. (1999). Human factors evaluation techniques to aid understanding of virtual interfaces. *BT Technology Journal, 17,* 128-141.

Kamel, N., & Davison, R. (1998). Applying CSCW technology to overcome traditional barriers in group interactions. *Information & Management, 34,* 209-220.

Kapferer, J. N. (1992). *Strategic brand management.* London: Kogan Page.

Karimi, J., & Konsynski, B. R. (1991). Globalization and information management strategies. *Journal of Management Information Systems, 7*(3), 7-26.

Kiesler, S., Siegel, J., & McGuire, T. W. (1984). Social psychological aspects of computer-mediated communication. *American Psychologist, 39,* 1123-1134.

Kim, Y. Y. (1988). *Communication and cross-cultural adaptation.* London: Multilingual Matters.

Knapp, M. (1984). *Interpersonal communication and human relationships.* Boston: Allyn & Bacon.

Konsynski, B., & McFarlan, W. (1990, September-October). Information partnerships-shared data, shared scale. *Harvard Business Review, 68,* 14-120.

Kraus, R. M., Apple, W., Morencz, N., Wentzel, C., & Winton. W. (1981). Verbal, vocal, and visible factors in judgments of another's affect. *Journal of Personality and Social Psychology, 40,* 312-320.

Kraut, R. E., & Lewis, S. H. (1984). *Communication by children and adults: Social cognitive and strategic processes.* Beverly Hills, CA: Sage.

Kraut, R. E., Lewis, S. H., & Swozey, L. W. (1982). Listener responsiveness and the coordination of conversation. *Journal of Personality and Social Psychology, 43,* 718-731.

Krippendorff, K. (1980). *Content analysis: An introduction to its methodology.* Newbury Park, CA: Sage.

Lambert, W. (1963). Psychological approaches to the study of language. *Modem Language Journal, 14,* 51-62.

Lea, M., O'Shea, T., Fung, P., & Spears, R. (1992). "Flaming" in computer-mediated communication: Observations, explanations, implications. In M. Lea (Ed.), *Context of computer-mediated communication* (pp. 89-112). London: Harvester-Wheatsheaf.

Lea, M., & Spears, R. (1992). Paralanguage and social perception in computer-mediated communication. *Journal of Organizational Computing, 2,* 321-341.

Lecraw, D. J. (1984). Bargaining power, ownership, and profitability of transnational corporations in developing countries. *Journal of International Business Studies, 14,* 27-43.

Li, M., & Ye, R. (1999). Information technology and firm performance: Linking with environmental, strategic, and managerial contexts. *Information & Management, 35,* 43-45.

Lievrouw, L., & Finn, A. (1990). Identifying the common dimensions of communication: The communication systems model. In B. Ruben & L. Lievrouw (Eds.), *Mediation, information, and communication* (pp. 37-65). New Jersey: Transactions.

Lim, P., & Facciola, P. C. (1988). *Social cognition on ICOSY: An examination of computer conferencing attributes and human perceptions.* Doctoral dissertation, University of Arizona.

Mantovani, G. (1994). Is CMC intrinsically apt to enhance democracy in organizations. *Public Relations, 47,* 45-62.

Martinez, Z. L., & Ricks, D. A. (1989). Multinational parent companies' influence over human resources decisions of affiliates: U.S. firms in Mexico. *Journal of International Business Studies, 20,* 465-514.

Martinsons, M., & Westwood, R. (1997). Management information systems in the Chinese business culture: An explanatory theory. *Information & Management, 35,* 215-228.

Mesdag, M. V. (2000). Culture-sensitive adaptation or global standardization—the duration of usage hypothesis. *International Marketing Review, 17,* 74-84.

Miller, J. M. (2000). Language use, identity, and social interaction: Migrant students in Australia. *Research on Language and Social Interaction, 33*(1), 69-100.

Munter, M. (1998). Meeting technology: From low tech to high tech. *Business Communication Quarterly, 61,* 80-87.

Newman, J., & Newman, R. (1992). Two failures in computer-mediated text communication. *Instructional Science, 21,* 29-43.

Nightly business report. (2000, May 5). Japanese women log on to new opportunity on the Internet [Online]. Available: http://www.nbr.com/trnscrpt.htm#STORY 4.

Oetzel, J. G. (1998). Explaining individual communication processes in homogeneous and heterogeneous groups through individualism-collectivism and self construal. *Human Communication Research, 25,* 202-224.

Olaniran, B. A. (1993). International students' network patterns and cultural stress: What really counts. *Communication Research Reports, 10,* 69-83.

Olaniran, B. A. (1994). Group performance in computer-mediated and face-to-face communication media. *Management Communication Quarterly, 7,* 256-281.

Olaniran, B. A. (1995). Perceived communication outcomes in computer-mediated communication: An analysis of three systems among new users. *Information Processing & Management, 31,* 525-541.

Olaniran, B. A. (in press). Computer-mediated communication and less developed countries. *Journal of South African Communication, 25.*

Perlmutter, H., & Heenan, D. (1974). How multinational should you managers be? *Harvard Business Review, 52*(6), 121-132.

Postmes, T., Spears, R., & Lea, M. (1998). Breaching or building the social boundaries? SIDE-Effects of computer-mediated communication. *Communication Research, 25,* 689-715.

Putnam, L. (1983). The interpretive perspective: An alternative to functionalism. In L. Putnam & M. Pacanowsky (Eds.), *Communication and organization: An interpretive approach* (pp. 31-54). Beverly Hills, CA: Sage.

Qureshi, S. (2000). Organizational change through collaborative learning in network form. *Group Decision and Negotiation, 9*(2), 129-147.

Redding, W. C. (1972). *Communication within the organization: An interpretive review of theory and research.* New York: Industrial Communication Council.

Rice, R. E. (1993). Media appropriateness: Using social presence theory to compare traditional and new organizational media. *Human Communication Research, 19,* 451-484.

Rice, R. E., & Aydin, C. (1991). Attitudes toward new organizational technology: Network proximity as a mechanism for social information processing. *Administrative Science Quarterly, 36,* 219-244.

Rice, R. E., Grant, A., Schmitz, J., & Torobin, J. (1990). Individual and network influences on the adoption and perceived outcomes of electronic messaging. *Social Networks, 12,* 27-55.

Rice, R. E., & Love, G. (1987). Electronic emotion: Socioemotional content in a computer-mediated network. *Communication Research, 14,* 85-108.

Rice, R. E., & Shook, D. (1988). Access to, usage of, and outcomes from electronic messaging. *ACM Transactions on Office Information Systems, 6,* 255-276.

Rogers, E. M. (1990). The emergence of information societies. In B. Ruben & L. Lievrouw (Eds.), *Mediation, information, and communi-* *cation* (pp. 185-192). New Brunswick, NJ: Transaction Publishing.

Schmitz, J., & Fulk, J. (1991). Organizational colleagues, information richness, and electronic mail: A test of the social influence model of technology use. *Communication Research, 18,* 487-523.

Scott, C. R. (1999). The impact of physical and discursive anonymity on group members' multiple identification during computer-supported decision making. *Western Journal of Communication, 63*(4), 456-487.

Short, J., Williams, E., & Christie, B. (1976). *The social psychology of telecommunications.* London: John Wiley.

Siegel, J., Dubrovsky, V., Kiesler, S., & McGuire, T. W. (1986). Group processes in computer-mediated communication. *Organizational Behavior and Human Processes, 37,* 157-187.

Sitkin, S. B., Sutcliffe, K. M., & Barrios-Choplin, J. R. (1992). A dual capacity model of communication media choice in organizations. *Human Communication Research, 18,* 563-598.

Spitzer, M. (1986). Writing styles in computer conferences. *IEEE Transactions on Professional Communication, 29,* 19-22.

Steingard, D. S., & Fitzgibbons, D. E. (1995). Challenging the juggernaut of globalization: A manifesto for academic praxis. *Journal of Organizational Change Management, 8*(4), 30-54.

Steinhoff, P. G., & Tanaka, K. (1988). Women managers in Japan. In N. Adler & D. Izraeli (Eds.), *Women in management worldwide* (pp. 103-121). New York: M. E. Sharpe.

Suomi, R., & Pekola, J. (1998). Inhibitors and motivators for telework: Some Finish experiences. *European Journal of information Systems, 7,* 221-231.

Tannen, D. (1993). The relativity of linguistic studies: Rethinking power and solidarity in gender and dominance. In D. Tannen (Ed.), *Gender and conversational interaction* (pp. 165-185). New York: Oxford University Press.

Tesch, R. (1990). *Qualitative research: Analysis stages and software tools.* New York: Falmer.

Ting-Toomey, S. (1988). A face negotiation theory. In Y. Kim & W. Gudykunst (Eds.), *The-*

ories in intercultural communication (pp. 213-235). Newbury Park, CA: Sage.

Triandis, H. C. (1995). *Individualism and collectivism.* Boulder, CO: Westview.

Turkle, S., & Papert, S. (1990). Epistemological pluralism: Styles and voices within the computer culture. *Signs, 16,* 128-157.

Verdin, J. A. (1988). The impact of computer technology on human resource information system users. In U. Gattiker & L. Larwood (Eds.), *Managing technological development: Strategic and human resources issues* (pp. 143-159). New York: Walter de Gruyter.

Walther, J. B. (1992a). Interpersonal effects in computer-mediated communication: A relational perspective. *Communication Research, 19,* 52-90.

Walther, J. B. (1992b). A longitudinal experiment on computer-mediated and face-to-face interaction. *Proceedings of the twenty-fifth Hawaii International Conference on System Sciences.* Los Alamitos, CA: IEEE Computer Society Press.

Walther, J. B. (1994). Anticipated ongoing interaction versus channel effects on relational communication in computer-mediated interaction. *Human Communication Research, 20,* 473-501.

Walther, J. B. (1997). Group and interpersonal effects in international computer-mediated collaboration. *Human Communication Research, 23,* 342-369.

Walther, J. B., Anderson, J. F., & Park, D. (1994). Interpersonal effects in computer-mediated interaction: A meta analysis of social and antisocial communication. *Communication Research, 23,* 3-42.

Walther, J. B., & Burgoon, J. K. (1992). Relational communication in computer-mediated interaction. *Human Communication Research, 19,* 50-88.

Watzlawick, P., Beavin, J. H., & Jackson, D. D. (1967). *Pragmatics of human communication: A study of interactional patterns, pathologies. and paradoxes.* New York: Norton.

Weisband, S. P. (1992). Group discussion and first advocacy effects in computer-mediated and face-to-face decision making groups. *Organizational Behavior and Human Decision Processes, 53,* 352-380.

Williams, F., Rice, R. E., & Rogers, E. M. (1988). *Research methods and the new media.* New York: Free Press.

Wood, R., & Bandura, A. (1989). Social cognitive theory of organizational management. *Academy of Management Review, 14,* 361-384.

Part II

Historical and Religious Struggles Within and Between Nations

Historical Struggles Between Islamic and Christian Worldviews

An Interpretation

ALI A. MAZRUI

Two major movements may impinge on the future relationship between Islam and the Western world. One is the *multicultural movement,* which seeks to sensitize policy makers, the media, publishers, teachers, and textbook publishers to the cultural diversity of each country. The other movement is the demand for *global studies,* which seeks to restore balance in the study of world history and the reporting of world affairs.

The multicultural movement in America, for example, seems to hold that whereas the United States has been the greatest asylum for diverse peoples, it has not been the greatest refuge for diverse cultures. The doors of transcultural communication have seldom been kept wide open in U.S. policy.

The American multicultural movement seeks to end Eurocentrism in the study of American history and culture. The United States as a pyramid was built not only by the pharaohs (or founding fathers) but by women as well as men, blacks as well as whites, non-Christians as well as Christians, immigrants as well as Native Americans. Historical recognition is communication across the centuries.

The global studies movement in the West also insists that world civilization is a product of many cultures—and not merely of the triumph of modern Europe. Civilization has always been a quest for creative synthesis.

Eurocentrism has its peculiar prejudices. Whereas the black man is the ultimate racial

AUTHOR'S NOTE: This chapter is partly based on a paper presented at the International Workshop on Islamic Political Economy and Capitalist Globalization: An Agenda for Change, held at Universiti Sains Malaysia, Pulau Pinang, Malaysia, December 12-14, 1994.

109

"Other" for the white man, a Muslim is often regarded as the ultimate religious Other for the Euro Christian. This is the crusade complex in the European psyche, historic Islamophobia.

Contrasting stereotypes are invented. Whereas Christianity is supposed to be peace loving, Islam is portrayed as fostering holy war *(Jihad)*. Whereas Christianity liberates women, Islam enslaves them. Whereas Christianity is modern, Islam is medieval. Whereas Christianity is forward looking, Islam is backward looking. Whereas Christians prefer nonviolence, Muslims easily resort to terrorism. Islam becomes the ultimate negative Other to the Christian tradition. That is the continuing theme of Islamophobia—the fear of Islam and the hostility toward it. Stereotypes are a form of miscommunication across cultures.

Often perpetrated in the media, in books, and in the classroom are two kinds of sins about the Muslim world and Muslim history, sins of omission and sins of commission. Sins of omission concern fundamental facts about Islam that are left out of Western accounts, omissions that seriously impede Western understanding of Islam. These are transcultural silences of omission.

Sins of commission are distortions of Muslim doctrine, Muslim practice, or Muslim history—particularly distortions that cause religious hostility and intolerance. Sometimes, those distortions are the result of ignorance rather than malice, but the consequences can still generate religious suspicions and antagonism. These are transcultural sins of perjury and falsification.

▶ The Abrahamic Sisters

One serious sin of omission in Western portrayals of Islam is omitting the simple fact that Judaism, Christianity, and Islam are sister religions that are closely related to each other. The three compose what is now called the Abrahamic religions.[1]

Few Westerners know that, in some matters, Islam is closer to Christianity than Judaism is; in some other matters, Islam is closer to Judaism than Christianity is. Let us take each of these, in turn. In what aspect is Islam closer to Christianity than Judaism is? Islam accepts a substantial part of the New Testament; Judaism does not.

Islam accepts Jesus as the messiah, whereas Judaism does not. Most Muslims accept the virgin birth of Jesus, whereas Judaism does not. Islam attributes more miracles to Jesus than to the Prophet Muhammad—healing the sick and reviving the dead with the touch of Jesus. Islam recognizes Jesus's sacred mission on earth, whereas Judaism does not. Most Muslims also believe that Jesus bodily and physically ascended to heaven on completion of his earthly mission. Islam and Christianity share important beliefs and doctrines.

There are some moving passages about Maryam (or Mary), the mother of Jesus, in the Koran. Moreover, across the centuries, many Muslims have married Christians without conversion under the doctrine of *ahl el kitab* (the people of the book). Some have married Jews without conversion under the same doctrine.

But in what aspects are Islam and Judaism closer to each other than either is to Christianity? Both Judaism and Islam have dietary laws, whereas most Christian denominations do not. In both Islam and Judaism, the pig is traditionally a special symbol of abomination in relation to diet and ritual cleanliness, whereas the pig is normatively neutral in most Christian denominations.

Both Islam and Judaism tend to emphasize a God of justice rather than love; therefore, both of them put a special premium on religious laws and divine ritual.

The divine attributes surrounding the God of Judaism and Islam tend to be what are culturally regarded as hard, masculine virtues—power, control, strength, even purposeful ruthlessness. This is the God of the Old Testament, the God of collective punishment and hard, inscrutable justice. On the other hand, the divine attributes surrounding the son of God in Christianity tend to be what were once culturally regarded as soft, feminine virtues—patience, meekness, submissiveness and ability to turn the other cheek.

Unlike Christianity, both Judaism and Islam require that male children be circumcised as a matter of compulsory ritual. Neither requires that female babies be circumcised or genitally mutilated, although some Muslim societies practice female genital excision for other cultural reasons.

Both Judaism and Islam are linguistically authentic in their use of original Semitic languages for ritual and for other religious purposes. Christianity, on the other hand, has become a religion in translation, a God in exile. Its leadership has moved from the Middle East to the Western world.

Even when the Roman Catholic church insisted on saying Mass in a particular language, the language chosen was not Aramaic, Jesus's mother tongue, but Latin, which Jesus might not have spoken at all.

To summarize, Judaism, Christianity, and Islam are sister religions. As with any three sisters, the question of which one is closer to which may vary according to which aspects of their relationship are being examined. As we indicated, Judaism and Islam are in some respects closer to each other than either is to Christianity. In some other respects, Islam has more in common with Christianity than Judaism has.

What Christianity has in common with Judaism is more familiar to Westerners. The Western rhetoric is full of references to the Judeo-Christian tradition. The real sin of omission is to forget mentioning that the Abrahamic legacy has three legs instead of just two. The missing leg in Western accounts has been the leg of Islam. It is time for this transcultural silence to be broken.

▶ Islam: The First Protestant Revolution?

There is a related tripartite character within Islam. This is the dynamic interplay between Judaism, Christianity, and what this chapter calls *Muhammadiyya* in a special sense. Our definition of Muhammadiyya restricts itself to those elements of Islam that are unique to the message of Muhammad and are not shared by either Judaism or Christianity. In other words, the religion of Islam as a whole consists of three legacies: the legacy of the Bible's Old Testament (duly amended or corrected), the legacy of the New Testament (duly amended or corrected), and the unique message that came with Muhammad himself. Muslims see the Prophet Muhammad as successor to Abraham, Moses, and Jesus, carrying the message of God to higher levels of perfection. This message, unique to Mohammad, is what this chapter calls Muhammadiyya.

Precisely because Islam conceived of itself in part as a restoration of the message of Jesus after it had been distorted, Muhammad's revolution was the first Protestant assertion in history. Like Martin Luther and John Calvin 900 years later, Muhammad felt that the message of Jesus had been perverted by his successors in the leadership of the flock.

In keeping with Calvinist reforms centuries later, Muhammad declared himself against a highly structured and hierarchical priesthood. Consistent with the lessons of both Luther and Calvin, Muhammad distrusted intercession between man and God and insisted on direct communication between worshiper and his or her maker. Like Calvin much later, Muhammad proclaimed the message of predestination and divine planning in human affairs. But the Prophet Muhammad was proclaiming this centuries before Calvin.

Luther and Calvin later denounced the Catholic church for having become too monarchical and too inclined toward pomp and splendor. Muhammad's Protestant revolution had occurred early enough to challenge this monarchical tendency at its source. The source was the conception of Jesus as a prince and as son of the almighty God. Muhammad insisted that Jesus had claimed no more than the role of messenger of God. All the alleged majesty of Jesus as a prince descended from the throne of God only led to the pomp of the church itself. The church struggled to do justice to a monarchical conception of its founder. Muhammad had gone further than either Luther or Calvin would do in challenging the royal and aristocratic tendencies of the legacy of Jesus in the hands of his successors.

What has all this to do with the Islamic mode of production? To some extent, we have to look at the later Protestant revolutions of Luther and Calvin to understand the earlier Protestant revolution of Muhammad. A whole body of literature has grown around the concept of the Protestant ethic and the origins and the underlying spirit of capitalism. Our understanding of the Islamic mode of production may draw from insights not only of Karl Marx but also of analysts such as Max Weber and his own paradigm of the Protestant origins of the capitalist revolution.

More important as a link between the origins of European Protestantism and the origins of Islam were doctrinal influences. On the economic front, the Prophet Muhammad's ideas on trade and commerce might indeed have been influenced by his personal experiences. The ideas that led to the rise of capitalism in the wake of the Protestant revolution in Europe may, in turn, have had their ancestry in the Islamic mode of production. European culture had been in contact with Islam for centuries. The Islamic economic mode could, in turn, have been profoundly influenced by both divine Providence and the Prophet's own experiences.[2]

That is why this chapter must begin with Muhammad's personal experiences before prophethood. Did they mold him as a political leader and policy maker? We know that in his childhood, he was poor enough for his condition to warrant a Koranic verse, a condition he shared with many others in centers of trade such as Mecca. In his youth, he entered into a relationship with the affluent merchant woman, Khadija, who probably owed her wealth to her two former husbands. The younger Muhammad was first an entrusted manager of her trade enterprises and later a husband whose love for his wife could not have been anything less than deep. How extensive Muhammad's trade experience was we are not sure, but it was certainly extensive enough for

him to have developed a special fondness for the profession, as a number of his statements, or *hadiths,* would seem to indicate. His early biography is relevant for understanding him as a great leader and policy maker.

Against this background, within the context of the then-prevalent mercantile economy with its market-oriented production that came under the regulation of customary laws, we may be able to understand Muhammad's own ambivalence toward the Arabian merchant class. Partly as a product of his childhood experience, he was sympathetic enough toward the "wretched of the earth" to render him critical, sometimes vehemently so, of the merchant class, especially during the early period of his prophethood. On the other hand, his personal links, first with Khadija and her trade engagements and later with influential merchant converts to Islam, such as Umar, produced sentiments that regarded trade as, perhaps, a very honorable profession and merchants as its honorable vanguard. From this duality, one could probably infer a desire on the Prophet Muhammad's part for an economic arrangement that would be just to both the rich and the poor. Great leadership sometimes demands compromises with historical realities.

Muhammad's own policy pronouncements on commerce would seem to suggest, however, that his views were more than tactical. His favorable portrayal of trade and merchants tends to betray an emotional attachment to trade, but with reservations. The Prophet was a human being with his own preferences. He was about to change the history of the human race itself.

What factors in the European Protestant revolution have been interpreted as aspects of the rise of capitalism? One was the rise of individualism. Because priestly intercession and confession in church were no longer necessary for salvation under Protestantism, man was held more directly accountable for his fate. Islam, too, had insisted that no intermediary was needed between believers and their Maker. In the religious sphere, there was emerging as a liberal doctrine the image of a person as ultimately his or her own advocate before the Almighty. This could become a principle of empowering people to be responsible for their own destiny. Such a concept was one day to become part and parcel of economic individualism and private enterprise.[3]

Yet, both Islam and Calvinism espoused a principle of predestination. If the fate of every human being was sealed in advance, why should people exert themselves?

Islam had one answer, Calvinism another. Islam, in the tradition of the Prophet, advised believers to behave, on the one hand, as if they were going to die tomorrow and, on the other, as if they were going to live forever. Believers were expected to strike a balance between the temporal and the spiritual, between the religious and the secular.

As a seemingly staunch believer in a free-trade economy, the Prophet Muhammad as a policy maker is said to have been opposed to price controls of any sort. Setting a price maximum was deemed unfair to the merchant. Muhammad seems to have trusted the forces of supply and demand to act as the only barometer on the basis of which the rightful price could be determined. Nonetheless, there was the institution of the *hisba,* something akin to a comprehensive ombudsman, which was charged with the responsibility of checking foul play, ensuring that no merchant was being dishonest by charging above the average price range at any one point.[4]

Two media of exchange existed side by side in Muhammad's day. They were money in the form of silver and, we believe, gold— the dirham and the dinar; and barter. Dealings in either of the two media, however, came under moral control, rules of the game.

Islam as the first Protestant revolution was laying the foundations of an Islamic mode of production in the centuries that were to follow. Was it also laying the foundations for the role of all three Abrahamic religions in the emergence of a world economy? A future Max Weber may be inspired to write a book entitled *The Abrahamic Religions and the Rise of Capitalism.*[5]

But Islam is not only about relations between producers and consumers. It is, of course, also about relations between men and women and between state and society. Let us turn to some of these aspects.

▶ Between Sexism and Violence

How sexist is Islam? An important sin of commission and cultural perjury concerns the portrayal of Muslim women in many books and films. The harem stereotype was illustrated in the American soap opera broadcast on CBS, *The Bold and the Beautiful,* in which the character Taylor Forrester lost her memory and was on the verge of being married as Laila under false pretenses to a despotic Moroccan prince. She was saved from a fate worse than death by the recovery of her memory in the nick of time.

The stereotype of the Muslim woman in the Western media is usually drawn not even from Morocco's real life experience but from even more conservative life experiences of the Arabian peninsula and the small gulf states. Heavily veiled, socially isolated Muslim women belong to a small minority of Muslim societies, but this is the dominant stereotype in most Western reporting.

How many Western observers are aware that just about the time Canada was briefly experimenting for the first time with a woman prime minister in 1993, three different Muslim countries had women prime ministers, and one of them also had a woman leader of the opposition? Here were cultural silences, sins of omission.

Pakistan, Turkey, and Bangladesh (all Muslim countries) have had women as chief executives, whereas the United States has had no woman president, Germany no woman chancellor, and Russia no woman president.[6]

Moreover, Muslim women executives lasted longer in power than did the Canadian woman prime minister of 1993, who was rapidly thrown out of office and her political party almost destroyed at the federal level.

Muslim countries that, in the past, have enlisted women into the armed forces include Libya, Algeria, and Siad Barre's Somalia. The number of women students in universities in Iran has doubled since the Iranian revolution of 1979. Indeed, a number of women are heads of research and other institutions in the Islamic Republic of Iran. Absence of such information in the West is a deliberate cultural silence, a sin of omission.

How much of a religion of peace is Islam? Another sin of commission concerns the relationship between Islam and violence. It partly depends on what kind of peace one is focusing on. Tehran is a city of 10 million people, about the size of New York City. Yet, in the 1990s in Tehran, I saw women and children picnicking in public parks at 10 p.m. or later. Indeed, in four different Iranian cities, I observed mothers at night with their children, sometimes without their menfolk, walking the streets seemingly without fear of being mugged or sexually assaulted. Does that qualify as a city at peace?

In a mosque in Tehran at nearly 11 p.m., a 12-year-old boy told his father that he was tired. The father (who was one of my hosts) said to the 12-year-old, "You may go home!" The father meant that the child was to walk home at nearly 11 p.m. The parent was not worried about the child's safety at that time of night, even if home was a mile away. In New York City, one hesitates to send one's dog out unaccompanied at that time of night. Which of the two cities has found peace?

On the one hand, Iranians are a people capable of collective and purposeful political violence. They have engaged in revolution and war. On the other hand, Iranians seemed to be less prone to petty interpersonal violence, such as mugging and rape, than Americans in big cities are.

Much of the explanation for the Iranian phenomenon is cultural, and Islam is an important part of this culture. Cairo is a city of 15 million people, and yet, it has only a fraction of the crime rate of Washington, D.C., a much smaller metropolis. Again, much of the explanation is cultural, with Islam playing an important role. By some definitions of *peace,* Islam is a more peaceful tradition than American culture.

But is not the low crime rate of Muslim cities due to their authoritarian governments and Draconian laws? If that were the reason, there would be very low crime rates in Lagos, Nigeria, and Nairobi, Kenya, where armed robbery, for example, is a capital offense. Strict laws in Lagos have not created the nonviolent environment of Tehran, although it is only half of Tehran's size. Johannesburg is a fraction of the size of Cairo, but by the standards of mugging and robbery, Johannesburg is more dangerous.

Nor must we jump to the other extreme and give Islam all the credit for the relative nonviolence of most Muslim cities. Extreme poverty and ethnicity can erode the pacifying power of Islam.[7]

But I cite Iranian cities and Egyptian cities to make the point that although some Muslims do engage in violence for political ends from time to time, they engage far less in day-to-day interpersonal violence for greed and sexual satisfaction.

Moreover, Muslim societies are far less likely to produce either drug abuse or alcohol abuse than are Western societies. The quality of ordinary life in traditional Muslim societies is, therefore, less likely to be violent on a day-to-day basis than the quality of life in major American cities.

With regard to this relationship between Islam and violence, the distorting sin of commission, therefore, lies in not recognizing that the streets of most major cities in the Muslim world are far less violent than comparable cities in much of the United States. Is Islam a religion of peace? There are senses of *peace* where Islam has been more successful in providing personal security than many other cultures and ways of life.[8]

▶ Seven Biases of Islamophobia

A number of underlying biases must be recognized as adversely affecting the study of Islam by non-Muslims. It is to these biases of Islamophobia that we must now turn. These truly interfere with transcultural communication.

There still is *the minaret bias*. This bias reduces Islam to a system of worship only. It overlooks the fact that Islam is also a body of accumulated philosophy in ethics, metaphysics, epistemology, and aesthetics. It ignores the fact that Islam is also a system of laws and precepts affecting matters that range from the basis of political obligation to laws of inheritance. Nor does it recognize Islam as a style of living encompassing literature, architecture, calligraphy, and the arts. Islam is, of course, also a basis of relationships between men and women, parents and children, intimates and strangers, Muslims and non-Muslims.

The minaret bias is in danger of overdramatizing the five prayers, very important as those are. Even among the pillars of Islam, all the prayers constitute only one pillar out of five pillars.

The second serious bias in the portrayal of Islam has been what might be called the *Arabesque bias*. I use the word *Arabesque* here not only in its artistic sense but also in reference to Islam as if it was still the religion only of the Arabs. Arabs ceased to be a majority of Muslims in the world at least 10 centuries ago. But the temptation to present Islam completely in Arab dress is still very strong in Western education, literature, and the media. This tendency includes portraying Islam as a religion of the desert, or even of the camel, the most reductionist of all.

Third, there is *the Jihad bias* in the portrayal of Islam. This is part of the crusade complex in the European psyche, still in search of Salahuddin (Saladin) and Richard the Lion Heart. Did Islam spread by the sword? Sometimes, it spread by conquest, even in Egypt and Persia. At other times, it spread by trade, as in most of sub-Saharan Africa. In any case, did not Christianity conquer by force of arms much of the New World, much of Africa, and parts of Asia? Was not the spread of Christianity in Europe itself originally due to newly converted Roman con-

querors, beginning with Constantine the Great?

The jihad bias in the second half of the 20th century sometimes portrayed Islam as a religion of terrorism. Islam is no longer spreading by the sword but seeks to halt Westernization through the barrel of the gun.

The *harem bias* in the portrayal of Islam is next. This is latter-day Shaharazade of the *Arabian Nights,* as she seeks to amuse the sultan with stupendous tales night after night to save her life.

There is a constant Western preoccupation with whether Islam is a particularly sexist culture. The Arabesque bias tends to reinforce the harem bias, because some of the most secluded women in the world are in the Arabian portions of the Muslim world, a small fraction of the total.

Among the sins of commission of the harem bias is the widespread belief that Islam requires female circumcision or female genital excision. A particularly difficult problem is posed here. Some Muslim countries practice female genital excision whereas others do not. Egypt practices female excision, whereas Algeria does not; Yemen practices female excision, whereas Saudi Arabia does not. Somalia practices female excision, whereas Zanzibar does not.

The explanation is quite simple. Those who practice female genital surgery were doing it long before the arrival of Islam. It is an ancient custom in Egypt, Sudan, Yemen, and Somalia, so ancient that it antedates the presence of Islam.

Among the Muslims of Malaysia, the custom is almost completely dead. In Indonesia, it is dying. In sub-Saharan Africa, the custom of female genital surgery has more non-Muslim practitioners than Muslim.

The harem bias sometimes claims that Islam favors sexual promiscuity for men. Although it is true that Islam is interpreted as permitting each man to marry up to four wives, we should also remember that Islam has the most Draconian laws against adultery of any culture. Sexual infidelity can be a capital offense in Islam. This is hardly encouragement of promiscuity, but it is rigid enforcement of marriage vows.

In any case, Muslim modernists argue that since the Koran permits polygamy (polygyny) only if a man can treat all his wives absolutely equally, and because this is humanly impossible, polygamy is in fact forbidden (rather than forgiven) by the Koran. No man can treat two women absolutely equally—and so he should not marry more than one.

This brings us to *the judicial amputation bias* in the portrayal of Islam. This bias emphasizes the enormous severity of punishment imposed by the Shari'a, including amputation of the hand of the thief and capital punishment for adultery. In fact, the rules of evidence demanded by the Shari'a before such punishments can be imposed are even more rigorous than the punishments themselves. In the case of adultery, the rules require four reliable witnesses who actually saw sexual penetration by the male into the female. Unless lovers were enjoying themselves in the marketplace for all to see, it is most unlikely that their sexual activity would be physically witnessed by four such observers.

In the case of amputation of the hand of the thief, it would have to be demonstrated that the theft was an act of pure greed and not of understandable need—and the entire economy of the country would have to be under the Shari'a before a single thief could lose a limb.

In any case, these Muslim laws were originally pronounced when Christian nations in the West were executing thieves rather than merely amputating their hands—and long before Henry VIII of England executed his wives on suspicion of adultery, at the same time that he inaugurated the Church of England in rebellion against the Church of Rome.

More recently, there has been the *anti-Semitic bias* in the portrayal of Islam. This bias deliberately obfuscates the fact that both Arabs and Jews are Semitic peoples, that Arabic and Hebrew are closely related, and that being anti-Zionist cannot possibly be the same as being anti-Jewish because many devout and religiously militant Jews are anti-Zionist or very critical of the Israeli state.

Moreover, across the centuries, the Muslim world had a better record in its treatment of the Jews than did Europe. Nor can Muslims ever be accused of a Holocaust against the Jews. The Holocaust was perpetrated in the middle of Christian Europe, by men and women most of whom professed to be Christians.

The seventh bias in the portrayal of Islam is the *exotic bias*. This overlaps with a number of other biases, but the central concern here is with the truly extraordinary about the Muslim experience, sometimes combined with the truly "cute." How sensuous is the Muslim paradise? How many *houries* will a devout male have? Is it true that women have no soul in Islam? If so, why should women pray, or fast, or go on pilgrimage?

Finally, there are Eurocentric biases that are wider than Islam but that inevitably also affect approaches to the study of Muslim history and culture. Because Europeans have dominated most branches of science for at least 300 years, many paradigms of *all* other cultures (not just Islamic) have been distorted by European perspectives. It is to these dimensions that we must now turn.

▶ The Geography of Space and Time

For illustration in this chapter, let us focus on the distinction between the geography of space and the geography of time. The geography of space, in our sense, is about continents, oceans, planets, and outer space at a given moment in time.

The geography of time, on the other hand, is about history and its periodization. Eurocentrism in the geography of space has gone so far that much of it may be irreversible. On the other hand, it may be possible to roll back Eurocentrism in the geography of time to a certain extent. Our concepts of ancient, medieval, and modern may still be deeply rooted in the paradigm of European history, but we may be able to struggle out of some of the shackles.

Although there is an Islamic calendar, the triumph of the Gregorian Christian calendar worldwide is so great that Muslims can no longer rely on the Hijriyya calendar alone. Great Muslim events such as the fall of Constantinople to the Turks are more likely to be remembered by their date in the Christian era than their date on the Islamic calendar.

But even when Muslims use dates in the Christian era as boundaries of their history, they need not, of course, be bound by European concepts of ancient, medieval and modern. One debate concerns the issue of whether Islam existed before the Prophet Muhammad. Were the two older Abrahamic religions (Judaism and Christianity) themselves Islamic? If there was Islam before Muhammad, what did Allah mean in the Koran when he said to the Prophet Muhammad and his followers the following: "On this day have I completed for you your religion, and perfected for you my bounty, and chosen for you Islam as your religion."

If there was Islam before the Prophet Muhammad, why does the Islamic calendar begin with the Prophet's migration from Mecca to Medina (the *Hijjra*)? If there was Islam before the Prophet Muhammad, why are the days before his mission deemed to be the era of *Jahiliyya* (the days of ignorance)?

However, a Muslim can argue that although the Prophet Muhammad was the last and greatest of the prophets, all the previous prophets were preaching different stages of the mission of Islam. This would include Moses and Jesus as prophets of Islam. Periodization in Islamic history might, therefore, include the following rather uneven epochs:

1. Islam before the Prophet Muhammad's birth
2. Islam between the birth of the Prophet Muhammad and the death of the Fourth Caliph, Ali bin Abi Talib

3. The era of the Umayyads
4. The era of the Abbassids
5. The era of global consolidation in Asia and Africa and decline in Spain
6. The rise of the Ottoman Empire
7. Islam in the shadow of European imperialism: Decline and the disintegration of the Ottoman Empire
8. Postcaliphate Islam: piety, patriotism, and petroleum

It is partly in this sense that the geography of time can be revised and made more relevant. Islamic periodization might be made to respond to the realities of Islamic history and belief.[9]

On the other hand, the geography of space, as bequeathed to the world by the West's hegemony, may be far less susceptible to modification or revision. The Eurocentrism in the geography of space may be more obstinate partly because it has been more effectively universalized.

Indeed, aspects of this Eurocentrism are virtually impossible to correct. To begin with, Europe *named* the world. She named the continents North and South America, Europe, and Antarctica. Africa and Asia have names that although non-European in origin, were applied to those land masses first and foremost by Europeans.

Europe also named the oceans: the Atlantic, the Pacific, the Mediterranean, the Arctic. Even the Indian Ocean could just as easily have been called the African Ocean, but for Europe's fascination with a sea route to India from European shores.

Europe *timed* the world, choosing a little place in Britain called Greenwich as the basis of a global standard time. Some broadcasting stations today call it Universal Time, but that is a euphemism for Greenwich Mean Time (GMT).

Europe also *positioned* the world on the map, making sure that Europe was above and Africa below. This was not an inevitable law of the cosmos but a convention chosen by Europeans. There was no spectator in outer space decreeing from which position planet earth was to be viewed.

Europe *christened* the majority of the countries of the world. Europeans determined either the names or national boundaries of perhaps up to 60% of the members of the United Nations. Quite often both name and borders were indeed determined by Europeans.

On top of all this, Europeans have been naming the *universe,* often with Euro classical names. The range includes Venus, Mars, Saturn, Pluto, and others.

How much of this Eurocentrism of geography is reversible? Although Muslim scholarship and civilization produced some of the earliest cartographers and map makers of modern history, and some of the earliest astronomers, the subsequent successes of European science and technology have left a more indelible impact on those disciplines. Much of the Eurocentrism of contemporary geographical knowledge is beyond repair.

▶ Conclusion

One of the most compelling *jihads* of the concluding years of the 20th century is a jihad against images and stereotypes of Islam that inform the media, the classroom, the mind, and general policy. Cultural silences and cultural perjuries need to be addressed. Against Islam, sins of omission and sins of commission are committed. Sins of omission (silences) deny the Muslim world positive portrayal and publicity; sins of commission (perjuries) include distortions at the expense of Muslim history, doctrine, and practice.

This chapter has identified seven recurrent biases in sins of commission: the Arabesque, the minaret, the harem, the jihad, the judicial amputation, the anti-Semitic, and the exotic biases.

But there are also wider biases affecting all other cultures, such as the Eurocentrism imbedded in the geography of space and the geography of time.

The more positive forces of history are Islam's links with the other two Abrahamic religions, Judaism and Christianity. In some matters, Islam and Judaism are closer together than either is to Christianity. In other respects, Islam and Christianity are closer to each other than either is to Judaism.

In relation to Christianity, Islam might have been the first Protestant revolution, the first effort to repair the message of Jesus after distortions. Were Islam and the later Protestantism of John Calvin and Martin Luther jointly involved in the genesis of capitalism and the world economy? Indeed, were all three Abrahamic religions (Judaism, Christianity, and Islam) the founding fathers of what Max Weber was later to call "the spirit of capitalism"?[10]

Clearly, there is a good deal yet to be done in reinterpreting Islamic history. There is a good deal yet to be done in the jihad against Eurocentrism. Muslims will need the wisdom to distinguish between what can be changed and what cannot. And Muslims will need the political and scholarly will to correct what does indeed need to be corrected as the population of the Muslim world begins its march toward becoming one quarter of the human race within the next decade or two.

▶ Notes

1. See, for example, Armstrong (1994). Consult also Gordis, Grose, and Siddiqi (1994).

2. Consult also Azzam (1979).

3. For a modern Islamic approach to economic development see, for example, Salleh (1992).

4. Consult also El-Awa (1980).

5. This section of the chapter has borrowed from Ali Mazrui's (1990) book, *Cultural Forces in World Politics.* See also Max Weber's (1988) *The Protestant Ethic and the Spirit of Capitalism.* On doctrinal issues, Ali Mazrui is also indebted for stimulation to Alamin M. Mazrui of Ohio State University, Columbus, and to Parviz Morewedge

of Binghamton University, Binghamton, New York.

6. For the rights of women in Islam consult, for example, Engineer (1992).

7. Consult also Mutalib and Hashmi (1994).

8. For violence and social decay in the United States, consult, for example, Bennett (1994).

9. For a future-oriented approach, consult Sardar (1987).

10. See Max Weber's (1988) *The Protestant Ethic and the Spirit of Capitalism.*

▶ References

Armstrong, K. (1994). *A history of God: The 4000-year quest of Judaism, Christianity, and Islam.* New York: Knopf.

Azzam, A. (1979). *The eternal message of Muhammad.* London and New York: Quarter Book.

Bennett, W. J. (1994). *The index of leading cultural indicators.* New York and London: Simon & Schuster.

El-Awa, M. S. (1980). *On the political system of the Islamic state.* Indianapolis, IN: American Trust Publications.

Engineer, A. A. (1992). *The rights of women in Islam.* London: C. Hurst.

Gordis, D. M., Grose, G. B., & Siddiqi, M. H. (1994). *The Abraham connection: A Jew, Christian, and Muslim in dialogue.* Notre Dame, IN: Cross Cultural Publications.

Mazrui, A. (1990). *Cultural forces in world politics.* Portsmouth, NH: Heinemann.

Mutalib, H., & Hashmi, T.-I. (Eds.). (1994). *Islam, Muslims, and the modern state: Case studies of Muslims in thirteen countries.* New York: St. Martin's.

Salleh, M. S. (1992). *An Islamic approach to rural development: The arqam way.* London: ASOIB International.

Sardar, Z. (1987). *The future of Muslim civilization.* London and New York: Mansell.

Weber, M. (1988). *The Protestant ethic and the spirit of capitalism.* Gloucester, MA: Peter Smith.

A Historiographical Survey of the Determinants of the North-South Divide in Sudan

AYMAN OMAR

As an Africanist scholar stated, "The question of national unity for the [post-independent] states of Africa stands at the center of their political problems" (Shepherd, 1966, p. 15). Immediately following their independence from colonial rule, most African states found themselves involved in the urgent task of integrating divergent ethnocultural groups into the new body politic. However, as the eruption of civil wars in many of these states soon revealed, the task of forging national unity in Africa was to prove very difficult indeed. At the heart of the difficulty of integration lay many divisions, even stratification, in African societies along ethnic and cultural lines. As George Shepherd (1966) noted, Africa, more than any other continent, "is troubled by the divisions between ethnic, racial, and religious groups" (p. 15), groups that found temporary consensus in the struggle against the common colonial enemy but that, having achieved independence, found it difficult to give up ethnic allegiances in favor of loyalty to the state.

The continent's endemic problems of national integration are perhaps best illustrated by Sudan's postindependence experience. Sudan is one of the world's most heterogenous societies, and its efforts to achieve national unity were viewed by fellow Africans as an example of how inter-ethnic cooperation might work in Africa (Voll, 1990). However, these efforts were soon overwhelmed by the country's divisions. Two years after independence in 1956, a civil war between north and south began over the issues of national identity and power sharing. After 17 years of fighting, Sudan succeeded in negotiating a settlement that, by granting the south autonomous rule, ended the first civil war in 1973. That success prompted many to hail the Sudanese model as "an example of creating national unity through acceptance of diversity" (Voll, 1990, p. 22). That peace, however, was short-lived, and war erupted anew in 1983, suggesting that the north-south divide is deeper than previously thought.

Given the persistence of an identity schism in Sudan that contributed to two civil wars, including one that continues today, this chapter will survey the literature on the historical factors that contributed to the evolution of two distinct identities in Sudan. As a survey study, the chapter will present the views and arguments these writings advanced as possible explanations for how these conflicting identities came into being and how they consequently have contributed to the north-south divide.

▶ Historical Setting and Description of the Problem

THE COUNTRY

Bilad al Sudan, The Land of the Blacks, was the name medieval Muslims gave to the belt of African territory south of the Sahara Desert and extending from the Atlantic to the Ethiopian plateau (Khalid, 1985). In the modern sense, however, the Sudan means the Republic of Sudan, formerly the Anglo-Egyptian condominium. The country stretches from latitude 22 North to latitude 4 North near the equator and from the Red Sea to Chad. Territorially, Sudan covers nearly 1 million square miles, an area roughly the size of Western Europe, making it the largest single country in Africa (Khalid, 1985). Lying wholly within the tropics, Sudan constitutes one vast plain, with the exception of the Sudd region in the south and some hilly districts in the east and

west. The Nile river and its affluents constitute the physiographic axis of the country. Geographically, Sudan varies tremendously. The extreme north is Saharan in its heat and aridity, whereas the south is composed of thickly forested and intensely humid jungle.

Ethnoculturally, the country is no less diverse, containing 597 tribes who speak more than 400 languages and dialects and practice a variety of religious traditions. Ethnically, the country's 22 million people represent a cross-section of all Africans, making Sudan "almost a microcosm of Africa" (Khalid, 1985). Of these people, Arab Muslims form 54% and live mainly in the north. About 25% are Nilotic peoples: Dinka, Nuer, Shilluk, Nilo-Hematic, and Bantu, all of whom live south of latitude 10 North and are mostly faithful to traditional beliefs, with 5% being Christians (Khalid, 1985). Among the remainder of the population, Nuba, animist Negroids who speak their own dialects, make up 5%, living in the south-central mountains. Beja, herders of obscure origin, are non-Arab Muslims who live in the northeast and constitute 6% of the population. Western tribes of Fur, Daju, Maslit, and Zaghawa account for the balance of the population, 10% to 12%, and are Muslim nomads who speak Arabic, although they retain their non-Arabic dialects.

It is generally accepted that the establishment of the Kushite kingdom about the 12th century B.C. marks the beginning of recorded history in Sudan (Lees & Brooks, 1977). Ending Egyptian occupation of north Sudan, the Kushite kingdom controlled most of north central Sudan and lasted until 330 A.D., when invading armies from Aksum brought Christianity to Sudan. Sudan remained Christian until the 7th century A.D., when waves of Arab Muslims infiltrated the country, initiating an Islamization process that reached full swing in the 15th and 16th centuries with the establishment of the Funji and Fur Sultanates. (Lees & Brooks, 1977).

The 1821 Turk-Egyptian conquest established Sudan, for the first time, as a single administrative unit. Oppressive and corrupt, Turkish rule inspired a militant revolt that resulted in the establishment of the Mahdist state (1885-1898). British reconquest of Sudan in 1889 ended the Mahdiyya and established an Anglo-Egyptian control over the country. The condominium was unique in colonial history. A British-headed government was to be administered by both Egypt and Britain, although in practice, "the government of Sudan was a British affair" (Lee & Brooks, 1977, p. 48). The condominium ended when Britain granted Sudan independence in 1956. Over the 38-year period following independence, Sudan was governed by eight regimes, alternating between civilian and military rule. The common denominator of these regimes was their professed commitment, and subsequent failure, to find a solution to the "southern problem," which erupted in civil wars in 1956 and 1983.

THE PROBLEM

Like the majority of African states, Sudan is essentially an artificial creation of European colonialism. Indeed, some historians argue that it is even "more recent than most" (O'Fahey & Spaulding, 1974, p. 234). Lacking a shared identity, the inhabitants of Sudan identified themselves by their tribes and subtribes or by their religion; they never thought of themselves as Sudanese (Al-Rahim, 1970). This diffused sense of loyalty found its profound expression in the current ethnocultural divide between north and south. Divided by religion, race, region, language, and history, the Arab-like Muslim north and the largely animist Negroid south have emerged as two distinct areas. They differ not only in racial and cultural systems but in all conceivable ways. The depth of the ethnocultural schism in Sudan is portrayed eloquently by a Southern leader, Jaden, who argued that "there is nothing in common between north and south; no shared beliefs; no identity of interests . . . and above all, the Sudan has failed to compose a single community" (Shepherd, 1966, p. 201). Thus, since independence, the African-Arab schism has

emerged as the fundamental problem that besets efforts at national unity and political integration in Sudan (Wai, 1981). This chapter will now turn its attention to the various scholarly opinions regarding the determinants of that divide.

▶ The Influenc of British Colonial Policy

Mayall and Simpson (1992) attribute the collapse of efforts to forge a sense of national unity in postindependence Sudan to what they term "the differential impact of colonialism" (p. 8). Noting that "nations need myths to live by" (p. 15), they argue that Sudan, like most former colonial states, lacks a shared sense of origin and destiny among its various ethnocultural groupings. Mayall and Simpson argue that the outcome of independence was determined largely by the differing impact of colonial policy on the degree of cultural cohesion among the country's two main ethnocultural groups. Adopting a distinctly different set of administrative policies toward the north and south, the British interregnum "reinforced an existing sense of separateness amongst ethnic groups" (Mayall & Simpson, 1992, p. 19) that left the south effectively sealed off from outside influence, whereas the north was encouraged to develop as Islamized Arabic identity.

Mayall and Simpson (1992) contend that, although southern resentment toward the northern Arabs predated the period of British administration (1898-1956), British colonial policy formalized the north-south divide. Through a British colonial policy that divided the country into two parts and treated each part differently, the condominium also widened the existing north-south divide. Thus, in the north, British policy allowed a form of Arab-Muslim nationalism to develop, whereas no such nationalistic development was encouraged in the south. There, the British relied heavily on Lugard's philosophy of indirect rule, forging a colonial policy that "militated against the unification of the country and the early development of a modern nationalist movement" (Mayall & Simpson, 1992, p. 20).

Under the provisions of this policy, Arabic was prohibited, and all Arabic names were removed. Christian missionaries were excluded from the north but permitted to preach in the south. Mayall and Simpson contend that the provisions regarding religious activity were particularly influential in enforcing religious divisions in Sudan. As a result of missionary activity in the south, they argue, "ethnic differences between northern Arabs and southern Africans were reinforced by a religious difference" (Mayall & Simpson, 1992, p. 21).

The view that the north-south divide was mostly the product of separatist British colonial policy is especially common among northern scholars. Khalid (1985), for example, charges that the colonial heritage "played a leading role in undermining the possibility of establishing . . . national unity" (p. 55). Khalid argues that British colonialists relied on the principle of divide and rule to facilitate the administration of Sudan and created a policy based on "treating the south and north as two separate parts" (p. 55). One particular aspect of that policy—the Closed Districts Ordinance—was particularly significant in facilitating the communal divide between the two regions. Implemented as early as 1922, this ordinance virtually isolated the south from any contact with northern values and, thus, hindered the emergence of political consensus between north and south (Khalid, 1985).

The northern view that the British colonial heritage bears the lion's share of responsibility for Sudan's schism is best articulated by Abd al Rahim (1970). Al Rahim attributes the influence of the colonial heritage to a British policy that was designed to "feed separatist particularism instead of Sudanese nationalism" (p. 237). According to Abd Al Rahim, British policy influenced the development of separate Sudanese identities in two distinct but related ways. In the first stage, British colonialists deliberately fostered a northern identity based on an Arab-Muslim symbolism. Fearful of neo-mahdist revivalism in the north, the British administration showed sensitivity to the Arab-Islamic sentiments of the north and even considered itself Islamic. Similarly, argues Al Rahim, the British encouraged the formation of a northern nationalist identity "in order to keep the Egyptians out of the country, so as to maintain Britain's control over the Sudan" (p. 239). By adopting the same symbolism that the Egyptians relied on to unite the Nile Valley under Egyptian rule, the British hoped to undercut Egypt's influence in Sudan. The end result of this aspect of British policy, argues Al Rahim, was the institutionalization of a northern nationalism that was different not only from that of Egypt but also, and even more so, from those nationalisms that existed in the south. There, the focus of colonial policy took a different aim; southern policy was to effectively keep the south insulated from northern influences. Introduced in the 1920s and vigorously pursued until 1946, the southern policy aimed at the "elimination of all traces of Muslim-Arabic culture in the south and the substitution of tribal customs, Christianity, and the English language" (Al Rahim, 1970, p. 239). The result of this policy was to accord the south "a character and outlook different from that of the country as a whole" (Al Rahim, 1970, p. 241). The outcome, Al Rahim explains, was consistent with long-term British policy, which aimed at separating the south from Sudan and lumping it together with British colonial possessions in Kenya and Uganda to create a great colonial East African Federation.

The northern view that British colonial policy bears the prime responsibility for the north-south divide lacks conclusive evidence. The literature presents considerable evidence that British colonial policy clearly militated against the emergence of a national consensus for unity in the south (Shepherd, 1966). As a prominent historian of British colonial policy in Sudan points out, the British "appeared content to ignore the southern Sudan," and thus, "little if any economic development had taken place" (Collins, 1961, p. 126). A southern scholar, Deng (1992), points out that British southern policy has "confirmed, reinforced and deepened the north-south dualism" (p. 71).

But although all this is true, it might be an oversimplification to conclude, as do Al Rahim and the majority of northern scholars, that the British colonial policy is the primary reason for the north-south divide. To the contrary, the British did not create the political, cultural, and religious differences between the peoples of the south and north. These differences, as Shepherd (1966) pointed out, "have a continuity over a long period of time" (p. 211). Needless to say, the British exploited these differences, even reinforced and deepened them, as Deng argued. As such, they do bear a considerable responsibility in the development of the communal divide in Sudan. But, contrary to northern views, such responsibility cannot be seen as the sole reason for the divide. To argue that point is to obscure the contribution of other relevant factors, such as insensitive attitudes in the north toward southern particularism and developmental needs. Whatever the extent of the damage that British policy caused, that policy cannot be extended to the period following Britain's departure from Sudan. Over that 38-year period of independence, northern practices might have confirmed and consolidated the north-south divide no less than British policy had.

▶ Influence of Postindependence Northern Policy

Some scholars argue that the postindependence northern elite's assault on diversity resulted in deepening the north-south divide. Specifically, proponents of this view suggest that separatism in southern Sudan was largely produced by southerners' fears of subjection by the dominant Arabic north that controls the state in Sudan. Thus, the Arabs' systematic attempts to absorb minorities are argued to have resulted in the formation of a dissident subnationalism in the south and the deepening of Sudan's communal divide.

The view that relates southern separatism to insensitive policies of northern govern-

ments is particularly prevalent among interpretations of southern scholars. Long victimized by northern elements, these scholars tend to view the south-north divide as a natural consequence of historical efforts by northern Arabs to subjugate and dominate the south. Specifically, they relate the current communal divide to the 19th century's practices of such men as Al Zubair Pasha Raham and other *jallabas* (Arab slave traders), who enslaved southerners in great numbers.

This group's views are perhaps best represented by Dunstan Wai (1981). A southern historian, Wai argues that the communal divide and militant separatism in the south are largely the product of a continual assault by successive northern governments on cultural diversity in postindependence Sudan. This school of thought argues that forcible efforts by successive northern governments to unify and integrate postcolonial Sudan have resulted in policies that threatened the southern African, non-Muslim identity. That is so because, according to Wai, successive northern regimes had a tendency to impose Arabic and Islamic values forcibly on the south, "giving the system an internal colonialist character" (Wai, 1981, p. 26). Subsequently, subordinate ethnic groups in the African south were pressured to accepted their north-determined lot at the bottom of the social pyramid. Threatened by the prospect of losing their ethnocultural identity, southerners not surprisingly opted to resist this cultural colonialism and to seek south self-rule, Wai argues.

Terming this tendency a "basic feature of northern cosmology," Wai (1981) quotes a former prime-minister, Sadiq El Mahdy, who stated in 1966 that "the dominant feature of our nation is an Islamic one and its overwhelming expression in Arabic" (p. 34). In light of such attitudes on the part of one of the north's most conciliatory leaders, Wai and others who share his view argue that it is hardly surprising that the communal divide between north and south has continued to widen. The tendency of northern elites to deculture the south, argues Wai, continued even during times of political reconciliation between north and south. Thus, after a 1973 peace accord that granted the south self-rule, the northern government of Gafar Nimeiri breached the Addis Ababa Accords by introducing Islamic laws, *Sharia,* to the largely non-Muslim south. The result was an intensification of southern fears of northern cultural imperialism and a subsequent renewal of a separatist insurgency.

In a different but related vein, Lesch (1990) and Shepherd (1966) argue that lack of effective power sharing between north and south was decisive in fueling southern separatism. Shepherd points out that postindependent governments were overwhelmingly north-dominated, with disproportionately low southern representation. Similarly, he argues that the southern share of economic resources was extremely low. For example, not only has the bulk of economic activity, including major commercial and manufacturing centers, been located in the central-north, but no similar efforts were undertaken in the south. Likewise, Shepherd points to the disproportionately small educational opportunities allocated to the south. For example, a full decade after independence, the south still had only 7 secondary and 27 intermediate schools, compared with 88 secondary and 175 intermediary schools established in the north. Given this terrible imbalance in resource distribution, Shepherd concludes that the north has marginalized the south economically. According to Shepherd, one aspect of such marginalization has been particularly influential in deepening southern resentment toward the north. Economically retarded, the south continued to be a major source of cheap labor to the north. Performing menial tasks at lower wages, these laborers live in poor conditions, and they exist in a hostile social climate (Shepherd, 1966).

Lesch (1990) also cities regionally imbalanced resource allocation as "fundamental to the conflict between north and south" (p. 414). She argues that the imbalances in postindependence distribution of resources fostered a southern dependency on financial aid from the north. Their autonomy being "compromised by this dependency,"

Lesch argues that southerners were particularly embittered by their failure to obtain a major share of natural resources located in their region. She argues that two development projects were particularly instructive regarding northern exploitation of southern resources without regard to the south's developmental priorities: The Jonglei Canal and the oil fields in Bantiu.

The first involved constructing a 360-kilometer canal to drain the extensive Sudd and increase the White Nile supply of water. However, the increase in water supply was to benefit mainly northern Sudan and Egypt, which bore half the construction cost (Lesch, 1990). Moreover, the proposed canal would have negative environmental and social impacts on the south, "disrupt[ing] grazing patterns for cattle [and thus] harming the livelihood of nomadic tribes nearby" (Lesch, 1990, p. 415). The other project, involving oil, "has been even more contentious" (p. 419). In 1997, major discoveries of oil in Bantiu (the Upper Nile) raised southerners' hope that oil would provide their region with a much-needed source of revenue to stimulate development. However, "they quickly became suspicious of the northern efforts to claim the oil for themselves" (Lesch, 1990, p. 421). These fears proved true when the government attempted to redraw boundaries so that Bantiu would be shifted to the north and announced its intention to refine the oil in the north, instead of producing on-site as economic logic would suggest. Despite southern denunciation of both the canal and the oil plan, the government went ahead, leading to southern militant harassment of production efforts in 1983, right before a full-scale civil war erupted again in the south. Successfully halting both projects, southern rebels demanded that "regional resources must be used to promote local development and raise deprived regions to the level of the favored areas" (Lesch, 1990, p. 423). Given the bleak reality of economic retardation in the south, the logic of this statement leaves nothing else to be said.

In a similar context, another scholar, Deng (1990, 1992) argues that the south's victimization by successive northern governments is not limited to economic deprivation; it extends to power sharing. Deng argues that inequalities in power sharing between north and south have been a consistent fracture in independent Sudan, confirming northern views of the south's subordinate role. For example, in 1955, 800 posts held previously by colonial personnel were turned over to Sudan citizens, but the south was accorded only 4 junior positions (Deng, 1989). The same pattern, Deng argues, continued steadily, with virtually all civilian governments being north dominated. The latest government, formed in 1988, included three southerners assigned to the least important portfolios: transport, labor, and water resources. The south's limited role in government decision making is further emphasized by the continued absence of southerners from critical national institutions such as railway and river transport authorities. Worse yet, even the head of Juba University, the only college in the south, has always been a northerner.

This northern dominance and disregard for the south's needs, Lesch (1990) argues, have "underlined the political and economic marginality of the south" (p. 424). Such northern dominance and southern marginalization, she reports, have played a crucial role in widening the north-south divide because southerners view their treatment as "a new dimension of the 'Jallaba mentality' that has seen the south as a source for the extraction of wealth but never as a real political partner in the future of Sudan" (Lesch, 1990, p. 424).

▶ The Religion Factor

According to Deng (1992, p. 2), the dispute over the relationship between religion and state "has emerged as the most controversial" dividing line between southern and northern perspectives on a Sudanese identity. One particular issue with regard to religion was identified by some scholars (Deng, 1992; Lobban, 1990; Voll, 1990) as the most crucial factor in crystallizing the postindependence ethnocultural divide between north and south Sudan. This issue pertains to the role of the

Sharia (Islamic laws), which, carried to its logical conclusion, means the creation of an Islamic state in Sudan.

Francis Deng (1992) reports that with regard to this role, a northern consensus has always linked the identity of Sudan to an Islamic character. Deng argues that this view, best articulated during the Mahdist state (1885-1898), dates back to the Funj Sultanate in the 16th century and carries on to the present day's northern vision of a Sudanese identity. Thus "the dominant political forces in the north . . . range from an almost absolute commitment to Sharia to ambivalent modifications in accommodation of the non-Muslim south" (Deng, 1992, p. 3).

Deng (1990) views the way in which Islam came to be identified with northern identity as the outcome of "a historical process characterized by stratification of races, ethnicity, cultures, religions in favor of Arabism and Islam" (p. 497). According to Deng, the stratifying process of Arabization dates back to the 7th century and was intensified by the coming of Islam to what is now Sudan. Economically advantageous and culturally coherent, northern Arabized Muslims soon "turned the system to their advantage" and prevailed over non-Muslim elements. As a result, Islam was established "as superior to the local religious beliefs and even to Christianity, which Islam recognized but was supposed to have superseded" (Deng, 1990, pp. 599-600).

In due time, the outcome of a dual process of Arabization and Islamization was the gradual transformation of north Sudanese identity into a society that is completely different from the rest of the country. Thus, in racial, cultural, and religious terms, the north became an integrated mold that is Arabic and "deeply religious in [its] indigenized version of Islam" (Deng, 1990, p. 602). Unlike many African countries with similar experiences, Sudan experienced an Islamization associated with Arabism as "a composite concept of race, ethnicity, and culture" (Deng, 1990, p. 602).

Arabic and Islamic cultural forces provided the north with an integrated community that was, according to Deng, decisive in the formation of northern identity. The same forces, however, also worked to hinder the reconciliation of northern and southern perspectives on a Sudanese identity. That is so, according to Deng, because the integrating Arabic and Islamic forces did not extend to the south. The south was physically isolated from Arab and Islamic influences and resisted them. Subsequently, the historical force that might have integrated north and south— Islamization and Arabization— worked only to produce a greater stratification between the two regions. Finally, racial division between north and south along class lines points to what many scholars (Deng, 1990; Johnson, 1989; Kasfir, 1990; Wai, 1981) have considered a lasting impact of the Arab slave trade in the South.

▶ The Influence of the Slave Trade

The view that the Arab slave trade in the south contributed to the south-north divide is perhaps best articulated by Nelson Kasfir (1990). The 19th-century slave trade is frequently mentioned by scholars as a historical factor that contributed to the emergence of hostility between north and south. Yet, Nelson Kasfir distinguishes his treatment by the racial and class elements he attaches to the slave trade. Kasfir suggests that the slave trade, which began in southern Sudan as early as 1841 and was largely the work of Arabs, resulted in the creation of social stratification between racial classes of servants and masters. Kasfir argues that the ideological basis for this cleavage was based only partially in Islamic traditions that permit the enslavement of non-Muslims captured in wars. The other justification, he seems to imply, must have been the Arabs' assumption of racial superiority vis-à-vis the conquered Negroid southerners. This was particularly the case during periods when the pretext of war could not have provided grounds for enslavement because southerners were in alliance with northern Arabs. Kasfir cites as case in point the large-scale slavery campaigns that took place during the Mahdist state. Despite the south-

ern support for the Mahdist revolt against the Ottoman rule in the 1880s, "the Mahdi's followers encouraged the slavery of 'infidels' more widely and ruthlessly than before" (Kasfir, 1990, p. 68). The end result of these practices, argues Kasfir, was to deepen the racial and class-based division between north and south in terms of region and religion. That was so, argues Kasfir, because the racially motivated violence of slavery "made race, religion, region, and ethnicity markers of social stratification long after slavery was prohibited" (p. 73). In other words, the Arab slave trade had the effect of institutionalizing Arabs' perception of racial superiority toward the Negroid southerners and resulted in the creation of permanent classes of advantaged and disadvantaged.

Douglas Johnson (1989) also cites the large-scale enslavement of southern people by northern traders as an important factor that contributed to postindependence difficulties of forging national unity in Sudan. Examining the impact of military slavery on social life in Sudan, Johnson argues that military slavery and institutions had a long history in precolonial southern Sudan. Johnson points out that military slavery in southern Sudan came into existence at the same time such practices disappeared from the Islamic heartlands, with the massacres of the Mamluks in Egypt in 1811. Johnson argues that, although military slavery acquired a vigor through Mohammad Ali's invasion of Sudan in 1820s, its existence predates that invasion, with "the independent Sudanese Kingdoms of Sennar, Funji, and Darfur all [having] used slave soldiers before the Egyptian conquest" (p. 76). Such practices also continued into the Mahdist state (1885-1898), whose standing army contained a significant proportion of slave soldiers, particularly in its rifle division, known as *Jihadiyyahs* (Johnson, 1989).

According to Johnson (1989), precolonial Sudanese recruited slaves for their armies in three ways. The first was through the agency of large, well-organized military campaigns that scoured the hinterlands of Sudan looking for slave military recruits. This was the pre-ferred method during the time of high demand for slave soldiers. When such demand for soldiers subsided, either because the states had secured enough slave recruits or were experiencing a relative peace, "the army played less of a role in raiding . . . and relied more on its nomadic subjects, who frequently had to pay their tribute in slaves" (p. 80). The third way in which precolonial Sudanese states in the north acquired slaves was through the "contribution" of northern slave merchants to the state's armies. This was particularly true during the Mahdist state, which enlisted the support of some *jallabas* (northern slave traders). When these jallabas joined the camps of the Mahdi, they brought along with them large numbers of slave soldiers they already "possessed." The jallabas acquired slaves through massive slave raiding from what are now the three southern provinces of the Sudan. These raids were undertaken by commercial companies who based themselves in armed camps, or *Zara'ib* (singular *Zariba*).

Even though the methods by which slaves were enlisted into the armies of precolonial Sudanese states differed, Johnson argues that the net impact was the same. Military slavery in precolonial Sudan was racially motivated and carried by and for state agencies. Through that racist practice, argues Johnson (1989), the northern states have long "defined . . . their relations with non-Arab groups or categories" (p. 82). What emerged from that definition, Johnson argues, was essentially a northern view that has always regarded southerners as former slaves and, hence, subordinates. As for their part, the descendants of former slave soldiers remain, in many ways, incompletely assimilated by the nation in which they now reside. Indeed, thousands of them have sought to escape the subordinating prospect of such assimilation by crossing the Sudan-Uganda border, obtaining Ugandan nationality, and joining the Ugandan army. Many thousands more remained behind, according to Johnson, continuing to feel alienated from a state that enslaved their fathers. This alienation, argues Johnson, was the lasting social legacy that

military slavery in precolonial Sudan has left behind: a group of people who, due to their past subordinate roles, found it extremely difficult, or altogether undesirable, to assimilate into "their" modern state. It is in this sense, argues Johnson, that military slavery by precolonial Sudanese states has contributed to the south-north divide.

▶ Conclusion

This chapter has attempted to survey the literature on the historiography of the north-south divide and the subsequent rise of militant separatism in southern Sudan. Testifying to the complexity of this phenomenon, the literature surveyed advances many possible explanations for the communal divide in pre-independence Sudan. These explanations range from the impact of a preferential British colonial policy on the administrative development of separate regional identities to the influence of more recent factors, such as insensitivity of northern authorities to the south's cultural particularism and developmental needs. Other factors cited as possible determinants for the African-Arab schism in Sudan include the role played by the 19th-century Arab slave trade in creating southern hostility and resentment, even suspicion of northern intents. The literature also points to the influence of a similar southern fear regarding the north's commitment to the creation of an Islamic state in Sudan.

This multiplicity of historical factors associated with the emergence and continuity of Sudan's communal divide also suggests the difficulty of resolving Africa's integration problems. Whereas some of these factors, such as northern assault on cultural diversity, are clearly identified and, hence, easy to remedy, other factors defy such straight answers. For example, the long-standing racially motivated exploitation of the south has left behind deep scars in the southern psyche, scars that are difficult to eradicate. Taken together, the multiplicity and complexity of these factors suggest that the resolution to Africa's integration dilemmas requires, short of a miracle, a political leadership that is willing to put the interest of the nation above sectarian and tribal calculation. Without such a political commitment to pluralism, Africa's communal divides are likely to persist, with considerable human and material costs.

As for shortcomings exhibited in the literature, perhaps the most serious is the tendency of some scholars to identify a single factor as the cause of the divide. Like all complex social phenomena, communal divides, including the one surveyed by this study, defy such monocausality. Most often, such issues are explainable, not by simple and single answers, but by a complex of causality. This does not imply that all factors weigh the same in explaining a historiographical phenomenon, leading to the other major shortcoming noticed in the literature surveyed. Although most of the works studied exhibit a tendency to identify more than one factor as possible reasons for the divide, few, if any, show serious efforts to synthesize and order them. This lack of synthesis points to the need for future scholarly efforts to fill this gap.

▶ References

Al Rahim, A. M. (1970). Arabism, Africanism, and self-identification in the Sudan. *Journal of Modern African Studies, 8*(2), 233-249.

Collins, R. O. (1961). Early British administration in the southern Sudan. *Journal of African History, 2*(1), 123-135.

Deng, F. M. (1989). The identity factor in the Sudanese conflict. In J. V. Montville (Ed.), *Conflict and peacemaking in multi-ethnic societies.* Lexington, MA: Lexington Books.

Deng, F. M. (1990). War of visions for the nation. *Middle East Journal, 44*(4), 597-609.

Deng, F. M. (1992, January 15). *Sudan: An action memorandum.* Unpublished paper prepared for the International Negotiation Network.

Johnson, D. (1989). The structure of a legacy: Military slavery in northwest Africa. *Ethnohistory, 36*(1), 72-88.

Kasfir, N. (1990). Peacemaking and social cleavages in Sudan. In J. V. Montville (Ed.), *Conflict and peacemaking in multi-ethnic societies.* New York: Lexington.

Khalid, M. (1985, July-August). Sudan: A plea for pluralism. *Africa Report,* pp. 53-57.

Lees, F., & Brooks, H. (1977). *The economic and political development of the Sudan.* Boulder, CO: Westview.

Lesch, A. M. (1990). Confrontation in the southern Sudan. *The Middle East Journal, 44*(4), 410-429.

Lobban, C. (1990). Islamization in Sudan: A critical assessment. *Middle East Journal, 44*(4), 610-625.

Mayall, J., & Simpson, M. (1992). Reflections on secessionism in the Third World: The cases of southern Sudan and Eritrea. *International Journal of Comparative Sociology, 32*(1-2), 5-25.

O'Fahey, R. S., & Spaulding, J. L. (1974). *The kingdom of the Sudan.* London: Methuen.

Shepherd, G. W. (1966). National integration and the southern Sudan. *The Journal of Modern African Studies, 4*(2), 193-212.

Voll, J. O. (1990). Sudan: State and society in crisis. *The Middle East Journal, 44*(4), 575-579.

Wai, D. (1981). *The African-Arab conflict in the Sudan.* London: Holmes & Meier.

An Analysis of Discourse
on the Spoken and Written Words

A Historical Comparison
of European and African Views

AMA MAZAMA

lthough most African people today are—at least in theory—no longer subjected to colonial rule, either in Africa or in the Americas, we find ourselves in a state of mental subjugation that prevents us from fully recovering our integrity. The reason for this is that colonization was not simply an economic enterprise but also a process of mental distortion and confusion that continues unabated. The end result is what Wade Nobles (1978, cited in Akbar, 1984, p. 396) has aptly referred to as "conceptual incarceration," that is, the disruption and displacement of our conceptual universe by European ideas. Furthermore, Europe's conceptual tyranny has been all the more effective in that it has gone unacknowledged.

Europeans have not hesitated to talk about a "European miracle" to describe their own development. It is, indeed, widely accepted that Europe, due to some unique quality, has rightly assumed leadership of the world, opening the path toward progress, that is, perfection and happiness for all. There is no agreement, however, about the nature of that unique European quality responsible for the European miracle. Different possible causes —sexual continence, biology, culture, the physical environment, the church, rationality, the family structure—have been suggested. The Eurocentric discourse on the word, written and spoken, plays a major part in the rationality argument.

It is this chapter's aim to contrast the European predilection for the written word with the African preference for the spoken word. Whereas the former is based on the fundamental epistemological assumption that one knows best through separation between what is to be known and the knower, the latter is generated by a worldview within which the spoken word, *Nommo,* has powerful generative powers.

However, because of the common European ethnocentrism mentioned above, the written word, that is, literacy, has often been presented as absolutely superior, whereas the spoken word, that is, orality, was, and still is to a great extent, associated with cognitive and social backwardness. This chapter argues against such a reductionist and poor understanding of orality by insisting that both literacy and orality must be understood within their proper cultural context, making relative the alleged superior effects of writing.

More generally, this chapter relates to the present volume as it takes a holistic approach to the language phenomenon. It is, indeed, impossible to appreciate the richness of language by simply dismissing orality. After all, only a few languages of the world are written. One can only ignore the importance of orality at the expense of a true appreciation of the depth of the human experience as expressed through the spoken word.

The discussion presented in this chapter will be organized as follows: European claims about the superiority of the written word will be reviewed, followed by an analysis of the arguments presented to support those claims. We will then proceed to examine the Eurocentric discourse on the written and the spoken word within its proper historical and cultural context. This section will be followed by a cultural analysis of the African understanding of the power of the spoken word.

▶ Writing as a Superior Tool

Writing, it is said, having some special effects on the brain, triggers and enhances rationality. Europeans are the most literate people, explaining their greater cognitive power and precocious progress. This is, needless to say, an ethnocentric position, according to which those "stuck" in orality cannot hope to progress, unless they become literate.

The idea that writing plays a special role in human development has permeated European thinking. Popper (1972), for instance, distinguishes between three Worlds, World I, the physical world; World 2, the world of our conscious experiences; and World 3, the world of the logical content of books, libraries, computer memories, and so on. World 3 is the world of theories and intellectual discoveries, in other words, of critical thinking. Popper further argues that without World 3, "full consciousness of self" (p. 74) can never be achieved. A similar point is made by Ong (1986): "Writing is utterly invaluable and indeed essential for the realization of fuller, interior, human potentials" (p. 25). The reason for this is that writing itself is responsible for logical and abstract thinking. We know, writes Ong (1986)

> that all philosophy depends on writing because all elaborate, linear, so-called "logical" explanation depends on writing. Oral persons can be as wise, as wise as anyone, and they can, of course, give some explanation for things. But the elaborate, intricate, seemingly endless but exact cause-effect sequences required by what we call philosophy and by extension scientific thinking are unknown among oral peoples. (p. 43)

The underlying epistemological assumption that one can know only through reason should be noted at this point. This unrestricted and rather naive faith in reason has characterized the Europeans at least since their so-called period of Enlightenment, and it should therefore be considered within their particular historical and cultural context. In other words, there is no particular reason to assume a priori that all the peoples of the world would or should place such a high emphasis on reason. The key issue here remains, however, whether or not writing has such a powerful cognitive effect, a question that I shall address later.

Writing, thus, is held responsible by many for European progress, starting with the Greeks and their supposed creation and generalized adoption of the alphabet:

> The development of an easy system of writing (easy both in terms of the materials employed and the signs used) was more than a mere precondition of the Greek achievement: It influenced its whole nature and development in fundamental ways. (Goody & Watt, 1963/1977, p. 67)

This view is widely shared, for example, by Havelock (1976) and by Ong (1986), for whom

> The invention of logic, it seems, is tied not to any kind of writing system but the completely vocalic phonetic alphabet and the intensive analytic activity which such an alphabet demands of its inventors and subsequently encourages in all sorts of noetic fields. (pp. 40-41)

Also, from Ong's perspective, "All formal logic in the world, down to that used for computers, stems from the ancient Greeks" (p. 41).

The alphabet is, indeed, deemed the best writing system ever created. This specific characterization was required, for white people, it is well known, did not invent writing. However, by crediting Europeans with the creation and use of an absolutely superior system, scholars might feel safe to argue that whites' late arrival on the scene of human civilization was compensated for by their technical superiority. Stubbs (1980, pp. 46-57), for example, went so far as to try to dismiss pictographic systems (such as Kemetic hieroglyphs) as not being "true writing systems," which comprise logographic (e.g., the Chinese system) and phonological (e.g., the Greek alphabet) systems, the latter being superior, needless to say. Goody and Watt (1963/1977, p. 38), for their part, have suggested grouping logographic and pictographic systems together, declaring that phonological systems are "unique." Such distinctions are highly arbitrary (and idiosyncratic), for in reality, there are no fundamental differences between pictographic, logographic, and phonological scripts: All are abstractions to the extent that they refer to something that is absent.

Without writing, and more specifically, without the alphabet, individual cognitive development is supposedly greatly hampered. According to Olson (1977), for example, "oral" people are unable to go beyond the Piagetian concrete operational stage, and this again because oral language "is an instrument of limited power to explore ideas" (p. 278). The oral mind is quintessentially "prescientific." In fact, mental/cultural primitiveness and orality go hand in hand. Writing, Parsons (1966) tells us, marks "the fateful development out of primitiveness" (p. 26). Or, as Olson (1977) puts it, "Speech makes us human, and literacy makes us civilised" (p. 258).

Those last statements, which explicitly link writing to civilization, lead us to consider the alleged effects of writing, not only at the individual level but also at the group level. By far the most dramatic effect that writing has on a particular community is said to be the entry of that community into history. History, it is commonly argued, starts with writing. Stubbs (1980) puts it squarely: "Without writing, science and history are inconceivable, since at one stroke, writing overcomes the limitations of human memory" (p. 193). Thus, any event taking place prior to or independent of the use of writing by a particular group is dismissed as "prehistorical" (Prieswerk & Perrot, 1978, p. xxi). In reality, it is rather simple: People without writing have myths. After writing has been introduced in their midst, they have history. Quite predictably, many people are still defined, in 2000, as mythical and prehistorical. This particular criterion—that knowledge

must be transmitted through a written medium—has often been used to dismiss the his-
toricalness of Africa, as pointed out by Keita
(1977).

> Until quite recently, it was generally believed
> that the concept of history was alien to African
> societies. Bearing unsubstantiated stereotypi-
> cal views about African society in general, evi-
> dence for the argument that African peoples
> were traditionally ahistorical was produced by
> pointing to the fact there was no tradition of
> written history in Africa. (p. 141)

The main reason why oral people are supposedly not historical—that is, they do not
move (forward)—is because each generation
of oral people must literally start anew. With
writing, Stubbs (1980) tells us, "accurate records can be kept of discoveries, inventions,
theories, and blind alleys, and each generation
no longer has to begin from scratch or from
what the previous generation can remember
and pass on" (p. 103). Ong (1986) further confirms that oral people are so busy remembering basic things that exploratory thinking is "a
luxury orality can little afford, for energies
must be husbanded to keep on constant call
the evanescent knowledge that the ages so la-
boriously accumulated" (p. 25). Hence, oral
people have a primitive and hopeless cyclical
conception of time. This combines with the
cognitive limitations of oral peoples to explain their mental, cultural, and historical
stagnation, as opposed to the spectacular and
brilliant evolution of the Europeans.

Orality, we are told by Europeans, further
accounts for the lack of complex social organization and administration in such cultures.
Indeed, Ong asserts (1986), "Administration
is unknown in oral cultures, where leaders
interact nonabstractly with the rest of society
in tight-knit, often rhetorically controlled,
configurations" (p. 40). In a similar fashion,
some have also suggested that a 40% literacy
rate is necessary for "take-off," that is, for "development" to occur. This was the rationale
behind UNESCO's push for "functional literacy" in the 1960s. In its search for solutions to
underdevelopment, UNESCO recommended
that underdeveloped adults be made at least
partially literate as a first and indispensable
step toward modernization.

▶ Arguments for the Superiority of Writing

Having reviewed the allegedly miraculous effects of writing on both individuals and the
group to which they belong, it is only fair to
expect some truly brilliant argumentation and
indisputable evidence from the literate minds
of the European scholars cited thus far. Unfortunately, such expectations are not met.
First, let me explain that my purpose here is
not to try to defend oral people, for they need
no such defense. To try to demonstrate that
oral people are not intellectually and culturally impaired would be to accept the Eurocentric universe of discourse, give up agency,
display a total ignorance of our past and present achievements, and entertain the idea of
African inferiority, all of which are unacceptable in my view. I would rather question the
internal consistency of the Eurocentric discourse on writing and analyze its epistemological premises.

The grandiose claims made about the impact of writing and literacy have not been con-
vincingly argued at all. Instead, most of the
time, a succession of strong statements like
those quoted above (as well as many others
not quoted here for lack of space) are presented without any proof to validate them, or
with very weak and confused justifications.

For instance, the main reason that writing
is supposed to play a key role in the development of critical thinking is that, as Ong (1986)
puts it, "Writing separates the known from the
knower" (p. 37). The written text is "objective," with a built-in, given, explicit, and immutable meaning, "whereas oral cultures tend
to merge interpretation with data" (Ong, 1986,
p. 38). Olson (1977) confirms that "an explicit
writing system [the alphabet] unambiguously
represents meanings—the meaning is in the
text" (p. 264). In fact, whereas written lan-

guage's main function is the communication of information, it is argued that oral language has a strong phatic function. In other words, through orality, people do not say anything meaningful, they simply establish contact with one another. On the other hand, by allowing people to distance themselves from what they read or write, writing supposedly promotes critical attitudes and objectivity. This is fantasy of the highest order, but one nonetheless quite consistent with the European belief in "objectivity," which can be obtained only through the separation of the knower and the known, coupled with the objectification of the latter. Marimba Ani (1994) has cogently written about this European epistemological emphasis on separation, which is clearly illustrated in Ong's (1986) statement that

> Between knower and known, writing interposes a visible and tangible object, the text. The objectivity of the text helps impose objectivity on what the text refers to (see Olson). Eventually, writing will create a state of mind in which knowledge itself can be thought of as an object, distinct from the knower. (p. 36)

Ong's arguments is, of course, unintelligible: Objectification (of the text) does not constitute objectivity.

Similarly, the idea that writing makes meaning ever stable, given, objective, and conserved through the ages is a ludicrous one. It has been very seriously undermined by Europeans themselves, in particular those belonging to the poststructuralist school of thought. Meaning is, indeed, the most elusive part of language, always subject to multiple interpretations and reinterpretations. The notion that a written text is value-free and purely factual is another European myth.

With particular respect to history, for which writing is supposedly responsible, and which is, therefore, supposedly based on facts (as opposed to "primitive myths"), it will be terribly devastating to our scholars to learn that "history is necessarily founded on value systems, without which there could be no selection of facts. By making a choice among available data, the historian grants importance, particular value, to the elements selected" (Prieswerk & Perrot, 1978, p. 123). According to the same authors, "The constant reevaluation to which 'historic' facts are subjected by succeeding generations is one of the clearest proofs of the relativity of historic accounts" (p. 121). Clearly, much of what passes for history—and the same could be said about science—are highly fictitious and deeply personal stories. Moreover, African people, whose experiences have been subjected to so many gross and malicious distortions by European historians, can only consider with much skepticism and suspicion any claim to "historical objectivity."

Finally, it is said that the superiority of the alphabet resides in its degree of explicitness, as opposed to the mystery and alleged ambiguity of pictographs, logographs, and syllabary. By spelling everything out (so to speak) in vowels and consonants, the alphabet supposedly renders meaning more concise and clear and, therefore, fosters critical thinking. Again, the shaky and mechanical reasoning behind such argumentation can only be understood within the gross positivistic context within which it emerged. In addition, it is not without internal dangers. What, for example, are the consequences of spelling inconsistencies, so common in European languages, on the brain of European literates? English, for instance, has no less than 11 different ways of spelling the sound *i*: *e, ie, ae, ee, eo, ei, ea, y, oe, ey,* and *i.* French is no better; the sound is spelled *en, ent, em, ents, ens, an, ant, ans, ants, am, amp, amps, anc,* and so on. One would expect that such confusion would interfere with the great analytical skills of English and French speakers. Also, English spelling was not codified until 1650. Until then, there was a great deal of variation. Can we safely conclude that this variation impeded the intellectual development of the British people prior to 1650? And what about the fact that the so-called Latin or Roman (derived from the Greek) alphabet is not purely alphabetic, but a mixture of logographic and alphabetic symbols? Should not the British and other Europeans rid their writing systems of all logographic symbols to become even smarter? All these are, within the simplistic universe created by the Eurocentric discourse on alphabetic writing, quite legitimate and important questions.

In the end, it seems as though the superiority accorded the alphabet by the Europeans is simply an additional attempt at the a posteriori justification of the belief in the superior achievements of the Greeks, that is, of white people. However, Greek civilization certainly was not as original and innovative as some would have us believe. As shown by James (1954/1992) and confirmed by Bernal (1987) more recently, it owed much to the African civilization that developed in Kemet. The very word *philosophy* is not even of Greek origin, but of Egyptian origin (Bernal, 1987, p. 102). This, of course, renders more than dubious the "invention" of philosophy by the Greeks under the influence of the alphabet. In fact, little historical evidence supports the correlation between the introduction of the alphabet in Greece and subsequent developments there (Street, 1984, p. 52). Ironically, prior to the great wave of racism that took over Europe in the 19th century, Europeans themselves, far from glorifying the alphabet, recognized the Egyptian and the Chinese writing systems as superior to their own. The hieroglyphs, in particular, were praised for their deep and rich symbolic meaning (Bernal, 1987, pp. 152, 164).

▶ The Eurocentric Discourse on Writing Within Its Proper Historical and Cultural Context

However, this dramatic change in European views on the respective worth of the different scripts should not be a surprise, for the 19th century witnessed the full development of *diffusionism,* a theory of pivotal importance about the nature and direction of cultural changes on a world scale. It is grounded, Blaut (1993) tells us, in two axioms:

(1) most human communities are uninventive. (2) A few human communities (or places, or cultures) are inventive and thus remain the permanent centres of culture change, of progress. At the global scale, this gives us a model of a world with a single center—roughly, Greater Europe—and a single periphery; as Inside and an Outside. (p. 14)

In its original and classical form, diffusionism argued that European colonialism was "scientifically natural, a matter of the inevitable working out of social laws of human progress" (Blaut, 1993, p. 24). In the 20th century, in particular in the 1940s and 1950s, diffusionism came to be known as *modernization.*

The assumptions and implications have remained the same: Europe, as Jones (1981, p. 257), one of the most ardent defenders of the European miracle thesis, has it, is "a peculiarly inventive society," constantly striving toward increased freedom and progress. Therefore, an imitation of Europe—modernization—is the sure key to salvation. Modernization entails development not only through (Western) science and technique but also through a change in attitudes and behaviors. For instance, people must discard their traditional, irrational attitudes to become "modern," that is, free, rational, and happy. The Indian philosopher Alvares (1979/1991) summarized the whole affair:

> We would be forced to be free, since we did not know the extent of our "bondage" to our past and our traditions. We would be forced to be free from an undue concern for human values of the shared identity of the community. Leading Western intellectuals told us what was wrong with our culture, and which old elements impeded economic development and needed to be discarded. (p. 154)

As one might suspect at this point, orality, and the primitive and prescientific mentality that it supposedly inevitably brings about and fosters, is precisely one of those weaknesses for which remedies are much needed, remedies in the form of literacy programs, language development and planning, and the use of the Roman alphabet (Mazama, 1994). The UNESCO functional literacy program, launched at the 1965 Teheran conference and discussed previously, is a good case in point.

It would be rather naive, however, to imagine that teaching writing (and reading) to "underdeveloped natives" simply entails the teaching of technical skills. In reality, let it be clear that writing (and reading) can never be reduced to the mere acquisition of technical skills; writing and reading also involve a social practice. Street (1984), in particular, has argued against what he calls the autonomous as opposed to the ideological model of literacy. He rightly insists that the act of reading or writing always takes place in a particular context, which ultimately determines its forms, function, and overall significance. In other words, people always read and write something, in a particular context, and for a particular purpose. The effects of literacy must, therefore, be considered within the particular context in which the act of writing and reading takes place. Thus, although it may be true, in some cases, that writing helps raise critical consciousness, a recommendation for which Paulo Freire is famous, most of the time writing and reading have been taught in an effort to domesticate. This was true of 19th- century Europe and North America, where new patterns of thought and behavior, compatible with industrial life (capitalism), had to be instilled in the masses: "To educate the workers was the problem. It was not an education in reading and writing, but rather the need to train them to a new work discipline, permeated with the middle class obsession with character and morality" (Graff, 1987, p. 66).

This link between learning to write and read and acquiring a new ethics became apparent in Africa when missionaries undertook systematic literacy programs. For instance, Frank Laubach, an American Christian missionary otherwise, was known as the "father of literacy" in the 20th century as a result of his relentless elaboration of alphabetic scripts for previously "undevelped" languages throughout the world (Jeffries, 1967). Laubach (1960) explained quite frankly that his work was aimed at protecting "international peace," in other words, the existence of a context favorable to world capitalism. Laubach stated, on one occasion, that

> It will be wonderful or terrifying, depending upon whether these vast multitudes awaken with their hearts full of Christ's love or with their hearts full of hate. They will bless or blast the world. That is why the church must step to the front and take a leading share in the mighty upsurge of the sunken half. We must not only help them rise but we must also put the right kind of reading in their hands; and that is the staggering task. (p. 14)

Laubach had no doubts, however, that the "natives" themselves appreciated his efforts and care. He describes his prospective African (adult) students as "trembling with hope," "hysterical," or "beaming like angels," at the prospect of learning to read and write and, in any case, being saved from "stark-nakedness" and "cannibalism" by white literacy and Christianity:

> The influence of this mission can only be realized when we recall that these lovely, well-dressed, cultured people were stark-naked cannibals a century ago. One of the Africans whom I heard pray in church said, "O God, we were once animals, but now we are people." (Laubach, 1960, p. 214)

Beside the activities of individual church agents like Laubach, the influential and very active Summer Institute of Linguistics, an American-based Christian organization, must be mentioned. The Summer Institute was specifically created in 1934 to deal "scientifically" with the development (including reduction to writing, standardization, and lexical modernization) of "undeveloped languages." The Summer Institute makes no mystery of its ideology: "It describes itself as conservative, evangelical, and fundamentalist. Most of its missionaries are whites from the Midwest and South. Their ideology suggests that Satan and Communism are one and that God, whites, and Americans are on the other side" (Laitin, 1992, pp. 98-99). In addition,

> Charges abound that [the Summer Institue] has, on numerous occasions, acted on behalf of one or another national government, particularly when that government's immediate interests have coincided with American foreign policy designs. Indeed, there are charges that [the Summer Institute] has gone as far as to put its resources at the disposal of U.S.-based multinational corporations and the CIA. (Newmeyer, 1986, pp. 60-61)

Today, the Summer Institute operates in 29 countries, many of which are in Africa: Ghana, Cameroon, Togo, Burkina Faso, Ivory Coast, Ethiopia, Sudan, Kenya, and Chad (Laitin, 1992, p. 99).

What this points to is a clear collusion between the much vaunted benefits of learning to read and write and the deliberate use of literacy as a means of indoctrination into modernity, that is—we may as well face it—into whiteness. The end result of this process of training in the European worldview has been an increased Westernization of the world (Latouche, 1992), whereby paradigms were discarded and at times lost, to be replaced by European ones. This was only possible because the Europeans, with their usual arrogance and ethnocentrism, were successful in invalidating all other people's experiences, while holding their own as superior and universal. The discourse on and teaching of writing, accompanied with the downgrading of orality, must be seen as an integral part of the Eurocentric enterprise of mystification and attempted conversion.

However, to what exactly are we supposed to convert? An analysis of the epistemological premises on which the European discourse on the word, spoken and written, rests is in order. By all accounts, the European understanding of language, of the spoken and written word, reflects the mechanistic paradigm that has dominated and informed European culture since the 17th century at least.

According to this paradigm, articulated by Descartes under the influence of Copernicus and Galileo, the whole world is a machine:

> To Descartes the material universe was a machine and nothing but a machine. There was no purpose, life, or spirituality in matter. Nature worked according to mechanical laws, and everything in the material world could be explained in terms of the arrangement and movement of the parts. (Capra, 1982, p. 60)

Having established a strict separation between the mind and the body, Descartes suggested that the human body itself was a machine. Hobbes, another influential Western philosopher, went a step further by arguing that the mind was another body in motion. In this view, "consciousness is interpreted as motion reducible to changes within the body system" (Brian, 1991, p. 21).

Thus, what resulted was a fragmented, one-dimensional understanding of life, reduced to its physical, visible manifestations. Positivism, the dominant epistemological mode in the West, rests on the exclusion of that which cannot be apprehended through the five physical senses identified by Europeans. Furthermore, distance between what is to be known and the knower is seen as indispensable for true knowledge to be gained. Likewise, language is described as a body made up of different components (phonemes, morphemes) that are connected according to specific rules that determine the structures of the language in question. This emphasis on the structural aspect was made at the expense of those who speak: people. It was felt that to achieve scientific status, the study of language, linguistics, ought not to preoccupy itself with life issues but should solely engage in the highly abstract exercise of decomposing and recomposing languages. Those who did raise the issue of language and power always did so in a materialistic sense, approaching language as a tool (i.e., external to human beings) used for or against others. In a similar vein, the elaboration of a script for a particular language is seen simply as "reduction to writing," whereas the script itself is presented as a "technical device" to be elaborated by "experts." This purely materialistic, mechanistic approach to language cannot be satisfactory to the Afrocentric person.

▶ The African Understanding of Nommo

It may be necessary, at this point, to remember that for Africans, one of the greatest challenges in life is the mastery of the word (Niane, 1998). Indeed, "through Nommo, the word, man establishes his mastery over things" (Jahn, 1961/1990, p. 132). The central importance placed on the word, on language, by African people has long been recognized as an African cultural characteristic. At the beginning of the world is the word: Diop (1981/1991) reminds us that "Ra is the first God, the first demiurge of history who created through the word" (p. 311). Words are literally the life force, creators and re-creators of reality. Throughout Africa, the metaphysical power of the spoken word, of utterances, has been amply documented, as Drewal (1989/1998) reminds us. For example, in Yoruba culture, "In certain contexts, . . . action verbs literally activate dynamic forces" (Drewal, 1989/1998, p. 256). In the same vein, it is clear that "the sound qualities of verbs, nouns, adjectives, and adverbs in Yoruba incantations often correspond to the dynamic qualities of actions in the natural environment" (Drewal, 1989/1998, p. 257). Generally speaking, Nommo is life force is rhythm, as well-understood by the Negritude poets: "The most salient and constant feature of black African's personality is a function of his conception of life and of the organization of the Universe and his way of reacting to these realities" (Ba, 1973, p. 110).

Given the power of the spoken word, it is not surprising that African people have created what is commonly referred to as an oral tradition of great complexity and magnitude. Djibril Tamsir Niane (1960) explains that the oral tradition represents an essential part of African culture, and he suggests the following typology:

1. Historical traditions, such as epics
2. Literary expressions, such as poems, fables, theater, riddles, and so on
3. Erudite traditions, such as genesis myths, prayers, initiation formulas, knowledge of plants, of the earth, the sky, the universe, and so on

Clearly, the oral tradition encompasses an extensive body of knowledge that only a few, the "Masters of the Word," will be able to master. The beauty and the power of orality can be astounding, as illustrated by the following story reported by Basil Davidson (1959). At the beginning of the 20th century in Africa, the Bushongo leaders told the story of their (oral) people to Torday, a European traveler:

> That was not in the least difficult for them, since remembering the past was one of their duties. They unrolled their story in measured phrases. They went on and on. They were not to be hurried. They traversed the list of their kings, a list of one hundred and twenty names, right back to the god-king whose marvels founded their nation. (p. 3)

It ought to be clear, at this point, that African people have not paid as much attention to the written word as Europeans have, due to our worldview and cultural inclinations. The written word is, to a large degree, lifeless. Indeed, it creates distance, not so much between a text and its author as between the writer and the reader, who may never have a chance to interact or even meet face to face. Ironically, what passes today for great strides in communication (e.g., the Internet) creates greater distance between those who are supposed to communicate. However, unlike Europeans, Africans have never privileged distance as our favorite epistemological mode. Much to the contrary, "our knowledge is direct and immediate. The mode of our epistemological method is participation, and relationship rather than separation and control" (Richards, 1989, p. 31). Hence, our definite preference and reverence is for the spoken word, which allows us to experience life in the most profound way. Consequently, the European interpretation of our African reality as lacking in rationality because of our orality/"ignorance" of writing speaks solely to European ethnocentrism. We now know that the mechanistic worldview espoused by the Europeans is suspect, for it rests on a conception of life and of matter in serious need of reconsideration, as made increasingly clear by the new physics. We have also learned, at our great expense, that the so-called European miracle has turned into a nightmare, rendering the very possibility of life on earth increasingly tenuous.

▶ Conclusion

In conclusion, African people, as well as others subjected to European ethnocentrism, have suffered from dislocation, as explained by Molefi Kete Asante (1988/1991, 1990/1992). By this, it is meant that, having lost sight of our agency, that is, of our capacity to project ourselves onto our own existence, we have lived on borrowed European terms. The time has come for relocation, for African existence based on the African interpretation of life, and this certainly includes an appropriate understanding and appreciation for language.

It is necessary, as argued above, that language be fully apprehended as a multidimensional phenomenon, not simply under its written form but also, and primarily, as a critical medium of oral expression. There is absolutely nothing that supports any claims of written superiority and/or oral inferiority. The arguments presented by the proponents of such a thesis are weak at best and certainly betray a high level of ethnocentrism, which has proven quite detrimental to a genuine dialogue between cultures.

▶ References

Akbar, N. (1984). Africentric social sciences for human liberation. *Journal of Black Studies, 14*(4), 395-414.

Alvares, C. (1991). *Decolonizing history: Technology and culture in India, China, and the West, 1492 to the present day.* New York: The Apex Press & Goa: The Other India Press. (Original work published 1979)

Ani, M. (1994). *Yurugu. An African-centered critique of European cultural thought and behavior.* Trenton, NJ: Africa World Press.

Asante, M. K. (1991). *Afrocentricity.* Trenton, NJ: Africa World Press. (Original work published 1988)

Asante, M. K. (1992). *Kemet, Afrocentricity, and knowledge.* Trenton, NJ: Africa World Press. (Original work published 1990)

Ba, S. W. (1973). *The concept of negritude in the poetry of Leopold Sedar Senghor.* Princeton: Princeton University Press.

Bernal, M. (1987). *Black Athena* (Vol. 1). New Brunswick, NJ: Rutgers University Press.

Blaut, J. (1993). *The colonizer's model of the world: Geographical diffusionism and Eurocentric history.* New York: Guilford.

Brian, M. (1991). *Western conceptions of the individual.* New York: Berg.

Capra, F. (1982). *The turning point: Science, society, and the rising culture.* New York: Simon & Schuster.

Davidson, B. (1959). *The lost cities of Africa.* Boston: Little, Brown.

Diop, C. A. (1991). *Civilization of barbarism.* New York: Laurence Hill Books. (Original work published 1981)

Drewal, M. (1998). Dancing for Ogun in Yorubaland and in Brazil. In A. Torres & N. Whitten (Eds.), *Blackness in Latin America and the Caribbean* (Vol. 2, pp. 256-281). Bloomington: Indiana University Press. (Original work published 1989)

Goody, J., & Watt, I. (1977). *The consequences of literacy: Literacy in traditional societies.* Cambridge, UK: Cambridge University Press. (Original work published 1963)

Graff, H. (1987). *The labyrinths of literacy: Reflections on literacy past and present.* London: Falmer.

Havelock, E. (1976). *The origins of Western literacy.* Toronto: Ontario Institute for Studies in Education.

Jahn, J. (1990). *Muntu: African culture and the Western world.* New York: Grove Weidenfeld. (Original work published 1961)

James, G. (1992). *Stolen legacy: Greek philosophy is stolen Egyptian philosophy.* Trenton, NJ: Africa World Press. (Original work published 1954)

Jeffries, C. (1967). *Illiteracy: A world problem.* London: Pall Mall Press.

Jones, E. (1981). *The European miracle: Environments, economies, and geopolitics in the history of Europe and Asia.* Cambridge, UK: Cambridge University Press.

Keita, L. (1977). Two philosophies of African history: Hegel and Diop. *Presence Africaine, 91,* 41-49.

Laitin, D. (1992). *Language repertoires and state construction in Africa.* Cambridge, UK: Cambridge University Press.

Latouche, S. (1992). *L'occidentalisation du monde.* Paris: Editions la Decouverte.

Laubach, F. (1960). *Thirty years with the silent billion: Adventuring in literacy.* Westwood, CA: Fleming Revel.

Mazama, A. (1994). An Afrocentric approach to language planning. *Journal of Black Studies, 25*(1), 3-19.

Newmeyer, F. (1986). *The politics of linguistics.* Chicago: Chicago University Press.

Niane, D. T. (1960). *Soundjata ou l'epopee mandingue.* Paris: Presence Africaine.

Niane, D. T. (1998, June 4). *The African oral tradition and epic.* Lecture given in the Department of African American Studies, sponsored by Nommo, Temple University, Philadelphia.

Olson, D. (1977). From utterance to text: The bias of language in speech and writing. *Harvard Educational Review, 47,* 257-281.

Ong, W. (1986). Writing is a technology that restructures thought: The written word. In G. Bauman (Ed.), *Literacy in transition* (pp. 23-50). Oxford, UK: Clarendon.

Parsons, T. (1966). *Societies: Evolutionary and comparative perspectives.* Englewood Cliffs, NJ: Prentice Hall.

Popper, K. (1972). *Objective knowledge. An evolutionary approach.* Oxford, UK: Clarendon.

Prieswerk, R., & Perrot, D. (1978). *Ethnocentrism in history: Africa, Asia, and Indian America in Western textbooks.* New York: NOK Publishers.

Richards, D. M. (1989). Toward the demystification of objectivity. *Imhotep, 1,* p.1.

Street, B. (1984). *Literacy in theory and practice.* Cambridge, UK: Cambridge University Press.

Stubbs, M. (1980). *Language and literacy: The sociolinguistics of reading and writing.* London: Routledge & Kegan Paul.

Part III

Socially Constructed
Racial Identities and
Their Consequences for
Transculturalism
in America

Multiple Identities

The Case of Biracial Children

CHEVELLE NEWSOME

Where do mixed race children and adults feel they belong in our world of European Americans, African Americans, Asian Americans, Hispanic/ Latino Americans, and Native Americans? How does society view intimate relationships between people from different races or ethnic groups? What ethnic categorization is given to those of mixed race? These are all questions that surround interracial couples and their offspring. Interracial marriage has traditionally been considered an indicator of assimilation. When a member of a minority group selects a spouse from the majority group, it suggests that societal and interpersonal barriers inhibiting interaction between the groups have been reduced. Although an ethnic minority group member's marriage to a person from the majority group

does not signify a decline in that person's ethnic identification (Cohen, 1983, 1988; Cross, 1991), the ethnic identity of the couple's offspring becomes more complex. The literature shows that children from these unions have a greater struggle in maintaining their ethnic minority group identity (Frideres, Goldstein, & Gilbert, 1971; Lieberson & Waters, 1988; Waters, 1990).

Despite the struggle that some biracial or multiracial individuals may face, the United States does provide these individuals with some racial identification options (Waters, 1990). These options are particularly available in multiethnic states such as California, Texas, and New York. Biracial children are usually provided information on their minority group heritage by the minority group parent, who usually has a greater degree of ethnic and racial consciousness than the majority group parent (Judd, 1990). According to Cohen (1983, 1988), biracial children do not automatically gravitate to the majority group parent's ethnic affiliation or racial identification preference. In fact, these children's racial identification can take varied courses, and the interaction with their parents, the ethnic diversity of the environment, and other socialization agents can affect their racial identification.

Assimilation into a culture can take three courses: Anglo conformity, cultural pluralism, and melting pot. The Anglo conformity model asserts that minority group individuals adjust to society by becoming absorbed in the culture of the dominant group. The cultural pluralist model suggests that minority group members in such societies continue to hold onto their culture while trying to adjust to that of the majority group. In this environment, cultural diversity is embraced, and minority group members are encouraged to express their ethnic identities. In the melting pot, the minority and majority groups are thought to merge and form a third unique culture, adjusting to and accepting the ideals and values of each group and creating a new system (Williams, 1992). These models are useful illustrators of the courses that ethnic identity can take, but they do not examine the impact communication messages, particularly those from family members, play in shaping which path a biracial child might embrace when exploring his or her racial identification.

In trying to understand the racial identification of biracial children from minority group and majority group parents, this three-path approach captures the different paths that are available to biracial children. The choice children make in their racial identification depends on the children's personal attributes, the parents' characteristics, and structural factors (Johnson, 1992). In reconciling the issues of being biracial, biracial children grapple with how to integrate two often divergent racial groups to which they belong. The result, theoretically, is the creation of a unified racial identity that encompasses both racial groups.

Over the last 30 years, scholars (Erickson, 1968; Jones, 1990; Mendelberg, 1986; Phinney, 1990; White & Burke, 1987) have conducted investigations into the identity of biracial children. However, few of the studies have investigated the communicative aspects within the family that shape the development of those identities. "Identity is inherently a communication process and must be understood as a transaction in which messages are exchanged" (Hecht, Collier, & Ribeau, 1993, p. 161). Our identity is largely shaped, and we are socialized, within the framework of a family. The association of racial attitudes between parents and children is thought to be highly complex. Although information from the socialization literature (Bowles, 1993; Herring, 1992) shows that parents are the primary socialization agents, the attitudes formed by children are subject to modification and intervention from forces outside the home, including peers and extended family members (Galvin & Brommel, 1996). Thus, future research from the field of communication should focus on the parents' communication about race and ethnicity with their children, as well as the children's conception of that information and the impact of societal influences. As a communication scholar studying the process of racial identification in biracial children, I seek to explore the transcultural realities of this group.

From the transcultural perspective, social interaction and dialogue are key to building an expanded worldview, one that embraces differences and respects the diverse cultures that shape human communication and social interaction. Biracial children exemplify the essence of transcultural realities. These individuals represent two different, often opposing racial and ethnic groups, which the children must integrate when forming their identity. A single racial or ethnic group label can be viewed as incomplete in describing an individual with two racial dimensions. Internally and through communication with their parents, biracial children exhibit a multiple centered perspective, where the racial identification and ethnic heritage of both parents must be respected to ensure the development of a positive racial identification.

Because of the diversity in California, where this study took place, it seems appropriate to investigate children from various multiracial backgrounds. Most of the research literature has focused on multiracial children with Asian and European American heritage (Saenz, Hwang, Aguirre, & Anderson, 1995; Verkugten & Kwa, 1996). The findings from these studies have offered some insights; however, children from African and Hispanic/Latino heritages are not included in these studies. Therefore, it is the goal of this project to include biracial children from a variety of racial backgrounds to gain further insight into biracial children's management of dual cultural realities.

IDENTITY: CONCEPT

Social science has long asserted that each individual has multiple identities based on gender, socioeconomic status, age, and ethnicity or race. Because racial or ethnic identity can motivate us, we must ask what happens when an individual belongs to two competing ethnic groups. Within the biracial person, how does the racial identification of the dominant group interact with the minority group identity in a given situation? Depending on the situation, a person's racial identification preference may become more prominent, or new compromises with or suppressions of the other identity may occur. Thus, the interplay of these competing racial identities is at the heart of this study. Hecht et al. (1993) assert that individuals have an option of when and in what context to assume or emphasize their identity roles. In this article, the degree to which a biracial individual must assert one racial identity over the other was explored. It is important to recognize the struggle that biracial children face when making a choice to

downplay the heritage of one parent in favor of the other to cope with everyday situations in American life. In the absence of an established social norm and a multiethnic category, biracial children and their parents are forced to choose one of the available racial categories for the biracial individual. Significant occasions where this option was exercised include past U.S. decennial censuses, birth certificate filings, school registration, and passport applications ("Multiple Race," 1998). Biracial individuals and parents of biracial children are beginning to demand the option of selecting more than one racial category; however, the inclusion of multiple racial categories for one individual is a recent phenomenon and is not a widely accepted practice in racial categorization.

Identity is multidimensional. The dimensions include a sense of belonging and self-identification. To measure identification, researchers usually ask the following question: "To what extent do you feel you belong to the following group?" Identification in this respect does not exclude ties to other groups but sets up a hierarchy of identities, with one dominant and others subordinate or of lesser importance. Identity may also be expressed in the form of negation. For example, a researcher may ask, "Do you feel you belong to a certain group?" The participants show identification even with a negative response to the inquiry. However, when these inquiries are centered on asking the participants to select between the majority and the minority groups to which their parents belong, a sense of betrayal and confusion can arise.

CHOICE OF ETHNIC IDENTITY

Referring to the ethnic identification of children from interethnic marriages and relationships, Hout and Goldstein (1994) purport that these relationships provide

an opportunity to exercise one's options. For some ethnic groups, intermarriage thins out the ethnic heritage because few offspring of mixed marriages remember ancestors from that group. For other groups, intermarriage is a recruitment opportunity because the offspring of mixed heritage often think of themselves as part of that group, simplifying their mixed heritage with a single mention or expressing the sense that they "feel closer" to one group than the other. (p. 71)

In this chapter, it is argued that the racial identification of biracial children with one parent from the majority group is, like Hout and Goldstein's (1994) definition about ethnic identification, a matter of option that is shaped by communication with parents and other agents in the socialization process. This is so because—in California, in particular—the number of interracial relationships and biracial children has been on the rise. Interracial relationships are not a recent phenomenon, but we are in a time when racial attitudes toward minorities have become more tolerant, and the number of minorities interacting with majority group members is at an all-time high for some in the minority community. Since the time of slavery, European Americans have used the "one drop" rule to identify the offspring of black-white relationships (Wilson & Davis, 1966). However, with other minority groups, that has not been the case, and even with the African American community, the prevalence of the "one drop" rule is waning. Thus, children of interracial relationships have an opportunity for more choice in respect to racial identification. However, other scholars would argue that choice of ethnic and racial identification does not freely exist for everyone (Courtney, 1995; Waters, 1990).

Lieberson and Waters (1988) contend that ethnic identity is much less a matter of choice for racial minorities in the United States. Waters (1990) argues that whereas whites have the freedom to select an ethnicity with which to identify, "Black Americans, Hispanic Americans, Asian Americans, and American Indians do not have the option of a symbolic ethnicity" (p. 49). For members of minority groups, social assignment of race overrides the importance of ethnicity. The choice of ethnicity is limited because of racial labels imposed by others in the dominant or majority culture. Again, the one-drop rule from the days of slavery defines as black any person who has a drop of black blood (Cose, 1995, 1997; Haizlip, 1995); thus, this rule negates choices in racial identification.

Race is a socially constructed category that distinguishes an individual based on physical appearance, whereas ethnicity is based on distinctions of national origin, language, religion, and other cultural markers (Cose, 1997; Jackson, 1999). The choice of ethnicity is far more flexible than the choices of race because of the observable physical characteristics that are used to determine race. There are numerous accounts of individuals who have opted to "pass" as a member of the majority group (Cose, 1995; Haizlip, 1995). Passing describes an attempt to achieve acceptability in one group, usually the majority group, by denying other elements that the person deemed undesirable. However, for the purposes of this study, the primary focus will be on racial identification of biracial children. Given the close relationship between racial identification and ethnic identification, it is important to review the literature on ethnic options in the study of biracial children. The communication that shapes the development of racial identification and ethnic identity merits our attention for research.

IDENTITY AND SOCIAL INTERACTION

One of the most fundamental units of human interaction is the family, and parents play the most crucial role in the transmission of culture and in the development of the racial identification of children. The literature presents conflicting evidence regarding which parent is the most significant in teaching children in the domain of culture. For example, it has been suggested that mothers represent the most important vehicle in the transmission of culture because they generally spend more time with the children compared to their husbands (Nelsen, 1990). On the other hand, Stephan and Stephan (1989) studied part-Hispanic college students in New Mexico and found that those Hispanic men married to non-Hispanic women tend to be more influential in establishing the cultural environment of the household, compared to Hispanic women married to non-Hispanic men, implying that fathers play a dominant role in shaping the environment for communication and development of racial identity.

Recent writings focusing on the ethnic identification of multiethnic people have suggested the need to introduce structural elements in examining the construction of ethnic identity (Johnson, 1992; Miller, 1992). Multiethnic individuals are at least potentially linked to different ethnic groups through their parents. However, societal factors, such as the size of the ethnic group, the ethnic diversity in the area, and the perception of communication, are elements that can shape the development of ethnic identity and racial identification of children of interracial couples. The literature shows a strong relationship between these societal factors and intergroup relationships (Bavelas & Segal, 1982; Miller, 1992).

The family plays an important part in the development of identity because cultural values and traditions are first learned and carried out in the home. Examinations of the role the family plays in racial identification development explores the tension or conflict that might exist in the family unit about ethnicity and racial identification. Ethnic and religious differences may add an element of conflict to marriages and relationships, as couples struggle over how the child should be identified ethnically and racially (Blau & Schwartz, 1984). An examination of communication between the parents and biracial children about race and ethnicity, from the biracial child's perspective, may provide some insight into the child's ethnic identity and racial identification development. The significance of communication and family dynamics can manifest itself in many ways. Some scholars argue that mothers have the primary responsibility for transmitting ethnic identity and racial identification to the children and speculate that biracial children will more strongly identify with their mother's race (Wilson, 1981). However, Waters (1990) argues that the father's ethnicity is more important than the mother's in determining the child's ethnic identity development and racial identification. Use of the father's surname is one of the principal cues of ethnicity, and it is potentially one reason ethnic identity is associated with fathers. However, racial identification is based more on physical characteristics, and other (social) factors may intervene in the identity process.

The family communication literature shows that conflicts can develop between children and their parents during adolescence. As children grow up, interactions with other external agents of socialization increase, and they may develop racial identifications that differ from the one selected by their parents. Children's new self-identification can then influence the parent's designation of the child's racial designation. The age of the child has a large bearing on this element. Thus, adolescence is the phase where the changes are the most likely to occur (Erickson, 1968; Phinney, 1990). Therefore, biracial children in this stage will be the focus of this investigation.

SELF-IDENTIFICATION

Ethnic identity is an individual's sense of self as a member of an ethnic group and the attitudes and behaviors associated with that sense (Phinney, 1990). It is a developmental process that takes the individual from an unexamined ethnic identity and through a period of exploration. Following the exploration process, an ethnic identity is achieved, according to Phinney (1990). Identification based on ethnicity involves a sense of shared substance with others based on the character and spirit of a cultural group linked through commonality of origin, beliefs, values, customs, or practices between group members. Racial identification is predicated on those same principles.

Individuals elect to identify with a racial group.

Each person has a self; being the self is defined by a person's own subjectivity. Acknowledgment of self includes statements that include the words *I, me,* and *myself.* The self is a dynamic, multidimensional entity that encompasses numerous self-conceptions. Hegel (1807/1967) explained, "Self-consciousness exists in itself, in that and by the fact that it exists for another self-consciousness" (p. 229). In other words, the self only recognizes itself in relation to other people, the end result being that the self encounters conflict between the public and private dimensions. Thus, as biracial adolescents struggle to define their selves and to establish identification with a racial group, they experience conflicts and struggles, juxtaposing their own views of their racial categorization with that of their families, their friends, and the larger society. During the racial identification process, the individual selects and incorporates information from the public, private, and social dimensions. This is a process that involves the concepts of identity, social interaction, and self-identification.

PURPOSE OF THE STUDY

Biracial children being reared in a culturally complex situation develop racial identifications that are shaped by family communication and other societal factors. According to Hecht et al. (1993), identity is relational because we learn to define ourselves in relation to others and in terms of our relationship with others (e.g., friend, child, spouse). In addition, the relationship itself takes on an identity. Throughout this relational process, the individual is being shaped by the messages received from others in the environment. The labels biracial children adopt (Verkugten & Kwa, 1996) and the socialization agents of biracial children (Galvin & Brommel, 1996) have been assessed. Studying the types of communication messages received can further our understanding of how biracial children

manage the divergent cultures to which they belong and develop their ethnic identity and establish racial identifications.

This study seeks to do the following:

1. Describe the nature of the communication received by those managing biracial identities (i.e., what biracial children state are the important communication message types, related to ethnic identity, received from parents)
2. Analyze the children's reports of parental messages related to ethnic identity and racial identification
3. Discuss biracial children's transcultural realities

The study was designed to allow participants to express information openly, using their own words, to share insights into experiences related to their reality.

▶ Method

The politics of racial identity are public and deeply personal. In recent opinion polls, there was a higher acceptance of interracial marriage and greater willingness to reside in ethnically diverse neighborhoods than at any other time in our history. However, biracial individuals feel invisible to the world because they are asked to choose between the heritages of their parents. In this study, I hope to stimulate a discussion into the process of ethnic and racial categorization and the development of biracial children's racial identification. Little is known about biracial children's identity from their perspective, about the communicative factors that influence it, and about the process by which it develops. A communication analysis of racial identification will consider how the subjects frame and enact their racial identities, and how their racial "identities are relationally and communally expressed, negotiated, and defined" (Hecht et al., 1993, p. 165). By talking with biracial individuals ages 13 to 18 about their communication related to racial identification and ethnic identity, I hope to discover information that will enable us to better understand their perspective and how the communication messages between parents and children influence biracial children's racial identification.

People have multiple identities, interpreted differently by individuals and subgroups, and as scholars, we need to analyze how biracial children align in various contexts. In this article, I will discuss how communication (messages from parents and other socialization agents) affects identities of adolescents (ages 13 to 18) who are biracial. To be included in the study, participants must have one parent of the majority group and the other from a minority group.

Research (Bowles, 1993; Galvin & Brommel, 1996; Herring, 1992) indicates that identity is a process of negotiation between the individual and those in the immediate social environment. The idea is that people must reconcile society's view of their social position with their own conception of self. The ideal method of studying ethnic identities and racial identification would be to observe and question the children and their parents in every situation where race and ethnicity were relevant, but this is clearly impractical. Thus, a more practical approach would be to administer a questionnaire and conduct in-depth interviews to get at the subjective conception of ethnicity held by the children and their racial identification. The questionnaire asked questions related to identity development and the communicative factors that might influence identity development. The interview focused on the communicative elements of transmitting information regarding ethnic identity and racial identification. This approach allowed the researcher to obtain an answer to the initial question, Where do mixed race individuals feel they belong in our world of European American, African American, Asian American, Hispanic/Latino, and Native American co-cultures? Closed-ended questions force individuals to make choices from predetermined categories. This question design stifles the descriptive information that open-ended questions afford the researcher (Babbie, 1999). Thus, this study aimed to understand the complex process of racial identification by allowing subjects to describe their ethnic identity development and racial identification without the imposition of predetermined choices. Instead, open-ended questions were used for both the questionnaire and the interview.

The present study investigated how biracial children develop their racial identification and the communication (messages) that affects that process. A survey was conducted, using the following questions as a guide to determine their sense of belonging and development of racial identification.

1. What did your parents or guardians teach you about racial differences? Which parent gave you this advice?
2. What do/did your parents tell you about handling situations where individuals assault you with verbal slurs or inappropriate ethnic or racial comments? Which parent provided you with this information?
3. Can you tell me some of the things you would do if someone called you a racist name or made inappropriate comments related to race or ethnicity? How do you think your parents (Mom and Dad individually) would react to your response? Does it fit in with what they taught you? Why or why not?
4. In your home, do your parents have pictures of people from various racial and ethnic groups, only European (white) people, or only people from one particular racial or ethnic group other than European (white)? Who decided to have those pictures, if you know?
5. As a small child, did you have play items that are characteristic of your minority co-culture or only of the dominant cultural group (European American)?

6. Did or do you see both your mother's and your father's sides of the family? Whose side do you see most? Why is that?

7. Do you feel comfortable with your relatives from your mother's side of the family? Why or why not? What words or behaviors affect your level of comfort?

8. Do you feel comfortable with your relatives from your father's side of the family? Why or why not? What words or behaviors affect your level of comfort?

9. What is your ethnic classification? When did you determine this classification? Do your parents (Mom and Dad individually) support this selection? Please explain why they do or do not support your ethnic classification? What did they say or do to make you aware of their feelings on this issue?

10. Do your friends and peers see you as a member of the ethnic group you identify with? What do they say or do to make you aware of their feelings about your ethnic identity?

Taking these questions into consideration, and looking at the development of racial identification of biracial children, three factors continue to be of importance: the individual's self-concept, family communication (particularly with parents), and societal factors (i.e., peers, geographical location). These factors were further explored in the follow-up interview session.

SUBJECTS

Participants were 72 students in junior and senior high schools from an ethnically diverse school district in northern California (34 males and 38 females with a mean age of 15 years). The sample reflected a racially diverse group for the region. Only self-identified biracial students with one parent from the majority group were included.

MEASURE AND PROCEDURE

To investigate the specific research questions and goals, the author developed an open-ended survey instrument to allow the subjects to record their responses. A demographic section was included, and then the content questions were posed. The survey was administered in a variety of school club and special meetings. In all cases, group administration was used. The instrument was explained and distributed after the consent forms had been collected.

Measuring identity is difficult, and all of the complexities of measuring this variable have not been sufficiently considered in the research. However, the survey coupled with the interviews allowed the researcher to collect data on a practical situation that could not easily be observed. Marshall and Rossman (1989) explained that "the researcher explores a few general topics to help uncover the participant's meaning perspective but otherwise respects how the participant frames and structures response" (p. 82). Thus, when the interview questions were posed to participants, the interviewer included words and phrases that the participant had included on his or her original survey sheet. Because identity also encompasses a sense of belonging, emotional elation, and pride in one's ethnic and racial group, the interview included questions such as, "Are you proud of your. . . . racial (ethnic) heritage?" The follow-up in-depth interviews allowed the subjects to clarify and explain their responses to the open-ended questions on the questionnaire. Probes in the interview were used to elicit detailed information on the participants' interactions with their parents and other socialization agents, to explore the major factors that affect racial identification.

DATA ANALYSIS

A latent content analysis was performed on the 72 surveys and interviews. In this type of analysis, "the researcher takes a voluminous amount of information and reduces it to certain patterns, categories, or themes and then interprets the information by using" characteristics of interest to the research (Creswell, 1994, p. 154). The categories were arrived at inductively by looking for similarities and differences in the situations described by the participants. As obvious themes emerged relating to communicative strategies that shape ethnic identity development and racial identification, this information was further categorized according to the questions and the focus of the research project. For example, the data were organized to examine the presence of choice in racial identification selection; categories for self and societal factors relating to racial identity formation were determined. Although information regarding ethnic and racial background was obtained for each subject, no major differences between the minority racial groups were found. Therefore, the compiled data are presented for all of the subjects, unless otherwise noted.

▶ Results

One of the issues important to the discussion of racial identification for biracial children is what parents communicate to their children about race and ethnicity. Examining the descriptive responses pertaining to biracial children's sense of belonging and development of identification with racial groups, it was apparent that the most frequently received messages were supportive communication messages. The messages were coded into six basic categories: comfortable, acceptance, happiness, annoyance, incompleteness, and disinterest. These categories were subdivided into two types: supportive (comfortable, acceptance, happiness) and disconfirming (annoyance, incompleteness, and disinterest) communication.

The data from the sample indicate that from the three courses of assimilation, the majority of the participants ascribe to the cultural pluralism model.

I can remember when I was growing up and I'd feel like I wanted to be a part of the group (Mexican heritage). I didn't betray my father's heritage by being with my Mexican friends. It's just who I am, a person with two lines of blood to be proud of.

This comment from one of the subjects typifies the sentiments of the majority of the participants (72%). From this perspective, the subjects remembered being encouraged to embrace their minority and majority ethnic and racial groups. The communication messages the subjects received were categorized as comfortable, acceptance, and happiness. These are all indicators of satisfaction with the communication interaction about the issue under discussion. There was a sense of sharing between the two group identities. Only 7% of the respondents reported that they were forced to accept their Caucasian identity over their minority group identity. The communication messages from these respondents were categorized as annoyance and incompleteness. These are characteristics of messages that illustrate dissatisfaction with the communication interaction. Three of the five students who were identified in this category identified their minority heritage as Spanish or Portuguese and had physical features that they believed allowed them to pass; this contributed to their ability and desire to conform to the majority culture. The remaining subjects (21%) were in the melting pot category.

As described earlier, in the melting pot category, minority and majority group identities are thought to merge and form a third unique culture, adjusting and accepting the ideals and values of each group and creating a new system. The communication messages these subjects reported were characterized to include both satisfaction and dissatisfaction; acceptance, disinterest, and incompleteness were the categories. The subjects who were in this category expressed the desire to have a multiracial category. "I am both white and black. I ought to be able to say I am mixed. To not say so is a lie." This response came from a male subject whose mother was African American and whose father was European American. In answering the question, "How does the ethnic identity of the dominant group interact with the other ethnic identity in a given situation?" the data show that the perspective on how to manage this situation is varied, but most subjects choose to embrace both minority and majority ethnic identities (cultural pluralism), and they reported characteristics of satisfaction for the messages they received from their family members and peers. Thus, racial identification is encouraged by messages of affirmation and support from parents and other people in the support network.

Although ethnic identity studies do acknowledge that an individual's social interactions influence identity development, most studies assume that the individual has a choice in selecting his or her racial group affiliation. From a communication perspective, identities are seen to be "enacted in social interaction through communication" (Hecht et al., 1993, p. 167). Thus, the subjects are not so much selecting their ethnic identities as they are selecting to communicate aspects of their ethnic identity in a given situation. Through their actions, the subjects are illustrating their racial identification. The majority of the subjects in this study (84%) admitted to adjusting their behavior to adapt to the different groups to which they belonged, based on racial composition of the group. When asked about whether they select their racial identity, the subjects indicated that they do, in fact, make a choice in their racial identification. The findings also support Waters's (1990) assertion that those from Hispanic/Latino and African American minority backgrounds were less likely to feel a choice in selecting their racial identity. One subject of Asian and European descent claimed that she could be a part of the majority culture and felt her choice in racial identity was hers alone to make. However, the majority of the subjects (56%) from Hispanic/Latino and African American backgrounds did not believe that they were free to select their ethnic identity: Their racial identity was already prescribed because of their physical features. However, the majority of

the subjects (93%) responded favorably to the question, "Do your friends see you as a member of the ethnic group you identify with?" The communication messages regarding this question all indicated satisfaction and acceptance. One subject indicated that her friends would include her in discussions on Afrocentric issues. She commented, "They're [her friends are] cool about it; they know my mom's white and they don't diss white people around me, and I think they know it helps me for them to be cool [about ethnic and racial issues]." The debate about choice in racial identity selection is not clarified by the data. However, the data do help to show that racial identities can be confirmed through social enactment and communication and that parents and other socialization agents can assist adolescents in their development of a racial identity by providing messages that are supportive and connote acceptance of the subjects' choices.

The results of previous studies indicate that racial identification is strongly influenced by relationships. As previously stated, ethnic identities and racial identification are socially constructed through interaction; from a communication perspective, this means that people's social behaviors are merged with the relational component of the interaction. "Identity is jointly constructed for participants, emerges out of social interaction, and is a property of the relationship" (Hecht et al., 1993, p. 168). Thus, for adolescents, their interaction with their parents helps to shape and develop their racial identities. The results indicate that 88% of the sample had a discussion with one or both of their parents about racial and ethnic differences. In the majority of the cases (61%), the mother was the parent who gave advice on how to handle racial or ethnic encounters and who discussed racial identification and ethnic identity with the subjects. One subject who was African American and European American described what her mother told her about being a biracial individual and how to handle inappropriate comments about race and ethnicity. The subject commented,

My mom is white, and she said I love you, honey, but the world will see you as black because you have brown skin like your dad's. Don't let that label define you. You are black, but you are also a part of me. If someone calls you the "N" word just tell them that they are one and that their use of the word shows their ignorance. She wants me to be me, and I see myself as black, but I am also part of my mom who happens to be white.

A range of societal factors affects the development of racial identification. The environmental and societal factors include friendships, presence or absence of minority groups in the geographical area, majority group influence, and geographical location in general. The subjects were asked about the negative encounters they had related to race and ethnicity, the type of diversity that was evident in their home environments, the types of stimulants they received related to ethnicity, and the type and amount of interactions they have with family members. These are all elements that affect the development of ethnic identity and the group with which one develops racial identification.

In describing their home environment, only a small number of participants reported having items of the minority ethnic or racial group present in their home (12%). The subjects were probed about photographs, wall hangings, or collectibles that represented the minority ethnic or racial group. The majority of the subjects did not view the lack of these objects in the home as a lack of ethnic or racial identity for the parent from the minority group. Of those who reported that these items were not present in their home, 28% had fathers who were the members of the minority culture. Thus, the gender of the parent did not have a bearing on whether or not these items of ethnic representation were present in the home. The trend of items representing the racial minority group was extended to the toys or play items the subjects reported that they played with as a small child. Only 8% of the females reported having dolls or books with representations of the minority ethnic group. One of those who reported having such items commented that the items were not presented by her parents but by her paternal grandmother, a member of the majority group. The subject commented, "It was a book with Chinese words for things like apple; I think it was like a[n] alphabet book. I liked it because it was Chinese and I wanted to speak it [the Chinese language]." This shows that ethnic identities have semantic properties that are expressed in core symbols and meanings. These items are representative of a culture and for that particular student, her grandmother's actions communicated acceptance of the subject's minority racial identity. Thus, the student was compelled to identify freely with the minority group, and the decision was arrived at without coercion or shame. None of the male subjects reported having play items representative of the minority racial group.

Because identity development is communal and identities prescribe modes of appropriate and effective communication, the subjects were asked about their relationships with members outside their immediate family. The findings show that when the mother is the member of the minority ethnic group, more than 63% of the subjects report an enjoyable relationship and positive interactions with the mother's family members. Also, 55% report that they spend more time with the mother's family than with the father's family, with no significant difference based on majority and minority group membership. When asked why they spent more time with the mother's side of the family, the subjects' responses (77%) indicated that female parents are more closely connected with their extended families. This finding may also help to explain why the subjects felt more at ease with their maternal family. They spend more time interacting with the individuals from the maternal side of their families. In this case, maternity seems to play a large role in creating ease of communication and developing the relational aspect of the communication. Therefore, there are more opportunities for communication satisfaction and identification with the minority cultural group when the mother is a member of the minority cultural group.

Identities are hierarchal, and we attribute meaning to self as an object in a social situation. In other words, we decide on our racial identity by prioritizing all of the other identities we are managing. We assess the social situation and then communicate our racial identity. This process helps to describe the complexity of the identity process. Thus, when asked to identify their racial identity, 51 of the 72 subjects identified themselves as being both their minority and majority racial identities. When these subjects were asked if they wanted to be placed in a biracial or multiracial category, the response mirrored the path of the cultural pluralist. The subjects categorized themselves as members of two groups and as people who enjoyed being part of both groups. From the cultural pluralist perspective, these individuals embrace diversity and enjoy being able to partake in the events of both groups. Sixteen students followed the melting pot path, and five subjects followed the Anglo conformist path.

When asked if their parents supported their racial classification, 92% reported that their parents did, in fact, support their racial classification and identity. Only 14% of the subjects reported that they changed their ethnic categorization and racial identity in the previous 2 years; the remaining subjects reported that their parents assisted or assigned them the identity and they embraced that identity. This finding again supports the notion that communication with the parents helps to influence a child's racial identification, and it supports that idea that communication in the family and social interaction assist in the development and reinforcement of racial identity for biracial children.

▶ Discussion and Conclusion

It is important to realize that people can achieve racial identification through language, whether it is the language they use to describe themselves or to describe others. Through language, the process of identification begins and is fulfilled. According to Burke (1969), the substance we share with others is the basis of identification, and we express the sharing of substance through language. The subjects in this study illustrate this point. Racial identification for the subjects was established through the social interactions they had with other people, particularly their parents. The decision about which racial group to identify with was made based on the language used by the parents to describe the child and the language used to support or disconfirm the ethnic identity and racial identification choice selected by the subjects. Through social interaction, the subjects begin to form a unique perspective on race; they learn to mesh the divergent issues into a view that reflects their heritage (Chen & Starosta, 1998).

Biracial children's identity, like all identities, is the result of individual interaction within society. In this research study, the goal was to make biracial children the primary subjects and to explore how language and parental communication affected the children's ethnic identity and identification with racial groups to which they belong. Biracial children begin to identify with the particular racial group to which they belong when they establish that race is an essential substance. Therefore, it was important in the study of biracial children's racial identification to allow the subjects to provide information on how they view themselves racially and how others perceived their views. In addition, it was key to examine the types of messages received from primary socialization agents, namely parents.

Through the use of open-ended questions on the survey and during the in-depth interviews, the biracial children expressed their insights and experiences, and through the content analysis, the messages the children received were categorized to describe the types of communication that occurred most often (i.e., supportive/satisfying, disconfirming/unsatisfying). Because of the analysis, we have a better understanding of the nature of the communication between parents and biracial children. We know that, based on this sample, parents of biracial children most often use supportive communication messages when discussing with the children their ethnic identity and racial identification. These findings are consistent with the arguments made by Diggs and Socha (1999).

In the content analysis of the communication messages the subjects received, I can infer that supportive messages from parents produced a high degree of satisfaction on ethnic identity and racial identification choices for biracial children. It is clear from the analysis that the biracial children who participated in this study have clear ideas about the importance of their ethnic identity and choices in racial identification. It is also clear that the supportive messages received reinforce the cultural pluralism model.

From the cultural pluralism perspective, the subjects expressed an understanding and appreciation of the complexity of their reality. As children of people from different racial groups, biracial children must decide whether or not to embrace and integrate both cultures or to suppress one of the cultures. In the tradition of pluralism, the two cultures are allowed to coexist. This ideology appears to be the one most confirmed by supportive communication from parents.

During the era of high immigration into the United States (1930-1970), the prevailing ideology on assimilation was the melting pot. The assumption of the melting pot view was that the mainstream culture and the co-cultures would merge to form a unique new culture. The analysis in this study revealed that this perspective still exists in our society today. However, reports of a mixture of satisfaction and dissatisfaction with the communication messages from this perspective indicate a shift further away from this concept of the melting pot. The respondents who expressed dissatisfaction and reported receiving unsupportive message types in this area indicated a strong desire to embrace the uniqueness of each racial group to which they belong and an unwillingness to make a racial preference, despite messages from their parents urging them to do so. When deciding with which racial group to identify, the consensus of biracial children was to embrace both. However, the observable characteristic of race did limit options in racial identification, according to the subjects' responses. Those with observable racial indicators were more likely to express dissatisfaction with the melting-pot view.

The majority of the biracial children in this study do share substance with a racial group, and their racial identification is validated not only by their parents but also by their peers. This is a key dimension to understanding how communication affects and helps to validate the formation of racial identification. The subjects reported receiving supportive messages from their parents and their peers. Supportive messages reinforce the individual's decision to identify with a racial group, and the affirmations further the development of a sense of shared substance with the chosen racial group.

For biracial children, a strong sense of racial identification with their minority racial group was not fostered by objects in the home that represented the ethnic group. Because identification includes the sharing of substance, one could assume that having in the home paintings, books, and other artifacts representing the minority group would assist in developing a strong racial identification with that minority group. However, the subjects from this study indicated that there were no significant objects representing the minority group in their homes. This finding further supports the importance of supportive messages regarding racial identification, particularly from the mothers, because the majority of participants indicated they received information pertinent to racial identification and ethnic identity from their mothers.

This research study was designed to add a communicative component to the study of ethnic identity and racial identification. Given the above results, what can we say about communication in relation to ethnic identity and racial identification? The research was based on the "assumption that ethnic culture is socially and historically emergent, is co-created and maintained as a function of identity, and is constituted as a system of interdependent patterns of conduct and interpretation" (Hecht et al., 1993, p. 160). Ethnic identity can be seen as consisting of three separate but interrelated elements: racial/ethnic awareness, racial/ethnic preference, and self-identification. Issues of identity become especially important during the period of early adulthood or adolescence. Overall, the results of this study point to the usefulness of the holistic communicative approach guiding the analysis for better understanding the complexities of ethnic identity and racial identification.

In general, the findings suggest that the majority of participants tend to enjoy their dual ethnic identity and do not find it to be particularly burdensome to manage their competing ethnicities. These positive findings can be attributed to the ethnically diverse environment to which the subjects have been exposed. The findings may be different if biracial children outside of California, Texas, or New York are studied. Also, societal factors, such as the positive social environment and support from peers, may have an impact on the results. These findings point to the need for further, more detailed research on ethnic identity and racial identification of biracial children and the messages received related to these issues. To focus more on the communicative factors, it may be beneficial to interview both parents and children to gain a full understanding of the communicative dynamics of the family and the relationships and to be able to compare the responses of the parents and their biracial children. Also the content component of the messages can be better studied by having comparative messages to analyze. With the rate of interracial marriage continuing to rise, the number of biracial children will, undoubtedly, increase; these individuals grapple with difficult personal and political issues. Thus, it is imperative that communication scholars continue to explore how communication affects the dimensions of racial identification and ethnic identity formation.

► References

Babbie, E. (1999). *The basics of social research.* Belmont, CA: Wadsworth.

Bavelas, J., & Segal, L. (1982). Family systems theory: Background and implications. *Journal of Communication, 32,* 99-107.

Blau, P. M., & Schwartz, J. E. (1984). *Cross-cutting social circles: Testing a macro structural theory of intergroup relations.* New York: Academic Press.

Bowles, D. D. (1993). Biracial identity: Children born to African-American and white couples. *Clinical Social Work Journal, 21,* 417-428.

Burke, K. (1969). *A grammar of motives.* Berkeley: University of California Press.

Chen, G. M., & Starosta, W. J. (1998). *Foundations of intercultural communication.* Boston: Allyn & Bacon.

Cohen, S. M. (1983). *American modernity and Jewish identity.* New York: Tavistock.

Cohen, S. M. (1988). *American assimilation or Jewish revival.* Bloomington: Indiana University Press.

Cose, E. (1995, February 13). One drop of bloody history. *Newsweek,* pp. 70-72.

Cose, E. (1997). *Color blind.* New York: HarperCollins.

Courtney, B. A. (1995, February 13). Freedom from choice. *Newsweek,* p. 16.

Creswell, J. W. (1994). *Research design qualitative and quantitative approaches.* Thousand Oaks, CA: Sage.

Cross, W. E. (1991). *Shades of black: Diversity in African American identity.* Philadelphia: Temple University Press.

Diggs, R. C., & Socha, T. J. (1999). *Communication, race, and the family: Exploring communication in black, white, and biracial families.* Mahwah, NJ: Lawrence Erlbaum.

Erickson, E. (1968). *Identity: Youth and crisis.* New York: Norton.

Frideres, J. S., Goldstein, J., & Gilbert, R. (1971). The impact of Jewish-Gentile intermarriages in Canada: An alternative view. *Journal of Comparative Family Studies, 11,* 268-275.

Galvin, K. M., & Brommel, B. J. (1996). *Family communication* (4th ed.). New York: HarperCollins.

Haizlip, S. T. (1995, February-March). Passing. *American Heritage, 46,* 46-53.

Hecht, M. L., Collier, M. J., & Ribeau, S. A. (1993). *African American communication: Ethnic identity and cultural interpretation.* Newbury Park, CA: Sage.

Hegel, G.W.F. (1967). *The phenomenology of mind* (J. B. Baille, Trans.). New York: Harper Torchbooks. (Original work published 1807)

Herring, R. D. (1992). Biracial children: An increasing concern for elementary and middle school counselors. *Elementary School Guidance & Counseling, 27,* 123-130.

Hout, M., & Goldstein, J. (1994). How 4.5 million Irish immigrants became 40 million Irish Americans: Demographics and subjective aspects of the ethnic composition of white Americans. *American Sociological Review, 59,* 64-82.

Jackson, R. L. (1999). *Negotiations of cultural identity.* New York: Praeger.

Johnson, D. J. (1992). Developmental pathways: Toward an ecological theoretical formulation of race identity in black-white biracial children. In M. P. Root (Ed.), *Racially mixed people in America* (pp. 37-49). Newbury Park, CA: Sage.

Jones, W. T. (1990). Perspectives in ethnicity. In L. Moore (Ed.), *Evolving theoretical perspectives on students: New directions for students services* (Vol. 51, pp. 59-72). San Francisco: Jossey-Bass.

Judd, E. P. (1990). Intermarriage and the maintenance of religio-ethnic identity, a case study: The Denver Jewish community. *Journal of Comparative Family Studies, 21,* 251-268.

Lieberson, S., & Waters, M. (1988). *From many strands: Ethnic and racial groups in contemporary America.* New York: Russell Sage Foundation.

Marshall, C., & Rossman, G. B. (1989). *Designing qualitative research.* Newbury Park, CA: Sage.

Mendelberg, H. (1986). Identity conflict in Mexican-American adolescents. *Adolescence, 21,* 215-222.

Miller, R. L. (1992). The human ecology of multiracial identity. In M. P. Root (Ed.), *Racially mixed people in America* (pp. 24-36). Newbury Park, CA: Sage.

Multiple race categories get green light. (1998, January). *Forecast, 18,* 12.

Nelsen, H. (1990). The religious identification of children of interfaith marriages. *Review of Religious Research, 32,* 122-134.

Phinney, J. S. (1990). Ethnic identity in adolescents and adults: Review of research. *Psychological Bulletin, 108,* 499-514.

Saenz, R., Hwang, S. S., Aguirre, B. E., & Anderson, R. (1995). Persistence and change in Asian identity among children of intermarried couples. *Sociological Perspectives, 38,* 175-194.

Stephan, C. W., & Stephan, W. G. (1989). After intermarriage: Ethnic identity among mixed-heritage Japanese Americans and Hispanics. *Journal of Marriage and Family, 51,* 507-519.

Verkugten, M., & Kwa, G. A. (1996). Ethnic self-identification, ethnic involvement, and group differentiation among Chinese youths in the Netherlands. *Journal of Social Psychology, 136,* 35-48.

Waters, M. (1990). *Ethnic options: Choosing identities in America.* Berkeley: University of California Press.

White, C., & Burke, P. (1987). Ethnic role identity among black and white college students: An interactionist approach. *Sociological Perspectives, 30,* 310-331.

Williams, T. (1992). Prism lives: Identity of binational Amerasians. In M. Root (Ed.), *Racially mixed people in America* (pp. 280-303). Newbury Park, CA: Sage.

Wilson, A. (1981). In between: The mother in the interracial family. *New Community, 9,* 208-215.

Wilson, R. L., & Davis, J. H. (1966). *Church in the racially changing community.* New York: Abington.

A Culturally Based Conception
of the Black Self-Concept

RICHARD L. ALLEN

In hating Africa and in hating the Africans, we ended up hating ourselves,
without even realizing it. Because you can't hate the roots of a tree, and not
hate the tree. You can't hate your origin and not end up hating yourself. You
can't hate African and not hate yourself.

El Hajj Malik Shabazz

The purpose of this chapter is to provide the historical context for an examination of African Americans' concept of self. It focuses on the major forces, with particular emphasis on enslavement, that have impinged on and fashioned the self-concept of this stigmatized and maligned group in American society. Extant traditional theorizing of the self is informed by an emphasis on European American cultural and social experiences. Thus, primacy is given to the independence of self from the collective as a fact and an ideal. This work provides an alternative viewpoint that states that the conception of self among Africans in the United States is interdependent and influenced by the collective. Du Bois's concept of double consciousness provides the foundation for this framework by specifying the unique experience of Africans in the United States, which has led to major psychological consequences. A model was developed to explore the implications of the double consciousness. It proposed that social structural variables, represented by location in the social structure, have an influence on the expression of symbolic social reality, and these factors, in turn, influence the self-concept. Three dimensions of the self are identified and theoretically and operationally defined: African self-consciousness, ethnicity, and black identity. The first is presented as an African-centered construct with a normative, evaluative component; the latter two are presented as non-African-centered constructs. Ethnicity is presented as an affective or emotional component with an avowed universal relevance. Black identity is presented as a cognitive component that makes reference to race or to being black. Hypotheses were generated and tested based on the similarity and differences among these self-concepts.

This chapter is compatible with the rest of the work in this book on three different levels. First, it points to the importance of culture in its many manifestations. For example, it defines and examines the importance of taking into account culture, broadly defined, in understanding socially significant outcomes. It suggests that even within the same geographic boundaries, different historical events can lead to demonstrably different cultures that have an identifiable and distinctive influence on the way people view the state of nature. Second, it speaks to the relevance of history in providing a context for understanding a social problem. Finally, it suggests an interdisciplinary analytical framework for integrating theory with research on a complex social problem.

▶ Background

To understand the contemporary state of the Africans in the United States, it is imperative to consider both the slave industry and the continuous and systematic forces that impinge on the lives of Africans today. Forcing individuals into bondage requires prodigious techniques and procedures. The attempt was to change an independent, self-supporting individual into a totally dependent appendage of the enslaver. These forces of oppression have left an indelible mark on the culture, socialization practices, and subsequent consciousness of Africans. Because of the brutality and the barbarity of these forces, the scholarly community has tended to gloss over some of the details of the peculiar institution called slavery and to underestimate the significance of its carryover companion, white supremacy (Huggins, 1991). Even many contemporary victims are inclined to downplay the relevance of these forces for many reasons, least of which is the hurt involved, and some make the fervent wish that these things are totally in the past. Moreover, given the nation's lack of political will to address the legacy and vestiges of the slave industry, many African Americans have considered it inappropriate or at least impractical to analyze the many impediments it imposed on the development of Africans past and present. Although many African Americans are sympathetic toward and knowledgeable about the oppression of others, they are often numb to their own. Perhaps, this is indicative of the degree to which they have been adversely affected.

The slave system contained both a physical and a psychological component. Aside from the whippings, burning mutilations, and death, strategies were developed to impress on the enslaved Africans that they were inferiors. They were taught to "know their place," to see themselves as symbols of subordination, and to identify with the enslavers' needs and interests (Anderson, 1995; Zinn, 1995). Karenga (1993) provided a graphic description of the slavery system when he asserted that it can be defined in terms of its brutality, its cultural genocide, and its machinery of control. Its brutality was expressed in physical ways (which included a variety of violence: mutilations, torture, food deprivation, and overwork). Psychological brutality often took the form of frequent humiliations and denial of African history and humanity. Sexual brutality took the form of "breeding" and rape, with women suffering the brunt of the maltreatment. The other defining characteristic of the slave system was the cultural genocide; there was a concerted effort to destroy the culture and the identity of the people, along with their capacity to further develop themselves. Last, the slave system is identified by several mechanisms of control: (a) laws, (b) coercive bodies, (c) religious institutions, (d) divide-and-conquer political techniques, and (e) plantation punishments.

The slave system laid the foundation for the present situation, for after the abolition of slavery, a new system was instituted that showed a striking resemblance to the past. Africans, having won their freedom, were thrust into a cash economy without any cash. Moreover, the promise of 40 acres and a mule was not honored. Thus, impending problems were initiated. In addition, the abuse of a racist system did not disappear. After Reconstruction, the Black Codes were formalized. Not only was the movement and opportunity structure of Africans restricted, but the psychological underpinning was to engender inferiority or self-hatred. That is, with government sanction, Africans in the United States were made to feel less equal than other citizens of the United States. Many restrictions on their mobility and access were legislated. The U.S. government was culpable in the perpetuation of inequality and white supremacy (Allen, 2001). Although there were opportunities for the government to foster a more equitable society, it was not up to the task. Steinberg (1989, 1995) pointed to the many lost opportunities to foster greater equality in the United States. Of particular importance to the contemporary setting was the recruitment of Europeans to participate in the Industrial Revolution in the United States at the exclusion of readily available African American labor. Steinberg contends that this was one of the more recent lost opportunities to create equity between African Americans and European Americans. Furthermore, he argues that had this opportunity been seized, it might have dramatically changed the economic and, relatedly, the political predicament of African Americans.

The dimension of oppression that I believe has received insufficient attention is the impact of the aforementioned psychological impositions, which have come to be known as inferiorization attempts. It is worth noting that there were a host of complementary detractors. Indeed, one need only examine the writings of prominent scholars and influential individuals during and well after slavery in the United States to see how endemic was the process and how overwhelming was this idea of African inferiority. Many scholars have traced some of the writings of these individuals (see, e.g., Gould, 1993; Harris, 1972; Hilliard, 1995). What is also revealing is the extent to which members of the scientific community were, and still are to a substantial degree, purveyors of ideas attacking the intelligence and even the humanity of African people (Harding, 1993). With uncanny consistency, the literature produced by many European Americans has created a number of stereotypes that have wide currency. Kern-Foxworth (1995) carefully analyzes these stereotypes in advertising over time. Brown (1969) traced the existence of various stereotypes and hideous images presented of Africans in white literature. Finkenstaedt (1994) elaborated on the ideas presented by Brown and extended the critique with an updated evaluation.

It is useful to think of the mass media as a

> system for communicating messages and symbols to the general populace. It is their function to amuse, entertain, and inform, and to inculcate individuals with the values, beliefs, and codes of behavior that will integrate them into the institutional structures of the larger society. (Herman & Chomsky, 1988, p. 1)

With respect to the majority mass media, they have been culpable in the onslaught on the African. Besides taking images created in the white literature and tailoring them to the different mass media, the mass media themselves have contributed substantially to the mix. Newspaper and magazine (the print media) treatment of Africans reflected little attention to their everyday activities but substantial attention to the sensational in the African American community. Indeed, it was this treatment that led Africans to start their own press. Similarly, the European American film industry had no place for Africans, except as comic characters totally subordinate to white characters and objects of ridicule. As with the press, a black film alternative was created. With the advent of television, there was initial hope for a better day or at least a better representation, hope that Africans would be an integral part of the new medium. But like the previous mass media, television relegated Africans to the periphery if they had any spot at all. For an insightful, in-depth and cogent analysis of network television's contemporary representation of blackness, see Gray (1995).

In summary, the pejorative portrayal of Africans has been a major trend across media, mass and otherwise, and was created and nurtured by several generations of white image makers. Although there have been marked changes in the presence and depiction of African Americans over time as a consequence of black contestation, a surprising vestige still remains (Dates & Barlow, 1993; Gray, 1995; MacDonald, 1992; Pierce, 1980; Riggs, 1988, 1991).

▶ Resistance to the Forces of Oppression

Ture and Hamilton (1992) observed that against the aforementioned forces, African Americans resisted and that the intensity of the struggle has varied depending on the level and intensity of the onslaught. They maintained that this reflects the law of human nature that "where there is oppression, there is resistance, and where oppression grows, resistance grows."

Physical resistance began on the African continent and continued unabated in the Caribbean and in the United States, where revolts and conspiracies were abundant (Aptheker, 1944; Bennett, 1966; Jackson, 1970). Acknowledging the impact of slavery on the African, Blassingame (1972, p. 6) noted that the personality and behavior of the African was strongly influenced by the interaction between universal elements of African culture, the institutionalized demands of plantation life, the process of enslavement, and the creative response to enslavement. He pointed to the following forms of cultural resistance: (a) cultural synthesis and retention, (b) cultural creation, and (c) maintenance and development of a family against all odds. He further iterated that the most distinctive retentions were dance, storytelling, music, magic, spiritual beliefs, and language patterns. Other scholars have elaborated on the nature and kinds of retentions and have also referred to their ability to make European forms serve African functions (Blassingame, 1972, pp. 21-22; Hilliard, 1995; Holloway, 1990; Thompson, 1984).

To a large degree, the communal culture differentiated Africans from the European majority and permitted them to adjust to a hostile environment; that culture serves today as an alternative to cultural domination. It is the strength of that culture that shielded African Americans from hostile forces and provided the foundation for consciousness raising. African Americans, the producers of the only indigenous American art form in their music, have as a group been placed outside the system. No matter how many of them do well individually and join the orthodox mainstream, African Americans have `achieved a sense of community that has little to do with that of pluralistic white groups that are included in the middle class.

> A feeling of solidarity is common to black folk from the South to the North, from the church to the bar, from the rural settlement to the slums. The fact that blacks complain about their race's not sticking together, a sentiment that is not common to ethnic associations, testifies to a strong consciousness of black solidarity. (Finkenstaedt, 1994, p. 12)

Referring to the African American's resistance to degrading images, Dates and Barlow (1993) called it a continuous "war of images" fought by African people, the essence of which was an ongoing movement to define themselves and to reclaim their history and identity from cultural terrorism (Ture & Hamilton, 1992). Black writers have been instrumental in providing an alternative (Baldwin, 1985; Neal, 1968). From many and diverse perspectives, these writers often spoke directly to African people's struggles and aspirations.

In reference to the mass media, the black press filled the void of black mistreatment or their absence in the majority press by creating its own. This press, however, was activist oriented, involved, and committed. Although not as prominent historically as the black press, an alternative black film movement surfaced in the late 1920s and the 1930s. After a nadir in the 1940s, black filmmakers emerged again in the 1980s and 1990s, displaying a general concern for contemporary social problems, the success of which has been hotly debated. Television, often touted as the most powerful of the mass media, has loomed large in the lives of African Americans, but the obstacles to obtain ownership are great. Thus, it has been difficult to create an alternative expression. African Americans have galvanized their forces to get this medium to better portray the life of the African. Such pressure has historically resulted in some concessions over time. Thus, today, it is not uncommon to find a few television shows with a large African American presence (a large percentage fitting into the category of situation comedies). Although the number of African Americans appearing on television has risen appreciably, the quality of the roles is limited (Pierce, 1980), and African Americans are still subjected to racial ridicule (MacDonald, 1992).

The great social thinker Du Bois (1961) captured the essence of the problem, which he referred to as double consciousness. Using this concept to encompass the essence of the phenomenon, he argued that the African engages in an ongoing struggle to maintain his or her sense of humanity in the light of persistent, powerful, and tenacious attacks from powerful adversaries. Du Bois credited these attacks with having profound effects, but he also saw that the embattled African, through struggle, manages to maintain a sense of self that fluctuates over time and historical circumstance. Many scholars have taken this insight and embellished it in the service of a further understanding of the black self-concept. It has been employed by those working within many different theoretical and ideological frameworks.

Gaines and Reed (1995) interpreted Du Bois's double consciousness along with his other ideas about the black personality as suggesting that African Americans could not develop without creating a profound internal division. Moreover, the

> process of becoming an African American involves becoming both an American and not an American, being both successful and unsuccessful, and being both proud and ashamed of the same acts and abilities because of the fundamental rift created by membership in a group socially defined as negative. If one is internally divided into loyalties, aspirations, and fears, then individual goal formation per se may be a divisive process. (p. 97)

Although a great deal of the behavior of African Americans is a reaction to living in a white-dominated world, a significant part of their time is also spent in a nonthreatening, often nurturing environment (Cross & Strauss, 1998).

▶ Nature of This Inquiry

So far, I have outlined the many elements that have a direct bearing on the present-day conception of the black self. I have tried to provide the historical context for asking the overarching question of how, in the light of the physical and social impediments, African Americans have managed to maintain their sense of identity and sense of well-being. What are the forces that come into play in elevating or diminishing the identity of African Americans? Does having a certain sense of self or identity lead to certain predictable outcomes? Do the different perspectives on the black self have different antecedents and lead to different outcomes?

Clearly, the research interest here is on the self-concept but in a broader sense than usual. The majority of past research inquiries have focused on the existence of a certain self-concept; only a paucity of that research has explored a range of predictors of the self-concept. A research question that has not received much attention pertains to the investigation of the antecedents and consequences of the self-concept. These questions may be posed as How does class position in a sociohistorical time (age) and spirituality influence sense of self? Moreover, how does symbolic reality, that is, interaction with the African American community and media behavior (black and non-black), influence the self? Of equal importance is the question of what influence the self has on ideas of appropriate behavior.

As I intimated above, the self-concept can have different meanings and may be conceptualized in various ways. One major distinction that has been cogently and forcibly argued by Cross (1991) is the distinction between what has been called the personal self-identity, which would include such constructs as self-esteem, self-worth, self-confidence, and the like, and reference group identity. The latter would include such constructs as racial identity, racial awareness, group identity, black identity, and so on. One of the major reasons for this distinction is the confusion in the empirical literature. That is, a researcher may report findings that used a variable that pertains to an individual's self- conception as represented by the personal identity construct, but that researcher may make inferences about one of the constructs falling under the reference group identity.

The argument is that whereas both are a reflection of the self-concept, the two categories of variables often have different sources of influence and African Americans relate to the two broad categories differently. Personal identity is thought to tap the universal component of human behavior and to exist in various degrees in all humans. Reference group iden-

tity is said to reflect the ethnographic dimension of the self-concept. In evaluating the reference group orientation, race or color is typically an explicit component of the stimulus condition.

An integral part of the psychological operation of ethnic groups (Broman, Neighbors, & Jackson, 1988; Cross & Strauss, 1998; Gurin & Epps, 1975), there are a plethora of conceptualizations of identity or more generally of the black self-concept. Using the concept *African American racial belief system,* which is similar to Cross's (1991) *reference group orientation,* the work of Allen, Dawson, and Brown (1989) clearly showed that the black group identity of African Americans is multidimensional.

Phinney (1990) explicated the concept of ethnic identity in three different ways: social identity reflecting ethnic identity, acculturation, and identity formation. It is ethnic identity as a component of social identity that is of concern to this investigation. As Phinney pointed out, ethnic identity has been variously defined. Some have referred to it as an aspect of a person's self-concept that emerges from his or her knowledge of membership in that group or groups, along with the value and emotional significance associated with that membership; it includes attitudes toward one's group, a sense of shared values, a feeling of belonging and commitment, language, behavior values, and knowledge of ethnic group history. Although it is generally assumed that group identification conjures up a sense of well-being (Lewin, 1948), the introduction of ethnic identity confounds this position. Concerning African Americans, there has been considerable theorizing about the effect of being a member of a disparaged or stigmatized group on identification with that group. Several theoretical orientations suggest that African Americans should have a less than sanguine view of the group. On the other hand, other formulations posit just the opposite. Although using a number of different theoretical frameworks, the empirical literature, which reflects a wide variety of measures of ethnic identity, demonstrates that African

Americans have a strong sense of the group (Allen, 2001; Baldwin, 1991; Cross, 1991; Porter & Washington, 1993).

Under the rubric of ethnic identity, there has also been a concern with the issue of an individual's participation in a dominating culture and a dominated culture, analogous to the questions raised in the double consciousness framework. Scholars have discussed the possible consequences on group identity of an individual being a member of a dominated group. In the aggregate, which identity is most often endorsed? Is it possible to develop a bicultural ethnic identity? In this study, black identity is more concrete than ethnic identity. It is a reference-based manifestation of how closely, both emotionally and cognitively, an individual is attached to African Americans as a group.

Another focus on the black self, the African-centered approach, is quite distinct from the aforementioned approaches by design, assumption, and definition (Akbar, 1995; Baldwin, 1991; Karenga, 1993). Although there is no one African-centered approach to the black self, all approaches share certain assumptions and emphases. Furthermore, many either explicitly or implicitly embody Du Bois's double consciousness conception. Using different terms and emphasizing different elements of this form of consciousness, many refer to the African being caught in the European cultural frame, which is in opposition to the African cultural frame. The struggle, then, is to bust out of this self-restricting mold and strive to be in tune with the African philosophical foundations of the self.

In a seminal article, Nobles (1991a) conceptualized the African self-concept as different from and much broader than the European American conception of self. Maintaining many of the vestiges of traditional African philosophy, African Americans, Nobles argues, link self-definition to the collective definition of their people. This philosophical tradition recognizes that only through one's people does the individual become conscious of his or her own being. Only through others do people learn their duties and responsibilities toward themselves and the collective self (tribe or people). Major emphasis is placed on the *we* as distinct from the *I*. In fact, the *I* is thought to be realized by the *we*. This is the essence of what Nobles considers the African self-concept, an extended self. Consistent with Du Bois's double consciousness, Nobles argues that to maintain a black self-concept is an enduring struggle. On the one hand, European American culture is presented as the only civilized culture and under certain conditions, the African American can be assimilated into it. However, to do so would require the African American to "deny historical roots" or "the grounding of self into the collective and social definition of one's people" (Nobles, 1991b, p. 303). In short, snared in the contradictions of two philosophical systems (i.e., the African and the European American), the African American would have to make psychological peace.

Other scholars have made similar points. For example, Akbar (1985) maintained that the main problem facing African Americans after more than 100 years of political emancipation is the urgency of psychological emancipation. Africans in the United States, after the experience of the holocaust of enslavement, have not yet managed to regain their inner selves. Rather, "we still listen only to the ideas, interpretations, explanations, and directions that are given to us outside of our community" (Akbar, 1985, p. 22). Building on the work of a multitude of scholars and leaders, Akbar goes on to say that it is crucial for African Americans to listen to their inner voice to recognize their identity. By *inner voice,* he means

the history of experiences, a multitude of determined ancestors who cherished freedom, and a culture that has developed out of the efforts to obtain and maintain freedom. The inner voice is a compassion for each other, a commitment to the Creator, a respect for nature's laws, and a spirit that has refused to be defeated. The inner voice is self-love and an appreciation for beauty and a being that goes back to the very origin of human time. (pp. 22-23)

With a similar emphasis, Myers (1993, 1998) contends that for African Americans to resolve the many problems concerning the self, they must move to an African-based understanding of the world. She argues that this is a move from a suboptimal level of understanding to an optimal level, which she terms an *Afrocentric view*. More specifically, she notes that the suboptimal worldview has wide currency and is the dominant view in the United States. It assumes a fragmented world in which the spirit and matter are separate. "Individualism, competition, and materialism provide criteria for self-definition as a natural consequence of a worldview in which a finite and limited focus orients us toward such disorder that we fight one another to sustain an illusion" (Myers, 1993, p. 11). Because the dominant culture is conceived of as suboptimal, and because African Americans are socialized into the culture, it is difficult for members to escape—but escape they must to realize themselves. The alternative is the optimal conceptual system, an African-centered worldview (i.e., it originated in Africa). It holds that reality is both spiritual and material; with the spiritual and material ontology, people lose the sense of individualized ego/mind and experience the harmony of the collective identity of being one with the source of all good. The optimal conceptual system assumes an interrelatedness and interdependence of all things and thus yields a worldview that is holistic. As with the double consciousness framework and other African-centered conceptualizations, there is a challenge and struggle to be waged. In this instance, the struggle is to break from the definitions derived from the powerful and pervasive suboptimal worldview to embrace the more elevating definitions derived from the optimal worldview. Although there are a number of variations on these African-centered themes, emphasizing one point more than another, I think their essence may be seen as a return to the source. I have not, however, pointed out any sharp differences between this concept of the self and the more common and older conceptualizations of the black self.

The different conceptions of the black self correspond to the different approaches to black psychology. Karenga (1993), summarizing the work of many different scholars, outlines the different overlapping perspectives under the titles of traditional, reformist, and radical. He describes the traditionalist perspective as defensive or reactive, supporting the Eurocentric model of psychology with superficial changes; it emphasizes changing the attitudes of non-Africans and presents only limited ways for Africans to overcome their psychological maladies. The reformist perspective retains the general concern for the attitudes of non-African Americans, yet it focuses more on changing public policy. Furthermore, it endorses certain aspects of an African-centered psychology but attempts to synthesize this with the traditional focus on change that would presumably benefit both blacks and whites. Finally, the radical perspective makes little or no appeal to whites but instead directs its attention to the analysis, transformation, and treatment of African Americans. This perspective fosters an understanding of the world and the self based on an African worldview, articulated as in opposition to the European worldview. It is this perspective that most often acknowledges the theorizing of Du Bois (Gaines & Reed, 1994, 1995).

From the above discussion of the black self, it becomes clear that certain distinctions have been made concerning the appropriate representation of the black self. One distinction, intimated above, needs to be further elaborated. It is the distinction between the African-centered and non-African centered approaches. One of the clearest distinctions was made by Kambon (1991). Arguing that there is substantial variation within the non-African centered approach to the black self, Kambon (1991) stated that generally those notions of the black self derived from the non-African centered approach rely on the conceptual framework of a European American worldview. That is, they tend to emphasize the reactive aspect of the black self, the vulnerability, abnormality, or defensiveness of the black self. Conversely, the African-centered approach employs the African worldview as the conceptual framework. This approach focuses on describing and explaining the natural and normal condition of African psychological function and behavior, apart from white/European supremacy and domination or racism and racial oppression. The fundamental assumption is that the "basic striving in the African personality is toward self-affirmation, self-determination, and self-fulfillment" (Kambon, 1991, pp. 33-41).

What might be gleaned from the variety of perspectives of the self is that different hypotheses, definitions, and measures would be used to explore the black self. A paucity of research, no matter the perspective, has been directed at finding the antecedents and outcomes or processes and effects of various black self-conceptions.

▶ The Antecedents

SOCIOSTRUCTURAL FACTORS

Religiosity has been referred to as an important indicator of identity formation. This construct has been shown to be a significant element in the black identity. Moreover, with the more restricted notion of religious involvement, Demo and Hughes (1990) suggested that the black church provides opportunities for African Americans to hold important positions denied them in white society and that having such positions enhances self-respect and the evaluation of African Americans. Allen (2001), after noting the pervasiveness of religion in the lives of African Americans, pointed out that the church served as an agency of social reorientation and reconstruction, a shield against the racist attacks on their self-worth, and an invisible spiritual community engaged in social struggle (see Karenga, 1993).

Age is an important predictor of identity in that it situates people in specific sociohistorical contexts (Demo & Hughes, 1990). Several social observers have referred to cer-

tain historical periods as exemplifying a more or less pronounced identity with the collective. On such period is the Civil Rights Movement. Thus, scholars have referred to the pre-civil rights era and the post-civil rights era. It is generally assumed that the identity of African Americans was positively enhanced as a consequence of the Civil Rights Movement.

SYMBOLIC SOCIAL REALITY

Media

Here, the term *symbolic social reality* refers to any symbolic expression of objective reality, which may take the form of art, literature, media content, or interpersonal communication (Adoni & Mane, 1984). In this designation, I have tried to include the major informational sources that influence how people interpret their life space. The mass media are the most predominant purveyors of images in the United States. They provide us with interpretations that include who is important, how they got to be important, what are the normative beliefs of the society, and how certain groups act and act up. In short, the media transmit the values and assumptions of the society in which they operate (Markus & Kitayama, 1994). Furthermore, the majority media fashion and reinforce certain racist perspectives by modifying, distorting, or tailoring history to accommodate the preferred image of the oppressive group and by presenting pejorative or distorted images of the oppressed group. The latent and not so latent message is that in the United States, reality as defined by certain people is of greater value than reality defined by others (Myers, 1993). Gray (1995) asserted that the contemporary representation of African Americans in majority network television can be usefully analyzed in terms of three kinds of discursive practices or types of shows. He refers to these as *assimilationist,* or shows that are characterized by the complete elimination or marginalization of social and cultural differences; pluralist or separate but equal, or shows that place black characters in a black world in circumstances parallel to those of whites; and *multiculturalism or diversity,* or shows that "attempt to explore the interiors of black lives and subjectivities from the angle of African Americans" (pp. 85-89).

The major thrust of the majority media has resulted in an imbalanced view of African Americans; the black media came into existence to correct this situation and to explore the full range of African life and culture. The black print media, especially, have taken an activist and advocacy role. Although there is considerable variability across the black media, the major focus has been to present more inspiring aspects of black life and a context in which to interpret the sordid physical conditions that disproportionately visit the African American.

BLACK INVOLVEMENT

Involvement in cultural rituals and events and the day-to-day struggles of African Americans provides a basis on which people make their assessment of the group and obtain their sense of self. This construct taps into the nature of the relationship that an individual has with the group: the interpersonal component of that contact. It is not necessary for other channels to provide the individual with an understanding of the group; the individual has a more reliable and valid representation through firsthand experience. Thus, the interpretations that may be presented in the omnipresent mass media may be interpreted through the experiences that the individual has acquired. Indeed, the experience may ward off the denigrating representations and interpretations provided in mass-mediated channels.

EFFECTS OR OUTCOMES

Much speculation exists concerning how possessing a sense of black identity influences other aspects of the individual's life. Many of the outcomes are psychological in origin. For example, identity has been credited with being related to well-being, life satisfaction, self-esteem or self-worth, delinquency, and activism, just to name a few. An outcome that bears consideration is the degree to which possessing a black identification is related to the endorsement of either an individualistic or collectivist philosophy.

Recent theorizing on the self-concept has addressed the issue that self-concepts may be usefully divided into Western and non-Western (Shweder & Bourne, 1982; Triandis, 1994). Markus and Kitayama (1991, 1994) contend that Western or European American theories of the self describe people as independent entities that consciously work to distance themselves from the group. Similarly, Nobles (1973, 1991b) maintained that the Western or European American worldview emphasizes the "survival of the fittest" or control over nature, which is shown in the emphasis placed on individuality, uniqueness, and difference. In this view, the individual is conceived to be against the collective (Allen, 2001).

In contrast to the European American concept, the African worldview puts emphasis on commonality, groupness, and similarity (Nobles, 1973). Akbar (1995) refers to the African self-conception as an unqualified collective phenomenon that acknowledges the uniqueness of the individual self as a component of the collectivity. As noted above, the theory that drives this study builds on the insight of Du Bois's double consciousness and its many modified versions and attempts to present an interrelated set of hypotheses to account for numerous conceptions of the black self. The theory also predicts the implications of having a black identity on the kinds of outcomes that it fosters.

The essence of the theory, which I call the double consciousness of the black self, is that African Americans operate from markedly different conceptions of the world, especially with respect to the self. African Americans are more collectivist-oriented as opposed to individualistically oriented. However, given that they live in a society that fosters the more individualistic conception, African Americans are in a constant struggle to experience the fruits of a society they were born into, which means in some way endorsing or adjusting to an individualistic conception of the world. At the same time, African Americans are trying to stay true to their roots, experience, and history, embracing a more collectivist conception of the world. This attempt at reconciliation creates major internal problems, resulting in African Americans being more or less in a struggle with themselves. Accepting an alien worldview that is in opposition to the self-realization of the group to which they belong will lead to major internal problems; embracing an indigenous worldview will lead to a curtailment of life chances and restrict material attainments and physical comforts. Acknowledging an ongoing struggle, with many casualties, this theory argues that the African in the aggregate opts for the latter. That is, African Americans remain fundamentally committed to the group.

According to this theory, African Americans will have a strong group attachment, and many factors determine the level of this attachment. Age, class standing (education and income), and spirituality are assumed to have an impact on the black self-concept; however, the different factors often have different relationships with different conceptions of the black self. The claim is made that class has no relationship with the African-centered conception of self (i.e., the self tied to traditional African philosophy) and a minor influence on the non-African centered conceptions of identity. Age, on the other hand, is thought to have a differential effect on the black self. Within this theory, religiosity is assumed to have powerful effects on the various conceptions of the black self.

Aside from these social structural antecedents, the variables within the symbolic social reality category are conceived as having an impact on the black self, with the majority media generally having a negative effect on the self, and the black media (especially print media) having a positive effect. Black involvement with black community cultural, social, and political activities is assumed to be an important and consistent influence on the black self, variously defined. Finally, this theory assumes that the black self-conception will influence a wide range of attitudes, behaviors, and beliefs. The outcomes under investigation here are abstract notions of individualism and collectivism. It is assumed that the black self-concept will be related either to the acceptance of collectivism or to the rejection of individualism.

Figure 10.1 presents a conceptual representation of the aforementioned theory. It incorporates all the variables that are subjected to statistical testing.

To minimize confusion, theoretical definitions are provided for the major constructs, starting with the social structural variables:

Age is defined as sociohistorical, which situates an individual in a particular historical period.

Class is defined as any group of people who have similar goods, services, or skills to exchange for income in a particular economic order and who therefore receive similar remuneration in the marketplace (Wilson, 1980).

Religiosity is defined as beliefs, values, and traditions shared by individuals who engage in regular social interaction.

The constructs under the domain of symbolic social reality are defined in the following way:

Black involvement is the degree to which an individual is engaged in different cultural, political, and social activities committed to the enrichment of Africans as a group.

African self-consciousness represents the conscious African survival impetus in African Americans. It is considered to be relational, with a collective and communal orientation (Kambon, 1991).

Ethnic identity is defined, borrowing from Tajfel (1981), as the aspect of an individual's self-concept that springs from knowledge of his or her membership in

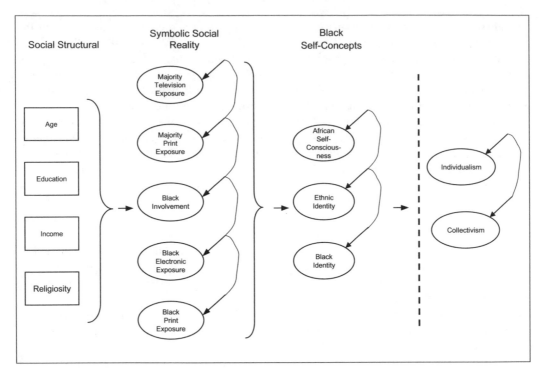

Figure 10.1. Conceptual Representation of the Black Self.

a particular social group, along with the value and emotional bond attached to its significance. In this case, when the object of inquiry is black, the ethnic identity becomes, in operational terms, black identity.

Individualism as a belief system puts priority on personal goals, even when they are in conflict with the goals of family, friends, and intimate others. Alternatively, collectivism is a set of beliefs that give priority to the group and its goals and aspirations.

HYPOTHESES

What follows are the many hypotheses embodied in Figure 10.1, along with the rationale for each.

SYMBOLIC SOCIAL REALITY

Hypothesis 1: Demographic and social structural variables are positively related to majority media exposure.

a. The older the person, the greater the majority television exposure.
b. The older the person, the greater the education, and the greater the income, the greater the exposure to majority print media.

Hypothesis 2: Demographic and social structural variables are related to black media exposure.

a. The younger the person, the greater the black television exposure and the greater the black print exposure.

b. The greater the education and the greater the income, the greater the black television exposure.
c. The greater the education and the greater the income, the more the black print exposure.

Hypothesis 3: Demographic and social structural variables are related to involvement in black activities. The older the person, the greater the education, and the greater the religiosity, the greater the involvement in black activities.

Because the influence of demographic and social structural factors on media exposure (majority and black) and black involvement or in short, symbolic social reality, has already been explored with the accumulated data in a much larger model (Allen, 2001), I repeat the supported hypotheses here. Because of several additional variables in the previous model, relationship may be affected, but because the outcomes were reasonable, I decided not to change the hypotheses. It is worth noting that certain background information, for example, demographic and sociostructural factors, depends on the media under investigation and their operationalization. Different demographic and social structural factors have different influences on media exposure. Although the direction of the effect varies, age has had a consistent effect. For certain types of content, it is the younger who attend more to the media; for other types of content, the older attend more often.

Hypothesis 4: Age influences the degree of ethnicity and black identity. Older people are more likely to have a higher ethnicity and black identity.

Concerning this hypothesis, the theoretical as well as the empirical literature has not always been consistent. For example, Allen et al. (1989) found that socioeconomic status or class was related to certain versions of black identity and closeness to black masses, although the effect was small. A recent study (Allen, 2001) using one of the measures of identity, ethnic identity, found class

(education and income) was not a factor in black identity, although the variable was operationalized differently. Given the content of the ethnicity scale, and especially the African self-consciousness scale, I hypothesize that class (education and income) and religiosity will have negligible effects. That is, across class designations and religious conceptions and actions, there will be no differences with respect to the sense of ethnicity and more broadly to the sense of the African self and group.

Hypothesis 5: Those who are more religious are more likely to embrace collectivism.

This hypothesis grows out of the role that religion has played in the betterment of the entire community and the degree to which individuals who are more religious endorse the principles of their religion. Thus, I assume that the more religious will be more drawn to the notions surrounding collectivism and its strong emphasis on sharing and caring for the less fortunate.

BLACK SELF-CONCEPT

Hypothesis 6: Symbolic social reality influences the different black self-concepts.

a. The greater the black media exposure, the greater the ethnicity and black identity.
b. The greater the black involvement, the greater the African self-consciousness, ethnicity, and black identity.

The idea underlying this hypothesis is that the more African Americans participate in activities and share life experiences with African Americans, the more likely that they will develop a sense of the group and will see their fate as being connected with the group (black identity, ethnic identity). In addition, they will be more willing to work in behalf of the group and to define that group in broader, more diasporic terms (African self-consciousness). Indeed, an argument could be made that the relationship between black involvement and African self-consciousness is reciprocal; I maintain that the dominant effect is from participation in various black cultural and social activities to the development of a certain consciousness. That is, consciousness and identity grow essentially out of actions or, more generally, struggle.

Although black media presentations are generally thought to have a positive influence on the black self-concept, life experiences are sufficient to invoke a positive sense of the black self. Again, as with all media presentations, their influence depends on the content examined. I assume that the content of the black media, especially the black print media, is compatible with a non-normative conception of the self, thus, ethnicity and black identity.

The relationship of black media is a bit more tentative. Theoretically, I defined black media as content that is written and produced by African Americans in the electronic media. The assumption is that work written and directed by African Americans for an African American audience would be more likely to present a more accurate, representative view of the complexity and challenges confronting this group. Moreover, those exposed to such content would more likely have a stronger sense of the black self. There is, however, a gap between this definition and the indicators used to measure it.

On the other hand, if black media or what might be called black-oriented media are defined in terms of the audience to which the fare is directed, without emphasis on the producer or content themes, then the hypothesis becomes more questionable. In this instance, it would be difficult to specify any relationship.

The issue is further complicated by the fact that for black-oriented media and even to some degree in the case of black media, the content produced may reflect varying representations of black life. That is, the content may incorporate either a predominately assimilationist, pluralist, or multiculturalist theme (Gray, 1995). The predominate theme

to which an individual pays attention will likely influence his or her sense of self. To obtain a better grasp of these issues and allow for more confidence in the predictions, it would have been advisable to assess the type of programs and thus the themes embodied in them. Unfortunately, the measures used did not allow that refinement.

INDIVIDUALISM-COLLECTIVISM

Hypothesis 7: The black self-concepts are positively related among themselves and differentially related to individualism and collectivism.

a. Those with a higher African self-consciousness, ethnicity, and black identity are more likely to have a negative attitude toward individualism.
b. Those with a higher African self-consciousness, ethnicity, and black identity are more likely to have a positive attitude toward collectivism.

I assume that the individual who identifies strongly with the African American community senses that his or her fate is aligned with the fate of African people as a whole. That is, identifying with the African American community means to think of more collective solutions to problems and all those attributes that foster such a result. Conversely, I assume that such individuals would therefore be opposed to the emphasis placed on individual solutions or the concept of separating the self-interest from the group interest. An integral part of African self-consciousness is coming together not only to talk about problems but also to solve some of them as a group. Thus, it is likely that those with this attribute would be both in favor of the collectivist conception and against the individualistic conception. I assume that even more than the identity construct, this African-centered conception of the world is compatible with collectivism and opposed to, rather than just neutral toward individualism. Within the confines of my model, this is where the phenomenon of double consciousness can be most graphically explored. If we assume that the essence of having black identity and African self-consciousness is having a sense of the collective, and if we assume that collectivity would therefore be in opposition to the dominant ideas of the larger dominant European society, it would be safe to assume that it would be difficult to embrace collectivism and individualism simultaneously. This would reflect two warring tendencies, to use Du Bois's terms. It would be less problematic if these individuals endorsed collectivism but had no particular relationship with individualism. An interesting situation could arise whereby the individuals with strong black identity and African self-consciousness do not support either collectivism or individualism. Or more confusing yet, these individuals might be negative toward collectivism and positive toward individualism. This would bring into question the construct validity of our identity and consciousness constructs.

▶ Data and Methods

The data were collected from African American adults living in the Detroit metropolitan area. The sample was selected to ensure a wide range of opinions and attitudes on a divergent group of social issues. This purposive sample was composed of respondents from identifiable social and religious groups. The sample included individuals from church groups (three different denominations), from a social self-help group, from undergraduates at a university, and from a professional social group. The sample was intended to be representative in age, income, and gender composition. From these various stratifications, 311 respondents where chosen.[1] This sample was the first stage of a larger final sample of 551 people.

The questionnaire was self-administered, which took about 40 minutes. Each individual received $10 for participating. The questionnaire covered such topics as self-esteem, social beliefs and opinions about contemporary

social issues, media behavior and attitudes, and basic background and other identifying information.

AFRICAN SELF-CONSCIOUSNESS

This scale was created by Baldwin and Bell (1985). It grew out of and is one operationalization of an African-centered approach to the self. Baldwin and Bell maintained that the full scale of 42 items tapped four competencies. They were (a) the awareness or recognition of one's collective African identity and origin; (b) priority placed on African survival, liberation, and proactive development; (c) priorities placed on African self-knowledge, African-centered values, rituals, customs, and institutions; and (d) attitudes of resistance and contestation to anti-African forces.

I selected a subset of only 18 items from these four areas, attempting to obtain the most representative elements in each category. Overall, the items reflected the evaluative component. The items used reflected all four of the aforementioned domains and were evaluated with a 5-point *agree* to *disagree* format. The Cronbach's alpha measure of internal consistency was .88.

ETHNIC IDENTITY

This ethnic identity scale may be deemed non-African centered in the way described previously. The author of this ethnic identity scale, Phinney (1990), attempted to provide a general conception of ethnic identity with universalistic applications. The assumption is that the scale is valid across racial groups. The items reflected the extent to which the respondents identify with their ethnic group, enjoy being in the company of the group, and have a sense of belongingness to the group. The items represented the affective or emotional dimension of identity. Respondents were asked to express how well each question described them: 1 = *does not describe me at all,*

2 = *describes me a little bit,* 3 = *describes me moderately well,* 4 = *describes me a lot,* 5 = *totally describes me.* The Cronbach's alpha measure of internal consistency was .85.

BLACK IDENTITY

The operationalization of this scale is such that it does not make the same claims embodied in the African-centered approach; thus, it would not be considered within that designation. This identity measure was used as race specific and reflected the cognitive component. It asks respondents to indicate the extent to which they identify with being black. Using pictures of circles at various levels of overlap, respondents mark the representation that best characterizes their position. There were eight different degrees of overlap, ranging from *far apart* to *complete overlap.*

INDIVIDUALISM/COLLECTIVISM

The individualism scale was composed of six items selected from a larger universe of items proposed by Triandis, McCusker, and Hui (1990). On a 5-point scale, where 1 = *strongly disagree* and 5 = *strongly agree,* respondents indicated the amount of agreement on the following items.

1. One should live one's life independently of others as much as possible.
2. I would rather struggle through a personal problem by myself than discuss it with my friend.
3. One does better working alone than in a group.
4. What happens to me is my own doing.
5. It is important to me that I perform better than others.
6. When faced with a difficult personal problem, it is better to advise yourself rather than follow the advice of others.

The Cronbach's alpha measure of internal consistency was .76.

The collectivism scale was composed of four items selected from the same larger universe of items with the same *agree* to *disagree* format. These items were

1. I would help within my means if a relative told me that he/she is in financial difficulty.
2. I enjoy talking to neighbors every day.
3. I like and live close to my good friends.
4. Aging parents should live at home with their children.

The Cronbach's alpha measure of internal consistency was .60.

The above items were coded to reflect a greater sense of the attribute in question.[2] Thus, for example, the higher the number for ethnic identity, the greater the ethnic identity.

BACKGROUND AND SOCIAL STRUCTURAL VARIABLES

Age was tapped by an item that asked the age at last birthday.

Class was tapped by two items: (a) the highest level of education completed, from 1 = elementary school to 7 = graduate degree; (b) total family income, using eight categories ranging from 1 = 0- $4,999 to 8 = $50,000 or more.

RELIGIOUS BACKGROUND (RELIGIOSITY)

The following six measures were used:

1. How often do you attend religious services? Response on a scale of 1 = *never* to 5 = every week.
2. How religious would you say you are? Response on a scale of 1 = *very much* to 4 = *not at all.*

3. How often do you read religious books or other religious materials? Response on a scale of 1 = *never* to 7 = *every day.*
4. How often do you listen to or watch religious programs? Response on a scale of 1 = *never* to 7 = *every day.*
5. How often do you pray? Response on a scale of 1 = *never* to 7 = every day.
6. How often do you ask someone to pray for you? Response on a scale of 1 = *never* to 4 = *very frequently.*

The Cronbach's alpha measure of internal consistency was .82.

SYMBOLIC SOCIAL REALITY

I selected only a sample of the many indicators of symbolic social reality.

Majority Television

1. How much time do you spend watching TV on an average day (in minutes)?

Majority Print

1. How many days during the week do you read the newspapers (number of days)?
2. How often do you read magazines? (7-point frequency scale, ranging from 1 = *never* to 7 = *very often*)

On a 5-point scale from 1 = *never* to 5 = *all the time,* respondents indicated frequency regarding the following:

Black Electronic Exposure

1. Watch black TV stations/shows
2. Go to black movies
3. Listen to black radio stations/programs

Black Print

1. Read black newspapers/magazines
2. Read books by black authors

Black involvement

1. Attend or participate in black festivals or celebrations
2. Practice customs or traditions unique to your black heritage
3. Teach your children about black history
4. Plan or desire to visit Africa

The Cronbach's alpha measure of internal consistency was .68.

▶ **Results**

Figure 10.1 is a representation of the relationships embodied in my theoretical model. The data were analyzed by structural equation modeling. A general program (LISREL) was used to estimate the unknown coefficients in a set of linear structure equations.

The first step in this analysis is to test the global model fit to determine whether the general theorizing is valid. This involves the investigation of the measurement aspect of the model. The second step is to estimate the many hypotheses and to find out the extent to which they are confirmed or disconfirmed. I provide a context for these above analyses by first presenting the summary measures. Table 10.1 presents the means for the self-concepts.

If we use any value above the midpoint as a measure of adequacy, Table 10.1 shows that African Americans are above this point on each of the black self-concepts and also on the individualism and collectivism scales. The table indicates that African Americans have an especially high ethnic identity and collectivist conception, followed by a strong African self-consciousness and black identity. Clearly, the smallest mean was evident for the individualism construct. One might conclude that African Americans feel a strong sense of ethnic identity, an African-centered consciousness, a heightened black identity, and a collectivist concept, but a comparatively weak individualistic orientation. These outcomes are consistent with the overall theorizing.

TABLE 10.1   Means for Black Self-Concepts and Individualism and Collectivism

Concept Name	Mean	(SD)
African self-consciousness (18 items, 5 points)	61.39	(3.41)
Ethnicity (12 items, 5 points)	45.25	(3.77)
Black identity (1 item, 8 points)	5.25	(2.30)
Individualism (6 items, 5 points)	16.32	(2.72)
Collectivism (4 items, 5 points)	14.28	(3.57)

TABLE 10.2   Correlation Among the Black Self-Concepts and Individualism and Collectivism

	African Self-Consciousness	Ethnicity	Black Identity	Individualism	Collectivism
African self-consciousness					
Ethnicity	42*	—			
Black identity	.21*	.37*	—		
Individualism	−.34*	−.28*	−.23*	—	
Collectivism	.24*	.26*	.15*	−.22*	—

*$p < .05$.

Table 10.2 provides a clear picture of the association among the various black self-concepts, collectivism, and individualism. As predicted, all the black self-concepts are positively correlated, and they were all statistically significant. Moreover, the measures of the black self-concept were positively related to collectivism and negatively related to individualism as hypothesized. The majority of the correlations were from moderate to fairly high in magnitude.

I now turn to the fit of the model. Indeed, a number of fit measures might be examined. I explored only a few of the generally accepted fit measures. Table 10.3 presents some of the major fit measures.

Looking at the χ^2 measure, which is affected by sample size, we see that this measure is statistically significant, thus suggesting a poor model fit. However, according to the other more appropriate measures, the fit is good. For example, the Comparative Fit Index (.94), the non-normed fit index (.91), and the root mean square residual (.04) all signify a good fit. With these results, we can feel comfortable in examining the component fit measures.

The factor loadings or the extent to which the indicators reflect their respective constructs were very good. The factor loadings ranged from .46 to .90. The magnitude of the standardized factor loadings was similar. The biggest discrepancy appeared for the black involvement construct, where the smallest value was .47 and the largest was .74. Furthermore, a considerable amount of the variance was explained in each of the self-constructs and the individualism/collectivism constructs: in or-

TABLE 10.3	Global Fit Measures for the Black Self-Concept Model

Measures	Estimates
χ^2	300.29
df	169
p	.00
χ^2/df	1.78
Root mean square residual	.04
Comparative fit index	.94

der of magnitude, 53% of the variance in ethnicity, 44% of the variance in African self-consciousness constructs, and 12% of the variance in black identity. More of the variance was explained in individualism as compared to collectivism, .28 and .19, respectively.

Figure 10.2 presents the amount of variance explained for each construct and the statistically significant estimates of the entire model. As you can see, many relationships are evident. The demographic and social structural variables have pronounced effects on the constructs that fall under the heading of symbolic social reality. I find that one's position in social history, or age, influences all of the social reality constructs. Those who were older watched more majority television and read more majority print media; they were also more involved in black events and activities. However, the younger respondents attended more to black-oriented television and black print media. The two indicators of class, education and income, had different effects, with income being more influential. Those with more income attended to the majority media and to black-oriented television more often. On the other hand, those with more education attended more to the majority media, but this education variable had no effect on majority television viewing or any other media variable. Education did, however, have a positive influence on the amount of black involve-

ment. Religion had only one effect on the social reality constructs, namely, black involvement, where the greater the religiosity, the greater the black involvement. A modest amount of variance was explained in the symbolic social reality constructs. For the majority media, 2% and 15% of the variance were explained for majority television exposure and majority print exposure, respectively. For the black media, 23% and 4% of the variance were explained for black-oriented television exposure and black print media exposure, respectively.

The social structural variables had no direct effects on the self-constructs in the model. There were indirect effects of age, education, and income transmitted by the black involvement construct. The results indicated that older African Americans have a greater sense of ethnicity, and those with higher incomes tend to have greater black identity. This latter relationship, however, is quite small.

Although the symbolic social reality construct was influenced by many social structural variables, these variables generally had little effect on the self-constructs. Majority television exposure had a positive influence on African self-consciousness. More exposure to majority television was linked with greater sense of African self-consciousness. Only one other variable within the social reality category had an influence on any of the self-concepts. This construct, black involvement, had a strong positive influence on all the self-constructs. Thus, those who were involved in activities of African people were more likely to have an African self-consciousness, greater ethnicity, and a greater black identity. The black self-constructs also had the greatest amount of variance explained in the entire model: 44% of African self-consciousness, 53% of ethnicity, and 12% of black identity were explained by the aforementioned variables.

Finally, we can see that the degree to which individualism or collectivism is embraced is influenced by a number of variables. Only one social structural variable had an influence, and that is the religiosity variable. Those who

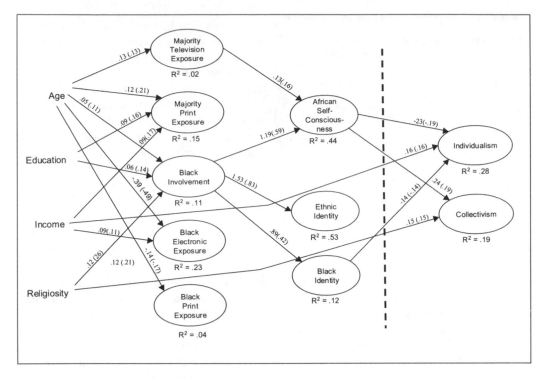

Figure 10.2. Statistically Significant Estimates of the Model of the Black Self.

were more religious were more likely to embrace collectivism. Only one social reality construct had an influence, and that was the variable of majority television exposure. The relationship was such that the more respondents were exposed to majority television, the less was their sense of collectivism. Although ethnicity had no influence on either individualism or collectivism, black identity had a negative influence on individualism. Those with greater black identity were less likely to embrace individualism. Only the construct of African self-consciousness influenced both individualism and collectivism. Those with a greater African self-consciousness not only were more likely to embrace collectivism but also were less likely to endorse individualism. A modest amount of variance was explained in collectivism (19%) and individualism (28%).

In sum, most hypotheses received some support. Specifically, Hypotheses 1a and 1b were fully supported. Older respondents were more likely to attend to majority television and majority print media, and the more educated and those with greater income were more involved with the majority media. Hypothesis 2 had only partial support: Younger people were more likely to attend to the black media, both print and electronic. Income did have an impact on the level of black electronic media exposure. As predicted by Hypothesis 3, the older, the more educated, and the more religious were more involved with black activities. Whereas Hypothesis 4 predicted age to influence both the degree of ethnicity and black identity, it had no direct influence. Hypothesis 5 was supported. Those who were more religious were more likely to embrace collectivism. Hypothesis 6 pertained to the influences of the symbolic social reality variables. As predicted, the greater the involvement in black activities, the greater the African self-consciousness, ethnicity, and black identity. The second part of the hypothesis suggests that the black media would influence ethnicity and black identity. This hypothesis received no support. There was no relationship between black print media and black-oriented television exposure and ethnicity or identity. Hypothesis 7 assumed that the black self-concepts would be positively related among themselves and that they would have a positive impact on collectivism. Support for these hypotheses was somewhat unclear. Looking at the association among the black self-concepts, they follow the assumed relationships, but only African self-consciousness influenced both collectivism and individualism. Although African self-consciousness had an influence on individualism and collectivism in the predicted direction, no other self-concept had an influence on collectivism and only one other self-concept, black identity, had an influence on individualism. That relationship was such that the greater the black identity, the less the individualism. Briefly, individuals with an African self-consciousness best reflect what one would expect from an African-originated sense of self—attachment to the collective and comparatively less emphasis on the individual self. Such an outcome seems more compatible with the resolution of double consciousness. Individuals having a black identity seem to be averse to individualism but have no particular tie to collectivism. It is noteworthy that those who endorse the nonrace-referenced ethnic identity have no relationship with either individualism or collectivism. Perhaps this indicates that although the various self-concepts are related, they have demonstrably different outcomes, with the race-based self concepts having more similar outcomes than the nonrace-based self-concept.

► Conclusion

In this study, I addressed two related questions of the self: namely, who am I? and where do I belong? These are questions of identity. Their complexity is exacerbated for African Americans, whose sense of self is under enduring attack. I relied heavily on the work of W.E.B. Du Bois, especially his ideas concerning the omnipresence of double consciousness. With this theoretical formulation and the many modifications made by contemporary theorists, I constructed a theory fragment called the double consciousness of the black self. I used it to predict and explain those elements that influence the black self and that are influenced by black self-concept. The essence of the argument is that African Americans on average have a high regard for and close attachment to their group and as a consequence have a strong collectivist orientation.

I emphasized the historical context and contemporary background for understanding the forces that impinge on the black self and how these important constructs affect the broader philosophical issues. I identified a wide range of antecedents to explain the outcome of an Africa-centered conception of self, African self-consciousness, and two non-African centered conceptions of the self, black identity and ethnic identity. Essentially, I maintained that people's placement in sociohistorical time, their class, and their religious experiences all influence their symbolic social reality, and these together influence their black self-concepts. Moreover, I employed these three black self-concepts to predict the extent to which they produce certain views of life, that is, individualistic and collectivistic, and I asserted that the different categories of identity (African-centered and non-African centered) have different influences on philosophical orientations toward life.

To summarize the major findings, age was an important predictor of exposure to certain kind of media content and participation in black activities and affairs. Older African Americans tended to pay more attention to majority media and to engage in more black activities, but the younger pay more attention to black media. In short, one's location in historical time, as age is defined, were distinctly different in level of exposure and participation. Interestingly, age had no appreciable effect on having an African self-consciousness.

Another antecedent variable, religiosity, influenced two outcomes, namely black involvement and collectivism. The more religiously oriented African Americans were more likely to be involved in activities directed at African Americans and tended to be more collectivist in orientation. Class, as reflected in level of education and family income, had differential positive impact on several media measures but had a positive influence on black involvement. However, this class variable did not have an effect on any of the black self-concepts. Income, but not education, had a positive effect on individualism. Those with more income tended to embrace individualism.

Out of all the variables in the symbolic social reality category, black involvement had the most pronounced effects on black self-concept. The effects were consistently positive and strong. That is, those who had greater black involvement in the black community possessed a stronger ethnic identity, black identity, and African self-consciousness.

Finally, only those who possessed an African self-consciousness are both in favor of collectivism and simultaneously against an individualistic orientation. Of the three self-concepts, the African self-consciousness construct was the only one explicitly developed to reflect an African-centered concept of the world. Whereas ethnic identity had an effect on neither individualism nor collectivism, black identity was negatively related to individualism. To facilitate an interpretation of these findings, it should be kept in mind that the black self-concepts were positively correlated among themselves. Furthermore, these black self-concepts correlated negatively with individualism and positively with collectivism. Also of interest in interpreting the adequacy of the theorizing is that a substantial amount of variance is explained in several of the black self-concepts, and these variables explain a sizable portion of the variance for the individualism and collectivism variables.

Several salient aspects of the theorizing should be noted. First, the distinction between the African-centered conception of the self and its less normative counterpart revealed basically the same antecedents as predictors and in the same direction. Indeed, there are few predictors of these self-concepts, the most notable being black involvement. This suggests that once black involvement is initiated through various social structural factors, it stimulates a strong black self-concept. It may be, however, that the two different categories of the black self-concept lead to different outcomes or lack thereof as shown in this study. Indeed, some of the literature suggests this outcome, but it needs to be more systematically explored with a wider range of theoretically derived outcomes.

Furthermore, the examination of these black self-concepts alerts us to the multi-dimensionality of the black self-concept and to the importance of clarifying the meaning and measurement of these constructs. A useful distinction has been made in the literature between personal self-esteem and reference group identity (Cross, 1991), but in addition, one needs to keep in mind the various concepts that might fall under this heading of reference group identity and its differing substantive significance. Very different processes may be in operation for the different constructs.

Although I found support for many hypotheses, some predicted relationships did not receive support. For example, the impact of the mass media is minimal. With the exception of the influence of majority television on an African self-consciousness, no media exposure measure produced any strong effects. I predicted that the black media especially would have a positive influence on two of the black self-concepts, black identity and ethnic identity. In some of the past literature (e.g., Allen, 2001; Allen & Hatchett, 1986), the black print media had positive effects on the sense of self-worth and one version of the identity measure, closeness to the masses. Again, this lack of relationship points to the importance of taking into account the specific dimension of the black self under examination. Moreover, it may be worthwhile to operationalize black media with respect to the ideological range of its content within both the print and electronic media. This strategy might extend to cover the different content types in the majority media, particularly in light of the positive relationship between exposure to majority television and having a sense of African self-consciousness. Finally, a debate in the literature suggests that class should have an impact on black identity, but the empirical literature has shown conflicting findings. With certain black self-concepts, a relationship exists, sometimes strong. With other black self-concepts, no relationship exists. Apart from the variance in the definition and operationalization of class, it sometimes looms as an important force and at other times it does not. In this study, class had only a modest influence on various indicators of symbolic reality and had negligible effects on the sense of self. The two indicators of class, education and income, often had relationships with different variables. Perhaps this is just further support for the argument that class takes a complex form in the lives of African Americans. Moreover, it suggests that African Americans' sense of self has an importance across various class groupings. Acknowledging the complexity of the class concept, it may be useful to explore certain segments of the African American community with respect to identity. For example, much discussion surrounds the so-called black underclass, or those most adversely affected by an oppressive system, and how they relate to the group. Many researchers assume that this segment, apart from their brethren who have managed to withstand the onslaught, are more prone to have less favorable views about the group and more likely to operate in ways detrimental to the group. This is an issue waiting to be systematically explored.

Although the model employed was compatible with the data, there are always many other models that might fit the data equally well. Thus, it would be helpful to examine the model with other data and in different settings

to increase our confidence in the model's viability. I must also add the proviso that the data were collected to be broadly representative of the African American community with respect to crucial social and demographic variables, but it was a purposive sample; thus, we must be cautious in our generalizations.

▶ Notes

1. With the full data set, I examined an expanded version of my conceptual model. Whereas the same variables were used in both studies under the headings of *social structural* and *social reality,* several additional variables were used to represent the black self-constructs. The analysis is provided in my forthcoming book, *The Self-Concept: African-American Identity and Self-Esteem.*

2. Some constructs in the model were composed of summed indicators. Religiosity was composed of six summed indicators. Also, each of the constructs falling under the heading of symbolic social reality was composed of non-summed indicators (i.e., individual items). The black self-concept constructs were composed of summed items, with the exception of black identity. It was a one-item construct. The African self-consciousness and the ethnic identity constructs were composed of three summed indicators. Finally, the individualism and collectivism constructs were each composed of a summed scale.

▶ References

Adoni, H., & Mane, S. (1984). Media and the social construction of reality: Toward an integration of theory and research. *Communication Research, 11,* 323-340.

Akbar, N. (1985). *The community of self.* Tallahassee, FL: Mind Productions & Associates.

Akbar, N. (1995). *Natural psychology and human transformation.* Tallahassee, FL: Mind Productions & Associates.

Allen, R. L. (2001). *The concept of self: A study in black identity and self-esteem.* Detroit, MI: Wayne State University Press.

Allen, R. L., Dawson, M. C., & Brown, R. E. (1989). A schema-based approach to modeling an African-American racial belief system. *American Political Science Review, 83,* 421-441.

Allen, R. L., & Hatchett, S. (1986). The media and social reality effects: Self and system orientations of blacks. *Communication Research, 13,* 97-123.

Anderson, S. E. (1995). *The black holocaust for beginners.* New York: Writers and Readers Publishing.

Aptheker, H. (1944). *American Negro slave revolts.* New York: International Publishers.

Baldwin, J. (1985). *The price of the ticket: Collected nonfiction, 1948-1985.* New York: St. Martin's.

Baldwin, J. A. (1991). African (black) psychology: Issues and synthesis. In R. L. Jones (Ed.), *Black psychology* (3rd ed., pp. 125-135). Berkeley, CA: Cobb & Henry.

Baldwin, J. A., & Bell, Y. R. (1985). An Africentric personality questionnaire. *The Western Journal of Black Studies, 9,* 61-68.

Bennett, L. (1966). *Before the Mayflower: A history of the Negro in America, 1619-1964.* Baltimore: Pelican Books.

Blassingame, J. (1972). *The slave community.* New York: Oxford University Press.

Broman, C. L., Neighbors, H. W., & Jackson, J. (1988). Racial group identification among black adults. *Social Forces, 67,* 146-158.

Brown, S. (1969). *The Negro in American fiction.* New York: Quadrangle.

Cross, W. E., Jr. (1991). *Shades of black: Diversity in African-American identity.* Philadelphia: Temple University Press.

Cross, W. E., Jr., & Strauss, L. (1998). The everyday functions of African identity. In J. K. Swim & C. Stranger (Eds.). *Prejudice: The target's perspective* (pp. 267-279). San Diego: Academic Press.

Dates, J. L., & Barlow, W. (1993). Introduction: A war of images. In J. L. Dates & W. Barlow (Eds.), *Split image: African Americans in the mass media* (2nd ed., pp. 1-21). Washington, DC: Howard University Press.

Demo, D. H., & Hughes, M. (1990). Socialization and racial identity among black Americans. *Social Psychology Quarterly, 53,* 364-374.

Du Bois, W.E.B. (1961). *The souls of black folk.* New York: Fawcett.

Finkenstaedt, R.L.H. (1994). *Face to face: Blacks in America: White perceptions and black realities.* New York: William R. Morrow.

Gaines, S. O., & Reed, E. S. (1994). Two social psychologies of prejudice: Gordon W. Allport, W.E.B. Du Bois, and the legacy of Booker T. Washington. *Journal of Black Psychology, 20,* 8-28.

Gaines, S. O., & Reed, E. S. (1995). From Allport to Du Bois. *American Psychologist, 50,* 96-103.

Gould, S. J. (1993). American polygeny and craniometry before Darwin: Blacks and Indians as separate, inferior species. In S. Harding (Ed.), *The racial economy of science: Toward a democratic future* (pp. 84-115). Bloomington: Indiana University Press.

Gray, H. (1995). *Watching race: Television and the struggle for "blackness."* Minneapolis: University of Minnesota Press.

Gurin, P., & Epps, E. G. (1975). *Black consciousness, identity, and achievement.* New York: John Wiley.

Harding, S. (1993). Introduction: Eurocentric scientific illiteracy—A challenge for the world community. In S. Harding (Ed.), *The racial economy of science: Toward a democratic future* (pp. 1-22). Bloomington: Indiana University Press.

Harris, J. E. (1972). *Africans and their history.* New York: Mentor.

Herman, E. S., & Chomsky, N. (1988). *Manufacturing consent: The political economy of the mass media.* New York: Pantheon.

Hilliard, A. G. (1995). *The maroon within us: Selected essays on African American community socialization.* Baltimore: Black Classic Press.

Holloway, J. E. (1990). The origins of African-American culture. In J. E. Holloway (Ed.), *Africanisms in American culture.* Bloomington: University of Indiana Press.

Huggins, N. I. (1991). The deforming mirror of truth: Slavery and the master narrative of American history. *Radical History Review, 49,* 25-48.

Jackson, J. G. (1970). *Introduction to African civilization.* Secaucas, NJ: Citadel.

Kambon, K.K.K. (1991). *The African personality in America: An African-centered framework.* Tallahassee, FL: Nubian Nation Publications.

Karenga, M. (1993). *Introduction to black studies* (2nd ed.). Los Angeles: University of Sankore Press.

Kern-Foxworth, M. (1995). *Aunt Jemima, Uncle Ben, and Rastus.* Westport, CT: Praeger.

Lewin, K. (1948). *Resolving social conflicts.* New York: Harper.

MacDonald, J. F. (1992). *Blacks and white TV: African Americans in television since 1948* (2nd ed.). Chicago: Nelson-Hall.

Markus, H. R., & Kitayama, S. (1991). Culture and the self: Implications for cognition, emotion, and motivation. *Psychological Review, 98,* 224-253.

Markus, H. R., & Kitayama, S. (1994). A collective fear of the collective: Implications for selves and theories of selves. *Personality and Social Psychology Bulletin, 20,* 568-579.

Myers, L. J. (1993). *Understanding an Afrocentric world view: Introduction to an optimal psychology* (2nd ed.). Dubuque, IA: Kendall/Hunt.

Myers, L. J. (1998). The deep structure of culture: Relevance of traditional African culture in contemporary life. In J. D. Hamlet (Ed.), *Afrocentric visions* (pp. 3-140). Thousand Oaks, CA: Sage.

Neal, L. (1968). And shine swam on. In L. Jones & L. Neal (Eds.), *Black fire: An anthology of Afro-American writing* (pp. 637-656). New York: William R. Morrow.

Nobles, W. W. (1973). Psychological research and the black self-concept: A critical review. *Journal of Social Issues, 29,* 11-31.

Nobles, W. W. (1991a). African philosophy: Foundations for black psychology. In R. L. Jones (Ed.), *Black psychology* (3rd ed., pp. 47-63). Berkeley, CA: Cobb & Henry.

Nobles, W. W. (1991b). Extended self: Rethinking the so-called Negro self-concept. In R. L.

Jones (Ed.), *Black psychology* (3rd ed., pp. 295-304). Berkeley, CA: Cobb & Henry.

Phinney, J. S. (1990). Ethnic identity in adolescents and adults: Review of research. *Psychological Bulletin, 108,* 499-514.

Pierce, C. M. (1980). Social trace contaminants: Subtle indicators of racism in TV. In S. Withey & R. P. Abeles (Eds.), *Television and social behavior: Beyond violence and children* (pp. 249-257). Hillsdale, NJ: Lawrence Erlbaum.

Riggs, M. (1988). *Ethnic notions* [Film]. San Francisco: California Newsreel.

Riggs, M. (1991). *Color adjustment* [Film]. San Francisco: California Newsreel.

Shweder, R. A., & Bourne, E. J. (1982). Does the concept of person vary cross-culturally? In R. A. Shweder & R. A. LeVine (Eds.), *Culture theory: Essays on mind, self, and emotion* (pp. 158-199). Cambridge, UK: Cambridge University Press.

Steinberg, S. (1989). *The ethnic myth: Race, ethnicity, and class in America.* Boston: Beacon Press.

Steinberg, S. (1995). *Turning back: The retreat from racial justice in American thought and policy.* Boston: Beacon.

Tajfel, H. (1981). *Human groups and social categories.* Cambridge, UK: Cambridge University Press.

Thompson, R. F. (1984). *Flash of the spirit: African & Afro-American art & philosophy.* New York: Vintage.

Triandis, H. C. (1994). *Culture and social behavior.* New York: McGraw-Hill.

Triandis, H. C., McCusker, C., & Hui, C. H. (1990). Multimethod probes of individualism and collectivism. *Journal of Personality and Social Psychology, 59,* 1006-1020.

Ture, K., & Hamilton, C. V. (1992). *Black power: The politics of liberation.* New York: Vintage.

Wilson, W. J. (1980). *The declining significance of race* (2nd ed.). Chicago: University of Chicago Press.

Zinn, H. (1995). *A people's history of the United States, 1492-present.* New York: Harper.

Communication and Social Scientific Discourse

Toward an Understanding of the Du Boisian Perspective

ANTHONY MONTEIRO

From 1892 to 1895, while completing research and studies at Harvard University and the University of Berlin that would eventually appear as his doctoral dissertation, W.E.B. Du Bois boldly projected the possibility of subjecting to scientific scrutiny the problem of race in the modern world. To achieve this end, he would have to confront not merely race but power. He would be compelled to rethink the language of social science as well as its methods. How, he would ask, to communicate with diverse and at times antagonist racial audiences about race? What discursive and linguistic strategies should be deployed? And finally, most significant, how

could one dislodge or at least weaken racist domination over intellectual and social scientific discourse? In the course of his long and creative career, Du Bois addressed these issues, leaving to us a profound legacy on which to build, one that challenges not only race as a conceptual category and thus a mode of discourse but also race power and the discourse that flows from it. Hence, the Du Boisian approach is the inverse of the postmodernist. It looks at reality as the context and foundation of discourse. Therefore, the point is not to change discourse first but to change reality. This chapter will explore Du Bois's path to an empowering African American/African-centered social science discourse, one that challenges the 20th century and leaves us the task of challenging the 21st.

In this chapter, I think about science as a site of cultural communication, with distinct codes and modalities of knowing. I argue that Du Bois, in attempting to construct a science of race and race relationships, sought to introduce new modalities of scientific communication, both within the social scientific community and among the general public. I also attempt to show that Du Bois ultimately understood that knowledge is inevitably interconnected with power. That is, those who control social and cultural power decide what is considered scientific knowledge. Hence, the Du Boisian intervention into extant scientific discourse can be considered part of an attempt to construct a transcultural discourse. On the one side stands the culture of the white male scientific community; on the other, the culture of black thinkers, who were marginalized and excluded from institutions of cultural power and denied the instruments of knowledge diffusion and legitimation. However, through his sociological laboratory at Atlanta University and the Atlanta University Conferences, Du Bois began to develop what I consider an alternative scientific discourse about race and thus redefined social scientific discourse. In this sense, it was a distinct scientific culture that was developed at Atlanta University, a discourse that he hoped might resonate on both sides of the color line. Yet—and this becomes the specifically scientific aspect of his enterprise—he wanted to equip the social sciences with new linguistic tools, cultural codes, and theoretical conceptualizations. The Du Boisian enterprise in this respect is viewed as transgressive, even disruptive, of existing relationships of cultural and scientific power.

In large measure, by looking at Du Bois's work as part of the sociology of scientific knowledge production, I at the same time contextualize his project as one of communicating to both the powerful and the powerless, speaking through science to both sides of the color line. His achievement, then, seems far more significant than to explain empirically the plight of black folk. Rather, it was to radically alter the culture of the social sciences. This project, located in Black, Africana, and Afro-American Studies departments and programs, continues to this day.

Unlike most of the white founders of academic sociology, Du Bois would contend, more forcefully in succeeding years, that the central object of a uniquely scientific American sociology would be the study of race. This, of course, would radically separate the American and European social scientific and intellectual projects. Turner, Beeghley, and Powers (1995) make clear that sociology, and the social sciences generally, emerged in the 19th century as intellectual endeavors to make sense of historical developments in Europe. "Sociology," they remind us, "was formed from theoretical questions about the European historical experience" (p. 1). Modernity, science, and reason became central issues for it to explain. Class, social status, prestige, and the relationship of the individual to society and the state emerged as dominant themes. The social universe was viewed as being exclusively European. To be human, and thus worthy of scientific consideration, meant being European. In the 19th century, European social scientists sought to organize themselves as branches of science and to model the social sciences on one of the natural sciences. In this respect, positivism, in the Comtean sense of metaphysical or general statements being tested against carefully collected facts, increasingly defined what it meant to be scientific in the social sciences.[1] Du Bois sought to apply scientific methods to the study of the African American people, with the intent of upsetting the prevailing notions of race superiority and inferiority.

Although this was not immediately clear, Du Bois's project challenged a fundamental assumption of Eurocentric social thinking: the idea that only Europeans and only European societies were worthy of scientific investigation. In 1897, Du Bois declared before the American Academy of Social and Political Sciences that the Negro is a member of the human race, and as one who, in the light of history and experience, is capable to a degree of improvement and culture, is entitled to have his interests considered according to his numbers in all conclusions as to the common weal. (Du Bois, 1940/1995, p. 60)

And he concluded, "The American Negro deserves study for the great end of advancing the cause of science in general" (p. 61). On this point, he became more tough minded over the years.

Africans, in the European mind, were objects of history and had not emerged beyond the state of nature. Social science as a study of human agency was, by definition, not concerned with Africans. Biology or anthropology were considered the appropriate fields for study of Africans. Du Bois challenged these assumptions from the start of his career. Science in the postbellum United States was the new intellectual fad. In the Progressive Era, it was being touted as the answer to most of the extant problems of white civilization. Du Bois (1940/1995), speaking of his education at Fisk, Harvard, and Berlin, said, "The main result of my schooling had been to emphasize science and the scientific attitude" (p. 50). Whereas the natural sciences were well on their way into the 20th century, the social sciences, Du Bois (1940/1995) observed, "were engaged in vague statements" (p. 51). Herbert Spencer's 10-volume *A System of Synthetic Philosophy* reflected the intellectual and scientific style of the age. Spencer sought to use biology as a methodological analogue for society. He agreed with Darwin that evolution is a process of adaptation of organisms to their environment. The mind, he argued, was a part of natural evolution. And as biological evolution had produced superior and inferior species and intelligences, social evolution had produced inferior and superior societies, races, and classes with distinct moral, physical, and intellectual capacities. William James, Du Bois's professor and friend at Harvard, passionately disagreed with Spencer's social Darwinism, opposing him from a Dar-

winian standpoint. James believed Darwin's theory implied that the mind's job is to select aspects of the world important for us to act on and thus assist in our adaptation to the world. James recognized that the core of Darwin's theory was the idea of local adaptation to specific conditions, rather than a grand theory of progress predicated on a linear notion of stages of development, wherein each succeeding stage is considered superior to what preceded it.

The biological analogy, although striking for its bold generalizations, would have to await Francis Galton's discoveries in statistics to be translated into what would pass for a scientific research program. Galton's contribution to positivist social science was inventing techniques that could measure social Darwinian principles. Statistics were his method of proving that through selective breeding, a superior racial stock could be created. In 1869, he published *Hereditary Genius,* designed to convince the skeptical public of the superior hereditary endowments of certain eminent British families. Smedley (1993) indicates, "Arguing that there is a physiological basis for psychological traits, he invented techniques for measuring what he thought was intelligence, along with the bell-shaped curve for demonstrating its 'normal distribution' " (p. 266).

Du Bois had experienced an even more lethal form of social Darwinism in Germany in the classes of the German ultranationalist and racist Heinrich von Treitschke. German academics combined normal social Darwinism with the Nietzschean concept of the superman. This was the 19th century's legacy to the 20th century on race: extending the positivist philosophical bent to measurement of human genetic inheritance.[2]

Du Bois, the young positivist, showed a profound opposition to social Darwinism. He recognized, as he indicates, that a real situation presented itself to him and, he hoped, to the social sciences. He would use science against scientific racism in the interest of reform and uplift, "but nevertheless, I wanted to do the work with scientific accuracy" (Du Bois,

1940/1995, p. 51). Du Bois subsequently turned his "gaze from fruitless word-twisting and fac[ed] the facts of my own social situation and racial world, I determined to put science into sociology through a study of the conditions and problems of my own group" (1940/1995, p. 51). Du Bois earnestly sought to discover, and then to equip the social sciences with methodologies appropriate to its object of inquiry. Yet, in so doing, he rejected the lures of reductionism, solipsism, and the pure objectivism of positivism. This, in the end, placed Du Bois in an irrevocable conflict with Spencerian social Darwinism and the hereditarian research program that accompanied it.[3] For most white Americans, these views expressed both commonsense and experience. They became the dominant ideological and research paradigms on race matters within Anglo-American social science and research of the time. The ideas related to Social Darwinism actively supported racism and class subordination; they were strongly anti-immigrant. Social structure and social behavior were viewed as the consequences of inherited genetic characteristics. As the official scientific explanation of their age, they dominated political and cultural discourse. Early in his career, Du Bois attributed this problem to society's lack of scientific knowledge, which he traced to the conceptual and methodological poverty of the social sciences. This was a situation he hoped to change.

What he failed to see early in his career was that it was not science but rather ideology driving this research program. Race and white supremacy were what Bourdieu (1977) calls structuring structures. That is, white supremacy shaped the intellectual space within which Anglo-American social thought and research operated. In the end, the irreducible element in the equation, ordering white intellectual space and operating as a springboard for shaping and reshaping its geography, was white supremacy. Race and white supremacy were elemental to the configuration of capitalism itself. Social Darwinism and the hereditarian research program, therefore, although constituting a "science" of race, were ideologically linked to capitalism and its relationships of production. Race, as an ideological category, was a decisive part of the ideological production of the social structure based on race and class inequalities.

▶ Early Sociology on Race Matters

When sociology appeared as an academic discipline in the 1890s, there was no rush to examine the race problem. Early white academic sociologists wrote no books on it and only a scattering of articles. McKee (1993) points out, "A few brief comments on race appeared in some books such as those by Franklin H. Giddings, E. A. Ross, and Lester F. Ward" (p. 28). Furthermore, little concerning race appeared in the first five volumes of the new sociological journal, *The American Journal of Sociology*. Ross (1991, p. 95) indicates that American social scientists of this era viewed themselves as an intellectual gentry. Coming from upper-class families, they were more concerned with the rise of working-class militancy and the specter of socialism. They saw class conflict as a threat to the Gilded Age's notion of American exceptionalism. Class, not race, was viewed as the problem of the age.[4] As a result of vast social and economic changes occurring in the 1890s, Ross (1991) points out.

> Many social scientists revised the idea of American exceptionalism. They argued that realization of American liberal and republican ideals depended on the same forces that were creating liberal modernity in Europe, on the development of capitalism, democratic politics, and science. (p. 50)

Schwendinger and Schwendinger (1974, p. 97) view these theorists as transitional thinkers, whose ideas manifested the transition from free market to monopoly capitalism. Whether in their laissez faire or monopoly capitalist expressions, the founders of American sociology adhered to the essentially conservative idea that social science had the object of finding the natural laws of social behavior necessary to integrate and stabilize society. These laws revealed themselves, the Schwendingers (1974) suggest, in "Ward's conception of genetic evolutionary processes, in Ross's assertion that inequality is functionally necessary for the survival of society, and in Small's conception of interest group relationships" (p. 97). Each of these thinkers drew on ideas developed by French reformers, going back to August Comte, and the German "socialist of the chair." The white founders of American sociology, moreover, agreed with the substance of social Darwinism, especially as it related to race. However, Ward, Giddings, Ross, and Cooley were what has been described as reform social Darwinists. Theirs was a modified racist view espousing guided or managed social evolutionary change to quicken evolutionary social developments in a reputedly "enlightened manner." Their views, although racist, still understood the central problem of American society to be social class, not race, and what they viewed as industrial violence.

The great gulf between their understanding and reality is recognized when one looks at the age objectively and, certainly, as Du Bois must have. The era began with the destruction of Reconstruction and the Hayes-Tilden Compromise of 1877, followed by the Supreme Court's declaring the equal accommodations provisions of the Civil Rights Act of 1875 unconstitutional (1883); it reaches its high point with the *Plessy v. Ferguson* (1896) decision. Rayford Logan refers to this period in African American history as the *nadir*. Class conflict was a crucial part of this moment; however, the race issue and its complex relationships to the entirety of class, gender, social, and political issues would prove to be the overarching and central question.

In larger historical and political economic contexts, the period 1896 to 1914 (the period when Du Bois produced his main sociological research) was a glorious period for world imperialism and racism. Between 1859 (when Charles Darwin's *Origins of the Species* was

published) and the Boer War of 1902, white Western men conquered, explored, fought over, and partitioned among themselves all of Africa south of the Sahara desert. In 1895, when Du Bois became the first African American to receive a Harvard Ph.D., the Great Abolitionist, Frederick Douglass, died, and the Great Accommodator, Booker T. Washington, delivered his Atlanta Compromise speech. These events occurred at the very moment when black leadership was passing from Douglass, the revolutionary democrat, to Washington, the politician of compromise. Of Douglass, Du Bois (1903/1993) said, "in his old age, [he] still bravely stood for the ideals of his early manhood—ultimate assimilation through self assertion, and on no other terms" (p. 44). Of Washington, he declared, "Mr. Washington represents in Negro thought the old attitude of adjustment and submission"; his program "practically accepts the alleged inferiority of the Negro races" (Du Bois, 1903/1993, p. 45).

Du Bois began his teaching and public careers at a time when the forces of reaction had achieved political, ideological, and cultural supremacy. He chose a path based on scientific rigor and an unbending partisanship to the cause of African American equality. In the process, he would redefine the social sciences, creating a new paradigm of race and race conflict. Du Bois's literary and research production is massive. Herbert Aptheker (1989) says it is on "a Dickensian scale." Du Bois published books and essays in magazines throughout the world. He edited or wrote for *The Nation, The Atlantic Monthly, The American Historical Review, The American Sociological Review, Fisk Herald, The Moon, The Horizon, The Crisis, The Journal of Negro History,* and *Phylon.* In addition, he contributed weekly columns to newspapers, including the *Pittsburgh Courier* and the *Chicago Defender* (see Aptheker, 1973).

In the remainder of this chapter, I will demonstrate the dimensions of the Du Boisian episteme by presenting how its development can be followed in several of his major works. I will look at *The Suppression of the African*

Slave Trade (Du Bois, 1896/1986), "On The Conservation of Races" (Du Bois, 1897/1995), *The Philadelphia Negro* (1903/1993), *The Souls of Black Folk* (1903/1986), *John Brown* (Du Bois, 1909/1987), and *Black Reconstruction* (1935/1992) as models. I will indicate the form and substance of a Du Boisian method of conducting social science.

▶ Du Bois's Epistemic Commitments

As Du Bois strode from Harvard to assume his place in the world, his motto might have been that of a fellow alumnus of University of Berlin, Karl Marx: "Until now, philosophers have only explained the world; our task is to change it." Du Bois was convinced early on that sociology must develop methods suitable to what was then considered scientific standards, methods that would allow social knowledge to be deemed scientific. He was, however, dissatisfied with the ways that the natural and social sciences were discussing race. He would, to alter this situation, invent a unique science of race. In this respect, he explored a wide and complex philosophical terrain. His Harvard and University of Berlin training had allowed him to become conversant in, and acutely sensitive to, the contending philosophical camps of his day. He intellectually engaged the competing claims of pragmatism and European epistemology. Scholars differ about where Du Bois came down philosophically. Robert Gooding-Williams (1992), David Levering Lewis (1993), and Shamoon Zamir (1995) argue that Hegel's *Phenomenology of Mind* exerted a strong and enduring influence on him. Arnold Rampersad (1976) and Cornel West (1989), on the other hand, claim that Du Bois remained a Jamesian pragmatist. As Rampersad (1976) contends, "the overall impact of William James was preeminent" (p. 30). Du Bois's sociological and historical studies demonstrate, however, what I consider a synthesis of several philosophical and methodological stances. He nonetheless brought a specific philosophical and methodological attitude to the understanding of race, one that acknowledged the plebian and existential orientation of pragmatism as articulated by Emerson and William James, along with its sense of contingency and specificity; the phenomenology and dialectics of Hegel; and the inductivist methods of his German professors of economic history, Adolph Wagner (1835-1917) and Gustav von Schmoller (1838-1917).[5] Du Bois, at the same time, remained committed to a version of positivism; that is to say, in sociological or historical research, he did not abandon hard data, be it official censuses, government documents, specific studies, or his own carefully gathered information, most times through well-constructed and -executed surveys. Du Bois was, at the same time, a masterful ethnographer. Through his ethnographic work, he sought to discover that uniquely human dimension of behavior and society: the nonmaterial, the psychological, and, if you will, spiritual dimensions. This would bring him into the domain of anthropology and cultural studies. Yet, Du Bois constructed not merely a distinctive methodological approach to the problems of race but a distinct episteme, a way of knowing and changing the world of race relations. Thus, his intellectual commitments can be best understood as more than merely methodological: rather, as epistemic commitments.

To understand these commitments, it is necessary to go beyond his academic influences. Alexander Crummell, his mentor in the American Negro Academy, is one such influence. Crummell was an Anglo-African nationalist. Moses (1978, p. 59) locates Crummell's Anglo-African nationalism in commitments to Christianity, the destiny of Africa, an authoritarian political style, and belief in separate black institutions. Du Bois, unlike Crummell and later Marcus Garvey, was not an Anglophile; but like them, he believed in a single destiny for black folk in Africa and the United States. In his 1897 paper delivered to the American Negro Academy, "The Conservation of Races," he argued that blacks must operate as one union of "200,000,000 black hearts beating in one glad jubilee" and that Negroes in the United States should take their place in the vanguard of Pan-Negroism. Present throughout Du Bois's work is a deep respect for the Haitian revolution, the slave uprisings of Gabriel Prosser and Nat Turner, and, significantly, mid-19th century nationalism. To this must be added his identification with Frederick Douglass's call for constant struggle. Here rest the ideological foundations of his theoretical and research projects. His identification not only with blacks but with the black struggle sets boundaries for the manner in which he conducted scholarship and thought about the world. This radical politics is asserted forthrightly by Du Bois (1903/1986) throughout *The Souls of Black Folk,* but especially in the chapter, "Of Booker T. Washington and Others" (see pp. 42-44).

In large measure, the disputes about where to place Du Bois intellectually and politically emerge from the fact that most commentators have failed to examine his effort in epistemic terms. Thus, without coming to terms with epistemic issues and perspectives inherent to his scholarship and political activity, it is not possible to accurately locate him and his project. In its broad outlines, Du Bois's episteme is holistic: It was nonreductive and sought to arrive at global or general principles to explain specific events. Hegelian concerns with world history are combined with an acute awareness of contingency and a sense of the significance of day-to-day events. This synthesis was first revealed in a paper, "The Large and Small-Scale System of Agriculture in the Southern United States, 1840-1890," done for Schmoller. He believed it would become his thesis for a Ph.D. from the University of Berlin. The paper looked at the land tenure system in the U.S. South from the bottom up. What we see here, from a methodological and philosophical point of view, are the influences of the German school of historical economics (headed by Schmoller and Wagner), which according to Du Bois's class notes, "tries as far as possible to leave the *Sollen* [what should be] for a later stage and study the *Geshehen* [what is actual] as other

sciences have done" (see Lewis, 1993, p. 142). This view that large patterns emerge only after determining the pattern of particular events mirrored what Du Bois had heard at Harvard from his professors William James and Albert Bushnell Hart.

On the political side, Marable (1986) contends that Du Bois was a radical democrat. Moses (1978) and Outlaw (1996) are also right in recognizing Du Bois's nationalism and Afrocentrism. On the other hand, Omi and Winant (1986) incorrectly locate Du Bois's *The Souls of Black Folk* in cultural nationalism, thus limiting the range of his nationalist concerns to cultural restoration in the tradition of Edward Wilmot Blyden. This is not to say that his nationalism did not have a definite cultural and, perhaps more accurately, a civilizational dimension. His sense of culture and African centrality, in significant ways, departs from modern day Afrocentrism in the tradition exemplified by Molefi Asante (1986). Modern-day cultural nationalists and Afrocentrists, including men such as Asante and West (1989), see Du Bois as a liberal cosmopolitan and integrationist unable to appreciate or understand black nationalism, whereas liberal integrationists such as Appiah (1992) see him as a racial essentialist and narrow nationalist. In some senses, all sides can find in Du Bois the Du Bois they wish to see. If one deconstructs the whole and separates the parts and the whole from their social and historical contexts, it is possible to come up with whatever one pleases.

In the late 1890s, Du Bois made an effort to combine often conflicting views of radical democracy, black nationalism, and liberal cosmopolitanism. He was, however, in the process of development, a process not unconnected to the real world of ideas and black oppression. It was, after all, a period of profound racism and reaction when the social sciences were that only in name and had very little to say to the nation or black folk. Du Bois came into the 20th century with a plan to change that. It is, however, with *The Souls of Black Folk* that Du Bois, the full and mature intellectual, arrives.

▶ Du Bois and the Philosophy of Knowing

Du Bois's philosophical sensibilities were firmly demonstrated in a term paper, "The Renaissance of Ethics: A Critical Comparison of Scholastic and Modern Ethics," for a course with William James at Harvard in the academic year 1888-1889. The paper demonstrates extraordinary sophistication and was a harbinger of Du Bois's future philosophical orientation. It has common elements with the paper from the University of Berlin, especially in handling the philosophical issues surrounding the mind-matter duality. Furthermore, it suggests that Du Bois and his idol William James diverged sharply on philosophical matters.[6] Rampersad (1976) contends that "The Renaissance" "is by no means a mature work" (p. 25). "Du Bois tried to be coherent and methodical," Rampersad argues, "but certain passages show an unsure grasp of his material, as well as attempts to conceal his uncertainty by bold assertions and ambiguous suggestions" (p. 26). Contrary to Rampersad, I would suggest that when working out complex problems, uncertainty need not be a curse; it can be a blessing. Rampersad would have had Du Bois affect a certain pose more characteristic of certain modern academics, who act as if they know what they see only through a glass darkly. Or perhaps he would have Du Bois imitate what logical positivists have perfected, the rush to reduce knowledge to logical statements and on this basis declare them truth.

Du Bois, even as an undergraduate, had better instincts than to make either of these mistakes, and he would avoid them for most of his life. Zamir (1995, p. 59) believes the strength of the work is in its attempt to resolve the late 19th-century dualism of psychology of mind and science by historicizing ethics and ethical choices. He sees Du Bois drifting from Jamesian ethical relativism to historicism. Du Bois, thus, combines a sense of agency with a beginning recognition of its restraint by history.

David Levering Lewis (1993) indicates that Du Bois approached the perennial mind-matter problem in a way not unlike Marx in *Kapital* and Engels in *Anti-Duhring*. Lewis argues,

> Marx and Engels maintained that the structure and laws of the world became revealed through the manipulation (engagement) of the forces of nature. Essentially, "The Renaissance of Ethics" waveringly arrived at the same conclusion: ethical imperatives arose out of the interaction of mind and matter, as both became transformed and purposive through willpower. (p. 95)

Commenting on the thesis of the paper, James said he believed there was an unbridgeable chasm between facts and ethical beliefs. Lewis insists,

> The philosophical distance between James and Du Bois would grow as the latter soon became committed to a program of finite investigation, incremental accumulation of data, and confidence that unity of knowledge and the discovery of truth, behind or beyond mere contingency of which he wrote in his Philosophy 4 essay, was with perseverance and intellect possible. (p. 95)

To understand Du Bois's approach to the social sciences and the methods he used in *The Suppression of the Slave Trade, The Philadelphia Negro* and *The Souls of Black Folk,* and in constructing the department of sociology at Atlanta University, these intellectual foundations are vital. In a certain way, they made his approach to the discipline profoundly unique. Throughout his sociological research, Du Bois asserts that right and wrong are involved in social matters and that scientific knowledge is a method of their discovery. The activist manner in which Du Bois (1903/1993) framed and conducted the research for *The Philadelphia Negro,* and his belief, stated there, that knowing should lead to action and public policies to correct wrongs, can be traced back in important ways to the beliefs he stated in "The Renaissance of Ethics." Indeed, there remained throughout Du Bois's sociology this uniting of research, theory, public policy, and practice.[7] Also, we discover in his work the notion that research should be purposeful and knowledge construction and research should be part of social transformative activity. That the social scientist is engaged and must be so, is part of the nature of social science. And thus, the sociologist is compelled by the nature of the discipline to a certain amount of intellectual engagement. Moreover, his intellectual practices are as significant as the texts themselves. And certainly, the "The Renaissance of Ethics" informed an intellectual practice that produced *The Suppression* and *The Philadelphia Negro.* The practice of engagement, therefore, was certainly not rooted in either pragmatism or Kantian rationalism and its transcendental approach to discovering ethical principles. Throughout his life, Du Bois would assert a praxis of mass involvement and a commitment to the African American people.

His most important works, moreover, have that rare quality of being paradigmatic; that is, setting the broad philosophical and conceptual outlines of disciplinary research. In this respect, his work in both sociology and history established an alternative research program to the dominant ones in the U.S. academy. His scholarship in history, sociology, social history, and political economy, as well as his artistic production of novels, plays, and poems, has that quality of taking on fundamental questions in a scientific and courageous manner. This gives a timeless quality to his most important work and many of his historical predictions. Of this kind is Du Bois's (1903/1986) brilliant prediction at the beginning of this century that "the problem of the 20th century is the problem of the color line" (p. 16). The lasting significance of this prediction is that in making it, Du Bois did not suggest that race would be the only problem of this century, nor did he separate race from the manifold problems that emerged in the 20th

century. Throughout his life, he continued to evolve and expand the notion of the color line. What his scholarship and research did was to verify the interactive relationship between race, class, and the multilevel configurations of the social structure of modern society. Of deep significance is how Du Bois conceptually arranged the race-class-social structure problem. His causal sequence places race in a determining position with respect to class and social structure. This would constitute a major break with previous social theoretic constructions of the problem. Furthermore, Du Bois articulated race in a global context. He connected it to the colonial and the world economic systems. He insisted that the 20th century could not be understood unless the issue of race was understood.

Whereas modern European social theory associates modernity variously with new class arrangements (Marx); the rise of new relationships of status, prestige, state and bureaucratic arrangements, and the centrality of the individual (Weber); and the appearance of anomie and normlessness (Durkheim); Du Bois contended that the central feature of modernity is race. He is, thus, the only major theorist of modernity to come to grips with race and race oppression as overarching in the formation of the modern world.

▶ Du Bois and the Early Roots of Sociology

Du Bois's skills as a researcher in sociology and history were magnificent. These were nowhere better demonstrated than in *The Suppression of the African Slave Trade,* his Ph.D. dissertation at Harvard, and in *The Philadelphia Negro.* Few sociologists would deny that he is one of American sociology's major pioneers. However, his place as an innovator is not as widely acknowledged, and a full recognition of the enormity of his contribution has not yet occurred. In a sense, sociology has dealt with him only in passing, assessing his contribution only superficially.

Green and Driver (1980, p. 39) insist that Du Bois rightly deserves a place among the giants of sociology for his work during the years 1896 through 1910, when sociology was being established as an academic discipline. Along with establishing a department of sociology at Atlanta University, he created a sociological laboratory, instituted a program of systematic research, founded and conducted regular sociological conferences on research, founded two journals (*Crisis* and *Phylon: A Journal of Race Relations*), and attempted to organize a sociological society in 1897, or 8 years before the American Sociological Society. Moreover, he established a record of valuable publications that has rarely been equaled by any sociologist.

Du Bois's department at Atlanta University was the second to be established in the United States. Albion Small set up the first at the University of Chicago in 1892. The sociological laboratory and the Atlanta University Conferences he directed made his department unique. The Atlanta Conference met annually between 1896 and 1914 and produced *The Atlanta University Publications,* consisting of 18 monographs. From 1896 through 1914, Du Bois published articles and sociological monographs based on research and spoke to audiences throughout the nation and around the world.

Unlike other sociology departments, Du Bois's was centered on black people and a strong anti-eugenics and anti-hereditarian program. In 1898, in an article entitled "The Study of the Negro Problems" in *The Annals of the American Academy of Political and Social Science,* he wrote,

> The present period in the development of sociological study is a trying one; it is the period of observation, research, and comparison—work always wearisome, often aimless, without well-settled principles and guiding lines and subject ever to pertinent criticism. (Du Bois, 1898/1980, p. 70)

He was convinced that the Negro was a worthy subject of serious sociological inquiry. He dreamed, as Lewis (1993) indicates, of a laboratory that could inform the wider public of the conditions of a "concrete group of living beings artificially set off by themselves" (p. 219). He anticipated that the Atlanta Conferences would bring together the best minds in the world and that his students, in the manner of a University of Berlin seminar, would devour bibliographies and data on the Negro. This annual meeting turned out some of the most influential research of its time and attracted the likes of Max Weber and Franz Boas.[8]

The research Du Bois headed was rigorous and based on the best scientific methods of its time. As he put it,

> The Atlanta Conference sought to apply to the study of the Negro problem the methods of sociological inquiry which the trained experience of the world has found most successful, and it seeks to interpret the results in the light of similar data obtained by students the world over. (Du Bois, 1985, p. 70)

In retrospect, Du Bois's scientific effort has prevailed over the research program of scientific racism. This is true in spite of the fact that scientific racism continues to rear its ugly head, as revealed in the publication of *The Bell Curve.*[9] Du Bois's emphasis on race, class, and social structure as primary causal factors of social behavior, social action, and social conflict subsequently propelled a tradition in American social science that stretches from Franz Boas to the Chicago School of Sociology and into the present. E. Digby Baltzell (1967) argues that Boas, in *The Mind of Primitive Man* (1911), was echoing the findings of Du Bois when he wrote that "the traits of the American Negro are adequately explained on the basis of his history and his social status . . . without falling back upon the theory of hereditary inferiority" (p. xxvi).

In a profound sense, American sociology still has not caught up to Du Bois. It remains a child of its Gilded Age beginnings and its reluctance to face head-on the issue of race and the complex interactions of race, class, and social structure. Nor has it successfully challenged the strictures of pragmatism and positivism. Du Bois's German education, especially regarding Hegel's *Phenomenology of Mind* and the political economic methods and theories of his German professors Schmoller and Wagner, along with his lifelong studies of the Black Belt South, gave him a strategic advantage over most sociologists of his time and even of ours.

▶ Suppression of the African Slave Trade and African Scholarship

The Suppression of the African Slave Trade to the United States of America, 1638-1870, according to Herbert Aptheker (1989), is "the first full-length product of Afro-American scientific scholarship; as such it is the seed" (p. 11). Furthermore, it has not been supplanted. Like *The Philadelphia Negro,* which was to follow it, *Suppression* adheres closely, as Zamir (1995, p. 81) indicates, to the empirical realism of Schmoller's idea of the social sciences and the methods Du Bois had encountered through Hart and others at Harvard. *Suppression,* Du Bois (1896/1986) tells us, is "a contribution to the scientific study of slavery and the American Negro" based on "a study of sources, [that is] national, State, and colonial statutes, Congressional documents, reports of societies, personal narratives, [and so on]" (p. 3).

Zamir (1995) argues,

> It is this emphasis on the centrality of primary documentation and the rigorously localized focus that put Du Bois's work at the forefront of contemporary developments in American historiography rather than with the more outmoded literary tradition of nineteenth-century historiography represented by figures like Macauly (whom Du Bois had read with relish as a child and then at Fisk), Carlyle, or the American George Bancroft, whose *History of the United States from the Discovery of America* (1834-1887) was informed by a nationalist

> mythology of heroic achievement and progress buoyed up with inflated liberal and nationalist sentiments. (pp. 81-82)

While seeking to adhere as closely as possible to what seems to be positivist methods, it is clear the work is subversive of American racism and its myth of racial progress. Rather than being presented as a narrative about the triumph of liberty, the history of the slave trade is narrated as a series of failures and of the triumph of self-interest over law. Du Bois points to consistent failures to enforce the 1808 act outlawing slave trading and the subsequent growth of the trade, especially after 1820; he notes the repeated calls for revival of the slave trade. Du Bois attacks America's continual bargaining and compromising with slavery. In the end, he offers a stinging rebuff to the normal view that American colonial and revolutionary history represented the rise of liberty and democracy. "No American," Du Bois (1896/1986) insists, "can study the connection of slavery with United States history, and not devoutly pray that this country may never have a simiiar social problem to solve" (p. 197). He continues with a forthright challenge to the ideology of American exceptionalism and progress:

> We have the somewhat inchoate idea that we are not destined to be harassed with great social questions, and that even if we are, and fail to answer them, the fault is with the question and not with us. Consequently we often congratulate ourselves more on getting rid of a problem than on solving it. (p. 197)

In *Suppression,* Du Bois evinces an approach to history writing that does not exclude advocacy or partisanship. In *Black Reconstruction,* Du Bois (1992/1935) comments on Charles A. and Mary R. Beard's *The Rise of American Civilization.* In their work, he argues, the impression is left "that nothing right or wrong is involved" (p. 714). Their approach manifested a strict historical positivism, which Du Bois would flirt with but reject. Moreover, in *Black Reconstruction,* Du

Bois indicates that two antagonistic systems developed in the North and South, and "they clash, as winds and waters strive" (p. 715). Du Bois disputed the Beards' "mechanistic" approach to history, which failed because human experience is not machinelike and humans are not machines. The slave trade and slavery were not inevitable. They manifested actual political and economic interests. These interests were regional, national, and international, connected to a world system of capital, slavery, and commerce in cotton. Du Bois (1896/1986) would contend that the course of U.S. history was determined by the "fatal rise of the slave labor large-farming system, which before it was realized, had so intertwined itself with and braced itself upon the economic forces of the industrial age" (p. 153). In the second quarter of the 19th century, the slave labor system changed from "a family institution to an industrial system," and it would take a "vast and terrible civil war" to displace it. In his dissertation, Du Bois was already indicating a point he would more fully develop in *Black Reconstruction*: that the slaves were in fact workers whose conditions of work after 1820 were of an industrial type. This would lay the foundation for his concept of the class struggle as the central dynamic of the antislavery struggle. However, he saw the class struggle as being shaped by race and slavery. This view, as we will later show, represented a profound inversion of Eurocentrist Marxism. Significant for what will become a Du Boisian explanation of U.S. history and society is his concept of the centrality of race to the formation of class and class relationships in the United States.

Suppression was widely and favorably reviewed in, among others, *The Nation, The American Historical Review,* and *The Atlantic Monthly.* According to Aptheker (1989), "One of the most discerning reviews . . . came from the pen of H. T. Kealing of Philadelphia, the editor of the AME Church Review" (p. 824). Kealing called the book "epochal" and drew attention to its emphasis on the role of Toussaint, leader of the Haitian revolution. Kealing found its emphasis on slave militancy

and rebellion valuable. Kealing's review contained the hope, with which most of Du Bois's work was received by the African American public, that it would help bury "the almost antediluvian conceit of exclusive Caucasian scholarship" (Kealing, cited in Aptheker, 1989, p. 8). *Suppression* was out of print for some 50 years, although it was cited thousands of time. At the same time, relatively recent works such as those of Staughton Lynd (1967) and Ronald Takaki (1971), although they cover the same terrain as Du Bois's *Suppression,* and do not supersede it, nevertheless totally ignore it. On the other hand, recent scholarship on the transatlantic slave trade, for example by Joseph Inikori (1992), Ronald Bailey (1992), and Clarence Munford (1991), has taken account of the work of Du Bois. *Suppression*'s was republished in 1954 by Social Science Press, headed by then-doctoral student Eugene Genovese. In this edition, Du Bois included a postlude, or what he saw as "a short explanation" regarding what he saw as the omissions in the book. These included what was in Du Bois's view a certain naivete with respect to human psychology, reflecting the pre-Freudian epoch of the book's production, and the Marxian analysis. Du Bois acknowledged the existing economic emphasis in the book and also the absence of the concept of class domination of the state, class struggle, and class interest as basic to the historical process. In 1954, he evaluated the book as a good one, which represented a conscientious effort.

▶ On the Conservation of Races: Toward a General Theory[10]

Between the publication of *Suppression* and *The Philadelphia Negro,* and while polishing the research and language of the latter, Du Bois delivered a paper before the American Negro Academy entitled "On the Conservation of Races." It can be viewed as a prolegomenon to a general theory of race. It seeks to provide a general concept of races, uniting the general concept of races, or large populations, with the particularity of the African or Negro race. The work proceeds from two compatible, yet not fully worked out notions: first, a populationist definition of races, that is, that races are large groups of people united on the basis of culture and phenotypical characteristics; and second, a genogeographical definition, which suggests that gene populations generally occupy certain geographic regions of the planet and that language and culture correlate with genogeographical populations. Both definitions are suggested in the work and provide a foundation for later conceptualizations of race, as seen in *Dusk of Dawn* (Du Bois, 1940/1995) and *The World and Africa* (1947/1995).

Suppression and *The Philadelphia Negro* provide enormous empirical and historical data to demonstrate the reality of race; "Conservation" seeks to generalize on that data. We witness Du Bois working from the concrete to the general, from specific knowledge to general explanation. Races as he articulated them are constituted on the basis of geography, genes, history, and culture. Race is a type of supranational community of people. The object of the paper, however, was to assert the civilization equality of the Negro race with other great races. Africans were one of Du Bois's eight major races. The paper was to become the basis of scientific research and political agitation for civil and political rights. Its foundational assumption was that Africans were civilized and, more, that Africa was where human civilization originated. Du Bois would insist that African Americans, only a little more than 30 years out of slavery, still brought much to the table of human culture. From the standpoint of the Du Boisian *oeuvre,* this paper should be viewed as an initial approximation of a more general theory of race and race construction and not his final statement. "Conservation" helps us understand Du Bois's *oeuvre* generally and to understand how each work was a further approximation and a deeper understanding of social complexity. His life's work should be viewed as a series of approximations, amendments, additions, revisions, and rethinkngs as new evidence and new argu-

ments and explanations come forward. And yet, Du Bois would always attempt to verify empirically the categories of his thinking. This paper was, however, given the time, competitively plausible and generally progressive. Like all of his scholarly and intellectual work, it was profoundly political. Responding to the racist and colonialist notions of world history, Du Bois was calling for Pan African unity, declaring that Africans have a unique contribution to make to civilization and humanity.

The reactionary political and racial climate that made such a work necessary is suggested in *Dusk of Dawn* (1940/1995, p. 98). This context helps explain "Conservation's" political and intellectual strategy. It assumes a militant nationalist voice not heard in either *Suppression* or *The Philadelphia Negro,* a voice explained, certainly, by the paper's audience, a black nationalist-led group. In *The Souls of Black Folk,* the militant and political tone in "Conservation" reappears. Du Bois proposes a conceptualization of races as culturally and historically distinct, while each—and significantly Negroes—has contributions to make to civilization. In the graduate schools at Harvard and Berlin, race became a matter of culture and cultural history. The history of the world was paraded before the observing students, Du Bois (1968) tells us in his autobiography. Comparative history was done for the sake of determining superior and inferior races and peoples. The white race, of course, had history and thereby civilization. There was some mention, Du Bois (1940/1995) continues, of Asiatic culture, "but no course in Chinese or Indian history or culture was offered at Harvard, and quite unanimously in America and Germany, Africa was left without culture and without history" (p. 98).

What most commentators have missed in assessing "Conservation" is that Du Bois was arguing for the conservation of races and peoples as distinct cultural entities, but not in a separatist, insular, or invidious ethnocentrist manner. What he was demanding was recognition of both the flowering of and pride among races and peoples, on the one side, and their coming together to form a better humanity on the other. Hence, revealed in Du Bois's thinking is recognition of a two-sided historical process among races, cultures, and peoples, a stance that he would champion throughout his life.

In *Black Reconstruction,* he would define race and the problem of race in far more radical terms. "His fight is a fight to the finish," Du Bois (1935/1992) says of the African American struggle.

> Either he dies or he wins. . . . He will enter modern civilization here in America as a black man, or he will enter not at all. Either extermination root and branch, or absolute equality. There can be no compromise. This is the last great battle of the West. (p. 703)

In *Dusk of Dawn,* Du Bois (1940/1995) looks at the African American race in robust cultural, historical, political, and ideological terms. He says,

> But the physical bond is least and the badge of color relatively unimportant save as a badge; the real essence of this kinship is its social heritage of slavery, the discrimination and insult; and this heritage binds together not simply the children of Africa but extends through yellow Asia and into the south Seas. It is this unity that draws me to Africa. (p. 117)

▶ The Philadelphia Negro: Empirical and Ethnographic Research

The Philadelphia Negro (Du Bois, 1903/1993) is the first major work of American empirical and urban sociology and remains unsurpassed in its methodology, research design, conceptualization, scope, and rigor. It should be viewed as the masterwork in the field. Although basically ignored by most scholars, it is the preeminent model in urban sociology. With it, Du Bois opened the field. Zamir (1995) argues that

Du Bois succeeded in deploying empirical practice against the alliance of pseudo-science, liberal optimism, and racism not only because his marginalized position fostered critical understanding but also because he enlarged his scientific training to include a more historical assessment of the evidence in his work. (p. 89)

A survey of the urban sociology literature from the Chicago School in the 1920s to the present indicates an enormous debt to Du Bois.[11] In an appendix to his famous study of the American race situation, *An American Dilemma,* Gunnar Myrdal (cited in Baltzell, 1967) discusses the need for further research on the black community:

> We cannot close this description of what a study of the Negro community should be without calling attention to the study which best meets our requirements, a study which is now all but forgotten. We refer to W.E.B Du Bois' *The Philadelphia Negro.* (p. ix)

The Philadelphia Negro can be considered part of a larger scientific project, which included Du Bois's Atlanta studies. Following his 15-month work on *The Philadelphia Negro,* Du Bois was hired as a professor at historically African American Atlanta University. What links Du Bois's sociological work between 1896 and 1910 (including the research on *The Philadelphia Negro* and the Atlanta studies) is its empirical orientation, combined with an up-close, in-the-trenches ethnography. Anderson (1995) argues that *The Philadelphia Negro* is perhaps the first major ethnographic study of an urban population and that its ethnography is its high point. Green and Driver (1980) say Du Bois "was firm in his commitment to the use of sociological measurement to describe and delimit social phenomena" (p. 37). Moreover, "Implicit in this belief was a more general belief in the worth of quantitative, empirically based sociology which, if properly practiced, would form the foundation of social policy" (Green & Driver, 1980, p. 37).

The Philadelphia Negro (Du Bois, 1903/1993) emerges from the social reform movement of the late 19th century. Du Bois's scholarship became a central part of that movement. The Settlement House and Social Gospel Movements in the United States stimulated early empirical sociological research. Reform- minded and activist women such as Jane Addams, founder of Hull House; Vida Scudder; Ellen Gates Starr; Dr. Jane Robbins; Susan Wharton; and Isabell Eaton were leaders of these early "uplift movements." The University of Pennsylvania sponsored Du Bois's research. Du Bois's biographer David Levering Lewis (1993) provides the intellectual and social context in which Du Bois found himself.

> Du Bois knew his sponsors held a theory about the race to be studied. The city was "going to the dogs because of the crime and venality of its Negro citizens." "Something is wrong with a race that is responsible for so much crime," the theory ran, and "strong remedies are called for." Another junior academic (and a minority scholar at that), given the chance to impress rich and pedigreed sponsors for future assignments and fellowships, might have been conscientious about fleshing out the data but neutral or even collusive about their implications. To believe Du Bois, however, he "neither knew nor cared" about the agenda of the reformers. "The world was wrong about race, because it did not know." He would teach it to think right. The task was "simple and clear-cut" for someone with his cutting-edge training in sociology. He proposed to "find out what was the matter with this area and why," and he would ask "little advice as to procedure." It was an opportunity—a mandate really—whose scientific and racial implications made the politics behind his appointment unimportant. (pp. 188-189)

Du Bois's anti-hereditarian beliefs defined and shaped not only the design of the study but also his goal to show that social conditions and previous servitude best explain the behavior and social situation of blacks. As Du Bois (1899/1995) states, "The final design of the work is to lay before the public such a body of information as may be a safe guide for all ef-

forts toward the solution of the many Negro problems of a great American city" (p. 1). In 1896, Du Bois understood what many conservative and liberal sociologists have yet not digested, that ghettoes and poverty are not the creations of the poor but the result of processes controlled by economic and political forces far removed from the ghetto and the poor themselves. Du Bois argued that poverty, ghettoes, and crime were finally symptoms of institutional and structural racism. Data and analysis in this work counter the "culture of poverty" and social pathology arguments that blame the poor for poverty and that have been reinvented in the 1980s and 1990s to justify conservative social and economic policies. Du Bois considered the situation of black folk in Philadelphia "a disgrace to the city—a disgrace to Christianity, to its spirit of justice, to its common sense." His judgment remains valid.

The Philadelphia Negro (Du Bois, 1903/1993) includes the belief, also found in "Conservation," that African Americans are part of the great Negro race based in Africa and that African Americans exhibit cultural and behavioral patterns found in Africa. For instance, in the section of *The Philadelphia Negro* devoted to the black church, Du Bois observes that in its organization, it repeats the communal pattern of African village life (p. 201). The idea of African survivals in the African American community, later asserted by Boas and Herskowitz and disputed by E. Franklin Frazier, has its roots in Du Bois's engagement with 19th-century black nationalism. It was his way of arguing that blacks should not be expected to behave like white Americans, although he would uphold a certain behavioral norm appropriate to civil society.

Elijah Anderson (1995) indicates that *The Philadelphia Negro* anticipates the research of the Chicago School of urban sociology headed by Robert Parks and was preceded by the works of Charles Booth and Jane Addams. Anderson (1995) points out that "the work of these authors probably served as models for Du Bois" (p. xviii). Du Bois used the same methods they did, including maps, census data, descriptive statistics, and in-depth interviews. Charles Booth's influence spread beyond London to New York, Pittsburgh, and Chicago, and

> The works of the Westside Studies and the Pittsburgh Survey, sponsored by the Russell Sage Foundation in 1914, resemble those of Addams and Booth as well as those of Du Bois. In this perspective, Du Bois may be viewed as a link in the empirical chain engaged in the central social scientific, if not ideological, work of the Settlement Movement. (Anderson, 1995, p. xviii)

However, the ideological link that ties Du Bois to Hull House and Booth may lead back to mid 19th-century Marxism. Aptheker (1989, p. 17) indicates that the radical critique of Marx and Engels propelled the reformist works of Jacob Riis in the United States in the 1890s and of Samuel A. Barnett and his Oxford and Cambridge university colleagues in England a decade earlier. The efforts of Barnett and others resulted in the founding of Toynbee Hall (1884) and the Fabian movement, which led to the studies of Charles Booth, especially *The Life and Labour of the People of London* (1889-1891), which grew into a massive 17-volume study completed by 1903. Among the researchers assisting Booth was the young Beatrice Potter (later Beatrice Webb). Jane Addams was a friend of Beatrice Potter, who visited London to observe Booth and his colleagues and was impressed with the work of Toynbee Hall. The Settlement House movement in Chicago, Boston, New York, and Philadelphia, therefore, traces its roots to Toynbee Hall and Fabian socialism. Thus, reformers and Fabian socialists shaped a significant part of the intellectual environment in which Du Bois worked. Environmental factors help explain aspects of the work.

Du Bois's study also parallels Engels's *The Conditions of the Working Class in England* (1845/1975). *The Philadelphia Negro*'s ethnography and advocacy have much in common with Engels's work. Du Bois, like Engels, examines the formation of a distinct urban population, for Engels the working class, for Du Bois Philadelphia's black community. Engels points to profound demographic changes that flow from changes in technology and class relationships; Du Bois sees the Philadelphia black community as a distinct population that grew as slavery grew and later declined. Both Du Bois and Engels advocate on behalf of those who are the object of their studies. Whereas Engels calls for socialism and militant class struggle, Du Bois was probably at this point a reformist or Fabian socialist.

Du Bois's (1903/1993) concept of class in *The Philadelphia Negro* is racial, social, economic, and cultural rather than only economic. Classes are defined on the basis of occupation, education, income, values, and behavior. In some ways, his concept is of a type of eth-class or race-class that was later articulated by certain sociologists of race and ethnicity. The top 10th were the educated elite, whom he felt were obligated to serve and lead. At the bottom were what he called the "submerged tenth." This was a declassé stratum. However, all classes among Philadelphia's black community were shaped by and determined on the basis of race oppression and discrimination. However, a sense of the dialectic of race and class is present in Du Bois's work, as well. The race-class phenomenon appears throughout his work. No scholar has explored this problem as consistently as Du Bois did. It would come close to a final resolution in *Black Reconstruction.*

In spite of his marvelous achievement (*Suppression* and *Philadelphia Negro* were finished by the time he was 30), a generation later, in a favorable review of Harris and Spero's *The Black Worker,* Du Bois (1932) critiqued his *The Philadelphia Negro* (1903/ 1993) for a certain "provincialism" that tended to view the oppression of black people "from the view of religion, humanity, and sentiment." What is undeniable is that *The Philadelphia Negro* made a significant contribution to the development of an American sociology. It cannot be overlooked that Du Bois operated in an intellectual environment where social scientific thought and practice were severely impoverished, lacking both methods and firm philosophical groundings to explain the American social structure, which was so securely rooted in race.

► The Souls of Black Folk: Toward a Philosophy of Race

Souls (Du Bois, 1903/1986) is a unique Du Boisian effort to philosophically address the problem of race and the failure of American pragmatism and positivism to provide a philosophical framework for a social science of race. In many respects, *Souls* can be viewed as a narrative with Hegel, where Hegelian idealism is inverted. Du Bois's narrative is based in action, manifested as a striving or struggle to achieve freedom. Freedom is understood as achieving a new stage in history. Du Bois rejects both the naive optimism of American exceptionalism and the idealism of Hegelianism. "The history of the American Negro," he says,

> is the history of this strife,—this longing to attain self-conscious manhood, to merge his double self into a better and truer self. In this merging he wishes neither of the older selves to be lost. He would neither Africanize America, for America has too much to teach the world and Africa. He would not bleach his Negro soul in a flood of white Americanism, for he knows that Negro blood has a message for the world. (p. 365)

Although many Afrocentrists have viewed the Du Boisian notion of double consciousness as a capitulation to whiteness and Eurocentrism, it is in fact a recognition of the reality of being black in a multiethnic state founded on race oppression. Yet, Du Bois also acknowledges in *Souls* the presence of the Native American civilization in America. In the beautiful and sociologically compelling last chapter, "The Sorrow Songs," Du Bois speaks of Africa and America. This understanding goes quite a way in explaining how he understood double con-

sciousness or multiple forms of social being in America. "Little of beauty has America given the world save the grandeur God himself stamped on her bosom," he says. The human spirit as manifested in the white American "expressed itself in vigor and ingenuity rather than in beauty" (Du Bois, 1903/1986, p. 536). Then comes the critical yet too often overlooked sense of the principal side of the dialectic of double consciousness as Du Bois uses it: He insists, "And so by fateful chance the Negro folk song—the rhythmic cry of the slave—stands today not simply as American music, but as the most beautiful expression born this side of the seas" (Du Bois, 1903/1986, p. 536). Du Bois (1903/1986) then reminds us, "it still remains as the singular spiritual heritage of the nation and the greatest gift of the Negro people" (pp. 197-198). This music of an unhappy people, "the children of disappointment," tells "of death and suffering and unvoiced longing toward a truer world of misty wanderings and hidden ways" (pp. 197-198). In "Of Our Spiritual Strivings," Du Bois (1903/1986) hints at but does not fully develop the intermixture of African and Native American culture: "There is no true American music but the wild sweet melodies of the Negro slave; the American fairy tales and folklore are Indian and African" (p. 15). The sense, therefore, of the doubleness and what he meant by America can be found here. He did not see America as white only but as a mixture of races and cultures. He insists on an America of Indian, African, and Caucasian and an African or Negro consciousness, expressed in the Sorrow Songs, which preceded America. Doubleness, then, is even more complex than merely twoness. It seems, from the ways that Du Bois unfolds the concept throughout *Souls,* that he is speaking of racial, social, and cultural complexity and the forms of African American consciousness in the midst of this complexity. The painful realities of black life in capitalist America are Du Bois's starting point.

In *Souls,* Du Bois (1903/1986) starts to come to terms with pragmatism. He would not (and did not) countenance self-edifying indi-

204 SOCIALLY CONSTRUCTED RACIAL IDENTITIES

vidualism. He demanded a commitment to the oppressed black masses. Whereas American pragmatists and Hegelians avoid real history, Du Bois confronts it head on and seeks to construct a philosophy of real history and of human action. When viewed in relationship to the research that preceded it, *Souls* is part of a Du Boisian challenge to the limits of the social sciences and philosophy of the time. How, Du Bois seems to ask, does one construct a social scientific and philosophical discourse on race at the start of the 20th century? Du Bois understood that the audience for *Souls* was wide and interracial. However, the text speaks in specific ways to the black talented tenth. He joins the attack on the compromise policies of Booker T. Washington. He locates the black freedom struggle in the long struggle for democracy and especially the Haitian revolution. In drawing on Hegel's *Phenomenology of Mind* and adapting its categorical grid to understanding the specificity of the United States, Du Bois gives U.S. social science the intellectual tools to understand the complexities of race. Zamir (1995, p. 117) suggests that Du Bois reworks Hegel's (1966) *Phenomenology.*[12] Most American 19th-century readings of Hegel were upbeat, justifying the idea of an organically united people with a historic mission. Du Bois's critical reading of Hegel is similar to the one that emerges from Marx or Sartre. "What Hegel's idealist philosophy makes available to Du Bois," Zamir (1995) insists, "is a complex model for thinking about the relationship of consciousness and history" (p. 117). And Du Bois makes a radical rupture with Hegel by anchoring his enterprise in actual history. Yet, like Hegel's *Phenomenology,* Du Bois acknowledges complexity, contradiction, striving, and movement in history and day-to-day events.

In *Souls,* Du Bois (1903/1986) rejects naive psychologism of the Jamesian and Deweyan types.[13] His examination of the collective souls of black folk is his way of historicizing psychology. He develops a historically contextualized and contingent notion of double consciousness and of black striving, suggesting a social psychology that argues

that black folk emerge from a history of oppression and resistance. In the last chapter of *Souls,* entitled "The Sorrow Songs," Du Bois locates the Negro spirituals within the context of that striving for freedom and justice and the realization of a collective self—a peoplehood. He, however, defines the Sorrow Songs as the central historical narrative of black folk. "They are," he tells us, "the music of an unhappy people, of the children of disappointment; they tell of death and suffering and unvoiced longing toward a truer world, of misty wanderings and hidden ways" (Du Bois, 1903/1986). Yet,

> Through all the sorrow of the Sorrow Songs there breathes a hope—a faith in the ultimate justice of things. The minor cadences of despair change often to triumph and calm confidence. Sometimes it is faith in life, sometimes a faith in death, sometimes assurance of boundless justice in some fair world beyond. But whichever it is, the meaning is always clear: that sometime, somewhere, men will judge men by their souls and not by their skins. (Du Bois, 1903/1986, p. 544)

And then he asks, "Is such a hope justified? Do the Sorrow Songs sing true?"

This engagement with the Sorrow Songs and Du Bois's locating them as the central narrative of the African American people is also part of his locating the role of the talented tenth. Chapter 12, entitled "Of Alexander Crummell," develops a notion of the centrality of the black masses. Crummell, an Anglican priest and ascetic, believed that the essential need of freedmen was moral uplift. Du Bois believed their essential need was freedom, civil rights, the vote, and education. Crummell believed the talented tenth were a civilizing tenth, which would bring Christianity and thus civilization to the former slaves. Du Bois believed the talented tenth were obligated to serve and that the freedmen, through the Sorrow Songs and the antislavery resistance, had demonstrated they were civilized. Crummell's notion of the sublime personality is thus countered by Du Bois's notion of the sublimeness of a people whose resistance to oppression has elevated them above their oppressors. Here, Du Bois emphasizes the mass and calls on the intellectuals to enter into an organic relationship to them. Here is found, finally, Du Bois's belief in an activist, practical, and engaged social science. Rather than becoming an intellectual gentry, social scientists have a moral and professional obligation to be part of the mass that they study.

▶ Black Reconstruction: Toward an Engagement With Marxism

The idea for a study of Reconstruction can be traced to themes Du Bois was writing on at the close of the 19th century and especially to an essay in *The Souls of Black Folk* (Du Bois, 1903/1986), "On the Dawn of Freedom." Of great significance to the formation of his ideas on Reconstruction was his 1909 paper, presented at the American Historical Association meeting, entitled "Reconstruction and Its Benefits," which was published in the 1910 volume of *The American Historical Review*. However, I believe the roots of the analysis go back to themes he was researching at the University of Berlin for his doctoral thesis, titled *The Large and Small-Scale System of Agriculture in the Southern United States 1840-1890*. The thesis, written in the Department of Economics under Gustav von Schmoller, looked at the farming system in the South from the bottom up; that is, from the standpoint of the peasantry and slaves. Clearly, while building on the work of Hart at Harvard, Du Bois was showing the influences of the German school of economics and history. The theories of the German Social Democratic Party and one of the many forms of Marxism whirling around him no doubt influenced him.[14] As well, his work was a response to the racist interpretation of Reconstruction as evidenced in the film, *Birth of a Nation*. By 1924, in *The Gift of Black Folk: The Negroes in the Making of America*, Du Bois (1992/1924) would begin to make the case that is more fully developed in *Black Re-*

construction: that the question of slavery and Reconstruction was, in the end, a question of labor. "The Negro still is the mightiest single group of labor force in the United States" (p. 64)." But he would also make the argument that the cause of the Civil War was slavery; it was not, in essence, as mainstream historiography had argued, a regional North-South conflict.

In this work, we glimpse Du Bois's methods of inquiry and presentation. Indeed, we get a sense of his unique scientific method. Du Bois worked collectively, actively engaging colleagues from the Niagara and Pan African Movements, as well as fellow academicians such as Rayford W. Logan and Anna Julia Cooper, principal of Washington, D.C.'s elite M Street High School.

John Brown (Du Bois, 1987/1909) is an important foundational work in the formation of Du Bois's notion of Black Reconstruction. While it is an interpretative biography of the white abolitionist who led the armed raid on Harper's Ferry in 1859, it is also a study of Jacobin or radical democracy. In some ways, John Brown plays a role in Du Bois's understanding of race, democracy, and opposition to slavery similar to the role played by Thomas Munzer, the early 16th-century German peasant leader, in Engels's conceptualization of German history. John Brown and Thomas Munzer were prototypes and metaphors to explain larger historical forces. Du Bois's study of John Brown was part of a larger research project that would result in *Black Reconstruction*. In a sense, Brown for Du Bois and Munzer for Engels were revolutionaries in what might be conceived of as prerevolutionary times. Both were defeated and executed.

The book *John Brown* tells what a leading black fighter for full freedom in the 20th century thought of the great martyr—himself white—in the struggle for freedom in the 19th century. Herbert Aptheker (1989) contends that Du Bois's interpretation portrays John Brown as a white man who had consciously divested himself of racism, uniquely in 19th-century America. In this sense, the story is part of Du Bois's larger antiracist research agenda. Brown himself becomes a metaphor for what was possible for white antiracists, yet what was seldom realized. In the preface to *John Brown,* Du Bois states,

> John Brown worked not simply for Black Men—he worked with them; and he was a companion of their daily life, knew their faults and virtues, and felt as few white Americans have felt, the bitter tragedy of their lot. The story of John Brown, then, cannot be complete unless due emphasis is given this. (p. 10)

This identification with African Americans led Brown to make the supreme sacrifice. More than a record, the book is a tribute to the white man who, Du Bois says, "has come nearest to touching the real souls of black folk." John Brown, Du Bois believed, was an exemplar of a white Jacobin tradition in U.S. history. He saw the quality that most African Americans seek out in their white fellow citizens. John Brown was also the product of profound historical forces and an example of the individual who fights to be on the correct side of history. Last, Du Bois drew attention to the manner in which John Brown led his life. Du Bois insisted, "He sought them [Black people] in home and church and out on the street and hired them in his business. He came to them on the plane of perfect equality—they sat at his table and he at theirs" (p. 10).

In *John Brown* Du Bois cites what became his life's motto: The cost of liberty was less than the price of repression (Aptheker, 1989). Du Bois praises John Brown's guiding principles, the Hebrew religion and the French revolution. Moreover, according to Aptheker (1989), Du Bois was, in this volume, 30 to 40 years ahead of U.S. historiography in demonstrating the insurrectionary and revolutionary spirit of the slaves, the significance of the slaves self-initiative and organization, and what would later appear in *Black Reconstruction,* the "deepest realities of slavery, the expansionism of the slave system, and the nature of Reconstruction and its overthrow in 1876" (Du Bois, 1935/1992, p. 94). By examining

the life of John Brown, Du Bois was exploring white consciousness and behavior on race. He would finally conclude that the majority of whites were not capable of such antiracist heroism as John Brown. Du Bois's *John Brown* was out of publication for more than 50 years, until 1962. Aptheker indicates that the white commercial press generally ignored its republication, although the African American public warmly received it.

In *Black Reconstruction,* his magnum opus, Du Bois theoretically develops the idea of the centrality of the struggle for African American equality to American democracy. Professor Stanley Aronowitz (1981) called Du Bois the greatest of the 1930s Marxist scholars and his *Black Reconstruction* a "pathbreaking historical treatment" in "the tradition of Marxist historiography" (p. ix). In this book, one gets a sense of the way Du Bois conducted scholarship, of how ideas germinated and were nurtured over years and how he finally developed and presented them. We furthermore witness how Du Bois's scholarship is connected to current social and political events. The radical tone of the work cannot be separated from the Great Depression and the radical politics of the time. In fact, the last chapter is boldly titled, "The Propaganda of History," contending that history has been used to advance certain racial and class positions over others. In many ways, *Black Reconstruction* can be compared with Frederick Engels's *The Peasant War in Germany.* Both are shaped to address politically pressing questions of the moment from the standpoint of an analogous political moment. For Engels, the German peasant uprising of 1525 was used to explain the German revolution of 1848-1850. Du Bois used the Civil War and Reconstruction to indicate the direction of U.S. history and to assert the centrality of the black struggle to democracy and revolutionary transformation in the 20th century.

Given the liberal tenor of the country in the 1930s, the book received a positive reception and an enthusiastic response from African American periodicals and journals. Du Bois's long-time associate in Pan African efforts, the eminent historian Rayford Logan, said that *Black Reconstruction* revealed Du Bois "as both the merciless critic and constructive historian." "The real value of this epoch making book" according to Logan, is that it is "the first Marxian interpretation of this crucial period" (cited in Aptheker, 1989, p. 239). Historian Charles Wesley portrayed Du Bois as a "lyric historian, the literary knight with the plumed pen" (cited in Aptheker, 1989, p. 242).

In *Black Reconstruction,* Du Bois emphasizes the momentous impact on the nature of American society, and therefore on world history, of the failure to democratize the South, which is what the defeat of Reconstruction signified for him. Du Bois also sought to make clear that Reconstruction was an episode in the worldwide struggle of the rich against the poor. Property and property relationships shape his thesis in the book. He emphasized not only the specifics of the land question in the South but the entire matter of property rights; indeed, he called one of the most pregnant chapters in this book, "Counter-Revolution of Property." Du Bois understood that the question of property was central to the State and democracy. "In this sense," Aptheker (1989) says, "Du Bois saw the story both of Emancipation and Reconstruction as an essential feature of the story of labor . . . in the generic sense of those who had to work to make ends meet" (p. 251). But chattel slavery turns blacks as human beings into property, not just into their labor power. What this produces is a situation where the race struggle inevitably shapes the class struggle. In this context, Aptheker raises important theoretical questions that are present in Du Bois's effort. For instance, Du Bois's notion of *radical reconstruction* included the possibility of a proletarian dictatorship. He later backed away from such a notion.

Herein rests the important question of the relationship of the struggles for democracy to struggles for socialism. It might even be suggested that Du Bois conceived of Reconstruction as a continuation of John Brown's armed activity in 1855 and raid on Harper's Ferry in 1859, perhaps assuming a generally proletarian revolutionary situation issuing out of the Civil War. What was clear is that Du Bois believed in a radical democratic or Jacobin solution to the race question in the South. And this undertaking, Aptheker (1989) forcefully argues, "would almost certainly require—like the Civil War—the shedding of much blood" (p. 90). Du Bois, no doubt, viewed himself as continuing in the Jacobin tradition of Nat Turner, the Haitian revolution, John Brown, and Frederick Douglass.

The theoretically most innovative and engaging chapter in *Black Reconstruction* is Chapter 4, "The General Strike." Here, Du Bois affirms a revolutionary agency for the black slaves, whom he defines as workers. What must, however, be acknowledged is that Du Bois was applying his massive genius to understanding Reconstruction as part of a scientific effort to discover the foundations of institutional and legal racism in the United States and its overturn. The race and class dialectic and their interpenetration in the formation of struggles for radical democracy are primary focuses of the work. His scientific accomplishment, therefore, should be placed in the context of his effort to define the logic of democratic transformation in the context of the race problem. Hence, this book seems to signal the full maturity of Du Bois as a theoretician of social change.

▶ Conclusion

This chapter views Du Bois as a seminal thinker in the social sciences. Moreover, it looks on his development of social theory and research, not as a trickle down from, or black face imitation of, white thinking. His intellectual and scholarly practices emerge from his racial, political, professional, and ideological positions within U.S. society. The ways that he thought about the world and attempted to resolve both theoretical and practical problems cannot be separated from these relationships. Du Bois's thinking emerged from an intellectually and politically hostile environment, where his status was always marginalized. Yet, he was more than a leader of protest against these circumstances; he critically analyzed and constructed theories to explain them. I differ, therefore, with Elliot Rudwick (1968) and August Meier (1963), who see Du Bois almost solely as a propagandist of protest and, in the process, misrepresent the depth of his contributions to social theory. Rudwick (1968) contends that Du Bois's *Philadelphia Negro* and the Atlanta studies "were lacking in systematic theory" (p. 49). Du Bois's research, he asserts, was essentially geared to propaganda. "The Atlanta studies," he tells us, "may not have improved the conditions of the race very much, but they probably did improve its morale." Francis L. Broderick (1959, p. 228), however, makes one exception. *Philadelphia Negro* represented, he tells us, Du Bois's only first-class scholarship. These writers exemplify the racist treatment that Du Bois's work has received from white academics.

Arnold Rampersad's (1976) *The Art and Imagination of W.E.B. Du Bois* takes Du Bois seriously as an intellectual, yet falls into the trap of searching out what are believed to be all of the white influences on him. Rampersad expresses the view that Du Bois, with differing levels of success and accuracy, reflects the ideas of one or another white theoretical or philosophical mentor. *The Souls of Black Folk,* Rampersad argues, is "the fruit of a secondary career of cultural commentary, based on history and sociology . . . a work of definitive importance to the future of Black culture" (p. 48). What Rampersad fails to acknowledge is that the work is foundational to the construction of a social science of race. Cornel West (1989), like Rampersad, views Du Bois as part of the history of American pragmatism. "Du Bois" West insists, "seems to have been attracted to pragmatism owing to its Emersonian evasion of epistemology-centered philosophy and his sense of pragmatism's relevance to the Afro-American predicament" (p. 139). To West, Du Bois was a Jamesian organic intellectual. Therefore, he is a less seminal thinker than the pragmatist

whom he allegedly followed. Reducing Du Bois within the frame of pragmatism or another European or Euro-American intellectual movement carries with it the idea that Du Bois was actually an intellectual utilitarian who eclectically, and without concern for their foundations, grafts ideas together to make a propaganda point. Hence, he was not a serious or critical thinker. Others, such as Marable (1986) and Moses (1978), see Du Bois almost solely from the standpoint of political activism and attempt to locate him politically, failing to locate the philosophical and theoretical foundations of his politics. Adolph Reed's (1997) *W.E.B Du Bois and American Political Though: Fabianism and the Color Line* attempts to locate the philosophical and theoretical foundations of Du Bois's politics. Reed contends, "little book-length scholarly work has concentrated on the theoretical dimension of Du Bois's political thought" (p. 4). Yet, Reed, like Rampersad and West, believes ultimately that it is impossible for Du Bois to stand on his own as a thinker. And when he does he usually falls on his face, Reed argues. For Reed, Du Bois not only operated within the political and intellectual context of his time but was basically not unlike white thinkers of the period.

Du Bois, however, has to be dealt with on his own terms. His work must be judged from the standpoint of the theoretical, philosophical, methodological, and ideological problems he sought to address and solve. He looked at the social universe very differently from white thinkers of his day (and even of most in our time). He saw what they did not see. But more than this, he developed a unique way of examining the world in the process. Du Bois placed race as the central dynamic of modernity. In so doing, he understood race as a set of complex global relationships including, as his studies of the U.S. South indicate, relationships of production. This I consider to be a major innovation in social thinking. In Kuhnian terms, it could be considered a paradigm shift, not only in U.S. letters but in the world's understanding of itself. This suggests that to one or another extent, European social theories of modernity in one way or another express false consciousness.

My basic contention in this chapter is that as a thinker, Du Bois stands on his own. However, his innovations in thought were not just a "black thing;" they were crucial to the world's understanding of itself. His insights, and the research program that flowed from them, developed over the course of more than 75 years of research, activism, and reflection. In the end, what was produced was a distinct episteme, which I call a Du Boisian episteme. The Du Boisian episteme is a distinct intellectual product that cannot be accounted for merely by, as most have done, talking about where he went to school, who his professors were, and how his views parallel those of dominant white thinkers. Moreover, through most of his life, his intellectual audiences, scientific environments, and colleagues were black. These organic ties have been poorly researched. They are, however, decisive in explaining and understanding his thought. Du Bois, rather than merely leaning on others, constructed an intellectual and scientific edifice on which others are now standing.

It behooves African American studies to examine and understand the foundations on which Du Bois stood because, in large measure, they are our intellectual foundations. We have, in the end, only barely begun to construct an organized understanding of the core of Du Bois's intellectual vision, from which his thought and life radiated. This chapter has been an effort to get at that core.

Du Bois's place in intellectual and political history must also be evaluated from the standpoint of how it can shape the future geography of ideas. It should not, as Reed (1997) has done, be limited to the Jim Crow period of American history. Du Bois's central contribution is to the conceptualization of race and modernity. His thinking constitutes a strategic break with the Eurocentric paradigm. His was a specific antiracist episteme, one that recognized social change as being rooted in the worldwide struggle to alter relations of racial oppression. The Du Boisian episteme lays the basis of a progressive research program that

should become the property of African American studies as it enters the 21st century.

But all of this indicates a challenge to the hegemonic discourse on race as constructed by white supremacy. To traverse the paths from white social science to a social science of African American liberation, Du Bois constructed an episteme, a linguistic strategy, and a discourse of black power.

▶ Notes

1. August Comte introduced issues of methodology into the discourse on the social sciences issues. Positivism came to be defined by its attempts to infuse the social sciences with methods that replicated those of the natural sciences (Frisby, 1969). Habermas defined this procedure as *scientism,* which is the conviction that science is not just one possible means of knowing but the means of achieving knowledge per se.

2. Although this virulent mixture occurred in the German academy, the most influential racist views came from England. Francis Galton, a cousin of Charles Darwin, pursued themes that dominated research about eugenics for decades. His research program came to be named the hereditarian research program. At its center were the ideas that biology determined social behavior, that non-whites were inferior to whites, and that Anglo-Saxons were superior to other white people. In pursuance of this agenda, Galton made significant contributions to statistics and originated mental testing.

3. Sociobiology is the latest expression of social Darwinism. In a sense, it can be termed *reformed social Darwinism* because it attempts to shed much of the rankest racist language associated with classical social Darwinism. There is, however, an openly racist trend even within contemporary social Darwinism. This is demonstrated in a renewed interest in the hereditarian research program and eugenics, as demonstrated in Richard Herrnstein and Charles Murray's (1996) *The Bell Curve.*

4. Du Bois (1903/1986), in *The Souls of Black Folk,* declared, "The problem of the twenti-

eth century is the problem of the color line" (p. 16). He insisted that Booker T. Washington's service to the white establishment was in removing race from national politics. Washington also came forward with a compromise whereby in return for philanthropy, blacks would relinquish their right to the vote and legal equality and black leaders would urge an abandonment of protest over lynching. Du Bois (1903/1986) eloquently summarized the moment and the nation's attitude to the Negro: "Mr. Washington came, with a simple definite program, at the psychological moment when the nation was a little ashamed of having bestowed so much sentiment on the Negroes and was concentrating its energies on Dollars" (p. 38).

5. Schmoller was the father of German historical economics. Du Bois did a paper for a seminar with him on U.S. agriculture in the South, titled *The Large and Small-Scale System of Agriculture in the Southern United States, 1840-1890* (cited in Lewis, 1993). In methodological disputes that arose in the German academy of the late 19th century, Schmoller stood for an approach that emphasized the inductive empirical over the abstract theoretical approach. He believed in economic stages based on constant improvement in technology. Wagner, on the other hand, was a Christian socialist and a spokesman for the antiradical trend within socialism, known as socialism of the chair, its English version being Fabianism.

6. William James (1890/1950) referred to his form of pragmatism as *radical empiricism*. His psychology flows from this radical stance. In the *Principles of Psychology,* he says, "thoughts and feeling exist and are vehicles of knowledge . . . psychology when she has ascertained the empirical correlation of the various sorts of thought or feeling with definite conditions of the brain can go no farther—can go no farther, that is, as natural science. If she goes farther, she becomes metaphysics" (p. vi). As Eugene Reed (1997, p. 6) suggests, James was urging psychologists to do their philosophy as properly as they did their science. Du Bois did not make such a severe division between science and metaphysics as James did, nor did he follow James down the path of methodological individualism. He did, however, echo James's argument that positivists, such as Herbert Spencer, were putting forward overtly philosophical and ideological theories and labeling them scientific. James considered the positivism of Spencer and others to be metaphysics, much in the way Du Bois did. In this respect, James and Du Bois shared common ground in their attacks on the antiscientific positivism of social Darwinism.

7. His commitment to knowing and action based on scientific knowledge became stronger over the years. In his commencement speech on the 20th anniversary of his graduation from Fisk University, Du Bois crystallized this commitment. The speech, entitled "Galileo Galilei," criticized Galileo for submitting to papal authority and renouncing the truth of his scientific discoveries. Du Bois (1908/1973) passionately insisted, "Science is a great and worthy mistress, but there is one greater and that is Humanity which science serves; one thing there is greater than knowledge and that the Man who knows. In the midst then of society whose life blood is faith, and in the name of Science which will know the truth that the truth may make it free, the verdict of civilization must be that not even the splendor of the service of Truth done by Galileo Galilei can wipe away the plot of his cowardly lie. By the lie civilization was halted, science was checked, and bigotry was more strongly enthroned on its crimson glory" (p. 24).

8. Max Weber participated in the 1904 conference on crime, and Boas took part in the 11th conference, on "The Health and Physique of the Negro American," and delivered a paper on the cultural basis of racial behavior (see Lewis, 1993, pp. 225, 351-352).

9. Barkan (1992, p. 24) suggests that racist theories reflect race conflict in society and that the high points of British racism and race theorizing were also the high points of British imperialism. In this respect, *The Bell Curve* perhaps heralds a new stage of race conflict in the United States.

10. This paper's meaning has become the source of significant and at times vitriolic debate among African American scholars. Most important to this debate are Lucius Outlaw (1996, Chapter 6) and Anthony Appiah (1992, pp. 28-46).

11. Important works in urban sociology that draw on Du Bois's methodology are St. Claire Drake and Horace Cayton's *Black Metropolis* (1946/1962), Kenneth Clark's *Dark Ghetto*

(1964), David Katzman's *Before the Ghetto: Detroit in the 19th Century*(1973), Kenneth Kusmer's *The Ghetto Takes Shape: Black Cleveland 1870-1930* (1976), and William Julius Wilson's *The Truly Disadvantaged* (1987).

12. It is clear Du Bois follows themes from the *Phenomenology of Mind.* For example, there are parallels in *Souls* to *Phenomenology*'s Chapter 3, "Force and Understanding: Appearance and the Supersensible World," especially the sections, "Independence and Dependence of Self-Consciousness: Leadership and Bondage" and "Freedom of Self-Consciousness: Stoicism, Skepticism, and the Unhappy Consciousness," to Chapter 4, and to the opening section of Chapter 6. Lewis (1993) points out that Du Bois had a genuine affinity for Hegel's *Phenomenology of Mind,* "and for all James's supposed pragmatic and empirical influence upon him, Du Bois found in the Hegelian World-Spirit, dialectically actualizing itself through history, a profoundly appealing concept" (p. 139).

13. James's and Dewey's psychological theories flowed from their pragmatic philosophy. In this sense, streams of consciousness that were in a continual state of flux, whose alterations reflected physiological changes within the individual, determined psychological states. Their stance, as with pragmatism generally, was a form of extreme methodological individualism and ahistoricism.

14. Du Bois (1968) says that while he was attracted to socialism as a student in Germany, he found the development of Marxism and the revisionism of Lassalle, Bernstein, and Bakunin "was too complicated for a student like myself to understand, who had received no real teaching along this line. I was overwhelmed with rebuttals of Marxism before I understood the original doctrine" (p. 168).

▶ **References**

Anderson, E. (1995). Introduction. In W.E.B. Du Bois, *The Philadelphia Negro: A social study.* Philadelphia: University of Pennsylvania Press.

Appiah, A. (1992). *In my father's house: Africa in philosophy of culture.* New York: Oxford University Press.

Aptheker, H. (1973). *Annotated bibliography of the published writings of W.E.B. Du Bois.* Millwood, NY: Krause-Thompson.

Aptheker, H. (1989). *The literary legacy of W.E.B. Du Bois.* White Plains, NY: Krause.

Aronowitz, S. (1981). *The crisis in historical materialism: Class, politics, and culture in Marxist theory.* New York: Praeger.

Asante, M. K. (1986). *Afrocentricity.* Trenton, NJ: Africa World Press.

Bailey, R. (1992). The slave(ry) trade and the development of capitalism in the United States: The textile industry in New England. In J. E. Inikori & S. L. Engerman (Eds.), *The Atlantic slave trade: Effects on economies, societies, and peoples in Africa, the Americas, and Europe.* Durham, NC: Duke University Press.

Baltzell, E. D. (1967). Introduction. In W.E.B. Du Bois, *The Philadelphia Negro: A social study.* New York: Schocken.

Barkan, E. (1992). *The retreat of scientific racism: Changing concepts of race in Britain and the United States between the wars.* Cambridge, UK: Cambridge University Press.

Bourdieu, P. (1977). *Outline of a theory of practice.* Cambridge, UK: Cambridge University Press.

Broderick, F. (1959). *W.E.B. Du Bois, Negro leader in a time of crisis.* Stanford, CA: Stanford University Press.

Clark, K. (1964). *Dark ghetto: Dilemmas of social power.* New York: Harper &Row.

Drake, St. C., & Cayton, H. (1962). *Black metropolis: A study of negro life in a northern city.* New York: Harper & Row. (Original work published 1946)

Du Bois, W.E.B. (1932, March). Book review. *The Crisis,* pp. 39, 102-103.

Du Bois, W.E.B. (1968). *The autobiography of W.E.B. Du Bois.* New York: International Publishers.

Du Bois, W.E.B. (1985). *Against racism: Unpublished essays, papers, addresses, 1887-1961* (H. Aptheker, Ed.). Amherst: University of Massachusetts Press.

Du Bois, W.E.B. (1986). *The suppression of the African slave trade to the United States of America 1638-1870.* New York: Library of America. (Original work published 1896)

Du Bois, W.E.B. (1986). The souls of black folk. In N. Huggins (Ed.), *W.E.B Du Bois: Writings.* New York: Library of America. (Original work published 1903)

Du Bois, W.E.B. (1987). *John Brown.* New York: International Publishers. (Original work published 1909)

Du Bois, W.E.B. (1992). *The gift of black folk: The Negroes in the making of America.* Millwood, NY: Krause-Thompson. (Original work published 1924)

Du Bois, W.E.B. (1992). *Black reconstruction in America 1860-1880.* New York: Atheneum. (Original work published 1935)

Du Bois, W.E.B. (1993). *The Philadelphia Negro: A social study.* Philadelphia: University Press. (Original work published 1903)

Du Bois, W.E.B. (1995). *Dusk of dawn: An essay toward an autobiography of a race concept.* New Brunswick, NJ: Transaction Publishers. (Original work published 1940)

Du Bois, W.E.B. (1995). *The world and Africa.* New York: International Publishers. (Original work published 1947)

Engels, F. (1975). The conditions of the working class in England. In K. Marx & F. Engels, *Collected works* (Vol. 4). New York: International Publishers. (Original work published 1845)

Frisby, D. (1969). *The alienated mind: The sociology of knowledge in Germany, 1918-1933.* New York: Routledge.

Galton, F. (1869). *Heredity genius.* London: Macmillan.

Gooding-Williams, R. (1992, Winter). Evading narrative myth, evading prophetic pragmatism: Cornel West's *The American Evasion of Philosophy. Massachusetts Review.*

Green, D. S., & Driver, E. D. (1980). Introduction. In D. S. Green & E. D. Driver (Eds.), *W.E.B Du Bois on sociology and the black community.* Chicago: University of Chicago Press.

Hegel, G.W.F. (1996). *The phenomenology of mind.* London: George Allen & Unwin.

Herrnstein, R., & Murray, C. (1996). *The bell curve: Intelligence and class structure in American life.* New York: Simon & Schuster.

Inikori, J. E. (1992). *The chaining of a continent: Export demands for captives and the history of Africa south of the Sahara, 1450-1870.* Mona, Jamaica: Institute of Social and Economic Research.

James, W. (1950). *Principles of psychology* (Vol. 1). New York: Dover. (Original work published 1890)

Katzman, D. (1973). *Before the ghetto: Black Detroit in the nineteenth century.* Urbana: University of Illinois Press.

Kusmer, K. (1976). *A ghetto takes shape: Black Cleveland, 1870-1930.* Urbana: University of Illinois Press.

Lewis, D. L. (1993). *W.E.B. Du Bois: Biography of a race 1968-1919.* New York: Henry Holt.

Lynd, S. (1967). *Class conflict, slavery, and the United States Constitution, ten essays.* Indianapolis, IN: Bobbs-Merrill.

Marable, M. (1986). *W.E.B Du Bois: Black radical democrat.* Boston: Twayne.

McKee, J. B. (1993). *Sociology and the race problem: The failure of a perspective.* Urbana: University of Illinois Press.

Meier, A. (1963). *Negro thought in America, 1880-1915: Racial ideologies in the age of Booker T. Washington.* Ann Arbor: University of Michigan Press.

Moses, J. (1978). *The golden age of black nationalism, 1850-1925.* New York: Oxford University Press.

Munford, C. J. (1991). *The black ordeal of slavery and slave trading in the French West Indies, 1625-1715* (Vol. 1). Lewiston: The Edwin Mellen Press.

Omi, M., & Winant, H. (1986). *Racial formation in the United States from the 1960s to the 1980s.* New York: Routledge and Kegan Paul.

Outlaw, L. (1996). *On race and philosophy.* New York: Routledge.

Rampersad, A. (1976). *The art and imagination of W.E.B Du Bois.* Cambridge, MA: Harvard University Press.

Reed, E. (1997). *W.E.B Du Bois and American political thought: Fabianism and the color line.* New York: Oxford University Press.

Ross, D. (1991). *The origins of American social science.* New York: Cambridge University Press.

Rudwick, E. M. (1968). *W.E.B Du Bois, propagandist of the Negro protest.* New York: Atheneum.

Schwendinger, H., & Schwendinger, J. R. (1974). *The sociologists of the chair: A radical analysis of the formative years of North American sociology (1883-1922).* New York: Basic Books.

Smedley, A. (1993). *Race in North America.* Boulder, CO: Westview.

Spencer, H. (1862). *A system of synthetic philosophy.* London: Williams & Norgate.

Takaki, R. T. (1971). *A pro-slavery crusade: The agitation to reopen the African slave trade.* New York: Free Press.

Turner, J. H., Beeghley, L., & Powers, C. H. (1995). *The emergence of sociological theory.* Belmont, CA: Wadsworth.

West, C. (1989). *The American evasion of philosophy: A genealogy of pragmatism.* Madison: The University of Wisconsin Press.

Wilson, W. J. (1987). *The truly disadvantaged: The inner city, the underclass, and public policy.* Chicago: University of Chicago Press.

Zamir, S. (1995). *Dark voice: W.E.B. Du Bois and American thought, 1888-1903.* Chicago: University of Chicago Press.

Social Cognition and Racial Stereotyping in Television

Consequences for Transculturalism

TRAVIS L. DIXON

In the first half of the 20th century, W.E.B. Du Bois proclaimed that America's most pressing issue is the "color line." This line epitomizes the racial hierarchy that relegates blacks to the lowest level of existence in American society. During the next 50 years, civil rights activists attempted to erase the boundaries presented by this line. They were successful to the degree that legislation designed to put an end to de jure discrimination in the United States was passed. However, prejudice, racism, and stereotyping remain commonplace in America, especially in educational and business opportunities (Bell, 1987; West, 1993).

The mass media may foster the racist conditions that confront African Americans. Although there have been examples of counter-stereotypical programming such as *The Cosby Show,* it can reasonably be argued that television still frequently portrays blacks in a stereotypical manner (Dates & Barlow, 1990; Evuleocha & Ugbah, 1989; Graves, 1993). For example, Dates and Barlow (1990) have reported that blacks are often portrayed as less competent than whites and have less serious roles than their white counterparts. Critics argue that these stereotypes can have the effect of communicating misinformation about blacks. This misinformation is then used by whites to make social judgments about African Americans (Graves, 1993).

The theme of this book is how we can promote transcultural realities that affirm diverse ways of knowing, communicating, and behaving that result in more positive intercultural and intergroup interactions. The primary thesis of this chapter is that creating these transcultural realities will be difficult as long as the stereotypical images that air on television persist. The present chapter seeks to understand the extent to which the mass media may contribute to the persistence of what W.E.B. Du Bois has called the color line by reinforcing stereotypical beliefs about African Americans that affect both black self-esteem and black interactions with whites and other racial groups. It is argued that theories of social cognition offer a useful paradigm for investigating these issues. Although the primary focus of this chapter will be on how television hinders the promotion of transcultural realities, it will also outline how television might be transformed to promote greater intercultural understanding. This discussion begins with an introduction to the theories of social cognition and stereotyping.

▶ Social Cognition and Stereotyping

The social cognition approach conceives of stereotypes as belief systems that characterize various social groups (e.g., Hamilton, Stroessner, & Driscoll, 1994). This perspective views stereotypes as cognitive structures or categories similar to other social schemas (Hamilton & Trolier, 1986). These cognitive structures affect the encoding and processing of information, particularly information pertaining to outgroup members.

A phenomenon known as the illusory correlation may be one psychological mechanism that explains how these stereotypes or cognitive structures evolve. Chapman (1967) and Chapman and Chapman (1969) conducted research demonstrating that when a relationship between two variables is expected, subjects often overestimate the degree of relationship that exists or impose a relationship when none actually exists. They found evidence that the same principles may account for this systematic error, regardless of the subject matter being observed, such that (a) words that have a strong associative connection are reported as correlated in their occurrence when they are not actually correlated, and (b) illusory correlations occur between distinctive stimuli. For example, although *bat* and *ball* may not have occurred together during the experiment, subjects would report seeing them together because they are typically associated with one another. In an application of the illusory correlation effect to the process of stereotyping, Hamilton and his colleagues found that even in cases where there is an equal distribution of stereotypical and nonstereotypical traits among an in-group and an out-group, out-group members are more likely to be associated with the stereotypical trait (Hamilton & Trolier, 1986).

Social cognition researchers believe that although old prejudicial attitudes have declined, prejudicial tendencies have evolved into more subtle responses. For example, Devine's (1989) dissociation model provides a social cognition explanation for why stereotypes persist despite efforts to eradicate them. This model emphasizes the idea that stereotypes and personal beliefs represent distinct cognitive structures or belief systems. According to Devine, stereotype activation and processing is automatic. It takes effort and cognitive capacity to stop prejudice-like responses. Nonprejudiced people have a personal belief system that is distinct from their stereotypes. Their personal belief system suggests that it is "bad" to give a prejudiced response, and this belief system requires intentional, controlled processes to work properly. According to Devine (1989), the dissociation model holds that although low-prejudiced people have changed their beliefs concerning stereotyped group members, the stereotype has not been eliminated from their memory system. In fact, the stereotype continues to be a well-organized, frequently activated knowledge structure. In short, the nonprejudiced belief system is not automatically activated, but the stereotype is automatically activated. The result is that when subjects cannot monitor their stereotype activation, they will give a prejudice-like response, regardless of their level of prejudice.

The implication of the social cognition perspective is that the only way to stop stereotyping is to prevent the cognitive mechanism from operating or to undermine its influence (e.g., Devine, 1989; Hamilton et al., 1994). This is a difficult task, especially when there is evidence to suggest stereotype activation is automatic (Devine, 1989). Hamilton and Trolier (1986) suggest that it is essential to attend to the cognitive processes involved in the stereotyping process to discourage the use of stereotypes.

SOCIAL COGNITION, THE STEREOTYPING PROCESSES, AND THE ROLE OF TELEVISION

In the relationship between the mass media and the theories of social cognition described above, the media serve primarily as cultivators of stereotypes. According to scholars working in the area of social cognition, the information that we gain from the mass media results in the production of stereotypes that help us simplify our environment. In other words, the media may act as a sociocultural agent or source of stereotypical information about African Americans (Hamilton et al., 1994). We might view the media as a source of social learning that essentially teaches and reinforces certain ideas about blacks. This learning function may be similar to the way that the media reinforce notions of violence (Hamilton & Trolier, 1986; Wilson et al., 1997).

The cognitive processing of African Americans as a group in stereotypical ways may be related to seeing them in consistently stereotypical roles on television over a long period of time. Hamilton et al. (1994) maintain that white South Africans' stereotypes about blacks arose from seeing them on a daily basis in particular roles. Thus, if white viewers continuously see blacks on television in certain roles, they may come to develop stereotypes that reflect these characterizations. To demonstrate what traits have been historically associated with blacks on television, it is necessary to review the relevant content analysis literature.

Black stereotypes learned from entertainment programming. There were only a handful of studies this author could locate that content-analyzed racial stereotypes on entertainment television. One of them was conducted by Lemon (1977), who found that blacks had more dominant portrayals in situation comedies than whites and were unfavorably portrayed in crime dramas. She also reported that compared to whites, blacks were more likely to be portrayed as criminals and as unable to adapt to white society.

Another study was undertaken by Reid (1979), who found that black women were portrayed as louder and more boisterous than white women when interacting with their family members. This study is complemented by Greenberg and Neuendorf (1980), who found that black families had a greater probability of being in conflict with one another compared to white families. Finally, Baptista-Fernandez and Greenberg (1980) found that blacks were less likely to have an identifiable job compared to whites, and they were also flashier dressers than whites.

Black stereotypes learned from news and reality programming. One could argue that news and reality programming contain even more stinging portrayals of black stereotypes than entertainment programming. One of the most significant problems with news and other reality programming is that they appear to portray African Americans as criminals and trouble makers. A few studies have examined depictions of blacks on local television news and reality-based programming and suggest that blacks are typically depicted as dangerous and destructive (Dixon & Linz, 2000; Entman, 1992; Oliver, 1994).

For example, Entman (1992) found that blacks accused of crime were much more likely than whites to be shown in the grip of a restraining police officer and were more likely than whites to have mug shots of them shown. A second study by Dixon and Linz (2000) used three indices of law-breaking portrayals to investigate black criminal perpetration in the news: intergroup measures (e.g., comparing black to white perpetrators), inter-role measures (e.g., comparing black perpetrators to police officers), and inter-reality measures (e.g., comparing the proportion of perpetrators portrayed on television news to crime reports). Their study revealed that black defendants are linked to criminal behavior based on all three indices. Finally, Oliver (1994) found that the black criminal stereotype was also prevalently depicted on reality-based programs, including *Cops, Top Cops, America's Most Wanted, FBI, The Untold Story,* and *American Detective.*

Social cognition and the content of television stereotypes. Social cognition suggests that viewers might learn stereotypical information from seeing the stereotypes featured on television. Content analyses of television news suggest that television is rife with portrayals of African American stereotypes. Entertainment and news and reality-based programming depict blacks as prone to conflict, flashy dressers, unable to adapt to white society, unemployed, and criminals. Based on theories of social cognition, as a result of such exposure, there can be a number of negative consequences for intergroup encounters.

SOCIAL COGNITION, TELEVISION, AND INTERGROUP ENCOUNTERS

The development of these cognitive categories or stereotypes from the media may have important implications for the way that out-group members encode and retrieve information about African Americans. If whites encounter blacks on television who are depicted as inept, unemployed, conflict-driven, and criminal, they will come to think of blacks outside of the television environment in these stereotypical terms. Linville, Salovey, and Fischer (1986) suggest that whites who obtain their information about blacks primarily from the media will be more likely to overestimate the number of blacks who are entertainers and athletes and to underestimate the proportion who are in other occupations, such as white-collar jobs. As blacks become associated with a stereotypical characteristic by way of the media, whites come to anticipate the presence of the television characterization in their social interactions with African Americans.

The anticipation of the stereotype may foster discriminatory behavior. According to Hamilton and Trolier (1986), when subjects are categorized into an in-group and out-group, even on a relatively arbitrary basis, their behavior reveals a clear preferential treatment for in-group members, even when direct self-interest is not a factor. One of the most robust effects of the categorization process is the belief that out-group members are more dissimilar than members of one's in-group. The out-group is seen as more extreme with regard to certain social attributes (Hamilton & Trolier, 1986).

Furthermore, exposure to depictions of blacks on television as either inept buffoons or people prone to conflict—even a small number of times—might reinforce common stereotypes about blacks as unintelligent or violent according to the illusory correlation effect described above. When asked to make judgments about blacks in other contexts, participants may believe that the trait of intellectual inferiority is present due to the expectation that it should be present.

In addition to affecting intercultural relations, media stereotypes may also shape the group identity of those who are negatively portrayed. Below, this possibility is examined by focusing on how negative stereotypes of African Americans on television might have an impact on black self-esteem.

MEDIA STEREOTYPES
EFFECTS ON BLACK SELF-ESTEEM

One of the premier concerns about negative stereotypes in the media is whether or not blacks come to have lowered self-esteem after viewing negative African American stereotypes. The scholarly work on stigmatization and self-esteem suggests an intuitively appealing hypothesis: The negative effects of media coverage of blacks will lead them to have lower self-esteem than whites. Contrary to expectations, tests of this hypothesis show that blacks have the same or a higher self-esteem than others (Crocker & Major, 1989). Graves's (1975) early study demonstrated that negative stereotypes of blacks had no negative impact on the self-esteem of African Americans. Her study showed that when children were exposed to media imagery presenting blacks, black self-esteem rose, regardless of the nature of the depiction (i.e., whether it was stereotypical or positive). However, negative depictions of blacks caused white children to see African Americans in more stereotypical terms. Graves concluded that because so few shows had black characters, any portrayal of African Americans was greeted in a positive manner by blacks. African Americans were simply thankful to see any reflection of themselves presented in the media.

Social psychologists have a different explanation for blacks' higher self-esteem. According to them, blacks can attribute negative feedback to white prejudice and protect their self-esteem (Crocker & Major, 1989). When African Americans make an attribution to white prejudice, their self-esteem is maintained because any negative feedback about their behavior can be construed as inaccurate. A second, complementary explanation is proposed by Steele and Aronson (1995), who have examined African American college students. They argue that African American self-concept is also protected by disengaging from activities that are likely to confirm stereotypes about black performance. Disengagement refers to the divestment of either time, emotion, or energy in some activity. In these cases, the self-concept is maintained because the African American students are able to avoid investing themselves emotionally in situations where they may be likely to receive negative feedback. When negative feedback is received, black self-esteem is also protected because disengaged African Americans can argue that their performance is a reflection of their lack of interest.

Both of the psychological explanations above are based on laboratory experiments that examine interpersonal interactions. Attributing negative feedback to prejudice when viewing mass media depictions may be more difficult because the source of the message is harder to ascertain. Is the negative message coming from the producers of the show or the actors? Or is the television station the source of the message?

Developmental differences may influence viewers' attributions regarding the source of stereotypical mass media messages. Compared to adults, children, particularly younger children, may be less likely to ascertain the source of the mass media's message. This suggests that black children's self-esteem may be more vulnerable than black adults' self-concept when confronted with stereotypical portrayals of African Americans. The adults may be capable of attributing negative media portrayals of blacks to the prejudice of white producers or writers. These adults would perceive the portrayal of African Americans as negative and would then claim that the stereotypical depiction is a result of racism. Children, on the other hand, may have trouble making that attribution and might interpret the negative depiction as an accurate indication of their self-worth.

If viewers are unable to attribute the negative messages to prejudice, it may be more difficult to protect themselves from the negative feedback unless they choose simply not to watch television. Ratings data suggest that blacks watch the same amount of or more television than whites (Greenberg & Brand, 1994); therefore, it does not appear that blacks are avoiding the media. Given Graves's (1975) speculation that African Americans responded to the media in a positive way because of the lack of characters in the 1970s and the fact that more television shows currently feature blacks (Randolph, 1995), it seems appropriate to re-examine the effect of black portrayals on self-esteem.

Although it has been argued thus far that the media may create and maintain negative stereotypes of blacks that have an impact on intergroup interaction and possibly on black self-esteem, it is also possible that the media can change stereotypes. This possibility is examined below.

ALTERING INTERGROUP ENCOUNTERS BY PORTRAYING MEDIA COUNTERSTEREOTYPES

The most intuitive method for eradicating stereotypes is to provide examples to the in-group of out-group members who strongly disconfirm the stereotype. For example, if one is trying to discourage a white person from thinking that blacks are athletes rather than scholars, one might try to expose them to examples of great African American scholars who lack athletic ability. However, the goodness-of-fit principle, articulated by social cognition scholars, suggests that strongly disconfirming examples might lead to the inadvertent maintenance of the stereotypical category (Rothbart & John, 1985). The goodness-of-fit principle suggests that viewing strongly disconfirming members of a category sustains the category because these people will be classified or assigned to a new category. For example, an affluent black might be recategorized or subtyped by in-group members as a "middle class black" instead of simply as black.

According to Rothbart and John (1985), for the disconfirming out-group member to be effective in discouraging the use of the stereotype, the observer must relate the out-group member to the superordinate category that represents the disconfirming member's group (such as blacks or African Americans). In other words, the disconfirming group member must be seen as a true representative of the out-group, instead of an exception to the out-group. Furthermore, the degree to which a disconfirming group member will be associated with a category is a function of the fit between the category and the out-group member (Rothbart & John, 1985).

Based on the contact hypothesis and the goodness-of-fit principle, to disconfirm the stereotype, an individual cannot be a strongly disconfirming instance. Otherwise, this person's behavior would not be generalized to other out-group members. Strongly disconfirming members of an out-group are more likely to be associated with a different, possibly counterstereotypic category. This represents a Catch-22 situation. To disconfirm the stereotype, one must interact with a disconfirming group member. However, if that member is too disconfirming, the disconfirming behavior will have no effect on that person's stereotype of the group.

The solution is to provide observers with examples of moderately disconfirming members of an out-group (Rothbart & John, 1985). These moderate disconfirmers should both be associated with the larger category and at the same time provide information about the out-group that is inconsistent with the stereotype. For example, a working-class black person who has a child in college might be considered a moderate disconfirmer. In this case, the person is not rich, so he or she would continue to be associated with the category of blacks. However, the fact that his or her child is in college would provide information that combats the stereotype of blacks as intellectually inferior.

The goodness-of-fit principle suggests that counterstereotypical black portrayals in the media that feature strongly disconfirming out-group members might do little to discourage whites' use of stereotypes about African Americans. For example, *The Cosby Show*'s middle-class characters might not be associated with the general category of blacks, and therefore, the disconfirming information contained in the program is not effective in eradicating stereotypes about African Americans. On the other hand, shows that present moderately disconfirming characters such as *Roc,* which features a garbage man with good character, might do more to discourage the use of stereotypes by observers because the characters would be associated with the general category of blacks.

INCORPORATING THE PSYCHOLOGICAL PERSPECTIVE INTO A COMMUNICATION RESEARCH PROGRAM

Whereas the social cognition approach helps us understand the mental processes associated with stereotyping, the communication perspective focuses our attention on the role of mass media messages in contributing to stereotyping. Given the conclusions outlined above, there are four major areas that should be explored in a program of research that incorporates both the social cognition and communication approach. The first is a series of content analyses that investigate whether or not there have been any changes in the frequency and intensity of African American stereotypes on entertainment television since the advent of the 1990s. The second is an investigation of how the media may be involved in stereotype creation through associative processes such as illusory correlation. The third is an exploration of how the media may have an impact on black self-esteem. The last is an investigation of how the media may be used to change stereotypes.

Black media images in the 1990s. Given that the content analyses of entertainment programming featuring African Americans is severely dated, it is possible that black media imagery may have undergone change since the advent of the 1990s and, more particularly, in the new millennium. To investigate this possibility, new content analyses of African American portrayals seem warranted. These studies should attempt to replicate

some of the earlier findings of communication scholars who suggested that blacks are largely segregated on situation comedies where they are depicted as inept, unemployed people likely to engage other family members in conflict. It is possible that more positive images have emerged. However, the frequency of these portrayals needs to be documented.

Media and stereotype creation. As a complement to these content studies, research should then be conducted to understand the influence of the psychological mechanisms related to the media's role in the creation and maintenance of racial stereotypes. Scholars using the social cognition approach argue that the media may operate as a sociocultural agent that provides information leading to the creation of stereotypes (Hamilton & Trolier, 1986). In addition, they have suggested that illusory correlation (i.e., the association of a group with a characteristic when little or no relationship exists) may be part of the process that leads to stereotype creation and maintenance. However, no study to the author's knowledge has examined this associative process when the media is the primary agent of information about both the group and the stereotypic characteristic. A program of research that examines how messages propagated in the media contribute to such an association would be beneficial. Some of the questions that would need to be answered include (a) What message characteristics found in the media about an out-group and some trait produce an illusory correlation effect? (b) Does salience of the television message make a difference? (c) What characteristics of mass media messages affect learning and recall of information about out-group members?

Media and black self-esteem. The relationship between blacks in the media and self-esteem needs further investigation. It seems necessary to test the idea that black self-esteem might be affected by media portrayals for two primary reasons. First, a replication of the Graves (1975) study seems in order because it has been more than 20 years since this initial research was conducted; arguably, there have been several changes in television programming over recent years (Randolph, 1995). Second, it seems necessary to test whether or not the self-esteem of African Americans is protected by attributing negative mass media messages to prejudice or by disengaging from (e.g., not viewing) negative mass media messages.

Conducting an experiment where portrayals of African Americans are varied and then measuring the self-esteem of African American observers would be a good direction to pursue. Part of the investigation should include an examination of what effect African American portrayals have on both white and black viewers.

Using the media to change stereotypes. The investigation of stereotype change through the media is yet another important prong of this research program. The contact hypothesis assumes that the information gained from an interaction with an out-group member will result in stereotype disconfirmation. Television might be a stand-in for interpersonal contact in the sense that viewing television results in the transference of information (Graves, 1993). Television's role as a medium of contact with out-group members is extremely important, considering that many whites lack other forms of contact with blacks.

To test the hypothesis that moderately disconfirming out-group members will have a larger impact on stereotype change, an experiment could be performed whereby white participants will be exposed to a strongly disconfirming, moderately disconfirming, or confirming TV segment containing blacks, and then they will be allowed to make trait judgments about a black target. It would be expected that moderately disconfirming members would provide the most stereotype change because they would continue to be associated with the category of blacks

yet they would not represent the prototypical stereotype.

▶ Social Cognition, Media, and Transcultural Realities

In conclusion, this chapter argues that theories of social cognition provide insight into the underlying psychological mechanisms related to the media's role in stereotyping. Content analyses of news and entertainment programs have revealed that blacks are mostly portrayed as conflict driven, inept, unemployed, and criminal. Theories of social cognition explain how these portrayals might be tied to the creation and maintenance of negative African American stereotypes. These stereotypes might influence viewers to interact with others not as individuals but as representatives of social categories. Media stereotypes may or may not also lower black self-esteem. More research is needed to understand these effects.

It was concluded that our knowledge on this topic can best be advanced by the development of a new research program. Specifically, researchers should undertake new content analyses of African American television portrayals, examine the role of the illusory correlation in a media context, study the role of the media in affecting self-esteem, and explore the role of the media in discouraging the activation of stereotypes.

The theme of this book deals with how we can promote transcultural realities that affirm diverse ways of knowing, communicating, and behaving that result in more positive intercultural and intergroup interactions. The theories of social cognition outlined in this chapter suggest that what we see on television can either contribute to this positive affirmation or inhibit it. As long as negative stereotypes of African Americans persist on television, the mass media will act as a sociocultural learning agent that discourages positive intergroup interaction and group identity. If the media can be transformed, it is possible that we could witness the emergence of mediated transcultural realities where positive group identity and intergroup interaction is affirmed.

▶ References

Baptista-Fernandez, P., & Greenberg, B. S. (1980). The context, characteristics, and communication of blacks on television. In B. S. Greenberg (Ed.), *Life on television* (pp. 13-21). Norwood, NJ: Ablex.

Bell, D. (1987). *And we are not saved: The elusive quest for racial justice.* New York: Basic Books.

Chapman, L. J. (1967). Illusory correlation in observational report. *Journal of Verbal Learning and Verbal Behavior, 6,* 151-155.

Chapman, L. J., & Chapman, J. P. (1969). Illusory correlation as an obstacle to the use of valid psychodiagnostic signs. *Journal of Abnormal Psychology, 14,* 271-280.

Crocker, J., & Major, B. (1989). Social stigma and self-esteem: The self-protective properties of stigma. *Psychological Review, 96,* 608-630.

Dates, J., & Barlow, W. (1990). *Split image: African Americans in the mass media.* Washington, DC: Howard University Press.

Devine, P. G. (1989). Stereotypes and prejudice: Their automatic and controlled components. *Journal of Personality and Social Psychology, 56,* 5-18.

Dixon, T. L., & Linz, D. (2000). Overrepresentation and underrepresentation of African Americans and Latinos as criminals on television news. *Journal of Communication, 50*(2), 1-25.

Entman, R. (1992). Blacks in the news: Television, modern racism, and cultural change. *Journalism Quarterly, 69,* 341-361.

Evuleocha, S. U., & Ugbah, S. D. (1989). Stereotypes, counter-stereotypes, and black television images in the 1990s. *The Western Journal of Black Studies, 13*(4), 197-205.

Graves, S. N. (1975). *Racial diversity in children's television: Its impact on racial attitudes and stated program preferences.* Unpublished doctoral dissertation, Harvard University, Cambridge, MA.

Graves, S. N. (1993). Television, the portrayal of African-Americans, and the development of children's attitudes. In G. L. Berry & J. K. Asamen (Eds.), *Children & television: Images in a changing sociocultural world* (pp. 179-190). Beverly Hills, CA: Sage.

Greenberg, B. S., & Brand, G. H. (1994). Minorities and the mass media: 1970s to 1990s. In J. Bryant & D. Zillman (Eds.), *Media effects: Advances in theory and research* (pp. 273-314). Hillsdale, NJ: Lawrence Erlbaum.

Greenberg, B. S., & Neuendorf, K. A. (1980). Black family interactions on television. In B. S. Greenberg (Ed.), *Life on television* (pp. 173-181). Norwood, NJ: Ablex.

Hamilton, D. L., Stroessner, S. J., & Driscoll, D. M. (1994). Social cognition and the study of stereotyping. In P. G. Devine, D. L. Hamilton, & T. M. Ostrom (Eds.), *Social cognition: Impact on social psychology* (pp. 292-323). San Diego, CA: Academic Press.

Hamilton, D. L., & Trolier, T. K. (1986). Stereotypes and stereotyping: An overview of the cognitive approach. In J. Dovidio & S. Gaertner (Eds.), *Prejudice, discrimination, and racism* (pp. 127-163). Orlando, FL: Academic Press.

Lemon, J. (1977). Women and blacks on prime-time television. *Journal of Communication, 27*(4), 70-79.

Linville, P. W., Salovey, P., & Fischer, G. W. (1986). Stereotyping and perceived distributions of social characteristics: An application to ingroup-outgroup perception. In J. Dovidio & S. Gaertner (Eds.), *Prejudice, discrimination, and racism* (pp. 165-208). Orlando, FL: Academic Press.

Oliver, M. B. (1994). Portrayals of crime, race, and aggression in "reality-based" police shows: A content analysis. *Journal of Broadcasting & Electronic Media, 38*(2), 179-192.

Randolph, L. B. (1995). The '95 TV season: Who's gone? who's new? who's back?: Black-oriented television programs for 1995. *Ebony, 50*(12), 94-98.

Reid, P. (1979). Racial stereotyping on television: A comparison of the behavior of both black and white television characters. *Journal of Applied Psychology, 64,* 464-471.

Rothbart, M., & John, O. P. (1985). Social categorization and behavioral episodes: A cognitive
analysis of the effects of intergroup contact.
Journal of Social Issues, 41(3), 81-104.

Steele, S., & Aronson, J. (1995). Stereotype threat
and the intellectual test performance of African
Americans. *Journal of Personality & Social
Psychology, 69,* 797-811.

West, C. (1993). *Race matters.* New York: Vintage.

Wilson, B. J., Kunkel, D., Linz, D., Potter, J.,
Donnerstein, E., Smith, S. L., Blumenthal, E.,
& Gray, T. (1997). Violence in television pro-
gramming overall: University of California,
Santa Barbara study. In Mediascope, Inc.
(Eds.), *National Television Violence Study:
Scientific papers 1994-1995,* (pp. I-1-I-171).
Studio City, CA: Mediascope, Inc.

Part IV

The Transformative Effects of Sojourning in Diverse Cultural Environments

Intercultural Adaptation

A Stranger But Not Strange

TONI-MOKJAETJI *HUMBER*

The purpose of this research is to address the process of intercultural adaptation and adjustment that sojourners make when traveling to the home of their ancestral origin. Stanfield (1994) calls for the creation of new paradigms and methodologies in qualitative research that are grounded in the experiences of people of color to gain more adequate knowledge about them. To shed additional light on the intercultural adaptation and adjustment of Africans in the Americas when traveling to Africa, the factors of ancestral origin and the positive psychological disposition and identification sojourners feel toward their ancestral homeland and its people will be introduced as significant elements in their adaptive process. To regard their sojourns as typical of other groups returning to

their homes of ancestral origin negates factors that brought people of African descent to the western hemisphere and negates their sociocultural histories in Africa and the Americas.

For African sojourners on their way to Africa, an analysis of the process of adaptation and adjustment must include a dimension of *African identity*. Living in a society dominated by sociocultural and political systems that overtly or covertly oppress them because of their Africanness has had a tremendous impact on how African Americans view themselves and *continental* Africans. Richards (1990) acknowledges this when she states,

Throughout their sojourn in America, Africans have been taught the separateness of themselves from Africa and Africans. The teaching

227

has been so ingrained that even in those communities which are "most African" there is the greatest scandal of "being African." (p. 207)

Developing a *positive African identity* (PAI)—or, according to Hilliard (1997), a declaration of *mental independence*—is essential to the psychological health of African people in the diaspora (Hilliard, 1997; Shujaa, 1996). Shujaa (1996) declares that for African people to evolve through the process of *coming home*—a conversion of their mental state—they must undergo a transformation, a *re-Africanization*. Re-Africanization is part of psychologically healing from enslavement and its residual effects. It requires conscious efforts by Africans in the Americas to confront African alienation and to "reject the world view perspectives of their former colonizers or former enslavers by assuming their own history" (Shujaa, 1996, p. 38). They must erase the internalized myths, lies, stereotypes, and claims of African inferiority that distort the sociocultural histories of African peoples. As part of the psychological transformation, many Africans in the United States and other countries in the Americas have journeyed to Africa to gain firsthand knowledge about their ancestral past, African culture, and traditions and to experience life in Africa.

I, too, have sought *mental independence* and *re-Africanization*. Two key elements have contributed to my psychological transformation and the development of my *positive African identity:* (a) efforts to *re-educate* myself about African history and culture and (b) travel to Africa. Both of these factors have been integral in the evolvement of my positive African consciousness. Each has caused me to develop a deeper understanding of who I am and an understanding of my significance as a person of African descent. Each has enriched my intercultural relations with *continental* Africans and other diasporan Africans. Finally, each has given me a broader view of the interconnectedness of African people.

This is an ethnographic study. The participant-observer method serves "to generate practical and theoretical truths about human

life grounded in the realities of daily existence" (Jorgensen, 1989, p. 14). Through interpreting the experiences of my life, I have found meaning as it relates to understanding intercultural adaptation. This chapter is autobiographical, in that my life experiences serve as a model for interpreting and generating meaning about how the desire to develop and the process of developing a positive African identity can lead to positive intercultural adaptation experiences for Africans from the Americas who travel to Africa. I have identified models that explain my positive African identity and intercultural adaptation while traveling in Africa, which I believe are germane to theorizing about and understanding the adaptive experiences of Africans from the Americas who make that sojourn.

The issue of intercultural adaptation presents an important point of discussion for Africans from the Americas who sojourn to Africa. One can ask, Did a common ancestral heritage and conscious efforts to identify with Africa provide elements that would make the adaptive process easier? This chapter will address how affinity can have an impact on the intercultural adaptation and adjustment sojourners make when traveling to a country vastly different from the country of their birth, yet a country that holds a historical, ancestral connection. Ultimately, this chapter will address and answer the following questions:

1. What does it mean when a sojourner travels to his or her country/region of ancestral origin?
2. Does this ancestral origin mean there will be better intercultural understanding and adaptation to the cultural differences that will be encountered?
3. Can a sense of ancestral connection and identification be strong enough for the sojourner to overcome culture shock and enable positive intercultural adaptation and adjustment?
4. Does the fact that people are of African descent ensure they will adapt well in African intercultural settings?

Over the past 10 years, intercultural scholars have studied the process of intercultural adaptation for newcomers to a country. In 1988, Kim and Gudykunst led the discussion with the publication of *Cross-Cultural Adaptation: Current Approaches.* According to Kim and Gudykunst, all visitors to a new country are strangers and, therefore, must cope with a high level of uncertainty and unfamiliarity inherent in being in a new cultural milieu. Intercultural newcomers share common adaptation experiences, and a major task for them is to acquire a degree of intercultural competence that enables them to function at a minimal level. Kim and Gudykunst use the term *cross-cultural adaptation* "in a broad and all-inclusive sense to refer to the complex process through which an individual acquires an increasing level of 'fitness' or 'compatibility' in the new cultural environment" (p. 10).

Furnham (1988) discussed the notion of *culture shock* and its relationship to intercultural adaptation. She noted the research of Oberg (1960), Bock (1970), Lundstedt (1963), and Hays (1972), which provided an analysis of the culture shock phenomenon. Bock (1970, cited in Furnham, 1988) "described culture shock as primarily an emotional reaction that is consequent upon not being able to understand, control, and predict behavior, which appears to be a basic need" (pp. 45-46). In general, culture shock occurs from unpleasant and stressful experiences the newcomer encounters in the new intercultural situation. While experiencing shock, the sojourner does not know the appropriate behavior for a situation, cannot anticipate appropriate behavior for a situation, has no control of the situation, and feels ill at ease in the cultural setting.

Culture distance is related to culture shock. When studying the intercultural adaptation of international students, Babiker, Cox, and Miller (1980, cited in Furnham, 1988) "hypothesized that the degree of alienation, estrangement, and concomitant psychological distress was a function of the distance between the students' own culture and the host culture" (p. 49). Furnham and Bochner (1983, cited in Furnham, 1988) found that the greater the difference between a student's culture and the host society, the greater the adjustment the student would have to make. "The stress experienced by foreign students was viewed largely as a result of their lacking the requisite social skills with which to negotiate specific social situations" (p. 49).

Kim (1995, cited in Martin & Nakayama, 1997) proposed the *communication-system model* for cross-cultural adaptation. Within the model, Kim noted that adaptation includes *acculturation,* learning new habits and cultural ways, and *deculturation,* unlearning old habits from the home culture that are not appropriate for the new situation. Cross-cultural adaptation includes *the stress-adaptation-growth dynamic.* Stress occurs when the sojourner's competence does not match the demands of the cultural setting. Coping with the ambiguities in the situation leads to adaptation and growth. The process is not static but cyclic and requires the continual resolution of internal stress.

Kim (1995, cited in Martin & Nakayama, 1997) also cites *preparedness* for the cross-cultural encounter as an important factor in adaptation. She defines preparedness as "mental, emotional, and motivational readiness to deal with the cultural environment including understanding of host language and culture" (p. 185). In addition, she defined *openness,* one's receptiveness to new information; and *strength,* "resilience, risk-taking, hardiness, persistence, patience, elasticity, and resourcefulness" (p. 186) as personality attributes that support positive cross-cultural adaptation.

According to Mansell (1981, cited in Chen & Starosta, 1998), sojourners experience four emotional and affective states in the process of intercultural adaptation. They are

Alienation: The sojourner rejects host culture and retains a strong identification with her/his own.

Marginality: The sojourner is caught between two cultures and experiences divided loyalties. He or she also may have an "uncertain self-identity" (p. 169).

Acculturation: The sojourner adopts the ways of the host culture. Consequently, "the primary culture loses its importance" (p. 169).

Duality: The sojourner develops biculturality. The sojourner accommodates "both the original and the host culture while living in a new environment" (p. 169).

The process of intercultural adaptation also has been described as following the *U-curve* (Adler, 1975; Chang, 1973; Deutsch & Won, 1963; Lysgaard, 1955; Morris, 1960; Oberg, 1960; Smalley, 1963; all as cited in Chen & Starosta, 1998) and the *W-curve* (Gullahorn & Gullahorn, 1963; Kohls, 1984; both as cited in Chen & Starosta, 1998) patterns. In general, the U-curve model identifies four stages of intercultural adaptation (Chen & Starosta, 1998). They are (a) an initial high point or honeymoon period, (b) a low point or crisis period, (c) an adjustment period, and finally (d) the development of biculturalism. The W-curve pattern describes the adjustments made when sojourners return to their home culture. On re-entry to the home culture, sojourners experience another culture shock and must, therefore, adjust to the home situation. During the adjustment to home, sojourners experience (a) a period of sharing their intercultural experience with friends and relatives; (b) a period of catching up on events missed, thus entering a stage of information seeking, (c) a period of joining social groups to gain more information and reconnect with home culture; and (d) a period of finding and associating with people who have international experiences or who originate from their intercultural host country (Kohls, 1975, as cited in Chen & Starosta, 1998).

Gudykunst's (1993, 1995) *Anxiety/Uncertainty Management (AUM) Theory* identifies *anxiety* and *uncertainty* as central factors that cause stress and inhibit effective intercultural communication. He extended the interpersonal research of Berger and Calabrese's (1975, in Gudykunst, 1993, 1995; Gudykunst & Kim, 1992) *Uncertainty Reduction Theory* to include intercultural situations. How well people handle anxiety and diminish uncertainty will determine the degree of adjustment and adaptation they make in the host society. Whereas uncertainty causes people to pose behavioral and cognitive questions—how should I behave, what do they think about me doing this?—anxiety is an affective response and "refers to feelings of being uneasy, tense, worried, or apprehensive about what might happen" (Gudykunst & Kim, 1992, p. 11).

For many Africans in the Americas, a journey to Africa can evoke great emotion in anticipation of finding family roots and answering the question, Who am I? Certainly, the notion of *stranger* coupled with *anxiety* and *uncertainty*—which Gudykunst and Kim (1992) and Gudykunst (1993, 1995) describe—and the notions of *culture shock* and *culture distance* are appropriate for the discussion of the African American's sojourn to Africa. However, for those who have consciously sought knowledge about Africa, who have positively identified with its people and many of their cultural ways, who have sought to develop an understanding of the African worldview, *stranger* is not the appropriate descriptor. Such people are *newcomers* in a land not so strange to them. Their knowledge and understanding of African culture and history, paired with intense feelings and expectations generated by returning to the place of their ancestral origin after generations of separation, add a significant dimension to their intercultural experiences.

The complexities of experiencing the *maafa* (Richards, 1989, 1990), "the terroristic interruption of African civilization that was occasioned by European and Arab slavery and cultural aggression" (Hilliard, 1997, p. 1), and being separated from their home of origin cause deep longings for connection among many Africans in the Americas. These feelings cause a longing to be embraced by

Mother Africa. For many, the sojourn to Africa represents a pilgrimage home with hopes of experiencing *ancestral healing.* The sociohistory of Africans in the Americas and their cultural dislocation from their homelands overshadow issues of being a stranger in a *foreign* land or traveling to some *exotic* place. Viewing the journey as merely adventure and exotic masks a significant element in understanding the traveler's experiences and intercultural adaptation: the need for identification and connection with Africa and African people.

Asante (1987) proposes that discussions and analyses of African people must be African centered, "which means, literally, placing African ideals at the center of any analysis that involves African culture and behavior" (p. 6). Asante (1990b) reminds us that studying Africans in the Americas "must be done with the idea in the back of the mind that one is studying African people, not 'made-in-America Negroes' without historical depth" (p. 15). Africans in the Americas know they are descendants from continental Africans. In this knowing, some may embrace that fact and feel positive about their heritage, but others may reject that fact and diminish the importance or deny any significance of being African descendants. Whatever the perspective, Asante (1987) says African continuities in African American culture are evident. For example, when analyzing the lyricism of the African oral tradition present in the United States, he notes, "Africa is at the heart of *all* African American behavior. Communication styles are reflective of the internal mythic clock, the epic memory, the psychic stain of Africa in our spirits" (p. 48). The notion of psychic stain is key to this discussion because it suggests that *Africanness* is indelibly etched into the psyche of Africans in the Americas.

The acknowledgment and/or recognition of one's *Africanness* and positive attitudes toward that acknowledgment or recognition provide a basis for describing *positive African identity. Positive African identity* can be identified among Africans in the Americas when they

1. Exhibit/demonstrate positive identification with continental Africans and Africans in the Americas
2. Actively seek to understand and enhance their knowledge about the African worldview and the cultures and histories of African peoples
3. Incorporate attitudes that reflect positive and truthful characterizations of African peoples
4. Support and participate in activities that celebrate the lives and accomplishments of continental Africans and Africans in the Americas
5. Support and participate in activities that reflect a positive identification with African peoples, their cultures, and struggles.

Positive African identity is viewed as an integral element for positive adaptive experiences for Africans in the Americas who travel to Africa. Therefore, this chapter proposes that *positive African identity* and the need for connection with Africa are more important to the intercultural adjustment of many African Americans traveling to Africa than would be the case if they were to travel to countries that have no strong African influence and ancestry. The central theses of this chapter, which support this proposition, are

1. Positive intercultural adaptation for many Africans in the Americas who travel to Africa can be attributed to the degree of *positive African identity* and personal knowledge sojourners have about African countries and their people.
2. Positive intercultural adaptation for many Africans in the Americas who travel to Africa can be attributed to experiencing an event or events that cause them to feel connected to their *homeland,* the continent of their ancestral origin.

We begin this discussion with an examination of reasons the journey to Africa may be different for Africans in the Americas than journeys to other parts of the world. This will be followed by discussion of the elements that lead to development of *positive African identity*. Reflections on my journeys to Africa, coupled with testimonies by a South African friend and a fellow traveler, will illuminate the significance of the connections Africans in the Americas and continental Africans can make, leading to positive intercultural experiences for African Americans. Finally, the concluding remarks will answer whether returning to their ancestral home ensures greater intercultural adaptation for Africans in the Americas and whether ancestral connection ensures positive intercultural adaptation.

▶ Finding the Source

The journey to Africa for many Africans in the Americas is about finding the source of their ancestral line. The longing to know who they are, where they come from, and who their people were can be likened to the quest of adopted children who seek information about their birth parents and birth families. The need for positive identification and connection with Africans and Africa by Africans in the Americas is an aspect of ethnic identification and intercultural adaptation that broadens discussions by Berger and Calabrese (1975), Gudykunst and Kim (1992), and Gudykunst (1993, 1995). This quest to know who they are is information seeking, but in a deeper sense than Berger and Calabrese suggest. This identification provides an answer to profound questions about their existence: Who are my people? How did they come to this land (the Americas)? and Who were the direct ancestors of my family? By piecing together the puzzle of one's ancestral story, which has been incomplete for more than 400 years, a sense of self-knowing and self-understanding evolves that previously had not existed. Such knowing and understanding have

the power to produce a psychic ease about one's ancestral heritage that heretofore had never existed. This psychic ease might account for positive intercultural adjustments, even though sojourners may encounter great cultural differences in the host country(ies).

In this quest for African connection, many Africans in the Americas hungrily embrace anything associating them with Africa by wearing traditional African clothing, jewelry, and/or hair styles. This may be their way to identify and say, "I am African!" Many are thirsty for information that gives clues to who they are. They may attend lectures and seminars and study cultural and historical materials about Africans, information that was never presented or discussed during their years of formal education. They may attend festivals and celebrations that incorporate African traditions: Kwanzaa, weddings, christenings, and funerals. However they do it, many Africans living in the Americas, especially the United States, find ways to proudly acknowledge their African heritage.

In contrast, many continental Africans living in the Americas give no outward appearance, through clothing or adornments, that they are from Africa. There could be two reasons for this: (a) to wear traditional African dress in this country would set them too much apart from the mainstream population, and it might cause differential treatment; (b) their Africanness—national allegiance, ethnic identification, cultural ways and/or orientations—has always been intact, and they therefore have no reason to overtly express what is. They just have *to be*. In that being, they *are* African.

Whereas continental Africans *know* their Africanness, many Africans in the Americas must overtly express their Africanness to counter the centuries of racism that have degraded their ancestral heritage. For many, the development of *positive African identity* becomes necessary for psychological well-being. *Positive African identity* does not just happen, and it cannot evolve by just living in the western hemisphere. Its development requires a course of action and requires people to make conscious efforts to respect, understand, and appreciate their African heritage in the face of entrenched values and beliefs that have been perpetuated in the Americas that are racist and denigrate Africanness. This entails deculturalization, which is different from Kim's (1995, in Martin & Nakayama, 1997) definition addressing the learning of new cultural ways in a new cultural setting. Africans in the Americas must *unlearn* devaluation in the Americas as part of their positive identity; doing so will enable them to adjust better to experiences in Africa. In the following section, I will address the issue of *positive African identity*. Baldwin and Bell (1985), Cross (1991), Cross, Parham, and Helms (1991), and Shujaa (1996) provide the theoretical perspectives from which we can understand the significance of *positive African identity*.

▶ Developing Positive African Identity

The process of developing *positive African identity* involves two phases. The first phase notes attributes of the Black personality that identify a positive regard for Africa and African people (Baldwin & Bell, 1985). The second phase describes stages that evolve during the development of *African American identity* (Cross et al., 1991), *Afrocentric identity* (Cross, 1991), or *re-Africanization*, "the path toward cultural centeredness" (Shujaa, 1996).

When African Americans have a positive regard for Africa and its people and have feelings of connection through "beliefs, attitudes, and behaviors which affirm African American life and the authenticity of its African cultural heritage" (Baldwin & Bell, 1985, p. 62), they reflect positive attributes of the Black personality. According to Baldwin and Bell (1985), *the African Self-Consciousness (ASC) system* is a core component of Black personality.

The African self-consciousness construct functions essentially as the organizing principle of the Black personality, and it follows a developmental pattern. Chief among the critical indices of the African self-consciousness construct are such attitudes and behaviors as the following:

1. The person possesses an awareness of his/her Black identity (a sense of collective consciousness) and African cultural heritage, and sees value in the pursuit of knowledge of Self (i.e., African history and culture throughout the world—encompassing African American experience).

2. The person recognizes Black survival priorities and the necessity for institutions (practices, customs, values, etc.) which affirm Black life.

3. The person actively participates in the survival, liberation, and proactive development of Black people and defends their dignity, worth, and integrity.

4. The person recognizes the opposition of racial oppression (via people, concepts, institutions, etc.) to the development and survival of Black people and actively resists it by any appropriate means. (Baldwin & Bell, 1985, pp. 62-63)

Baldwin and Bell's work suggests a "reliable relationship between positive (self-affirming, efficacious) psychological functioning and behavior and high levels of African Self-Consciousness among Black people" (p. 65).

Whereas Baldwin and Bell (1985) identified the characteristics and attributes necessary for positive *African self-consciousness*, Cross et al. (1991) outlined the essential stages that lead to the development of a *positive African American identity*. Cross (1991) called it an *Afrocentric identity*, and Shujaa (1996) identified it as *re-Africanization*. According to Cross et al. (1991), two competing processes have dominated the social history of African Americans: (a) *deracination*, an attempt to obliterate Black consciousness; and (b) *nigrescence*, the development of an African American identity. Addressing the sociohistory of African Americans, Cross et al. state,

> Given the ubiquity of the White emphasis on deracination, it comes as no surprise that within African American history are accounts of Blacks who, having first been successfully deculturalized, experienced revitalization through the process of nigrescence. Nigrescence is derived from French and means "to become Black." (p. 320)

Historically, African Americans have experienced a "Negro-to-Black identity conversion" (p. 320), a search for an Afrocentric identity (Cross, 1991) or re-Africanization (Shujaa, 1996). A resocialization process—transforming attitudes, behaviors, practices, and identities that have been culturally and psychologically alienating—is at the core of nigrescence and re-Africanization. Cross (1991) proposes that "nigrescence is a *resocializing* experience" (p. 190) that incorporates five stages of identity development for African Americans. They are described below.

STAGE 1: PRE-ENCOUNTER

The continuum for those at the pre-encounter stage ranges from (a) *low salience,* attaching little or no importance to their Blackness or Africanness, experiencing feelings of shame about their Blackness or Africanness, and feeling that their race is a stigma; to (b) anti-Black feelings, being alienated from people of African descent, harboring racist attitudes toward them, perceiving their Blackness/ Africanness as a mark of oppression, and feeling they are captives in a body and community they hate.

Pre-encounter Blacks cross socioeconomic lines, and their attitudes have evolved from both White oppression and Black success. They have not moved beyond their *miseducation* to learn more about their heritage, Africa's role in world civilization and culture, and "the role of Blacks in the evolution of American culture and history in particular" (Cross et al., 1991, p. 192). They are more

likely to adapt a European cultural perspective by valuing a European aesthetic over an African one; however, they may listen to music and appreciate art reflecting the Black/ African aesthetic, but these artistic expressions may be looked on as *ethnic* and less valued than cultural expressions that reflect European "*high culture.*" People in this stage also may exhibit *spotlight anxiety,* or nervousness and anxiety about appearing "too Black" in settings where Whites are present. Their race conflict-resolution perspective is one that favors assimilation-integration themes rather than placing demands on Whites to change racist attitudes, practices, and institutions.

STAGE 2: ENCOUNTER

At this stage, an event or a series of events jars and "shatter[s] the person's current feelings about himself/herself and his or her interpretation of the condition of Blacks in America" (Cross et al., 1991, p. 324). During this stage, two things happen: "(a) the old identity seems inappropriate, and (b) the proposed new identity is highly attractive, the person throws caution to the wind and begins a frantic, determined, obsessive, and extremely motivated search for Black identity" (p. 324). This stage begins the journey toward a new identity.

STAGE 3: IMMERSION-EMERSION

Stage 3 represents the "vortex of psychological nigrescence" (Cross, 1991, p. 202). This is a period of rebellion against the old identity and the larger society and is characterized by shedding vestiges of the old thinking, consciously working to incorporate the new frame of thought and being, and conforming to what are viewed as the attributes of African consciousness. Thus, *immersion* "into Blackness and liberation from Whiteness" (p. 203) is characteristic of this stage, and a person becomes involved in activities and align with people and institutions that reinforce their evolving *Africanness.* This is an in-between stage because the person "lacks knowledge about the complexity and texture of the new identity and is forced to erect simplistic, glorified, highly romantic speculative images of what he or she *assumes* the new self will be like" (p. 202). People evolving through this stage feel the need to prove their level of Blackness/Africanness for the new group, and they may demonize White people and White culture. They have yet to internalize the values, attitudes, and understandings of the Black/African-conscious person. During the final segment of this phase, *emersion* enables one to analyze more critically what it means to be Black/African, noting weaknesses, strengths, and oversimplifications in his or her perspective. A person emerges from being one who has an *either-or, Black-or-White* view of life to having a broader perspective.

STAGE 4: INTERNALIZATION

The internalization stage signals the resolution of conflicts between the old Negro identity and the *new Black consciousness/ Afrocentric identity*. People at this stage reflect "ideological flexibility, psychological openness, and self-confidence about their Blackness . . . in interpersonal transactions" (Cross et al., 1991, p. 326). Because they understand their Blackness, people at this stage are free to broaden interests and concentration of issues. They have moved from a state in which race consciousness had little significance or low salience to a position where they place high salience "on Blackness in everyday life" (Cross, 1991, p. 212). This is reflected in social networks, memberships, and associations in groups and causes, socialization of children, cultural and artistic preferences, and cultural and historical perspectives.

STAGE 5: INTERNALIZATION—COMMITMENT

This stage recognizes the elements of commitment and sustainability of the identity. Over time, some people's interests may not be

as strong in affairs and issues related to African people as they once were. Consequently, Parham (cited in Cross, 1991; Cross et al., 1991) suggests there is a need for *recycling* the stages because of new encounters that may call for rethinking one's Blackness.

Shujaa's (1996) *Personal Transformation/ Re-Africanization Methodology Model* provides another path for achieving *positive African identity*. Transformation is necessary to heal psychological and spiritual alienation from the African self, which has occurred as a result of experiencing the *maafa* and its residual effects, enslavement and colonization. Transformation occurs by acquiring knowledge about African cultural history and gaining clarity and understanding of the African worldview. *Worldview* is defined as "the way people perceive their relationship to nature, other people, and things. [It] constitutes our psychological orientation in life and can determine how we think, behave, make decisions, and define events" (Sue, 1978, in Cross et al., 1991, p. 334).

Shujaa's (1996) model uses a deconstruction-reconstruction-construction (D-R-C) methodology to understand the transformation process. It recognizes that these elements, as well as resignation, represent modes of knowledge integration. *Resignation* is the acceptance of information without critically analyzing its truth or validity; it is characterized by the unquestioning acceptance of information about African worldview and African cultural history. *Deconstruction,* the opposite of resignation, represents critical analysis of information to determine the extent to which it "is congruent with the African worldview and . . . is consistent with wisdom derived from knowledge of Africana cultural history" (Shujaa, 1996, p. 61). This process parallels the immersion-emersion stage of the Cross (1991) model. Here, a person questions what has been understood as prevailing truth regarding African people and their cultural histories. *Reconstruction* is the process of re-explaining information that has been incongruent with the African worldview, content that "is inconsistent with wisdom that is grounded in the knowledge of the African experience" (Shujaa, 1996, p. 62). *Construction* acknowledges the process of creating "new concepts that are congruent with African world view perspective and consistent with wisdom produced by knowledge of African cultural history" (Shujaa, 1996, p. 62).

The *Transformation Model* recognizes that *re-Africanization* is ongoing and takes conscious effort and self-monitoring. The process has different rates of development, and throughout the process of developing new consciousness, people's perceptions about themselves continue to change because they have developed a deeper knowledge of their African ancestry and a clearer understanding of the African worldview. *Re-Africanization* "includes applying values and beliefs that are consistent with wisdom derived from knowledge of African cultural history and congruent with the African world view perspective to lifestyle" (Shujaa, 1996, p. 64).

Having a positive regard for African people, having an appreciation and understanding of African history and culture and its connections with Africans in the Americas, and countering anti-Black/African ideologies are key attributes of the Black personality inherent in *African self-consciousness* (Baldwin & Bell, 1985). These attributes enable the development of a *positive African American identity* (Cross et al., 1991), *Afrocentric identity* (Cross, 1991), and *re-Africanization* (Shujaa, 1996). They ensure psychological well-being and strength, necessary elements for functioning in a racist society.

I have often thought about the ideological transformation I have made as an adult and as an educator, a change that has heightened my love for things African and that has inspired me to continue studying about and traveling to African countries. Since my first trip to Africa in 1972, I have sought information to enrich my knowledge base about Africa and its people. Travel and independent study, coupled with my passion to know more about my ancestral heritage, reflect my conscious efforts to develop a strong and positive African consciousness. In the following section, I will address how the development of my *positive Af-*

rican identity and my feelings of connection with African people factored into positive intercultural adaptation experiences for me when traveling to African countries.

▶ Journeys to Africa

On my first journey to Africa, I visited Ghana and Nigeria. I was on a study tour and traveled with university students from California and Ohio. During the trip, I confronted the stereotypes I had learned about Africans and Africa throughout my life in the United States. As a child, I had never heard of the magnificence of Kemet (ancient Egypt), the kingdoms of West Africa, or the struggles of African people to rid themselves of colonial intruders. I was raised in a time when *King Kong, King Solomon's Mine, Tarzan,* and *Rama of the Jungle* were typical of the grossly distorted images of African people I saw at the movies or on television. I knew very little about Ghana and Nigeria and had never heard of Accra or Lagos until I signed up for my trip. I was not familiar with the political struggles these countries had experienced. Even though I was a university graduate, I was ignorant of anything positive about Africa and its people. I visited Nigeria shortly after the Biafran war ended. I had heard about the war but had no knowledge of why it was fought or of its ramifications in Nigeria. I began my first trip to Africa very naive. All I knew was I was going *home!*

The plane ride to Accra, Ghana, signaled that something very special was about to happen. We were close to 200 jubilant Africans from the United States on our way to the *homeland,* and we were about to immerse ourselves in *Africanness.* We were hungry at the prospect of finding our roots. Many of us carried containers to bring back soil from the homeland. Had Cross (1991), Cross et al. (1991), and Shujaa (1996) been on that plane, they would have said our group was deep in our *Black/Afrocentric/re-Africanization* identity development. Out came the picks (cake cutters used as combs for natural hair styles) to comb and braid our Afros for the long plane ride. On came the Aretha Franklin, Marvin Gaye, Stevie Wonder, Bill Withers, and War tapes. Choruses of *Respect* and *What's Going On, My Cherie Amour, Lean on Me,* and *Everyday People* could be heard throughout the plane. One *brotha* named Ben walked the aisle playing improvised jazz on his flute as he was accompanied, spontaneously, by beats on tray tables. The celebration was on. We had embarked on a journey that we knew—or hoped—would change us profoundly.

As a result of my 6-week journey, I fully understood the meaning of culture shock and culture distance. There were real cultural differences between my life in the United States and what I was experiencing in West Africa. Languages, customs, food, and social behaviors differed enough for me to realize that I had adjustments to make. I experienced frustration because I did not have some of the creature comforts I was used to at home. I found being of African descent was not enough to ensure intercultural adjustment. The levels of poverty in the cities I saw, coupled with the deep emotional pain I felt while visiting Cape Coast Slave Dungeon, caused frustration and anger—anger and frustration for my ancestral separation from this land and for the traumas of European colonial rule. As I recall, one student in our group—who had lived a marginalized life in the United States, not feeling accepted by African Americans or by Whites—had great difficulty adjusting and returned to the United States by the end of the first week. From my conversations with those who interacted with him, he experienced more than culture shock; he experienced trauma. The journey to Africa exposed us to historical realities that were haunting. Although the rest of the group members did not experience cultural trauma, we surely experienced an emotional upheaval and had to deal with the myths and lies we had learned about Africa from our U.S. education. Africa was diverse in more ways than we could have realized. We did not see jungles and wild animals. We traveled to traditional societies and villages as well as to modern urban centers.

Despite the adjustments I had to make traveling through Ghana and Nigeria, I had many powerful moments that touched my soul and let me know I had come home. First, I was awed to be surrounded by so many African people. I found myself staring at the beautiful black and blueberry-black hues of continental Africans. It took a while for me to get used to seeing Africans in every administrative and authoritative position I encountered. That was empowering!

During a welcoming ceremony, my group members and I were encouraged to join the celebration and dance. We knew the steps. Joining in the dancing that day erased 400 years of separation and sealed our connection. Through this journey, I had emotional experiences coupled with profound pride. I felt a sense of belonging that I could never feel in the United States; however, I was very aware of the fact that I was from the United States.

On my first excursion with friends, I sat on a curb waiting for a bus to take us to the Akosombo Dam along the Volta River in Ghana. A gentleman sat next to me as we waited. After a brief conversation, he looked at me and said, *"Welcome home, sister!"* That welcome eased frustrations that arose because Ghana and Nigeria were not the United States, and they were not functioning as such. His greeting signaled to me that I was embarking on a journey that was quite different from my travels through Europe 3 years earlier. I was indeed *home.*

I was fully immersed in Africa in a way that would never have happened in the United States. I had to view African countries as *subject* and not as *object,* meaning I saw *myself* and heard *my* stories in Ghana and Nigeria. My people had been captured, raped, and enslaved at Cape Coast Slave Dungeon. My ancestors sold other Africans into slavery at Badagri, Nigeria. This was not some impersonal place that held only a passing interest for me. These were not some colored spaces on a map for which I had no connection. These countries held the stories of my ancestors and provided links that helped me understand who I am in the United States. When I touched the ground in one of the dungeons at Cape Coast, it was damp, as if still damp with the blood of *my* ancestors. I could not experience Africa and return to the United States the same person who had left it 6 weeks earlier. For me, a great psychological transformation had begun.

Although the 6 weeks proved to be difficult, that did not change my determination to get the most out of my experiences. Turning moments of anxiety and confusion into meaningful reflections and understandings about Ghanaian and Nigerian cultural ways enabled me to broaden my perspectives about African people and myself. However, this was not the case for everyone in my group. What distinguished me from one friend on the trip was that I vowed to spend the rest of my life returning to Africa when I could, and she vowed never to return. The differences in our perspectives about the trip had to do with how well we dealt with the cultural and life differences that affected our personal comfort levels, how we viewed African people and Africa in general, and how important the trip was in terms of finding ancestral connections. I believe my friend participated in the trip as something to do for the summer rather than as a quest to identify, understand, and connect with Africans and, in turn, learn more about herself.

On returning to the United States after such an emotion-filled journey, I experienced another culture shock. I had gone from the sights and sounds of an all-African world to the hustle and bustle of Kennedy Airport, where I saw very few African faces, especially going through customs. Flying from New York back to Los Angeles provided me with time to ease back into the United States and to reflect on how drastically my first African journey had changed my life. I had bathed in the richness of my ancestral heritage. My African consciousness had been awakened. My thirst for knowledge about Africa had been stimulated. I had seen, felt, and experienced a connection that linked me to my ancestral home. *I had been endarkened and had seen the light.* Now,

I was "back home" in the United States. Being home sent me into culture shock because I was living again in a predominantly European world. I had to adjust to the ignorance of people who would ask, "So, how were the natives?" and "Do Africans wear clothes?" I was subject to all of the negativity associated with those who were very ignorant about Africans and Africa.

For me, this first trip typified the U-curve and the W-curve intercultural adjustment patterns. I had gone from a high in the excitement of taking the trip to a low because of adjustments and the deep pain I felt at Cape Coast to another high when I realized how profound the trip was. On re-entry into the United States, I experienced another low period. I had to adjust to being back home and going through the process of dealing with the ignorance of others and my personal conflicts: wanting to return to Africa but realizing that my life was in the United States. The final high came when I fully appreciated what the trip had done for my self-concept and my knowledge base. I was a better and stronger person as a result of that trip. I had gained a respect for my African ancestry that I could never have gotten in the United States, and I had many opportunities to share my experiences and teach the lessons I learned from my journey. I sought opportunities to interact with those who had made the *pilgrimage* home. When meeting continental Africans, I would let them know I had been to Africa, and if appropriate, I would extend a greeting in their language, if I knew it. I found a special comfort, connection, and understanding that could only be found among those who had been to Africa and who had had *an experience,* made a connection, and/or felt something very profound about their experiences.

Between that first trip in 1972 and my last in 1995, I traveled to Africa three other times. In 1983 and 1984, I traveled to Egypt. Those trips were awe inspiring and touched me at the core of my African-centered knowledge base. I was where Asante (1987, 1988, 1990b) said African-centered thought should begin, in

Kemet. In 1986, I returned to West Africa and visited the Francophone countries of Cameroon, Togo, Benin, and Senegal. Again, this West African journey caused a powerful connection with my ancestral past. My visit to Goree Island off the coast of Senegal echoed the pain I felt at Cape Coast Slave Dungeon: a site where millions of enslaved Africans passed through its portals and where 6 million of them died.

In 1995, I was selected to be a Fulbright-Hays scholar to South Africa along with 13 other educators. Because this was my fifth trip to the African continent, I was a well-seasoned traveler and no longer felt like such a stranger to Africa as I had two decades earlier. Traveling to an African country that was new to me was an exciting prospect. Compared to West Africa or Egypt, South Africa held another type of magnetism for me. It was a country engaged in a struggle that closely paralleled the struggles of *my* people in the United States.

Traveling as Fulbright-Hays scholars afforded members of our group amenities that did not exist for me during my first journey to Africa. On my first trip, my group stayed in college dormitories that had no hot water for showers. On this fifth trip, we stayed in some dormitories (with hot water) but also in hotels. We even stayed in a Holiday Inn. As a result, the compromises and the adjustments that travelers have to make in a new country were not as great and not as challenging physically nor psychologically as were my experiences 23 years earlier. That in itself led to an easier adjustment period. However, the length of the journey—5 weeks—factored into fatigue and missing home.

The issue of race is as topical in the United States today as it was 400 years ago. The arguments have changed over time, but the undergirding beliefs of European superiority over African and *other* inferiority are very real today. I viewed the Afrikaner regime in South Africa as a cousin to the historical and present-day racism in the United States. The opportunity to travel to the *new* South Africa

was one I had never expected to have because of apartheid. That in itself stimulated great intellectual curiosity.

Considering my four previous journeys, I asked myself, would I really be a stranger in South Africa? According to Gudykunst's (1995) definition,

> Strangers represent both the idea of nearness in that they are physically close and the idea of remoteness in that they have different values and ways of doing things. Strangers are physically present and participate in a situation and at the same time, are outside the situation because they are members of different groups. (p. 10)

Given this definition, I would have been considered a stranger entering South Africa, one who would be subject to the anxieties, uncertainties, and ambiguities inherent in new intercultural encounters (Gudykunst, 1993, 1995; Gudykunst & Kim, 1992). In my mind, however, Africa and South Africa were not *strange* to me. I was not a stranger because, after all, I was a long-lost child who was coming home *again*. Home to me—an African diasporan—was any place in Africa. In each country I had previously visited, I was identified with many of the ethnic groups. In West Africa, I was told that I looked like the Bambara and Fulani. I was called a *Nubian* American in Egypt. I claimed all of these. I expected to identify with the Xhosa and Zulu in South Africa. After all, I was traveling to the land of Shaka Zulu and the Mandelas, who were Xhosa.

This time, I had different expectations for what I would experience and had a knowledge base infinitely stronger about Africa and its people. In 1972, I had an Afro hairstyle and exhibited external identification with Africa through clothing, jewelry, and the decor of my house; 23 years later, I had reached Cross's (1991) Stage 4, the internalization of attitudes, beliefs, and values that demonstrate strong positive regard for Africa. I had placed an understanding and an appreciation of African culture and history at the center of my intellectual pursuits, echoing Shujaa's (1996) Re-Africanization Transformation. Deep inside, I felt a kinship to African people and had a deep respect for my historical roots and those ancestors who survived the Middle Passage. I had positive associations with continental Africans and sought opportunities to have interpersonal relationships. My professional and personal life affirmed that I would have scored well on Baldwin and Bell's (1985) *African Self-Consciousness Scale.*

Now, I was on my way to South Africa. I had been following the movement since the middle 1980s, when Randall Robinson, founder and president of TransAfrica, picketed the White House. I was in Washington, D.C., when Nelson Mandela was released from prison. I was among the many thousands who flocked anxiously to see Nelson and Winnie Mandela when they first toured the United States in 1990. I sat in Metropolitan African American Methodist Church (Frederick Douglass's church) when Winnie Mandela and Jacqueline Jackson (Jesse Jackson's wife) embraced one another during an electric afternoon of celebration. I was there when the city greeted the Mandelas at the Washington Convention Center, and I was there in October 1994 when Howard University conferred an honorary doctorate on *President* Mandela.

I knew South Africa—or so I thought. From what I had read, I felt as though I were about to enter Alabama or Mississippi after the Civil Rights Movement of the 1960s. I had been to rallies led by Maxine Waters in Los Angeles and attended vigils in Washington, D.C. I had read *Part of My Soul Went With Him* by Winnie Mandela (1984), as well as *No Easy Walk to Freedom* and *Long Walk to Freedom* by Nelson Mandela (1985, 1994). I had seen *The Last Grave at Dimbaza, Sarafina, Dry White Season, Cry Freedom,* and *Bopha.*

I had more political information about this destination than about any other African country I had visited. Was I really *a stranger, a newcomer?* I knew that I would cross the Atlantic and enter a world that had different ethnic groups, languages, and cultural ways. However, I did not feel my adjustment would

be great in comparison to other members in the group who had never been to Africa, because through many international travels, I felt comfortable talking to, interacting with, and negotiating with international people. I felt my personal knowledge and previous travel experiences had given me the *preparedness, openness, and strength* that Kim (1995) had identified as attributes contributing to intercultural adaptation.

I wondered: Could South Africa be so different from my West African experiences? On the journey, I found the answer. I was moved to find close historical parallels between the struggles of Africans in the United States and Indigenous South Africans. While in South Africa, I met a remarkable woman, Lindiwe Myeza, activist and lay minister, who told her life story to me. As she recounted the events in her life, I noted the uncanny parallels between human rights and civil rights struggles in both countries and noted parallels in our people's struggles.

▶ South African Connection: Parallel Struggles

Lindiwe Myeza ignited a great curiosity in me about the parallel histories we shared. In 1996, I wrote *Lessons from South Africa,* in which I chronicled events in her life. The following is an excerpt from that article.[1] From it, one can get a glimpse into the parallel struggles for human rights and civil rights Africans in the United States and *African* South Africans share. From it, one can understand the strong sense of connection I feel toward *African* South Africans.

> On the eve of my departure from South Africa, through the life of this extraordinary woman, I gained a deeper understanding of what it really meant to fight against apartheid and what it meant to fight for the full empowerment and dignity of all South Africans. Of all of the things Lindiwe told me . . ., two events stood out clearly in my mind. They were her descriptions of what it was like to finally be able to

cast her vote in South Africa's first democratic elections and the account of Sophiatown—the community of her birth—being razed, bulldozed by the Afrikaner government in 1955. The story of Sophiatown provided a period in South African history that paralleled a time when African Americans also were embroiled in a struggle for human dignity and civil rights.

Lindiwe spoke of Sophiatown with great pride. It was a thriving community nestled on the slope of a hill four miles west of Johannesburg. It represented all that the South African government hated: politically astute and active Africans living independently of the apartheid restrictions that forbade Africans from owning land. Even though many residents were unskilled laborers and workers, many residents managed to own property.

Sophiatown was very ethnically diverse with Coloureds, Indians, Chinese, and all of the African ethnic groups living together. It housed "[t]he most talented African men and women from all walks of life—in spite of the hardships they had to encounter. . . . The best musicians, scholars, educationists, singers, artists, doctors, lawyers, [and] clergymen" (Tlali, 1975, in Lodge, 1983, pp. 94-95) lived in Sophiatown. Lindiwe's family was representative of that thriving middle class. Her grandparents had been missionaries; her mother, Emma, worked as a domestic worker, and her father, Albert, worked for a pharmacist.

The African National Congress (ANC) was very influential in Sophiatown, and the government considered this area one of the "hotbeds of African resistance" (Lodge, 1983, p. 99). It was among the many African communities throughout South Africa that were labeled *black spots*. According to Lindiwe, being a *black spot* meant the area was a place for *White* people only, and no Blacks were allowed to live in the White South Africa. . . . Such labeling justified the forced removal and relocation of millions of *Black* South Africans, the *razing* of their communities, and the stripping of prime land from them *for* Whites. The South African government initiated its plan to demolish and relocate the residents of Sophiatown to diffuse the social and political networks of this thriving community. Its destruction took place over a five year period, but, certainly, 1955 is pivotal to Lindiwe because that is the year her home and community surrounding her home were destroyed.

When Lindiwe talked about Sophiatown, I immediately thought about parallel events in United States history: segregationist polices and the turbulence of the Civil Rights Movement during the 1950s and 1960s. I also thought about how 1955 held memories of great joy, tragedy, and fear for me. I remember the first day of summer that year because my best friend's mother was killed in a car accident. This was the first death and first major tragedy I had encountered as a child. To counteract the sorrow of this tragedy in our family, there was excitement and joy with the anticipation of and birth of my sister, Janet.

As the summer of 1955 progressed, Disneyland opened, and my best friend's father, who worked on the construction of the *Magic Kingdom,* took my brother, Richard, and me along with his three children to Disneyland. The world of Disney with its powerful media images produced and still produces fantasy, magic, and happiness for millions of children and their families, yet it holds such contradictions because of its history of fostering policies of racial exclusion in employment and its promotion of racially stereotypical images, particularly in its animated movies so dearly loved by everyone. As I loved *Bambi, Dumbo, Cinderella, Fantasia, Snow White,* and so many other productions, I was unaware of the cultural stripping it was doing to me and other children of African descent in this country and worldwide. Even as I traveled throughout South Africa in 1995—forty years after the opening of Disneyland—books, toys, and dolls from *Pocahontas, The Lion King, Aladin,* and *Beauty and the Beast* were readily available. I was saddened to see that these images were more sought after than toys that reflected the culture and images of Black South African children.

The world of Disney then as it does now permeates the media and contributes to shaping a reality for children that presents perspectives that are often both racist and sexist. With the opening of Disneyland, 1955 ushered in a major period in the globalization of Disney *consciousness*. It contributed to the notion that *Mirror, mirror on the wall, who's the fairest of them all*? certainly was not an African American girl like me from Watts, California, nor a South African young woman from Sophiatown like Lindiwe. Positive cultural images for Africans in the United States and Africans in South Africa were nowhere to be found!

As I traveled through *Fantasyland* during that summer, one of the most heinous crimes of the Civil Rights Movement and surely one of the crimes that magnified the degradation and brutality that the *Negro* faced in this country occurred: the murder of Emmett Louis Till, a fourteen-year-old teenager from Chicago. Till was visiting his relatives in Mississippi when he was alleged to have whistled at a White woman. For that *offense,* he was abducted, tortured, and brutally murdered. The pictures of his mutilated body were featured in *Jet* and *Ebony* magazines. As a child, the picture of his battered face stayed with me, as it does even today. The death of Emmett Till terrified me and other young Black children around this country. We must have wondered, "What did he do to make them hate him so much? Why are Black people so hated?"

On the [heels] of the Emmett Till murder came two events in December 1955 which catapulted Martin Luther King, Jr., into the leadership role in the Civil Rights Movement—Rosa Parks refusing to give up her seat to a White man on that bus in Birmingham, Alabama, and the consequent bus boycott in that city. The death of Emmett Till along with the Rosa Parks incident and the Birmingham bus boycott were significant events in this country's history of race relations. Even as a child, those events left a profound impression on me. . . .

In this country, while 1955 ended with a major movement in civil rights history and the growing fight against racism and oppression, across the Atlantic Ocean, it ended with *Black* South Africans engaged in struggles to save their communities from being destroyed by the racist Afrikaner regime, and it ended with *Black* South Africans engaged in a long battle against the human rights offenses imposed by apartheid. Just as Sophiatown and the events of that year are indelibly etched into the psyche of Lindiwe and her fellow South Africans, so are the events of 1955 etched in my mind and those of many African Americans. What irony I found in that connection—a connection which enabled me to see that the South African story was my story too! The story of Sophiatown provided for me the first event that connected our struggles together—the struggles against apartheid in South Africa and *apartheid* in the United States. (Humber, 1996, pp. 10-12)

The historical parallels in South Africa that I became aware of did not end with Lindiwe's story. Our group had the honor of meeting Mrs. Winnie Mandela at her home in Soweto. That meeting was one of the highlights of the trip. One of the things Mrs. Mandela did during the meeting with us was to thank us, as Americans, for our support of the fight against apartheid. She profoundly connected our mutual struggles when she said,

> Our liberation is the liberation of the continent of Africa and your liberation. Your roots are here! Your navel is here! For us to be totally free, we need to liberate each and every one of you as well. Those bones that are buried in the Mississippi River are our bones too! We will not feel totally free unless we make this country your country as well! (Humber, 1996, pp. 42-43)

My time in South Africa awakened an understanding of the depth of connections that Africans in the Americas have with continental Africans. Recognizing the parallel struggles for human and civil rights of African South Africans and Africans in the United States was one of the most profound insights of the journey for me. The words of Mrs. Mandela rang in my ears as I returned home. I kept hearing her say, "Those bones that are buried in the Mississippi River are our bones too!" (Humber, 1996, p. 43). Her words spoke to an unbroken linkage between continental Africans and Africans in the Americas.

► Cultural Parallels

The Chinese proverb, "A fish doesn't know it's wet," is appropriate to explain the *invisible* cloak of culture that surrounds us. We do not realize our culture and its influences are there until we have to leave them. Traveling to another country causes us to emerge from our cultural waters and enter the waters of other cultural groups. When sojourners are going through the period of recognizing cultural differences and adapting and adjusting to those differences, they may often note similarities in their own cultural ways. For African American sojourners returning to the source of their ancestral heritage, there often comes a recognition: "That is why I act, dance, sing, dress, wear my hair, and behave as I do. I can now see the roots of my being. I am aware of how African I really am." Thus, sojourners recognize cultural ways that previously had been understood as distinctly southern or particular to Black folks now as reflecting African continuities. This recognition of continuities can deepen the impact of the journey, strengthen an identification with African people, and nurture feelings of belonging and coming home.

In my African travels, I saw myself, family members, and friends walking the streets and roads of many of the places I visited. I heard music and felt rhythms, though new to me, that sounded and felt familiar. There were times when I felt as though I were experiencing the culture I knew at home in the United States. There were times I felt a familiarity that transcended my historical separation from Africa.

Scholars have been researching African retentions in the culture and language of Africans in the Americas for more than 50 years. We can look to the following works for documenting the unbroken cultural and linguistic continuities existing between continental Africans and Africans in the Americas: *The Myth of the Negro Past* by Melville J. Herskovits (1941), *Africanisms in the Gullah Dialect* by Lorenzo D. Turner (1949), *Black Culture and Black Consciousness: Afro-American Folk Thought From Slavery to Freedom* by Lawrence W. Levine (1977), *The Bantu Speaking Heritage of the United States* by Winnifred K. Vass (1979), *Slave Culture: Nationalist Theory and the Foundations of Black Culture* by Sterling Stuckey (1987), "The African Essence in African-American Language" by Molefi Kete Asante (1990a), and *Africanisms in American English* by Joseph E. Holloway and Winnifred K. Vass (1993). In 1991, Joseph E. Holloway edited *Africanisms in American Culture,* a collection of research that makes a major contribution in documenting African continuities in the Americas. *Africanisms* includes the following chapters: "The Origins of African-American Culture" by Joseph E. Holloway, "African Elements in African-American Language" by Molefi Kete Asante, "The Case of Voodoo in New Orleans" by Jessie Gaston Mulira, "Gullah Attitudes Toward Life and Death" by Margaret Washington Creel, "African Religious Retentions in Florida by Robert L. Hall, "Sacrificial Practices in Santeria, an African-Cuban Religion in the United States" by George Brandon, "Kongo Influences on African-American Artistic Culture" by Robert Farris Thompson, "Africanisms in African-American Music" by Portia K. Maultsby, "Africanisms and the Study of Folklore" by Beverly J. Robinson, and "The African Heritage of White America," by John Edward Philips.

To those who question and doubt African continuities in the Americas, Asante (1990a, 1991) notes that no cultural group has experienced cultural dislocation without retaining some elements from its home culture. That also is the case for Africans in the United States. The connections might not always be evident; nevertheless, continuities exist. He says

> That something of the African backgrounds of Black Americans survived is not difficult to argue despite intense efforts to prove that Blacks were incapable of cultural retention because of slavery. No displaced people have ever completely lost the forms of their previous culture.

The specific artifacts may differ from those employed in a prior time, but the essential elements giving rise to those artifacts are often retained and produce substantive forms in the new context. (Asante, 1990a, p. 235)

In Holloway's *Africanisms,* Mulira's (1991) research focused on voodoo, "a functional religious system in West Africa" (p. 35), and its influence in New Orleans. According to Mulira, Africanisms have been more obvious in the Caribbean, Brazil, Haiti, and the southern United States, where large numbers of Africans lived together. She noted,

It is more difficult to measure and evaluate the persistence of African culture elsewhere, especially in the United States outside the core areas of New Orleans and the Sea Islands. In many "pocket areas" in southern states and in cities and towns through the United States, remnants of African culture abound: in language patterns and vocabulary, in literature, in techniques of storytelling, in folktales such as Brer Rabbit and Tar Baby, in music and dance forms, singing and rhythm, in foods, and in ways of eating certain foods. The extended-family concept and respect for elders in many rural areas were African transplants. Africanisms are of course most prevalent among Black southerners because the South was the heart of the slavery system in the United States. (pp. 35-36)

Maultsby (1991) also affirmed African retentions in the Americas when she wrote,

The continuum of an African consciousness in America manifests itself in the evolution of an African-American culture. The music, dance, folklore, religion, language, and other expressive forms associated with the culture of slaves were transmitted orally to subsequent generations of American Blacks. (p. 185)

Vass (1979), Holloway (1991), and Holloway and Vass (1993) noted the impact of Bantu culture on continental Africans and that

impact in the United States. They discussed the merging of Bantuisms with other African cultures and the continuation of the Bantu influence in the United States. In Africanisms, Holloway (1991) said,

Once the Bantu reached America they were able to retain much of their cultural identity. Enforced isolation of these Africans by plantation owners allowed them to retain their religion, philosophy, culture, folklore, folkways, folk beliefs, folk tales, storytelling, naming practices, home economics, arts, kinship, and music. These Africanisms were shared and adopted by the various African ethnic groups of the field slave community, and they gradually developed into African-American cooking (soul food), music (jazz, blues, spirituals, gospels), language, religion, philosophy, customs, and arts. (p. 17)

The wealth of research supporting African continuities reinforces my position that for many Africans from the Americas who travel to Africa, the journey may be new to them in many obvious ways, but they also may have experiences that remind them of *southernisms* or *Africanisms* in their upbringing. These experiences can engender feelings of connection and familiarity. The languages and cultures of the people may be different, but the rhythms, practices, movements, and ways of the people can be reminiscent of their lives back home in the United States.

What I was not prepared for on my South African journey was to find South Africa so European and so U.S. American. The itinerary for the group had us spending more time in the urban areas than in townships and rural areas. Staying in the cities could leave one with the impression that South Africa is not too much different from Europe and the United States. South Africa appears so European and American in its outward appearances that I often wondered if I was really in Africa. However, I, along with other Fulbright-Hays scholars, knew there was an *African* South Africa that we had yet to see. Had I not experienced a naming ceremony at Mapela, a rural community 4 hours north of Johannesburg, a northern Ndebele community, I would have missed the sights, sounds, rhythms, and harmonies of Africa that I longed for. I would have missed the *soul* of South Africa, which linked me to the *heart* of Africa.

Four weeks into the journey I, along with three other African American women, was given the opportunity to participate in a naming ceremony. We traveled through the countryside to get to Mapela.

> There I heard the sounds, heard the songs, heard the language, and felt the rhythms of Africa!! It was there that I was a child who had come home. It was there that I was embraced by a Northern Ndebele community and given my African name, *Mokjaetji Langa.* My first name means *Angel, Spirit of Africa,* and my surname means *The Sun!* (Humber, 1996, p. 39)

The full impact of that day and how African my life has been in the United States did not really hit me until I returned to the United States and discussed the events of that glorious day with my new Ndebele sister, Lovonya DeJean. Lovonya, our other Ndebele sisters, and I experienced a connection with South Africa at the *soul* level. Our naming ceremony added a depth to our journey that tied us to South Africa forever. Uncertainties because of our cultural and language differences were erased that day. We were welcomed into a community and found a new family: a family whose ways were different yet very familiar to our own in the United States.

▶ African Continuities at Mapela: Lovonya DeJean's Story

In remembering our experiences at Mapela, Lovonya recounted the parallels she found between her life growing up in Lake Charles, Louisiana, and our South African journey (in a 1997 personal interview with me, excerpted here).[2] She recalled that she saw, heard, and experienced some of the things her great-

grandmother, a former enslaved African, had told her and taught her. What she had considered to be *southern hospitality* was really *African hospitality,* an extension of African cultural ways in the United States. The following are Lovonya's reflections and recollections of her South African experience and the parallels to her life in the United States.

One of the things that struck me most at my naming ceremony at Mapela was the reconnection of what my great-grandmother told me. My great-grandmother was born into slavery about 1856 and lived to be 98 years old. She was between ten and twelve years old when slavery ended. I was about the same age when she died.

My grandmother raised me. When I say this, I have to be clear because people have the tendency to think that if my great-grandmother raised me, my mother and father did not. Today, there is a big tendency for grandparents to take on the responsibility of raising their grandchildren. That was not the case for me. My entire family lived in a compound kind of area close to the way many Africans live. I was always at my great-grandmother's house, and she had a tremendous influence on me. When I began to study African culture, especially when I experienced the naming ceremony at Mapela, I realized I had learned several things from her that could be identified as coming from Africa.

I remember my great-grandmother teaching me about *eldership* and talking about *ancestors.* I was told to respect elders and told who the elders were. She talked about honoring people *who went before us.* She would not name anyone specifically, but she would talk about them in a collective sense *as family members who went before me.* When I began studying African culture, I learned how important the respect for elders and the revering of ancestors are to African societies. I clearly saw this importance carried out at Mapela.

My great-grandmother also loved to tell us stories. She always told them at night. I remember Lindiwe [our South African friend] telling us that when she was growing up, stories were told at night. She said it helped to build character, and it entertained the children.

The day's activities at Mapela reminded me of special occasions growing up in Lake Charles, Louisiana. We were the honored guests for the day. Even though we were more than an hour late, everyone waited for us to arrive before the ceremony and festivities began. When we arrived, I noticed women had a huge role in taking care of the needs of the celebration. That is very true of how we do things in the South.

We first were taken to meet Chieftanness Langa. She was in the kitchen area of the community center helping with the preparation of food for the day. She had on her apron and worked along with the other women. When the ceremonies got underway, she emerged in her *Sunday best* dressed in a vibrant pink dress and hat. She would have been well dressed for any Black church in my community.

The activities began with the singing of the South African National Anthem. Testimonies were given, gospel songs were sung, and the woman's group that was honored for the day sang inspiring songs. The ceremony had the feel of African American churches in the United States and did not look a lot different from what I would experience at an eleven o'clock service at my church in Vallejo, California.

During the naming ceremony, I noticed that the children had a place. Even in the sitting arrangements during the ceremony, the children in the choir were sitting in a designated area. I also noticed the children were one place and the adults were someplace else when conversations were going on. This reminded me of when my great-grandmother and her friends were talking. We were never allowed to be a part of *grown folks' conversations*. From this separation of children from adults at Mapela, I may have seen the reason my great-grandmother dismissed us from adult conversations.

When our turn came for the naming ceremony, the senior elder woman performed the libation ceremony and called upon the ancestors to receive us. After we were given our Ndebele names, we were dressed in Ndebele traditional dress by women of the community. They surrounded us, sang songs to us, and included us in their circle to dance with them. After picture taking, there was a feast. We, as guests of honor, were served first. That is how my family would have treated special guests back home. I honor that practice today.

In the South, if we visited someone's home, we could not *eat and run*. That would be considered bad manners. Before we left the festivities, we went to the home of Chieftanness-Mother Langa to thank her for the day and to formally tell her good-bye. She offered us cookies to eat and then gave us some to take with us. That was exactly what would have happened at my mother's or my great-grandmother's house. We would have *toted*. It was typical for them to give us fried chicken, baked sweet potatoes, cookies, and teacakes to take with us after a visit. [Smitherman (1977) identified *tote* as a word that is a direct survival from West African languages. While its etymology may be West African, the practice of toting may be common to African societies in general.]

Had I not experienced the naming ceremony at Mapela by my new Ndebele family, I would have missed seeing and feeling some of the African continuities I did not know existed in my southern upbringing. If I had stayed in the cities—Johannesburg, Cape Town, and Durban— my South African experience would have been one of seeing the disparity that still exists between Black and White South Africans and seeing a country that is obviously European dominated, but I would have never really seen *African* South Africa. Mapela let me know I was really in Africa and that I had come home.

The direct connections that Lovonya made between what she learned as a child from her great-grandmother, her closest link to African tradition, and our naming ceremony echoed the findings of scholars who have identified Africanisms in culture, language, religion, folklore, storytelling, folkways, kinship practices, and naming practices in the Americas (Asante, 1991; Herskovits, 1941; Holloway, 1991; Holloway & Vass, 1993; Levine, 1977;

Maultsby, 1991; Mulira, 1991; Smitherman, 1977; Stuckey, 1987; Turner, 1949; Vass, 1979). The major points of connection that Lovonya identified are as follows:

1. Communal living and child rearing
2. Respect for elders
3. Remembering ancestors
4. Children not in *grown folks* conversations
5. Importance of women preparing for a celebration
6. Putting on *Sunday* best for special occasions
7. Spiritual connection through the libation ceremony and prayers
8. The importance of storytelling and telling stories at night
9. The practice of not *eating and running*
10. The practice of *toting.*

Experiencing the naming ceremony at Mapela opened a channel of understanding for Lovonya DeJean that brought great significance to her journey. Prior to her trip to South Africa, she would have been identified as a person who has *positive African identity.* Her life's journey had caused her to value African culture and history and to seek information and experiences that brought a greater understanding of her African self and an appreciation of Africa and its people. Although her purpose as a Fulbright-Hays scholar initially might have been a quest to look at culture, history, education, and the new South African government, her experiences enriched her life in ways unforeseen and connected her to South Africa in a most profound way. She experienced the *new* of an intercultural sojourner, yet some of the new was very familiar to her because of the Africanisms inherent in the lives and cultures of Africans living in the Americas.

► Conclusion

Intercultural adaptation of travelers in international settings has been a major topic of re-

search in intercultural communication for the past decade. Kim and Gudykunst (1988) were in the forefront of the discussions through their research in cross-cultural adaptation. Gudykunst (1993, 1995) proposed the notion of *stranger* to address the phenomenon of being a newcomer in a cultural setting and enlarged the research of Berger and Calabrese (1975) to include intercultural communicative events. He proposed that intercultural sojourners experience *anxiety* and *uncertainty.* How well they cope with these will determine the degree of their intercultural adaptation. In addition, sojourners will more than likely experience *culture shock* (Furnham, 1988) and feel *culture distance* (Furnham & Bochner, 1983, cited in Furnham, 1988) in settings that differ considerably from their own where they lack the linguistic and cultural competence to negotiate comfortably in a new cultural environment. They will more than likely experience the *U-curve* (Adler, 1975; Chang, 1973; Deutsch & Won, 1963; Lysgaard, 1955; Morris, 1960; Oberg, 1960; Smalley, 1963; all cited in Chen & Starosta, 1998) in the adaptive process and the *W-curve* (Gullahorn & Gullahorn, 1963; Kohls, 1975; Kohls, 1984; all cited in Chen & Starosta, 1998) when returning to the home culture. Kim (1995) suggested that cross-cultural adaptation includes the *stress-adaptation-growth dynamic* and that *preparedness, openness,* and *strength* are among the attributes necessary to enable intercultural sojourners to adapt to their new cultural experiences and settings.

When considering the experiences of Africans from the Americas, Asante (1987, 1990a) and Holloway (1991) propose that one must consider the significance of African continuities present in the Americas and their impact on African American behavior and culture. Asante (1987) placed Africa at the heart of all African American behavior. Understanding the connection to and affinity for Africa and its people that many diasporan Africans have consciously developed is integral to understanding intercultural adaptation and adjustment for them. For this discussion, *positive African identity*—positive identification with continental Africans and Africa, participation in activities that celebrate African heritage, and seeking of knowledge about the culture, history, and struggles of African people—was introduced as an integral element in understanding the adaptive process. *Positive African identity* embodies both the African *Self-Consciousness* system of the Black personality (Baldwin & Bell, 1985) and the stages of developing *positive African American identity* (Cross et al., 1991), *Afrocentric identity* (Cross, 1991), and *re-Africanization* (Shujaa, 1996). Baldwin and Bell (1985) identified the *African Self-Consciousness system* as reflecting positive attributes of the Black personality. These attributes incorporate a positive regard for African culture and history, positive associations with people of African descent, and support for causes of African peoples in the face of institutionalized racism. Cross (1991) and Cross et al. (1991) identified the stages of developing *positive Afrocentric/ African American identity* and proposed that internalizing *positive Afrocentric/ African American identity* is significant to generating psychological well-being and strength necessary for functioning in a racist society. Shujaa (1996) proposed that the relationship between developing a strong knowledge base of Africana cultural history and understanding the African worldview helps diasporan Africans find their way home and leads them to *re-Africanization:* personal transformation to end the alienation of their African selves and to heal the effects of experiencing the *maafa.*

Africans from the United States and the Americas are not immune to the stages of intercultural adaptation when traveling to Africa. The central theses of this chapter propose that *positive African identity* and *personal knowledge* that sojourners have about Africa and its people, coupled with *experiencing* an event or events that caused them to *feel* connected to Africa, would contribute to their intercultural adaptation and adjustments. This research asked and responded to the following questions:

1. What does it mean when a sojourner travels to his or her country/region of ancestral origin?
2. Does this ancestral origin mean there will be better intercultural understanding and adaptation to the cultural differences that will be encountered?
3. Can a sense of ancestral connection and identification be strong enough for the sojourner to overcome culture shock and enable positive intercultural adaptation and adjustment?
4. Does the fact that a person is of African descent ensure she or he will adapt well in African intercultural settings?

All people of African descent who live in the United States and other American countries are not going to share *positive African identity.* Some may have little interest in Africa, Africans, their culture, history, and struggles and may find little or no need for connection with Africa or Africans. Moreover, some who travel to African countries for a *vacation,* much like going to Hawaii, Mexico, the Caribbean, and Europe, will have difficulties in adjusting to the cultural differences there. However, for some Africans in the Americas, the connection to the motherland has a greater significance. For them, the journey is more than an *exotic* adventure. When African sojourners from the Americas find a point of identification with the struggles of continental Africans and/or experience a significant event(s) that causes the recognition of their *Africanness,* the experience is profound, and there evolves a strong connection and identification with Africa that might not occur when traveling to other international settings. The experiences, in turn, might cause greater awareness of who they are and provide better opportunities to cope with the cultural differences that can cause culture shock and feelings of culture distance, thus enabling better intercultural adaptation and adjustment. Ultimately, African sojourners journey to a land where their *Americanness* makes them *strangers* but their *Africanness* makes intercultural encounters *not so strange.*

► Notes

1. This passage from Humber, 1996, "Lessons from South Africa," published in *Vitae Scholasticae: The Journal of Educational Biography, 15,* 9-46, is reprinted with permission of the publisher.

2. This passage from an interview with Lovonya DeJean is reprinted with permission of DeJean.

► References

Asante, M. K. (1987). *The Afrocentric idea.* Philadelphia: Temple University Press.

Asante, M. K. (1988). *Afrocentricity: The theory of social change.* Trenton, NJ: Africa World Press.

Asante, M. K. (1990a). The African essence in African-American language. In M. K. Asante & K. W. Asante (Eds.), *African culture: The rhythms of unity* (pp. 233-252). Trenton, NJ: Africa World Press.

Asante, M. K. (1990b). *Kemet, Afrocentricity, and knowledge.* Trenton, NJ: Africa World Press.

Asante, M. K. (1991). The African elements in African-American language. In J. E. Holloway (Ed.), *Africanisms in American culture* (pp. 19-33). Bloomington: Indiana University Press.

Baldwin, J. A., & Bell, Y. R. (1985). The African Self-Consciousness Scale: An Africentric personality questionnaire. *The Western Journal of Black Studies, 9,* 61-68.

Berger, C., & Calabrese, R. (1975). Some explorations in initial interaction and beyond. *Human Communication Research, 1,* 99-112.

Brandon, G. (1991). Sacrificial practices in Santeria, an African-Cuban religion in the United States. In J. E. Holloway (Ed.), *Africanisms in American culture* (pp. 119-147). Bloomington: Indiana University Press.

Bock, P. (Ed.). (1972). *Culture shock: A reader.* New York: Knopf.

Chen, G., & Starosta, W. J. (1998). *Foundations of intercultural communication.* Boston: Allyn & Bacon.

Creel, M. W. (1991). Gullah attitudes toward life and death. In J. E. Holloway (Ed.), *Africanisms in American culture* (pp. 69-97). Bloomington: Indiana University Press.

Cross, W. E., Jr. (1991). *Shades of black: Diversity in African-American identity.* Philadelphia: Temple University Press.

Cross, W. E., Jr., Parham, T. A., & Helms, J. E. (1991). The stages of black identity development: Nigrescence models. In R. L. Jones (Ed.), *Black psychology* (pp. 319-338). Berkeley, CA: Cobb & Henry.

Furnham, A. (1988). The adjustment of sojourners. In Y. Y. Kim & W. B. Gudykunst (Eds.), *Cross-cultural adaptation: Current approaches* (pp. 42-61). Newbury Park, CA: Sage.

Gudykunst, W. B. (1993). Toward a theory of effective interpersonal and intergroup communication: An Anxiety/Uncertainty Management (AUM) perspective. In R. L. Wiseman & J. Koester (Eds.), *Intercultural communication competence* (pp. 33-71). Newbury Park, CA: Sage.

Gudykunst, W. B. (1995). Anxiety/Uncertainty Management (AUM) theory. In R. L. Wiseman (Ed.), *Intercultural communication theory* (pp. 8-58). Thousand Oaks, CA: Sage.

Gudykunst, W. B., & Kim, Y. Y. (1992). *Communication with strangers: An approach to intercultural communication.* New York: McGraw-Hill.

Hall, R. L. (1991). African religious retentions in Florida. In J. E. Holloway (Ed.), *Africanisms in American culture* (pp. 98-118). Bloomington: Indiana University Press.

Hays, R. (1972). Behavioral issues in multinational operations. In R. Hayes (Ed.), *International business.* Englewood Cliffs, NJ: Prentice-Hall.

Herskovits, M. J. (1941). *The myth of the Negro past.* Boston: Beacon.

Hilliard, A. G., III. (1997). *SBA: The reawakening of the African mind.* Gainesville, FL: Makare.

Holloway, J. E. (Ed.). (1991). *Africanisms in American culture.* Bloomington: Indiana University Press.

Holloway, J. E., & Vass, W. J. (1993). *The African heritage of American English.* Bloomington: Indiana University Press.

Humber, T. C. (1996). Lessons from South Africa. *Vitae Scholasticae: The Journal of Educational Biography, 15,* 9-46.

Jorgensen, D. L. (1989). *Participant observation: A methodology for human studies.* Newbury Park, CA: Sage.

Kim, Y. Y. (1995). Cross-cultural adaptation: An integrative theory. In R. L. Wiseman (Ed.), *Intercultural communication theory* (pp. 170-193). Thousand Oaks, CA: Sage.

Kim, Y. Y., & Gudykunst, W. B. (Eds.). (1988). *Cross-cultural adaptation: Current approaches.* Newbury Park, CA: Sage.

Levine, L. (1977). *Black culture and black consciousness.* New York: Oxford University Press.

Lodge, T. (1983). *Blood politics in South Africa since 1945.* New York: Longman.

Lundstedt, S. (1963). An introduction to some evolving problems in cross-cultural research. *Journal of Social Issues, 19,* 1-9.

Mandela, W. (1984). *Part of my soul went with him.* New York: Norton.

Mandela, N. (1985). *No easy walk to freedom.* London: Heinemann.

Mandela, N. (1994). *Long walk to freedom.* Boston: Little, Brown.

Martin, J. N., & Nakayama, T. K. (1997). *Intercultural communication in contexts.* Mountainview, CA: Mayfield.

Maultsby, P. K. (1991). Africanisms in African-American music. In J. E. Holloway (Ed.), *Africanisms in American culture* (pp. 185-210). Bloomington: Indiana University Press.

Mulira, J. G. (1991). The case of voodoo in New Orleans. In J. E. Holloway (Ed.), *Africanisms in American culture* (pp. 34-68). Bloomington: Indiana University Press.

Oberg, K. (1960). Culture shock: Adjustment to new culture environments. *Practical Anthropology, 7,* 197-182.

Philips, J. E. (1991). The African heritage of white America. In J. E. Holloway (Ed.), *Africanisms in American culture* (pp. 225-239). Bloomington: Indiana University Press.

Richards, D. (1990). The implications of African-American spirituality. In M. K. Asante & K. W. Asante (Eds.), *African culture: The rhythms of unity.* Trenton, NJ: Africa World Press.

Richards, D. M. (1989). *Let the circle be unbroken: The implications of African spirituality in the Diaspora.* Trenton, NJ: Red Sea Press.

Robinson, B. J. (1991). Africanisms and the study of folklore. In J. E. Holloway (Ed.), *Africanisms in American culture* (pp. 211-224). Bloomington: Indiana University Press.

Shujaa, M. (1996). Coming home again: Re-Africanization as personal transformation. In E. K. Addae (Ed.), *To heal a people: Afrikan scholars defining a new reality.* Columbia, MD: Kujichagulia Press.

Smitherman, G. (1977). *Talkin and testifyin: The language of black America.* Boston: Houghton Mifflin.

Stanfield, J. H., II. (1994). Ethnic modeling in qualitative research. In N. K. Denzin & Y. S. Lincoln (Eds.), *Handbook of qualitative research.* Thousand Oaks, CA: Sage.

Stuckey, S. (1987). *Slave culture: Nationalist theory and foundations of black America.* New York: Oxford University Press.

Sue, D. (1978). World views and counseling. *Personnel and Guidance Journal, 56,* 458-462.

Thompson, R. F. (1991). Kongo influences on African-American artistic culture. In J. E. Holloway (Ed.), *Africanisms in American culture* (pp. 148-184). Bloomington: Indiana University Press.

Turner, L. D. (1949). *Africanisms in the Gullah dialect.* Chicago: University of Chicago Press.

Vass, W. K. (1979). *The Bantu speaking heritage of the United States.* Los Angeles: UCLA, Center for Afro-American Studies.

The Impact of Cultural Dynamics on the Newcomer to the Organizational Environment

EMEKA J. OKOLI

The domain of business is rapidly moving beyond national boundaries. . . . Global competition in the 1990s makes parochialism self-defeating. No nation can afford to act as if it is alone in the world. . . . The United States economy is inextricably linked to the health of other economies. Like businesspeople the world over, Americans must now compete and contribute on an international scale.

Adler, 1991, p. 13

Adler (1991) takes the position that failure or success in the 21st-century organization depends largely on the organization's ability to develop strategies for survival in a high-energy environment. The end of the Cold War; rapid social, political, and cultural changes all over the world; and the need to provide answers to perceived economic challenges from Asia and Europe exert enormous pressure on organizations and countries to change and adapt. Many organizations have responded to this challenge by making their internal environments more culture-sensitive and -friendly. Others have gone beyond a friendly internal climate to seek global stability through the creation of strategic partnerships that span the globe. With global reach, however, comes the need to attract and retain the best people from around the world. For most of these organizations, the human resource problem begins as recruiters negotiate with the would-be organizational member. Two pivotal dimensions to the assimilation process, both of them based in the self-interests of the organization and the individual, characterize this boundary event. On its part, the organization seeks to attract the best and most qualified individuals who will contribute to the organizational goals and dreams. The individual, on the other hand, attempts to modify and leverage the new organizational environment to better satisfy his or her needs (Jablin, 1982; Schein, 1968; Van Maanen, 1975). This unique transcultural interaction between the organization and the individual and the events that follow constitute the focus of this chapter. The transcultural dimension of this experience makes an examination of culture and its impact on the interacting parties necessary.

> Culture is the total accumulation of an identifiable group's beliefs, norms, activities, institutions, and communication patterns. (Dodd, 1991, p. 41)

Dodd's definition of culture is favored in this study for its simplicity and comprehensiveness in its scope. His definition agrees, to a large extent, with those of other researchers (Bormann, 1983; Hall, 1977; Herkovitz, 1955). Herkovitz (1948) defined culture as "the man-made [sic] part of the human environment" and as "essentially a construct that describes the total body of belief, behavior, knowledge, sanctions, values, and goals that make the way of life of a people" (p. 625). For Luzbetak (cited in Hasselgrave, 1978), "culture is a design for living. It is a plan according to which society adapts itself to its physical, social, and ideational environment" (p. 68). In his thesis on the comprehensiveness of culture, Hall (1977) said that "culture is man's [sic] medium; there is not one aspect of human life that is not touched and altered by culture" (p. 14). Hall further posited that culture affects

> how people express themselves (including shows of emotion), the way they think, how they move, how problems are solved, how their cities are planned and laid out, how transporta-

tion systems function and are organized, and how government systems are put together and function. (p. 14)

Hall's definition, like Dodd's (1991), makes culture an extremely complex and pervasive concept that reaches into every aspect of life. Samovar and Porter (1991) echoed the same sentiment when they stated that, culture is our "invisible teacher" (p. 47) and that it "dictates who talks to whom, about what, how, when, and for how long" (p. 48). Keesing (in Gudykunst & Kim, 1992) viewed culture as "a system of knowledge, shaped and constrained by the way the human brain acquires, organizes, and processes information and creates internal models of reality" (p. 12). Schein (1968) defined culture as

> a pattern of shared basic assumptions that the group learned as it solved its problems of external adaptation and internal integration, that has worked well enough to be considered valid and, therefore, to be taught to new members as the correct way to perceive, think, and feel in relation to those problems. (p. 12)

From the above, one can easily infer that people's cultural orientation affects both their understanding of a communication act and what they see as the "correct" behavior within the context of the act. This assumption is valid in view of the ways researchers have conceptualized communication vis-à-vis culture. To Bormann (1983), communication referred to "the human social processes by which people create, raise, and sustain group consciousness" (p. 100). He sees culture as "the sum total of ways of living, organizing, and communing, built up in a group of human beings and transmitted to newcomers by means of verbal and nonverbal communication" (p. 100). Gudykunst and Kim (1992) tied these conceptualizations of culture and communication neatly together in their definition of intercultural communication. The authors define intercultural communication as "communication between people from different societal cultures" (p. 16). Their definition applies to all situations where individuals from different cultural backgrounds interact with each other. In particular, their definition covers the complex dynamics of organizational or cross-cultural entry, socialization, assimilation, or exit, activities that constitute the crux of this present chapter. A detailed discussion about the concept of culture from intercultural and organizational perspectives is outside the scope of this study. An attempt will, however, be made to highlight and examine the impact of cultural dynamics within the environment on acculturation.

▶ Environmental Influences on Acculturation

In the course of everyday living, people constantly make adaptations to their environment, which is constantly in a state of change. . . . They adapt by using any of four strategies: reconstructing their perception of the environment, adapting their behavior to the demands of the environment, or changing the environment, either by reshaping it or moving to a more congenial one.

Taft, 1988, p. 150

The environment in which communicative acts take place influences both the interactants and the outcome of the interaction (Lewin, 1936). Lewin recognized this effect when he included the environment as one of the factors that affect behavior in the formula

$$B = f(P, E)$$

where B = Behavior, P = Person, and E = Environment.

This means that our behavior at any time is a function of who we are and the environment in which the interaction is taking place. Kuhn (1975) echoes the same thought when he says, "human beings are controlled systems behaving in an environment" (p. 112). Kim (1991) indicated that

Each person is an "open system" with a fundamental goal of adapting to its environment through its inherent homeostatic drive to maintain equilibrium, both internally and in relation to the environment (including the other person). When the system is challenged by the environment, its internal equilibrium is temporarily disturbed as the person-environment symmetry is broken. (p. 268)

Kim notes that the resultant situation is stressful and causes the individual to make necessary adjustments in an effort to regain internal equilibrium. *Acculturative stress* refers to a kind of stress in which the process of acculturation is identified as the source (Berry, 1990). Berry and Kim (in Berry, Kim, & Boski, 1988) found "the nature of the larger society" (p. 74) was one of the five moderating factors in the relationship between acculturation and stress.

The systems framework, recommended by researchers such as Kim (1991), makes it possible to conceive of the individual and the environment as two interdependent systems that have vital links to each other. The individual receives necessary inputs from the environment while generating outputs to the environment. In discussing the relationship between a person's frame of reference, behavior, and environment, Grove and Torbiorn (1985) declare, "the environment is affected by a person's frame of reference because the frame recommends behaviors; these, in turn, directly and immediately affect what is occurring in the environment" (p. 209). They further observe,

As a person notices what is occurring in his [*sic*] environment and the extent to which his behavior is in harmony with that of others, the facts and evaluations thus acquired are fed back into his frame of reference to become part of his total accumulation of values, attitudes, opinions, ideas, knowledge, and so forth. (p. 209)

The implication of this can be far-reaching in the sense that the type of feedback can affect our view of others, the environment, and our-selves. Pandey (1992) identifies three major domains of the environment:

Natural environment: Includes geograph-ical features, landscapes, wilderness, di-sasters, pollution, flora and fauna, and so on

Built environment: Buildings, architec-ture, technology, cities, and so on

Social environment: Territory, crowding, space, and so on (p. 181)

Pandey (1992) is of the opinion that each indi-vidual has a unique relationship with the envi-ronment at all levels. It is, however, necessary to indicate that this conceptualization of the environment becomes more complex when the subjective dimension of culture is super-imposed on these domains of the environ-ment. There is the element of culture that in-cludes "people's perceptions, values, norms, and behaviors" (Pandey, 1992, p. 255) and that underlies Pandey's three domains and goes further to touch on issues that are much deeper than the physical environment. Al-though there are countless definitions of cul-ture, we will adopt these: "a body of knowl-edge that is drawn upon as a resource for explaining and making sense of new experi-ences" (Pacanowsky & O'Donnel-Trujillo, 1982, p. 123); the accumulation within an identifiable group of beliefs, norms, activities, institutions, and communication patterns (Dodd, 1991), which the groups teach "to new members as the correct way to perceive, think, and feel" (Schein, 1968, p. 12). Deetz and Kersten's (1983) description of organizational (and cultural) reality as embracing two struc-tures can also be applied to the larger host en-vironment. The authors distinguish between surface and deep structures of organizational (and cultural) reality. They define surface re-ality as

the world in which members self-consciously live, where things are rational and are made rational, where the guidelines are clear and get clarified, and where individuals are seen as having and exercising power. Meaning here is

largely taken for granted so that work can be done in an apparently efficient manner. (p. 157)

Pandey's (1992) three domains of the environ-ment belong in this level of appreciation. The deep structure, on the other hand, includes "the unexamined beliefs and values upon which the taken-for-granted surface structure rests" (Deetz & Kersten, 1983, p. 158).

Our idea of the environment (this can be the cultural environment of the host country or the organization) is further complicated by the fact that the individual stranger imports into the situation environmental variables that may be totally different from that of the host. An organizational newcomer, therefore, will be faced with three levels of the environment at any one time, the surface structure, the deep structure, and the individual's culture.

THE SURFACE STRUCTURE
OF THE HOST ENVIRONMENT

The surface structure includes several ele-ments.

Values. These provide the evaluational basis that organizational members use for judging situations, acts, objects, and people. Values reflect the real goals, ideals, and stan-dards—as well as sins—of an organization and represent members' preferred means of resolving life's problems. They represent a people's understanding of "what ought to be" (Cummings & Huse, 1989) in the organiza-tion or society.

Norms. A group norm is "the standard by which the group judges behavior . . . [it] is what is expected and what usually occurs" (Van Fleet, 1991, p. 137). Norms compose an unwritten code of behavior that tells members how to behave in particular situations. Van Fleet suggests that "norms result from the tra-ditions of the group, individual members' personalities, the situation, and the task" (p. 138). He identified four basic functions of group norms:

1. Norms ensure group survival by discouraging behaviors that threaten the group's existence.
2. Norms create an atmosphere that reduces uncertainty within the group.
3. Norms restrict members' behavior to acceptable limits.
4. Norms distinguish one group from the others.

Artifacts: Artifacts and creations of the group are at the highest level of cultural awareness and represent visible levels of the other cultural elements of the group. Schein (1968) brought under this classification "all that one sees, hears, and feels when one encounters a new group with an unfamiliar culture" (p. 17). He indicated that this level of culture (or the environment) is "easy to observe but hard to decipher" (p. 17). For a newcomer to any organization, decoding the group's classificatory system for its artifacts is a function of time and socialization.

THE DEEP STRUCTURE

This structure encompasses the basic assumptions in the host culture and lies at the deepest levels of cultural awareness. From its dictates, members of the host culture or organization perceive, albeit unconsciously, what to think, how to think, and how to respond to situations. At this level, the out-of-awareness assumptions about the environment, human nature, and activities are stored to be referred to as the need arises. This description of the deep structure agrees with Pacanowsky and O'Donnel-Trujillo's (1982) definition of culture as a body of knowledge that is used to explain and make sense of new experiences. Assumptions are unconscious underpinnings, that is, the implicit, abstract axioms that determine the more explicit system of meaning. Basic assumptions stored up in the deep structure are so taken for granted that people are reluctant to examine them, thus making change difficult. Schein (1968) attributed this reluctance to the fact that "reexamination of basic assumptions temporarily destabilizes our cog-

nitive and interpersonal world, releasing large quantities of basic anxiety" (p. 22). To avoid dissonance that may arise from incongruities between a group's basic assumptions and reality, therefore, members tend to deny and distort reality to suite their assumptions (Schein, 1968, p. 22).

THE INDIVIDUAL'S CULTURE

This is the sum total of the individual's initial culture of socialization. Researchers agree that cross-cultural contacts pose special problems for the individuals involved (Bochner, 1982; Church, 1982; Westwood & Barker, 1990).

▶ Dealing With Initial Contact With a Host Environment

For the persons proceeding to an unfamiliar culture, mundane, everyday interpersonal encounters with members of the host society, e.g., in the streets and in shops, factories, and bars are often a major source of stress due to the person not knowing the rules and conventions that apply to these episodes in the receiving culture.

Bochner, 1982, p. 159

Bochner (1982) lends support to the long-held notion that awareness of the dynamics within the environment of socialization makes adaptation easier for the newcomer. However, to properly articulate a position on the impact of environmental factors on cross-cultural or interorganizational transition, it is necessary to examine the relevant literature as it relates to the cross-cultural experiences of the organizational newcomer from the intercultural and organizational communication perspectives. Sojourner studies began in the late 1950s and early 1960s. One of the earliest such studies was by the Committee on Cross-Cultural Education of the Social Sciences Research Council in the early 1950s (Gudykunst, 1977). Gudykunst credited this committee with creating a positive research situation that yielded several monographs, out of which came many studies on student sojourners (Beals & Humphrey, 1957; Bennet, Passin, & McKnight, 1958; Lambert & Bressler, 1956; Morris, 1960). Since this beginning, sojourner research has examined several facets of the experience, such as personal characteristics of the sojourner (Cleveland, Mangone, & Adams, 1960; Mottram, 1963). Other researchers (Adler, 1991; Du Bois, 1956; Oberg, 1960) chose to examine the stages that sojourners go through during the adjustment period in a host culture. Oberg (1960), who is credited with the introduction of the term *culture shock,* identified four stages of sojourner adjustment. The first period, the honeymoon stage, covers the first 6 months of the sojourn. According to Oberg, this period is characterized by fascination with everything in the host culture. The second stage is characterized by hostility toward the host culture and increased identification with fellow sojourners. Increased knowledge of the host language and more fluidity in relationships with host nationals characterize the third stage. In the fourth and final stage, the newcomer either settles into the new culture and continues the adjustment process or begins the exit process. Other researchers examined the role of communication in the adaptation process (Abe & Wiseman, 1983; Gudykunst & Hammer, 1984; Kim, 1976, 1977, 1978). Research on the adaptation of international students did not really take off until the late 1950s and early 1960s. Early studies in this area include Baylin and Kelman (1962), Davis, Hanson, and Burner (1961), Deutsh and Won (1963), Morris (1960), Schild (1962), and Veroff (1963). Researchers (Coelho, 1958; Gullahorn & Gullahorn, 1963; Lysgaard, 1955) examined student adjustment by extending Oberg's (1960) *culture shock* hypothesis to student sojourners. Lysgaard (1955) studied 200 Norwegian Fulbright winners visiting the United States for periods of 0 to 6 months, 6 to 18 months, and more than 18

months. He discovered that the students adjusted better during the first and third periods than during the second stage. Despite the weaknesses of the U-curve hypothesis, it has led to further research (Becker, 1968; Coelho, 1958; Spaulding, Flack, Tate, Mahon, & Marshall, 1976). Pruitt (1977) notes that the paucity of research on foreign students in the mid 1960s was compensated for by renewed interest in the subject since the late 1960s (Becker, 1968; Brislin & Penderson, 1976; Coelho, 1972; Eide, 1970; Golden, 1973). In particular, Pruitt (1976, 1977) found that prior knowledge about the host culture has an impact on adjustment. Others found that adjustment is positively correlated with satisfactory academic achievement (Rising & Capp, 1968; Sharma, 1971). Sofola (1967) found that Nigerian students in the United States showed slightly more negative attitudes toward the United States in the middle of their stay than at the beginning.

Of particular interest to this discussion is what happens to organizational outsiders when they first establish contact with the host environment. Researchers agree that organizational newcomers frequently encounter culture shock (Church, 1982; Westwood & Barker, 1990) and many other problems that arise during the transition from one environment to the other. Some of the problems encountered by African students on entry into the United States probably apply to newcomers in any organization (Pruitt, 1977). Pruitt lists communication, discrimination, homesickness, loneliness, depression, irritability, and tiredness as some of the key problems that confront newcomers.

As outsiders in an environment different from their culture of socialization, organizational newcomers have to cope with the same problems common to every other member of the cultural environment. However, they must also deal with the additional problems that arise from being in an unfamiliar environment. For newcomers, therefore, success does not depend entirely on preparedness and inner resources. To a large extent, success is also determined by their adjustment to new environmental demands and the people with whom they must interact. Westwood and Barker (1990) listed some of the concerns and difficulties encountered by foreign students (and which may well apply to organizational newcomers):

1. Information overload and lack of familiarity with the educational institution (or organizational culture)
2. Faulty decisions and bad judgments arising from initial problems with culture shock and from lack of awareness about the requirements.
3. Negative evaluations of the newcomer by the host society arising from initial mistakes.

These initial impressions, especially among key organizational operatives, can haunt newcomers throughout their tenure in the new environment.

From the foregoing, one may safely conjecture that the environment has far-reaching impact on the performance of its members. It follows that the type of environment can affect the individual's ability to function effectively. One can even stretch this line of thinking further to argue that a negative or hostile environment can hamper an individual's ability to communicate effectively. This, in turn, may lead to entropy (Kuhn, cited in Ruben & Kim, 1975, p. 115) and thus frustrate newcomers' *acculturative motivation* Kim (1976), leading to a decision to quit. Conversely, as Kuhn (cited in Ruben & Kim, 1975, p. 115) argued, an individual in an open system with positive feedback may develop greater differentiation and thus the need to stay on.

▶ The Concepts of Entry, Socialization, Assimilation, and Possible Exit in Organizational and Intercultural Communication

Organizational entry refers to several processes that take place as new members enter organizations (Wanous, 1977). For this cur-

rent discussion on the assimilation of newcomers into the host environment, the word *organization* is used in its broadest sense to include "a group of people working together to achieve a common goal" (Van Fleet, 1991, p. 474). It also includes the host society or environment as a cultural entity. Wanous presented two perspectives on organizational entry: the organizational and the individual's perspectives. He posited that the major difference between the two perspectives "stems from the different goals or objectives pursued by the individuals as opposed to organizations during entry" (p. 601). According to Wanous, the typical organization is primarily concerned with the ability or competence of newcomers to perform satisfactorily. The individual, on the other hand, is concerned with satisfying personal needs through the agency of the organization. An example of this relationship between the organization and the individual is seen in the admission process at most universities and colleges. Like any organizations, universities and colleges admit only students who have the potential to succeed. Students, on the other hand, want to use the opportunities offered by universities to achieve their personal goals.

Wanous (1976) examined the organizational entry process in three stages: prior to entry (the individual is an outsider), shortly after entry (newcomer), and after more experience (insider). Jablin (1985) calls the first stage *anticipatory socialization,* which he suggests has two phases: (a) the process of vocational choice/socialization and (b) the process of organizational choice or entry. Researchers agree that occupational socialization precedes organizational choice and entry, especially for workers in their first full-time job (Jablin, 1987; Wanous, 1977). Organizational entry is the final step in what Crites (1969) calls *the exclusion process,* a process during which the individual constantly narrows the range of organizational choices until a decision is made. In his review of specific topics in organizational entry, Wanous (1977) raised three questions that are relevant to the purpose of this discussion:

1. How do individuals develop preferences and choose new organizations?
2. How accurate and complete is the information that outsiders have prior to actual entry?
3. What is the impact of recruitment activities on an individual's organizational choice and on post-entry attitudes and behavior?

Researchers identify three stages of organizational socialization (Louis, 1980; Wanous, 1977), which are described next.

ANTICIPATORY SOCIALIZATION AND ORGANIZATIONAL CHOICE

Anticipatory organizational socialization is primarily concerned with the ways in which individuals seek and transmit information about jobs, make employment decisions, and develop expectations of what "life" will be like in the organization in which they are considering employment. The impact of pre-entry socialization on post-entry performance will be discussed briefly later. It is, however, necessary to mention that research supports the correlation between realistic anticipatory socialization and satisfactory post-entry socialization and performance on the job (Wanous, 1976, 1977). Louis (1980) defined organizational socialization as "the process by which an individual comes to appreciate the values, abilities, expected behaviors, and social knowledge essential for assuming an organizational role and for participating as an organizational member" (p. 230). Jablin (1987) said that when babies are born, they begin to absorb the values of, first, the immediate family, then friends at school, and finally society at large. He suggests that during this process of growth from childhood to young adulthood, individuals gather several pieces of information that are used in making occupational decisions later in life. Jablin (1985) lists a number of likely sources through which people acquire information during this stage of the socialization process: (a) family mem-

bers, (b) educational institutions, (c) part-time job experiences, (d) peers and friends, and (e) the media. These five sources apply directly to outsiders who are planning to enter any organization. At this stage, outsiders anticipate their experiences in the new culture or organization that they are about to enter. Several studies in this area suggest that individuals often know very little about the organizations they plan to enter and that their expectations are largely unrealistic (Wanous, 1977). The question that needs to be answered at this stage relates to how an individual finally arrives at a choice in the face of many alternatives. From Wanous's (1977) study, some researchers (Swinth, 1976) view the organizational choice process as one of "unprogrammed decision making." This unprogrammed decision-making process, according to Wanous (1977), "views individuals as using only a few criteria to screen alternatives and make an implicit choice" (p. 604). Of interest to this discussion is the application of expectancy theory (Wanous, 1977) and what Crites (1969) describes as an exclusion process. The exclusion process, as already indicated, presupposes the fact that an individual starts out having many choices that are consistently reduced until the final choice is made.

Lawler's study (cited in Wanous, 1977) indicated,

> According to expectancy theory, two psychological considerations determine the attractiveness of an organization: (a) expectations about the organization and (b) the valence, or desirability, of each characteristic for each person . . . these two components are multiplied for each characteristic considered, and the products are then summed for all characteristics. (p. 608)

Wanous posited that the particular organization that emerges with the highest rating stands a good chance of being chosen. Jablin (1987) suggested two basic sources of information for organizational outsiders: (a) organizational literature and (b) interpersonal interactions with other applicants, organizational interviewers, current employees, and the like (p. 685). Louis (1980) raised three pertinent questions regarding pre-entry expectations relevant to this study:

1. How do newcomers cope with unrealistic unmet expectations?
2. How do newcomers cope with early job (or school) experiences?
3. How do they come to understand, interpret, and respond in and to an unfamiliar organizational setting?

These questions lead to the second stage in the organizational entry process.

THE ENCOUNTER STAGE AND TRANSITION SHOCK

The encounter or "breaking-in" period of organizational assimilation is often a traumatic one for the new employee. During this phase . . . the new employee's cognitive scripts and schemas must be redefined and recalibrated and attributional models created to explain why people behave and think as they do in the new work environment.

Jablin, 1982, p. 266

During this stage, newcomers' anticipations are tested against the reality of their new cultural or organizational experience. Differences between anticipations and experiences (including unmet expectations) become apparent and contribute to transition or reality shock. Transition shock is a state of loss and disorientation precipitated by a change in one's familiar environment that requires adjustment (Bennett, 1977). Hughes (1958, cited in Louis, 1980) described the experiences of newcomers to an organization as *reality shock*. Louis (1980) stated,

Reality shock is the phrase . . . used to characterize what newcomers often experience in entering unfamiliar organizational settings. Time

and space become problematic at the moment of entry. At that particular time, all surroundings, that is, the entire organizationally based physical and social world are changed. There is no gradual exposure and no real way to confront the situation a little at a time. Rather the newcomer's senses are inundated with many unfamiliar cues. It may not be clear to the newcomer just what constitutes a cue, let alone what the cues refer to, which cues require response, or how to select responses to them. Time and space remain problematic until . . . the newcomer is able to construct maps of time and space specific to the new setting. (p. 230)

Interorganizational transfers may have the same effect on transferees that cross-cultural entry has on newcomers. Hughes's description of this experience agrees with those of other researchers (Adler, 1991; Bennett, 1977; Lysgaard, 1955; Oberg, 1960). Kahn et al. (1964, cited in Berlew & Hall, 1966) suggested that when new managers first enter the organization, the portion of their life-space corresponding to the organization is blank. According to Kahn and his colleagues, the manager will

feel a strong need to define this area and develop constructs relating himself [sic] to it. As a new member, he is standing at the boundary of the organization, a very stressful location, and he is motivated to reduce this stress by becoming incorporated into the "interior" of the company. (cited in Berlew & Hall, 1966, p. 210)

At this stage of the entry experience, many newcomers to the organization or culture decide whether to continue the acculturation process or quit (Dodd, 1991, p. 307). Dodd suggests that people at this "everything is awful" stage of entry respond to the psychological stress in one of four ways:

Fight: The tendency to look down on the culture of the host country and act ethnocentrically

Flight: The urge to leave for home shortly after arrival to the host culture

Filter: The tendency to deny reality; newcomers may deny any differences between their home culture and the host culture, glorify their culture by extolling only the good things, or "go native"

Flex: The decision to understand and adapt to the foreign ways of the host culture

Besides the very stressful experience of culture shock, Zaharna (1989, p. 502) argued that a degree of self-shock is an integral part of the overall transition package. This is that aspect of psychological confusion that arises during culture contact and affects the individual's relationship with him- or herself. Zaharna said, "self-shock is the intrusion of new and, sometimes, conflicting self-identities that the individual encounters when he or she encounters a culturally different Other" (p. 511). In other words, both the individual's cognitive maps and self-identity are affected during organizational entry.

ORGANIZATIONAL ADJUSTMENT AND ASSIMILATION

If newcomers resist the urge to become a "voluntary turnover" (Louis, 1980) or to engage in flight (Dodd, 1991, p. 307), both of which speak of premature exit, they begin the adjustment process within the culture or organization. This process involves learning the functionally defined elements of the organization (the mission, values, strategy, artifacts, and the basic assumptions) as well as the network of shared symbols of meaning that members use to make sense of their environment. Geertz (1973, cited in Griffin, 1991) writes, "man [sic] is an animal suspended in webs of significance that he himself has spun" (p. 254). Geertz pictures culture as those webs. To travel across the strands toward the center of the web, an outsider must discover

the main strands that support the web (Figure 14.1). Culture, according to Griffin (1991), is "shared meaning, shared understanding, shared sense making" (p. 254). By direct application, the culture in an organization can be likened to a web, the center of which holds the future of the outsider or new member within the organization. The strands of this cultural web include the surface structure and the deep structure (Deetz & Kersten, 1983, p. 157) of the organization or environment. Jablin (1987) defines organizational assimilation as the process by which an individual becomes integrated into the reality of the host culture or culture of the organization; this is a process by which organizational members become a part of, and are absorbed into, the culture of an organization (Jablin, 1982, p. 256). It is the transition from outsider to newcomer to insider (Wanous, 1976). Jablin sees two reciprocal dimensions to the assimilation process: (a) deliberate and unintentional efforts by the organization to socialize employees (Van Maanen, 1975) and (b) workers' attempts to individualize or modify their roles and organizational environment to better satisfy their needs, ideas, and values (see Schein, 1968). The process of adjustment to a new environment poses for newcomers (students, cross-cultural managers, or immigrants) the fundamental alternatives of adapting to meet environmental requirements or manipulating the environment to meet individual needs (Nicholson, 1984). Louis (1980) notes that it is after the entry stage that newcomers really begin to "learn the ropes" and experience a series of surprises that enhance the development of cognitive maps suitable for sense making and survival in the new environment. Using the cognitive complexity-simplicity template, it is possible to have two types of newcomers to the new environment: the *sideliners* and the *active players*. The sideliners are those newcomers whose main motivation is to get by and meet their basic life needs. They are satisfied with basic membership privileges and accept the status quo as satisfactory, if not ideal. Sideliners are overwhelmed by any effort to draw them into the active life of the new environment and would rather maintain non-challenging relationships or networks outside the new environment. The social life of this type of newcomer is often limited to pre-entry friendships and networks. These individuals are nativistic (Chang, 1972, p. 15) in their approach to acculturation into the new environment and tend to resist any change in the status quo. At the other end of the spectrum are newcomers who want to be active players in the new environment. These people belong to one of Chang's remaining acculturation types: the bicultural movement. In this process, newcomers combine the cultural elements of their first culture of socialization with the culture of the new environment to form a new cultural whole. In *cultural assimilation,* individuals literally abandon the old culture for the new. Newcomers who are active players readily immerse themselves in existing networks and, through these, tap into the basic assumptions, norms, and sense-making mechanisms in the new environment. Such individuals find it a lot easier to adapt effectively to the realities of the new environment.

ORGANIZATIONAL EXIT AND THE QUALITY OF ORGANIZATIONAL INFORMATION AVAILABLE TO OUTSIDERS

Organizational entry researchers agree that the expectations outsiders have of organizations are largely unrealistic and inflated. Others found that individuals know very little about new organizations they join until they are inside them (Wanous, 1976). Jablin (1987) suggested two basic sources of information for organizational outsiders: (a) organizational literature and (b) interpersonal interactions with other applicants, organizational interviewers, current employees, and the like (p. 685). He further posited three approaches adopted by researchers in examining the above sources:

1. The relative effectiveness of various information sources in recruiting/attracting newcomers
2. The realism or accuracy of job/organizational expectations that result from contacts with each source
3. The role of employment interviews as a recruiting and selection device

To better understand how pre-entry expectations of organizational newcomers affect their performance within the organization, it is necessary to examine the realism and accuracy of information given to outsiders by organizational agents and recruiters. The kind of organizational information given to outsiders and the method of passing on the information are blamed for the unrealistic expectations of outsiders (Wanous, 1977). Part of the problem is that, to be legitimized by their environments, organizations present a public relations image, a view of the organization that tells the world everything is OK for the organization; this image is projected to their "important others." In an effort to make their organization look good, recruiters fail to distinguish between two levels of outsiders: those without any interest in becoming insiders and those who are interested. The resultant effect of this is that an inflated image of the organization is presented to job seekers or those outsiders who are genuinely interested in becoming insiders (Okoli, 1991). However, as Jablin (1987) has found, newcomers recruited informally through employee referrals tend to stay with the organization longer than those recruited through formal means. Also, certain aspects of organizational life are better experienced than explained. How would the recruiter explain issues such as organizational culture, informal networks, and all the other nuances that constitute life within the organization to an outsider? Some recruiters may themselves be in need of such information. Researchers agree that voluntary turnover among newcomers is attributable to "unrealistic or inflated expectations that individuals bring as they enter organizations" (Louis,

1980, p. 227). Citing other researchers, Louis attributed early turnover to the differences between newcomers' expectations and early job experiences.

► Conclusion

This chapter attempted to highlight and examine the impact of cultural dynamics within the environment on acculturation. Central to this effort was the impact of the organizational environment on the decision of newcomers either to assimilate into the organization or to exit prematurely. It became obvious that outsiders seeking entry into an organization want to use the organization to meet their own needs. On its part, the organization must hire individuals it considers most suited to the attainment of its needs. Researchers agree that the initial contact between these two levels of need is usually very stressful, owing to unrealistic expectations among outsiders and the inability of organizational agents to paint a more realistic picture of the organization at job interviews. Efforts are currently being made by both researchers and organizations to bring the expectations of outsiders in line with organizational reality. Some researchers have suggested various ways to better prepare people for "the unpleasant aspects of the new environment" (Wanous, 1977, pp. 612-615). Wanous and others also proposed realistic job previews as one alternative. In previews, candidates for jobs are presented with a realistic picture of the organization. It is generally believed that this will lower outsiders' expectations, making them more realistic and attainable. Ilgen (as cited in Louis, 1980, p. 227) hypothesized that met expectations lead to satisfaction, and satisfaction is inversely related to turnover. Wanous (1976) also suggested the need to reexamine the dynamics of organizational (and cross-cultural) entry, socialization, and assimilation (or exit) from the perspective of the individual. His suggestion echoes the position of this chapter. The author

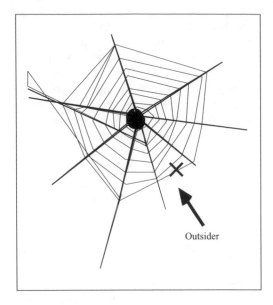

Figure 14.1. Cultural Web and the Outsider.

sees the point of entry into another culture or organization as a clash of cultures. From the discussion so far, it appears that at the point of entry into the organization or new environment (represented by the letter X in Figure 14.1), the individual's initial culture of socialization and the culture of the new environment join in mortal combat for supremacy. From the chapter, it also seems safe to conclude that in this contest between cultures, the individual involved in the transition makes the decision as to which of the two cultures wins. If the pull factors within the new culture or organization overwhelm the homebound, nativistic factors, the individual may decide to assimilate. If, on the other hand, the outward-bound pull factors prove stronger, premature exit or turnover occurs.

► References

Abe, H., & Wiseman, R. A. (1983). A cross-cultural confirmation of the dimensions of intercultural effectiveness. *International Journal of Intercultural Relations, 7,* 53-67.

Adler, P. S. (1991). The transitional experience: An alternative view of culture shock. *Journal of Humanistic Psychology, 15,* 13-23.

Baylin, L., & Kelman, H. C. (1962). The effects of a year's experience in America on the self-image of Scandinavians: A preliminary analysis of reactions to a new environment. *Journal of Social Issues, 18,* 30-40.

Beals, R. L., & Humphrey, N. D. (1957). *No frontier to learning: The Mexican students in the United States.* Minneapolis: University of Minnesota.

Becker, T. (1968). Patterns of attitudinal changes among foreign students. *American Journal of Sociology, 73,* 431-442.

Bennet, J., Passin, H., & McKnight, R. K. (1958). *In search of identity: The Japanese overseas scholar in America and Japan.* Minneapolis: University of Minnesota.

Bennett, J. (1977). Transition shock: Putting culture shock in perspective. In N. C. Jain (Ed.), *International intercultural communication annual* (Vol. 4, pp. 45-52). Falls Church, VA: Speech Communication Association.

Berlew, D. E., & Hall, D. T. (1966). The socialization of managers: Effects of expectations on performance. *Administrative Science Quarterly, 11,* 207-233.

Berry, J. W. (1990). Psychology of acculturation: Understanding individuals moving between cultures. In R. W. Brislin (Ed.). *Applied cross-cultural psychology.* Newbury Park, CA: Sage.

Berry, J. W., Kim, U., & Boski, P. (1988). Psychological acculturation of immigrants. In Y. Y. Kim & W. Gudykunst (Eds.), *Cross-cultural adaptation: Current approaches.* Newbury Park, CA: Sage.

Bochner, S. (1982). *Cultures in contact: Studies in cross-cultural interaction.* New York: Pergamon.

Bormann, E. (1983). Symbolic convergence: Organizational communication and culture. In L. L. Putnam & M. E. Pacanowsky (Eds.), *Communication and organization: An interpretive approach.* Beverly Hills, CA: Sage.

Brislin, R., & Penderson, P. (1976). *Cross-cultural orientation programs.* New York: Gardner.

Chang, W. H. (1972). *Communication and acculturation: A case study of Korean ethnic group in Los Angeles.* Unpublished doctoral dissertation, Graduate College, University of Iowa, Iowa City.

Church, A. (1982). Sojourner adjustment. *Psychological Bulletin, 91,* 540-575.

Cleveland, H., Mangone, G. J., & Adams, T. G. (1960). *The overseas Americans.* New York: McGraw-Hill.

Coelho, G. V. (1958). *Changing images of America: A study of Indian students' perceptions.* Glencoe, IL: Free Press.

Coelho, V. A. (1972). *Students from India in the United States: An exploratory study of some cultural and religious attitudes.* Doctoral dissertation, Loyola University of Chicago.

Crites, J. O. (1969). *Vocational psychology.* New York: McGraw-Hill.

Cummings, T. G., & Huse, E. (1989). *Organization development and change* (4th ed.). St. Paul, MN: West Publishing.

Davis, J. M., Hanson, R. G., & Burner, D. R. (1961). *Institute of international education survey of the African student: His achievements and problems.* New York: LSE.

Deetz, S. A., & Kersten, A. (1983). Critical models in interpretive research. In L. L. Putnam & M. E. Pacanowsky (Eds.), *Communication and organizations: An interpretive approach.* Beverly Hills, CA: Sage.

Deutsh, S. E., & Won, G.Y.M. (1963). Some factors in the adjustment of foreign nationals in the U.S. *Journal of Social Issues, 19,* 115-129.

Dodd, C. H. (1991). *Dynamics of intercultural communication.* Dubuque, IA: William C. Brown.

Du Bois, C. A. (1956). *Foreign students and higher education in the United States.* Washington, DC: American Council on Education.

Eide, I. (1970). *Students as links between cultures: A cross-cultural survey based on UNESCO studies.* Oslo, Norway: Universitetsforlaget.

Golden, J. S. (1973). Student adjustment abroad: A psychiatrist's view. *International Education and Cultural Exchange, 8*(4), 28-36.

Griffin, E. (1991). *A first look at communication theory.* New York: McGraw-Hill.

Grove, C. L., & Torbiorn, I. (1985). A new conceptualization of intercultural adjustment and goals of training. *International Journal of Intercultural Relations, 9,* 205-233.

Gudykunst, W. (1977). Intercultural contact and attitude change. In N. C. Jain (Ed.), *International and intercultural communication annual* (Vol. 4). Falls Church, VA: Speech Communication Association.

Gudykunst, W. (1983). Toward a typology of stranger-host relationships. *International Journal of Intercultural Relations, 7,* 401-413.

Gudykunst, W., & Kim, Y. Y. (1992). *Communicating with strangers: An approach to intercultural communication.* New York: McGraw-Hill.

Gudykunst, W. B., & Hammer, M. R. (1984). Dimensions of intercultural effectiveness: Cultural specific or cultural general? *International Journal of Intercultural Relations, 8,* 1-10.

Gullahorn, J. T., & Gullahorn, J. E. (1963). Extension of the u-curve hypothesis. *Journal of Social Issue, 19,* 33-47.

Hall, E. T. (1977). *Beyond culture.* Garden City, NY: Anchor, Doubleday.

Hasselgrave, D. J. (1978). *Communicating Christ cross-culturally.* Grand Rapids, MI: Zondervan.

Herkovits, M. (1948). *Man and his works.* New York: Knopf.

Herkovits, M. (1955). *Cultural anthropology.* New York: Knopf.

Jablin, F. M. (1982). Organizational communication: An assimilation approach. In M. E. Roloff & C. R. Berger (Eds.), *Social cognition and communication.* Beverly Hills, CA: Sage.

Jablin, F. M. (1985). An exploratory study of vocational organizational communication socialization. *Southern Speech Communication Journal, 50,* 261-282.

Jablin, F. M. (1987). Organizational entry, assimilation, and exit. In F. M. Jablin, L. L. Putnam, K. H. Roberts, & L. W. Porter (Eds.), *Handbook of organizational communication.* Newbury Park, CA: Sage.

Kim, H. J. (1991). Influence of language and similarity on initial intercultural attraction. In S. Ting-Toomey & F. Korzenny (Eds.), *Cross-cul-*
tural interpersonal communication. Newbury Park, CA: Sage.

Kim, Y. Y. (1976). *Communication patterns of foreign immigrants in the process of acculturation: A survey among Korean population in Chicago.* Unpublished doctoral dissertation, Northwestern University, Evanston, IL.

Kim, Y. Y. (1977). Inter-ethnic and intra-ethnic communication: A study of Korean immigrants in Chicago. In N. Jain (Ed.), *International and intercultural communication annual* (Vol. 4, pp. 55-68). Annandale, VA: Speech Communication Association.

Kim, Y. Y. (1978). A communication approach to acculturation process: Korean immigrants in Chicago. *International Journal of Intercultural Relations, 2,* 197-224.

Kuhn, A. (1975). Social organizations. In B. D. Ruben & J. Y. Kim (Eds.), *General systems theory and human communication.* Rochelle Park, NJ: Hayden.

Lambert, R. D., & Bressler, M. (1956). *Indian students on an American campus.* Minneapolis: University of Minnesota Press.

Lewin, K. (1936). *Principles of topological psychology.* New York: McGraw-Hill.

Louis, M. R. (1980). Surprise and sensemaking: What newcomers experience in entering unfamiliar organizational setting. *Administrative Science Quarterly, 25,* 226-251.

Lysgaard, S. (1955). Adjustment in a foreign society: Norwegian Fulbright grantees visiting the United States. *International Social Science Bulletin, 7,* 45-51.

Morris, R. T. (1960). *The two way mirror: National status in foreign student's adjustment.* Minneapolis: University of Minnesota Press.

Mottram, R. (1963). *The selection of personnel for international service.* New York: World Federation for Mental Health.

Nicholson, N. (1984). A theory of work role transition. *Administrative Science Quarterly, 29*(21), 172-191.

Oberg, K. (1960). Culture shock: Adjustment to new cultural environment. *Practical Anthropology, 7,* 177-182.

Okoli, E. (1991, May). *Organizational entry and the information-seeking needs of the outsider.*

Paper presented at the 21st annual communications conference, Howard University, Washington, DC.

Pacanowsky, M. E., & O'Donnell-Trujillo, N. (1982). Communication and organizational cultures. *Western Journal of Speech Communication Monographs, 46,* 115-130.

Pandey, J. (1992). The environment, culture, and behavior. In W. B. Gudykunst & Y. Y. Kim (Eds.), *Readings on communicating with strangers.* Newbury Park, CA: Sage.

Pruitt, F. J. (1976). *The adaptation of African students to the United States.* Paris: International Institute for Educational Planning, UNESCO.

Pruitt, F. J. (1977). *The adaptation of African students to American education.* Washington, DC: U.S. Department of State, Bureau of African Affairs.

Rising, M. N., & Capp, B. M. (1968). *Adjustment experiences of non-immigrant foreign students at the University of Rochester.* Rochester, NY: University of Rochester.

Ruben, B. D., & Kim, J. M. (Eds.). (1975). *General systems theory and human communication.* Rockel Park, NJ: Hayden.

Samovar, L. A., & Porter, R. E. (1991). *Communication between cultures.* Belmont, CA: Wadsworth.

Schein, E. H. (1968). Organizational socialization and the profession of management. *Industrial Management Review, 9,* 1-16.

Schild, E. O. (1962). The foreign student as a stranger learning the norms of the host culture. *Journal of Social Issues, 1,* 41-54.

Sharma, J. A. (1971). *A study to identify and analyze adjustment problems experienced by foreign non-European graduate students enrolled in selected universities in the states of Carolina.* Unpublished doctoral dissertation, University of North Carolina at Greensboro.

Sofola, J. A. (1967). *American processed Nigerians: A study of the adjustment and attitudes of the Nigerian students in the United States of America.* Unpublished doctoral dissertation, American University, Washington, DC.

Spaulding, S., Flack, J. M., Tate, S., Mahon, P., & Marshall, C. (1976). *The world's students in the United States: A review and evaluation of research on foreign students.* New York: Praeger.

Swinth, R. L. (1976). A decision-process model for predicting job preferences. *Journal of Applied Psychology, 61,* 242-245.

Taft, R. (1988). The psychological adaptation of Soviet immigrants in Australia. In Y. Y. Kim & W. Gudykunst (Eds.), *Cross-cultural adaptation: Current approaches.* Newbury Park, CA: Sage.

Van Fleet, D. D. (1991). *Behavior in organizations.* Dallas, TX: Houghton Mifflin.

Van Maanen, J. (1975). Breaking in: Socialization to work. In R. Dubin (Ed.), *Handbook of work, organization, & society,* (pp. 67-120). Chicago: Rand McNally.

Veroff, J. (1963). African students in the United States. *Journal of Social Issues, 19,* 48-60.

Wanous, J. P. (1976). Organizational entry: From naive expectations to realistic beliefs. *Journal of Applied Psychology, 61*(1), 22-29.

Wanous, J. P. (1977). Organizational entry: Newcomers moving from outside to inside. *Psychological Bulletin, 84*(4), 601-618.

Westwood, M. J., & Barker, M. (1990). Academic achievement and social adaptation among international students: A comparison group study of the peer-pairing program. *International Journal of Intercultural Relations, 14,* 251-263.

Zaharna, R. S. (1989). Self-shock: The double-binding challenge of identity. *International Journal of Intercultural Communication, 13,* 501-525.

Research and Training in Cross-Cultural Readjustment

Recommendations for Advancements

CHUKA ONWUMECHILI
JOY OKEREKE-ARUNGWA

About a decade ago, several scholars lamented the lack of literature in the field of intercultural readjustment, which is the process of readjusting to one's home culture after an extended sojourn abroad (Martin, 1984; Sussman, 1986). Undoubtedly, few studies have focused on cultural readjustment when compared to the plethora of studies that investigate adjustment to foreign cultures. Fortunately, the field of cultural readjustment has grown recently, both in quantity and quality. For example, the quality of studies has improved from those that merely describe problems encountered by returning sojourners to those that now explain why such problems are encountered.

However, various issues still need to be adequately addressed, despite this recent good news. For example, research on more diverse populations and improvements in training strategies still urgently need to be addressed. Improved research and training strategies are among the critical issues in the forefront of transculturalism. Transcultural reality presumes cultural globalism, particularly in this era in which broadcast media have popularized diverse cultural images. Such popularizations have not eased the adjustment problems that travelers encounter. For example, travelers who re-enter their own culture after a sojourn in a foreign place encounter adjustment problems that are of great interest to those who conceptualize transculturalism. After all, the perspective of transculturalism requires that the intersection of cultures during reentry adjustment and the varied experiences of the intersecting cultures should be well understood. That is the task of research and training.

These issues, as well as others that are discussed in this chapter, are critical because incidents of cultural readjustment are more frequent than we often assume. Edmonston (1996) has noted that an increasing number of immigrants eventually return home and thus are faced with issues related to readjustment. Furthermore, cases of intercultural readjustment are complex because returning sojourners do not expect their home culture to have changed, and their home friends do not expect the returnee to have changed. This often presents puzzling and sometimes difficult situations for the returnee.

The purpose of this chapter is to point out avenues for advancing knowledge in the field of intercultural readjustment. Suggestions for advancing knowledge in this field are made in the hope of encouraging better services for those who confront intercultural readjustment. The chapter begins by discussing early research and the current status of the field. The intent is to use those discussions to point the field to new directions.

▶ Early Work in the Field

Most of what we classify as early work in the cultural readjustment field was done before the late 1970s. That period was guided by assumptions proposed in the W-curve hypothesis. Only in the last two decades have research findings begun to reject the early fundamental tenets of the W-curve hypothesis.

Interest in intercultural communication began shortly after the World War II as a way to prepare people for participation in postwar government-exchange programs. Most participants in the early research studies were exchange students and Peace Corps volunteers who spent short periods in foreign countries. The early studies focused on identifying factors that help people to adapt to a host foreign culture. Such studies included Bennett (1977) and Brislin (1981). Other studies focused on identifying the process of adjustment in a foreign culture. For instance, Lysgaard's (1955) seven-page article in the *International Social Science Bulletin* on the adjustment process signified a landmark in this era. Lysgaard based his article on interviews conducted with 200 Norwegian students who had received Fulbright travel grants and had stayed in the United States before returning to Norway in 1953.

Lysgaard concluded from his study that the process of adjustment follows a U-curve. He observed a wide experience of the Norwegians and found that they were elated during the early period of their arrival to the United States. This elation stemmed from feelings of excitement and pleasure in meeting new people, who were falling over themselves to satisfy the visitors. A few weeks after, the excitement of welcome began to wear off as the hosts returned to the demands of their daily lives, and the Norwegian sojourners began to encounter the realities of the host culture. This reality exposed cultural differences between the sojourners and the host culture. The bridge of cultural differences is not easily crossed, and the shock it presents is a psychological setback for sojourners. Fortunately, this negative period wears off gradually as sojourners begin to adapt to the values of the host. Thus, the process of adjustment culminates in a sense of comfort and satisfaction for sojourners.

Gullahorn and Gullahorn (1963) later observed that the process of cultural adjustment, as just described, is also experienced by sojourners on return to their homeland. This led to their W-curve hypothesis. Thus, the W-curve hypothesis is an extension of the U-curve hypothesis.

Some of the early works in cultural readjustment help us differentiate it from cultural adjustment, even though scholars such as Landis and Wasilewski (1999) continue to ask whether or not the two experiences are different. This is important because the seminal work by Gullahorn and Gullahorn (1963) on the W-curve did not significantly differentiate one from the other. Instead, the W-curve simply extended the U-curve and thus created the impression that both types of adjustment were similar. But Brislin and Pederson (1976), Sussman (1986), Rogers and Ward (1993), and Martin and Nakayama (1997) have pointed out several important differences. These differences include the following: (a) returnees don't expect re-entry problems; (b) returnees are often unaware that they have changed; (c) returnees have fixed notions about an unchanged home country; (d) family, friends, and colleagues expect an unchanged returnee; and (e) people at home have a general lack of interest in the sojourner's experience.

Regarding the unexpectedness of re-entry problems, prospective sojourners often prepare psychologically for cultural differences that they will encounter in a foreign culture. For instance, Africans who are about to immigrate to the United States often engage in discussions about life in the United States and how different it is from life at home. This prepares the immigrants for cultural adjustment in the United States. However, the process is different when the sojourners prepare to return home. Sojourners are elated about returning to a culture they are "used to." Problems begin when returnees arrive home and suddenly realize unexpectedly that they are, in fact, not used to being home.

This unexpected realization of not being used to home is a function of changes in returnees as a result of life in the foreign country. Returnees are usually unaware of those changes. Gaw (2000) recently measured the symptoms of these changes, which he called *reverse culture shock*. Gaw found that shock existed for all returnees but that the degree differed with the returnee's level of shyness.

Bochner (1973) and Sussman (1986) found that the more successful sojourners are in adapting to a foreign country (thus, undergoing major changes), the more difficult it will be for them to adjust during re-entry into the home country. This is in sharp contrast with adjustment in a foreign country, where sojourners are conscious of their own cultural values as they enter the foreign culture.

The above discussions have touched on the returnee's fixed notion of an unchanged home country. Sojourners, while still in the foreign country, carry in their mind a picture of life at home. That picture is usually created by their own experience prior to leaving home. That picture remains real for them until they re-enter the homeland and discover that it has changed. The ability to cope with such a notion varies with the returnee's level of concern for adjustment (Gaw, 2000). For instance, the ability to cope weakens as adjustment concerns rise.

Sojourning in a foreign country includes awareness that one has to meet strangers and establish a network of new friends. Therefore, the process of adjustment in a foreign country includes attempts to develop such a network. Studies establish the fact that the degree of interaction with members of the host country is associated with the type of adjustment outcome that sojourners achieve (Berry, Kim, & Boski, 1987). Those with more interactions become adjusted or assimilated whereas those with fewer interactions are marginalized or become culturally separated. On the other hand, returnees from a foreign sojourn expect to re-establish old ties with family, friends, and colleagues. Unfortunately, studies find that this is not often successful (Gama & Pederson, 1977; Gaw, 2000; Gullahorn & Gullahorn, 1963). Family, friends, and colleagues expect an unchanged returnee just as the returnee expects an unchanged home. In actuality, returnees have often changed, and this creates a gulf between them and family, friends, and colleagues.

To make matters worse, people at home have little interest in listening to sojourners' experience abroad. Some interest is shown early during re-entry, but it dies down as colleagues, friends, and family begin to see the returnee as one of them. Returnees' urge to share their experience leads to frustrations. Again, this is different from the experience of sojourners in a foreign country. Sojourners are continually seen as symbols of a foreign culture, and thus, their knowledge of the foreign culture is continually sought during relationships with hosts. This brings its own frustrations, but such frustrations are different from those experienced by returnees back in their homeland.

Most of the early studies went beyond differentiating cultural adjustment from cultural readjustment. Some focused on providing in-depth studies of problems encountered by returnees from study abroad. For instance, both Pearson (1964) and Stolley (1965) found that difficulties included role and value conflicts. Although these scholars studied American Peace Corps volunteers on their return to the United States, the issue of role or value conflict also affects non-U.S. students on return to their homelands (Isogai, Hayashi, & Uno, 1999; Yashiro, 1995). Researchers found, for example, that students who had studied in the United States adopted a more liberal position on several social issues, and this was in conflict with expectations in their homelands. In addition, some students also assumed values regarding equality of the sexes and freedom of speech. Unfortunately, these values are not universally appreciated. Thus, these students largely experienced frustration on return to their homeland.

Other issues, such as changes in attitude (Pruitt, 1978) and general frustration (Gama & Pederson, 1977), could also be classified as changes in the sojourner. Changes in financial status (Howard, 1980), structural difficulties (Murray, 1973), objective changes in home environment (Opubor, 1974), and home cultural characteristics (Hatzichristou & Hopf, 1995) have also been identified as issues for returnees.

Opubor (1974), Pruitt (1978), Sussman (1986), Hatzichristou and Hopf (1995), and Isogai et al. (1999) identified changes in sojourners as critical in their readjustment to the homeland. Pruitt's study of 26 African students in the United States found that many experienced attitude changes, as shown by a decline in religious observance and adoption of more liberal ideas. Furthermore, many students were not conscious of these value changes. The combination of such changes and the individual's lack of consciousness about them makes readjustment difficult. In fact, Opubor concludes that the combination of changes in the returning person and in the home environment is the most important factor in re-entry adjustment.

Change in the financial status of returnees was widely observed among corporate employees who had returned from corporate-sponsored training abroad. The employees' stay abroad is often supported by their organization. However, the employees lose those benefits on their return home, marking an abrupt change in lifestyle that becomes a variable in readjustment.

Structural difficulties focus on facilities that directly affect the returnee's ability to function as a professional worker. Facilities at home may contrast sharply with the quality of facilities available abroad. Thus, a large discrepancy in these facilities triggers structural readjustment problems.

Opubor (1974) and Sussman (1986) identify changes in the home culture (while the returnee was away) as another source of adjustment problems. This variable has not been clearly identified in the re-entry literature. However, recognizing that changes take place in the home culture reminds us that cultures are dynamic and not static. Unfortunately, there is little to go on here because the concept has been largely unoperationalized. Instead, the literature merely reminds us that changes in the home culture while sojourners are away help alienate them on their return. Sussman (1986), however, suggests that such changes can be found in the political, economic, social, or corporate cultural spheres.

Isogai et al. (1999) discussed the last category, home cultural characteristics. Their article identified several studies of returning Japanese students and noted that Japanese at home had very little tolerance for returnees who exhibited values or behaviors outside Japanese norms. Thus, such returnees were under immense pressure to conform to the norms of a homogenous Japanese society.

Asuncion-Lande (1976), Martin (1984), and Martin and Nakayama (1997) have also studied various types of difficulties experienced by returnees, including those noted above. Asuncion-Lande suggests six areas in which such difficulties are often expressed: academic, professional, social, cultural, linguistic, and political.

A summation of the early work in the area of cultural readjustment is captured in this quote from Brislin and Pederson (1976):

> The readjustment back home is likely to be even more difficult than going abroad in the first place, all the more since this adjustment is frequently unexpected. Not only has the trainee (returnee) changed, but the back home culture has likewise changed, making it doubly difficult to readjust. (p. 16)

▶ Current Status of the Field

By 1983, Austin identified as many as 350 works in the field of cultural readjustment. Most of these works were descriptive and nonempirical. Although the number was surprisingly large at that time, there was general agreement that far more literature and training information were needed in the field (Martin, 1984; Sussman, 1986). Much more important, empirical literature was needed as well as studies designed to integrate the diverse opinions and findings from the previous era. The field responded to these needs by moving forward on four fronts: (a) testing the W-curve, which had formed the core assumptions on which earlier readjustment studies were based; (b) launching much more in-depth work on critical variables in the readjustment field; (c) expanding the types of research design used in the field; and (d) ex-

panding the literature on training. We will discuss each of these fronts below.

By the late 1970s, scholars had begun to conduct a few empirical studies. Very few of these studies produced findings to support the W-curve hypothesis, which had been assumed to provide an accurate description of the process of readjustment. Klineberg and Hull (1979), Adler (1981), and Brislin (1981) were unable to find support for the W-curve in their research investigations. Only in a few cases did researchers find support for the W-curve. Kealey's 1989 study was one that found partial support for a linear process of adaptation like that proposed in the W-curve. Kealey found that 10% of his study participants followed the undulating and linear process for cultural adaptation, whereas the majority of participants showed very little change in satisfaction throughout the adjustment period.

It is also important to note that both the U-curve and the W-curve, which had earlier typified cultural adjustment and readjustment processes, respectively, are no longer considered accurate descriptions of adjustment processes. In their places are new concepts that propose multiple outcomes for both sojourners and returning sojourners. Berry et al. (1987) proposed a model that describes outcomes such as marginalization, integration, separation, and assimilation in cultural adjustment in a foreign country. In the readjustment field, Adler (1981) has proposed outcomes that lead to a proactive, resocialized, alienated, or rebellious returnee. White (1980) also proposed alternative outcomes that lead to reassimilators, adjusters, or internationals.

Nancy Adler conducted two major studies in 1976 and 1981 that helped her make conclusions about readjustment outcomes. In 1976, she studied 35 returning Peace Corps volunteers, and in 1981, she published a study of about 200 workers who were returning from a sojourn in Canada. She found that some of the returnees were proactive. They did not simply sit back in the face of frustrations they encountered on their return. Instead, these returnees took matters into their own hands by seeking various ways of making their return satisfactory. Others, who were unable to resocialize, either continued to feel alienated or simply rebelled against the cultural system.

On the second front, most criticisms of earlier work centered on the lack of empirical studies in the readjustment field. Most earlier studies focused on describing the process of readjustment as well as the problems encountered by the returnees. The effect of those criticisms has been an increasing number of empirical studies that test various variables in the field. The aftermath is that there is a better understanding of the field.

Church (1982), Martin (1984), and Uehara (1986) have provided leadership in this area by providing a comprehensive list of variables assumed to affect a returnee's ability to adjust to the home culture. Uehara's list includes the following: age, length of sojourn, value change, desire to return home, amount of information about the home country, level of satisfaction in foreign country and at home, past experience of travel abroad, motivation of foreign sojourn, and personal character (p. 418).

Uehara (1986) tested some of the variables in a study of 58 overseas sojourners whom he compared to 74 domestic travelers. The overseas sojourners were found to have more severe adjustment problems on their return. The major predictor of adjustment problems in that study was the extent of value change in the sojourner.

Adler (1981) has also investigated "desire to return home" as a predictor of readjustment problems. She found that returnees who had high or low desire to return home experienced more adjustment problems than those who had only a moderate desire to return home. At first reading, it is surprising that those with high desire to return home will have adjustment problems. However, this can be explained by noting that a high desire to return home may lead to the sojourner expecting that home is unchanged. In addition, sojourners may not be aware that they have also changed. On return, the reality sets in, and returned sojourners become disappointed.

Many studies have investigated the effects of age on readjustment. Most of them find that adults are quicker to adjust than children (Enloe & Lewin, 1987; Hatzichristou & Hopf, 1995). This is quite different from adjustment to a foreign culture, where children are better adjusters than adults. Enloe and Lewin (1987), for example, found that children had more difficulties in readjustment than did their parents. Enloe and Lewin's study focused on 21 families (including 40 children) who returned to Japan after an overseas sojourn.

There is also evidence to support Uehara's (1986) suggestion that the amount of information about the home country affects readjustment of returnees. Studies have shown that older sojourners in a foreign country are often marginalized, that is, they often withdraw into a network of fellow nationals residing in a foreign country rather than developing a network of host country friends. In this network, fellow nationals periodically share information about their homeland and may continue to practice the cultural norms, values, and rituals of their homeland. In addition, Brabant, Palmer, and Gramling (1990) found that "cultural shock may not be as universal as generally assumed in the literature [and] may be alleviated by visits home" (p. 387). This information, obtained within the network of nationals in a foreign country and through frequent home visits, prepares sojourners for a less severe adjustment on permanent return to the homeland.

Several scholars have tested gender as a predictor variable in readjustment (Baty & Dold, 1977; Brabant et al., 1990; Gama & Pederson, 1977). The findings have mostly indicated that females have more problems readjusting to the homeland on return. Brabant et al. (1990) found this in a study of 96 foreign students who had studied in the United States before returning to their home countries. Gama and Pederson's (1977) study found similar results in a study of Brazilian students who returned after 13 to 46 months in the United States. The primary adjustment problems for these females centered on the diffi culties they experienced after they returned to a more conservative homeland that had substantial restrictions on female behavior, compared to the liberal U.S. environment.

On the third front, more diverse research methods are appearing in the field. There are more attempts to use repeated measures rather than the cross-sectional ones that were prevalent in the earlier years. Rogers and Ward (1993), for example, used repeated measures in testing 20 secondary school students who returned to New Zealand after a stay of 10 weeks to 1 year in North America, Europe, and Asia. They tested the students before the students departed for their overseas stay and then tested them again on their return to New Zealand. It is encouraging that results from Rogers and Ward's study produced some insights into the re-entry adjustment field. Surprisingly, they found no significant relationship between expectations and readjustment experiences. This finding is at odds with several studies in the field, including Gullahorn and Gullahorn (1963) and Klineberg and Hull (1979). Findings by Rogers and Ward should be accepted with caution, however, because they used a very small sample, and the response rate in their study was less than 25%. More important, the rigor of their method points to a variable—expectations—that needs further study.

Fourth, several re-entry training programs as well as other relevant programs that broadly address adjustment have been developed in the last two decades. Such programs have been discussed or suggested by Westwood (1984), Sussman (1986), Ptak, Cooper, and Brislin (1995), Gudykunst, Guzley, and Hammer (1996), Dahlen (1997), Gannon and Poon (1997), and Goldstein and Smith (1999). Most of the effective training programs employ role-play, group discussions, and experiential exercises. For instance, Weaver and Uncapher (1981) reported the effectiveness of role-play in a project sponsored with USAID funds and involving Nigerian students who were preparing to return home after sojourning in the United States. The role-play was re-

ported as helpful in changing student expectations from a "fixed and an unchanged home" to a "realistic and changing home." Gannon and Poon (1997) found that cultural trainees reported a significantly higher level of cultural awareness than others and that experiential approaches to training were effective in stimulating positive cultural reactions in trainees. Westwood's (1984) handbook is also widely used in the field, and it provides a range of options for trainers including group activities, guided fantasy, and visuals. In essence, several effective programs are now available for re-entry training. However, room for improvement remains in the programs that are now available, and we will provide suggestions in the following section.

▶ New Directions

Several previous discussions of the readjustment field stopped at presenting the status of the field. However, others, such as Martin (1984) and Landis and Wasilewski (1999), published in the *International Journal for Intercultural Relations,* went a step further by outlining directions for the future. Our intent is to provide suggestions that will help advance the field. We will suggest new directions by addressing all the critical aspects of the field. This will be done by answering the questions of who, what, when, and how. In addition, we will provide suggestions for improving training programs. This way, we hope our suggestions will address a broad spectrum of topics within the field.

Why is a question addressed in the opening pages of this chapter, where we provided reasons for advancing the knowledge in the field. *Who* focuses on who should be the target of study in the field. A majority of the present studies in the field have focused on the United States, Israel, and Japan (Landis & Wasilewski, 1999). This has severely limited the scope of knowledge. The few studies focusing on returnees from or to other countries, particularly in Latin America and Africa, have exposed this limitation in the scope of readjustment studies. For instance, most studies in the field found that returning American females experience more readjustment problems than males, but a study of U.S. returnees from Mexico found exactly the opposite: Males experienced more readjustment problems on their return to the United States after a 1-month stay in Mexico and some locations in the American Southwest (Baty & Dold, 1977; Rohrlich & Martin, 1991). A close examination of that study showed that the males had experienced stranger cultural encounters during their sojourn than did the females, who largely stayed indoors during their sojourn in Mexico. Mexico, according to Hofstede's (1984) cultural studies, values low individualism, high power distance, and strong uncertainty avoidance, whereas the United States values high individualism, low power distance, and low uncertainty avoidance. Other studies that found females experiencing more readjustment problems (Gama & Pederson, 1977) studied students who had sojourned in the United States and then returned to a more male-dominant homeland. It would be interesting to find out the extent of readjustment problems that are experienced by U.S. returnees from Africa or by African returnees from the United States. Africa is culturally distant from the United States, which means that there is a wide divergence in cultural values between the two cultures. The distance between American and African culture is such that U.S. returnees from Africa may have difficulty readjusting to American values after experiencing the strange but constant pull toward conformity and a close-knit relationship network in Africa. Furnham and Alibhai (1985) and Gudykunst (1988) stressed cultural distance as a predictor of the extent of cultural adjustment problems that sojourners will experience. The cultural distance index (CDI), which is widely used in measuring the cultural distance concept, predicts the severity of adjustment problems in a foreign culture. For instance, the CDI identified that students from Africa experienced more adjustment problems in England when compared to their

American and Canadian sojourning colleagues (Furnham & Alibhai, 1985). However, these measures have been few and far between. Thus, the cultural readjustment field needs additional CDI measures, drawn from comparisons of groups of foreign students who are returning to and from different homelands or comparisons of returning students who stayed in locations that are significantly different from each other.

In addition, most of the readjustment studies have been focused on returning students or Peace Corps volunteers (Sussman, 1986). In a few other cases, scholars have investigated returning corporate employees. However, an increasing number of returning sojourners are refugees or others who participated in extended sojourns. Readjustment studies should focus on those emerging groups. The breakup of eastern Europe and crises in other regions have created major refugee situations. Crises in Africa and the Middle East have produced additional refugees. Liebkind (1996) notes that refugees go through "traumatic experiences before and during flight, refugees experience high levels of unpredictability, stress, and powerlessness, leading to higher incidences of depression, anxiety, and psychosomatic complaints" (pp. 161-162). Primarily, refugees are on a traumatic sojourn whereas others are on intended sojourns. This difference portends a different reaction for both groups during the return home.

Both returning refugees and returning extended sojourners or re-migrants are groups that have been understudied. Both groups usually spend more than 5 years in a foreign country. In fact, most participants in readjustment studies have lived just 1 to 5 years in a foreign country. In most cases, they spent less than 1 year abroad. It is generally assumed that the longer sojourners stay in a foreign country, the more likely they will adopt foreign values and thus the more difficult it will be for them to re-enter the homeland successfully. Martin (1984) has suggested that scholars in the field extend their research focus to other groups, such as returning military personnel, diplomats, missionaries, technical workers, and children. This way, the knowledge gaps in the field would be narrowed.

There are additional knowledge gaps in the field of cultural readjustment. Clearly, much of the present work in the field was done in the last two decades, but a lot of necessary work remains. For instance, work needs to be done in the continued study of some important but vaguely understood readjustment variables as well as in the discovery of new variables. These constitute the question of *what* should be the focus of the field.

Variables such as the effect of expectations on cultural readjustment need to be further studied. Rogers and Ward's (1993) study on expectations, which we discussed earlier, is only a beginning. Studies of similar variables are needed, such as the readjustment relationships between returnees and their family, friends, and colleagues. Early studies found the relationship to be strained, but Martin's (1986) study of 173 U.S. students returning from a sojourn in Germany and Turkey found negative relationships with friends but positive relationships with both parents and siblings. Why the differences? Is there a confounding variable lurking somewhere? These inconsistent findings can only be resolved with more studies testing diverse contexts as well as additional variables.

Perhaps, exploring the effects of different contexts on cultural readjustment can uncover new variables. Asuncion-Lande (1976) has provided a list of contexts such as academic, professional, social, cultural, linguistic, and political. This list is by no means comprehensive, but it provides a starting point for discovering new variables and relationships. The examples, provided in this section, lend credence to the importance of the cultural context. It is ironic that so many scholars continue to reify findings of intercultural studies conducted in the United States to universal levels. These are scholars who ordinarily study the contact of different cultures. Furthermore, a sprinkling of findings caution us about these quick generalizations. These studies, for example, those on U.S. student returnees from Mexico, have challenged the appropriateness of unwarranted generalizations. The lesson is that the field will grow from knowledge, that there is still much to discover if only scholars would take those cautions to heart.

Some scholars (Martin, 1986; Nwanko & Onwumechili, 1991) have also proposed a move toward refocusing cultural adjustment studies within the framework of communication. Martin points out that a communication-centered approach "emphasizes sojourner change and conceptualizes reentry as the sojourner's interpreting changes through interaction, providing a rationale for investigating the role of communication in sojourners' close reentry relationships" (p. 6). Martin (1986) and Rohrlich and Martin (1991) have also pointed out that the field lacks theoretical grounding; they suggest that a search for an integrative communication theory is paramount. Rohrlich and Martin (1991) suggest Kim's communication-centered model for sojourner adjustment as a theoretical starting point for a cultural readjustment theory. The next stage is to test this model's applicability as a guide for cultural readjustment studies.

When studies should be conducted is an additional concern in the field. Koester (1983) has suggested that the process of cultural readjustment begins in the minds of prospective returnees while they are still in the foreign country and not at the point of physical re-entry into the homeland. This suggestion has implications for the timing of cultural readjustment studies. At present, cultural readjustment studies are conducted after the returnees have re-entered their home country. Following Koester's suggestion, studies should begin when sojourners are preparing to return to the homeland. Others have also observed that adjustment is a dynamic and continuous process rather than a static state. Africans who have returned home after a sojourn in places such as England and the United States have confided in friends about bumps in the road to readjustment. Most left for home without thinking of the readjustment problems, only to gradually encounter problems a few days after their return. They point out that the adjustment never ends. In fact, some cut short the process and return to their initial foreign host. Thus, it would be best to spread readjustment studies across time rather than following the present focus on cross-sectional research. Readjustment training should be conducted around the same timetable to provide continuous skill support to returnees.

This brings us to how studies should be designed. Church (1982), Martin (1984), and Landis and Wasilewski (1999) have pointed out several design problems with present studies. These include a wide use of limited samples and the lack of control groups. Also, Landis and Wasilewski call for the development of adequate scales for measuring adaptation. They point to numerous low-reliability scores produced by today's scales as a demonstration of weaknesses.

In any case, remedies should not only focus on those weaknesses. In addition, more longitudinal studies are needed to monitor the readjustment process more completely. Earlier, we noted that the process of readjustment is lengthy, and this makes it more conducive to use longitudinal methods. Fortunately, some studies are now using longitudinal or repeated measures in recognition of the fact that cultural readjustment is a process and not a fixed state. However, there is a general agreement that more of such methods should be in use. In addition to longitudinal measures, more qualitative and observational methods should be applied. These measures will bring more insight and diverse explanation to cultural readjustment than the largely quantitative measures that are now used in the field for empirical studies. Some cultures, such as those in Africa, are more amenable to qualitative than quantitative methods. African values project hospitality to strangers. As a result, African research participants may provide positive answers to surveys in the hope of making the researcher "comfortable and happy." In qualitative studies using observation techniques, researchers would live among African participants, and their true feelings might be more easily distinguished. This way, qualitative methods have a better

chance of measuring readjustment phenomena and perhaps generating new variables and hypotheses.

We have mentioned the increasing effectiveness of training programs in an earlier section. At this point, it is important to note that such programs have room for improvement, particularly in the following areas: timing/scheduling of training, individualization of course content, adaptation of training to student values, and training evaluation.

Most training is scheduled a few weeks or days before the sojourners' departure for home; instead, such re-entry training might be integrated with a series of adaptation workshops throughout the sojourning period. Integration, as well as long-term training, will better prepare returnees to become knowledgeable about the important link between acquiring adjustment skills in the host country and acquiring readjustment skills on return home. A one-time or short-term workshop misses this subtlety. In addition, readjustment training would continue to be necessary during and beyond the early period after return home. At present, training in the field does not include the periods suggested above.

Second, Sussman (1986) suggests that training should include "design [of] individualized coping schemes for returnees" (p. 245). This is difficult to implement, but it has the potential to produce a quantum improvement in the effectiveness of the returnee's readjustment because it takes into account the differences among returnees. A suggestion is to design a manageable number of different coping modules to fit the most common returnee personality types.

Third, Sawadogo (1995) and Richmond and Gestrin (1998) have both noted value differences that make the present cultural training ineffective in certain contexts. For example, Sawadogo notes that most training models have been Western-based, incorporating linear presentation of materials, trainee participation, and feedback. Sawadogo advises that "trainers who use African languages in their training will be better equipped to express themselves in less linear fashion with message structure that is based on high repetition and that utilizes narrative and critical incidents" (p. 290). Both Sawadogo and Richmond and Gestrin note that Africans value passivity, which makes explicit participation difficult during training. Thus, African trainees are more apt to observe, reflect, and imitate in deference to the trainer, who represents a symbol of authority. Sawadogo suggests that a more effective feedback strategy in such cultures is the use of peer-intermediaries outside the training environment. Obtaining feedback otherwise will lead to a positively skewed response, which denotes respect for the trainer rather than providing a true measure of the training or trainer's effectiveness.

The fourth suggestion concerns the need for more rigorous evaluation of training. At present, most evaluations are focused on workshop feedback and cross-sectional post-studies or reports. Also needed are rigorous pre- and posttests, as well as longitudinal tracking of the readjustment process of returnees. Furthermore, training models need to be tested against each other, as was recently proposed by Landis and Wasileswki (1999). This makes it easier to clearly identify the most effective models within specified contexts.

▶ Conclusion

We have focused our discussion on reiterating the importance of the cultural readjustment field. Our hope is that more studies are conducted to advance our knowledge of this important intercultural field. In addition, we have reviewed the trends of research studies and training programs in the field by dividing them into two periods: (a) the earlier period covered studies that were conducted between the World War II and the late 1970s and (b) later studies and training programs that define the current status of the field. Finally, we ended by suggesting various directions for the future in the field. Those suggestions have focused on the target groups for study, what needs to be studied, when studies should be carried out, research methods that need to be applied, and improved training programs. These suggestions should help us achieve the goals of transculturalism.

▶ References

Adler, N. (1981). Reentry: Managing cross-cultural transitions. *Group and Organization Studies, 6*(3), 341-356.

Asuncion-Lande, N. (1976). Inventory of reentry problems. In H. Marsh (Ed.), *Reentry/transition seminars: Report on the Wingspread Colloquium*. Washington, DC: NAFSA.

Austin, C. (1983). *Cross-cultural reentry: An annotated bibliography*. Abilene, TX: Abilene Christian University Press.

Baty, R., & Dold, E. (1977). Cross-cultural homestays: An analysis of college students' responses after living in an unfamiliar culture. *International Journal in Intercultural Relations, 1*(1), 61-76.

Bennett, J. (1977). Transition shock: Putting culture shock in perspective. In N. Jain (Ed.), *International and intercultural communication annual* (Vol. 4). Falls Church, VA: Speech Communication Association.

Berry, J., Kim, U., & Boski, P. (1987). Psychological acculturation of immigrants. In Y. Kim & W. Gudykunst (Eds.), *Cross-cultural adaptation: Current approaches* (pp. 62-89). Newbury Park, CA: Sage.

Bochner, S. (1973). *The mediating man: Cultural interchange and transitional education*. Honolulu, HI: East-West Center.

Brabant, S., Palmer, C., & Gramling, R. (1990). Returning home: An empirical investigation of cross-cultural reentry. *International Journal in Intercultural Relations, 14*(4), 387-404.

Brislin, R. (1981). *Cross-cultural encounters*. New York: Pergamon.

Brislin, R., & Pederson, P. (1976). *Cross-cultural orientation programs*. New York: Gardner.

Church, A. (1982). Sojourner adjustment. *Psychological Bulletin, 91*(3), 540-572.

Dahlen, T. (1997). *Among the interculturalists: An emergent profession and its packaging of knowledge*. Stockholm, Sweden: Gotab.

Edmonston, B. (Ed.). (1996). *Statistics on U.S. immigration: An assessment of data needs for future research*. Washington, DC: National Academy Press.

Enloe, W., & Lewin, P. (1987). Issues of integration abroad and readjustment to Japan of Japanese returnees. *International Journal in Intercultural Relations, 11*(3), 223-248.

Furnham, A., & Alibhai, N. (1985). Value differences in foreign students. *International Journal in Intercultural Relations, 9*(4), 365-375.

Gama, E., & Pederson, P. (1977). Readjustment problems of Brazilian returnees from graduate study in the United States. *International Journal in Intercultural Relations, 1*(4), 46-57.

Gannon, M., & Poon, J. (1997). Effects of alternative instructional approaches on cross-cultural training outcomes. *International Journal in Intercultural Relations, 21*(4), 429-446.

Gaw, K. (2000). Reverse culture shock in students returning from overseas. *International Journal in Intercultural Relations, 24*(1), 83-104.

Goldstein, D., & Smith, D. (1999). The analysis of the effects of experiential training on sojourners' cross-cultural adaptability. *International Journal in Intercultural Relations, 23*(1), 157-173.

Gudykunst, W. (1988). Uncertainty and anxiety. In Y. Kim & W. Gudykunst (Eds.), *Theories in intercultural communication* (pp. 123-156). Newbury Park, CA: Sage.

Gudykunst, W., Guzley, R., & Hammer, M. (1996). Designing intercultural training. In D. Landis & R. Bhagat (Eds.), *Handbook of intercultural training* (2nd ed.). Thousand Oaks, CA: Sage.

Gullahorn, J., & Gullahorn, J. (1963). An extension of the U-curve hypothesis. *Journal of Social Issues, 19*(3), 33-47.

Hatzichristou, C., & Hopf, D. (1995). School adaptation of Greek children after remigration: Age differences in multiple domains. *Journal of Cross-Cultural Psychology, 26*(5), 505-522.

Hofstede, G. (1984). *Culture's consequences: International differences in work-related values*. Beverly Hills, CA: Sage.

Howard, D. (1980). The expatriate manager and role of the MNC. *Personnel Journal, 59*, 838-844.

Isogai, T., Hayashi, Y., & Uno, M. (1999). Identity issues and reentry training. *International Journal in Intercultural Relations, 23*(3), 493-525.

Kealey, D. (1989). A study of cross-cultural effectiveness: Theoretical issues, practical applications. *International Journal in Intercultural Relations, 13*, 387-428.

Klineberg, O., & Hull, W. (1979). *At a foreign university: An international study of adaptation and coping*. New York: Praeger.

Koester, J. (1983, May). *Intercultural reentry from the viewpoint of communication*. Paper presented to the International Communication Association, Dallas, TX.

Landis, D., & Wasilewski, J. (1999). Reflections on 22 years of *International Journal of Intercultural Relations* and 23 years in other areas of intercultural practice. *International Journal in Intercultural Relations, 23*(4), 535-574.

Liebkind, K. (1996). Acculturation and stress: Vietnamese refugees in Finland. *Journal of Cross-Cultural Psychology, 27*(2), 161-180.

Lysgaard, S. (1955). Adjustment in a foreign society: Norwegian Fulbright grantees visiting the United States. *International Social Science Bulletin, 7*, 45-51.

Martin, J. (1984). The intercultural reentry: Conceptualization and directions for future research. *International Journal in Intercultural Relations, 8*(2), 115-134.

Martin, J. (1986). Training issues in cross-cultural orientation. *International Journal in Intercultural Relations, 10*(1), 103-116.

Martin, J., & Nakayama, T. (1997). *Intercultural communication contexts*. Mountain View, CA: Mayfield.

Murray, J. (1973, Summer). International personnel repatriation: Culture shock in reverse. *MSU Business Topics*, pp. 59-66.

Nwanko, R., & Onwumechili, C. (1991). Communication and social values in cross-cultural adjustment. *The Howard Journal of Communications, 3*(1 & 2), 99-111.

Opubor, A. (1974, October). *Intercultural adaptation: Resocialization versus reacculturation*. Paper presented for the NAFSA Wingspread Colloquium on Reentry/Transition Seminars.

Pearson, D. (1964, October 17). The Peace Corps volunteer returns: Problems of adjustment. *Saturday Review,* pp. 54-56, 74-75.

Pruitt, F. (1978). The adaptation of African students to American society. *International Journal in Intercultural Relations, 2*(1), 90-118.

Ptak, C., Cooper, J., & Brislin, R. (1995). Cross-cultural training programs: Advice and insights from experienced trainers. *International Journal in Intercultural Relations, 19*(3), 425-453.

Richmond, Y., & Gestrin, P. (1998). *Into Africa: Intercultural insights.* Yarmouth, ME: Intercultural Press.

Rogers, J., & Ward, C. (1993). Expectation-experience discrepancies and psychological adjustment during cross-cultural reentry. *International Journal in Intercultural Relations, 17*(2), 185-196.

Rohrlich, B., & Martin, J. (1991). Host country and reentry adjustment of the student sojourners. *International Journal in Intercultural Relations, 15*(2), 163-182.

Sawadogo, G. (1995). Training for the African mind. *International Journal in Intercultural Relations, 19*(2), 281-293.

Stolley, R. (1965, March). Reentry crisis: Return of the Peace Corps volunteer to the United States. *Life,* pp. 98-100.

Sussman, N. (1986). Reentry research and training: Methods and implications. *International Journal in Intercultural Relations, 10*(2), 235-253.

Uehara, A. (1986). The nature of American student reentry adjustment and perception of the sojourn adjustment. *International Journal in Intercultural Relations, 10*(4), 415-438.

Weaver, G., & Uncapher, P. (1981, March). *The Nigerian experience: Overseas living and value change.* Workshop presented at the 7th annual SIETAR conference, Vancouver, Canada.

Westwood, M. (1984). *Returning home: A program for persons assisting international students with the reentry process.* Ottawa: The Canadian Bureau for International Education.

White, M. (1980). *Stranger in his native land: Group boundaries and the Japanese international returnee.* Unpublished doctoral dissertation, Harvard University.

Yashiro, K. (1995). Japan's returnees. *Journal of Multilingual and Multicultural Development, 16*(12), 139-164.

Part V

Toward the Fundamentals of Transcultural Research

Toward an Ethic of Intercultural Communication Research

JUDITH N. MARTIN
RUTH LEON W. BUTLER

We come to this discussion of ethics from different backgrounds, one an African American scholar beginning an academic career in interdisciplinary approaches to rhetoric and social ethics, the other a white tenured faculty member in mid-career engaged in social science research on issues of ethnicity and communication. Although we come from different vantage points and locations, we have both had experiences working on multicultural research teams and are both particularly concerned with ethical issues in research that describes communication patterns of "others."

A review of previous literature revealed some discussion of ethical intercultural communication practice (Barnlund, 1982; Bruneau, 2000; Casmir, 1997a, 1997b; Gilchrist, 1997;

Howell, 1981, 1982; Johannesen, 1990; Kale, 1994; Martin, Flores, & Nakayama, 1998; Metzger & Springston, 1992; Shuter, 2000) but few explicit guidelines for conducting ethical intercultural communication research (Davis, Nakayama, & Martin, 2000; Jandt & Tanno, 1994; Triandis, 1983).

In this chapter, we describe three research traditions within intercultural communication, each of which investigates communication of others. We identify the ethical concerns in each tradition and then propose a framework and several guidelines for conducting ethical intercultural communication research.

It must be noted at the outset that we recognize the complexity and difficulty of developing ethical guidelines that could apply to the variety of cultures and methodologies in intercultural communication scholarship. Therefore, our goal is modest: simply to continue the dialogue on this topic. The enormity of such a project probably explains the dearth of scholarship addressing ethical issues. In addition, culture and communication research in the United States is in the midst of a paradigm shift, and many of the current debates relate to ethical issues in research (Martin & Nakayama, 1999). Numerous research paradigms and methods enrich the field but make consensus on ethical issues particularly difficult. Discussions with our colleagues lead us to believe that we are not alone in grappling with these issues. Although these issues are acknowledged in informal discussions, they have not been systematically addressed in the literature. As F. L. Casmir (1997b) observes,

> We, as communication scholars, have undoubtedly been slow when it comes to dealing with ethic- and value-systems that need to be renegotiated and built *across* the dividing lines of culture and the boundaries of states—or *inter*culturally and *inter*nationally. But as the need for such an effort becomes clearer in our minds, communication scholars surely do have an important role to play. (p. 5)

▶ Ethics and Intercultural Communication Research

In the broadest sense, ethics may be recognized as a philosophical discipline primarily concerned with evaluating and justifying norms and standards of personal and interpersonal behavior, the science of morality (Karhausen, 1987). However, as Homan (1991) points out, when applied to professional conduct, it is more narrowly conceived as the "prescription and regulation of human behavior, a system of standards established within the profession for the conduct of its members" (p. 1). Is there such a system of ethical standards that could guide our research conduct, particularly in investigations of others' communication?

What makes ethics an especially challenging topic for intercultural communication re-searchers is that it brings into focus the intersections of three systems of prescriptive behavior: the cultural norms of the researcher, the cultural norms of those being researched, and also the professional and paradigmatic norms of researchers in the intercultural communication field. These various cultural norms sometimes seem nontransferable, creating ethical dilemmas in intercultural research situations. There has been much discussion about universalist versus relativistic approaches to ethics, and one could argue that in the early 21st century, ethical guidelines have shifted from rigid codes created by formalist institutions to pragmatic situational norms based more on sensibilities than on interpretation of laws (Fullbrook, 1990; Wellman, 1988). However, B. J. Hall (1997) argues against adopting a totally situational ethic; although doing so creates an image of sensitivity and tolerance, such an ethic can quickly degenerate into an ethics of personal desires that ultimately destroys the very basis of community (p. 13). Hall rejects the universalist-relativist dichotomy and argues for a more complex, dialectical, and emergent vision, supporting Popper's (1976) view of ethics as an adjustable response to changing issues, problems, and dilemmas—an imagining of new values in response to moral dilemmas, a progressive ethical project. This more flexible approach to ethics presents great opportunity for intercultural research but also great challenges.

There are at least three different research paradigms or traditions of intercultural communication research: The functionalist paradigm, the interpretive paradigm, and more recently, the critical paradigm (Martin & Nakayama, 1999). How do scholars within these three traditions characterize and respond to ethical challenges involved in the study of cultural others?

FUNCTIONALIST RESEARCH

Functionalist research assumptions (ontological, epistemological, and so on) have been described ad nauseam in communication literature and can be briefly described as emphasizing objectivity, an assumption of an external reality so that the researcher is not intimately involved with those researched (Martin & Nakayama, 1999; Mumby, 1997). Research in this tradition often conceptualizes culture as an independent variable, operationalized by value frameworks (e.g., individualism-collectivism) or other theoretical notions (e.g., low/high context) that influence communication (Gudykunst, 1995; Gudykunst & Nishida, 1989; Gudykunst & Ting-Toomey, 1996; Gudykunst, Ting-Toomey, & Nishida, 1996; Hall, 1992; Ting-Toomey, 1994).

These research programs generally explore cross-cultural comparisons of communication patterns within an *etic* (universal, researcher-imposed) framework using quantitative, quasi-experimental methods (pretested instruments, standardized measurements of theoretical notions, self-report attitude questionnaires) or interviews, borrowing heavily from research and theory in psychology and sociology (Gudykunst & Nishida, 1989; van de Vijver & Leung, 1997).

The ethical concerns of this research tradition, although not discussed in the literature, seem to center around the protection of subjects, a concern borrowed from psychological research. The ethical guidelines in psychology, in turn, are based on medical ethics or the Nuremberg Code (Homan, 1991, p. 10). The overriding concern for many years was that no harm should be done to research subjects. The most recent American Psychological Association Code of Ethics (adopted by its Council of Representatives in August 1992) reflects concern for the general welfare of research participants. The following guidelines are included: (a) participants have a right to know the procedures involved in research (informed consent); (b) their participation should be voluntary; (c) the purpose of the research should be humanitarian, with concern for the dignity and welfare of the participants; (d) appropriate protections should be in place for the rights and welfare of participants; (e) researchers should be qualified to conduct the research; and (f) subjects must be free to withdraw at any time.

There has been a great deal of discussion about these ethical issues in social science research, and specific guidelines have been established (Bower & de Gasparis, 1978; Diener & Crandall, 1978; Heller, 1986; Herring, 1988; Hook, Kurtz, & Todorovich, 1977; Sieber, 1982, 1992; Sjoberg, 1967). Most universities have human subjects' review boards based on these principles, and communication scholars generally adhere to these guidelines (McEuen, Gordon, & Todd-Mancillas, 1990).

However, there are many issues in intercultural communication research (e.g., motivation of researchers, ownership of data, how others are represented, and so forth) that are not directly covered by ethical guidelines in this research tradition. These issues are not seen as involving ethical decisions and are not included in human subjects' guidelines. As noted earlier, intercultural communication scholars have seldom addressed these issues, and this has resulted in an increasing skepticism and resistance in cultural communities to participation in traditional intercultural communication studies (Stanfield, 1993a). Therefore, it seems timely to expand the boundaries of ethical responsibilities in the functionalist-research tradition and to join in exploring ethical guidelines further (Davis et al., 2000).

INTERPRETIVE RESEARCH

The second intercultural communication research tradition for investigating others, cultural-communication research, is conducted from an interpretive or subjective perspective (Martin & Nakayama, 1999; Mumby, 1997). Among many interpretive approaches (e.g., textual, rhetorical), the most relevant to this chapter are the cultural communication studies based on Hymes's (1974) ethnography of communication and developed by Philipsen and colleagues (see Carbaugh, 1990; Gonzalez, Houston, & Chen, 2000; Hall, 1997).

In this ethnographic tradition, culture is conceptualized as dynamic, and the relationship between culture and communication is seen as reciprocal. Culture is performed and constructed as well as reflected through communication. Generally, cultural communication researchers are more involved with those being researched than are those in the functionalist tradition. There is an explicit relationship between the researcher and those researched. The goal of this research is to describe communication patterns representing the subjective and lived experience of various cultural groups through qualitative methods (e.g., participant observation, structured, semistructured and unstructured interviewing) often associated with fieldwork and borrowed heavily from anthropology. Researchers in this paradigm are generally interested in an *emic* perspective (describing emergent patterns within one particular cultural community), but some are explicitly interested in extending their research to intercultural interaction and in making theory-based, cross- cultural comparisons (Carbaugh, 1990; Fitch, 1994; Lindsley, 1999).

It should be noted that ethnographic researchers have long been concerned with ethical issues concerning the relationship between researchers and those being researched (Denzin, 1996; Hammersly, 1992, 1995; Lincoln & Guba, 1985; Lindlof, 1995; Rosaldo, 1989). Both the American Anthropological Association (AAA) and the American Sociological Association (ASA) have established codes of ethics to guide professional conduct in doing fieldwork. These issues go beyond a concern for not harming research participants and address some of the issues identified earlier, for example, researchers' motivations in pursuing cultural information, ways to gain access and acceptance from others, responsibility to respondents during and after fieldwork (Glazer, 1982, p. 48), and ethical issues in interviewing (Kvale, 1996, pp. 109-120).

Some would argue that interpretive research is more ethical than functionalist research because the relationship between the researcher and researched is comparatively more symmetrical and harms and benefits are relatively minimal although difficult to measure (Cassell, 1982, p. 21). As Margaret Mead (1969) rather optimistically stated, "Anthropological research does not have subjects. We work with informants in an atmosphere of trust and mutual respect" (p. 371).

Other scholars have stressed that all researcher-researched relationships are asymmetrical, but the size of the power distance between the two varies, as does the amount of power and control the researcher has over the other. Wax (1982) describes various models along this continuum. The most asymmetrical relationship, in which the researcher is most powerful, is the "verandah" model (where the fieldworker sits on the verandah of the government station and sends for a native who will be subjected to several hours of systematic questioning about indigenous language and customs). The next is the noblesse-oblige model, where researchers install themselves in relatively opulent environments while studying "natives." These are very similar to what Hall (1997) terms the "zoo approach" to studying intercultural communication, "as if we were walking through a zoo admiring, gasping, and chuckling at the various exotic animals which we observe (p. 14). There is also the "going-native" model, where the researcher becomes friends with those studied, the undercover agent model, and the most symmetrical: the advocate model (Wax, 1982, p. 15).

Cassell (1982) points out that there is a difference between participants being wronged and being harmed. Participants may be wronged while not being harmed. Being wronged may be the result of the researchers' deception or manipulation of the community (e.g., revealing information not for public knowledge). There has been an extensive and heated discussion in sociology over the propriety of deceptive research, sparked by the admission of sociologist Carol Ellis (1986) that her award-winning study of a rural South Carolina fishing community was conducted without telling those in the community that she was a researcher. As Allen (1997) summarizes the debate, some scholars agree that community members should be informed when they are the objects of a study, and some defend deception from a cost-benefit perspective, arguing that deception on the part of the researcher is often the only way to get information from deviant or marginal groups and is acceptable as long as no one is hurt very much and the payoff in data is high (p. 32).

There are no easy answers for ethical fieldwork, and fieldworkers have few grounds for sentiments of moral superiority. Cassell (1982) suggests three guidelines: (a) reflecting in advance on what may occur, (b) making every possible effort to avoid both harming and wronging, (c) not only avoiding harming but attempting to benefit those studied.

More recently, anthropologists and ethnographers have extended the discussion of ethical issues. Much has been written about the ethical dilemmas involved in forming intimate and reciprocal relationships with informants while maintaining some neutrality and distance (Andersen, 1993; Facio, 1993). Another ethical issue is the challenge of conducting fieldwork across race and class lines (Andersen, 1993; Rosaldo, 1989; Stanfield, 1993b). Dennis (1993) discusses ethical dilemmas in participant observations: the need to be reflective about why people share information. He provides specific guidelines for protecting informants and respondents in publications and also describes ethical issues involving validity and reliability.

Intercultural communication scholars have only recently joined in the discussion of ethical concerns in interpretive studies of others (Davis et al., 2000). For example, Jandt and Tanno (1994) propose an alternative way of working with others in research. They suggest that researchers should view the others as a coproducer of knowledge (so that ethnographic fieldwork becomes a collaborative effort by researcher and researched); as a participant, someone who "possesses the ability, means, and willingness to participate in creating and understanding knowledge" (p. 41); and as an audience that should have access to research results.

More recently, Gonzalez (2000) outlined guidelines for appropriate relationships between researcher and those researched. She encourages ethnographers to respect others: "We listen to others who have gone before us

and know of the culture. They can help us to identify the rules . . . research does not entitle us to be able to enter, ask, or do as we wish" (p. 641). And she suggests that researchers let the indigenous participants in the culture teach researchers how to function as human beings in their world. "This is not in order to understand them as subjects, but to fully participate as one's self in their world (p. 644). Finally, she encourages students of culture to search their own hearts concerning their motivations and to think about the impact they have on their host culture, suggestions further elaborated by scholars in the third tradition, critical research.

CRITICAL RESEARCH

The third research tradition for investigating others is critical ethnography (Conquergood, 1991), which is influenced by European critical theory and postmodernism (for a distinction between modernist-critical theory, see Mumby, 1997; see also neo-Marxists, Gramsci, 1971; Lukacs, 1971; Frankfort School scholars, Horkheimer & Adorno, 1988; Habermas, 1981, 1984, 1987; and postmodern scholars, Baudrillard, 1988; Foucault, 1980, 1988; Lyotard, 1984). Critical researchers focus on power relations in popular culture and see culture as a site of power struggle where various representations and meanings are negotiated (Grossberg, 1985; Hall, 1985; Hegde, 1998).

This relatively recent (within the field of intercultural communication) research tradition shares many of the metatheoretical assumptions, methods, and ethical concerns of the ethnography of communication researchers described in the previous section. However, critical ethnographers differ in two ways: in their focus on the centrality of power relationships and the focus on macro contexts. Critical scholars contend that all relationships are characterized by power and power differentials, including those between researcher and researched. The responsibility (indeed the goal) of scholarship is to locate, identify, and make explicit these power differentials, including those between researcher and researched, to better understand and ultimately liberate (Clifford, 1988; Clifford & Marcus, 1986; Conquergood, 1991, 1992; Fiske, 1991; Said, 1994).

Second, critical scholars hold that the human experience (and therefore human communication) cannot be understood without examining *all* contexts in which this experience is lived. Whereas cultural communication scholars also emphasize the importance of micro contexts (Carbaugh, 1990; Katriel, 1995), the interest of critical scholars extends to most macro contexts (social, political, economic, and historical). Therefore, critical ethnographers maintain that scholars need to understand how contexts have shaped their own lives and discourses as researchers; that researchers need to examine and explicate how their training and experiences influence the way they see the world and the ways in which they see and describe others.

These two notions, power and context, lead specifically to a third issue, a debate about who can speak for others, which is directly related to ethical issues in intercultural communication research. Because researchers are shaped by political and social forces (contexts) that predispose them to see the world in a particular way, regardless of academic training, how can any researcher appropriately represent (or speak about) the lived experience of another?

The question is even more problematic when there is a power differential between researcher and researched. As Linda Alcoff (1991) observes,

> The practice of privileged persons speaking for or on behalf of less privileged persons has actually resulted in many cases in increasing or reinforcing the oppression of the group spoken for—and is coming more and more under criticism from members of those oppressed groups themselves. (p. 7)

Many intercultural communication researchers, representing all three paradigms, are engaged in speaking for others when they describe/predict communication patterns of those in various cultural groups. The issue of speaking for another seems to be at the heart of many ethical issues in intercultural communication research and, as noted earlier, has led to resistance by others to participating in research. For example, our own quantitative and qualitative research efforts (e.g., intercultural dating study) have met with resistance among various university and community groups (Hispanic, African American) to participating in research projects. These groups are resisting being spoken for by researchers. Because of researchers' lack of attention to these issues, there are limited findings in our field, a poverty of interpretation and applications (Jandt & Tanno, 1994; Nishida, 1996; Rosaldo, 1989; Stanfield, 1993b), and the marginalization of minority groups in the academy (Allen, Orbe, & Olivas, 1999). Exploring the question of who has the right to speak for others can illuminate our search for guidelines for ethical research investigating others.

► Who Can Speak for Whom?

Alcoff (1991) maintains that speaking *for* and speaking *about* are closely related, and she critiques the range of responses to the question of who can speak for whom. One response is the *reductionist response,* which says if researchers describe their location, readers can understand the meaning of the research. For example, if J. Martin describes her location thoroughly as a researcher (e.g., white, female, middle-aged, middle-class, professor), readers will be able to interpret her description of others' (e.g., African American) communication patterns. This position requires that white researchers doing research on ethnicity/race and communication examine self-consciously the influence of institutional racism and the way it shapes the formulation and development of their research (Andersen, 1993, p. 43; Rowe, 2000).

Alcoff (1991, p. 17) rejects this "charge of reductionism" response because it assumes a direct relationship between location and meaning/truth. She argues that location is not a fixed essence; rather, there is an uneasy, underdetermined, and contested relationship between location and meaning; the evaluation of the speaker (researcher) cannot be reduced to an identification of the speaker's location.

A second alternative is the *retreat response*: simply to retreat from all practices of speaking for anyone and never to make claims beyond one's own individual response, a favored position of many researchers. This position applies particularly to research that crosses class, racial, and gender boundaries. Researchers often use standpoint theory to support this position. Standpoint theory explores how specific societal positions, the results of one's field of experience, serve as a standpoint from which one views and evaluates the world (Orbe, 1998). Using standpoint theory, feminist scholars explore specific ways in which gender and the research context intersect and thereby influence research outcomes, privilege some communication, and/or marginalize others (Allen et al., 1999; Arliss & Borisoff, 1993; Hegde, 1998; Houston & Kramarae, 1991; Rowe, 2000). Similarly, members of subordinated groups have unique viewpoints that cannot be represented or understood by members of dominant groups; only minority scholars can produce knowledge about racial or gender communication (Andersen, 1993, p. 43).

Alcoff (1991) rejects an extreme retreatist position:

> A retreat from speaking for will not result in an increase in receptive listening in all cases; it may result merely in a retreat into a narcissistic yuppie lifestyle in which a privileged person takes no responsibility for her society whatsoever. (p. 17)

She points out that, in addition, such a position limits possibility for political action and may be motivated by a desire to be immune to criticism, that is, if one speaks only for oneself, no one can criticize this position.

The response advocated by Alcoff is based on a *speaking to and with* position rather than speaking *for* others. This notion is borrowed from Gayatri Spivak (1988), who according to Alcoff

> criticizes the "self-abnegating intellectual" pose that Foucault and Deleuze adopt when they reject speaking for others on the ground that it assumes the oppressed can transparently represent their own true interests. But Spivak is also critical of speaking for others that engages in dangerous representations. In the end, Spivak prefers a "speaking to," in which the intellectual neither abnegates his or her discursive role nor presumes an authenticity of the oppressed, but still allows for the possibility that the oppressed will produce a "counter-sentence" that can then suggest a new historical narrative. (pp. 22-23)

The impetus to speak for must be carefully analyzed and, she would say for academics, sometimes squelched. In addition, speaking for should carry accountability with it. This position speaks to the ethical issues raised in our own and other researchers' experience and offers a framework with which to develop ethical guidelines in studying others. It is also commensurate with a communication-practice ethic that is meaning- and collective-centered rather than individual-centered (Casmir, 1997a, 1997b; Deetz, 1990) and the ethics of caring (Bruneau, 2000; Metzger & Springston, 1992; Steiner, 1997).

Conquergood (1992), in his review of three critical ethnographies, reflects on what it means to do ethnography *with* and not *of* a people. The first explores the ongoing process of an ethnographer trying to understand day-to-day meanings with a theater troupe in postcolonial Africa (Fabian, 1990):

> It occurred to me that the group's work—giving form to everyday experience in the urban-industrial world of Shaba—was not in essence different from my own groping for an

ethnography of work and language. My "method" had always been to rely on recordings and texts. Now I realized that their plays and sketches would make documents of the kind I tried to produce but would be superior in their linguistic quality. (p. 42)

In a second ethnography, political scientist Scott (1990) challenges assumptions of traditional ethnographic characterizations of the poor as passive in the face of oppression. He studies "hidden transcripts," the discourse of the disempowered that occurs away from the public's (and researcher's) eye, a "zone of constant struggle." He shows how to locate counterpublics and listen for and think about the "voice under domination" (p. 136). A third example is Lavie's (1990) research with Bedouins who live in the south Sinai in the midst of the Arab-Israeli conflict, in a land that is governed alternately by Jews and Arabs, a people subject to a "cultural dizziness." As Conquergood (1992) describes the strength of Lavie's work,

> The account of how she delicately opened communication, negotiated rapport, and came to live with a people who had every reason to see her as the enemy is one of the great human stories of ethnographic fieldwork. [She] builds into her scholarship a clear and precise account of the circumstances under which the knowledge was produced. (p. 94)

These are all accounts of fieldworkers grappling with specific power differentials. What would a research ethic look like that was based on speaking *with* and *to* others?

▶ Guidelines for Ethical Research

Taking Spivak and Alcoff's position, we propose the following guidelines for ethical research in all paradigms. This position calls for functionalist-quantitative research to go beyond the traditional guidelines borrowed from psychology and biomedical research and for interpretive research in ethnography

of communication to further explore issues of power and context in research methodology.

ETHICAL RESEARCH IS PARTICIPATORY

Intercultural-communication research should continue to increase participation by the group being studied at various points in the research process. This could apply to functionalist, interpretive, and critical research. As Jandt and Tanno (1994) suggest,

> We must begin thinking of the "other" as someone who possesses the ability, means, and willingness to participate in creating and understanding knowledge. We must acknowledge that the "other" can contribute not only the data upon which we impose our methodologies, but also the questions that guide our research, the interpretation of data and the validation of conclusions. (p. 41)

We should move away from thinking of individuals as passive sources of data (replace *subjects* with *participants*). Sociologist Stanfield (1993a) observes that social-science research is one of the last areas in U.S. society where social inequality is unquestioningly accepted and warns

> If the social sciences are going to be of any relevance in the next century their human creators and maintainers must democratize how they structure, interpret, and distribute their work. No longer can social scientists hide behind the ivy-covered walls of academia and their research laboratories, assuming they can study whomever they want to, whenever they please. (pp. 32-33)

Participation can occur at various points in functionalist as well as in field research: in developing research questions and instruments and in interpreting data (Houston, 2000; Lincoln & Guba, 1985; Lindlof, 1995; Rosaldo, 1989). Advocates of participatory action research (PAR) provide a number of useful strategies for involving others at all phases of research, as both researchers and communities work together to promote change (Carr & Kemmis, 1986; Greenwood, White, & Harkavy, 1993; Heller, 1993; Kemmis & McTaggart, 1988; Reason & Rowan, 1981; Whyte, 1991). Founded on traditional action research, which engages "subjects" as active participants in the research process and looks for practical outcomes related to lives of participants, more recent PAR scholarship has taken a critical and postmodern turn (Stringer, 1996). Participation is a core element of successful community-based action research and, according to Stringer, is most effective when it involves significant levels of active involvement and deals personally with people rather than their representatives (p. 38). Although these strategies have traditionally been employed by interpretive researchers, functionalist research could benefit from them as well (Orbe, 2000).

One participative strategy is to conduct member checking, where the researcher takes findings back to the community being studied for their interpretation (Lincoln & Guba, 1985). For example, in one quantitative project investigating Hispanic communication competence, we developed a traditional social-scientific framework but member-checked our findings and interpretations by conducting focus groups with Chicano students. They provided invaluable information and strengthened our interpretations (Martin, Hammer, & Bradford, 1994). Another example is Hecht, Ribeau, and Alberts's (1989) strategy of alternating between survey research and interviews/focus groups in their studies of ethnicity and communication.

Another strategy for increasing participation is through collaborative research teams, including members and nonmembers of the cultural group being studied. Researchers from all paradigms are emphasizing the benefits of this approach (Gudykunst & Nishida, 1989; Martin, Krizek, Nakayama, & Bradford, 1996; Ting-Toomey & Chung, 1996). The findings and interpretations concerning culture and communication are richer (and more ethical) than if the study was conducted by any one researcher from any one research paradigm.

Ethical challenges are also raised concerning participation by those helping with research. A common model of academic research in the United States is a white tenured professor conducting research on minority groups' communication, employing graduate and undergraduate assistants from the ethnic minority groups being studied. The asymmetrical relationship between faculty researchers and student assistants often brings challenges of role definition and boundaries, responsibilities, and obligations; but the relationship with minority assistants brings with it particular ethical challenges.

Minority students are sometimes used as a way to gain immediate access to the community of interest. These students go into communities, and the (usually white) professors are spared the intense, time-consuming work of establishing relationships in the community. Furthermore, these assistants are then placed in the position of interpreting their community to the senior researchers, of speaking for a community that is assumed to be monolithic. Their interpretations may put them in a tenuous position within their community (Stanfield, 1993a, p. 31), and their position as "outsiders within" can make them vulnerable in the academy as well (Allen et al., 1999).

We are not suggesting that minority assistants should not participate in research; rather, senior researchers should acknowledge and meet the ethical challenges from a speaking-with-and-to position. First, senior researchers should acknowledge the value of the assistants' contribution and ensure that the students understand the importance of this contribution, that their involvement provides a particular value and lends authenticity to the project, which may be impossible to achieve without their cooperation. Senior researchers may need to explain explicitly the professional rewards associated with research: that completing such research results in convention papers and publications that lead directly to promotion or tenure as well as other professional rewards (e.g., increased status, leadership roles in organizations, research awards).

Second, senior researchers should help the students reflect on their role in the project. What will their participation mean for their own professional development and their cultural identity? How will their participation affect relationships in their community? They could be encouraged to keep a journal or a record of their thoughts and observations about their participation in the project.

Finally, senior researchers should also think carefully about appropriate rewards for the students' assistance. Providing access to an otherwise inaccessible community, providing member checks, and interpreting research data are research commodities that go beyond the usual research assistant responsibilities and should be rewarded accordingly. Depending on the professional goals of the students, senior researchers may play a mentor role, helping the student enhance research skills (e.g., interviewing, data collection, analysis) and scholarly writing (e.g., co-authoring papers and publications that result from the project or helping the student to develop a separate paper or publication from the same research project under the student's name).

ETHICAL RESEARCH IS RECIPROCAL

Those studied should benefit from the research. There are many kinds of reciprocity and many ways in which individuals and communities can benefit from participating in research projects (Lincoln & Guba, 1985; Lindlof, 1995; Stringer, 1996). The particular form of reciprocation should be determined by the participating group and the researchers through open and honest dialogue. Stringer's (1996) guidelines for effective communication in PAR are instructive: listen attentively, accept and act, be truthful and sincere, act in socially and culturally appropriate ways, and regularly advise others about what is happening. Inclusion and reciprocity mean involvement of all groups, inclusion of all relevant issues, and ensuring that all relevant groups benefit from activities (p. 38). It should not necessarily be assumed that a community will (or will not) want particular rewards for cooperating in a research project.

For example, in a study on intercultural dating, we obtained the participation of minority student groups on our campus by engaging in discussion and offering reciprocation: by sharing our research findings and also offering to conduct cross-cultural training for their groups. They told us that we were the first researchers who offered this. Through dialogue with the group, we determined that the appropriate reward was to share our findings with them.

In ethnographic studies, researchers can help participants in many ways, from helping with daily activities (help participants move, give rides, run errands, help deal with bureaucratic red tape) to educational assistance (tutoring, helping with language practice) (Andersen, 1993).

ETHICAL RESEARCH EMPLOYS A BROAD INTERPRETATION OF INFORMED CONSENT

Informed consent should be extended to include participants understanding the important role they are playing in the researchers' success. This is particularly important in research involving exploited communities. As noted above, research participants often do not realize that they have important information—a valued research commodity—that is needed by the researcher (Stanfield, 1993a, p. 31). Without their help, the research project may not be seen as valid or may not even be completed.

This means that questionnaire instruments should include a description of the importance of the information being requested, along with the usual informed consent paragraph. In interview and participant-observation studies, researchers should carefully explain the assistance's importance and specifically how the researchers will benefit, as described previously (e.g., conference papers, books, tenure, promotion).

ETHICAL RESEARCHERS ARE SELF-REFLECTIVE ABOUT THEIR MOTIVATIONS

Researchers need to consider why they are conducting research with particular communities and should share the reasons with participants (Gonzalez, 2000). Questions about why research is wanted in this particular community should be explicitly confronted by any scholar who studies the communication patterns of others. Is it because the researcher worked previously in this community (e.g., Peace Corps) and it's an easy way to complete a study or a dissertation? Is it because knowledge about this particular cultural group can lead to lucrative consulting jobs? Or perhaps the motivation is to find ways to empower our own communities. On the other hand, the reason may be primarily professional advancement rather than personal learning.

Also, it may be easier for white middle-class researchers to put the focus on other groups rather than their own, in a form of culture envy or appropriation (Gonzalez, 1998). This is not to say that in any of these instances, the research should *not* be conducted. It means only that we need to question our motivations. Who benefits from our research? What are the implications of our research to this community?

ETHICAL RESEARCHERS ARE SELF-REFLECTIVE ABOUT THEIR POSITIONALITY

According to Alcoff (1991), the first step in attaining a speaking-with-and-to position is for researchers to be self-reflective. To recognize and articulate power and contextual influences, researchers need to examine the position from which they are speaking and their location with respect to the other being researched. As many scholars point out, researchers are almost always in positions of power, due to advanced education and the concomitant privileged social position (Allen et al., 1999; Hammersly, 1992; Hegde, 1998; Rosaldo, 1989; Said, 1989, 1994; Stanfield, 1993b).

Researchers must think about the bearing of location and context on what they say, first, to articulate the possible connections between location and what they are saying (but not as a disclaimer). It may be time for all researchers, even functionalists, to include a description of their positions in their research reports, enabling readers to assess the research conclusions better.

In functionalist research, researchers should consider how their position may influence the implementation of the research project. Will participants cooperate only because researchers are in a position of authority? Or will the participants resist because of the power differential? If they participate, will respondents answer truthfully on questionnaires and interviews?

In examining positionality, researchers should not be afraid to turn the research spotlight ón themselves. For example, white researchers are beginning to examine the explicit construction of white identity and communication patterns in the United States (Martin et al., 1996; Rowe, 2000). This research stands in contrast to the research that focuses on communication of whites without naming it that.

ETHICAL RESEARCH ATTEMPTS VALID INTERPRETATIONS

This is not as obvious as it seems. Valid interpretations are those that make sense to the others being studied, depends on their participation, and is not as easily achieved as the methods textbooks say. As one scholar observed, "Many researchers would be surprised, if not angry, if they could see the Afro-American respondents who so politely answered their questions and then kindly closed the door after them, only to have a good laugh" (Stanfield, 1993a, p. 31).

The style of reporting should also be appropriate to the community. In an ethnographic study of the sharing of spiritual traditions between Indians and non-Indians, Gonzalez (1998) describes her realization that "traditional academic writing would distort what had been shared with me in ways that would very likely offend or hurt . . . the dialectic tension would be removed by reporting units of knowledge rather than present both the positive and negative" (p. 488). She then decided to write the ethnography in poetry, because "poetry enabled the dialectic tension to be maintained, and allowed for the experience of the spiritual through poesies" (p. 488).

As noted earlier, one way to increase validity and ensure appropriateness is to involve members of the community. There are guidelines for member checking, whether the research is a survey, a personality inventory, or an interview/participant-observation study (Hammersly, 1992; Lincoln & Guba, 1985). We might go so far as to suggest that those publishing research on others report member checks, regardless of research paradigm.

► Conclusion

In summary, this chapter represents a continuing dialogue about ethical issues in research on culture and communication. It has been pointed out that functionalist researchers have contributed a concern for not harming others; interpretive cultural communication researchers extend this discussion to concern for not wronging and suggestions that others should benefit, that researchers should rethink their relationship to others. Critical researchers contend that relationships between researchers and research—and research positionality—should be examined and included as part of the research reporting. To bring the discussion full circle, we propose that all intercultural communication research be based on an ethic of speaking with and to, taking into account cultural and paradigmatic norms.

► References

Alcoff, L. (1991). The problem of speaking for others. *Cultural Critique, 20,* 5-32.

Allen, B. J., Orbe, M. P., & Olivas, M. R. (1999). The complexity of our tears: Dis/enchantment and (in)difference in the academy. *Communication Theory, 9,* 402-429.

Allen, C. (1997). Spies like us: When sociologists deceive their subjects. *Lingua Franca, 7* (9), 30-39.

American Psychological Association. (1992). *American Psychological Association ethics code.* Washington, DC: Author. Available: www.apa.org/ethics/code.html (Accessed November 22, 2000)

Andersen, M. L. (1993). Studying across difference: Race, class, and gender in qualitative research. In J. H. Stanfield II & R. M. Dennis (Eds.), *Race and ethnicity in research methods* (pp. 39-52). Newbury Park, CA: Sage.

Arliss, L. P., & Borisoff, D. J. (Eds.). (1993). *Women & men communicating: Challenges and changes.* New York: Holt, Rinehart & Winston.

Barnlund, D. C. (1982). The cross-cultural arena: An ethical void. In L. Samovar & R. E. Porter (Eds.), *Intercultural communication: A reader* (3rd ed., pp. 378-383). Belmont, CA: Wadsworth.

Baudrillard, J. (1988). *The ecstasy of communication.* New York: Semiotext(e).

Bower, R. T., & de Gasparis, P. (1978). *Ethics in social research: Protecting the interests of human subjects.* New York: Praeger.

Bruneau, T. (2000). Peace communication: The ethics of caring across cultures. In L. A. Samovar & R. E. Porter (Eds.), *Intercultural communication: A reader* (9th ed., pp. 455-463). Belmont, CA: Wadsworth.

Carbaugh, D. (Ed.). (1990). *Cultural communication and intercultural contact.* Hillsdale, NJ: Lawrence Erlbaum.

Carr, W., & Kemmis, S. (1986). *Becoming critical: Education, knowledge, and action research*. Philadelphia: Falmer.

Casmir, F. L. (1997a). Ethics, culture, and communication: An application of the third-culture building model to international and intercultural communication. In F. L. Casmir (Ed.), *Ethics in intercultural and international communication* (pp. 89-118). Mahwah, NJ: Lawrence Erlbaum.

Casmir, F. L. (Ed.). (1997b). *Ethics in intercultural and international communication*. Mahwah, NJ: Lawrence Erlbaum.

Cassell, J. (1982). Harms, benefits, wrongs, and rights in fieldwork. In J. E. Sieber (Ed.), *The ethics of social research: Fieldwork, regulation, and publication* (pp. 8-27). New York: Springer-Verlag.

Clifford, J. (1988). *The predicament of culture*. Cambridge, MA: Harvard University Press.

Clifford, J., & Marcus, G. (Eds.). (1986). *Writing culture: The poetics and politics of ethnography*. Berkeley: University of California Press.

Conquergood, D. (1991). Rethinking ethnography: Toward a critical cultural politics. *Communication Monographs, 58,* 179-194.

Conquergood, D. (1992). Ethnography, rhetoric, and performance. *Quarterly Journal of Speech, 78,* 80-97.

Davis, O. I., Nakayama, T. K., & Martin, J. N. (2000). Current and future directions in ethnicity and methodology. *International Journal of Intercultural Communication, 24,* 1-12.

Deetz, S. (1990). Reclaiming the subject matter as a guide to mutual understanding: Effectiveness and ethics in interpersonal interaction. *Communication Quarterly, 38,* 226-243.

Denzin, N. (1996). *Interpretive ethnography: Ethnographic practices in the 21st century*. Thousand Oaks, CA: Sage.

Diener, E., & Crandall, R. (1978). *Ethics in social and behavioral research*. Chicago: University of Chicago Press.

Ellis, C. (1986). *Fisher folk*. Lexington: University of Kentucky Press.

Fabian, J. (1990). *Power and performance: Ethnographic explorations through proverbial wisdom and theater in Shaba, Zaire*. Berkeley: University of California Press.

Facio, E. (1993). Ethnography as personal experience. In J. H. Stanfield II & R. M. Dennis (Eds.), *Race and ethnicity in research methods* (pp. 75-91). Newbury Park, CA: Sage.

Fiske, J. (1991). Writing ethnographies: Contribution to a dialogue. *Quarterly Journal of Speech, 77,* 330-335.

Fitch, K. (1994). A cross-cultural study of directive sequences and some implications for compliance-gaining research. *Communication Monographs, 61*(3), 185-209.

Foucault, M. (1988). The ethic of care for the self as a practice of freedom. In J. Bernauer & D. Rasmussen (Eds.), *The final Foucault* (pp. 1-20). Cambridge: Massachusetts Institute of Technology Press.

Fullbrook, K. (1990). *Free women: Ethics and aesthetics in 20th century women's fiction*. Philadelphia: Temple University Press.

Gilchrist, J. A. (Ed.). (1997). *Proceedings of the 4th National Communication Ethics Conference*. Washington, DC: National Communication Association.

Glazer, M. (1982). The threat of the stranger: Vulnerability, reciprocity, and fieldwork. In J. E. Sieber (Ed.), *The ethics of social research: Fieldwork, regulation, and publication* (pp. 49-71). New York: Springer-Verlag.

Gonzalez, M. C. (1998). Painting the white face red: Intercultural contact presented in poetic ethnography. In J. N. Martin, T. K. Nakayama, & L. A. Flores (Eds.), *Readings in cultural contexts* (pp. 485-495). Mountain View, CA: Mayfield.

Gonzalez, M. C. (2000). The four seasons of ethnography: A creation centered ontology for ethnography. *International Journal of Intercultural Relations, 24,* 623-650.

Gonzalez, A., Houston, M., & Chen, V. (Eds.). (2000). *Our voices: Essays in ethnicity, culture, and communication* (3rd ed.). Los Angeles: Roxbury.

Gramsci, A. (1971). *Selections from the prison notebooks* (Q. Hoare & G. N. Smith, Trans.). New York: International.

Greenwood, D. J., White, W. F., & Harkavy, I. (1993). Participatory action research as a process and as a goal. *Human Relations, 46,* 175-192.

Grossberg, L. (1985). Strategies of Marxist cultural interpretation. *Critical Studies in Mass Communication, 1,* 392-421.

Gudykunst, W. B. (1995). Anxiety/uncertainty management (AUM) theory: Current status. In R. L. Wiseman (Ed.), *Intercultural communication theory* (pp. 8-58). Thousand Oaks, CA: Sage.

Gudykunst, W. B., & Nishida, T. (1989). Theoretical perspectives for studying intercultural communication. In M. K. Asante & W. B. Gudykunst (Eds.), *Handbook of international and intercultural communication* (pp. 17-46). Newbury Park, CA: Sage.

Gudykunst, W. B., & Ting-Toomey, S. (1996). Communication in personal relationships across cultures: An introduction. In W. B. Gudykunst, S. Ting-Toomey, & T. Nishida (Eds.), *Communication in personal relationships across cultures* (pp. 3-16). Thousand Oaks, CA: Sage.

Gudykunst, W. B., Ting-Toomey, S., & Nishida, T. (Eds.). (1996). *Communication in personal relationships across cultures.* Thousand Oaks, CA: Sage.

Habermas, J. (1981). Modernity versus postmodernity. *New German Critique, 22,* 3-14.

Habermas, J. (1984). *The theory of communicative action: Reason and the rationalization of society* (Vol. 1) (T. McCarthy, Trans.). Boston: Beacon.

Habermas, J. (1987). *The theory of communicative action: Lifeworld and system* (Vol. 2) (T. McCarthy, Trans.). Boston: Beacon.

Hall, B. J. (1992). Theories of culture and communication. *Communication Theory, 1,* 50-70.

Hall, B. J. (1997). Culture, ethics, and communication. In F. L. Casmir (Ed.), *Ethics in intercultural and international communication* (pp. 11-42). Mahwah, NJ: Lawrence Erlbaum.

Hall, S. (1985). Signification, representation, ideology: Altusser and the poststructuralist debates. *Critical Studies in Mass Communication, 2,* 91-114.

Hammersly, M. (1992). *What's wrong with ethnography?* New York: Routledge.

Hammersly, M. (1995). *The politics of social research.* Thousand Oaks, CA: Sage.

Hecht, M. L., Ribeau, S., & Alberts, J. K. (1989). An Afro-American perspective on interethnic communication. *Communication Monographs, 56,* 385-410.

Hegde, R. S. (1998). A view from elsewhere: Locating difference and the politics of representation from a transnational feminist perspective. *Communication Theory, 8*(3), 271-297.

Heller, F. (1986). Another look at action research. *Human Relations, 46,* 1235-1242.

Heller, F. (Ed.). (1993). *The use and abuse of social science.* Newbury Park, CA: Sage.

Herring, M. Y. (1988). *Ethics and the professor.* New York: Garland.

Homan, R. (1991). *The ethics of social research.* New York: Longman.

Hook, S., Kurtz, P., & Todorovich, M. (Eds.). (1977). *The ethics of teaching and scientific research.* Buffalo, NY: Prometheus.

Horkheimer, M., & Adorno, T. (1988). *Dialectic of enlightenment* (J. Cumming, Trans.). New York: Continuum.

Houston, M. (2000). Writing for my life: Community-cognizant scholarship on African American women and communication. *International Journal of Intercultural Relations, 24,* 673-686.

Houston, M. S., & Kramarae, C. (1991). Speaking from silence: Methods of silencing and of resistance. *Discourse & Society, 2,* 387-399.

Howell, W. (1981, November). *Ethics of intercultural communication.* Paper presented at the 67th meeting of the Speech Communication Association, Anaheim, CA.

Howell, W. (1982, November). *Carrying ethical concepts across cultural boundaries.* Paper presented at the 68th meeting of the Speech Communication Association, Louisville, KY.

Hymes, D. (1974). *Foundations in sociolinguistics: An ethnographic approach.* Philadelphia: University of Pennsylvania Press.

Jandt, F., & Tanno, D. V. (1994). Redefining the "other" in multicultural research. *The Howard Journal of Communications, 5,* 36-45.

Johannesen, R. L. (1990). *Ethics in human communication* (3rd ed.). Prospect Heights, IL: Waveland.

Kale, D. W. (1994). Peace as an ethic for intercultural communication. In L. A. Samovar & R. E. Porter (Eds.), *Intercultural communication: A reader* (7th ed., pp. 435-444). Belmont, CA: Wadsworth.

Karhausen, L. (1987). From ethics to medical ethics. In S. Doxiadis (Ed.), *Ethical dilemmas in health promotion* (pp. 25-33). New York: John Wiley.

Katriel, T. (1995). From "context" to "contexts" in intercultural communication research. In R. Wiseman (Ed.), *Intercultural communication theory* (pp. 271-284). Thousand Oaks, CA: Sage.

Kemmis, S., & McTaggart, R. (1988). *The action research planner.* Geelong, Australia: Deakin University Press.

Kvale, S. (1996). *Interviews: An introduction to qualitative research interviewing.* Thousand Oaks, CA: Sage.

Lavie, S. (1990). *The poetics of military occupation: Mzeina allegories of identity under Israeli and Egyptian rule.* Berkeley: University of California Press.

Lincoln, Y. S., & Guba, E. G. (1985). *Naturalistic inquiry.* Beverly Hills, CA: Sage.

Lindlof, T. R. (1995). *Qualitative communication research methods.* Thousand Oaks, CA: Sage.

Lindsley, S. L. (1999). A layered model of problematic intercultural communication in U.S.-owned maquiladoras in Mexico. *Communication Monographs, 66,* 145-167.

Lukacs, G. (1971). *History and class consciousness: Studies in Marxist dialectics* (R. Livingstone, Trans.). Cambridge: Massachusetts Institute of Technology Press.

Lyotard, J. F. (1984). *The postmodern condition: A report on knowledge* (G. Bennington & B. Massumi, Trans.). Minneapolis: University of Minnesota Press.

Martin, J. N., Flores, L. A., & Nakayama, T. K. (1998). Ethical issues in intercultural communication. In J. N. Martin, T. K. Nakayama, & L. A. Flores (Eds.), *Readings in cultural contexts* (pp. 455-462). Mountain View, CA: Mayfield.

Martin, J. N., Hammer, M. R., & Bradford, L. (1994). The influence of cultural and situational contexts on Hispanic and non-Hispanic communication competence behaviors. *Communication Quarterly, 42,* 160-179.

Martin, J. N., Krizek, R. L., Nakayama, T. K., & Bradford, L. (1996). Exploring whiteness: A study of self labels for White Americans. *Communication Quarterly, 44*(2), 125-144.

Martin, J. N., & Nakayama, T. K. (1999). Thinking dialectically about culture and communication. *Communication Theory, 9,* 1-25.

McEuen, V. S., Gordon, R. D., & Todd-Mancillas, W. R. (1990). A survey of doctoral education in communication research ethics. *Communication Quarterly, 38,* 281-290.

Mead, M. (1969). Research with human beings: A model derived from anthropological field practice. *Daedelus, 98,* 361-386.

Metzger, J. G., & Springston, J. K. (1992). The skillful, the loving, and the right: An analysis of ethical theories and an application to the treaty rights debate in Wisconsin. *The Howard Journal of Communications, 4,* 75-91.

Mumby, D. K. (1997). Modernism, postmodernism, and communication studies: A rereading of an ongoing debate. *Communication Theory, 7,* 1-28.

Nishida, T. (1996). Communication in personal relationships in Japan. In W. B. Gudykunst, S. Ting-Toomey, & T. Nishida (Eds.), *Communication in personal relationships across cultures* (pp. 237-262). Thousand Oaks, CA: Sage.

Orbe, M. P. (1998). *Constructing co-cultural theory: An explication of culture, power, & communication.* Thousand Oaks, CA: Sage.

Orbe, M. P. (2000). Centralizing diverse racial/ethnic voices in scholarly research: The value of phenomenological inquiry. *International Journal of Intercultural Relations, 24,* 603-621.

Popper, Sir C. (1976). *Unended quest: An intellectual autobiography/Carl Popper* (rev. ed.). LaSalle, IL: Open Court Press.

Reason, P., & Rowan, F. (Eds.). (1981). *Human inquiry: A sourcebook of new paradigm research.* New York: John Wiley.

Rosaldo, R. (1989). *Culture and truth: The remaking of social analysis.* Boston: Beacon.

Rowe, A. M. (2000). Locating feminism's subject: The paradox of white femininity and the struggle to forge feminist alliances. *Communication Theory, 10,* 64-80.

Said, E. W. (1989). Representing the colonized: Anthropology's interlocutors. *Critical Inquiry, 15,* 205-225.

Said, E. W. (1994). *Representations of the intellectuals.* New York: Pantheon.

Scott, J. C. (1990). *Domination and the arts of resistance: Hidden transcripts.* New Haven, CT: Yale University Press.

Shuter, R. (2000). Ethics, culture, and communication: An intercultural perspective. In L. A. Samovar & R. E. Porter (Eds.), *Intercultural communication: A reader* (9th ed., pp. 443-450). Belmont, CA: Wadsworth.

Sieber, J. E. (Ed.). (1982). *The ethics of social research: Fieldwork, regulation, and publication.* New York: Springer-Verlag.

Sieber, J. E. (1992). *Planning ethically responsible research.* Newbury Park, CA: Sage.

Sjoberg, G. (Ed.). (1967). *Ethics, politics, and social research.* Cambridge, MA: Schenkman.

Spivak, G. (1988). Can the subaltern speak? In C. Nelson & L. Grossberg (Eds.), *Marxism and interpretation of culture.* Urbana: University of Illinois Press.

Stanfield, J. H., II. (1993a). Epistemological considerations. In J. H. Stanfield II & R. M. Dennis (Eds.), *Race and ethnicity in research methods* (pp. 16-36). Newbury Park, CA: Sage.

Stanfield, J. H., II. (1993b). Methodological reflections: An introduction. In J. H. Stanfield II & R. M. Dennis (Eds.), *Race and ethnicity in research methods* (pp. 3-15). Newbury Park, CA: Sage.

Steiner, L. (1997). A feminist schema for analysis of ethical dilemmas. In F. L. Casmir (Ed.), *Ethics in intercultural and international communication* (pp. 59-88). Mahwah, NJ: Lawrence Erlbaum.

Stringer, E. T. (1996). *Action research: Handbook for practitioners.* Thousand Oaks, CA: Sage.

Ting-Toomey, S. (Ed.). (1994). *The challenge of facework: Cross cultural and interpersonal issues.* Albany: State University of New York Press.

Ting-Toomey, S., & Chung, L. (1996). Cross-cultural interpersonal communication: Theoretical trends and research directions. In W. B. Gudykunst, S. Ting-Toomey, & T. Nishida (Eds.), *Communication in personal relationships across cultures* (pp. 237-262). Thousand Oaks, CA: Sage.

Triandis, H. C. (1983). The essentials of studying culture. In D. Landis & R. W. Brislin (Eds.), *Handbook of intercultural training* (Vol. 1, pp. 82-117). New York: Pergamon.

van de Vijver, F., & Leung, K. (1997). *Methods and data analysis for cross-cultural research: Cross-cultural psychology* (Vol. 1). Thousand Oaks, CA: Sage.

Wax, M. L. (1982). Research reciprocity rather than informed consent in fieldwork. In J. E. Sieber (Ed.), *The ethics of social research: Fieldwork, regulation, and publication* (pp. 33-48). New York: Springer-Verlag.

Wellman, C. (1988). *Ethics and morals* (2nd ed.). Englewood Cliffs, NJ: Prentice Hall.

Whyte, W. F. (1991). *Participatory action research.* Newbury Park, CA: Sage.

Afrocentric Empiricism

A Model for Communication Research in Africa

DONALD S. TAYLOR
PETER O. NWOSU

Afrocentrism provides essential structures through which a unique consciousness that is rooted in African history, African traditions, and the core value boundaries of African culture can be explored (Asante, 1980, 1989). The need for such an approach in the study of human and mediated communication processes and patterns in Africa has been apparent in communications research for quite some time (Nwosu, Taylor, & Blake, 1998).

Any cursory review of the available research will show that our knowledge of how Africans communicate in purely African settings is, at best, fragmentary, unsystematic, and largely Eurocentric in orientation. Several

reasons have been suggested for this paucity of knowledge. Among them are these: the universality of elements in the communication process (e.g., source, message, channel, receiver) has produced equally universal assumptions about communication possibilities; the tendency is to study African communication processes as opposed to African patterns of communication in ways that are culture sensitive; unsuitable Western concepts and measurement tools are applied to examine communication behaviors in African environments; and a viable African-derived method that offers a necessary basis to understand individual and collective motivations is presumed to be absent (Blake, 1993b; Drake,

1973; Mbiti, 1975; Mukasa & Becker, 1992; Nwosu et al., 1998; Nwosu, Taylor, & Onwumechili, 1995; Obeng-Quaidoo, 1985, 1986).

Even though some Afrocentric perspectives have emerged in the writing of some Africanist scholars, as a whole, they have never been integrated into any systematic model for conducting communication research in Africa. For instance, much of the work done in Africa in the area of intercultural communication and communication and national development has emphasized the value of culture and interpersonal networks for effective communication strategies. Consider, for example, that Ugboajah (1986), Sonaike (1987), Mudariki (1990), McLean (1992), and others have emphasized the resiliency of African culture such that only people-centered communication policies emphasizing oral traditions were found to be effective. Note also that Rogers (1983) and Mowlana and Wilson (1990) have advocated the saliency of culture and the social system to explain why innovations either succeed or fail.

Similarly, there is an abundance of research that illustrates the difficulty of applying Western-derived concepts and empirical approaches to African communication research. This research discusses the failure of the dominant paradigm of communication and national development (Hagen, 1962; Lerner, 1958; McClelland, 1961; Schramm, 1964; and others); an acceptance that the transfer of technology brings particular value systems that may create conflicts with existing indigenous systems (Beltran, 1976; Hedebro, 1982); the futility of cultural dependency on national development (Beltran, 1976; Schiller, 1978); the notion that African media philosophies are antithetical to Western media principles (Katz & Wedell, 1977; Wilcox, 1973); the value of integrating folk media into Western mass media, including the concept of *oramedia* (Ugboajah, 1986); the suggestion that Western intervention efforts in Africa have, in some ways, been the source of the problem (Frank, 1970; Rodney, 1972); and the need for

indigenous communications systems to be part of the global conversation on communication (UNESCO, 1980), to name a few of the studies that have offered glimpses into what we do not know about how Africans communicate.

Another area of frustration has centered around the challenges of employing Western empirical procedures for observation, conceptualization, and measurement. For instance, survey research techniques typically elicit a respondent's opinion about attitudes, beliefs, and behaviors; yet, expressing personal opinions is not a common feature of African communication processes. Opinions are often influenced by group norms, status, gender, and the like (Nwosu et al., 1995; Obeng-Quaidoo, 1986).

Other problems have also been identified. They include difficulties with translation in regard to such things as language equivalencies in a continent where there is a high illiteracy rate in the major international languages (Gwebu, 1977; Taylor, 1991); difficulties with asking sensitive and taboo questions, especially those related to sex, income, age, and other personal issues (Nwosu et al., 1995); the absence of data sources from which relevant samples may be drawn; and the difficulties associated with applying a range of variations between extremes (e.g., forced-choice items in survey research) in settings where people may think in dichotomous terms (e.g., agree vs. disagree) (Nwosu et al., 1995; Taylor, 1991).

As a result of these misassumptions, scholars have struggled with problems of validity, arriving at conclusions that are inadequate to advance theory and describing African behaviors from the prism of Western rationality. Through these discourses, a clear need has been established for advancing a method to conduct communication research in Africa with the goal of increasing our knowledge of African communication processes and patterns. Against this background, the Afrocentric framework is presented as a viable basis on which to commence any such inquiries. The framework is reflective of the transcultural theme of the book because it offers another viable approach to knowing from the prism of African rationality.

Asante (1989) and others have argued that the Afrocentric framework considers that the way Africans have been socialized also determines how they will conceptualize various phenomena. As Harris (1992) observed, "the way one constructs reality, one's place in it, and the way one validates knowledge determines one's life chances" (p. 58). This need to understand how Africans interpret reality becomes the indispensable starting point for studying communication in different contexts in Africa. At a minimum, it presents a new imperative of integrating an understanding of the core value boundaries that guide African rationality into communication problem solving in that setting. Any assumptions of universal or homogenous African processes and patterns are considered in relation to cultural variability, unique cultural experiences, and environment-specific factors that make Africans similar but yet different in their communication experiences.

In this chapter, then, we respond to this felt need by proposing an African-centered model for conducting communication research in Africa. The assumptions we make are:

1. Existing Western concepts and tools are inadequate to understand unique and complex African communication environments.
2. The core value boundaries that make up African rationality must accompany explanations of African communication phenomena.
3. Afrocentric assumptions are necessary to build a model that has a better capacity to understand how Africans communicate.

The discussion is organized into three main parts. The first is an examination of the epistemological foundation of Afrocentrism, including a discussion of some of the challenges that non-Afrocentric perspectives face in seeking valid interpretation of African communication phenomena. The second is an overview of several components of the African-centered model proposed here and its utility.

▶ Structuring an African-Centered Epistemology

Discussions about epistemology focus on how we know and how we know that we know. When approached from purely Western reasoning, the search begins with seeking to establish proofs that, in an empirical sense, explore cause and effect relations in mechanistic and linear ways. Events are directly observed and are presumed to be objectively measured against "universal" (read Western) yardsticks of probabilistic determinism. The individual is the unit of measurement and becomes the basis for understanding phenomena. Any interpretation, then, must be grounded in a rational theory that advances or dispels the original observation.

The Afrocentric paradigm, on the other hand, is predicated on the humanistic principles of "interconnectedness and interdependency of natural phenomena" (Schiele, 1990, p. 146). In a very practical way, it accepts the collective consciousness of the African and uses that to insulate interpretations of African communication behavior. Asante (1990) asserts that under this paradigm, the quest for proof about observations must derive from "language, myth, ancestral memory, dance- music-art, and science" to arrive at shared perceptions, attitudes, and predispositions (p. 10).

Phoenix (1991) in his essay *Toward an Afrocentric Way of Knowing* eloquently illustrates how this African worldview is deeply rooted in symbols that go much deeper than words. Specifically, "one knows not just through counting and measuring nor through just reasoning alone, but ultimately, one knows through the symbolic, through rhythm and through shared feelings" (p. 29). The relationship then between the symbols (rhythm, shared feelings, time, and so on) are at the superstructure of the African rationality. Understanding the interdependencies between these elements requires going beyond the surface structure. It also requires researchers to be equipped with the ability to adequately decode symbols rooted in the deep structure of what is being observed, for therein lies the meaning. Consequently, Asante has argued that Afrocentric investigators must devise methods that engage researchers in cultural and social immersion into the African environment where they become familiar with the history and philosophy of the people under study. Specifically, "this is an interactive rather than a distant, sterile, abstract, isolated, and non-contact model. This method finds its strength in the cooperative and integrative function of human experiences" (p. 26).

Drawing from these propositions, several Afrocentric researchers have advanced some basic assumptions that underlie the perspective. Covin (1990) synthesized the available body of knowledge to offer the following five measures of Afrocentric inquiry:

1. People of African descent share a common experience, struggle, and origin.
2. The infusion of European values into African societies has a nonmaterial effect on African culture. Thus, African cultures are resistant to assault on their traditional beliefs and norms.
3. The value of modernization processes must be linked to the core African values of harmony with nature, humaneness, and rhythm.
4. An African way of knowing and of interpreting the world can be developed.
5. Communalism undergirds the production and distribution of wealth.

These postulates clearly encapsulate the essential perspectives on which to build a parsimonious model for the study of communication phenomena in Africa. Such a model would include elements that relate to core African values, distinguish between communication processes and patterns and their interdependence with core African values, and build an Africalogical methodology that identifies the process and patterns for studying communication in African settings. According to Afrocentric notions, the model would also be sensitive to exploring traditional beliefs, even in situations where Western influences are evident; it should relate such concepts as harmony with nature, rhythm, and communalism to explain the deep structure of the African communication experience.

Clearly, such a humanistic perspective would be at variance with mainstream empirical approaches and may, in some respects, be thought too subjective for scientific conclusions. Herein lies the challenge: to break new frontiers in explaining what we know about how Africans communicate. The need to inject an African-derived epistemology into the research process requires familiarization with new tools, new forms of rationality, and a new lexicon of discourse. These are embodied in what Asante (1990) has called "the soul of method" in Afrocentric research. He asserts that

There is nothing mysterious in this type of appreciation of the human process of activating Afrocentric research. . . . In research, the scholar must understand that everything is potentially active, powerful, and possible, and it is up to the scholar to access the vitality of the project. . . . Soul, as a concrete motive force, activates research by engaging the researcher in an effort to explain human functioning by relating to concrete human conditions and cultural factors" (p. 108).

From this perspective, it becomes immediately apparent why existing research attempts have been insufficient to understand African communication phenomena. In the next section, we offer a model for conducting communication research in Africa.

The model depicted in Figure 17.1 encompasses three key elements: the core set of African values, the communication units of

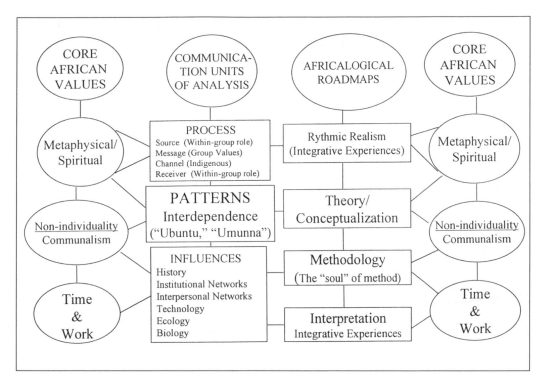

Figure 17.1. Afrocentric Empiricism: A Model for Communication Research in Africa.

analysis, and elements of an Africalogical empiricism.

▶ The Afrocentric Model

Although some might perceive the central components of this model as ultimately succumbing to a linear-empirical paradigm, in reality, a proper application of this model shifts it much more within the domain of a nonlinear framework. An essential pillar on which this nonlinear expectation lies is the requirement that for each element of the model, integration of core African values must guide conceptualization, methodology, and interpretation. Thus, it is quite conceivable that in some African settings, the application might be more nonlinear than it is linear, whereas in some other African settings, the application might produce more linear than nonlinear associations. This is what lends credence and

vitality to the model's transcultural nature. Indeed, it is against this background that careful examination of the model must be assessed.

The central component of the model is the core set of African values. These core values include the African's relationship to the metaphysical and spiritual world, the relationship to time and work, and the relationship to the group and one's role and place in it. These core values generally inform social discourse and interpersonal interactions in Africa. We argue that to competently study and meaningfully analyze African communication discourse, researchers not only must be aware of but must equally be guided by some understanding of African philosophical thought discussed in the previous section and the core value boundaries of African culture that emerge from that philosophy.

Several African scholars have written about these values (Mbiti, 1975; Obeng-

Quaidoo, 1986; Onwubiko, 1991; Sofola, 1982). Obeng-Quaidoo (1986), for instance, identifies four such values: the metaphysical/spiritual value, the relationship to time, work, and the person. The metaphysical/spiritual dimension of the African demonstrates the relationship of Africans to a supreme god and lesser gods; the concept of personhood demonstrates the relationship of Africans to one another in the context of communalism or individualism; and the concepts of time and reincarnation, as well as the concept of work, demonstrate how Africans relate to nature and the cosmos as well as how they view work. Although these value boundaries are found around the continent and among Africans, there are within-group differences from region to region. Each of these core value boundaries is implicated in communication activities in African settings.

Obeng-Quaidoo (1986) notes that the African worldview is both metaphysical and spiritual, evolving around one Supreme Deity (called different names by different groups on the continent) and lesser gods. The lesser deities, it is believed, have a supernatural connection with the Supreme Deity. Because the Supreme Being is held so high but seems so far away, it is very common for Africans to consult the representatives (priests) of lesser deities to seek solutions to the challenges of daily life. In African rationality, God is the Great Force in a hierarchy of forces that begins with spirits and ancestors, followed by living men, then animals, vegetables, and minerals. In African thought these beings have an intimate ontological relationship. As a result, Africans feel themselves to be part of a hierarchy of forces (Obeng-Quaidoo, 1986).

Clearly, the above dynamic conception of being in African rationality essentially differs from the metaphysics of Western philosophy, which has long been based on a static conception of being. More important, it helps us understand role differentiations within African societies. This understanding is critical when researchers begin to develop the unit of analysis for a study. Should the focus, for example, be on the individual per se, or should it

be on individuals as they function within the group? We shall return to this point later.

Related to the conception of being is the second core value boundary of African culture, the concept of communalism. Although somewhat similar to Hofstede's (1980) concept of collectivism, the African concept is not necessarily the same. Communalism as a construct captures the full essence and the "core of social life" in Africa. Just as the concept of individualism has been elevated to the status of a national religion in the West (Stewart & Bennett, 1991), the same can be said of the concept of communalism in Africa. Whereas individualism represents commitments to independence, privacy, self, and the all-important *I,* communalism represents commitment to interdependence, community affiliation, others, and the idea of *we* (Nwosu et al., 1998). As Awa (1988) notes,

> Communalism is the soul and fibre of work, activity, and social life in Africa. It is a testament to the nonindividuality of the African, a vital part of the African cultural ethos . . . [providing] social security for the less fortunate members of a community. It is, in a sense, an outward expression of the empathy of the African—the impulse to show concern for others. (p. 136)

Communalism is manifested, for example, through the extended family system, which has been well documented (see Anyaegbunam, 1995; Awa, 1988).

Anyaegbunam (1995), drawing, for example, on the life experiences of Igbos of eastern Nigeria, notes that the Igbos treasure kinship solidarity so much that they often say

> *Onye ya na Umunna ya n'akwuro ga eli onwe ya* (A person who is not with the members of his extended family must bury himself). In fact, group solidarity is manifested in every aspect of Igbo life—at birth through death; in peace and in war; in marriage and in family. The Igbo social structure rests on the family, the extended family. (p. 7)

The kinship relationship is a vital force in the Igbo social system, in that it shapes the behavior of the individual toward the others. The underlying principle here is found in the Igbo saying, "I am because we are, and since we are, therefore I am." The Igbo concept of *Umunna* (extended family group or kindred) typifies the emphasis on communalism or interdependence rather than individualism as a vital part of the African cultural ethos. In South Africa, the Zulu word *Ubuntu* also signifies the African emphasis on group solidarity or interdependence. The underlying principle of *Ubuntu* is that a person can only be a person through others (Mbiti & Maree, 1995).

Overall, the African believes that he is a part of a wheel of interacting forces, a part of the larger community of individuals, and that how he behaves has an impact on those individuals and affects the full functioning of the community. The African believes that his life belongs not to himself, but to his elders, his ancestors, and his God. This simple principle serves to guide his relationship with other members of the community. Therefore, what he chooses to do and what he chooses not to do have direct impact on preserving the community's social ethos and stregthening its fabric and fiber.

A third core value boundary of African culture, crucial to our model, is the attitude toward time and reincarnation. First, the African concept of time is fundamentally different from the way time is structured and perceived in Western societies. Time is central to all activities in Western societies—business and social; time is not central to life in Africa. Awa (1988) notes that

> African concepts, structure, perceptions of time are dictated by nature. People wake up to the crowing of the cock, which happens at the crack of dawn. Dawn may be anytime from 5:30 to 6:00 a.m. If a paramount chief summons his cabinet through a messenger to convene at daybreak and some arrive at 5:30 a.m. and others at 6:00 a.m., none will be perceived as late. Decisions by "chiefs-in-council" require full representation and participation of all

section heads, and such decisions are generally preceded by a social event—the ritual breaking of kola note, a prolonged libation ceremony—deliberately calculated to allow time for a quorum to be attained. (p. 139)

Obeng-Quaidoo (1986) notes that subsumed in the concept of time (in some African societies) is the concept of reincarnation:

> Death, for the African, means the death of the physical body, but the real essence of the human being lives on and would be born again into the same family or clan. Added to this is the view that the African never accepts death as a natural phenomenon. There is always a reason for death; whether it comes to the youth or to the aged, and this explains the African's preoccupation with necromancy and visits to the priests and shrines to find out why someone is dead. (p. 93)

Furthermore, physical death does not mean spiritual death. When elderly people die, for instance, it is believed that their spirits live on to join those of other departed ancestors of the land, where they continue to offer protection to the extended family or the clan. This explains why Africans first call the spirits of the departed ancestors to guide and protect them, in addition to the Supreme Deity and the other lesser gods, whenever they offer supplications during different occasions.

Blake (1993a) notes,

> African societies share certain fundamental values that guide the day-to-day life of inhabitants in traditional African settings. . . . There are, for example, certain "rules" that guide discourse in the deliberative, forensic, and epidiectic genres. The "rules" are grounded in values such as respect for elders; acceptance of the supremacy of hierarchical structures; performance of certain rituals for various occasions ranging from farming to death and burial ceremonies; sibling relationships, etc. . . . the values, some of which are mentioned above, are critical in our efforts to understand communication philosophies, ethics, processes, struc-

tures and genres in traditional African settings. (p. 3)

A final core value that shapes the model proposed here is the African concept of work. Among Westerners, work is seen as an end in itself, a duty central to one's existence because it has some eternal reward. For the African, work is seen not as a duty that has some eternal reward but as a means to an end, a necessary but not a sufficient condition for survival.

The African communication profile includes communication patterns that demonstrate the core value boundaries of African culture. Thus, to study communication discourse in African settings, researchers must first understand the philosophical underpinnings and the core value boundaries of the African communication profile. In addition, the units of analysis must derive from an understanding of the process and patterns of human communication in African settings, as well as the forces that shape such transactions. Similarly, the investigative tools and the method employed should also reflect that understanding. Let us discuss the units of analysis for conducting communication research in Africa.

▶ The Communication Units of Analysis

In addition to understanding the core value boundaries, the model proposed requires an understanding of the units of analysis in African communication settings.

The unit of analysis in African communication contexts is the individual within the framework of group identity. Institutions around which the individual functions must also be analyzed within the same framework.

From our model, the communication unit of analysis consists of three main elements: process, patterns, and influences. The first element relates to process. The communication process contains four basic characteristics that are universal. These characteristics are *the source,* which is the generator of the message; *the message* itself, which includes both verbal and nonverbal codes that give content and meaning to ideas; *the channels,* which are the mechanisms and situations through which messages are distributed or shared; and *the receiver,* or the person receiving/decoding the message. In essence, when scholars conduct research on communication events, they typically study one or a combination of these characteristics. In Western scientific tradition, when researchers study the source, for example, they are generally interested, for example, in examining the psychological, sociological, and demographic attributes of the individual in terms of source credibility. Sociological attributes would include such things as whether people are single or married and the associations or clubs to which they belong; psychological attributes would include matters related to gender, age, income, and the like. When Western researchers study source credibility, the investigation is conducted within a cultural context, a Eurocentric context. After all, as Wisemann and Koester (1996) note, how scholars go about approaching, conceptualizing, measuring, and studying any or a combination of the elements in the process is informed by a set of cultural rules.

Thus, in examining the communication process in African settings, the elements of the process can only be considered and analyzed from their relationship with cultural patterns that derive from the core value boundaries in Africa. Meaning lies, for example, in exploring the relationship between source and the set of core values or cultural patterns that govern the communication environment in which the source operates and functions in Africa.

The second element of our model deals with *patterns.* Cultural patterns are shared mental perceptions about values, beliefs, and norms that provide meaning to communication events/activities in specific contexts. Individual roles and behaviors in such contexts are, therefore, shaped by these patterns. Gudykunst and Kim (1983) suggest that people behave consistently because their culture provides norms, rules, and values to guide action. This consistency allows for generalizations and predictions about the particular culture, although such generalizations must be viewed as approximations, not absolutes, essentially because some people in the specific context may be atypical of the prevailing values, beliefs, and norms in that context.

Intercultural research suggests four dimensions of values that drive cultural patterns in Africa. These are the relationship to the physical and metaphysical world, the relationship to the group and to the individual, the relationship to time, and the relationship to activity or work. Again, the African's sense of the relationship with these core value boundaries generally informs the nature and climate of social discourses in human interaction processes and must be the focus of analysis in communication research in African settings.

Lustig and Koester (1999) suggest that the forces shaping cultural patterns include history, ecology, biology, technology, institutional arrangements, and interpersonal networks. Consequently, different scholars, because of their cultural backgrounds, will begin their research with different assumptions, different motivations or goals, and different methodologies. Yet, in conducting research in African settings, these assumptions, motivations, and methodologies are assumed to be universal.

In studying African communication processes, one cannot ignore the influence of colonialism on African history, leading, for example, to the scramble for and partition of the continent. The emergence of Francophone and Anglophone Africa, a consequence of colonialism, has had a strong impact on linguistic groupings and communication on the continent. In addition, the impact of the trans-Saharan and trans-Atlantic slave trades and age-old ethnic conflicts cannot be ignored in understanding communication processes and cultural patterns in Africa.

In terms of ecology, the African environment offers an opportunity for understanding the African's relationship to nature, the nature of work, and attitudes toward work. For the most part, the African environment has encouraged such professions as fishing, agriculture, herding, and so on. The clothing styles, the food patterns, and the way houses are built are a function of the ecology.

Although Africans are generally racially homogenous, there are differences in physical attributes depending on the region. In North Africa, for example, there is a large presence of fair-skinned groups, in contrast to sub-Saharan Africa, a region with predominantly dark-skinned groups. More work is needed to establish the extent to which such biological differences affect communication in Africa. However, research has shown that physical attributes do alter our perceptions of each other and thus have a major influence on human interaction processes.

With regard to institutional arrangements, such things as religion, system of governance, marriage, and so on emerge. Consider, for example, religion. Although African spirituality is not based on mass worship, the indigenous belief systems that draw on various notions of spirituality provide a basis for the values that most Africans hold. The extent to which a person holds a particular value provides a more accurate reading of the rhythm that gives meaning to the communication event.

Most traditional African societies have customary structures of governance that shape a person's attitudes toward interpersonal interactions. Thus, how we relate to people in authority or people who are old and how we relate to peers, whether male or female, whether the message is direct or indirect, is a function of the customary structures of governance designed to promote harmony in social discourses in African settings.

Our position is that in approaching, conceptualizing, measuring, and studying the units of analysis for communication processes and patterns in Africa, researchers must pay close attention to the forces or influences that shape those processes and patterns. Individual roles and behaviors within the context of communication processes in Africa are shaped by these patterns and influences.

Consider, for example, the Maasai of East Africa. Their worldview and approach to communication have been shaped by (a) their history of conflict and warfare against invaders, which has made them suspicious of strangers; (b) their view of nature, which requires every Maasai person to live in harmony with nature; and (c) their institutional arrangements, in which age determines one's role and place in the community. Thus, in Maasai logic, young people cannot know the truth until they become old. The institutional arrangements in Maasai culture also place great value on children. In this context, then, marriage is seen as a communal duty to be performed by each Maasai, and the man with the most children is considered the wealthiest (Skow & Samovar, 1991).

Central to interaction processes among the Maasai is loyalty to the group. This group loyalty, well grounded in the concept of interdependence, suggests a lesser emphasis on loyalty to self. Such things as personal freedom, self-assertiveness, and individual entitlements become secondary to filial piety and group identity. To study communication activities among the Maasai requires researchers first to understand the relational arrangements and the forces that shape such arrangements.

▶ Research Steps: Navigating the Africalogical Roadmap

The third major component features the research steps. It is understood at the outset that Afrocentric empiricism is grounded in a humanistic, generally qualitative research approach. Afrocentric researchers differ from one another in terms of the specific methodology they select to investigate a phenomenon, provided that theories, concepts, data gathering techniques, and interpretations describe the African context according to uniquely African characteristics. The principal steps to consider, then, in conducting an Afrocentric

empirical-humanistic study are as follows. The African communication experience is a complex phenomenon. We need to emphasize discovery rather than validation of existing knowledge.

DEFINING THE PROBLEM

1. Do not conduct a literature review first. Immerse yourself in the phenomenon under investigation with an open mind. Be guided by core African values and the communication unit of analysis to form your own understanding of the nature of the problem before reading others' perceptions and interpretations.

2. Note how things are related to each other, exploring a holistic rather than a particularistic phenomenon.

3. Develop the problem statement only after a careful evaluation of the several dimensions that may emerge so that you can focus on a clearly stated and well defined problem.

DATA TYPE

1. Observe actual communication phenomena with information from indigenous participants to explain and relate to values. What is the meaning of the event to the culture? How has that meaning changed over time?

2. Arrange group settings for interviews, recognizing the power-distance relations that govern group discussion (e.g., the role of chiefs, elders, women, men, children, etc.)

3. Use individual interviews to obtain a pattern of responses, incorporating language and concepts offered by the informant. Only when its meaning is fully grasped should translation of the concept or behavior be undertaken.

DATA ANALYSIS

1. Develop and use a coding system that identifies main themes from the events and behaviors observed. These themes must be identified from an African-centered perspective (e.g., Ubuntu).
2. Be guided both by the logical and humanistic elements that are interconnected with communication units of analysis as well as the core values.
3. Identify the repetitive interrelationships.
4. Conduct a literature review to assess prevailing perceptions and interpretations of what you have observed and how these mirror or deviate from your emerging conclusions.

INTERPRETATION

1. Tell the story of the phenomenon as you understand it, taking care to distinguish between analysis and perception. How will those who were studied view themselves?
2. Identify alternative interpretations and clearly show the value of your analysis over that interpretation.
3. Suggest how your interpretations can be independently confirmed.

▶ Conclusion

It should be apparent from the steps outlined above that the goals of Afrocentric empiricism are to discover and illustrate how African-centered explanations help to enhance our understanding of African communication phenomena. Some may ask then, of what functional utility is such a model? Some uses are readily identifiable.

First, the model will enable researchers to explore the cultural warrants embodied in the persuasive discourse patterns of Africans. Second, researchers will accurately provide insights into any unique patterns of how Africans think, feel, and act and by so doing develop effective strategies for conflict management and intercultural communication competence. Third, the model is viable to examine how Africans actually construe their own experience with, for example, the mass media, interpersonal relationship development, effective leadership styles, and gender communication.

The challenge, however, lies in the apparent subjectivity and flexibility of the approach. This difficulty is minimized by the stubborn consistency of core African cultural values, the pillars on which this approach stands.

▶ References

Anyaegbunam, J. (1995). *Igbo traditional marriage and Christian marriage: Toward inculturation.* Unpublished master's thesis, University of Nigeria.

Asante, M. (1980). *Afrocentricity: The theory of social change.* Trenton, NJ: Africa World Press.

Asante, M. (1989). *Afrocentricity.* Trenton, NJ: Africa World Press.

Asante, M. (1990). *Kemet, Afrocentricity, and knowledge.* Trenton, NJ: Africa World Press.

Awa, N. (1988). Communication in Africa: Implications for development planning. *Howard Journal of Communication, 1*(3), 131-144.

Beltran, L. (1976). Alien promises, objects, and methods. *Communication Research, 3,* 107-137.

Blake, C. (1993a). Development communication revisited: An end to Eurocentric visions. *Development, 3,* 8-11.

Blake, C. (1993b). Traditional African values and the right to communicate. *Africa Media Review, 7*(3), 201-216.

Covin, D. (1990). Afrocentricity in Omovimento Begro Unificado. *Journal of Black Studies, 21*(2), 126-144.

Drake, H. (1973). Research method or culture bound technique? Pitfalls of survey research in Africa. In W. O'Barr, D. Spain, & M. Tessler (Eds.), *Survey research in Africa: Its applications and limits* (pp. 58-69). Evanston, IL: Northwestern University Press.

Frank, A. G. (1970). The development of underdevelopment. In R. I. Rhodes (Ed.), *Imperialism and underdevelopment.* New York: Monthly Review.

Gudykunst, W., & Kim, Y. (1983). *Communicating with strangers.* Newbury Park, CA: Sage.

Gwebu, T. (1977). *Migration and the dynamics of a space economy: An investigation of spatial development in Sierra Leone.* Unpublished doctoral dissertation, Kent State University.

Hagen, E. (1962). *On the theory of social change.* Homewood, IL: Dorsey.

Harris, N. (1992). A philosophical basis for an Afrocentric orientation. *Western Journal of Black Studies, 16*(3), 154-159.

Hedebro, G. (1982). *Communication and social change in developing nations: A critical view.* Ames: The Iowa University Press.

Hofstede, G. (1980). *Culture's consequences: International differences in work related values.* Beverly Hills, CA: Sage.

Katz, E., & Wedell, G. (1977). Broadcasting in the third world: Promise and performance. London: Macmillan.

Lerner, D. (1958). *The passing of traditional society.* New York: Free Press.

Lustig, M., & Koester, J. (1999). *Intercultural competence: Interpersonal communication across cultures.* New York: HarperCollins.

Mbiti, J. (1975). *African religion and philosophy.* London: Heinemann.

Mbigi, L., & Maree, J. (1995). *Mbutu: The spirit of African transformation and management.* Pretoria, South Africa: Knowledge Resources (PTY) Ltd.

McClelland, D. (1961). *The achieving society.* Princeton, NJ: Van Nostrand.

McLean, P. E. (1992). Radio and rural development in Swaziland. *Africa Media Review, 6*(3), 51-65.

Mowlana, H., & Wilson, L. J. (1990). *The Passing of modernity: Communication and the transformation of society.* White Plains, NY: Longman.

Mudariki, T. (1990). Literacy and social development in Zimbabwe. *Media Development, 37*(1), 13-14.

Mukasa, S., & Becker, L. (1992). Toward an indigenized philosophy of communication: An analysis of African communication educational resources and needs. *Africa Media Review 6*(3), 31-50.

Nwosu, P., Taylor, D. S., & Blake, C. (1998). Communication and development: Imperatives for an Afrocentric methodology. In J. Hamlet (Ed.), *Afrocentric visions: Studies in culture and communication* (pp. 229-246). Thousand Oaks, CA: Sage.

Nwosu, P., Taylor, D. S., & Onwumechili, C. (1995). Search for appropriate research methods in the African context. In P. Nwosu, C. Onwumechili, & R. M'Bayo (Eds.), *Communication and the transformation of society: A developing region's perspective* (pp. 397-426). Lanham, MD: University Press of America.

Obeng-Quaidoo. I. (1985). Culture and communication research methodologies in Africa: A proposal for change. *Gazette, 36,* 109-120.

Obeng-Quaidoo, I. (1986). A proposal for new communication research methodologies in Africa. *Africa Media Review, 1*(1), 89-98.

Onwubiko, O. (1991). *African thought, religion, and culture.* Enugu, Nigeria: Shaap Press.

Phoenix, J. K. (1991, Fall). Towards an afrocentric method of knowing. *New Essence.*

Rodney, W. (1972). *How Europe underdeveloped Africa.* Washington, DC: Howard University Press.

Rogers, E. M. (1983). *Diffusion of innovations* (3rd ed). New York: Free Press.

Schiele, J. H. (1990). Organizational theory from an Afrocentric perspective. *Journal of Black Studies, 21*(2), 145-161.

Schiller, H. (1978). *Communication and cultural domination.* New York: International Arts and Sciences Press.

Schramm, W. (1964). *Mass media and national development*. Stanford, CA: Stanford University Press.

Skow, L., & Samovar, L. (1991). Cultural patterns of the Maasai. In L. Samovar & R. Porter (Eds.), *Intercultural communication: A reader.* Belmont, CA: Wadsworth.

Sofola, J. (1982). *African culture and the African personality.* Ibadan, Nigeria: University of Ibadan Press.

Sonaike, S. A. (1987). Going back to basics: Some ideas on the future direction of third world communication research. *Gazette, 40(2),* 79-100.

Stewart, E., & Bennett, M. (1991). *American cultural patterns.* Yarmouth, ME: Intercultural Press.

Taylor, D. S. (1991). *Application of the use and dependency model of mass communication to development communication in the western area of Sierra Leone.* Unpublished doctoral dissertation, Kent State University.

Ugboajah, J. (1986). Communication as technology in rural development. *Africa Media Review, 1*(1), 1-19.

UNESCO. (1980). *Many voices, one world: Communication and society, today and tomorrow.* New York: Author.

Wisemann, R., & Koester, J. (1996). *Intercultural communication competence.* Thousand Oaks, CA: Sage.

Wilcox, D. (1973). *Mass communication in black Africa: Philosophy and control.* New York: Praeger.

Frameworks for Assessing Contact as a Tool for Reducing Prejudice

DONALD L. RUBIN
PAMELA J. LANNUTTI

The fundamental premise of the contact hypothesis, as articulated for about a half century now, is that intergroup prejudice could be reduced if only members of opposing groups could get to know each other better (see reviews in Amir, 1976; Brown, 1995). The appeal of this thesis to the liberal conscience is obvious. People are not naturally hateful. They are merely frightened by the unknown. The task for social policy makers and administrators, therefore, is simply to devise programs that encourage contact. In the warm glow of positive intergroup interactions, people will naturally see that their anxieties about out-group members are groundless. They will experience epiphanies about the essential unity of interests among all humankind.

Intergroup contact of one kind or another occurs in numerous guises and situations, each characterized by greater or lesser degrees of deliberate social engineering. Thus, for example, relatively little programmatic intervention characterizes the everyday, casual social encounters that may under certain circumstances result in reduced prejudice of heterosexuals toward identified gay men and lesbians (Herek & Capitanio, 1996). In contrast, the great social experiments surrounding housing desegregation (Robinson & Preston, 1976) or liberalized immigration policies (Pettigrew, 1997) typically entail deliberate social engineering of intergroup mixing but often lack any provision for third-party facilitation to enhance the quality of the communication between the groups brought thus into contact. Similarly, racial and ethnic integration of public schools (at least in the United States) has too often been unaccompanied by any human relations programming to facilitate constructive interaction between groups. As a result, the kinds of interracial contact that actually take place at purportedly integrated public schools may be quite limited indeed (Grant, 1990).

On the other hand, high levels of both deliberate intergroup mixing and third-party facilitation do characterize the encounter workshops and training programs that have been established in some especially intense and protracted conflict situations (Bar & Eady, 1998). Some of these workshops involve grassroots participants—local youth and other neighborhood residents—who are on the front lines of hostile contact situations (e.g., Bargal, 1992). Other genres of structured workshop intervention may involve community elite and government leaders (e.g., Neu & Volkan, 1999), some of whom may be engaged in formal negotiations (e.g., Kelman, 1998).[1]

The problem with the contact hypothesis is that human social cognition is in situ wondrously more complex, more variable, and more resistant to change than the ideal supposed in the romantic liberal vision of intergroup relations. A vignette captured in the video documentary *Beyond Hate* (Moyers, 1991) shreds any naive faith in the power of interpersonal contact:

Two teenagers—Ariel, an Israeli Jew, and George, a Palestinian Arab—have spent 6 weeks at a summer camp in Maine as part of a facilitated intergroup encounter. By the end of the session, the two boys have grown patently close. Throughout an interview, George solicitously shoos away from Ariel's face an annoying fly that buzzes persistently about his friend. Yet, in counterpoint to this idyllic solicitude, Ariel earnestly accuses Arabs as a group of threatening to kill Jews. George, for his part, allows that in a few years, when Ariel comes to his village as a soldier in the Israeli army, Ariel will not be the same boy with whom he has shared this summer respite; he will be just one more enemy occupier.

If blind faith in intergroup contact as a panacea for prejudice and hostility is naive, so is it unwarranted to abandon contact as a necessary (if not sufficient) element in building toward multicultural harmony (Biernat & Crandall, 1994; Brewer & Miller, 1988; Herek & Capitanio, 1996). The purpose of this chapter is to place the contact hypothesis under close scrutiny so that program developers and policy makers can extract some frameworks for assessing the likelihood of change ensuing from particular contact situations. We begin by considering the variables and factors that mitigate against contact as a force for dissolving stereotypes. We then discuss some of the conditions that tend to increase the potency of contact for prejudice reduction. Next, we consider some of the models and mechanisms that have been proposed as underlying effects of contact on social perceptions. Finally, we observe that previous discussion of the contact hypothesis has largely ignored the various functions that prejudice serves for individuals and groups. We conclude by suggesting that effects of intergroup contact can best be anticipated and engineered when one considers the functions of those prejudices that are targeted for reduction.

▶ The Limits of Contact as a Tool for Reducing Prejudice

In the context of prejudices between Arabs[2] and Israeli Jews, it is generally accepted that those Jews who immigrated from Arab or Muslim nations, or who have Arab or Muslim ancestry, tend to be politically more right-wing and hawkish with regard to Arab affairs; they harbor more *negative* prejudices against Arabs than their compatriots with European backgrounds. In that case, then, historically high contact between ethnic groups is directly proportional to—rather than inversely associated with—prejudice. In a parallel fashion, increased contact with Jews has been associated with decreased tolerance on the part of Arab Israelis (Yogev, Ben-Yehoshua, & Alper, 1991). Similar patterns, wherein high contact leads to increased rather than decreased prejudice, have been detected with disconcerting frequency in other social settings as well (e.g., adverse impact of racial desegregation in U.S. schools on children's social attitudes; Schofield, 1991).

MERE PROPINQUITY

One reason why programs for encouraging intergroup contact have often failed to reduce—and, in some cases, apparently have exacerbated—prejudice is that groups can be in physical proximity (contact) while yet engaging in remarkably limited interpersonal interaction (Hewstone & Brown, 1986). Such is the case for groups that formally proscribe intimate intergroup contact as a measure to preserve in-group ethnolinguistic vitality, such as Amish sects in Ohio and Pennsylvania (Fishman, 1988). Such groups may erect linguistic, dress code, or other symbolic barriers to enforce taboos against interactions more personal than service provider-customer exchanges, even in the midst of crowded multicultural neighborhoods (witness Hasidic enclaves in Brooklyn, N.Y.; Shaffir, 1995).

But propinquity also fails to lead to interpersonal penetration in cases where a history of intergroup hostility and distrust militate against any but the most superficial interaction. Only one in seven Israeli Jews has ever visited an Arab home, by way of illustration, despite the fact that none of the former group dwells more than a few miles away from the latter (Bard, 1998). Similarly, one Protestant resident of Northern Ireland, where 35% of the population is Catholic and opposing groups live in contiguous neighborhoods, exclaimed after attending an encounter session, "You know, I've never really had a conversation with a Catholic before" (Doob & Foltz, 1973, p. 504).

This same reasoning helps explain why massive social programs such as racial desegregation of public schools often lead to disappointing results with respect to prejudice reduction (Schofield, 1991). Even a casual observer cannot fail to see that U.S. public schools with multiethnic demographic profiles still remain essentially segregated socially. All one need do is to visit a school cafeteria at lunchtime, especially at upper grade levels where peer pressure militating against out-group mixing is strongest. Grant (1990) calls for more active facilitation of contact if school integration is to bring about attitude change.

RESISTANCE OF PREJUDICE TO DISCONFIRMATION

Moreover, left to their own devices, individuals in contact situations tend to seek mainly information that confirms their pre-existing stereotypes of the other; they may be oblivious to disconfirming information (Fiske & Taylor, 1991). Neuberg (1994) summarizes several social cognitive impediments that must be overcome if contact is to yield information with even the potential for disconfirming prejudices:

- ▶ Because of time limitations or other lack of resources, perceivers adopt the efficient strategy of seeking out primarily prejudice-confirming information about the other.
- ▶ Perceivers fail to attend to individuating information about the other, information which might otherwise demonstrate that the perceiver is operating on the basis of overgeneralizations about the out-group.
- ▶ Perceivers tend to interpret ambiguous information about the other in prejudice-confirming ways.
- ▶ Perceivers "leak" their negative feelings toward the other through nonverbal and verbal behaviors, and the other

reciprocates by behaving in prejudice-affirming ways.

Neuberg's (1994) account of the vicious cycle of prejudice-affirming information processing, and the concomitant tendency to ignore or discount prejudice-disconfirming evidence, is well-illustrated in the recent best-selling novel, *Snow Falling on Cedars* (Guterson, 1995). A major theme of the novel is the fundamental distrust of many Euro-American citizens toward Japanese Americans, even those who have been their long-term neighbors, dwelling among them for generations. This distrust became officially sanctioned and especially virulent against the historical backdrop of World War II and in the geographic setting of the Pacific Northwest. In one especially telling vignette in the book, the defendant in a murder case, Kabuo Miyamoto, explains to his own defense attorney why he chooses to withhold potentially exonerating information. "You figure because you're from Japanese folks, nobody will believe you anyway," observes the attorney. Kabuo replies,

> I've got a right to think that way. Or maybe you've forgotten that a few years back the government decided it couldn't trust any of us and shipped us out of here. . . . We're sly and treacherous. . . . You can't trust a Jap, can you? This island's full of strong feelings . . . people who don't often speak their minds but hate on the inside just the same." (Guterson, 1995, p. 391)

Kabuo's assessment seems—unfortunately, for the outcome of his case—right on target. The author narrates,

> Kabuo Miyamoto rose in the witness box so that the citizens in the gallery saw him fully—a Japanese man standing proudly before them. . . . The citizens in the gallery were reminded of photographs they had seen of Japanese soldiers. . . . And there was nothing akin to softness in him anywhere, no part of him that was vulnerable. He was, they decided, not like

them at all, and the detached aloof manner in which he watched the snowfall made this palpable and self-evident. (Guterson, 1995, p. 412)

This scenario of suspicion and self-fulling expectation is replicated in countless cross-cultural interactions. It is consistent with Rothbart and John's (1985) well-articulated explication of social categorization and the reasons why it is so difficult for casual contact to devolve stereotypes. The Rothbart model postulates that three factors dictate the degree to which a stereotypic trait is susceptible to disconfirmation via intergroup contact:

▶ Is an observed behavior (e.g., the stolid industriousness of Japanese-American berry farmers) clearly inconsistent with some negative trait (e.g., murderous treason)?

▶ How many instances of the behavior must observers witness to disconfirm a stereotype? (e.g., in *Snow Falling on Cedars,* the captain of the high school baseball team apparently has seen enough instances of camaraderie on the part of Japanese American teammates to dispel his prejudices; after a school dance, he blithely hands out honorary team letters to those teammates who will miss the remaining season because they are being "relocated" to internment camps.)

▶ What is the likelihood that a particular contact setting will provide opportunities to evince prejudice-disconfirming behavior? (e.g., when federal agents invade Japanese American households to search for evidence of sedition, the situation is not a likely occasion for demonstrations of patriotic disclosures of incriminating information.)

Prejudice-affirming interaction patterns. The third factor identified by Rothbart and John (1985), the notion that social contexts themselves either engender or suppress stereotype-confirming behaviors on the part of out-group members, is especially useful in understanding why "the political is the personal" in intergroup relations. For example, a classic study of cross-gender communication found that women's verbal behavior in telephone conversations was discernibly less sociable if the male caller was led to believe (through experimental manipulation) that he was speaking to an unattractive female (Snyder, Tanke, & Berscheid, 1977). In other words, the women in this study behaviorally conformed to the male's expectations of them, expectations that the males communicated no doubt through subtle nuances of discourse features and vocal inflection.

In a similar vein, if a society is structured such that members of a particular nondominant social group are routinely denied voice and efficacy in their interactions with the mainstream, then members of the subordinated group may quite naturally begin enacting roles that are perceived by the mainstream culture as underhanded, conspiratorial, or sullen (Rothbart & John, 1985). In such a society, forthright communication on the part of the subordinate group is either foreclosed or else patently counterproductive. Thus, each interaction produces yet additional behaviors on the part of subordinate group members that simply confirm the dominant group's subtly (or not so subtly) communicated prejudices. The converse is also likely: Members of the dominant group begin to conform behaviorally to the negative expectations that minority group members hold toward them. As Hamilton, Sherman, and Ruvolo (1990/ 1992) note, "We can imagine an interaction in which each person 'becomes' what the other expects of him or her" (p. 150). Given this syndrome, it is easy to see how contact situations can go awry, reinforcing rather than erasing negative stereotypes. It is easy to see why prejudice is often so intractable.

Moreover, even if a contact situation can be engineered in which a potentially stereotype-disconfirming behavior (a) *is* elicited and (b) is patently incompatible with the stereotyped attribute, and even (c) is observed by prejudiced individuals on several occasions,

Rothbart and John (1985) contend that the stereotype is nonetheless likely to persist. That is because the bigot's last recourse against stereotype disconfirmation is to defend his or her stereotype by disassociating a particular performer from the out-group of which the performer is a member. "Oh, he's not like those others of his kind," rationalizes the bigot.

PRINCIPLED OBJECTIONS TO CONTACT HYPOTHESIS-BASED INTERVENTIONS

Even if contact was sufficient to induce prejudice reduction, some authorities have pointed to political and ethical reasons why this could actually be an undesirable state of affairs. If positive affect between members of opposing groups is the primary outcome of a contact encounter, it might delude those participants into a false sense of conflict resolution. That is, in the warmth of the camaraderie that contact participants have forged together, they might forget that the sociopolitical conflict that originally positioned them as opponents is far less tractable than any set of interpersonal relationships (Bar & Eady, 1998). Indeed, Kelman (1998) argues that the best practice when facilitating contact among negotiators from opposing groups is to *prevent* them from establishing positive interpersonal affect, lest that sentimentality impair the negotiators' abilities to bargain forcefully enough to devise a resolution that can endure.

Finally, some ethical objections to typical contact-hypothesis interventions warrant a serious hearing. Many intergroup contact activities are designed primarily to help modify or train members of the majority/dominant culture. They do little to assist minority group participants (Bar & Eady, 1998), nor to promote better relations between members of one minority and members of other minorities (Grant, 1990). Smith (1994), by way of illustration, found that the sheer amount of interracial contact had greater impact on Euro-Americans than on African Americans (see also Sigelman & Welch, 1993, for similar findings). For contact to exert comparable impact on attitudes of African Americans, the intergroup interaction needed to be characterized by conditions of social justice, such as equal status and mutually beneficial outcomes. Thus, a great many intergroup contact situations, in which these conditions unfortunately do not prevail, may inadvertently reproduce rather than overcome social inequities.

▶ Conditions for Prejudice-Reducing Contact

In fairness to the contact hypothesis, it should be acknowledged that dating at least from its most well-known formulation by Allport in 1954, the ameliorative effects of contact were hypothesized to be contingent on a number of accompanying conditions. Indeed, identifying and elucidating the facilitative conditions for contact has consumed prodigious research efforts in the intervening years. Although different authorities use varying terms and highlight different constellations of these conditions (e.g., Brown, 1995; Desforges, Lord, Pugh, & Sia, 1997; Forbes, 1997; Neuberg, 1994; Pettigrew, 1997; Smith, 1994), they can be broadly categorized as follows:

▶ The contact situation ensures equal status for members of the different groups.

▶ The contact rules of engagement impose egalitarian decision making.

▶ The groups are working toward common goals in the contact situation.

▶ The contact tasks require cooperative interdependence between members of the groups in contact.

▶ The contact is endorsed and supported by acknowledged authorities or institutions.

▶ Participants in the contact situation are given sufficient time and are relieved of other stresses.

▶ The contact situation provides a high potential for interpersonal acquaintance between members of the different groups.

▶ Participants are readily seen as being typical rather than atypical of their groups.

The conjunction of all these conditions in any single contact program constitutes a tall order. For example, it requires considerable finesse to manage both sponsorship by authority figures or institutions and also a sense that participants are truly representative of their constituencies. Experience with opinion leaders in the dissemination of innovations across cultures (e.g., new agricultural techniques, family planning) indicates that once a community member is selected for participation in an externally sanctioned program or workshop, that person's authenticity credentials (i.e., perceived homophily) can become suspect to the very in-group he or she is supposed to serve (see discussion in Dodd, 1993).

No available empirical evidence points to the pre-eminence of any one of the conditions over the others. Certain theoretic positions, however, do accord primacy to particular conditions among them. Most prominently, realistic group conflict theory, formulated by Sherif (1966; see review in Jackson, 1993), emphasizes the importance of the cooperative principle of intergroup contact. That is, realistic group conflict theory holds that the most important factor for reducing intergroup hostility is establishing superordinate goals that transcend opposing groups' own competing needs. In fact, the theory is sometimes cast as contradicting the contact hypothesis, because competition-fueled conflict between groups can apparently be quite heated, even when group members' attitudes are not especially prejudiced—for example, some findings regarding interracial school busing (Bobo, 1983). Moreover, realistic group conflict theory explicitly rejects *interpersonal* contact as a means for reducing conflict; useful contact must take place between groups not individuals. Yet, the theoretic rift between real-istic group conflict theory and the contact hy-pothesis is not unbridgeable (Jackson, 1993), and the insistence that contact situations must be designed to reduce competition between groups and provide for mutually satisfying shared outcomes has become a bedrock of current thinking about contact hypothesis.

Several of the conditions for effective con-tact can be simulated in laboratory studies but have proved extremely difficult to operationa-lize in field settings. In fact, the condition of noncompetition between groups is one such problematic factor (Brewer, 1996). In applied settings, such as labor disputes or the com-mercial incursion of one ethnic group into the residential enclave of another, project facilita-tors generally must overcome participants' skepticism that their groups really do share common goals (Billig, 1976). Equal status among participants is another condition that often breaks down in practice outside the lab-oratory. It can be extremely difficult to shield even high-intervention and often artificial workshop and encounter group exercises from the eventual invasion of realpolitik power dif-ferentials (Bargal & Bar, 1994; Yogev et al., 1991).

Similarly, establishing the typicality or representativeness of out-group participants in contact encounters has proved rather intrac-table (Desforges et al., 1997). That is because when individuals encounter out-group mem-bers who disconfirm their stereotypes, they tend to preserve their stereotypes and instead distinguish the disconfirming members as ex-ceptions to their groups. The net effect of this process is that even positive intergroup con-tact experiences may result in much mutual liking among direct participants but still fail to generalize prejudice reduction toward the out-group as a whole (cf. Hamburger, 1994). However, when perceivers can be convinced that the out-group member with whom they have experienced positive affect is indeed typ-ical, those positive feelings may generalize to the entire out-group (Wilder, 1984).

► Mechanisms by Which Contact Reduces Prejudice

The literature on the contact hypothesis posits at least four alternative mechanisms by which contact may, under the right conditions, re-duce prejudice:[3]

Stereotype disconfirmation: Contact de-stroys inaccurate prejudices by provid-ing information that disconfirms nega-tive expectations about the other (Pettigrew, 1997).

Anxiety reduction: Contact reduces anxi-eties about the other by providing pleasant, gratifying experience in inter-group interaction (Stephan & Stephan, 1992).

Decategorizing: Contact allows partici-pants from one group to individuate participants from the other group, thus unlinking the other from negative gen-eralizations toward the out-group iden-tity (Brewer & Miller, 1988).

Recategorizing: Contact leads participants to recategorize members of the out-group under a mutual identity, an umbrella identity effacing previous in-tergroup boundaries (Gaertner, Dovidio, & Bachman, 1996).

Stereotype disconfirmation is most funda-mental to the contact hypothesis. The notion is that contact brings greater knowledge of the other and that more accurate knowledge of the other will contradict stereotyped beliefs. Ear-lier in this chapter, however, we discussed a number of sources of resistance of stereotypes to disconfirming evidence (Rothbart & John, 1985). Indeed, surprisingly little empirical ev-idence demonstrates the fundamental premise that intergroup contact does, in fact, increase knowledge and thus diminish stereotyping. One study of the effects of contact over time on stereotypes of various college subgroups (e.g., football players, sorority members) indi-cated that contact with members of those sub-groups may not lead to acquiring more knowledge about them, but such contact does seem associated with greater conformity to consensual perceptions of those groups (Biernat & Crandall, 1994). Moreover, some theoreticians challenge the view that stereotypes are necessarily inaccurate. Rather, stereotypes can vary in their accuracy. Knowledge about the other acquired through intergroup contact will not diminish stereotyping if those stereotypes are accurate to begin with (Jussim, McCauley, & Lee, 1995).

CONTACT AND AFFECT

Stephan and Stephan (1992) delineate four types of negative consequences of contact that can cause intergroup anxiety. These consequences are (a) psychological (frustration and loss of control), (b) behavioral (exploitation), (c) evaluative on the part of the out-group (disdain, prejudice), and (d) evaluative on the part of the in-group (ostracism, rejection). When these sources of anxiety are eliminated, intergroup contact can lead to reduced prejudice and conflict. The intergroup anxiety-reduction model is based in part on the simple premise that positive contact is rewarding. Indeed, Cook (1984) attributed the success of many contact interventions to participants' sense that encountering the other was pleasant, satisfying, and fun.

The mechanism of uncertainty reduction (Gudykunst & Nishida, 1984) seems also related to the construct of anxiety reduction. Uncertainty is endemic to all interactions but especially to cross-cultural ones. All other factors held equal, people seek to avoid uncertainty and, hence, would tend to avoid potentially stressful intergroup contact. On the other hand, personal disclosure that accompanies contact can reduce uncertainty, and in many (but not all) cases, reduced uncertainty leads to greater relational comfort and satisfaction. Thus intergroup contact that reduces uncertainty, and concomitantly anxiety, no doubt reduces hostility as well. Strategies for reducing uncertainty/anxiety in intergroup settings include question asking and familiar-

izing oneself with scripts and procedures for interacting in that other culture.

EFFACING GROUP IDENTITY

The decategorization process renders the other's group identity nonsalient, subordinate to personal identity ("They're not so different from us, you know. Some hate, others don't. It isn't all of them," says one Japanese American protagonist in *Snow Falling on Cedars,* just prior to deportation to Manzanar; Guterson, 1995, p. 200). The recategorization process creates a common, transcendent group identity ("We are the world . . . "). Brown (1995; Hewstone & Brown, 1986) takes issue with the general precepts of both these models. According to Brown's critique, both decategorization and recategorization transform contact situations from the realm of intergroup to the realm of interpersonal. Positive interpersonal contact may very well result in warm, satisfying affect among all immediate participants, but it obviates any possibility of generalizing that positive feeling to the other's social category as a whole (see also Jackson, 1993). After all, in both decategorization and recategorization, the other's association with outgroup identity has been dissolved. Terkel (1992) presents a dramatic case study of a Euro-American women in Chicago who admits to increasing prejudice against African Americans over a 20-year period. She believes that African Americans tend to be lazy and criminal. She excepts from this stereotype her African American coworkers (she is a federal peace officer), whom she has individuated and decategorized from her prejudiced view. Amazingly, it turns out that this individual is a faithful member of a virtually all-black church. She has recategorized the African American members of the church as members of her extended family, and thus, they too are exempt from her prejudice.

It appears, then, that for contact to bring about a generalized mitigation of a group prejudice, elements of group distinctiveness must be preserved in the contact encounters. Brewer (1996) takes up this challenge by proposing the concept of *optimal group distinctiveness*. Brewer's formulation begins with the assumption that "social psychological solutions to intergroup relations problems must start with a deep respect for the powerful influence of in-group identification on individual behavior" (p. 295). Thus, group boundaries must not be effaced. At the same time, groups must be induced to regard themselves as mutually interdependent. Optimally distinct group identities remain salient during contact situations but never overwhelm the cooperative enterprise in which participants are engaged. Participants are "the same, but different." To achieve this goal, Brewer proposes "cross-cutting task structures" for intergroup encounters. Such structures team together individuals from differing groups. However, care is taken to provide the members of the different groups with divergent rather than identical roles to play in the cooperative intergroup enterprise. Thus for example, on an interracial camping expedition, African Americans might be teamed with Euro-Americans to cook a meal together. African Americans might be designated campfire tenders, while the Euro-American partners are selected as pot tenders.

No doubt, in any particular contact situation, more than one of the four prejudice-reduction mechanisms—likely all of them simultaneously—come into play. For example, Stephan and Stephan (1992) found an interaction between available information (knowledge acquisition) and intergroup anxiety. In this case, intimate contact in which little information about the out-group was made available brought on increased anxiety. Not surprising, in the absence of adequate information about out-group characteristics, highly intimate intergroup contact produces lots of anxiety and hence is likely to backfire by exacerbating prejudices.

▶ Functions of Prejudice

Neuberg (1994) attempts to systematize findings regarding stereotype-confirming or disconfirming interactions by imposing a functional analysis. What are the perceiver's impression-formation goals, for example, to acquire accurate information about the other or to acquire information quickly and with little effort? What are the target's own self-presentation goals, for example, to ingratiate the perceiver? to alienate the perceiver?

In a parallel manner, social psychologists have considered the functions of prejudices themselves. Snyder and Miene (1994) note that stereotypes in general (and prejudices more particularly) can be considered from three perspectives. From a cognitive perspective, stereotypes serve "the function of cognitive economy by helping their holders to reduce incoming information to manageable size, thereby lending predictability to the social world" (p. 36; see also Jussim et al., 1995). From a psychodynamic perspective, prejudices against out-groups help members of the in-group feel superior about themselves; their egos or their collective esprit is supported. And from a sociocultural perspective, prejudices about out-groups promote identification with the in-group and reinforce common in-group values (e.g., Maoz, 2000; Neu & Volkan, 1999). These three broad functions of stereotypes map nicely onto the well-known functional typology developed by Brislin (1981, pp. 42-43).

Ego-defensive function: Some prejudices serve to protect the self-esteem of in-group members from threats to face, often by scapegoating the out-group.
Value-expressive function: Prejudices are a means of expressing the superiority of the in-group, especially in terms of its achievements and forms of expression.
Knowledge function: Prejudices help in-group members construct a (generally inaccurate) representation of the world and the role of various groups within it.

Implicit in the functional analysis of prejudice is the notion that the very same attitudinal posture may stem from one function for Individual A and stem from another function for Individual B. For example, anti-Semitism

TABLE 18.1   Conditions and Mechanisms of Intergroup Contact in Light of the Functions of Prejudice

Dominant Function of the Prejudice to be Reduced	Most Important Conditions of Contact	Primary Mechanisms of Prejudice Reduction
Utilitarian/adjustment	institutional/authority support, equal status, acquaintance potential	decategorizing, recategorizing
Ego defense	common goals, cooperative interdependence	anxiety reduction
Value expression	institutional/authority support, representative participants	stereotype busting, recategorizing
Knowledge	time/resources, acquaintance potential, representative participants	stereotype busting

served a knowledge function for many devout Christians, who held Jews as a race responsible for the death of Jesus. For Nazi true believers, on the other hand, anti-Semitism played a value-expressive role. By the same token, the functional basis for identical prejudices can vary across situations and across differing group targets of prejudice. Thus, for example, anti-Arab prejudices held by many Israeli Jews could serve utilitarian and value-expressive functions during times of peace and more of a knowledge function during times of war. By the same token, it is conceivable that anti-Palestinian prejudices held by some Israeli Jews serve more of a utilitarian function (i.e., a sort of litmus test for approbation in certain social and political circles), whereas anti-Egyptian prejudices (where active competition is less current) could meet value-expressive needs.

ASSESSING CONTACT-HYPOTHESIS INTERVENTIONS IN LIGHT OF FUNCTIONS OF PREJUDICE

If prejudices serve varying functions for different individuals, in different situations, and for different out-group targets, then it stands to reason that conditions and mechanisms of contact that apply in any given set-

ting will also vary. Optimal strategies for engineering prejudice-reducing intergroup contact experiences, therefore, will also differ according to the function of that prejudice (Snyder & Miene, 1994). Table 18.1 encapsulates recommendations for selecting contact conditions and mechanisms according to function of the prejudice being treated.

Consider, for example, based on the relations encoded in Table 18.1, the recommended design of a program for reducing anti-Jewish prejudices among Arab citizens. When intergroup competition is rampant, ego defense is likely to be a dominant function (Snyder & Miene, 1994). This is no doubt true for many Palestinians (e.g., Jews are connivers and bullies. Were they not, our economic infrastructure would be more developed). Engineering a contact situation involving common goals and cooperative interdependence would demonstrate to participants that they are *not* in fact threatened by the outgroup; in this case, that Jews as a group are not responsible for thwarting Arab aspirations. If the contact situation could establish these conditions, then intergroup anxieties would be reduced and, in turn, so would prejudices. For Jewish participants, on the other hand, the knowledge function of anti-Arab prejudice may dominate over the other functions; such would be typical for targets for whom the only intergroup interaction occurs in brief service encounters (e.g., No wonder the Palestinian Authority can't organize an effective police force. Arabs are never willing to follow instructions!). In this case, administrators of the prejudice-reduction program would want to create highly interpersonal contact situations with typical Arabs extending over relatively long periods of time (multiple encounters).

Such are precisely the design features of successfully evaluated prejudice-reduction programs for Arabs and Jews. Kelman (1979), for example, describes workshop encounters in which cooperative interdependence conditions prevail and that consequently result in decreased intergroup anxieties. He states, "The parties need each other if creative new ideas are to evolve—ideas for solutions that are responsive to each party's fundamental needs and anxieties" (p. 108). At the same time, high acquaintance-potential interaction results in stereotype disconfirmation, with the intent of mitigating knowledge-function prejudices. "Social interaction in the context of a workshop takes place among individuals. The procedures are directed at the individual participants' affective and cognitive processes" (Kelman, 1979, p. 111).

ECLECTICISM IN CONTACT HYPOTHESIS-BASED PROGRAMS

The program described by Kelman (1979) is eclectic rather than a pure example of any of the mechanisms we have described. The program described by Neu and Volkan for inoculating against hostilities between ethnic Estonians and ethnic Russians in Estonia is similarly eclectic. The functions of prejudices between the two groups are multiple. For example, the belief that Russians are brutish serves a knowledge function for Estonians, helping them explain their country's domination during the Soviet era. For ethnic Russians, who in independent Estonia can thrive only through the "indignity" of learning the Estonian language, anti-Estonian prejudice surely serves an ego-defensive function. The

prejudice-reducing mechanisms invoked by those facilitating the intergroup contact are primarily knowledge acquisition (i.e., allowing members of the two groups simply to learn more about each other) and perhaps also establishment of optimal group distinctiveness (both groups share a common destiny as residents of Estonia, but their distinct histories and conditions need to be respected). Conditions for contact that have been carefully cultivated include high acquaintance potential (lots of time for relatively unstructured interpersonal interaction) and sponsorship by authorities in both camps.

The very point of the analysis we present here is that alternative modes of contact should be selected depending on the functions of the prejudice to be treated. In complex situations, no doubt, prejudice serves several functions simultaneously, with varying degrees of intensity. Accordingly, effective prejudice-reduction programs will employ mixed strategies for engendering contact. These strategies may emphasize certain of the facilitative conditions of contact more than others and certain of the mechanisms. But successful programs deriving from the contact hypothesis will be multidimensional in character.

▶ Notes

1. Some authorities distinguish these high intervention workshops and encounter programs from pure contact situations (see, e.g., Bargal's 1992, p. 54, discussion of *facilitative conditions* versus *conflict management workshops*). We find that line of demarcation rather arbitrary, however, and so long as intergroup contact is the key ingredient in such facilitated encounters, we include them under the contact-hypothesis rubric.

2. We are aware that names and labels have profound implications for identity, and identity is the crucial issue in intergroup conflict. Some individuals might prefer to self-identify as Palestinian Israelis or as Palestinians, rather than as Arabs. However, we are using the name *Arab* at this point in its more inclusive sense, encompassing Pales-

tinians, North Africans, and other members of Arab nations.

3. If one accepts the distinction between workshop approaches and contact hypothesis-inspired experiences, then it is reasonable to attribute a unique mechanism of change to the workshop method (Bargal & Bar, 1994). In workshops, participants directly address the nature of their intergroup conflict and learn skills and techniques for conflict communication. Borrowing from the perspective of Kurt Lewin (1947), the mechanism by which such workshops act to reduce prejudice may be termed *re-education*. Participants are taught new analytic frames and acquire new behavioral repertoires.

▶ References

Allport, G. W. (1954). *The nature of prejudice*. Reading, MA: Addison-Wesley.

Amir, Y. (1976). The role of intergroup contact in change of prejudice and ethnic relations. In P. Katz (Ed.), *Toward the elimination of racism* (pp. 245-308). New York: Pergamon.

Bar, H., & Eady, E. (1998). Education to cope with conflicts: Encounters between Jews and Palestinian citizens of Israel. In E. Weiner (Ed.), *The handbook of interethnic coexistence* (pp. 514-534). New York: Continuum Publishing.

Bard, M. G. (1998). The variety of coexistence activities in Israel: Lessons for the United States. In E. Weiner (Ed.), *The handbook of interethnic coexistence* (pp. 468-489). New York: Continuum Publishing.

Bargal, D. (1992). Conflict management workshops for Arab Palestinian and Jewish youth: A framework for planning, intervention and evaluation. *Social Work with Groups, 15,* 51-68.

Bargal, D., & Bar, H. (1994). The encounter of social selves: Intergroup workshops for Arab and Jewish youth. *Social Work with Groups, 17*(3), 39-59.

Biernat, M., & Crandall, C. S. (1994). Stereotyping and contact with social groups: Measurement and conceptual issues. *European Journal of Social Psychology, 24,* 659-677.

Billig, M. (1976). *Social psychology and intergroup relations*. New York: Academic.

Bobo, L. (1983). Whites' opposition to busing: Symbolic racism or realistic group theory? *Journal of Personality and Social Psychology, 45,* 1196-1210.

Brewer, M. B. (1996). When contact is not enough: Social identity and intergroup cooperation. *International Journal of Intercultural Relations, 20,* 291-303.

Brewer, M. B., & Miller, N. (1988). Contact and cooperation: When do they work? In P. Katz & D. Taylor (Eds.), *Eliminating racism* (pp. 315-326). New York: Plenum.

Brislin, R. W. (1981). *Cross-cultural encounters: Face-to-face interaction*. New York: Pergamon.

Brown, R. (1995). *Prejudice: Its social psychology*. Oxford, UK: Blackwell.

Cook, S. W. (1984). Cooperative interaction in multiethnic contexts. In N. Miller & M. B. Brewer (Eds.), *Groups in contact: The psychology of desegregation* (pp. 155-185). Orlando, FL: Academic Press.

Desforges, D. M., Lord, C. G., Pugh, M. A., & Sia, T. L. (1997). Role of group representativeness in the generalization part of the contact hypothesis. *Basic and Applied Social Psychology, 19,* 183-204.

Dodd, C. (1993). *Dynamics of intercultural communication* (3rd ed.). Dubuque, IA: William C. Brown.

Doob, L. W., & Foltz, W. J. (1973). The Belfast workshop: An application of group techniques to a destructive conflict. *Journal of Conflict Resolution, 17,* 489-512.

Fishman, A. (1988). *Amish literacy: What and how it means*. Portsmouth, NH: Heinemann Educational Books.

Fiske, S. T., & Taylor, S. E. (1991). *Social cognition* (2nd ed.). New York: McGraw-Hill.

Forbes, H. D. (1997). *Ethnic conflict: Commerce, culture, and the contact hypothesis*. New Haven, CT: Yale University Press.

Gaertner, S. L., Dovidio, J. F., & Bachman, B. A. (1996). Revisiting the contact hypothesis: The induction of a common ingroup identity. *International Journal of Intercultural Relations, 20,* 271-290.

Grant, C. (1990, September). Desegregation, racial attitudes, and intergroup contact: A discussion of change. *Phi Delta Kappan, 72*(1), 25-32.

Gudykunst, W., & Nishida, T. (1984). Individual and cultural influences on uncertainty reduction. *Communication Monographs, 51,* 23-36.

Guterson, D. (1995). *Snow falling on cedars.* New York: Vintage.

Hamburger, Y. (1994). The contact hypothesis reconsidered: Effects of the atypical outgroup member on the outgroup stereotype. *Basic and Applied Social Psychology, 15,* 339-358.

Hamilton, D. L., Sherman, S. J., & Ruvolo, C. (1992). Stereotype-based expectancies: Effects on information processing and social behavior. In W. B. Gudykunst & Y. Y. Kim (Eds.), *Readings on communication with strangers* (pp. 135-169). New York: McGraw Hill. (Reprinted from *Journal of Social Issues, 46*(2), 35-60, 1990).

Herek, G. M., & Capitanio, J. P. (1996). "Some of my best friends": Intergroup contact, concealable stigma, and heterosexuals' attitudes toward gay men and lesbians. *Personality and Social Psychology Bulletin, 22,* 412-424.

Hewstone, M., & Brown, R. J. (1986). Contact is not enough: An intergroup perspective on the "contact hypothesis." In M. Hewston & R. J. Brown (Eds.), *Contact and conflict in intergroup encounters* (pp. 1-44). Oxford, UK: Basil Blackwell.

Jackson, J. W. (1993). Realistic group conflict theory: A review and evaluation of the theoretical and empirical literature. *Psychological Record, 43,* 395-414.

Jussim, L. J., McCauley, C. R., & Lee, Y.-T. (1995). Why study stereotype accuracy and inaccuracy? In L. J. Jussim (Ed.), *Stereotype accuracy: Toward appreciating group differences* (pp. 3-27). Washington, DC: American Psychological Association.

Kelman, H. C. (1979). An interactional approach to conflict resolution and its application to Israeli-Palestinian relationships. *International Interactions, 6,* 99-122.

Kelman, H. C. (1998). Informal mediation by the scholar/practitioner. In E. Weiner (Ed.), *The handbook of interethnic coexistence* (pp. 310-331). New York: Continuum Publishing.

Lewin, K. (1947). Frontiers in group dynamics. *Human Relations, 1,* 143-153.

Maoz, I. (2000). Power relations in intergroup encounters: A case study of Jewish-Arab encounters in Israel. *International Journal of Intercultural Relations, 24,* 259-277.

Moyers, J. D. (Executive Producer). (1991). *Beyond hate.* New York: Public Affairs Television, Inc. and International Cultural Programming, Inc.

Neu, J., & Volkan, V. (1999). *Developing a methodology for conflict prevention: The case of Estonia.* Atlanta, GA: The Carter Center.

Neuberg, S. L. (1994). Expectancy-confirmation processes in stereotype-tinged social encounters: The moderating role of social goals. In M. P. Zanna & J. M. Olson (Eds.), *The psychology of prejudice* (The Ontario Symposium, Vol. 7, pp. 103-130). Hillsdale, NJ: Lawrence Erlbaum.

Pettigrew, T. F. (1997). Generalized intergroup contact effects on prejudice. *Personality and Social Psychology Bulletin, 23,* 173-185.

Robinson, J., & Preston, J. (1976). Equal status contact and modification of racial prejudice. *Social Forces, 54,* 900-924.

Rothbart, M., & John, O. P. (1985). Social categorization and behavioral episodes: A cognitive analysis of the effects of intergroup contact. *Journal of Social Issues, 41*(3), 81-104.

Schofield, J. W. (1991). School desegregation and intergroup relations: A review of the research. *Review of Research in Education, 17,* 335-409.

Shaffir, W. (1995). Boundaries and self-presentation among the Hasidim : A study in identity maintenance. In J. S. Belcove-Shalin (Ed.), *New world Hasidim: Ethnographic studies of Hasidic Jews in America.* Albany: SUNY Press.

Sherif, M. (1966). *Group conflict and cooperation: Their social psychology.* London: Routledge & Kegan Paul.

Sigelman, L., & Welch, S. (1993). The contact hypothesis revisited: Black-white interaction and positive racial attitudes. *Social Forces, 71,* 781-795.

Smith, C. B. (1994). Back to the future: The intergroup contact hypothesis revisited. *Sociological Inquiry, 64,* 438-455.

Snyder, M., & Miene, P. (1994). On the functions of stereotypes and prejudice. In M. P. Zanna & J. M. Olson (Eds.), *The psychology of prejudice* (The Ontario Symposium, Vol. 7, pp. 33-54). Hillsdale, NJ: Lawrence Erlbaum.

Snyder, M., Tanke, E., & Berscheid, E. (1977). Social perception and interpersonal behavior: On the self-fulling nature of social stereotypes. *Journal of Personality and Social Psychology, 35,* 656-666.

Stephan, C. W., & Stephan, W. G. (1992). Reducing intercultural anxiety through intercultural contact. *International Journal of Intercultural Relations, 16,* 89-106.

Terkel, S. (1992). *Race: How blacks and whites think and feel about the national obsession.* New York: New Press.

Wilder, D. A. (1984). Intergroup contact: The typical member and the exception to the rule. *Journal of Experimental Social Psychology, 20,* 177-194.

Yogev, A., Ben-Yehoshua, N. S., & Alper, Y. (1991). Determinants of readiness for contact with Jewish children among young Arab students in Israel. *Journal of Conflict Resolution, 35,* 547-562.

The Kemetic Paradigm

An Afrocentric Foundation for Rhetorical Theory

CYNTHIA L. LEHMAN

In an essay titled, "Developing Rhetoric as a Modern Discipline: Lessons From the Classical Tradition," Charles W. Kneupper (1985) states that

> A modern discipline should be concerned with rhetoric as basic to human life; a discipline which applies to all levels and spheres of communication as well as to all media by which messages are transmitted and all subject matters upon which human knowing and choosing is concerned. It should be a discipline committed to making the best of each person's potentials, of better human culture and of doing this through bettering the substance, style, and form of communication. It should be a discipline uniting wisdom and eloquence. (p. 110)

This statement explains Kneupper's (1985) disdain for a modern communication discipline that all too often ignores its classical roots and a discussion of ethics in favor of regimented studies on the skills of persuasion (p. 108).

Kneupper's emphasis on a return to elements of classical Greek rhetorical theory reflects the earlier position of Richard M. Weaver (1953), a prominent theorist in the discipline. Weaver and Kneupper both believe in the higher moral nature of the study of rhetoric. However, when one wishes to explain, evaluate, and analyze African-derived communication, whether it is written or spoken, there is a significant lack of scholarship on the classical African foundations of oratory. In this regard, scholars of African communication systems need to look to the moral discourse deriving from the African world, particularly Egypt (Kemet), and not to the development of Greek philosophy and ethics. In a review of the literature, there is an abundance of research on the subject of ancient Kemetic civilization, history, philosophy, and religion; but there are no resources that posit specific descriptions of a canon of Kemetic discourse theory, which would prove useful in analyzing communication practices in the African world.

Thus, this chapter will provide a centered (Kemet-centered) African approach to the examination of human communication within the African world. Because of the interconnectedness of all human cultures and the rapidity at which distances in our present global community are shrinking, a Kemet-centered approach has merit not only for modern African cultures but also for the global cultures that interact with Africa. The reality of transcultural interaction is such that all cultures involved are part of a process of give and take, borrowing from and influencing the cultures with which they interact. The necessity in the discipline of communication, then, becomes the affirming of a variety of worldviews, ways of knowing, and value systems that inform human communication on a global scale. Using a culturally centered approach to construction of communication theory assures that each culture, *on its own terms,* will have the power to develop and define systems of communication relevant to its own worldview, ways of knowing, and value system.

The importance of such a cultural perspective in the study of rhetoric is evident in Richard M. Weaver's (1948) definition of culture. Weaver recognizes that "a culture defines itself by crystallizing around . . . feelings which determine a common attitude toward large phases of experience. . . . They originate in our world view, in our ultimate vision of what is proper for [humans] as higher beings" (p. 117). He further notes that

Rhetoric is able to serve as a bond for members of a culture because it is a storehouse of universal memory for a culture. . . . By embodying the experiences and meanings of words of all individuals, rhetoric is suprapersonal; it operates beyond the single individual to unite all the minds of the culture in their quest for the attainment of the tyrannizing image. (Weaver, 1970, p. 35)

The overwhelming body of scholarly research on ancient Kemetic civilization and history makes it possible to examine the philosophical basis of oratory in ancient Kemet, which will aid in the development of Afrocentric rhetorical theory. As Cheikh Anta Diop (1981/1991) emphasizes, "the return to Egypt [Kemet] in all domains is the necessary condition for reconciling African civilizations with history, in order to be able to construct a body of modern human sciences, in order to renovate African culture" (p. 3). The aim of this chapter is to outline the rhetorical ideals of "good speech" that are embedded in the culture, philosophy, religion, and literature of the classical period in Kemet.

► Methodology

The methodological posture which the communication field must take is that all sectors of a society and all societies can be explored, analyzed, and questioned on the basis of their contribution to the human personality.

Asante, 1993, p. 181

Thus, this study of an ancient Kemetic canon of discourse is significant because it advances an Afrocentric analysis of essential themes of rhetorical theory, which can then be used by scholars to develop new models and methods of criticism that reflect an African cultural orientation.

The research methodology will involve an Afrocentric analysis of the *Book of Khun-*

Anup, a Middle Kingdom text that illustrates ancient Kemetic cultural, philosophical, and religious concerns that have direct bearing on Kemetic ideals of public speaking. As Asante (1987) states, Afrocentricity requires "placing African ideals at the center of any analysis that involves African culture and behavior" (p. 6). Afrocentricity provides a framework for generating research questions, conducting research, and interpreting data.

As a research methodology, Afrocentricity does not preclude a researcher from using any particular research tool, that is, survey research, interviews, ethnography, and so on. The distinction between an Afrocentric and a Eurocentric methodology lies in the original purpose for doing research, the subject(s) under examination, the questions asked during research, and the final evaluation of data derived from the research. Therefore, in using content-analysis procedures in an Afrocentric research study, the researcher needs to incorporate conceptual frameworks that ensure that units of analysis, content categories, and data evaluation all reflect African-derived values and cultural orientations.

Most scholarship on classical theories of rhetoric begins with an examination of ancient Greek ideals; this chapter will present a new interpretation and analysis, arguing that ancient Kemetic philosophy is more valid in generating models and methods of criticism for oratory in the African world. Although this study focuses on one possible classical Kemetic model, the implications of Afrocentric research will lead the way to the promotion and appreciation of other African-centered models and rhetorical theories.

In the history of the Western rhetorical tradition, there is an extensive array of theories, models, and focuses, all sharing the same European/Western cosmological, epistemological, axiological, and aesthetic framework. Afrocentric scholarship will also promote an unlimited number of theories, models, and interpretations based on a cosmological, epistemological, axiological, and aesthetic framework derived from the African experience.

▶ Research Procedures

The method of data collection will be a content analysis of the text, in English translation, to generate a grounded-theory coding system based on the themes prevalent in the text. As information is being collected via a thorough examination of the *Book of Khun-Anup,* themes pertaining to spoken discourse will be recorded. As the recording of information is being conducted, the researcher will attempt to devise categories or ideals of spoken communication that reflect the concerns and traits most prevalent from the Kemetic worldview. These ideals will continue to evolve throughout the reading of the text. In the data-analysis phase, alternative interpretations and concerns will also be discussed as they reflect a divergence or interruption of selected themes from earlier historical periods in Kemet.

▶ Classical Rhetorical Theory

A sampling of the most widely respected work on the subject of classical theory reveals that what is termed *classical* has its origins in ancient Greece. *Webster's Dictionary* (1991) defines *classical* as "standard. . . . authoritative, traditional. . . . of or relating to a form or system considered of first significance in earlier times" (p. 246). The term *classical rhetorical theory,* which does not incorporate a discussion of any theory prior to the ancient Greeks, denies any historical/intellectual legacy from ancient Kemet. Also, these sources fail to recognize African intellectual heritage and do not address the cultural foundations of contemporary African communication.

Although this chapter exclusively examines the *Book of Khun-Anup,* a wealth of documents are relevant to the discussion of rhetoric in Kemet. Relevant texts for this discussion of themes related to spoken discourse include Kemetic philosophical, religious, and literary materials. The philosophical documents include what Karenga (1984/1989, 1994) calls the *Sebait (Books of Kagemni, Kheti, Khun-Anup, and Ptah-Hotep)*. The *Book of Khun-Anup,* also known as the *Story of the Eloquent Peasant,* is significant as a philosophical text because it represents a statement on Maatian ethics that is unparalleled in any of the other purely literary works of ancient Kemet. The story employs narrative form, and the oratorical style of the main character's appeals indicates earlier concerns in the Old Kingdom for truth and justice. These philosophical texts, while attributed to an individual thinker, reflect societal ideals and were usually written down years after they had been taught orally at the various temple schools.

The religious documents include the Old Kingdom Pyramid Texts and the Middle Kingdom Coffin Texts. Finally, literary documents include narratives, poems, inscriptions, autobiographies, and prose. Taken together, these philosophical, religious, and literary texts reveal to us the spirituality, cosmology, epistemology, axiology, and aesthetics of classical Kemet.

Based on a survey of the surviving texts from the Old and Middle Kingdom periods, several themes are apparent in regard to Kemetic rhetorical ideals. These themes are

Respect through proper speech
Respect for one's elders/leaders
Remembrance through proper speech
Purity
Absence of arrogance
Nonthreatening speech
Absence of gossip
Submission to authority (following of orders)
Pursuit of truth
Attainment of justice
Generosity
Self-control
Impartiality
Avoidance of hasty speech
Masking one's inner feelings
Good listening skills

These themes, which are socially constructed notions, reflect the connection between public speaking, leadership, and proper moral conduct.

▶ Kemetic Philosophy and the *Book of Khun-Anup*

The *Book of Khun-Anup,* also known as the *Story of the Eloquent Peasant,* is a moral narrative that displays how "fine speaking was made to serve the defense of justice. . . . In its display of fine speech, this work, more than any other, made extensive and successful use of metaphors and other poetic imagery" (Lichtheim, 1973-1980, vol. 1, p. 10; see also Karenga, 1984/1989, pp. 29-35).

The *Book of Khun-Anup* survives on four partial papyri from the Middle Kingdom (P. Berlin 3023, P. Berlin 3025, P. Berlin 10499, and P. Butler 527/P., British Museum 10274). Clayton (1994) believes the story is an actual event from the reign of King Nebkaure Akhtoy, the last king of the Tenth Dynasty (end of the First Intermediate Period). It is included here as a Middle Kingdom text, because most literary scholars on ancient Kemet point to its surviving in written form during this time and because there are no established dates for Nebkaure's reign. The text is written in narrative form and includes nine sections of orational material. "The mixture of seriousness and irony, the intertwining of a plea for justice with a demonstration of the value of rhetoric, is the very essence of the work" (Lichtheim, 1973-1980, vol. 1, p. 169).

The story begins with Khun-Anup's journey to the capital, Heracleopolis Magna, to buy food for his family. On the way, he meets a stranger, Nemtynakht, who blocks his path on the road. To continue on his journey, Khun-Anup attempts to maneuver around Nemtynakht's obstruction, and one of Khun-Anup's donkeys accidentally eats some barley from Nemtynakht's field alongside the road. Nemtynakht seizes the donkey as compensation, over Khun-Anup's protest. Outraged, Nemtynakht beats Khun-Anup and takes all of his possessions. Khun-Anup's pleas for the return of his possessions go unanswered, so he travels to the capital to speak directly with the High Steward, Rensi, a magistrate under King Nebkaure. The magistrates believe Khun-Anup to be a serf in service to Nemtynakht, so they dismiss his pleas for justice. In the context of Khun-Anup's mistreatment and continued unanswered pleas for justice, he speaks eloquently and passionately on the subject of Maat (the presence of truth, justice, harmony, peace, and balance within society) before the High Steward, Rensi, while enduring even more beatings at the hands of the magistrates. During his repeated appeals for justice, Khun-Anup moves from glowing words in praise of the magistrates to an outright call for justice, citing the tenets of good speech and proper ethical conduct (Maat).

> . . . Earth's rightness lies in justice!
> Speak not falsely—you are great,
> Act not lightly—you are weighty;
> Speak not falsely—you are the balance,
> . . . . Not great is one who is great in greed.
> . . . . If you avert your face from violence,
> Who then shall punish wrongdoing?
>
> (Lichtheim, 1973-1980,
> vol. 1, p. 176)

Khun-Anup is then beaten by the High Steward Rensi's guards, yet he continues in his criticism and his pleas for justice. He warns the magistrates that their refusal to pursue justice will backfire on them. In the Fifth Petition, Khun-Anup again chastises the magistrates.

> It is to hear cases that you were installed, to judge between two, to punish the robber. But what you do is to uphold the thief! One puts one's trust in you, but you have become a transgressor! (Lichtheim, 1973-1980, vol. 1, p. 178)

In his Sixth Petition, Khun-Anup stresses the pursuit of justice and attacks the magistrates' failure to correct his unjust treatment, making the magistrates accomplices to the injustice.

> He who lessens falsehood fosters truth,
> He who fosters the good reduces [evil],
> . . . . Now see for yourself:
> The arbitrator is a robber,
> The peacemaker makes grief,
> . . . . But he who cheats diminishes justice!
> Rightly filled justice neither falls short nor brims over.
> . . . . You are learned, skilled, accomplished,
> But not in order to plunder!
> You should be the model for all men,
> But your affairs are crooked!
>
> (Lichtheim, 1973-1980,
> vol. 1, pp. 178-179)

In this case, inaction in the face of evil intent is equated with the evil act itself. In this regard, Khun-Anup reflects the Old Kingdom philosophy of Ptah-Hotep. Khun-Anup mentions the criteria of justice and proper conduct as central to the theme of truth. Like Ptah-Hotep (Old Kingdom), Khun-Anup explains that proper ethical conduct and speech will result in achieving immortality and remembrance from the living.

In his Ninth Petition, Khun-Anup makes a final, eloquent appeal for justice.

> Do not rebuff one who beseeches you.
> Abandon this slackness,
> Let your speech be heard.
> Act for him who would act for you,
> Do not listen to everyone,
> Summon a man to his rightful cause!
>
> (Lichtheim, 1973-1980,
> vol. 1, p. 182)

At this point, the High Steward Rensi takes Khun-Anup before the king to repeat his charges. Khun-Anup believes that his death is imminent because of his repeated accusations against the magistrates. However, after the reading of the charges to the king, a royal order is issued granting all of Nemtynakht's possessions to be redistributed to Khun-Anup. This text illustrates how eloquent speaking is speaking on behalf of justice. The aesthetic of beauty and eloquence is that which assures proper ethical conduct in human affairs. Truthful speech that seeks to promote Maat is also speech that is passionate, eloquent, and beautiful.

► Maatian Ethics

Many researchers have expounded on the centrality of Maat in Kemetic society (Asante, 1990; Baines, 1991; Frankfort, 1948/1961; Karenga, 1984/1989, 1986, 1989, 1994; Lichtheim, 1992; Morenz, 1984; Obenga, 1996; Teeter, 1990; Tobin, 1987; Wilson, 1956). Their research notes the place of Maat as the moral ideal in ancient Kemet and as a philosophical and spiritual concept of the divine. As such, Maat is life giver, goddess figure, cultural artifact, foundation of order and responsibility, central philosophical construct, epistemological center, and the basis for human, supernatural, and ecological concerns.

Maat holds a special relationship to reality. As Obenga (1996) explains, five spheres of reality are related to Maat: the divine, cosmos, state, society, and the human being. Within each of these spheres, he notes, are five dimensions of reality: the religious, cosmic, political, social, and anthropological (Obenga, 1996, p. 93).

It means that because of Maat, the sacred world must be balanced to itself, to the cosmos, to the state, to the society, and to humans. The cosmos must be balanced to the divine world, to itself, to the state, to the society, and to humans. The state must be balanced to the sacred, to the cosmos, to itself, to the society, and to humans. The society must be balanced to the sacred, to the cosmos, to the state, to itself, and to humans. The humans must be balanced to the divine world, to the cosmos, to the state, to the

society, and to themselves. (Obenga, 1996, pp. 93-94)

Maatian ethics speaks to the entire realm of human possibility. Maat exists in everything and is useful in all situations to harmonize society. Even in the midst of conflict or chaos, the Kemites believed that Maat was present and only needed to be reactivated to restore truth, justice, peace, harmony, and balance in society. In ancient Kemet, there existed a duality in every situation (good and bad), and it was up to the individual and to society at large to ensure that the good (Maat) prevailed in all areas.

As a central philosophical and ethical construct, Maat exists in Kemetic thought from the Old Kingdom onward. Kemetic records that survive from this period are the earliest body of evidence for the existence of a social moral code.

In this period we are watching the higher aspects of an evolutionary process that cannot be observed at so early a stage anywhere else in the career of man. We are contemplating the emergence of a sense of moral responsibility as it was gradually assuming an increasing mandatory power over human conduct, a development which was moving towards the assertion of conscience as an influential force. (Breasted, 1934, p. 122)

► Maatian Ethics and Communication

The importance of proper speech and doing Maat is also expressed beautifully in the Kemetic ideal of *Maa-kheru* (Maat-kheru is the feminine determinative), an epithet applied to the deceased. This concept, which translates as "true of voice, justified," is evidence of the importance of proper moral conduct through speech in Kemetic society. After death, the deceased had to go before the tribunal—Maat, Djehuty, Osiris, and Anubis—and be judged on the basis of their actions while alive. On successful completion of the "weighing of the heart against the feather of Maat," the deceased became linked with Osiris, obtained the epithet of Maa-kheru, and could gain entry into the next world (Faulkner, 1994; Obenga, 1996, p. 81).

From the standpoint of Maatian ethics, one can begin to posit a possible example of a Kemet-centered (Afrocentric) approach to the study of rhetoric. Ancient Kemet, being a largely oral society, naturally would be among the first civilizations to develop criteria and standards for the promotion of public speaking. As discussed earlier, Kemetic society valued speech that addressed the themes of respect, remembrance, purity, absence of arrogance, nonthreatening speech, absence of gossip, submission to authority, pursuit of truth, attainment of justice, generosity, self-control, impartiality, avoidance of hasty speech, masking of one's inner feelings, and good listening skills. Naturally, with Maat as the guiding and life-giving force in Kemetic society, Maat would also function as a standard for the evaluation of good speech. In this regard, public speaking is intertwined with morality and human conduct. Any such model of classical Afrocentric rhetorical theory must include such an emphasis.

Operating from the standpoint of classical theory, whether it be classical Greece or classical Kemet, gives one direction for future research, provides interpretation, and prompts one to ask different questions. In the ancient Greeks, Aristotle in particular, one sees the emphasis on teaching people to argue both sides of an issue. Obviously, some issues only have one truthful, just argument. In this case, then, Aristotle and the classical Greek model are promoting a position in which rhetoric is devoid of morality and ethics. Such a position is untenable within the Kemetic paradigm. In his rhetoric, Aristotle teaches people to persuade others on the basis of appeals to logos (logic), ethos (emotion), and pathos (concern for humanity). In this case, one sees the dichotomy of logic and emotion common to the Western or Eurocentric paradigm in all disciplines. Also, one notices the discrepancy between a concern for humanity, on the one hand, and a potentially untruthful, unjust position on the other hand. How can one profess a concern for humanity when at the same time one promotes and persuades people to a cause or position that does not have the best interests (justice, righteousness) of that society at heart? These discrepancies are difficult to find in a classical African or classical Kemetic paradigm of rhetoric because these societies function, at their core, on the basis of Maat: justice, harmony, balance, peace, truth, and righteousness.

With this in mind, a starting point in the discussion of classical Afrocentric rhetorical theory is the place of ethics in the evaluation and promotion of the ideal leader and public speaker. All Aristotelian notions of arguing either side, including immoral or unjust causes, would be absent in this Afrocentric orientation to human communication. How an individual relates to the supernatural, the ancestors, the living, and nature is crucially important in evaluating discourse. An individual may have great oratorical skill, but if that same individual disrespects his/her leaders, elders, ancestors, other humans, and nature, then this person could not be considered the possessor of good speech. This metaphysical component to discourse/human conduct is at the core of classical Kemetic and contemporary African worldviews.

The Kemetic ideals of rhetoric are useful in that they help society begin to construct new theories, models, and methods of criticism that address core cosmological, epistemological, axiological, and aesthetic concerns among African cultures. With Kemet as a starting point, one can look to other African societies for similarities and/or differences in rhetorical strategies and practices. With the ground-breaking research by Cheikh Anta Diop (1978) and Théophile Obenga (1995), scholars are aware of the profound linguistic commonalities on the African continent, specifically owing to the vocabulary of ancient Kemet. Because language derives from a particular worldview and cultural practices, it can be advanced that these linguistic patterns reflect a deeper philosophical and cultural unity among African cultures. Thus, the Kemetic paradigm essentially becomes a classical point of reference for rhetorical theory developed to understand and critique communication practices throughout the African diaspora.

► References

Asante, M. K. (1987). *The Afrocentric idea*. Philadelphia: Temple University Press.

Asante, M. K. (1990). *Kemet, Afrocentricity, and knowledge*. Trenton, NJ: Africa World Press.

Asante, M. K. (1993). An Afrocentric communication theory. In M. K. Asante, *Malcolm X as cultural hero & other Afrocentric essays* (pp. 171-185). Trenton, NJ: Africa World Press.

Baines, J. (1991). Society, morality, and religious practice. In B. E. Shafer (Ed.), *Religion in ancient Egypt: Gods, myths, and personal practice* (pp. 123-200). Ithaca, NY: Cornell University Press.

Breasted, J. H. (1934). *The dawn of conscience*. New York: Charles Scribner's Sons.

Clayton, P. A. (1994). *Chronicle of the pharaohs*. New York: Thames and Hudson.

Diop, C. A. (1978). *Cultural unity of black Africa*. Chicago: Third World Press.

Diop, C. A. (1991). *Civilization or barbarism: An authentic anthropology* (Y.-L. M. Ngemi, Trans.). New York: Lawrence Hill Books. (Original work published 1981)

Faulkner, R. O. (Trans.). (1994). *The Egyptian book of the dead, the book of going forth by day*. San Francisco: Chronicle Books.

Frankfort, H. (1961). *Ancient Egyptian religion: An interpretation*. New York: Harper Torchbooks. (Original work published 1948)

Karenga, M. (Ed.). (1989). *Selections from the Husia: Sacred wisdom of ancient Egypt*. Los Angeles: University of Sankore Press. (Original work published 1984)

Karenga, M. (1986). Restoration of the Husia: Reviving a sacred legacy. In M. Karenga & J. H. Carruthers (Eds.), *Kemet and the African worldview* (pp. 83-99). Los Angeles: University of Sankore Press.

Karenga, M. (1989). Toward a sociology of Maatian ethics: Literature and context. *Journal of African Civilization, 10*(1), 352-395.

Karenga, M. (1994). *Maat, the moral ideal in ancient Egypt: A study in classical African ethics*. Unpublished doctoral dissertation, University of Southern California.

Kneupper, C. W. (1985). Developing rhetoric as a modern discipline: Lessons from the classical tradition. In C. W. Kneupper (Ed.), *Oldspeak/newspeak: Rhetorical transformations* (pp. 108-118). Arlington, TX: Rhetoric Society of America.

Lichtheim, M. (Ed.). (1973-1980). *Ancient Egyptian literature* (Vols. 1-3). Berkeley: University of California Press.

Lichtheim, M. (1992). *Maat in Egyptian autobiographies and related studies*. Frieburg, Switzerland: Universitäts Verlag.

Morenz, S. (1984). *Egyptian religion*. Ithaca, NY: Cornell University Press.

Obenga, T. (1995). *A lost tradition: African philosophy in world history*. Philadelphia: The Source Editions.

Obenga, T. (1996). *Icons of Maat*. Philadelphia: The Source Editions.

Teeter, E. (1990). *The presentation of Maat: The iconography and theology of an ancient Egyptian offering ritual*. Unpublished doctoral dissertation, University of Chicago.

Tobin, V. A. (1987). Ma(at and △IKE: Some comparative considerations of Egyptian and Greek thought. *Journal of the American Research Center in Egypt, 24*, 113-121.

Weaver, R. M. (1948). *Ideas have consequences*. Chicago: University of Chicago Press.

Weaver, R. M. (1953). *The ethics of rhetoric*. Chicago: Henry Regnery.

Weaver, R. M. (1970). *Language is sermonic: Richard M. Weaver on the nature of rhetoric* (R. L. Johannesen, R. Strickland, & R. T. Eubanks, Eds.). Baton Rouge: Louisiana State University Press.

Wilson, J. (1956). *The culture of ancient Egypt*. Chicago: University of Chicago Press.

Index

About the Authors

Richard L. Allen is professor of communication studies at the University of Michigan, Ann Arbor. He has published in a wide range of journals and a number of different disciplines. His areas of interest include communication and the self-concept, African identity and the mass media, and methods of analysis in communication.

Molefi Kete Asante is professor in the Department of African American Studies at Temple University, Philadelphia. Founder of the Afrocentric philosophical movement, he is author/editor of 45 books and has published more than 200 journal and magazine articles. His most recent works include *Ancient Egyptian Philosophies, The Painful Demise of Eurocentrism, Scream of Blood,* and *The African American Atlas.*

Ruth Leon W. Butler is a doctoral student in the School of Justice Studies at Arizona State University, where she is also a research associate and trainer in residential life. Her publications include research on African American oral traditions and intercultural communication; her current research centers on communication, ethics, womanism, and justice in the workplace.

Guo-Ming Chen is professor of communication at the University of Rhode Island. His primary research interests are intercultural and organizational communication and conflict management. He is coauthor/coeditor of two books, *Foundations of Intercultural Communication* and *Communication and Global Society.* His writings have appeared in several journals.

Travis L. Dixon is assistant professor of communication studies and a faculty associate at the Institute for Social Research at the University of Michigan. His primary research interests are in mass media effects in the context of the African American population.

Toni-*Makjaetji* Humber is associate professor in the Ethnic and Women's Studies Department at California State Polytechnic University, Pomona. Her research interests focus on African and African American culture and history, as well as ethnic studies, sociolinguistics, Ebonics, and intercultural communication.

Min-Sun Kim is professor in the Department of Speech at the University of Hawaii at Manoa. Her research interests focus on the role of cognition in conversational styles among people of different cultural orientations. She has conducted extensive research in this and related areas and has published more than 40 research papers. She currently serves as Associate Editor for *Communication Reports* and also as a reviewer for various communication journals.

Pamela J. Lannutti is a doctoral student in speech communication at the University of Georgia. Her area of specialization is affective processes in interpersonal perception and communication. Her publications appear in *Human Communication Reasearch* and other journals and books.

Cynthia L. Lehman is an assistant professor of African American Studies at the University of Illinois at Springfield. She received her Ph.D. in African American Studies from Temple University, with a dissertation on ancient Kemetic (Egyptian) philosophy and religion and its use in building an Afrocentric foundation for the study of African oratory.

Judith N. Martin is professor of communication at Arizona State University. She has coauthored several books on intercultural communication and on white identity. She has taught at the University of Minnesota and

the University of New Mexico. Her research interests include intercultural adaptation and communication, ethnic identity, and communication competence.

Ama Mazama holds a Ph.D. degree in linguistics from the University of La Sorbonne, Paris. She is currently an associate professor in African American studies at Temple University. Her research interests include African and African American studies, Afrocentrism, and cross-cultural relations.

Ali A. Mazrui is Albert Schweitzer Professor in the Humanities and director of the Institute of Global Cultural Studies at Binghamton University, State University of New York. He has published more than 20 books and hundreds of scholarly articles and essays. His research focuses on African politics, international political culture, and North-South relations.

Virginia H. Milhouse is Associate and Fulbright Professor of human relations studies and diversity management at the University of Oklahoma. Her research interests include international human relations studies and holistic education. She completed her Fulbright studies at the University of Potchefstroomse in South Africa in 1996-97 and continues to work with several South African universities in human relations training. She has authored and coauthored over five books and 20 research articles.

Anthony Monteiro is associate professor of sociology at the University of the Sciences in Philadelphia. He has written and lectured widely on W.E.B. Du Bois and the construction of social scientific knowledge and organizes the annual W.E.B. Du Bois Conferences. He has published more than 100 articles related to race, Black Studies, Marxism, and the sociology of knowledge.

Chevelle Newsome is a professor of communication studies at California State University, Sacramento. Her research has primarily focused on the political aspects of gender and race, political activism, and interethnic communication. She is research editor of *Communication Studies* and a member of the editorial board, *Western Journal of Communication.*

Peter O. Nwosu is professor of intercultural and international communication at California State University, Sacramento, and a consultant on multicultural issues, training, and development. His research interests focus on human communication processes and patterns across cultures. He has published in various journals and is coauthor of *Communication and the Transformation of Society: A Developing Region's Perspective.*

Joy Okereke-Arungwa is assistant professor of communications at Bowie State University. She has presented conference papers and has conducted several training workshops. Her research involves intercultural adjustment and gender studies. Her contributions to gender studies include an analysis of the intersection between naming and gender in African culture.

Emeka J. Okoli is associate professor in the Department of Mass Communication and Journalism at Norfolk State University, Norfolk, Virginia. His research interests include mass media, transcultural leadership development, and organizational dynamics.

Bolanle A. Olaniran is associate professor of communication studies in the College of Art and Sciences at Texas Tech University, Lubbock, Texas. His research focuses on computer-mediated communication, technological change crisis management, and cross-cultural issues.

Ayman Omar is a doctoral student in human relations at the University of Oklahoma. His area of interest is international human relations. He has presented papers at several international and national conferences as well as conducted workshops on the postindependence assault on diversity in Sudan.

Chuka Onwumechili is associate professor of communications at Bowie State University. He has presented and published peer-reviewed papers in intercultural communications, with a focus on adjustment studies. His recent work is in the area of cultural transiency and readjustments.

Donald L. Rubin is professor in the Department of Speech Communication and Language Education and in the Program in Linguistics at the University of Georgia. His research areas include studies of language and attitude and evaluations of international instructors. He has written on gender and language and relations between oral and written language.

Donald S. Taylor is professor of communication studies at California State University, Sacramento. His research and consulting focus on complex research design, analysis, and evaluation of human interaction processes in interethnic and intercultural settings. He has published several chapters, refereed journal articles, and book reviews.